Thales
To
Dewey

Books by Gordon H. Clark

Readings in Ethics (1931)
Selections from Hellenistic Philosophy (1940)
A History of Philosophy (coauthor, 1941)
A Christian Philosophy of Education (1946, 1988)
A Christian View of Men and Things (1952)
What Presbyterians Believe (1956)[1]
Thales to Dewey (1957, 1989)
Dewey (1960)
Religion, Reason and Revelation (1961, 1986)
William James (1963)
Karl Barth's Theological Method (1963)
The Philosophy of Science and Belief in God (1964, 1987)
What Do Presbyterians Believe? (1965, 1985)
Peter Speaks Today (1967)[2]
The Philosophy of Gordon H. Clark (1968)
Biblical Predestination (1969)[3]
Historiography: Secular and Religious (1971)
II Peter (1972)[2]
The Johannine Logos (1972, 1989)
Three Types of Religious Philosophy (1973, 1989)
First Corinthians (1975)
Colossians (1979, 1989)
Predestination in the Old Testament (1979)[3]
I and II Peter (1980)
Language and Theology (1980)
First John (1980)
God's Hammer: The Bible and Its Critics (1982, 1987)
Behaviorism and Christianity (1982)
Faith and Saving Faith (1983)
In Defense of Theology (1984)
The Pastoral Epistles (1984)
The Biblical Doctrine of Man (1984)
The Trinity (1985)
Logic (1985, 1988)
Ephesians (1985)
Clark Speaks From the Grave (1986)
Logical Criticisms of Textual Criticism (1986)
First and Second Thessalonians (1986)
Predestination (1987)
The Atonement (1987)
The Incarnation (1988)

[1] Revised in 1965 as *What Do Presbyterians Believe?*
[2] Combined in 1980 as *I & II Peter.*
[3] Combined in 1987 as *Predestination.*

Thales
To
Dewey

Gordon H. Clark

The Trinity Foundation
Jefferson, Maryland

ISBN 0-940931-26-5

Cover: David, Jacques Louis (1748-1825)
    The Death of Socrates
    The Metropolitan Museum of Art, Wolfe Fund, 1931.
    Catharine Lorillard Wolfe Collection.
    (31.45)

FOREWORD

When *Thales to Dewey* first appeared in 1957, published by a major academic publisher, it met with immediate acclaim as "brilliant" and "masterly." Gordon H. Clark, then Chairman of the Department of Philosophy at Butler University, was already recognized as one of the nation's most competent interpreters of ancient philosophy, and his exposition and analysis of medieval and modern philosophy were equally incandescent. *Thales to Dewey* quickly became a standard college text in both Christian and non-Christian institutions.

Now this second edition is being issued, with minor corrections made by the author himself, in the hope that it will once again become a standard text for college students. Anyone who opens the book and reads the first arresting sentence will be enthralled by both Clark and philosophy.

There are very few histories of philosophy written by Christians, and it is fair to say that the book you hold in your hands is the only such history in English that has escaped the corroding influence of secular philosophy, especially the philosophy of empiricism. In recent years others have attempted to write histories of philosophy, but they are neither so familiar with the subject as was Clark, nor so rigorous in their understanding of Christianity. The result is that *Thales to Dewey* stands alone among one volume histories of philosophy. It is eminently readable, consistently entertaining, unfailingly accurate, and uncompromisingly Christian. It deserves to be consulted continually by both the first year philosophy student and the aging professor.

When The Trinity Foundation began publishing and republishing

Gordon Clark's books in 1980, it was with the hope that they would be used by God to raise up a new generation of Christian intellectuals who are unafraid of studying, debating, and refuting the secular philosophies that so many of their fathers either feared to discuss or thoughtlessly embraced. That hope has not been disappointed.

For too long the phrase "Christian intellectual" has had an odd sound, almost a contradiction in terms, at least an oxymoron. Now, however, by the grace of God, the situation is changing, and a generation of new intellectuals, Christian intellectuals, is rising. The publication of this second edition of *Thales to Dewey* is in response to their demand for a reliable guide to the history of philosophy.

At the end of this volume we have appended an essay on the influence of philosophy on civilization: "The Crisis of Our Time." We have also added a list of Clark's other works in philosophy and theology that are now in print and which may be of interest to the reader. The outline of Clark's philosophy may be seen in *Thales to Dewey*, for it forms the framework for his analysis of secular philosophers, but the complete statement of that philosophy must be found in his other books. We hope that *Thales to Dewey* will not be the end of the reader's interest in philosophy, but merely the beginning. But whether end or beginning, no better introduction to philosophy could have been chosen than *Thales to Dewey*.

John W. Robbins
February 14, 1989

PREFACE

There are many good histories of philosophy, but they are not all good for the same purpose. Obviously, Uberweg's *Grundriss* is unsuitable as a college text and exceeds every normal notion of "Grundrisse." Other works of long and high standing, complete, profound, professionally admirable, fail to excite college undergraduates.

Within the college field the various authors solve their problems in various ways. One may decide to take note of every philosophic writer, major and minor, and the result is a sort of encyclopedia. Such a book may contain valuable précis of a hundred or even two hundred philosophers; but it would seem that the breadth of coverage adds to the depth of confusion, if a student tries to cover the whole in one year. Another author may try a different method. Not only will he reduce the number of names, but he will also try to bring philosophy down to the level of the student's understanding. This process of dilution can go and has gone to the extent of suppressing the subject matter. Something may be thus brought to the level of the student, but it is not philosophy; and education has become a façade of dilettantism.

The present volume, rather than trying the impossible — bringing philosophy down to the student's level — makes the difficult attempt of bringing the student up to philosophy's level. Two principles of restriction control the procedure. To avoid confusing the students with a multiplicity of strange names, the number of men discussed has been kept to a near minimum. Then, too, the subject matter has been restricted. There was not even a temptation to cover all the theories of any one philosopher. If, in the case of Aristotle, for example, a few lines are given to his logic, a paragraph to his physics, a bit of explanation for his *De Anima*, a footnote on the *Metaphysics*, a brief mention of ethics and politics, and the whole concluded with a flourish of poetry, the chapter, if accurate, would be unintelligible, or, if inaccurate, as is more likely, would not be worth reading.

In opposition to these horrible possibilities, the aim here has been to give a fairly thorough comprehension of a few major issues. On the principle that a reasonably clear grasp of one problem is better than a dim and faulty memory of a hundred, it might be said that the present work is predominantly concerned with questions relating to the problem of knowledge. At certain points, of course, as in the case of the Sophists, St. Augustine, and modern Pragmatism, ethics comes to the fore because the epistemology of these men is in one way or another determined by their ethics. And thus, for what seemed good reasons, several subjects were interwoven with the main epistemological theme.

The restriction of names and of subject matter is easy enough. Providing the student with an opportunity for thorough comprehension is far more difficult. To the best of my ability I have used the simplest and clearest language consistent with precision; illustrative material to encourage the casual student has been developed over years of teaching; expressions of opinion were included to provoke the instructor; and like any other author I can only hope that the result will meet with a measure of success.

Acknowledgment is made to the President and Board of Directors of Butler University for a sabbatical leave during which this book was brought to completion.

G. H. C.

CONTENTS

PART ONE

Greek Philosophy

CHAPTER 1

The Presocratics

Greek philosophy began on May 28, 585 B.C. at six-thirteen in the evening.

What Is Philosophy?

Behind this partly serious and partly facetious assertion lurk several puzzling problems that require some introductory remarks. The beginning student asks, What is philosophy? Is it true that there was none before 585 B.C.? And for what mysterious reason did it begin at precisely 6:13 P.M.?

The first two questions are intimately related. Assuredly something that had not existed previously was in evidence after 585; but whether or not this new something was philosophy is a matter of definition. Popular opinion usually connects the word "philosophy" with a manner of life. The phrase in which, more than in any other, most people have come across this word is the phrase, "a philosophy of life." Ordinarily this means anything from the habitual thoughtless living of the least intelligent individuals, through the principles deliberately chosen by men of affairs, on to the convictions of those who resolutely turn their backs on the interests of this world and retire into monasteries or gain the reputation of Seer by practicing Yoga. In this meaning Solomon and Abraham had a philosophy; it was not something new in 585 B.C.

Probing to recall other meanings and phrases which occur in literature, one thinks of the philosopher's stone, of alchemy, of magic, and the secrets of nature. Philosophers are reputed to be learned men. They know a great deal. But the men who know a great deal about plants are called botanists rather than philosophers. Physicists know a great deal too. Therefore the knowledge that characterizes philosophers must be of matters other than botany, chemistry, or political science. But if one should set aside all the special subjects of knowledge, would anything remain to be the subject matter of philosophy? Geology is a study of rocks. Theology studies God. What object then is left for philosophy? Is philosophy the knowledge of nothing? Since this is disrespectful, perhaps philosophy is the knowledge of everything. But no; something is still wrong. Even in early Greece, when there was not so much to be known as now, it is not likely that anyone knew everything. Certainly no one knows everything now, and yet there are philosophers. At least there are men who write books about philosophy. What is it then?

Perhaps the least misleading definition would be that philosophy is what this book discusses. It includes geology, astronomy, chemistry, and theology. In a sense the subject matter of philosophy is indeed everything. This includes a philosophy of life too. But a philosopher is not supposed to know all the details of everything. Rather he studies general principles and connects the special sciences with each other. The man who knows all about plants is not expected to know how botany affects political science; the chemist pays no attention to chemistry's relation to linguistics; a good psychologist need not be expert in economics. Yet all these sciences are related in some way to each other. And this is one preliminary way in which to describe philosophy.

Another way comes from Aristotle. One of the very greatest philosophers of all time, Aristotle discussed logic, physics, psychology, biology, ethics and politics; but he also had a volume on First Philosophy. Each of the particular sciences treats of certain objects or beings and ignores others; i.e., the particular sciences study being as qualified in particular ways. But First Philosophy studies being as such, unqualified, simple being. Aristotle's editors later renamed it Metaphysics. If philosophy be defined as what the present volume discusses, philosophy will include both metaphysics, and astronomy and psychology as well.

Another introductory question is this: If philosophy has continued from 585 B.C. to the present, why should not one begin with philosophy as it is now, rather than wasting time over antiquated theories? Why should one study the history of philosophy, when one can study philosophy itself. If the subject concerns the interconnections among the various sciences, why not study those relationships as they actually are, instead of as they used to be two thousand years ago? The answer is that the history of philosophy is not a waste of time. From a cultural point of view, quite aside from its usefulness to the graduate student in philosophy, a smattering of Plato and Aristotle is a pleasant thing to have. From a pedagogical viewpoint the history of philosophy enables the student to see the problems in their simplest form. These problems have become exceedingly complex in modern times, too complex for first lessons. Although pupils in grammar schools and high schools do not realize it, they learn mathematics in its historical development. Arithmetic and geometry were the first parts of mathematics to be worked out. They were started by the Greek philosophers. Analytic geometry and calculus came in the seventeenth century. Modern mathematics, most college students never get to know; and those who do, could not have learned its complexities without first having studied what the Greeks discovered five centuries before Christ. Further, just as arithmetic and geometry are quite up to date in spite of their Greek origin, so too the problems of philosophy, whether in their extremely complex modern form or in their simpler Greek dress, are the same problems. To say that the study of philosophy should be preferred to the study of the history of philosophy, is a false disjunction. The history of philosophy is philosophy.

THE MILESIANS

What was it then that existed after 585 B.C. but not before, and began at the ridiculous hour of 6:13 P.M.? It was on that day that there occurred an eclipse of the sun. Of course, solar eclipses had been occurring for some time, but the new characteristic was that this had been predicted by Thales, an astronomer of Miletus in Ionia. Records of celestial phenomena had been kept for centuries by the Eastern sages, but now for the first time Thales had discerned a regularity in these occurrences, had formulated a law, and had tested his formulation by a successful prediction.[1] Together with Thales' other speculations this is called philosophy. It had not existed previously.

Unity and Multiplicity

In a later age, the age of Kepler for instance, the formulation of an astronomical law would have been set down as a triumph of astronomy but would hardly have been called philosophy. One reason for this is that philosophy has given birth to the special sciences. When these grow to maturity, become specialized, and increase in detail, they leave the parental home and set up for themselves. At the time of Thales, however, there were no special sciences, and it was his fortune to initiate both science and philosophy.

The law by which solar eclipses can be predicted is itself an example of both. For while this law, directly applicable to sun, moon, and earth, was indubitably astronomy, yet more fundamentally it was a *law*, an instance of universalizing; and it is this characteristic which sets it apart as the great event of the age. The sages of the east had collected astronomical data in profusion, but they had never reduced these disconnected items of information to an orderly, unitary form. Philosophy begins with the reduction of multiplicity to unity.

The sciences, too, reduce their multiplicities to unity. Kepler had data on the positions of all the planets at many times. His genius consisted in arranging this mass of detail so that a uniformity would emerge. He showed that all planets move the same way — in ellipses with their radius vectors sweeping out equal areas in equal times. This is a unification of multiplicity. If the subject is sufficiently set apart, it is called science; if it is still general in comparison with the state of knowledge at the time, it is called philosophy. Thales therefore was the originator of both.

If Thales had speculated on nothing besides eclipses, perhaps his

---

[1] Modern astronomers calculate that this eclipse began after 6:00 P.M. in Asia Minor. It is not to be supposed that Thales predicted the minute, the hour, or even the day. If he had specified the month, he would have done remarkably well.

tory would have listed him as an astronomer only, even though the idea of law is of such wide significance. But Thales also attempted to impose unity on the multiplicity found throughout the entire universe. Besides the sun there are the planets and stars; on earth there are mountains, seas, and human beings; there are storms, earthquakes, and seasons; there is life, sensation, and death; and in addition, all the variety of common qualities from the taste of olives to the rosy-fingered dawn or the weight of Achilles' shield. Multiplicity, without doubt. Is there any unity at all?

The question that seemed most obvious to Thales and his more immediate successors was, How did this orderly multiplicity come to be? What is it all made of? The world seems to be made of an infinite variety of things — plants, animals, clouds, and mountains; but obviously many of these things are similar in composition. Since men eat plants and animals, the human body must contain the same materials that plants and animals are made of. Plants and animals, as well as men, drink water; and even the wood of trees is ninety-eight per cent water. When water boils, the steam feels very much like fire; the lightning that sets a tree on fire must be the same sort of thing as the fire in the hearth that makes the water boil. And if our bodies are warm, they must contain fire or hot water too. Could it be that all things are made of just one elemental stuff?

True, it does not at first seem so. But suppose that the universe were composed of several elements, perhaps ninety-four. Could there in this case be any reason for precisely ninety-four? Why not sixty-one or a hundred and fifty-two? Should there not be a reason? If there were no reason, the universe would be unreasonable, irrational, and in that case it could not be understood. Only the rational is capable of being understood; and to understand is to reduce multiplicity to unity. Eclipses are understood when the law is formulated, and the law is the unity found in all the instances. It follows then that the universe must, rationally must, be made of just one stuff.

The principle that explanation depends on the reduction of a multiplicity to unity and the notion that the universe is composed of but one type of element are broad, general, philosophical positions. But when it comes to the identification of the material element, it is hard to say, in this twentieth century, whether the subject is philosophy or speculative physics. The old theory of ninety-four elements used to be taught under the name of chemistry; but with the advent of the quantum theory and the splitting of the atom, what name shall we give to the supposition that the universe is composed, not of material, discrete particles, but of energy or a field of force?

A good old-fashioned name is *cosmology*. This modern cosmology is very similar to the view of Thales in that there is one pervasive substance out of which all things come, but the identification of that substance is much more naïve with Thales than it is for our own sophisticated century. Thales did not select energy or electricity, of which he knew nothing; he selected water.

Although it is difficult if not impossible to draw a line between speculative physics and philosophy, and although the history of philosophy is philosophy, Thales' identification of the world-stuff as water is an item of physical and historical information which one may well consider unimportant. Some educators give the impression that all facts are unimportant. They deprecate the transmission of information from teacher to pupil. Not the acquisition of facts by catechizing and cramming, but independent thinking is the goal of education.

Now, it is true that an ability to think is more valuable than a collection of disjointed bits of historical information. And the study of philosophy in particular should give the student exercise in thinking, and not merely in memorization. The best way to study philosophy is to argue; argue with the professor in class and argue with fellow-students outside. Arguing, serious arguing, is philosophizing. But there remains a question whether a student can think or argue seriously with an empty mind. If it is clear that a layman cannot argue intelligently about the cause and cure of cancer, it is hardly less clear that one who is ignorant of the military disposition and resources of the enemy is unable to argue seriously about international strategy and tactics. So too the quickest way to be introduced to philosophy is to be furnished with a few facts. And it is a fact that Thales thought he had discovered the fact that all things are made of water.

A Principle Must Explain

While the fact that all things are made of water is no more important than the fact that all things are made of energy, the reasons and motives behind these assertions cannot be dismissed. Thales was attempting a comprehensive explanation of the universe. Whatever element he chose, it would have to be a plausible source of all the force displayed in natural phenomena; and can anyone who has been tossed in a small boat by a storm on the Mediterranean deny that the ocean is a source of great power? Again, if water underlies all things, and lies under the earth also, as one can see by digging a well, the storms of this subterranean ocean would account for earthquakes. Again, if the universe and all its phenomena are to be explained by one stuff, the original stuff must be capable of transforming itself into the visible things of common experience. That water can produce earth is seen in the fact that when water evaporates from a dish, a little earth is left behind. Evaporation also shows how water can produce air. And in the lightning and the rain there is a connection between water and fire. Hence there is no impossibility in assuming that all things can come from water. But still further, not only are physics, chemistry, and meteorology to be explained by water; botany, zoology, and psychology also must be amenable to the same type of explanation. Philosophy cannot neglect any part of the world.

How then can water explain life? Well, in the first place, it is obvious that life cannot exist without water: plants soon die of drought, and when dead they dry up. Men likewise, though they can live a long time on water alone, cannot long go without it. Then again it seems that water can produce living things because when pools begin to dry up, little wigglers are found in the wet mud. Still further, water could not support life, or surely water could not produce life, if it itself were dead. To reduce multiplicity to unity, one must show either that what appears animate is basically dead or that all things are alive. The latter is by far the more promising tentative. One stuff to explain all the world has to be living stuff. The distinction between the animate and the inanimate is a later development. In modern times, particularly since the seventeenth century, the idea of the inanimate has been thought inescapable; some thinkers have denied the existence of a soul or life principle and have tried to explain plants, animals, and human beings on a materialistic basis; others believed that a soul was necessary, and, because they could not deny the existence of inanimate matter, asserted a dualism. But Milesian philosophy acknowledged a single, living, corporeal stuff — a theory to which is given the name of *hylozoism*.

This view can be stated in more universal and more fundamental terms. Earthquakes and the appearance of wigglers in pools, as well as the revolution of the planets and stars, are special instances of motion. Motion is no doubt the most universal of all natural phenomena, and hylozoism is an attempt to explain motion. The original cannot be set in motion by something more original; it must move itself. And in common experience those things which cause themselves to move are most obviously alive. Spontaneous change is the criterion of life. Motion therefore is an original characteristic of original being. To seek for some other principle would be a denial of the monistic motivation; it would lead to dualism. Spontaneity therefore is an inherent quality of body.

This is important theory; the followers of Thales, Anaximander and Anaximenes, also citizens of Miletus, furnish more facts. They even suggest a subsidiary principle or two; but their views are fundamentally the same, and therefore the three of them are grouped as a school under the name of Ionian nature philosophers, or simply the Milesian school.

Problems of Thales' Disciples

These two disciples of Thales, particularly Anaximander, added facts about astronomy. Several questions were pressing, all involving the relation of the earth to the sun. The alternation of day and night can be easily explained by supposing what is so evident to the senses — that the sky revolves about the earth once in twenty-four hours. But the succession of the seasons, their lengths, and the northward and southward motion of the sun, are more difficult problems. A great many college students today do not know whether the four seasons are of equal length or not; and when asked how they would find out, they reply that they would ask an astronomer or look it up in a book. The Ionians had neither astronomers nor books of reference. Nor did they have two-hundred inch telescopes. How then could they have answered this question? Obviously if they were going to measure the length of the seasons, they would have to use some device for the measuring of time; in fact, they might have to invent an instrument if none of the common objects of their culture would do. What simple instrument could they have used? How could they have determined the beginning and the end of a season? This will be left as an exercise in ingenuity for the student, with the hint that along the way he will have to determine the direction of north. (No, the answer is not a compass.) Another astronomical problem of the age was found in those peculiar celestial "wanderers," the planets. Sometimes they travel from east to west like the fixed stars, and then at other times they go from west to east like the sun. How can their motions be explained? There are still other problems, and the development of astronomy in Greece was rapid; its history is interesting but since this is not a history of astronomy, the student must choose between imitating a Greek philosopher and working it all out for himself, or going to his trusted source of all wisdom, the textbook, to ascertain the facts.

Anaximander was not satisfied with water as the single element of the universe. To him water seemed to be on a level with earth, air, and fire: these are all the results of natural processes, the developed things, and not the source from which things come. The source cannot be any one of them, but must somehow contain them or at least contain the qualities from which they can be developed. Accordingly, Anaximander posited an element which he called the "boundless" or the "unlimited."

Theophrastus, a pupil of Aristotle, said that the term *boundless* indicated a stuff that was limitless or infinite in extent. And to this is joined the notion that our solar system is but one of the infinite number of worlds scattered throughout infinite space. A century and a half later, it is true, the pluralists propounded this idea; but it is doubtful that the sixth century had yet arrived at the notion of infinite space; and it is incongruous that the early emphasis on unity should have resulted in the assertion of many simultaneous worlds. Another interpretation is at least possible. In Greek, the term *boundless* or *unlimited* is applied to things that have no divisions, no beginnings, or ends. For example, a smooth ring is unlimited; likewise a circle of women around an altar, a seamless robe, and a sphere are unlimited.[2] In these cases there is no suggestion of infinite extent. Therefore Anaximander's boundless, without being infinite in quan-

[2] Cf. F. M. Cornford, *Principium Sapientiae* (Cambridge University Press, 1952), pp. 171–178.

tity, may still be the inexhaustible source of the cosmos because it is a sufficient source for the production of all things. As a reservoir it may be depleted with the emergence of each thing, but it is constantly replenished as each thing is dissolved into it again. Thus it might be infinite in time, though not necessarily infinite in space.

Anaximander's original stuff was boundless also in the sense that it was not limited or made definite by any particular quality. Water is wet and fire is hot. But the boundless is — perhaps we should not say neither wet nor hot, but rather both wet and hot, cold and dry. These four basic qualities are all somehow thoroughly mixed in the original element, for if they were not there, how could wet and hot things like water and fire arise from it? Just what a stuff can be that is cold, hot, wet, and dry, perhaps strains the imagination; but there were later philosophers who, relying more on thought than on imagination, also posited original beings quite strange to ordinary experience: Plotinus excluded all qualities from his ineffable and perfectly simple being, from which differences proceeded in a mysterious manner; Spinoza, on the other hand, not only made his being both mental and material but also ascribed to it an infinite number of other unknowable qualities. Philosophers do strange things. But then it is a strange world.

Anaximander tried to make intelligible the process by which earth, air, fire, and water arose from this boundless. Apparently he had in mind something like a cream separator: the boundless whirls around and the qualities separate, with the result that water appears in some places and fire in others; and the cosmos we know comes into form. Since this whirling is connected with the courses of the stars and planets, astronomy and cosmology are explained by the same principle.

Anaximenes, the third member of the Milesian school, found it hard to credit an unperceived boundless. How could anyone know there was such a thing? An empirical substance seemed more reasonable to him. And of empirical substances, air seemed more reasonable than water. For one thing, the most obvious difference between a living animal and a dead one is not the amount of water in the body, but the amount of air. Air therefore is more plausibly the principle of life. And again, water, if unsupported, spills and falls; earth too cannot support itself; but if you put a cubic foot of air in a room, it stays put, without support. Therefore, since air is more stable than water, air is a better explanation of the fact that the planets do not fall down. Air holds them up because it can hold itself up. "As our soul which is air holds us together, so breath and air encompass the universe."

The selection of air by Anaximenes is an unimportant and perhaps even uninteresting fact; the reasons in favor of air are plausible modern guesses; but this method of explaining how water, earth, and fire come from air is more important and perhaps constitutes his chief claim to originality. A cream separator is intelligible enough on a dairy farm, but whether it would work on a questionable boundless is doubtful. The method of producing differences of quality from air is indubitable. Open your mouth wide and blow gently against the palm of your hand — the air is warm; almost close your lips as if to whistle and blow hard — the air is cold. Condensation and rarefaction therefore explain the generation of qualities. And condensation and rarefaction are strictly mechanical processes. Temperature and density are thus connected mechanically. And mechanical explanation, even though it may seem to be out of place in hylozoism, plays an important role in the history of philosophy.

In evaluating these very early philosophers it is impossible to determine whether to credit them with more or less. How profoundly did they understand their own principles? Did they foresee the future? Or are we reading back into them what we have learned from their successors? Philosophical mechanism was not clearly and explicitly enunciated until a century later; but on the other hand modern writers of textbooks with their lesser abilities may withhold proper credit because they measure these early philosophic minds by their own lack of penetration. The risk of underestimating the breadth and profoundity of the Milesians and other Presocratics is increased by the historical accident that their books have all been lost. Knowledge of this period must be pieced together from quotations and discussions by Plato, Aristotle, and much later writers. If Kant were known only through one page from each of six or eight twentieth-century authors, could we consider him a greater philosopher than Anaximenes? Undoubtedly these men had a very well integrated worldview. Its essential points have all been mentioned. All the phenomena of the entire universe without exception are to be explained on the basis of a single corporeal principle. Since this body is the origin of all things, it must be everlasting, without beginning or end. And the process by which this body takes on the forms of common objects is at once a living and a mechanical process. It is mechanical in description; it is living in that the original element causes itself to move — nothing starts it moving, it moves spontaneously. The Ionian philosophy is thus not far removed from twentieth-century naturalism.

However, while the modern historian should generously credit them with more rather than with less insight, there is one consideration that never crossed their minds. At least all evidence and plausibility are against it. Dominating Milesian thought was the principle of corporeal monism. They may have considered and discarded the possibility of a plurality of elements; they may have thought and thought absurd the absolute origin and final destruction of an element; they may have balanced the claims of a finite against an infinite universe; and they may possibly have wondered whether there was an alternative to spontaneous motion; but if explanation is in some sense the reduction of multiplicity to unity, they apparently never thought of anything other than a corporeal unity.

Cultures in Isolation

That the Ionians should have attempted an explanation of the universe in terms of bodies seems to be a natural way for philosophy to begin. It is so in accord with common sense that the very first thinkers cannot be expected to have thought of any other possibility. But in addition to this individual psychology there was a cultural isolation that hid from them a radically different type of view. This cultural isolation continued for many centuries and was not restricted to the early Ionian age. Even those of their successors who eventually came to the notion of an incorporeal reality never thought of reducing the multiplicity of the universe to the creative act of an almighty, personal God. This Hebraic concept was first introduced into Greco-Roman civilization by the spread of Christianity. Of course the Greeks thought of gods; in fact Thales is reported to have said that all things are full of gods; but these gods, sometimes scientifically but unhistorically interpreted as personifications of natural powers, were corporeal beings who like other hylozoistic persons had come into existence through natural processes. They were not eternal but had been born; they could be overthrown and possibly destroyed. The idea of Almighty God was entirely foreign to the Greeks. All the more so was the concept of creation. That an Almighty God could call the world into being from nothing was not a thesis that they rejected; it was something they had never thought of. Creation is an idea found only in Hebrew thought. Even as late as Lucretius, when he denies that anything has arisen by divine power, there is no indication that anyone in the pagan world had heard of creation. Lucretius merely means that the gods of the Greeks and Romans produce no effects in this world. Of course, Lucretius would have repudiated the Hebrew idea of creation if he had known of it; the point is simply that the pagans had never thought of such an idea.

This is not said for the purpose of disparaging Thales, Plato, or even Lucretius who with some expenditure of effort might have learned of the Jews. The purpose is twofold — pedagogical and logical. A contrast between two radically opposite views throws each into sharper relief. And while an appeal to Hebrew-Christian ideas anachronistically anticipates the chapter on the Middle Ages, the Western culture of our times has been so largely impregnated with Christian concepts that some polite acquaintance with them may be taken for granted. The logical purpose is to point out that in any system of philosophy the axioms assumed and the method used determine the nature of the conclusions. More than once from Thales to John Dewey, intricate difficulties will be put aside as inconsequential because the real trouble lies in the starting point. Unquestioning acceptance of an original position, either through ignorance of alternatives or through refusal to consider them, not only leads to foregone conclusions — any set of axioms does that — but it leads to the acceptance of a system without taking into account several weighty objections that ought to be faced. Though a given philosophic method may allow for some choices and may reply to some objections, it may at the same time ignore and thus prejudge others. In this way opposing systems are not given a fair hearing. The point of departure has prevented their consideration.

There is, however, at least one advantage of studying philosophies written in cultural isolation. A few pages back the value of ancient philosophy was defended on the ground that it was simpler and easier than modern philosophy. Centuries of profound reflection are bound to produce complications. This is true even within the Greek period, for Aristotle was far more intricate than the Ionians. But modern civilization, in addition to this source of complexity, has inherited the Hebrew tradition as well as the Greek, and is a blend of the two. Now, it can be plausibly maintained that any blending of such radically different points of view must result in confusion. Karl Marx and Friedrich Nietzsche would like to remove the confusion by restoring the purity of paganism, while Christian fundamentalists prefer the purity of the other tradition. Thomas Aquinas, the great medieval thinker, did not believe that the mixture of pagan and Christian ideas results necessarily in confusion. Therefore he aimed to integrate the best conclusions of Greek speculation with the Christian world-view. Particularly in Aristotle he believed he saw what the human mind was capable of learning without the help of divine revelation. For example, although it is possible to prove the existence of God, the doctrine of providence is beyond unaided human reason, for if it could have been demonstrated, Aristotle would have given us the demonstration. Now, perhaps it is not necessary today to hold Aristotle in quite such high esteem, nor even to suppose that Greek philosophy as a whole has exhausted human ingenuity. Yet if there are conflicts between paganism and Christianity, and if doubt arises whether Hegelianism, pragmatism, and contemporary humanism are entitled to include in their systems the Christian virtues of love, mercy, and justice, which are based on the conception of Almighty God, or whether with Spinoza and Nietzsche some or all of these virtues must be regarded as vices, the purity of Greek philosophy, together with the indispensable logical analysis, can prove to be a useful canon of judgment for the evaluation of the thought of our own age.

HERACLITUS

Closely conjoined with the Ionians in general outlook was Heraclitus, who lived in Ephesus about 525–475 B.C. Only geography prevents us from calling him a Milesian: his theory is essentially the same. From a scientific point of view he may even seem to be inferior to his predecessors, for he asserted that there is a new sun every day and that it is a foot in diameter. If this amazing remark is not to be taken literally, on the ground that his oracular style abounds in aphorisms and dark sayings to mystify the public, surely he meant to pour scorn on polymathy and detailed information. A mind crammed with facts like a telephone directory, and perhaps not even alphabetically arranged, was not Heraclitus' notion of wisdom. His views were lordly and grandiose, and what difference does it make whether the sun is new every day or whether the same sun reappears? In contrast, his untrammelled view is seen in the theory of the cosmic cycle. Just as day and night alternate, and as the seasons come and go, so too the universal process repeats itself in a cosmic cycle. Our present world therefore is, as it were, but one showing of a reel of film; when the reel comes to its end, it will be shown over and over again forever.

Yet Heraclitus was not entirely indifferent to natural phenomena. If the motions of the planets and sun are matters too detailed and insignificant, motion, just motion itself, requires all the more attention. When he rejected water and air and identified the single original element as fire, the quickest of all bodies, he was no doubt motivated by the desire to select a suitable basis for motion. That there were motions in the world was nothing new, but to Heraclitus belongs the distinction of centering attention on motion in general. Without motion, without the alteration of qualities, without the opposition and balancing of antagonistic forces, there could be no world. It is the struggle between hot and cold that makes the seasons; it is the forward and backward pulls on the bow that make the arrow fly; tension is necessary to the lyre; sickness makes health pleasant, and toil rest. Life is a struggle, and war is the father of all. Poets may lament the change and decay of time and the passing of the ancient golden age; Homer wished that strife might cease, and old

men wish that youth had been permanent. Such a bemoaning of
time and change results from a limited human viewpoint. For God
all things are fair and good and just, but men suppose that some
things are just and others are unjust. In this world, in any *world*, all
things must change.

From a promontory above a mighty river as it flows down a valley,
the river between a frame of trees seems to stand still as in a picture.
We know that it moves, but we cannot see its motion. Sensation is
too feeble and clumsy to see things as they are, and hence common
opinion holds that some things do not move. On the contrary, all
things flow. No man can ever step twice into the same river. How
could he? The second time he tried to step, new waters would have
flowed down from upstream: the water would not be the same.
Neither would the bed and banks be the same, for the constant ero-
sion would have changed them too. And if the river is the water, the
bed, and the banks, the river is not the same river. Strictly speaking,
there is no river. When common opinion names a river, it supposes
that the name applies to something that will remain there for a time
at least; but the river remains there no time at all. It has changed
while you pronounce its name. There is no river. Worse yet, you
cannot step into the same river twice because *you* are not there twice.
You too change, and the person who stepped the first time no longer
exists to step the second time. A person is also a river, a stream of
consciousness, as William James called it; and the stream of consciousness never has the same contents, the same bed or banks.
Persons do not exist.

For when anyone says that something exists, the meaning is that
something does not change. An object that is real must be an object
that stands still. Suppose a clever sculptor takes a lump of children's
modeling clay and begins to work it rapidly. It shortly takes on the
appearance of the child's teddy bear, and if the sculptor should stop,
we could call it a teddy bear. But he does not stop; his nimble fingers
keep working and the momentary bear turns into a small statue of
Zeus, only quickly to disappear into the form of the Empire State
Building. What is it? we ask. The answer is not that it is a bear, or a
god, or a building. Under these circumstances all we could say is that
it is modeling clay. And we call it clay because the clay remains the

same throughout the changes. But if the clay itself never remained the same, if it changed from clay to wax to papier mâché and never stopped changing, we could call it nothing. Nothing; that is, it does not exist, it is unreal.

But if everything is unreal, if everything changes, no names at all are possible. If nothing exists, there is nothing to be known. Knowledge therefore must be the correlate of the immutable; and the immutable is what is meant by reality. Although Heraclitus said all things flow, he admitted that there was one thing that did not change; only it was not a "thing." It was a law, the law of change. The Greek word that Heraclitus used is *Logos*, a word later taken over by the Stoics, then adopted by Philo, and with the help of John's Gospel utilized in the Christian patristic period. The word *Logos* can mean nearly any expression of thought: it means book, word, ratio, theory, or argument. Accordingly, one of Heraclitus' fragments may be translated either "this theory, though it is always true, men do not understand"; or, "this Logos, although it exists always," etc. In either translation there is something always, something that does not change, whether it is a truth or a law or a mysterious Logos. At any rate, it is not an individual thing.

However, Heraclitus was still a hylozoist; he could not distinguish between an immaterial law and corporeal fire. If we today question him too closely, our questions are likely to become anachronistic. Fitting awkwardly into nineteenth-century categories, the Logos is a material intelligent energy — an idea perhaps not far removed from some twentieth-century speculations. In this light, phrases from Heraclitus can be given a clearer meaning: wisdom is to understand the intelligence that steers all things, an intelligence that wills and does not will to be called Zeus; the order of the universe always has been, is now, and ever shall be an ever living fire, kindled and extinguished in fixed mathematical ratios.

There is much more information that could be detailed about Heraclitus; for example, he was a prohibitionist, for since fire is the original element, a dry soul is wisest and best. However, Heraclitus was not interested in detailed information. The mention of universal change proceeding in fixed mathematical ratios is an indication that other philosophical influences, beyond the Ionian school, had been at work. No doubt Anaximander had some dim perception of the need of mathematics in physical theory, but a more thorough study of number was the contribution of the Pythagoreans.

THE PYTHAGOREANS

Since the men so far studied were exponents of hylozoism and corporeal monism, a comparative method would make it tempting to picture all the early Presocratics as sharing this dominant view. Then when Parmenides' analysis exposed the absurdities and implications of his predecessors, the later Presocratics were forced to adopt corporeal pluralism. That this is the general course of the history, there can be no doubt; and the earliest Pythagoreans, who were certainly corporealists, may also have been monists. Even though their basic categories are arranged in a table of contrary pairs, which seems to favor a dualism, odd and even are both categories of number, and one is the source of number, so that an underlying monism cannot be ruled impossible. But inasmuch as the Pythagoreans are a school with a long history, and not a single man whose life can be placed between that of his teacher and his disciples, it is difficult to insert an account of them into Presocratic history and at the same time maintain a smooth chronological development. Moreover, the information that has been preserved comes largely from late sources which may not have had early Pythagoreanism in mind or may not have reported it accurately. Even with the help of Aristotle's accounts it is difficult to distinguish between pre- and post-Parmenidean Pythagoreanism.[3] But since Pythagoras himself antedated Heraclitus and may have given him the notion of a mathematical ratio, it is permissible to discuss the Pythagoreans at this juncture.

Homeric and Mystery Religions

The Pythagorean school with its center in southern Italy was intellectually as it was geographically at the other end of the Greek-speak-

[3] The delicacy of historical investigation and the divergence of opinions can be seen by comparing the works of F. M. Cornford and J. E. Raven.

ing world. To be sure, Pythagoreanism was not far enough removed
as to have left the Greek outlook and to have shared the Hebrew
conception of an Almighty Creator, but it had a religious motivation
and a desire for salvation that was entirely absent from the other
philosophy. If the common Greek religion, which the Pythagoreans
tried to improve upon, was not naturalistic in the modern, virtually
atheistic, meaning of this term, still it differs from the Hebrew in
being a natural religion. The gods may have spoken to men occasionally, and such conversations might be called revelation, but the
Greeks had nothing like an authoritative Bible. When Homer is
called the Bible of the Greeks, the expression must be taken in an
extenuated sense. The stories of the gods were not supposed to be
accurate information, and where there were different versions of a
genealogy or exploit, there seems to have been no insistence that one
form was orthodoxy and another heresy. In the next place, Greek
religion may be called natural because the gods themselves were very
much like men. They were finite in power and often immoral in
conduct. Worshipping them therefore put no strain on human frail-
ties, and provided little incentive to moral living. The Greeks of
course had some notion of right and wrong, of a good and bad life;
but they lacked the Hebrew idea of sin, of human depravity, and
failed therefore to see any need of regeneration. They did not admit
to having a heart of stone and hence could not ask God to give them
a heart of flesh. The fullest development of man's natural abilities
rather than the birth or implantation of a new nature was their program and ideal. The Homeric concept of the future life is similarly
devoid of moral motivation. Virtually all men, good, bad, and indifferent, meet the same fate. A very few, exceptionally wicked criminals, who perpetrated special crimes against the gods, will be tortured
like Tantalus and Sisyphus in Tartarus; a few exceptional heroes will
be made demigods; but everybody else spends eternity in Hades.
Hades is not a place of punishment; it is simply the abode of the
dead where flit the shades of worn-out men. Memory remains, but
reason is extinct. Dismal darkness has replaced the sunlight and joy
of the upper world. The Homeric religion is often pictured as one of
happy enthusiasm in the vigorous game of life, but it can remain
happy only through thoughtlessness. If one perchance thinks of the

future, or if hardship, national decay, and foreign aggression interrupt the game, the happiness evaporates.

These calamities all occurred. In the case of personal hardship, the common religion had little to offer in the way of divine solace. With the rites taking on the nature of a state function and being more a matter of political loyalty than of personal conviction, the deterioration of the Greek cities and the later Roman aggression tended to make Homeric observances empty and perfunctory. It is not surprising therefore that many individuals, even in the earlier centuries, sought something better.

These defects provided an opportunity for the mystery religions. A mystery is a secret rite in which sacred objects are exhibited and information is imparted which could not safely be seen or known by the worshipper before he had been purified in the initiation ceremony. One of the mysteries was the worship of Dionysus. On the mountain side at night the worshippers worked themselves into a frenzy by wild music and dancing around a bull, which was their god. When sufficiently worked up, they would fall on the bull, cut him up, and eat his raw flesh. In this way they had their god inside of them. This was indeed real contact and communion with the god. The initiates were also promised a happy future life. Orphism was a more sober mystery; it stressed education rather than drunkenness and it showed a better moral sense in that it preached, not only future rewards, but also future punishments for the wicked. There were other mystery religions also.

All these mysteries, in contrast to the Homeric religion, were methods of obtaining a happy immortality. The sense of need and the desire for salvation increased as time went on, and from 200 B.C. to A.D. 100 there were great waves of religious propaganda.

The Pythagoreans early recognized the need of salvation and the desirability of a blessed immortality. To secure it, they observed certain taboos: for example, they would eat neither beans nor white roosters and would wear no woolen but only linen clothes. They also memorized a poem of directions as to what to do when they arrived in the next world. In addition to these curious taboos, they insisted on a life of virtue, especially of friendship; and it is from Pythagoreanism that the story of Damon and Pythias comes. But chiefly they held that salvation comes by knowledge, and their search for knowledge resulted in mathematics.

Mathematics

One of the solid triumphs of Pythagoreanism is geometry. Pythagoras personally is credited with working out the Pythagorean theorem; and if a college student who has had plane geometry in high school cannot remember how to reproduce the proof, it is clear that the discovery of the proof without the aid of instruction was a success that called for the sacrifice of a bull to the gods.

Besides geometry, they developed what we now call number theory. Certain questions intrigued them. First of all, what is a number? Even the question, What are the numbers? is more difficult to answer than one might at first suppose. Of course, two, three, and four are numbers. But is one a number or is it the source from which numbers come? Is zero a number? Fortunately for the Greeks they never had to face the question, Is the square root of minus one a number? Once the series of numbers is determined, there are questions about each number individually. Is two just the number that comes after one, as Jim follows Jack at bat in baseball; or is it an abstract concept that includes all instances of pairs? And aside from the question whether each number is a class concept or not, there is the question whether there are classes of numbers and what their various properties are.

The last question is not so difficult. Obviously there are two classes of numbers, the odd and the even. Since odd numbers cannot be divided in half, the concept of odd is related to the concept of limit, while the concept of even is unlimited. Now the limited or definite is good, and right, and masculine; while the unlimited or chaotic is evil, left, and feminine. In this way a table of ten pairs of opposites was formed, and these basic oppositions explain the conflicting multiplicity that is harmonized in each thing.

In addition to odd and even numbers, there are square numbers, obtained by adding the successive odd numbers. That is, one plus three is four; one plus three plus five is nine; and so on. There are also oblong numbers, obtained by adding the successive even numbers. Then there are prime numbers whose only factor (aside from the number itself) is one. Perfect numbers are those whose factors, when added, result in the number itself. Six can be divided by one, two, and three, the sum of which is six. With these classifications the Pythagoreans discovered a relationship between prime numbers and perfect numbers. Construct a series starting from one by doubling each previous number: one, two, four, eight, sixteen, and so on. Begin adding the series. Whenever the sum is a prime number (as one plus two is three, and three is prime), this prime multiplied by the last number added will be a perfect number (as three, the sum, by two gives six). One plus two plus four is seven, a prime; and seven times four is twenty-eight, a perfect number. Add eight, and the sum is not prime. Add sixteen and the sum is thirty-one, a prime; thirty-one times sixteen is four-ninety-six. See if its factors add up to it.

All this is brilliant enough, but the Pythagoreans went further. Mathematics became the key to cosmology. In our present Einsteinian age the value of mathematical physics is not disputed, but the Pythagoreans made use of numbers in ways that Einstein has neglected to follow. For them the world is not made of water or fire, but of numbers. Numbers were not regarded as abstract class concepts, or as mere formal symbols; numbers were spatially extended entities, and bodies were mixtures of numbers. Chemical, mathematical formulas for bodies are routine today, but we use the numbers to indicate the amount of hydrogen or some stuff in the compound. For the Pythagoreans the numbers not only indicate the proportions, but they are themselves the stuff. And they indulged the hope of applying this type of number theory to social problems as well, in that they made justice four, a square number; and marriage five because it is the union of the first odd or male and first even or female number.

Where is the dividing line between the superstitions of numerology and sober mathematics? Is there some deep secret in the fact that musical harmonies are easy fractions like one-half, one-fourth, and one-fifth; while discord is found in awkward fractions like eight-ninths and fifteen-sixteenths? And what would your reaction be if the best estimate of the distances between the planets showed the same proportions as the notes of the scale? Would not the harmony of the spheres seem divine?

As always, there is interesting material that must be omitted. It would be instructive to see how zero became a number, and how, much later, the square root of minus one became a number. But this would be the history of mathematics. Or, one could trace the Neopythagoreanism of 50 B.C. and onward, possibly through the Middle Ages into *Romola*, the novel by George Eliot. But such interesting side-paths must be renounced in order to study the greatest of the Presocratics, Parmenides.

PARMENIDES

The Eleatic school had its headquarters on the western coast of southern Italy. Some of the motivation out of which Parmenides developed his imposing system was earlier originated by Xenophanes, who, born in Colophon in Asia Minor, wandered throughout the Greek world and may have ultimately arrived in Elea. The burden of his poetry was the stupidity and impiety of polytheism. "Those who assert that the gods have been born are just as impious as those who say they will die, for both agree that there is a time when the gods do not exist." He stressed the absurdity of mortal conceptions of the gods so pointedly that Rupert Brooke stole his thunder in the poem *Heaven*. Positively, Xenophanes taught that the origin of the gods is inconceivable and that there is but one God. If this be simplified or generalized so as to say that origin is inconceivable and that there is but One, Parmenides' thesis appears.

Xenophanes was very early; he was born before 590 B.C. But he lived to an extremely old age, at least to ninety, so that it was possible for Parmenides, when a youth, to have known him. Parmenides' main work is to be dated about 475 B.C.

Logic and Nonsense

Parmenides continued and intensified Xenophanes' insistence on unity; but perhaps his deepest conviction was that a philosopher should not talk nonsense. If the world is rational, an explanation of the world must be rational; but if explanations are irrational and all the theories are absurd nonsense, what hope can there be for philosophy? Absurdities describe nothing real. Try to think of a nice round circle which has four ninety-degree angles at its corners. It cannot be thought. Thought requires an object, and what cannot be thought cannot exist. If one tries to think of something that does not exist, e.g., a square circle, one thinks of nothing; and to think of nothing is not to think. Regardless of how elaborate or how learned a theory may appear, if its objects do not exist, it is a thinking of nothing. A geometry of square circles is nonsense.

Now, claims Parmenides, the previous philosophers talked nonsense and tried to think of nothing. Thales had said that fire and earth are (really) water; and Heraclitus said that earth and water are fire. Both men were talking about square circles. Examine the assertion that fire is water. The barest examination shows that it is false: fire obviously is not water. Since the word *fire* means one thing and the word *water* means something else, what could be clearer than that they do not mean the same thing? And if they are not the same, how can anyone assert their identity and say that water is fire?

So motivated by the logical difficulties in the previous theories, Parmenides drove still further. It might seem that there is at least one predicate that can be attached to both water and fire. Could not one say that water is existent and that fire is existent? Unfortunately the conclusion will be that water is not existent; for since the word *water* means one thing and the word *existent* means something else, what could be clearer than that they do not mean the same thing? It is nonsense therefore to say that water exists.

But can it not be maintained that water is water? Surely, water is water; who can deny it? Parmenides can. For although in this case the first water and the second water mean the same thing, attention must be directed to the verb *is*. The assertion says, Water is. It makes little difference what water is, whether it is fire or merely water; the trouble lies in the notion that water is. The previous part of the argument showed that water does not exist. And if water is not, then water is not even water.

Does this logical analysis result in denying all existence? Not at all. The existent exists. Being is. Being is being. Is it not crystal clear that what exists exists? In fact, only that which exists exists. What does not exist does not exist. Non-being is not; only being is.

Absolute Unity

More importantly, being is one. If being were not one, but were many; that is, if there were several beings, these several beings would have to differ from each other. If they did not differ, they would be the same being and would not be several. But if they are several and differ, they will differ with respect to being or with respect to non-being. There is no other respect in which they could differ. But they cannot differ with respect to being, for this is the assumed point of similarity — they are all supposed to be beings; accordingly they cannot differ with respect to being. Yet it is less possible that they should differ with respect to non-being, for non-being does not exist, is nothing, and cannot support differences. It follows inexorably therefore that the several beings are not in reality different. Therefore there are not many beings; there is but one being only.

Consistently with this, being cannot have originated. Anything that originates must come from something else or from the same thing. Being cannot come from something else, for anything else is non-being; and non-being does not exist for anything to come from. But being cannot come from the same thing, being, for being already is and no coming is needed. It follows that origin is inconceivable and that being is eternal.

If being cannot come from anything, neither can it pass into anything, for there is nothing else for it to change into. And since there are no differences of any sort, being must be entirely motionless and changeless. Being is completely immutable.

At this juncture modern college students and ancient Greeks begin to protest that Parmenides' being does not look much like a world. We can see differences of color; we can hear differences of sound; and the planets move. There must be something wrong somewhere. Yes, replies Parmenides, something is wrong somewhere; but it is necessary to indicate where. The objections of common sense rely on sensation; the argument has relied on reason. Irrespective of what we imagine we see, there is no justification for talking nonsense. Any theory that says the non-existent exists must be false; and the fact that the theory may be nicely phrased and agree with sensory experience does not make it any less absurd. When you *see* rabbits jumping out of a hat or a man climbing a rope hanging from nothing, you *know* it is not so. When reason and sensation conflict, sensation must give way.

Reason, however — at least the reason of those who have just met Parmenides for the first time — demands some further description of this Being. What is it? To say that Being is Being, and to say nothing more, seems to reduce Being to a mere word, a sound signifying nothing. Apparently Parmenides thought so too, for he made a desperate attempt to describe it, even running the risk of talking nonsense. It must be remembered, at this point, that Parmenides was a Presocratic and not completely emancipated from the opinions of his day. Under the influence of corporeal monism, he too shared the view that only body could be real. Therefore his Being must be a body, a solid, homogeneous, extended body. It had to be homogeneous, if there were to be no differences of any sort. For the same reason, it had to be completely symmetrical; that is, extended equally on both sides of every axis. This condition could be met by a body infinitely extended; but for the Greeks infinity carried the unpleasant connotation of indefinite and unfinished. Therefore Parmenides chose the only other possibility and pictured his Being as a sphere, a solid impenetrable atom of matter. How this conception influenced the latter Presocratics will soon be seen. But first a short summary.

The Meaning of "Is"

Of all the Presocratic philosophers Parmenides is undoubtedly the most important. He was the first to recognize that there are basic questions of logic involved in any physical or cosmological theory. He was arrested by the problem of predication. What is the significance of attributing a predicate to a subject? When one thing is said to be another, are they not said to be the same thing? Does not the verb *is* assert identity? And does it not also assert existence? If, when we say that water is fire or that Thales is an Ionian, we mean neither that they are one nor that they exist, are we not talking nonsense? At any rate, to discover and to defend some other significance for the verb *is*, will require considerable ingenuity. This matter of logic forced Parmenides to distrust sensation and to adopt a procedure that may be called rationalism. Similar views reappear in Plato, in

Spinoza, in Hegel, and were indeed anticipated in Heraclitus, for Heraclitus too distrusted sensation; but Parmenides followed this path more consistently than the earlier philosopher and with greater singleness of purpose than the later.

Consistent Monism

Parmenides' outstanding importance is seen also in that his attention to logic brought out the necessary implications of corporeal monism. A universe made of one stuff, a stuff that is really one, must be a unity such as Parmenides describes. Since unity is such an important philosophic principle, in fact since explanation was earlier defined as a statement of unity, a rational theory could admit the existence of differences only as a confession of failure. Have not the Presocratics been searching for a unitary reality? Their mistake was to suppose that this reality could both change and remain the same. Water became fire and all other visible objects, but it still remained water all the time. Even Heraclitus, who said "All things flow," hinted that the real could not change. Parmenides' pre-eminence rests on his logical consistency: he saw clearly what the others had but dimly dreamed. Unity excludes multiplicity.

The urge toward unity is strong, and later philosophers also tried to penetrate to the One. Plotinus, for example, claimed to have a mystic experience of a One so pure and simple that it excluded even the distinction between subject and predicate. But he also tried, as Parmenides did not, to derive from this pure unity all the intricacies of the common world. Succeeding generations have been wondering ever since how a simple One, devoid of every difference, could generate plurality. It must be asked therefore whether Parmenides has not shown for all time that if unity is basic, motion, plurality, and differences cannot possibly exist. If one starts with unity, does not one end with unity, and unity alone?

THE PLURALISTS

For Parmenides, then, only Being is, and origin, motion, and differences do not exist; but for the other Greeks this conclusion seemed as absurd as it does to modern common sense. However, if Parmenides' theory is the logical outcome of corporeal monism, then either we must accept the conclusion or reject corporeal monism. The Greeks who immediately followed Parmenides decided to reject corporeal monism. Accordingly, if the world could not be explained on the basis of one body, obviously it is necessary to explain it on the basis of more than one body. Yet Parmenides' work did not go entirely for nought. He had shown clearly (what was inherent in the Milesians) that origin is inconceivable; and therefore, if there are many bodies, each of them must be eternal. In fact each of these bodies must be a small edition of Parmenides' Being, save only for motion. That is, each body must be impenetrable, solid, eternal, and unchangeable except in place. Another of Parmenides' conclusions also had to be preserved. He had shown that differences could not originate. But, asserted the pluralists, differences exist, and they must be accounted for. In some way or other the immense variety of experience must be made rational. It was this attempt to explain the qualitative distinctions of phenomena that required pluralism to appear in three and in only three forms. The history of philosophy is not haphazard, and under the conditions of this period it was a foregone conclusion that there would be exactly three forms of pluralism.

Empedocles

Empedocles gave pluralism its first form. He believed that if one began with four qualitatively different types of body, everything could be explained. Essentially this is the precise position of nineteenth-century chemistry. Whether there are four types or ninety-four is theoretically immaterial; in both cases the world is to be explained in terms of a finite number of differences. Lead, gold, sulphur, hydrogen, and so on are indestructible, qualitatively distinct elements. The atom cannot be split. All the great variety of common experience is to be derived from combinations of these elements. Tastes, colors, odors, and all but the particular qualities of the elements are produced by varying the formulas. The taste of roast turkey comes from combining hydrogen, carbon, and a few other things which obviously do not by themselves taste like turkey. The weight, consistency, and physical characteristics of common materials are the result of other combinations. Of course, Empedocles had no notion of hydrogen and carbon; he had only four elements — earth, air, fire, and water; but the theory is the same, and he attempted to give formulas for things. Bone is two parts water, four parts fire, and (apparently) two parts earth: $W_2F_4E_2$.

In addition to this notion that the things of experience with their qualities come into being through a process of mixing elements, the pluralists were forced by the Eleatic philosophy to consider another crucial problem. The elements, atoms, or roots as Empedocles called them, were small editions of Parmenides' Being: each atom was unchangeable. But the more the immutability of each atom was asserted, the less their mixing and motion could be explained. How do these things come to move?

It is at this point that a distinction familiar to us comes to view for the first time. The preceding philosophers were in general hylozoists: for them matter was alive. But the post-eleatic atoms were dead, or, more accurately, inanimate, for their motion could no longer be spontaneous. Pluralism therefore must find a new way to explain life. Life is characterized by two phenomena, motion and sensation; and while these pluralists did not neglect sensation, the more important part of their contribution had to do with motion. Motion rather than sensation, in the light of the historical situation, was the crucial point because, prior to any elaborate theory, sensation might possibly be the result of mixings and combinations like other qualities and functions are, but motion cannot be the result — it must be the cause of the mixings. Therefore, if the world is composed of immutable atoms, how can motion be accounted for?

The answer seemed very obvious to Empedocles. If the four roots cannot move of themselves, there must be some other reality in the universe, some other principle or power. In fact, there must be two principles: one to cause the mixings and a second to cause the separations. These two he called Love and Hate. At one stage of the world process Love dominates and everything is so thoroughly mixed with everything else that nothing stands out distinctly: there is no cosmos. Then as Hate begins to exert force and separate parts of this mixture, things as we know them begin to appear: during this stage a cosmos exists. But when Hate has become all powerful, everything is separated from everything else, all the water is in one place, all the earth in another, and so on, so that again there is no cosmos. Then Love gradually regains control, and the universal cycle goes on forever.

But can philosophers invent new realities just because their theories need them? Do Love and Hate really explain anything? Love and hate between human beings is something we understand; but then human love and hate occur in the cosmos and are results of prior forces; this love and hate do not explain universal motion, but they themselves require explanation. What are that Love and Hate which need no explanation and which explain universal motion? Surely the ancient philosophers are indulging in mythology by appealing to such meaningless words. Perhaps so; but if the ancients indulged in meaningless words, the moderns sometimes follow their example. In physics there is talk of attraction and repulsion, and the law of gravitation is expressed as an attraction between two particles of matter according to a certain proportion. But is attraction any more intelligible than Love? When one particle of matter attracts another in proportion to the product of the masses and inversely as the square of the distance, are we to suppose that one atom puts on lipstick to attract another and that propinquity increases the attraction? What can Sir Isaac Newton have meant by the attraction of gravity? Undoubtedly some ancient philosophers sometimes talked nonsense; but modern scientists are human also.

Anaxagoras

In Empedocles' system, however, there were two flaws which Anaxagoras, his younger contemporary, wished to remove. Not that he rejected the basic position of pluralism: on the contrary, he agreed that the world of appearances required the postulation of many bodies, that these bodies move, mix, and separate, that the elemental realities themselves must be unchangeable, and that absolute origin is inconceivable. But because he held to these so firmly, especially to the last, he was unable to believe that the amazing variety of qualities in the world could be derived from so few as four. Think of all the tints of the sky and the shadows of the mountains, all the smells and sounds of a fishing fleet, and all the tastes of wines, oils, and grains.

To suppose that this infinite range of differences could result from the combination of only four elements is equivalent to the supposition that something comes from nothing. The only adequate assumption, since there is no theoretical difference between a chemistry of four elements and a chemistry of ninety-four, is the original and underived existence of an infinite number of qualitatively different types of element. Earth, air, fire, and water are not elements at all; they seem to be such because they are such homogeneous mixtures that their ingredients cannot be detected. But the real elements are hair, fingernails, bones, flesh, and so on. And there is some of every element in everything. This also seems to be required by the principle that absolute generation is unthinkable. If water becomes ice and also becomes steam, and if what is nonexistent cannot come into being, then the ice and the steam must pre-exist in the water. Any quality that appears in the processes of generation cannot be thought to arise from nothing: it must have been there all along and just now have come to the surface, as it were. Since nature is so rich in its generative processes, since there is no limit to the qualities that may appear in any thing, it is most reasonable to assume that there is something of everything in everything. In this way each particular thing reproduces the entire universe on a small scale — a conclusion on which Aristotle makes some interesting comments later. And no matter how things may be divided, each part still reproduces the universe. There is no least of what is small, for there is always a less; and there is always a greater than what is great.

The second flaw which Anaxagoras wished to remove from Empedocles' formulation concerns the cause of motion. Naturally, this new concept of an inanimate particle of matter demands the existence of a principle of motion; but it does not demand two principles. One is sufficient because every mixing is at the same time a separation: the water from the beautiful golden ewer is poured into the silver mixing bowl, and the bits of bread and meat are separated from the suitors' portions to mingle in the beggar's wallet. Similarly in the universe generally, if some of one stuff is mixed with some of another, it had to be first detached from its prior position. Anaxagoras was also clearer than Empedocles in his description of this moving principle. Instead of using metaphor and calling this power Love or Hate, he called it Mind. Apparently the source of his inspiration was the plausible analogy between the universe set in motion by a supreme Mind and the control our minds exercise over our bodies. The universal Mind, necessarily, is omniscient and omnipotent. It began the rotation of the stellar system (though consistently there should be no literal beginning) by producing a small vortex that has now grown large and will continue to grow. All things, past, present, and future, the Mind arranges in order. Unfortunately, these ideas, in particular the idea of an order imposed by Mind, were too strange and pregnant for the times; Anaxagoras himself hardly understood what he said and, as both Plato and Aristotle complained, failed to develop the implications. With later Christian ideas in view one is tempted to see in Anaxagoras an incipient theism; but so foreign to the historical context would theism be, that it is difficult to credit Anaxagoras with such an intention. More in keeping with the fifth- and fourth-century philosophy is a dawning of teleological explanation; i.e., explanation in terms of purpose. And rather than any theistic theology it is the stillborn teleology that caught Plato's and Aristotle's attention: stillborn because the working out of the system was entirely mechanical. Mind may have initiated the original vortex from which the cosmos grew, but it grew by an expanding rotation; and it is the mechanical action of the rotation, after the pattern of Anaximander and Anaximenes, that caused the separation of the qualities. Purpose plays no part.

However, it is not so much the absence of purpose as it is the presence of Mind that fits awkwardly into the pluralistic world-view. Up to this time reality has always been conceived as corporeal: it might be alive, but it was a body. Now the dialectic of history was forcing a distinction between the bodies moved and the force moving them. The same considerations that necessitated a moving principle also necessitated the conclusion that this force is not a body. In Empedocles, as might be expected of the first man to have such conceptions, the sharp separation between body and moving principle was not clearly expressed. He described Love and Hate in terms that could be used of bodies. But Anaxagoras said that while all bodies are mixtures of elements, the moving principle is completely unmixed. It exists alone by itself, for were it not by itself its complete power over everything else would be diminished. These phrases, which barely miss stating that Mind is incorporeal, follow the logic of the situation; for the more inanimate and inert the ultimate particles are made, the less a moving principle can be a body. Yet pluralism hoped to explain all reality in terms of bodies. A third and final attempt to make pluralism self-consistent must therefore be anticipated. And at the same time, it will be an improvement if this third attempt can rid itself also of the fanciful supposition that hair and fingernails are elements.

Democritus

Accordingly, instead of positing four types of element and instead of an infinite number of types, one may say that all the atoms are qualitatively identical. This was the view of Leucippus and Democritus. Democritus was born in Thrace about 460 B.C. and lived almost a century. No one, even in modern times, has given a more classic expression to atomism or mechanism. The motivation of materialistic or mechanistic systems is to explain all phenomena in terms of mechanism; that is, the only original differences allowed to the elements are strictly geometrical, plus the motion in space necessary to alter their positions. For Democritus therefore two principles explain everything: atoms and empty space. The atoms are infinite in number, they differ in size and shape, but qualitatively they are all alike. Or, it would be more accurate to say that the atoms individually have no qualities: their characteristics are strictly mechanical or geometrical. In the first place, each atom is indivisible. The word *atom* itself means indivisible; it was for this reason that Democritus invented the term *atom* and applied it to his elements. Atoms cannot be split for the simple reason that anything that can be split is not an atom. Recent nuclear physics has not succeeded in splitting an atom; it has only shown that what the nineteenth-century chemists thought were atoms are not atoms at all. The little bits of lead or gold or hydrogen, until recently thought indivisible, are in reality compounds. For only compounds can be split. Democritus made his atoms indivisible, not by reason of their smallness, but by reason of their solidity. There is no nucleus, there are no electrons or protons, there is no empty space in a Democritean atom. Conceptually, as Anaxagoras' theory might have suggested, it is possible to divide anything no matter how small it is. So long as a piece of matter has some extension, one can think of half of it. Physically to divide it, however, is quite a different affair; and the reason Democritus' atoms could not be divided was that they were solid. Indeed, his atoms were not necessarily small. They not only varied in size, but some of them were decidedly big. One of the ancient sources says that Democritus admitted that an atom could be as large as the world. This somewhat surprising statement can be explained on the ground that all variations must be possible if the only original characteristics are to be some size and some shape. Possibly there could be a view in which all atoms are perfect spheres equal in radius. But for the explanation of sensible qualities Democritus needed differences in shapes; and it would be without reason to deny differences in size, and further without reason to restrict the amount of the difference.

But the distinctive feature of the theory is that these underived, imperishable, unchangeable atoms have no qualities. Anaxagoras thought that the range of sensory qualities was too wide to be explained on the basis of a finite number of original qualitative differences; nothing less than an infinite variety of differences had to be assumed to avoid the impossibility of deriving something from nothing. For Democritus, though, even a finite number of original differences was too much: the atoms are all alike in that they have no qualities. They do not even have the quality of weight.

At first it seems incredible that a solid particle should have no weight; but when one stops to think, it appears as the only reasonable position. What is weight? Modern students are familiar with the idea that they would weigh less on the moon than they do on the earth. The smaller the body on which one stands, the less one weighs. Now, suppose that a man or a particle should stand on nothing: does it not follow that it would have no weight? Having weight is similar to having a brother. No man can be a brother by himself. It takes two to make one. Weight then is a type of relationship such that a single atom by itself cannot weigh anything. Or, to speak a little more accurately, weight is a tendency to move in a certain direction. On the earth's surface bodies tend to move downward; on the moon they would tend to move toward the center of the moon. But for a single atom in infinite space, there is no downward — there is no direction; nor could there be, for this solitary atom, any distinction between rest and motion, for this distinction requires a difference in distance between two or more bodies. The Democritean atom therefore has no tendency to move. If it is bumped, like a billiard ball, it will move off; but by itself it has no reason for going in one direction rather than in another. Since now weight is a tendency to move, it follows that a single atom has no weight. Only in combinations can weight appear.

Differences in weight between two bodies of equal size, such as a cubic inch of cork and a cubic inch of iron, i.e., specific densities, are explained by the proportion of atoms to empty space in the bodies. If the proportion of atoms is high, the body is heavy; if there is relatively more empty space, the body is light. Other qualities also must be reduced to a strictly geometrical or mechanical basis. To explain the difference between a solid and a liquid body, one should say that the atoms in the solid are relatively at rest, while those in the liquid are moving around. Rest resists motion, so that if you try to force your hand through a piece of wood, you only hurt your hand; but it is easy to force your hand through water. The atoms in the wood are at rest; the atoms in the water are in motion, and for this reason they permit the motion of your hand. Note too that liquid and solid are not the same as heavy and light. Mercury is a liquid, but it is heavy; cork is solid, but it is light. Mechanical or geometrical characteristics must also explain the difference between hot and cold. A hot body is one in which the sharp edges and points of the atoms are facing the surface; if the atoms present their smooth sides, the body feels cold.

The genius of atomism or materialism is to reduce the plurality of the universe to the smallest number of mechanical determinations; and since there are no fewer than the geometrical ones that Democritus specified, later materialists cannot hope to improve on Democritus in theory. All the qualities of common experience he claims to have reduced to quantitative arrangements. Atoms and space alone are real; other things exist only by convention, that is, they are merely thought to exist. But while modern materialists cannot surpass Democritus, they can and have imitated him. From the begin-

ning of modern science in the seventeenth century various thinkers
have claimed that life and sensation are not real: they are simply
particular motions of combinations of atoms. Sight is a chemical
reaction on the retina plus a few wiggles in the cortex. The chemical
reaction is real or natural; the sight is phenomenal, illusory, or at
least not so real as the chemistry. Color does not really exist, but
ether vibrations do; sound does not exist, but there are waves in the
air. All qualities must be reduced to quantities. Water is not wet
or liquid; water is H_2O.

Now, the simple facts of chemistry offer material for thought to
the materialist and the nonmaterialist alike. Is it or is it not true
that qualities can be reduced to quantities? Litharge or lead monox-
ide, PbO, is a dull yellow-orange powder; mixed with glycerine it
makes a cement. But if an extra quantity of lead or oxygen be added,
other qualities appear. PbO_2, and PbO_3, while they simply have
"more" of the same substance, have decidedly different qualities. A
more common comparison would be water and peroxide, which is
just water with an extra bit of oxygen added. But peroxide does not
taste like water, and water does not bleach like peroxide. What is
still more puzzling, a single substance, a lead oxide, sulphur, or carbon appearing as graphite and diamond, may exist in crystalline and
noncrystalline forms; yet though they are the same chemical substance, their physical properties are noticeably different; and these
differences depend simply on the geometrical arrangements of atoms
or ions. Does this mean that qualities have been reduced to quantities? What is meant by reduction? Does this mean that sensory
qualities are not real? What is meant by real? And if qualities are
sensory, are sensation and life merely quantitative distinctions that
happen to be a bit more complicated than the others? And, finally,
what does quality mean, anyhow? Sixty or seventy years later Aristotle attempted to answer some of these questions.

In addition to such important general problems, Democritus also
studied many particular phenomena. Magnetism attracted him, and
the salinity of the sea; he gave an explanation of earthquakes, thunder and lightning, the floating of metal objects on water, and besides
sensation, various matters of botany and zoology.

Inescapable Motion

But there is one other point, more general and more important than these many particularities. Whatever be said of the reality of sensory qualities, their origin through combinations of mechanical variations requires motion. The atoms must move. And how can motion be explained? By Love and Hate? Or by Mind? On this point Democritus is sure that the previous pluralists have wandered astray. Parmenides had shown that the universe cannot be explained on the basis of one body; therefore it must be explained on the basis of many bodies; but the introduction of Love and Hate, or Mind, is an appeal to something that is not corporeal. This goes beyond the limits of the basic principle. Now, if it could be shown that the universe cannot be explained on the basis of many bodies, possibly one could talk of something noncorporeal. Or, perhaps one would be forced to say that the universe is inexplicable. For what an incorporeal reality might be is completely unimaginable. But it will be premature to talk about the failure of corporeal pluralism, if Democritus can succeed within its conceptual limits. All that remains to be done is to show the cause of motion. In discussing weight it was said that the atoms individually have no tendency to move. They are like billiard balls on the table. And like billiard balls, if one of them is hit, it moves.

To explain the motion of this atom before us therefore, one need only indicate which atom struck it. Impact is the explanation. But if this atom before us was struck by another atom, what caused this other atom to move? The answer is simple: a third atom. And the fourth atom had previously hit the third. And so on back, forever. But what started motion in the first place? What happened at the beginning of this series? These questions arise only through failure to understand what Democritus is saying. There is no first motion. Motion has always existed. There is an infinity of atoms and through all time some of them have been colliding with others. In this way each particular motion can be explained. Therefore no mysterious moving principle is required. No divine mind directs the universe; no purpose or goal is in view; all things happen by necessity, and the universe is a vast mechanism.

ZENO

But what if motion is impossible? What if this concept is absurd? Because the latter half of the fifth century was one of great philosophical ferment and because the lives of these philosophers overlapped, it is difficult to give a strictly chronological account of these decades. Even though Democritus lived far into the fourth century, it is permissible to conclude this section with a younger man who claimed the last word among the Presocratics. Zeno, the Eleatic, a disciple of Parmenides, notwithstanding the lack of any further positive theory, directly attacks the atomists with remarkable arguments of his own invention. In his attempt to defend the thesis that Being is One, he sought to show that motion is impossible, that sensation is impossible, and that space does not exist. In modern eyes such a program may seem hopeless, but Zeno succeeded at least in getting all subsequent history to face and often to stumble over his arguments.

The first argument against motion comes in the form of a story. Achilles was the track star of antiquity, and the tortoise was not. But what the tortoise lacked in speed, he more than made up in intelligence. Relying therefore on his brilliance, he challenged Achilles to a race. It was in the terms and conditions that the tortoise knew he could get the best of Achilles. These terms were, simply, that the tortoise be given a head start of a certain distance, and that Achilles should not be considered the winner unless he could overtake the tortoise. At the crack of Zeno's pistol the two racers were off. Now, when Achilles by fleetness of foot arrived at the point from which the tortoise started, very obviously the tortoise was no longer there; during the time that had elapsed the tortoise had gone ahead a little bit; there is no denying that it was only a little bit, but there is no denying that the tortoise was ahead. However, the race did not slow up, as we must slow up in order to explain the situation; the runners kept on with their same speeds. Now, when Achilles, fleet of foot, arrived at the point at which the tortoise was when Achilles was at the point from which the tortoise started, very obviously the tortoise was no longer there; during the time that had elapsed the tortoise had gone ahead a little bit; there is no denying that it was only a little bit, but there is no denying that the tortoise was ahead. However, the race did not slow up, as we must slow up in order to explain the situation; the runners kept on with their same speeds. Now, when Achilles, whose fleetness of foot did not equal the tortoise's intelligence, arrived at the point at which the tortoise was when Achilles was at the point where the tortoise was when Achilles was at the point from which the tortoise started, very obviously the tortoise was no longer there. Well, to shorten a long story, every time Achilles got to the point at which the tortoise was, the tortoise was not there. And if Achilles failed to reach the tortoise every time, then there was no time at which the atomistic Achilles overtook his Eleatic rival. The moral of the story, aside from the fact that it is better to be an intelligent tortoise than a stupid athlete, is that the concept of motion leads to absurdity.

That Achilles' defeat lay in the terms the tortoise imposed can be seen from a second argument that divests itself of picturesque trappings and goes straight to the mathematics involved. Instead of athletes, consider a point or an atom, and see what difficulty it would have in trying to move from here to there. Before the atom can cover the entire distance, it must go halfway; and before it could reach the halfway mark, it would have to traverse a quarter of the distance; and before it covered this quarter, it would have to move an eighth. This also is a long story; but the moral is plain. Before the atom could even start from its original position, it would have to exhaust an infinite series. Unfortunately for the concept of motion, an infinite series is inexhaustible. And the atom cannot start. No wonder Achilles could not reach the tortoise: granted that the tortoise could not move, Achilles could not move either; and the tortoise was bright enough to trick Achilles into allowing him to be placed ahead at the beginning.

There is a third argument. It would be incumbent on Democritus to define rest and motion. Is a passenger on a train at rest? Is a man in bed at rest when the earth is moving at eighteen miles a second? Common opinion would answer these questions in the affirmative. This means that a body is at rest when two of its points are fixed against two points of its immediate surroundings. Now, consider the flight of an arrow. At any moment of the arrow's flight its extreme points are coincident with two points of space. That is, at any moment of its flight, it is at rest. And since this is true of any and every moment, it follows that the arrow is always at rest. It never moves. Motion is an absurdity. No doubt we see things move, but even Democritus admits that sensation and sense qualities are not real. And anyway, should not one trust his intelligence rather than his senses?

However, when Democritus deprecates sense qualities, he grants them enough reality to need reducing to atoms in motion. But, replies Zeno, on the atomistic theory, there could be no sensation at all, not even a little bit to reduce. For, suppose one stood on the rock-bound coast of Attica or Maine. A storm at sea sends waves crashing against the rocks, and their thunder is tremendous. But is it? If one were standing there as a tiny bit of spray, a mere atom of a wave, hit the shore, how much sound would be heard? Even such relatively gigantic things as a bit of chalk dust make no noise when they drop to the floor. A speck of mist would therefore not be heard at all; there would be no noise. And to this zero of sound, the next speck of spray adds its zero. Again to shorten a long story, the addition of zeroes forever gives zero; and yet the wave is the addition of the atoms of water. Democritus' theory therefore, if consistently applied, renders absurd the reduction of sensory qualities to quantitative determinations because the qualities, such as sound, could not have been produced in the first place.

Then too, space, in which the atoms are and move, is an impossible concept. If there must be a space for the atoms to exist in, then, if space exists, it too must exist in something — a space prime. And if space prime exists, it must exist in space double prime; and there comes another of these long stories. The best method of shortening such long stories as these is never to begin. Therefore space does not exist.

And lastly, the concept of a pluralistic universe is self-contradictory. If Being were many, it would have to be both infinitely small and infinitely great. It would have to be infinitely small because every plurality is a collection of unities; but true unity is indivisible; and what is indivisible has no magnitude; therefore a plurality of indivisible or unextended particles, when added together, would produce a world of no extension. But if the world and its parts are to have extension, each part must be separated from the next part; but the part that does the separating must itself be separated by another part, and so on, with the result that the world is infinitely great. In fact, since this argument can be applied to each atom, each atom is both infinitely small and infinitely great. And what more absurd conclusion could be derived from any theory.

Too often these arguments produce a laugh and no further thought; but they are not just funny stories. They not only point to the delicate problems of infinity and continuity, matters that still tax the abilities of philosophers, physicists, and mathematicians; but also it may very well be maintained that these absurd conclusions are in fact validly drawn from the premises of pluralism. In this case, Eleaticism has had the last word, and Presocratic philosophy has reached its end.

CHAPTER 2

The Sophists, Socrates, and Plato

THE RISE OF SKEPTICISM

The course of scientific or cosmological thought, now traced to the end of the fifth century, seems to have a clear-cut outcome. Unless the Eleatic rationalism be judged acceptable, the early attempt to understand the universe in terms of one body was a failure. The next group of philosophers, trusting their senses rather than their reason, attempted to explain the world in terms of many bodies; but Zeno was able to expose this as an even greater failure. Now, if one body cannot explain the universe, and if many bodies cannot explain the universe, and if sensation and motion cannot be abandoned, it follows rigorously that the universe cannot be explained. All attempts to arrive at truth have been proved to be failures, and therefore truth is unattainable.

Mathematical Irrationality

In the meantime the Pythagoreans had stumbled over a factor that enforced the same conclusion, for mathematics as well as physics had arrived at absurdities. Plato transmits the information in his dialogue *Meno*, relating how Socrates questioned a slave boy about a square drawn in the sand. The square is two units on a side, and when Socrates connects the mid-points of the opposite sides, the boy easily sees that such a square contains four square units. Since squares can be drawn of any size, it is quite possible to have a square exactly twice the area of the original square; that is, there can be a square containing eight square units. After eliciting this information from the boy, Socrates asks him how long must be the side of a square twice the area of the original square. The boy answers freely to the effect that if the square is twice the area, the side must be twice as long. When Socrates extends the sides of the original square to twice their length, the boy sees that there are not just eight but sixteen square units. The new square is not twice, but four times the size of the first square.

At this the boy corrects his answer: if doubling the side of the first square to four units makes it too long, the answer must be less than four. Since the first square was two inches on a side, the answer must be more than two. Now, obviously, the only number more than two and less than four is three. What could be simpler! But unfortunately a square three units on a side is more than twice the size of the original square. This is unfortunate, not for the slave boy, but for Pythagorean number theory that had specified the numbers as one, two, three, four, and so on. Socrates by skillful questioning succeeds in showing the boy that a square of eight square units can be constructed on the diagonal of a square of four square units. That is, the length sought for is the square root of eight. But who ever heard of a number called the square root of eight? There can be no such number — a number more than two and less than three! Yet there has to be such a number, for a square of such size is possible. It is a number, a number as exact as any number can be, and yet it is a number that cannot be measured by the unit. Three is precisely three units, and four four. But the square root of eight is not even two and a half. Expressible by no fraction at all, it seems to have no relation to unity. And how can mathematics be developed if the concept of unity be thus violated? It seems indeed that mathematics as well as physics has been shown to be impossible.

This discovery of incommensurable exact quantities spells the defeat of atomism in mathematics as Zeno's arguments did in physics. But while the mathematics involved is simple, the notion of incommensurables still puzzles people. Such a matter as calendar reform flounders on incommensurables. If a given day (the rotation of the earth) and a given month (the revolution of the moon) and a given year (the revolution of the earth), like three runners on a track, should start off at the same instant, then never again throughout all time would the runners come abreast of each other: a day, a month, and a year would never again begin at the same moment, for there is no unit which evenly divides these lengths or speeds. This discovery of incommensurables by the Pythagoreans threw arithmetic and geometry into confusion. Irrational numbers? Mathematics must be insane and knowledge impossible.

History and Politics

Such is the neat, streamlined development of science and mathematics, here traced without reference to social and political conditions that were also causing upheavals in Greece. Science is not the whole of philosophy. In certain epochs philosophy seems to be able to limit its interests, to retire to an ivory tower, and let the rest of the world go by. But a genuine philosophy that tries to understand all phases of the world cannot forever avoid moral and political problems. In times of upheaval, when the whole edifice of civilization caves in, philosophers, or if not philosophers, politicians are called upon to solve all problems at once. The old-fashioned virtues, the time-tested procedures, the dependable patterns of living, the ideals and spiritual values of a society, all collapse together; and until someone can rebuild, there is chaos. So it happens that the cultural conditions of the fifth century reinforced the skeptical conclusions of mathematics and physics.

The more Greek history one has in mind, the better can one understand how the rise of Sophism was necessitated. A few facts, all too few, must suffice to stimulate further study. In the Homeric period the governments of the Greek states were combinations in which the executive power was in the hands of kings, who were advised by a council, and these submitted their judgment to an assembly of citizens. Greek history then is to be partially described as a struggle among these three groups for more power. In Macedonia the power of the kings increased, and centuries later when the southern states had ruined themselves, Philip and Alexander were ready to conquer the world. In Sparta something like the original form of government was stabilized in a military state that reduced its western neighbors to slavery and ruled them cruelly. In Athens, however, a long struggle between the aristocracy and the lower classes of free citizens may be said to have resulted in victory for democracy and ruin for the state. Naturally, economic forces played a part in this struggle. The extension of commerce and colonization, the invention of money to replace barter, the mortgaging of farms at a high interest rate, and the enslavement of debtors led to a demand for better government. Draco (621 B.C.) and Solon (592 B.C.) attempted to meet the situation, and one result was the inaugurating of fixed written laws. Draco's laws may have been severe, but the establishment of written laws was an immense advantage. Solon extended some civil rights to the lower classes of citizens and prepared for the later development of democracy.

Toward the east in the latter half of the sixth century, the power of Persia appeared as Cyrus took over the Greek cities in Asia Minor. When they revolted, Athens sent them aid, and at their defeat Darius resolved to punish Athens. In the first half of the fifth century two Persian expeditions were sent against Athens, with the military result that Persia was decisively defeated. But there were other results. To defeat the Persians, Athens had formed a league of Greek states and levied taxes on them for the common defense. By the end of the wars these states found themselves in the form of an Athenian empire. Athens had led in war; now she would lead in peace as a democratic, imperialistic, naval power. Thucydides opposed both the democracy and the imperialism in favor of the conservative, isolationist aristocracy. But Pericles' grandiose plans to establish colonies, to beautify the city, to build a navy, and to submerge the nobility, all paid for by taxes collected from the subjugated states, won the applause of the masses. Eventually the oppressed cities appealed to Sparta for help, and the Peloponnesian war began in 431 to end with Athens' defeat in 404.

War, taxes, economics, legislation, public works, party rivalry, all mean intense political activity. And it is on the political and moral issues of this ferment that philosophy, heretofore so scientifically aloof, impinges. As the old aristocratic virtues of a stable society disintegrated under the pressure of changing conditions, and as changing conditions opened opportunities to those who wished to fish in troubled waters, all the accepted standards had to be reappraised. If laws are not divinely given or honored by immemorial custom, but are the changing products of democratic procedure by which forceful leaders work toward chosen ends, there is nothing sacred about them, and, it would seem, they need not be obeyed.

Thrasymachus, whose views are given in the first book of Plato's *Republic*, held that laws are the devices of a few, strong rulers to exploit the masses. If some of the legislation seems to benefit the people, it is similar to the shepherd's fattening the sheep for slaughter.

Callicles' theory, seemingly so different, and reported in the *Gorgias*, was that laws are made by the mediocre masses to hold the superior strong men in check. But both theories produce the same results. If law is the will of tyrants and dictators, they are justified in their irresponsible course; and if law is the fearful and envious attempt of the mediocre to restrain the better and more intelligent, these latter are thereby invited to throw off the ignominy of such despicable restraints.

Law, both civil enactments and moral law, had in the earlier days been considered "natural." People did not question the law's authority; they took it for granted. But democratic politics with its sudden and frequent changes in the cities' constitutions undermined the notion of the law's sacredness, as similarly contact with the Persians showed the Greeks a different set of social customs and led to a questioning of morality. Instead of thinking of law as natural, people began to think of it as conventional; law is only the arbitrary enactment of shifting majorities in the assemblies. Moral law would likewise be the conventional but equally arbitrary and uncritical habits of society. But if law is arbitrary rather than natural, universal, and rational, where is the compulsion to obey civil law or to honor moral custom? The tragedies of the theater, based as they were on conflicts among the traditional virtues, increased the popular confusion; and in the welter of argumentation the common mind lost its way. Ambition and lust for power did the rest.

The Educators

In these circumstances there appeared confident educators who claimed to teach ambitious young men virtue: not the old virtue, but the new — the virtue or power to succeed in the business of life. These men were not interested in natural science, nor (with the exception of Protagoras and Gorgias) in the logical and epistemological problems it raised; rather they were the modern counterparts of the wise old poets who had taught the people the sound, somewhat naïve maxims of popular wisdom. The new teachers were also wise men: they called themselves Sophists. Their wisdom, however, was not a matter of old-fashioned adages and dignified, stuffy advice fit only for a farmer's almanac; it was up-to-date and met the needs of the new day. Social effectiveness and an integrated personality was their ideal. What the young man needed was vocational training. The Sophists could instruct aspiring politicians in the tricks of the trade, the devices of oratory, the knack of swaying audiences, the secrets of gaining votes, and how to make the worse appear the better argument. Education was their business, progressive education, education for citizenship. The study of nature, dignified by the attention of impractical philosophers, had neglected life, the actual life of the city. Stars and atoms are equally remote from democratic struggle. Know then thyself; presume not God to scan; the proper study of mankind is man. Man is the measure of all things: man, not as a cold, bare, futile intellect, but as an active, living will. Life is a matter of willing a goal, and success is the standard of wisdom.

In search of students to whom to give instruction, most of the Sophists traveled from city to city. Plato later complained that this showed a lack of civic responsibility. The Sophists also boasted of how much money they made in fees; and this too was a scandal to the aristocratic tradition. But there was one "Sophist" who, though he neither traveled nor accepted fees, was considered worse than all the others. The others gave understandable lessons: anyone with a modicum of intelligence could learn how to confuse an opponent, how to change the subject when in a tight place, how to construct a pleasing speech. Moreover, even if they were sometimes agnostic with regard to the gods, they were entirely self-confident in their own line. They may have taught young politicians how to confuse their opponents; but they did not confuse the young politicians. This other "Sophist," however, lacked all self-confidence; he never knew anything; and instead of answering all questions, he only asked them. His sole aim in life, so it seemed, was to confuse those who talked with him. Now, this was hardly cricket. The voting public is fair game; but it is downright impolite to badger your friends in the market place. And Socrates did nothing else.

Plato heard these conversations in which Socrates punctured the pride of the democratic politicians, with the result that when Plato was ready to write, he used a dialogue form in which Socrates had the leading role.[1] Although a few scholars disagree, there will be no harm in assuming that the early simple dialogues give us a fair picture of Socrates, while in the later and more elaborate dialogues Socrates has become the mouthpiece for Plato's own philosophy.[2]

KNOWLEDGE AND MORALITY

One of the earliest and least polished dialogues, the Minos, discusses the subject of Law. From a philosophic standpoint it is rather elementary, but this turns out to be an advantage because it discloses certain Socratic ideas that Plato was later to utilize on a large scale.

Socrates asks an unnamed companion what is Law. The first vague answer is that law is what is customarily accepted as lawful. Socrates then draws an analogy between law and the senses: sight is not the things seen, nor is hearing the sounds heard; similarly law should not be the things customarily accepted, but a power for accepting such things, a power of discovering the lawful. Apparently the companion thinks that the power for discovering the lawful must be the state, and he next defines law as the positive enactments of the assemblies. That is, law is the state's opinion.

At this Socrates makes use of a line of argument that was from then on to be a mainstay of the Platonic philosophy: the wise are wise because of wisdom — wisdom is something they have that makes them wise; similarly, the just are just by reason of justice — justice

---

[1] Socrates was executed in 399 B.C. Plato's dates are 427–347.

[2] Werner Jaeger, *Paideia* (Oxford University Press, 1939), Vol. II, p. 96, writes, "When he wrote the first words of his Socratic dialogue, he knew the whole of which it was to be a part." Surely this is extreme.

is some real existing entity that makes these people just; therefore law must also be some reality which would be the cause of lawfulness.

Since wisdom and justice and law are noble and good, and since the positive decrees of states are often evil, it follows that these decrees cannot be law; there must be some resident quality in the good decrees to make them lawful, a quality absent from the evil decrees. Positive enactments or traditional customs obviously vary from time to time and from place to place. The Athenians do not offer human sacrifices, but the Carthaginians account it holy and legal. Even in Athens the burial customs have changed from what they were in earlier generations. These changes and disagreements show that people have not discovered the reality. People do not change their opinions as to the fact that just things are just, or that heavier things weigh more, and that base things are not noble. These opinions are held everywhere, always, by everybody. But changing opinion shows that the reality has not been grasped.

Therefore there ought to be a science of jurisprudence (as there is a science of geometry), with experts whose opinions do not change. As a farmer is an authority on farming, the statesman or king is an authority on law. Such an expert statesman was Minos of Crete, and we Athenians, Socrates concludes, should be ashamed not to know the benefits which a King can provide not merely for the bodies but also for the souls of his subjects.

In this very early dialogue there are at least three themes that Plato makes great use of. First, ethics is now a subject for philosophic study. This is not to say that the Presocratics never gave any thought to ethics, but it is true that they gave it little systematic thought. Second, there is the hint of a new kind of reality: justice and law, and other things to be discussed in other dialogues. And third, both government and personal conduct should be controlled by knowledge rather than by the arbitrary volition of a democratic assembly or of a dictator. But just here is the rub. Knowledge still seems to be impossible.

Lesser Hippias

The early Socratic dialogues do not solve the problem of knowl-edge, but for the first time in Greek thought they examine with great care the relation of knowledge to ethics. And the examination leads to surprising results. One of the most famous of these little dialogues is *Lesser Hippias*. Hippias, a confident Sophist, ready to teach anybody anything, is like his modern counterpart who has had all the courses in Education but has never bothered much with the content material. Socrates, poor man, not only is completely ignorant, but also he is cursed with queer ideas: he thinks that anyone who does wrong willfully and designedly is a better man than one who does wrong involuntarily. For example, the wily Odysseus who engaged in deliberate deception and never intended to keep his promise was a better man than the straightforward Achilles who went back on his petulant threat to desert the army. Hippias defends common opinion and points out that the laws punish the willful wrongdoer more severely than the involuntary offender.

Then Socrates by a series of questions forces Hippias to admit that in the world of sports the voluntary imperfection can be found only in the better athlete. A sprinter who voluntarily runs slowly is a better sprinter than a man who cannot help running slowly. A wrestler who permits himself to be thrown is a better wrestler than the victim who is thrown against his will. The same is true in intellectual pursuits also. The accountant who can voluntarily add up the figures incorrectly is a better accountant than the man who gets the wrong answer involuntarily. In fact this latter might get the right answer involuntarily and not know it. Or, to use a modern illustration, a college professor is safe in promising an A to any student who gets zero on a true-false quiz. The student who can get zero voluntarily is obviously the better student. And if this line of reasoning carries through all the other phases of activity, "then he who willingly does wrong and commits shameful and unjust acts, Hippias, if there be such a man, would be no other than the good man." Hippias stubbornly refuses to make the inference, but he can give no reason for his refusal. He simply says, "I cannot agree with you on that, Socrates." Then Socrates concludes, "Nor I with myself, Hippias, . . . but I wander up and down these matters and they never seem the same to me; but that I or any other ordinary man should be confused is not surprising; but if you wise men (sophists) are confused, that is most unfortunate for all of us."

This sort of conversation was well calculated to earn for Socrates the reputation of being the worst of the Sophists and the great corrupter of Athenian youth. His conduct is no example of how to make friends and influence people in your own favor. No wonder he came to a sad end. Superior intelligence always provokes egalitarian democrats. And Socrates was superior; despite his ironic admission of confusion, he was never so confused as was Hippias and those whom Hippias educated so confidently.

The key to the dialogue, found in the quotation above, is the words, "if there be such a man." This phrase is the veil that hides deep convictions, for Socrates is very certain that there cannot be such a man. Let Thrasymachus and Callicles hold that morality is only a social convention to be disregarded by those who wish to be successful; Socrates and Plato will try to prove that justice is intrinsically good and that the victim of injustice is less miserable than the perpetrator. Ambitious politicians try to appear just before the public so as to deceive them; but however much ambitious politicians prefer the appearance of justice to its reality, no one prefers the mere appearance of good to what is really good. Who would choose the appearance of health with a real case of smallpox rather than an appearance of smallpox with actual good health? Everyone wants what is really good. From this it follows that when anyone does not obtain the good, it must be by reason of ignorance. If he knew what the good is, he would get it. Perhaps the man who can commit the worst crime voluntarily is the best man; but though he can, he will not, for he knows that injustice is not really good. The voluntary wrongdoer does not exist. Ignorance then is the cause of crime, and knowledge insures virtue. Men need to be taught. But unfortunately for the Greeks the teachers were long on Education but short on knowledge and clear thought.

SOCRATES AND PROTAGORAS

The ridiculous position of the Sophists is skillfully portrayed in the last, the greatest, and the most artistic of the Socratic dialogues, the *Protagoras*. The scene opens in the very early morning with a young man, Hippocrates, pounding on Socrates' door to tell him that Protagoras is in town. Hippocrates has never seen or heard Protagoras, but he wants to study under him. Socrates, restraining the young man's exuberance and delaying until Protagoras has had time to get out of bed, inquires what Hippocrates hopes to learn. If he had wished to study under his namesake, Hippocrates of Cos, he would have learned medicine and would have become a physician. If he had wanted Phidias as a teacher, he would have studied art and become a sculptor. Now, Protagoras is a Sophist; does that mean that Hippocrates wants to become a Sophist? At this suggestion Hippocrates is taken aback, for he would be ashamed to be a Sophist; but with Socrates' help he remembers that when he took music lessons, he did not aim to become a professional musician but merely a cultured gentleman. Still, a music teacher teaches music; what does a Sophist teach? When Hippocrates guesses that Sophists teach their pupils how to speak forcefully and persuasively, Socrates points out that the music teacher will teach his pupils how to speak about music, and repeats the question as to what the Sophist will talk about. Hippocrates therefore has to admit that he wants to take a course without knowing what the subject-matter is. This is not only ridiculous, but Socrates warns of its danger also. The disciple of the Sophists must to some extent at least have his character modified by the instruction, and one's character or soul is of all things most important. Hippocrates therefore seems to be aiming to change his character without knowing whether the change will be an improvement or a deterioration. In such a predicament the only thing to do is to ask Protagoras himself what it is that he claims to teach.

Socrates and Hippocrates proceed to the home where Protagoras and several other prominent Sophists are staying. The scene in the cloister and courtyard, vividly portraying the fame and honor of these itinerant teachers, is a triumph of Plato's dramatic and literary ability. After polite introductions and a little ado, the question is put as to what result Hippocrates might expect from becoming Protagoras' disciple. When Protagoras sees that it is not sufficient to say that he will make Hippocrates better, for, as before, he will not make him a better musician, he puts forward the claim to teach civic virtue.

Can Virtue Be Taught?

At this Socrates professes to accept the common Greek opinion that civic virtue cannot be taught. When the Athenians, who of course are supremely wise, are perplexed about questions of medicine or navigation, they do not allow just anyone to speak, but they seek the advice of technicians who have been taught their knowledge. But in the Assembly when the debate concerns public policy, morals, justice, the administration of the State, instead of seeking advice of a technician, they allow anyone to speak. This implies that there are no technicians in civic virtue and that virtue cannot be taught. If indeed virtue could be taught, good fathers would put their sons under competent tutors of virtue, as they put them under competent tutors of music. But Pericles, so successful himself in public life, neither taught his sons personally nor had them taught in this subject by others. They were left to graze at will like sacred oxen and pick up whatever they could by chance. Apparently, virtue cannot be taught.

Protagoras' reply is a long, beautiful, persuasive speech that completely misses the mark. First, he explains why anyone is allowed to speak in the Assembly. Epimetheus, so the myth goes, gave strength, swiftness, and means of protection to the animals in such abundance that there was little left for man. To remedy this misfortune, Prometheus gave man fire and technical skill; but since men had no sense of justice they were constantly engaged in a war of all against all. No cooperation was possible. Then Zeus sent Hermes to give men a sense of justice. Since this was given to all men, anyone and not merely a technician is allowed to speak in the Assembly.

In the second place, and in spite of the fact that all men are innately endowed with a sense of justice, Protagoras declares that virtue can be taught. Natural defects, ugliness, and results of accidents do not subject a man to condemnation; but the lack of qualities he could acquire, does. Since therefore we hold men responsible for the lack of virtue, virtue must be teachable. In fact criminals are punished, not for irrational revenge, but to make them better and to provide a warning to others. This is teaching virtue.

And in the third and last place, not only do fathers teach their sons virtue, but the nurses, tutors, and masters in school teach the child virtue; and all society teaches virtue to adults. That the sons of eminent men are sometimes wicked should occasion no surprise, for the son of a good flutist is not necessarily an expert in music. Each son learns according to his ability. The confusion in common opinion with respect to the teachability of virtue lies in the fact that all this teaching goes on so constantly that it is unperceived. Everybody is a teacher of virtue just as everybody is a teacher of Greek; naturally some teachers are better than others, and I, Protagoras, am one of the best.

Thus the argument opens with Socrates denying and Protagoras affirming that virtue can be taught; if one should read through to the end, it would be discovered that the two men have apparently exchanged their positions, with Socrates asserting and Protagoras denying that virtue can be taught. This humorous touch of Plato's skill depends on the meaning of virtue, and it is the meaning of virtue that makes Protagoras' initial speech an irrelevant answer to Socrates' opening question. Socrates had been using music and navigation as examples of subjects that could be taught. These were definite bodies of knowledge; their technicians or teachers were recognizable; their methods could be explained to any intelligent person. Socrates therefore in his original question was demanding that Protagoras teach virtue as one teaches navigation or geometry. Ethics, if teachable, should be a definite body of knowledge that not only Athenians could learn but that Thracians and Persians and anyone else with enough intelligence to grasp navigation could learn.

But Protagoras could not satisfy the demand. In the first part of his speech, where he speaks of Prometheus and Hermes, he admits Socrates' contention that there are no technicians of virtue as there are of music. Zeus has given all men a sense of justice sufficient to enable them to speak in the Assembly; but whatever sense of music, or navigation, or geometry a man may be born with, he must study with recognized teachers before people will listen to his opinions on these subjects. Yet virtue is teachable, so the last part of the speech insists, for nurses, tutors, and all society are constantly teaching it in the same manner that they teach Greek.

Here is seen more clearly what Protagoras means by virtue. A child is born with the ability to speak, as it were a gift from Zeus; but whether the child speaks Greek or Persian depends on which society he is born into. The ability to speak and the sense of justice may be natural and common to all men; but as the rules of grammar change from place to place so also on this analogy, the particular moral rules depend on the customs of the different societies. In Greek it is right to use a singular verb with a neuter plural subject; in Greek it is right to abandon unwanted babies to die. Socrates, however, is seeking for a system of morals which, like the theorems of geometry or the laws of navigation, does not change, but is natural and common for all men. If virtue should be knowledge, then and only then would it be teachable. Custom is not knowledge, it is a knack; and the claim of a foreign teacher to teach Athenian customs to the Athenians better than the Athenians can, is impertinent.

But what if knowledge is impossible? Obviously, if there is no knowledge, and if a universal moral obligation is a matter of knowledge, it follows that there can be no virtue. Once more the argument is driven to epistemology.

Anticipatory Comment

However, before the problems of epistemology are outlined, a further anticipation of the medieval period may be made. Just as the Presocratic cosmological speculation developed without reference to an Almighty Creator, so too with respect to morality the antithesis between conventional and natural theories was framed without giving thought to a sovereign moral Law-giver. In the dialogue *Euthyphro* the question is raised whether pious acts are pious because the gods like them or whether the gods like them because the acts are pious. Here the blinding power of cultural isolation is seen at its strongest. That the Presocratics should not have anticipated Christian conceptions was to be expected; but that Plato, the greatest philosophic genius of all time, should have been blinded is more remarkable. To be sure, he notes the logical possibility that pious acts are pious because the gods like them; but instead of arguing against such a view, he merely brushes it aside as unworthy of consideration. To his thoroughly Greek mind it seemed obviously absurd. But if the gods like pious acts because the acts are pious, it follows that there is a standard, a norm, or a quality of piety superior to the will of the gods. The existence of such a standard independent of the will of the gods is of course consonant with Greek presuppositions. The Greek gods were limited beings, and since they had not created the universe, it would be incongruent to ascribe to them sovereign legislative power. Even though Plato so brilliantly transcended prior Greek conceptions, as we shall see, he never freed himself from the idea that the personal Maker of the world was subordinate to laws existing independently of him. It follows therefore that the antithesis between conventional morality and natural moral law may be an incomplete disjunction, and that a third possibility may be closer to the truth. In particular since the modern twentieth century widely rejects Platonism as a magnificent but unfortunately deceptive dream and has in very large measure accepted the social theory of morality advanced by Protagoras, it may be useful to remember that one is not forced to accept Platonism in order to defend universal obligation against contemporary humanism, but that the presupposition of a sovereign Law-giver presents an alternative that should not be dismissed without examination.

SOPHISTIC EPISTEMOLOGY

But is knowledge possible? Here there is no third possibility. Even if one wishes to base morality on a Law-giver, one must provide for the possibility of knowledge. And the Sophists, checked by the failures of science and mathematics, excited by the rewards of politics, freed from scruples by the paradoxes of morality, and intoxicated to argumentation by logic, but befuddled as to conclusions, declared that nothing could be known. All alleged knowledge, i.e., every proposition, is composed of a subject and a predicate; but Parmenides had shown that predication is impossible. Although Protagoras could not compare with the noble Parmenides, yet the Parmenidean theme is put in the mouths of Sophists who stand far below the rank of Protagoras. In the *Euthydemus* Plato ridicules the sharp, shallow Sophists who learn their elementary lessons rapidly but who lack all seriousness and profundity. In contrasting their brittle smart-

ness with the earnest purposefulness of Socrates, Plato assigns them
even some Socratic and Platonic themes which we cannot believe he
meant to repudiate. What they do with those themes is pitiful. So
ridiculous is the content of their arguments that the tremendous
importance of the problem of predication can easily be missed and
the dialogue taken merely as an exposé of sophistic chicanery.

Queer Logic

At one point in the dialogue the Sophists dispute the possibility
of telling a lie. To tell a lie means, of course, to tell what is not so;
and to tell the truth is to tell what is. When one tells the thing
about which one is telling, one tells a single thing distinct from
all other things that are; in other words he tells something that is,
not something that is not; and hence he must be telling the truth.
To tell a lie is to tell something that is not. And the things that
are not, cannot be anywhere or in any manner. A man who speaks
is speaking or doing something; and because he cannot do or speak
the non-existent, for in that case he would be doing nothing, it follows that he is speaking things that are, or, in others words, the truth.

The argument with a mixture of broad comedy begins to get hot,
and one of the auditors ventures to contradict the Sophists. At this
they question the possibility of contradiction. Each thing has its own
description, and no one can speak of a thing as it is not. Therefore
if two men speak the same description of a thing, obviously they
are not contradicting each other; if, however, neither of them gives
the description of the thing, just as obviously they cannot be contradicting each other, since in this case, neither of them would have
touched on the subject at all; but then finally, if one of them give
the description of the thing while the other give a description of a
different thing, they cannot contradict each other, for they are not
talking about the same thing. Contradiction therefore is entirely
impossible.

Toward the end of the dialogue comes one of the wildest arguments of all. The situation depends on the fact that Patrocles was
the brother of Socrates by the same mother but not by the same
father. This means that Patrocles was both brother and not-brother.
Similarly the father of Patrocles was Chaeredemus; of Socrates, Soph-

roniscus. Since Sophroniscus is father, and Chaeredemus is other than Sophroniscus, it follows that he is other than father; for if anything other than stone is no stone, anyone other than father is no father. On the other hand, a stone is a stone, always, everywhere. It would follow then that a father would be a father always and everywhere. Accordingly, if Chaeredemus is truly father, he must be the father of fish, puppies, and pigs. Or, conversely, if a dog is a father, and if the dog is the auditor's dog, the dog must be his father.

In the *Euthydemus* and in all the early Socratic dialogues where Plato attacks Sophism, there appear simple problems of logic. Protagoras himself, in the dialogue of the same name, boasts that he is aware of the inconvertibility of the universal affirmative judgment: he had said "all *a* is *b*," and it should not be understood as "all *b* is *a*." That it was a boast indicates the slight development of logic at the time; that it was a Sophist who boasted indicates that some elementary progress had become common knowledge. However, it is not always the Sophists who argue invalidly; sometimes Socrates makes apparent blunders; and we are left to guess whether Socrates also knew no better, or whether we have missed the point, or whether Plato intended to have a little fun with us. Underlying it all is the problem of predication. How can one thing be another? Must it not always be itself? A stone is a stone; and a father is a father; and to recall earlier thoughts, water is water. Then water cannot be fire, a stone cannot be something else, and a father cannot be not-father. The difficulty inherent in this problem for the Greeks becomes clearer when the predominant corporealism or materialism is emphasized. If all reality is corporeal, how indeed can one body be another body which it is not? This difficulty becomes more acute when negative predication is examined. For if we say that a father is not father, are we not in reality denying the existence of the subject? This too was pointed out by Parmenides, and it troubled Plato through most of his life, until in a late dialogue he gave it a solution. But, first, complete justice has not yet been done to the Sophists. In the *Euthydemus* Plato makes the Sophists look silly; in the *Protagoras* they are pictured as confused; but in the *Theaetetus* Plato acknowledges that Protagoras, whatever faults he may have had —

and Plato intends to expose those faults — nevertheless had a well developed theory that merited a thoroughgoing analysis.

THE MAN–MEASURE THEORY

Unlike some of the other Sophists, whose inspiration derived from Parmenides, Protagoras had adopted the viewpoint of Heraclitus. One of his primary assumptions was universal flux: all things are constantly changing. Not wishing to relinquish the word *knowledge*, Protagoras sought for something in the universal flux to which it could be applied; and he plausibly identified it with perception. Now, when constantly changing perception is taken to be knowledge, one is forced to accept the *Homo Mensura* or Man-Measure theory: man, every man, "is the measure of all things, of the existence of the things that are and the nonexistence of the things that are not."

No One Can Be Mistaken

The example that Plato attributes to Protagoras in the *Theaetetus* is the wind. When the wind blows, it will be perceived as chilly by a man with a fever, but to another man the same wind will appear exhilarating. This example, because it stands for all cases of sensory perception — the perception of brown or red, bitter or sweet, rough or smooth, shrill or soft — raises the problem of the relation of attributes or qualities to the real things in which they inhere; or, one may say, it raises the question whether qualities inhere in real things at all. If the wind appears chilly to one man and exhilarating to another, what quality belongs to the wind in itself? This is a puzzling question and it will be discussed from several points of view by the later philosophers. At the moment Protagoras wishes to say no more, and no less, than that perception is infallible. No one can be mistaken. This not only ties in with the impossibility of contradicting anyone, as was argued in the *Euthydemus*, but in itself it is highly plausible. Is it not true that the man with the fever was really chilled by the wind? Surely he was not mistaken about that. And if oysters and olives taste delicious to me, while you do not like them at all, can either of us be in error? Likewise if I see that grass is green, but you who are an artist see it purple, do we not both see what we see? And lastly, is it not pleasant, tolerant, and democratic to adopt a theory by which all people are equally infallible?

Everyone Is Mistaken

But another interpretation of the phenomena is possible. Plato suggests that the previous construction was what Protagoras told his audiences, flattering them by the conclusion that they could not be mistaken, but that he had a secret doctrine for his intimate disciples. The reference to secrecy may be a hint that this second interpretation goes beyond what the historical Protagoras actually said.

At any rate, it does not go beyond the logic of the matter. Suppose that some one in opposition to Heraclitus and Anaxagoras should deny the possibility of contrary qualities inhering in the same object. The wind, really and in itself, cannot be both agreeable and disagreeable. A coin, no matter how it may appear from different perspectives, could not itself be both circular and oval. Grass would appear green merely to me and purple merely to the artist. The wind would seem chilly to the man with the fever. But the wind itself would not be chilly. Did a wind ever put on an overcoat because it was chilly? Chilly and exhilarating, green and purple, oval and circular are effects produced in the sensitive organism; they are not qualities existing objectively in things. There are certain motions outside the sense organ which collide or combine with other motions originating within the organ, and this combination is the perceived quality. Obviously therefore the combination formed by my sense organ with the external motions and the combination formed by your sense organ and the external motions cannot be the same combination. This explains why the wind is chilly to one man and the grass purple to another. Two men cannot have the same sensation, for the sensation exists solely in the organ sensing. For this very reason therefore the quality cannot belong to some external thing. The wind itself is not chilly. The quality exists only in the percipient.

But whereas the first interpretation made everybody democratically infallible, this understanding of the matter shows that everyone is democratically in error. No predication is true. The wind is not chilly; the grass is not green; the coin is not round. In fact, the wind is not anything; the wind itself is not; that is, the wind does not exist. Nothing exists.

Now, this conclusion is not so far-fetched as it may at first seem. How could anything exist if everything is constantly changing? Though the wind is not, yet the wind becomes and becomes chilly if I perceive it so. I too become and do not exist. Persons as well as things do not exist in and of themselves: they too become, and they come to be only in relation. Therefore one man's sensation is on a level with another's; each man is the sole judge of his own perceptions. Do you know how oysters or rollmops taste to me? Have you ever felt my toothache?[3] Can you judge my sensation? No, I am the sole judge of my condition and you are the sole judge of yours. Therefore, because all things change, man is the measure and knowledge is perception.

Perception, for Protagoras, is a word of greater extent than the common meaning of sensation. In addition to the five ordinary senses, Protagoras includes not only the perceptions of pleasure, pain, heat, desire, fear, and innumerable others, but also opinions of all sorts. These too must be explained on the same principles. If the sensory qualities of green and oval are relative; concepts also, such as equality, more and less, justice and morality, are as they appear to a man and no one can dispute his perception. Neither in politics nor in medicine is the truth of an opinion of any importance, for all opinions are equally true, each to him who holds it.

Objections and Answers

When a student, ancient or modern, first reads a strange theory, various objections to it come easily to his mind. A second reading of the book may reveal that the objections do not apply. Or, should he have the opportunity of discussing these with the author of the theory, the answers will give the student a deeper understanding of what was meant. In the dialogues Plato gives us the illusion of conversing with such authors. Therefore certain criticisms are raised against the Man-Measure theory, not because they refute it but because they open a fuller explanation of Protagoras' meaning.

For example, men have dreams, and when insane they have hal-

[3] This toothache recurs in the final chapter on John Dewey, p. 522.

lucinations; surely these are not knowledge. To this Protagoras can reply that the situation is not essentially different from that in which one man perceives green and another purple. The point is that there are two men, and the insane man perceives his hallucination just as truly as the artist perceives his purple. Quite naturally different men have different perceptions; and the more different the men are, the greater difference among the perceptions. Dreams and hallucinations therefore do not disprove the theory.

Another objection occurs when an illiterate person sees a printed page or when one hears a foreign language. If knowledge is perception, should we say that since he hears the foreign language or sees the print, he therefore understands and knows; or should we say that since he obviously does not understand, he does not see or hear? This objection is not hard to answer. The person in question knows the print he sees or the sounds he hears; but all that grammarians have said about the language, he does not know because he has never heard lessons in grammar. Had he once perceived grammar, he would have understood this also. This answer, however, provokes another question. If to know is identical with to see, and if the objects of memory are not present and seen, then no one knows what he remembers. Or, if men know what they remember, though they do not see it, it follows, since seeing is knowing, that they both know and do not know the same thing. Yet, how can anyone both know and not know the same thing?

Although this objection may seem impressive to those who have not considered sufficiently, Protagoras solved the puzzle easily enough. In the first place, seeing is indeed knowing; but so is all other perception. The theory does not limit knowledge to sensation. Remembering is a kind of perception too. And from this one may conclude that there is no great difficulty in both knowing and not knowing the same thing. Within the limits of sensation, one can know and not know, see and not see, the same thing at the same time by simply shutting one eye. Outside of the limits of sensation, the case is somewhat more complicated. It still remains true that one can both know and not know the same thing: that is, he can know Protagoras whom he has not seen for several years because he remembers him, but at the same time he does not know Protagoras because he does not see him now. Further, it should also be noticed that the memory, the memory image, which is a present experience, is not the same thing as the past experience, the sensation, which was the image of Protagoras when we saw him. Still further, the ground can be cut from under all such superficial objections by making clear that just as the wind is not but becomes, so too percipients are not but become. The person who saw Protagoras some time ago is not the same person who sees Protagoras today. Persons like things are constantly changing, and any objection based on the notion that the same person cannot do thus or so fails because no person remains the same for two consecutive moments.

There is, however, another objection. If a "person" is but a stream of consciousness and never remains the same, and if every perception, memory, opinion is infallibly true, at the moment it occurs and to the momentary person who has it, then why should anyone pay tuition fees to Protagoras? He already knows as much as Protagoras and can learn nothing more true than he already knows. Since this view puts all men on a level, why should Protagoras be thought wiser than other people or be called a Sophist?

In answer to this objection, and the objection surely seems to have weight, Protagoras gives the final statement of his philosophy. He reasserts that every man is the measure of what is and what is not; but far from eradicating all differences and putting all men on a level, this view maintains that there are great differences among men. One man thinks the wind is chilling, another that it is invigorating, and so on. Now, the chilling wind is a bad appearance, as the man himself will admit, and a physician is wise and deserves his fee because he can make good things appear to the man who is suffering from bad appearances. In education too, a fine teacher, although he can never make a pupil who previously thought what is false think what is true—for it is not possible to think what is false—can nonetheless substitute in the pupil's mind better thoughts than the ones he at first entertained. And the pupil, presumably, will admit that the new thoughts are better after he has experienced them. Similarly a wise politician, though he can never advocate policies more just or right than those the community at first holds —for all policies are equally just—can nonetheless persuade the citizens of better or more advantageous opinions. And in this way some men are wiser than others and are worthy of their fees, even though no one ever thinks falsely and everyone is a measure.

The Protagorean philosophy has not been confined to antiquity, but has again become prominent in contemporary thought; and the last chapter of this history will examine the matter once more. At that time the student should review Plato's refutation of the ancient version.

Plato's Reply

If man is the measure of all things, then every opinion is true; in fact Protagoras says explicitly that whatever seems true to anyone is true for him to whom it seems so. Now, everyone, even Protagoras, believes that some men are wiser than others; but the difference between most men and Protagoras lies in the fact that most men believe the wise are wise on account of the truth of their opinions, and the unwise are ignorant on account of their false opinions. But if all opinions are true, as Protagoras says, and if the majority holds the opinion just now attributed to them, then this opinion — namely, that some beliefs are false — is true; and thus Protagoras is convicted of contradicting himself. What is more embarrassing: most people believe that Protagoras' theory is false, and since he admits that their opinion is true, he admits that his theory is false. And further, while Protagoras admits that their opinion is true, even if only for them, they do not admit that his theory is true even for him; and if all opinions are true, then Protagoras' theory is not true even for him.

The next step in Plato's refutation of Protagoras concerns the physician or statesman who changes bad appearances to good. Let it be granted that one medical theory and one political proposal is as true or just as any other. Yet where there is a prediction that one treatment will produce healthy appearances, or that one policy will produce prosperity, who could assert that the State's enactment of the policy will certainly make it advantageous. If opinion made it so, then everyone would always be healthy and prosperous. No plan could ever fail. And certainly Protagoras himself thought that his procedures for making young men better were truer predictions of the future than the claims of less distinguished teachers. In this he assumes that he is a more reliable measure than anyone else.

These two steps, the logical absurdity of Protagoras' admitting the falsity of his thesis and the *ad hominem* reply based on Protagoras' claim to greater accuracy in prediction, may be taken as a sufficient refutation not only of the ancient doctrine that all opinions are true but also of all the modern dilettante relativism that dismisses important controversies as merely a matter of opinion. Superficial minds still think that a proposition can be divested of its authoritative truthfulness and reduced to the innocuous level of all nondescript beliefs by castigating it as somebody's opinion. And, of course, in a democratic society, one opinion is as good as any other.

But there was a second way in which Protagoras explained his theory. To his intimate disciples he said that all opinions are false, and this interpretation was based on the Heraclitean doctrine of universal flux. Plato caustically describes the disciples of Heraclitus as faithful to their own theories and therefore in perpetual motion. They can never stand still long enough to hear an objection, to answer a question, or engage in orderly debate. They take care to leave nothing settled either in discourse or in their own minds for fear of admitting something stationary in the universe. This description itself contains the main idea of the refutation of Heracliteanism, but Plato is willing to dignify the discussion with particular detail.

First, Plato distinguishes between motion from one place to another and motion in the sense of qualitative change. The Heracliteans must be understood as asserting that all things are constantly changing in both these ways, and any others if such there be; for otherwise something, perchance a quality, would remain fixed and stable. From this it follows that white things, hot things, chilling winds and green grass do not remain white, hot, chilling, or green. Since the qualities are constantly changing it is impossible to name them accurately. The grass is not green nor is it any other fixed color. It is impossible to name any quality or state. Then what shall be said of seeing and hearing? Since they too cannot remain the same, the condition of hearing is no more hearing than it is not-hearing. Seeing is equally not-seeing. Therefore, perception is also non-perception and knowledge is not-knowledge. If all things are in change, any answer can be given to any question: it is so and it is not so.

To understand the development of Plato's thought, one must see that Plato is not trying to prove that sense qualities remain fixed or that perception is not constantly changing. As a matter of fact Plato accepts the view that the physical world is in continual flux. The point Plato is making, and he is making it for a later application, is that if the changing physical world is all of reality, then knowledge is impossible. There must be something that remains fixed, even if that something is not green, hot, or visible at all.

Plato's Further Reply

Underlying some of Protagoras' assertions was the notion that a man could at the same time both see and not see if one eye were open and the other shut. This is consistent enough with Protagoras' general philosophy, but it involves a view of man which Plato wishes to show is untrue.

What Protagoras calls a man reminds Plato of the wooden horse of Troy. In it several Greek soldiers were hidden, and one of them may have looked out of the horse's left eye, while another could see through the hole in the horse's right ear. When the latter soldier was not looking, Protagoras could say the horse saw and knew in the left eye but at the same time did not see and know through the right ear. Plato argues that the horse really did not see at all. Similarly with man: if it is the eye that sees and the ear that hears, then the man neither sees nor hears — he is nothing but a wooden horse with senses scattered here and there.

For Plato it is the man himself who sees and hears. He sees through his eyes, or even through one eye; and he hears through his ears; but it is the man himself and not the sense organ that sees, senses, or knows. In other words, in addition to the organs or instruments, there is something else, a knowing subject, a man, a soul, a mind. And it is this coordinating mind that completely escaped Protagoras' attention.

To press this important point still further: it is clear that the eye is not the organ or instrument of hearing, nor is the ear the organ of seeing. But if the eye cannot sense sound and the ear cannot grasp color, what organ is it, if any, that grasps a thought about both color and sound at once? There are such thoughts. For example, both seeing and hearing are sensations; they both use organs; they both exist. Existence is a quality that is common both to color and sound. What organ, then, if any, grasps the thought of existence? And there are the notions of difference and sameness; there are the thoughts of odd and even, unity and number. No part of the body, i.e., no organ, grasps these thoughts; but the mind itself is its own instrument for contemplating these common terms that apply to everything. These items therefore clearly show that knowledge cannot be restricted to or equated with perception. The hardness of something hard and the softness of something soft is perceived by the mind through the sense of touch; but the existence of something hard and its contrariety with or difference from something soft are notions of the mind that do not come through perception but through reflection on the perceptions. Perception begins with birth, and is found in men and animals, but reflection requires a long process of education. Unless this process reaches existence, it does not reach truth; and since perception cannot reach existence—on this point both Plato and Protagoras agree—it is clear that it never reaches truth. But if it never reaches truth, then the theory itself is not true.

Such is the fate of all relativistic theories, ancient or modern. They are self-destructive because self-contradictory. When a pragmatist asserts the impossibility of attaining the absolute, when an instrumentalist with his emphasis on change deplores the dogmatism of unchanging truth, or when a Freudian dismisses conscious reasoning as hypocritical rationalization, he means to except his own view. It is absolutely true that we miss the absolute; it is a fixed truth that nothing is fixed; it is validly reasoned that reasoning is hypocrisy. Objections to dogmatism are always dogmatic, and relativisms are always asserted absolutely. For this reason the Man-Measure theory must be rejected, and knowledge is shown to be other than perception.

Incorporeal Reality

The entire Presocratic development, with the exception of the Eleatic philosophy, falls with the Man-Measure theory. Sophism, perhaps even more clearly than Zeno, showed that pluralism had incorrectly located the cause of earlier difficulties. The pluralists had thought that the trouble with corporeal monism lay in the monism; therefore they developed corporeal pluralism; but now that this too is discredited, it is clear that the trouble lay in the corporealism and its attendant sensationism or perceptionism. If all existing things are sensory objects, the universe is subject to universal flux and knowledge is impossible.

It was at this point that Plato had the exceptional brilliance to make a very simple logical deduction. By contradicting and interchanging the premise and conclusion, it follows that if knowledge is possible, there must exist unchangeable, suprasensible realities. Throughout most of his dialogues Plato is trying to tell what these incorporeal realities are and how we know them. There is no one dialogue in which the theory is systematically explained, but rather it is assumed, referred to, and used to solve the more practical problems of politics, ethics, or life in general. To preserve some of the original Platonic flavor, though nothing takes the place of reading the dialogues themselves with their incidental remarks and acute reflections on related subjects, the argument will be developed by following a summary of the *Phaedo*.

THE PHAEDO

On the morning of Socrates' execution, as his friends come to visit him in jail, he is rubbing his legs where the chains, just now removed, have chafed them. This gives opportunity for some remarks on pleasure and pain, and the approaching execution turns the conversation toward death and the immortality of the soul.

The Care of the Soul

Socrates, calmly confident that he is about to enter a better world, contrasts the common fear of death with the lifelong philosophic practice of dying. To understand this paradoxical statement, death must be defined as the separation of the soul from the body. At this point in the *Phaedo* there is no argument to show the existence of a soul; some considerations can be obtained from the refutation of Protagoras where Plato shows that there must be something of a mind or soul, distinguishable from the bodily senses, whereby we think thoughts relative to disparate sensations. Other dialogues supply other considerations and the *Phaedo* itself soon emphasizes thoughts that are not perceptions. There is then a soul as well as a body and death is the separation of the two. The philosopher in contrast with the common man is concerned with his soul rather than with his body; he is not anxious about the pleasures of eating and drinking, or magnificent garments and ornaments. On the contrary, he is concerned about wisdom. But wisdom finds the body a hindrance, for the bodily senses are neither accurate nor clear; and when the soul attempts to learn truth in conjunction with the body, it is led astray. Knowledge of realities must be attained by reasoning, not by sensation. And the soul reasons best when it is not disturbed by contact with the body, with sight or hearing, or the distractions of pleasure.

With only an apparent break Socrates then asks the question, Do we say that justice itself is something or nothing? In the Presocratic development the real was something that occupied space and the argument kept close to atoms, or a universal stuff; but this question shows that in the discussions between Socrates, or at least Plato, and his companions, it had been maintained that justice itself is something — Justice exists; and this is the existence of a reality not discernible by sense. Socrates immediately adds other examples: beauty and goodness, magnitude and health, and the essence or reality of all such things. If we are looking for noncorporeal realities, these are they. For while we may have seen magnitudes, we have never seen magnitude; or, as one scholar explained it, we can draw approximately, elliptical lines; but we cannot even approximately draw the general conic.

Incidentally, this section indicates the nature of philosophy and marks an advance [4] over the earlier dialogues. In the *Rivals* philosophy was a kind of universal knowledge not clearly described; in *Alcibiades* philosophy was defined by the Socratic concept of self-knowledge, but the meaning was not too precise; here in the *Phaedo* philosophy is knowledge of reality, the realities, called Ideas or Forms,

[4] Cf. footnote 2, p. 50.

obtained by fleeing the blandishments of sense; and hence knowledge is closely related, as it was not in the Presocratic period, with morality.

The connection between epistemology and morality is seen in the fact that the body subjects us to innumerable hindrances. Diseases, desires, fears, and fancies, disturb calm reflection; the love of luxury and repute turns our attention to gaining wealth and leaves us no leisure for thought. It follows therefore that if we are to know anything purely, our moral task is to separate ourselves, that is, our soul, from the body and contemplate the realities themselves by the soul alone. This is wisdom, and this is what was meant by saying that the philosopher all his life practices dying.

For this reason Socrates is confident and without fear in the face of his approaching execution. Popular courage considers death an evil, and while it may face death, it does so because it is afraid of greater evils. But it is absurd to be brave through cowardice. Similarly, ordinary temperance, which foregoes pleasures through the fear of consequent pains, is a species of self-indulgence. True virtue, on the other hand, can exist only with wisdom; and where wisdom is lacking, as it is with the mass of mankind, there can be no true virtue. Socrates throughout his life left no means untried, but to the utmost of his ability sought wisdom and purification. "Whether I have endeavored rightly," Socrates concludes, "and what success I have attained, I shall know clearly upon my arrival over there, if it please God, and that will not be very long now, as it seems to me."

Immortality

Socrates' confidence, obviously, can be justified only if the soul survives death. But Cebes, one of Socrates' companions, is troubled by the possibility that, as many people believe, the soul after death perishes, vanishes like smoke, and no longer exists anywhere. Socrates willingly accepts the invitation to discuss the matter.

In all cases of generation, Socrates begins, that which comes to be comes from the contrary state. When anything becomes greater, it must first have been smaller; the weaker is generated from the stronger; if a man becomes just, he was previously unjust. This process between contraries works in both directions: it is the warm that becomes cold and the cold that becomes warm. Now, it is obvious that death is the contrary of life, and no one denies that it is the living who die. Does it not therefore follow that it is the dead who come to life? If this were not so, but if to use an illustration, people awake fell asleep and no one asleep awakened, soon everyone would be asleep. That is, if generation from opposites worked only in one direction, soon all generation would cease. The conclusion is that the living come from the dead, and this implies that souls exist apart from the body, waiting to be reborn.

Reminiscence

Another argument to prove the pre-existence and therefore the immortality of the soul is more closely connected with the problem of knowledge. In the *Meno,* as explained at the beginning of this chapter, a slave boy under Socrates' questioning was able to construct a square twice the area of a given square. Aside from the mathematical significance previously turned to account, the illustration shows that the least educated person can of himself, without being given information, bring up the truth from the recesses of his soul. Knowledge lies dormant and innate, awaiting a stimulation that produces a state of mind best described as recollection or reminiscence.

That this knowledge is properly called reminiscence may be seen from ordinary experience. For example, on a happier day in the market place Socrates may not have been thinking of Simmias, but when he saw Cebes, he would be reminded of him. And he would think of the extent to which Cebes resembles Simmias, and how far they differ. Not only does the sight of Cebes remind Socrates of Simmias, but even the lyre that Simmias plays, so different in outward appearance from the musician, may cause the same recollection. But this recollection and comparison would be impossible, unless Socrates had previously known Simmias.

Now to apply the illustration: equality exists, not the equality of one stone with another, but equality itself, abstract, absolute equality. There is such a thing, and we know it. In a way we learn equality from seeing logs or stones that are approximately equal, more or less equal, equal in some respects but not in others. Equality itself, however, never appears more or less equal, or equal in some respects only. It is absolutely equal, and therefore equality itself is not the same as equal things. But if it is not the same, then the equal things must have reminded us of equality as a lyre might remind Socrates of Simmias. More conclusively, since we recognize that things are only approximately equal, and this recognition depends on judging the things by the absolute standard, we must have known the standard before the time we first saw equal things and judged that they approached but fell short of equality itself. The original knowledge of equality cannot have come from experience because equality never appears in experience. Experience has only approximately equal things. Since we get these approximations through sensation, and since sensation begins at birth, we must have had knowledge of absolute equality before our birth. Because we were not conscious of this knowledge in childhood, it is evident that we had forgotten it, and that learning is therefore recollection.

This argument applies not only to equality, but with equal force to beauty in itself, good in itself, and justice and holiness and all those things which we seal with the term of absolute existence. We must have known all these things before we were born.

The Objects of Knowledge

The theory of reminiscence, particularly the notion that knowledge is inborn or innate, is extremely important; but the assertion that there exist absolute ideas as the objects of knowledge is still more so. It has already been indicated that Plato accepted Heraclitean flux as characteristic of the sense world. And within this world all that Protagoras had to say about the appearance of sensory qualities and the impermanence of perception is true. From this it follows, as the *Theaetetus* made abundantly clear, that there can be no knowledge of perceptible things. They are momentary and fleeting; they have no stability that could make them definite objects of any sort. Statements about sense objects, such as, this tree is exactly thirty-two feet, three and one-quarter inches tall, or, this boy weighs eighty-four pounds, seven and a third ounces, are false before they can be completed.

Yet if knowledge is to be possible there must be an object to be known, a definite object about which something definite can be said. From Socrates Plato had learned of something unchanging. In those market-place conversations it became clear that while particular examples of courage, or of beauty, or of equality, vary indefinitely, courage in itself, beauty per se, and absolute equality always remain the same. These unchanging items were in Socrates' dialectic the definitions he was seeking.

Plato advances beyond this apparently simple result. For him the Socratic definitions were not to be considered as the fancy or fabrication of an individual mind. The men in conversation did not manufacture or formulate the definition: they discovered it. Plato gave it an ontological status. It was real. These definitions of Ideas were the realities composing the real world. Or, conversely, the real world, in contrast to the unreal world of perception, is composed of fixed, unchanging, absolute entities, called Forms or Ideas. Unless there are such entities, knowledge will be impossible. This theory of Ideas is Plato's greatest contribution to the history of philosophy, and every passage in the *Phaedo*, or in any other dialogue, where the Ideas are mentioned, must be examined with care.

Souls Akin to Ideas

The immediate topic, however, was reminiscence and the immortality of the soul. Cebes, professing to be satisfied that the theory of reminiscence is well founded and carries with it the pre-existence of the soul, doubts whether pre-existence guarantees immortality. Perhaps the soul, though it existed before we were born, may still vanish like smoke after death.

To this objection Socrates replies that the argument on generation from opposites has already covered this point: if souls at death dispersed, the source of souls would soon be exhausted, and no more births would occur. But if one wishes to make very sure, there is also another argument in favor of the immortality of the soul. Obviously, that which can be dispersed or disintegrated must be a composite or compound. What has not been put together of parts or elements cannot be taken apart. Conversely anything that is subject to flux must be a compound. This is the principle that the pluralists were forced to accept from Parmenides. Now, reality itself is unchangeable. Equality per se, for example, never changes; so too absolute beauty and the other realities are always the same and never suffer any variation. But equal things and beautiful things never remain the same from one moment to the next. These latter are visible, tangible, or sensible; but the former, the realities, are suprasensible. The body, like all other visible things, constantly changes. But the soul is not visible or sensible; from which it ought to follow that the soul is not a compound, but a simple, unchangeable substance, and therefore indestructible.

However, before drawing the conclusion, Socrates reminds his companions that when the soul examines sensible things, and is thus employing the body, it becomes confused; whereas, when it considers the things in themselves, the pure, the immortal, the unchangeable, it escapes confusion and achieves wisdom. It would appear therefore that the soul is more akin to the suprasensible, unchangeable, and therefore immortal than it is to the visible and disintegrating. That the soul is more divine than the body is corroborated also by the fact that during our earthly existence the soul rules the body, and the body is subservient. If all these considerations do not quite prove the immortality of the soul, at least they show that the soul is more nearly indissoluble than the body; and since the body continues intact for a time after death, parts of it a long time, and in Egypt with their embalming an incredible time, the soul must continue almost indefinitely.

Philosophy for Life and Death

This theory obviously has ethical implications, for the doctrine of immortality gives confidence in face of death, but only to the man who has lived the life of a philosopher. The souls of other men are riveted to the body by pleasures and pains, hates and fears, errors and desires. So tainted, these souls must wander as ghosts and be subject to reincarnation in animals of the same low habits. Good souls will be reincarnated too, but into peaceful and clean animals, or even into gentle human beings again. It is philosophy that teaches us to abstain from bodily desires, to contemn the popular honors and disgraces as well, and to attend to nothing but that which absolutely and really exists in itself alone. Thus may true virtue and a blessed future be attained.

Plato from the very beginning took a serious interest in morality;

for him philosophy was first of all a way of life. And after he came to believe in the immortality of the soul, nothing is more natural than the conjunction of these two themes. But although the ostensible subject of the *Phaedo* is the immortality of the soul, the basis of all the argument is the real existence of incorporeal, unchangeable objects that can be known. Since no question on any subject, be it astronomy, medicine, or morality, can be answered unless knowledge is possible, the crucial factor in any system of philosophy is its epistemology.

After Socrates' powerful speech, the group sat in thoughtful silence for a long time; then, continuing the dialogue, Simmias, who had started to converse quietly with Cebes, indicates his hesitation, in these circumstances, to advance any doubts. With the encouragement of Socrates, however, he emphasizes the importance of the problem and hopes that it may be examined from every angle. Unfortunately, since there is no divine revelation of the truth, we must be satisfied with what is probable and sail through life, as it were, on a raft. Two objections, like rocks and rapids, may make the journey turbulent.

The Harmony

The first is the fact that the argument from invisibility to immortality would apply to the chords and harmonies of a lyre. Music is invisible, incorporeal, and indeed divine; but the lyre itself is a body, and when it is broken, the music dies. Now, that theory of life is very probable which holds that the soul is the functioning of the complex bodily organism. As digestion is the function of the stomach, and as sight is the activity of the eye, so life or soul is not a thing or substance but simply the activity of the body as a whole. In this case, it is clear, the soul or function will cease with the dissolution of the body.

The Weaver's Coat

Cebes does not agree with Simmias that the body produces the soul; it is rather the soul which produces the body; and yet he has a second objection to immortality, similar to what he had said previously. The soul may not be a function of the body; it may have existed before birth; it may be stronger, superior, and more durable than the body; indeed, like a weaver weaving a coat, the soul may manufacture and control the body; nonetheless, while the weaver may outlast many of the coats he weaves, and while we may produce and outlast many bodies — some say we have a completely different body every seven years — still there comes a time when the weaver weaves his last coat; similarly the body may remain, even a long time like the mummies in Egypt, but the soul will be no more. Confidence in the face of death requires, not merely that the soul should survive one, or two, or several deaths, but that it should be absolutely immortal and survive all.

These objections produced great distress in the company; not only is the personal fate of Socrates put in doubt, but if Socrates' previous arguments, which seemed so convincing when first given, can be overthrown by these equally convincing objections, then it will not be possible to trust any arguments whatsoever on any subject. Socrates, however, remained calm and warned the group not to become misologists as some men become misanthropes. Hatred of men is engendered by trusting the wrong men, and then concluding that no man is trustworthy; hatred of reason comes by trusting invalid arguments, and when disillusioned, concluding that no argument is sound. This is a danger that we must avoid. Socrates then proceeds to refute the objections.

Epiphenomenalism

The first objection, to the effect that the soul is a harmony — epiphenomenalism in modern terminology — is disproved by the arguments on recollection and the pre-existence of the soul. Simmias admits that this theory of knowledge is well founded, firmly established; but the harmony theory is merely probable, and must therefore be discarded. Furthermore, the harmony theory would empty moral distinctions of all significance, and is inconsistent with the obvious fact that the soul controls the body rather than the body the soul.

Natural Science

The refutation of Cebes' objection, however, is not such an easy matter, for it requires a thorough investigation of the causes of generation and dissolution: nothing less in fact than a theory of nature and science. When Socrates was a young man, he was very curious about these questions, and now he recounts his experience for the benefit of his friends and for its bearing on the argument. Presumably the questions here enumerated reflect the interests of science during the middle of the fifth century. Socrates had tried to discover whether chemical combinations explain life; whether it is the blood by which we think, or whether it is the brain that produces perceptions, memory, and opinion. But his studies puzzled him so greatly that not only was he convinced of his ignorance on these points, but also on other points he had never questioned previously. He had thought he knew that growth is the result of eating and drinking, and that a man becomes large by the addition of bulk. He also thought he knew that a tall man or horse, standing beside a short one, was taller by a head; and he had never doubted that ten was more than eight by two.

Yet as he was forced to consider these matters, they came to seem very doubtful indeed. Consider the simplest thing: when one is added to one, is it the one to which the addition was made that becomes two, or do the one which was added and the one to which the addition was made become two together? For, when each of these was separate, each was one; but when they came near together, it seems that the union made them two. But if union is the cause of two, how can it be that division is the cause of two? For, if a stick is broken, the one stick becomes two by being divided and separated from itself. How can union and separation be the cause of the same result? As a matter of fact, Socrates was unable to explain why one is one, or why anything is produced, or perishes, or exists. He was completely baffled.

Mechanical and Teleological Explanation

Underlying these difficulties is the problem of the nature of explanation. What sort of an account is it that satisfies a questioner? The Presocratics were deficient, not merely because their particular mechanical descriptions were factually incorrect, but because they had failed to understand the nature of explanation and were making statements which even if true would not have explained.

One day Socrates was told that Anaxagoras offered a different type of explanation. The cause of the universe, and the particular ordering of each thing in the universe, so it was said, is a regulating intelligence, a Mind. If such is the case, if a Mind orders each thing, then when anyone wishes to discover the cause of some existence or why something is produced or perishes, he must show that it is best for that thing to exist, to perish, or whatever. The earth would be flat or round because it is better that it should be such. The positions and the velocities of the sun, moon, and planets could be explained by showing that these are the best possible arrangements. For if the parts of the universe are set in order by Intelligence, no other cause can be assigned than that it is best for them to be as they are. Intelligence certainly would not choose the worst, nor would it act without any reason; and the only reason that could motivate Intelligence is what is best.

To Socrates' great disappointment, as he eagerly read through the book, he found out that Anaxagoras made no use of Intelligence. It was the same old Presocratic theme of air, water, ether, and other absurdities. "He appeared to me to be very like one who should say that whatever Socrates does he does by intelligence, and then, attempting to describe the causes of each particular action, should say, first of all, that for these reasons I am now sitting here: because my body is composed of bones and sinews, and the bones are hard, and have joints which separate them, and the sinews are capable of tension and contraction and cover the bones, together with the flesh and skin which contain them. The bones, therefore, suspended in their sockets, with the sinews relaxing and tightening, enable me to bend my limbs, as I now do, and this is the cause of my sitting here bent up. Or if, again, he should posit other similar causes for my arguing with you, assigning as causes voice, and air, and hearing, and ten thousand other such things, but omitting to mention the real causes: viz., that since it appeared better to the Athenians to condemn me, I therefore thought it better to sit here, and more just to remain and submit to the punishment which they have ordered; for, by the dog! I think these sinews and bones would have been long ago either in Megara or Boeotia, borne thither by an opinion of what is best, if I had not thought it more just and honorable to submit to whatever sentence the city might order than to flee and run away. But to call such things causes is very absurd. Of course, if anyone should say that without possessing such things as bones and sinews, and whatever else I have, I could not do what I please, he would speak the truth; but to say that I do what I do because of them, and that I act by intelligence but not from the choice of what is best, would be a great and extreme disregard of reason. For this would be inability to see that the real cause is one thing, and that without which a cause could not be a cause, quite another." [5]

How the Ideas or real existences are to be related to this account of the nature of explanation is yet to be determined, but the significance of these pages with reference to theories of causality needs emphasis. The Presocratics had proposed mechanical causes for all things: the universe was made of water; the earth remains in position because it is at the center of a vortex; and sensation is the passage of effluxes of particles through the pores of the sense organs, or even the physical impression of an image on a wax-like brain.

In the nineteenth century of our era also mechanism was a popular philosophy: a lever raises heavy weights because the product of the mass and distance on one side of the fulcrum equals the product of the two on the other side; or, a body falls to the earth and the earth revolves around the sun because every two particles of matter attract each other as the product of their masses and inversely as the square of the distance. In the section on Empedocles the meaninglessness of attraction was noticed; here the very principle of mechanical explanation itself is considered unsatisfactory.

Plato notes that Socrates could not sit in prison without bones, sinews, and so on; there is no denying the physical conditions; but instead of these conditions' being the explanation of anything, they are precisely the material that needs to be explained. Hence a different type of explanation or causality is needed — a causality in terms of intelligence and what is best. Teleological terminology must replace mechanical. When a mind is said to act for a reason, the reason is a purpose; and it is only in terms of purpose that anything can be understood.

[5] *Phaedo*, 98–99.

The Method of Hypothesis

Unfortunately, although Socrates saw the deficiency in Anaxagoras, he was unable to supply the necessary teleology, but was forced to make do with a second-best explanation. His method in any investigation was to lay down the reason, cause, explanation, or hypothesis which seemed most satisfactory. In general, this hypothesis was the existence of an absolute reality: beauty in itself, magnitude in itself, or whatever the subject required. For example, if we are studying triangles, the object of our science will not be the individual triangle that Socrates drew on the sand for the slave boy; the object of science is never an individual sense object, but rather an unchanging universal. Strictly Socrates did not draw a triangle on the sand, for his lines were crooked, and they also had a breadth; but the real triangle is bounded by straight lines that have no breadth whatever. The individual objects are changing, unreal, and indeterminate; the objects of all sciences have the opposite characteristics. Or suppose we wish to explain the beauty of a woman or statue. Obviously the cause cannot be her tall stature or light complexion, for if such qualities were the cause of beauty, every woman with those qualities would be beautiful; but there are many tall women of light complexion who are not beautiful. On the contrary, the cause of beauty, wherever it may appear, can be only the presence in the object or the communication to it of absolute beauty in itself. And likewise large things are large by participating in magnitude.

It is impossible that one man should be taller by a head and that another should be smaller by a head. The same cause or explanation cannot apply to opposite effects. Ten is not more than eight by two; and when one is added to one, it is not the addition that causes two. But just as beauty explains the beautiful object, so two is two because it partakes of duality, and one is one because of unity. Admittedly these answers are insufficient, for this is only a second-best explanation; but though insufficient, these answers are true and pertinent; and until more complete teleological answers are developed, they are the safest, and to them we must adhere.

When any hypothesis is accepted, the first thing to do is not to consider direct attacks against it; rather one must first deduce from it as many consequences as possible. If these consequences are incompatible among themselves, the hypothesis is refuted; if, however, they are mutually consistent, it is time to give a reason for or explanation of the hypothesis. This is done by assuming a superior hypothesis from which the previous one is an implication. This process is repeated until one arrives at a superior principle that is sufficient.

In the *Phaedo* Plato does not say what this sufficient principle is, and interpretations may differ; but it is plausible to suppose that in an investigation of the beauty of a statue, the first hypothesis is the existence of beauty in itself; the existence of this reality is an implication of the general theory of Ideas — that is, beauty in itself is but one of the many absolute realities. But if the theory of Ideas is only a second-best attempt, there must be one or several superior hypotheses. The highest of all, so it would seem, is the distinction between the true and the false, or, better expressed, the possibility of knowledge. If knowledge is impossible, then nothing can be either affirmed or denied; all opinions are of equal value and the value is zero. Any objection to the theory of Ideas would on this basis be literal nonsense. But if the possibility of knowledge implies the existence of suprasensible realities, there can be no more coercive demonstration of their existence.

The Problems Solved

Socrates therefore, having established the existence of the Ideas to the satisfaction of the company, explains that Simmias is taller than himself, not by a head, nor even because he is Simmias, but because of the presence in him of tallness. Simmias is also shorter than Phaedo, not by a head, but by reason of shortness. There is no contradiction in the colloquial statement that Simmias is both short and tall. Contrary attributes often appear in what people call the same thing. Such contrary empirical judgments, which formed so much of the Sophists' stock in trade, are possible because the thing is not strictly the same thing: either the contrary predicates are not simultaneous or the judgment is conceived under different relations. The sensible thing constantly changes; but the predicates are immutable. Simmias can be both tall and short, but short cannot be tall nor can tallness be shortness. Simmias can be both tall and short, but not at the same time or in the same relation. When standing next to Socrates, Simmias partakes of magnitude; but when shortness appears the magnitude withdraws. This is consistent with the theory of the generation from opposites: the tall Simmias becomes short. But tallness never becomes short.

Furthermore there are some sensible things that cannot admit both of two contraries. For example, snow is cold and it cannot become hot. Heat and coldness are a pair of opposites between which the generation of snow is impossible. If heat approaches, not only does the cold withdraw, but the snow vanishes as well. White snow may become dirty; but cold snow never becomes hot. Similarly the number three is always odd, it can never become even; and yet three is not identical with odd. These examples show that not only do contraries exclude each other, but also that there are things which exclude certain predicates.

The final conclusion is now prepared for. Since heat is the necessary, inseparable attribute of fire, we can say that a body is hot, not only because it participates in the Idea heat, but also because there is fire in it. And a body is alive, not merely because it participates in Life, but because there is a soul in it. For the attribute of soul is life, just as the attribute of snow is cold. Now, the contrary of life is death, as the contrary of cold is heat. But as snow cannot permit the approach of heat, so too the soul, when death comes near, withdraws: it can never accept the predicate of dead; it always preserves the predicate of life. But if the predicate of life attaches always, the soul never dies and is therefore immortal.

The theory of reincarnation, at least the notion of men being reborn as animals, though it is mentioned in more than one dialogue, may be intended as nothing more than a myth — Plato frequently indulged in picturesque fancies; but there is no reason to question his serious acceptance of immortality. Future rewards and punishments are an essential part of his moral theory. Although the early dialogues including the *Protagoras* contain no hint of immortality, from the *Gorgias* on it becomes a recurring and dominant note. Serious though it may be intended to be, whether it is a valid argument or not is quite another question. Justin Martyr in the middle of the second century of the Christian era was converted to Christianity after he became convinced that the arguments in favor of the natural immortality of the soul were invalid. But however interesting the question of immortality may be, and whatever bearing it may have on a theory of morals, the most important material in the *Phaedo* concerns the possibility of knowledge and the nature of the objects known.

THE PARMENIDES

The Platonic theory of Ideas, since it is the work of a man of genius as he reflects on the most profound problems of philosophy, is no simple, easily understood theory. From the time of its original promulgation down to the twentieth century it has not only found friends, but it has made enemies as well. Objections very difficult to answer have been raised against it. But strange to say — or in view of Plato's profundity is it strange at all? — Plato himself foresaw every type of objection that has since been raised against it. He outlined them briefly in a tremendously difficult dialogue, the *Parmenides*.

Ideas of Mud?

In the first place, if the theory of Ideas is to be made completely explicit, it will be necessary to state the extent of the Ideal world. Plato has admitted Forms or Ideas of Beauty, of Good, and other honorable concepts, but in the dialogue the venerable Parmenides asks the young Socrates whether there are Ideas of man, fire, and water. And more embarrassing is the question whether there are Ideas of hair, mud, filth, and other disgusting things. While an aristocratic Greek and high-minded philosopher might disdain such barnyard difficulties, Parmenides points out the inconsistency of refusing to posit Ideas for every type of thing. Parmenides in this place does not mention the problem of positing Ideas for instances of relation. A man is a "thing" or visible object; but "father" is a relationship and not a "thing." Must there be also Ideas of relationships? Is there an Idea of negation? Of deprivation? These are indeed difficult questions.[6]

---

[6] Cf. Aristotle, *Metaphysics*, 990 a 34–991 a 8 and 1078 b 32–1079 b 10; also L. Robin, *La Théorie Platonicienne*, pp. 121–198.

Participation

A second enigma is the precise connection between the Idea and the sense object. Does each sense object share, participate in, receive (or whatever term may finally seem best) the complete, whole, and undivided form, or only a part of it?

Since a horse is a complete horse, and not half a horse, it would seem more reasonable to suppose that each sense object possesses the whole Idea and not just a half-Idea. Besides, an Idea is a unit, and cannot be divided in half or separated from itself. Yet, if each sense object has the whole Idea, the Idea in one place will be separated from itself in another place. Or, to paraphrase Aristotle, who took his own objections to Plato from Plato himself, if the Idea animal is singular, and is the same both in the species man and in the species horse, how can this singular Idea be in both man and horse without being fragmented or separated from itself?

To this type of question the young Socrates of the dialogue replies that the day, or the daylight, is one and single, and yet it covers all men without being separated from itself. But this answer is unsatisfactory. Parmenides points out that this is essentially the same as covering a group of men with a tent. They are all under the tent, to be sure; but more strictly each one is under a part of the tent; and this analogy would return us to the untenable position that each man participates in a fraction of the Idea man — which means that a man is not a complete man, but only a fraction.

Why Plato chose to construct a dialogue between the venerable Parmenides and a young Socrates who gives thoughtless answers can only be surmised. Perhaps Plato wanted to indicate that he himself did not know the correct answers. Perhaps on the other hand he thought that the answers were so easily discoverable that it was not necessary to state them. Only one thing is sure: Plato was entirely aware of all the objections to the theory of Ideas, and they did not cause him to relinquish it. At any rate a satisfactory answer to this second objection is more easily made than to some of the others, for the objection rests on a spatial, materialistic analogy. A single body cannot be in several places at once, but any number of men throughout the world can have the same thought at the same time; and if, as is surely the case, the Ideas are more of the nature of thought than of body, the objection is convicted of a false analogy.

The Third Man

The next objection has been given the name of the Third Man Argument. The motive, or one of the motives, for accepting the theory of Ideas is the fact of common qualities. There are a number of objects, very similar to each other, and we name this group of objects men. Another multitude of objects we group under the one name of horse; and so on. We do so because each one of the group has the same quality as every other one. What can such a common quality be? Obviously it cannot be one of the group, for if Plato is absolutely identified as Man, then Socrates and Zeno, since they are not Plato, would not be men. Nor can this common quality be the totality of the group, for just as obviously neither Plato, nor Socrates, nor Zeno, is that totality. It must therefore be something in itself, and to it Plato gave the name Form or Idea. But here the difficulty appears. If the similarity among Plato, Socrates, and Zeno necessitates the positing of the Idea man; the similarity between men and the Idea man would necessitate the positing of a Super-Idea man (the Third Man), and so on ad infinitum. Opponents of the Ideal theory would say that it is better not to begin such an endless process.

Parenthetically, attention might be called to discussions in modern logic which are essentially the same. Some logicians identify and some logicians distinguish between the "inclusion" of an individual in a class, like Socrates in the class man, and the "inclusion" of a class in a higher class, like man in the class living being. The discussion naturally involves the problem of defining "class," and the arguments become quite complicated.

Nominalism

The fourth objection — in reality it is a totally different type of philosophy offered as a substitute for Platonism — is introduced by the young and not so brilliant Socrates in his attempt to escape the Third Man argument. The infinite regress would be avoided, Socrates claims, if the Ideas or Forms should be thoughts in someone's mind. If the Idea of man exists nowhere else than in the mind of the person who is thinking about men, it would retain its undivided unity and be immune to all the difficulties above.

Since the type of philosophy envisaged by the remark occupied the attention of many of the medieval philosophers, and since nominalism, as it is called, is in some form or other widely accepted today, this objection, foreseen by Plato himself, may be the most important of all seven. If so, we are fortunate to have Plato's own reply, for this is the only one which Plato does not leave without an answer. The portion of the dialogue (*Parmenides*, p. 132 b, c.) is as follows:

"How so?" he said. "Is each thought one, and yet a thought of nothing?"

"That would be impossible," replied Socrates.

"It is a thought of something?"

"Of course."

"Of something that exists, or of something that does not exist?"

"Of something that exists."

"Is it not of one something which that thought thinks as present in all the instances — a certain, single characteristic?"

"Yes."

"Then will not this that is thought to be one be a Form, always the same in all the instances?"

"Yes, that seems necessary."

"Well, then," replied Parmenides, "does not the necessity which compels you to say that things participate in Forms force this choice on you: either everything is composed of thoughts and everything thinks, or being thoughts they do not think."

The first part of this section is relatively clear. When men are engaged in the activity of thinking, they are thinking something; and the something is different from the mere activity itself. If, for example, I think equality, equality is not to be identified with my individual, subjective cerebration. And since equality or whatever may be the object of thought is a common quality, a norm not perfectly realized in sensation, an unchangeable object, the Forms or Ideas must be recognized as independently existing realities. Up to this point Plato the author has not left nominalism unanswered; but then Parmenides adds a statement, curious in its intention, that seems to overturn the whole Platonic theory.

The participation of things in Ideas implies that everything is composed of thoughts; but if this is so, then one of two alternatives follows. First, a thing composed of thoughts is naturally assumed to be a thinking thing, and so, everything would think; yet it seems untenable to maintain that equal stones think. The other alternative is that things do not think, even though they are thoughts. But what nonsense is unthinking thoughts! Young Socrates is puzzled.

Plato's Foresight

Far be it from a modern interpreter to read into Plato's lines more than was intended; but may he also be spared the much greater danger of understanding too little. The alternatives proposed by Parmenides are not so absurd as to have no supporters. Plotinus, the Neoplatonist who brought Greek philosophy to its culmination, adopted what is essentially the first view, though the proper qualifications cannot be put in one sentence. And in modern times Leibniz, Fichte, (and should we add Hegel?) also said that all things think. David Hume accepted the other alternative: that all things are composed of thoughts, impressions, and ideas, but that nothing thinks.

An oracular professor of logic once told his class, as they opened to the first page of the textbook, that they could not understand the first chapter until after they had understood the last chapter. The students indulgently considered such a queer statement as the prerogative of a half-cracked philosopher. But it is the sober truth in logic, and even more inescapably true for the history of philosophy. It is even necessary to know something about the twentieth-century instrumentalists, for, omitting the fifth difficulty, the sixth and seventh, complements of each other, are themes which F. C. S. Schiller in his *Studies in Humanism* has used against Plato.

But Can Ideas Be Known?

The first part of this double objection is that men would be unable to know the Ideas. Consider Ideas of relations. The slave boy is not the slave of the Idea master, and his master is not the master of the Idea slave. It is the man and the boy who are master and slave. But mastership and slavehood exist as relations only between two Ideas. Now, there is another Idea of relation, where this condition must hold also. Knowledge is a relation between a knower and a known. But if the Idea knowledge exists in relation only to the Idea known, and if our human knowledge relates only to human affairs, then the Ideas are not known by us. To avoid this difficulty Schiller aims to "humanize" knowledge. And even though other dialogues teach that before birth the soul contemplated the Ideas and was then born with an innate knowledge of them, here the young Socrates admits at least three times that the Ideas are not in us, we cannot have them, and the various Ideas are known only by Absolute Knowledge which we do not possess.

The second part of this objection, Parmenides says, is still more formidable. If Absolute Knowledge exists, then, since it is far superior to human knowledge, there is no one more likely than God who could have it. But if God has Absolute Knowledge, he must be ignorant of human affairs. The Ideas are not relative to our world and our world is not relative to the Ideas; hence if God dwells in the higher world, he has no relation to us: he cannot be our master, we cannot be his slaves; he cannot know us, and we cannot know him.

These difficulties and many more can be raised against the Forms; and at first nearly everyone thinks that they are convincing. Yet, concludes Parmenides, "a very brilliant man will be able to understand that there is a genus for each thing and an absolute reality per se. . . . But if anyone denies the existence of Ideas of things, because of the objections above and similar ones, and refuses to posit a Form for each individual thing, he will not know how to conduct his thought, for he has denied that an Idea of each reality is always the same, and thus he completely destroys the possibility of argumentation."

It is clear therefore that Plato was aware of all the objections to the theory of Ideas; whether he could have satisfactorily answered all of them remains in doubt; but no doubt remains of his conviction that the only alternative to Ideas is skepticism.

THE TIMAEUS

Let it be assumed that the theory of Ideas has now been successfully established. Admittedly, Plato developed it in much greater detail than the previous pages indicate. In particular, the world of Ideas was not a haphazard aggregation. It was an organized cosmos. Supreme among the eternal realities was the Idea of Good. In the *Phaedo* Socrates had complained that Anaxagoras failed to fulfil his promises of a teleological explanation of nature; and he himself, equally unable to develop a teleology, offered the theory of Ideas only as a second-best attempt. In the *Republic*, however, Plato asserts that each other Idea is known through the Idea of Good. To know what a horse or what a watch is, one must know what it is good for. That is to say, all classes are to be defined in terms of purpose. Mechanical definitions are impossible. For example, the class concept chronometer cannot be defined mechanically because a pocket watch, Big Ben, an electric clock, and a sun dial have no common mechanism — no blueprint describes them all. But a statement of purpose does so: they are all instruments for keeping time. Therefore we know the Idea chronometer through the Idea of Good. Not only is knowledge dependent on the Idea of Good, existence is too. For, a horse and a watch exist only so long as they fulfil their purposes. When a watch breaks down, one might say that it was a watch, but one cannot correctly say that it is a watch. A watch is what keeps time; but this thing is not a watch because it cannot keep time. The watch does not exist. Of course, the watch case and even a wheel or two may be good for something, and these *are* what they are good for. But something that is literally good for nothing *is* nothing. The supreme Idea of Good therefore is the cause both of knowledge and of existence.

However, the wheel and the watch in these illustrations are taken to be class concepts or Ideas, and while they are in some way related to sensible things, there remains to be given a more particular account of the physical world. It was difficulties concerning the world of sense that had in the first place led to Sophism and turned attention from science to epistemology. Plato, unwilling to pass over the earlier problems of science and cosmology, now toward the end of his career believed himself ready to discuss them in the dialogue *Timaeus*.

Being and Becoming

Basing this account of science on what he has constantly reiterated, Plato begins by dividing the sum total of things into two classes. There is the Being that always is and never becomes, and there is that which is always Becoming but never is. The first part, Being, is apprehended by reason and can be expressed in definite statements because it is always the same; but the second part, Becoming, is the object of opinion with irrational or inexpressible sensation, for it is constantly changing.

This second part is the sphere of science — science in its modern sense of physical investigation, not science in the Platonic sense of absolute knowledge of Ideas. The recognition that physical hypotheses are not absolute knowledge but are merely opinions subject to constant revision distinguishes Plato from Aristotle and many other scientists through the ages. Twentieth-century theories of science are returning to the views of Plato. The senses, even when aided by instruments, cannot perceive very small differences; there are sources of constant error as well as errors of observation; and there is always the possibility of finding new data which would overthrow established results. These factors forever prevent science from obtaining the absolute truth. But the most important factor, according to Plato, is the flux of the material itself. Things are constantly changing and cannot be grasped by a fixed formula. Hence one must recognize two states of mind, each appropriate to its object: absolute knowledge of the immutable Ideas and scientific opinion relative to the sphere of Becoming.

Becoming and Causation

In this lower sphere the first thing to be noted is that whatever becomes requires a cause. Socrates in the *Phaedo* had distinguished between secondary causes or concomitants and the real causes. He sat in prison, not because of bones, muscles, and sinews, but because of his decision regarding the Good. For Plato causality is not to be found in mechanical conditions or preceding events. A cause is a living agent operating for a purpose, and all explanations are teleological.

Inasmuch as Plato is preparing to identify the cause of the visible world, he must classify this world under the category of Becoming. In doing so, however, he asks a question in a form easily misunderstood by those later ages which came under the influence of Christianity. Plato's words are, "First we must see whether the world always was, having no beginning of generation, or whether it has been generated, beginning from a starting point." To Christian thinkers this phraseology about a starting point might seem to indicate that Plato was considering a theory of creation by which the world had a first moment. To some of the Greeks it might have suggested the possibility of a series of worlds, each one with a first moment but without a temporal beginning of the series. Even Aristotle took some such view of Plato's intention, but the preponderant tradition in the Academy was opposed to a temporal beginning of the world. The words *beginning* and *starting point* are better translated *principle*; and Plato's question simply means, Is the physical universe to be classed under Being or Becoming? Plato's short answer, obviously inadequate if a series of worlds or a temporal creation is under consideration, is quite sufficient for his actual argument. He wrote, "It has become, for it is both visible and tangible, and corporeal; all such things are sensible, and sensible objects, apprehended by opinion with sensation, are obviously objects of becoming and birth." [7] As such, the world must have a cause or Maker.

There is, however, a prior question. Why did the Maker, God, or the Demiurge make any world at all? The Ideas existed in purity and perfection — what was the necessity for bringing an imperfect copy to birth? To a mechanist like Democritus the question is silly. The world just is; its existence is a brute fact; neither a Maker nor an explanation is needed. But then a philosophy of brute fact and ultimate plurality has other bothersome problems. The later Christian philosophy faced a double irrationality: that God should create

---

[7] *Timaeus* 28 b. Though the answer may be sufficient for the actual argument, A. E. Taylor in his *Commentary* questions the argument. Does the conclusion require the world as a whole, and not merely some of its parts, to be visible? No one has seen the world as a whole.

a world seems to be an unmotivated choice, and that he created it at a given moment rather than sooner or later also puzzled the Christian thinkers.

But the problem for Plato is at least superficially easy. In addition to the world of Ideas as an eternally existing reality that can serve as a model for a physical universe, the Maker or Demiurge, also an independent and eternal existence, is confronted with another independent principle: chaotic matter. Plato therefore proposes a world-view with three eternal and independent principles. These may not be all equally supreme, for the Ideas are highest, the Demiurge is second, and matter is lowest. But though not equally supreme, they are independent: no one of them is the cause of another. Now, if the existence of chaotic matter be granted as a principle or brute fact without explanation, then Plato's answer to the question, why God made a world, is easy and adequate. God was good and free from envy; he wished to bring the chaotic matter to as high a degree of perfection as possible; therefore, using the Ideas as a model or blueprint, he fashioned the matter into a beautiful physical universe.

But is not the ultimate plurality of three principles as philosophically objectionable as Democritus' atoms? What would Parmenides have said? This problem was considered with great care by Plotinus, the Neoplatonist.

Scientific Detail

To follow Plato through the interesting details of his cosmology would require lengthy exposition. He explains that the world is a living being, as the model is. The soul of the world has been composed with mathematical care so that, surprising as it may be, the eight-note musical scale — probably Plato's own remarkable invention — corresponds to astronomical distances between the planets. An intricate geocentric theory of the solar system is outlined, and at least two orreries were constructed. In this connection it is also essential to record that Plato in his extreme old age discovered the possibility of a heliocentric system, brought to a fine state of perfection by Aristarchus, and then forgotten until Copernicus rediscovered him and tried to take the credit. The *Timaeus* continues with a short discussion of time which provoked much longer discussions as history

continued. Then along with an analysis of the four common elements, earth, air, fire, and water, into elementary triangles, so that
fire, for example, is composed of four equilateral triangles in the form
of a pyramid, Plato, more closely examining that matter on which the
Demiurge imposed order, asserts that this third principle of the universe is space. And space like time has continued to be a standard
topic of philosophic debate to the present day. There follows a
further section on physiology and medicine.

But all this science is only tentative. Based on observation of the
world of flux, dependent on the deceptive processes of perception,
science cannot transcend its base to attain the Ideas. At best it may
approximate the truth, but it can never really know the truth. The relation between science and truth between the sense world and the
Ideal World, and in a way the motivation and summary of all Platonic
philosophy are found in three short quotations which may appropri-
ately conclude this chapter. In the *Timaeus* (p. 51 d) Plato says, "If
mind (intellectual intuition) and true opinion are generically different, then most certainly absolute realities exist, Forms which we cannot grasp by sensation, but only by the mind. If, however, as some
people believe, true opinion in no way differs from mind, all that we
perceive through the body must be admitted to be most certain."
From the *Republic* (p. 477), these phrases may be chosen: "As to
what really is, then, is there not knowledge, and as to that which is
completely non-existent, is there not of necessity ignorance? And for
that which is between these, we must seek for something between
ignorance and knowledge . . . Do we say then that opinion is anything? . . . And it is plain that we have found opinion to be a different
thing from knowledge." The late dialogue *Timaeus*, and the *Republic* from the middle part of Plato's productive career, only echo the
guiding principle that he had set down in the relatively early *Meno*
(p. 98 b): "That there is a difference between right opinion and
knowledge is not at all a conjecture with me, but something I would
particularly assert that I knew." And on this basis the great Platonic
philosophy was built.

CHAPTER **3**

Aristotle

It is an amazing coincidence of history that Plato and Aristotle (384–323 B.C.) lived in the same century and that the latter was the pupil of the former. No other century can boast of such an amount of genius; no other pupil had such a teacher, and no other teacher had such a pupil. Extreme enthusiasm for Kant or Hegel might place the one or the other nearly on a level with Plato or Aristotle, but sober judgment fails to find an equal combination anywhere. Coincidences of history, however, may be of little significance. It is the clash of ideas that is important.

In the last chapter, in the section on the *Parmenides*, it was stated that Aristotle accepted the objections which Plato raised against his own theory. And there are others also. Accordingly, Aristotle considered the world of Ideas as a useless duplication of this world: useless, quite aside from the apparently intolerable difficulties involved in Platonism, because skepticism and all the troubles inherited from the Presocratics can be satisfactorily removed without its dubious aid. The student should be forewarned that Aristotle is not building on unaltered Platonic foundations; but precisely what Aristotle accepts from Plato and what he rejects, and how he combines and modifies the several factors, is a long and intricate story which makes Aristotle one of the hardest philosophers to understand. Then, too, his dull and methodical style does not cheer the flagging spirit. Plato was a vigorous and stimulating writer; he could combine the subtleties of epistemology, the excitement of politics, and the mathematical awe of astronomy all in one dialogue. The interrelations of the subjects, he constantly keeps before our eyes. Aristotle, on the contrary, carefully devotes one book to Logic, another to Physics, another to Psychology, and so on. This method undoubtedly has advantages, but the interrelations, which still exist, are hidden from view and must be sought out.

THE LAW OF CONTRADICTION

It is most appropriate to begin an account of Aristotle with some reference to his views on logic because the books on logic are logically put first in the corpus, and because his discussion of the fundamental laws of logic — the law of contradiction and the law of excluded middle — though taken from the *Metaphysics*, Book Gamma, forms a firm connection between earlier philosophy and the body of Aristotelian thought. For if Aristotle rejects the essential principles of Platonism, we should see at once how he will avoid the skepticism of Protagoras. Also it is at this point that the connection between logic and natural philosophy in general can be most clearly seen. For although logic aims to discover the principles on which all true judgment depends, it is not a merely formal science of thinking; but rather, since truth requires a relation to reality, the laws of logic must be, not only the laws of thought, but the laws of reality as well.

Logic and Reality

Aristotle introduces the topic by questioning whether logic and reality are the objects of the same science or of two different sciences. In view of the fact that the truths of logic and the principles of reality apply universally and are not restricted to any special field of study, Aristotle concludes that they belong to the same science. The truths of botany or of geometry, on the other hand, do not apply universally: geometry concerns being in so far as it occupies space, and botany is limited to being as it exhibits nutrition and growth. Yet all the special sciences make common use of the laws of logic because these laws hold for all reality, and not merely for that part of reality that the special science studies. But the special sciences use logic without discussing it. It would be incongruous for a botanist or an astronomer to discuss the nature of truth and the law of contradiction. No doubt some of the Presocratics did so, and their inclusion of this material is perhaps defensible on the ground that they thought they were discussing the whole of reality. But in this they were mistaken; for nature is only one genus of reality, and physics, while it is a kind of wisdom, is not the first kind. Therefore there must be a still more universal science that deals with primary being, and to this science Aristotle sometimes gives the name of First Philosophy. As the botanist or physicist is responsible for the most general principles within his special sphere, principles applying to the particular kind of being that forms the subject matter of that science, so the philosopher must state and explain the principles that apply to being without qualification, to all being without exception, to being *qua* being — principles that are absolutely universal without any restriction at all. It is therefore the prerogative of philosophy, and not of botany or any other special science, to study the most general principles of all existence.

The most certain of all principles is the law of contradiction, for it is impossible to be mistaken about it. It is not an hypothesis, a tentative by which to rise to something more general, for a principle which everyone must have who knows anything about being cannot be so characterized. The principle is this: the same attribute cannot attach and not attach to the same thing in the same respect. Or, otherwise, contrary attributes cannot belong to the same subject at the same time. This principle, be it noted again, is stated not merely as a law of thought, but primarily as a law of being. The ontological form is basic, the purely logical is derivative: it becomes a law of thought because it is first a law of being. If anyone should object to the law of contradiction and should assert, as Heraclitus is supposed to have done, that contrary attributes attach to the same thing, it would be necessary to conclude that he cannot believe what he says. For if we have shown that the number three cannot be both odd and even, and that a stone cannot be both heavy and light, and so on, then it follows that no one can think that three is both odd and even, even though he verbally makes such an assertion. Anyone who pretended to believe that contrary attributes attach to the same subject would be affirming two contrary opinions at the same time; and these two opinions would be as it were two contrary attributes attaching to him as a subject. But this is what the law of contradiction makes impossible.

Indemonstrable Axioms

Not only has the Heraclitean coexistence of contraries been maintained, but there are some writers who, thinking that the above derivation of psychological from ontological impossibility is circular, demand that the law of contradiction be formally demonstrated. This demand, however, evinces their ignorance. The demonstration of a proposition, such as any theorem in geometry, is completed only when it is referred back to the axioms. If the axioms in turn required demonstration, the demonstration of the proposition with which we began would remain incomplete, at least until the axioms could be demonstrated. But if the axioms rest on prior principles, and if these too must be demonstrated — on the assumption that every proposition requires demonstration — the proof of our original theorem would never be finished. This means that it would be impossible to demonstrate anything, for all demonstration depends on indemonstrable first principles. Every type of philosophy must make some original assumptions. And if the law of contradiction is not satisfactory, at least these Heracliteans fail to state what principle they regard as more so. Nonetheless, though the law of contradiction is immediately evident and is not subject to demonstration, there is a negative or elenctic argument that will reduce the opposition to silence.

Significant Speech

The negative method avoids the charge of begging the question, for it is the opponent and not oneself who makes the assertion. Of course this depends on the opponent's willingness to say something. The proof aims to show the opponent who attacks the law of contradiction that so soon as he says anything at all, he is recognizing the principle. If he should say nothing, we have neither an opponent nor an objection to face. Nor need we insist that he make some tricky admission that plays into our hands. All that is required is that he say something significant for himself and for us, for this is the presupposition of every understanding between two persons, or even of one person's understanding himself. Let the opponent then say something: that three is an odd number or that Socrates is a man. It will always be of the form, x is y. Now, in the first place, the word *is* has a definite meaning and does not mean *is not*. Therefore Protagoras was mistaken when he said that everything is and is not.[1] But perhaps the argument will be clearer if we consider the x and the y.

In any sentence the predicate, the y, must have a single, definite meaning; and when we say that x is y, or that Socrates is a man, we are asserting of Socrates the meaning of *man*, whatever it may be — two-footed animal, perhaps. Thus we assert something definite. The remark that words have several meanings will not damage this contention, provided the meanings are limited in number. Suppose the word *man* had ten different meanings: it would be possible to invent ten different terms so that each term would stand for a single meaning; and once more the predicate and the assertion as a whole would be definite. If, however, terms had an infinite number of meanings, then all reasoning would come to an end. For if a word is to convey a significance, it must not only mean something, it must also not mean something. If it had all the meanings of all the terms in the dictionary, it would be useless in speech. Therefore if terms had an infinite number of meanings, no term would have one meaning; and not to have one meaning is to have no meaning; but if words have no meaning, it is impossible to argue with other people or even to reason privately within oneself. If we do not think one thing, we think nothing; but if we can think of one thing, then we can assign to it a single unambiguous term. On this basis it is impossible that *being a man* should mean precisely *not being a man*, or that perception should be nonperception, or that a wind should be both y and not-y. And this is in reality a justification of the law of contradiction.

The Sophists, both of antiquity and of the present, ignoring the ontological basis of this argument, attempt the reply that what one person calls a man, another may call a mouse and not a man. Hence the same thing would be both man and not-man. But this is elementary ambiguity. The question is not whether a subject can be man

[1] Cf. *Theaetetus*, p. 183 a.

and not-man in name, but whether it can be so actually or ontologically. If man and not-man mean two different things, as was indicated above, and if man means two-footed animal, it follows that anything that is a man must be a biped. But if this must be so, i.e., if this is necessary, the contrary is impossible: it is impossible that the subject should not be a two-footed animal, and hence the same subject cannot possibly be both man and not-man.

Denial of Substance

Further to refute his opponents, Aristotle plunges into logical and ontological complexities that will try the most ambitious student. Those who argue against the law of contradiction must also deny substance and reality. To explain how this is so and why it is absurd requires reference to the theory of categories, later to be explained. To anticipate, however, it may be briefly stated that a category is a predicate; or, more precisely, the ten categories are the ten types of possible predicates. For example, of Socrates it may be said that he is a man, he is ugly, he is wise, he is short, he is heavy, and perchance he is a musician. But of these, the predicate *man* holds a favored position. Heavy and musical are accidental predicates; that is, it is not necessary or essential to being a man that one should be heavy or musical: there are men who are frail and unmusical. These predicates and other accidental predicates fall under the categories of quality, quantity, relation, or others. But the predicate *man*, when one says that Socrates is a man, is no accident: man is what Socrates essentially is. The predicate *man* falls under the category of substance or reality. And the category of substance is basic because there can be no quality or quantity unless there is a substance that it is the quality of.

The Sophistic opponents of logic, however, do away with substance, for they must say that all attributes are accidents, and that no subject is essentially man. The line of reasoning behind this is as follows. To be essentially and substantially man is incompatible with being not-man or not being man, for when we say that Socrates is essentially man, we are designating his substance; and to designate a thing's substance, essence, or reality is to deny that it is essentially or really something else. The skeptical relativists must say therefore that nothing can be defined and that all attributes are accidental. But if all predication is accidental, there will be no reality of which the predication is made, and predication would be endless. This, however, is impossible, because, far from being endless, not more than two terms can be joined in accidental predication. We may say that the musician is blond or even that the blond is musical; but the accidental conjunction of blond and musical is possible only because they are both accidents of the same reality — Socrates perhaps. In the absence of an underlying subject of which both are predicates, blond could not be predicated of musical nor musical of blond. Now, when we say that Socrates is musical or that Socrates is blond, the predicate is not related to its subject as in the previous predications, for, while blond and musical were equally accidents of an underlying reality, Socrates and musical are not thus on the same level as accidents of some third subject. Socrates is not a predicate at all, and hence there cannot be an infinite series of predicates: every series must end with a reality.

As this section of Aristotle is somewhat subtle, and as its importance has been seen in Plato's refutation of Protagoras, it will be well to elaborate a little. Aristotle may be willing to admit that the law of contradiction as stated does not hold for accidental predication. The musician can be white; yet since white is "not-musical," the musician can be "not-musical." But with substantial predication, the case is different. Suppose we ask the opponent if A is a man. He could answer, Yes, but he is also white and musical, and these are not-man, hence A is man and not-man. This answer is correct to the extent that a subject may have an indefinite number of accidents; but so understood the answer is beside the point. Our original question was, Is A essentially a man? If the opponent ignores the "essentially," as he did in the answer just given, he should list all the accidents — all, and that includes the negative as well as the positive ones. He should therefore say A is man, musical, white, not-green and therefore blue, not-ship and therefore house. For, if it is true that man is not-man, as the opponent claimed just above, it is all the more true that man is not-ship; but since house is not-ship and since on this theory contrary accidents attach, the man must be both a house and also a ship. Such a list of accidents would be infinite. Yet, if the opponent begins to list these accidents, he ought to continue with them. Let him give all or none. There is no reason for specifying only three or four. From which it follows that if he begins and continues, he will take so long that we shall be spared the trouble of answering him. In other words, if the opponent depends on accidental predication, if he repudiates the distinction between substantial and accidental predication, discussion ends. On this theory no predicate is definitive, and the metaphysical implication is that reality does not exist.

Now, to repeat a thought previously stated near the beginning of this analysis of the law of contradiction: this analysis or "proof" is a negative or elenctic one. It is not a demonstration based on more original principles. A careless reading might conclude that the law is demonstrated from the principle that every word must have a single meaning. But the truth of the matter is quite the reverse. Aristotle is saying rather that every word must have a single meaning because the principle of contradiction holds. He is applying the law to this particular case. And the particular case is chosen for the purpose of showing that an opponent cannot carry through his own theory. He becomes tangled in an infinite regress and must drop out of the argument. Therefore, if anyone, including the opponent, wishes to argue, reason, discuss, or say anything meaningful, he must presuppose the law of contradiction. Hence, this law is not demonstrated from some higher principle, but Aristotle shows that it must be presupposed by anyone who wishes to speak intelligibly.

The inanity of skeptical relativism was hinted at in the remark above that the musician must be a not-ship and therefore a house. This has a further ontological implication. If contradictory statements are true of the same subject at the same time, evidently all things will be the same thing. Socrates will be a ship, a house, as well as a man; but then Crito too will be a ship, a house, and a man. But if precisely the same attributes attach to Crito that attach to Socrates, it follows that Socrates is Crito. Not only so, but the ship in the harbor, since it has the same list of attributes too, will be identified with this Socrates-Crito person. In fact, everything will be everything. Therefore everything will be the same thing. All differences among things will vanish and all will be one. Such is the metaphysical nonsense to be derived from Protagoras or anyone else who denies the law of contradiction.

An Ethical Anticipation

Aristotle continues in this vein for a few pages, stressing the *ad hominem* aspects of his remarks. Only one of these remarks will be included here. It is singled out partly because, together with other points in the argument, it shows Aristotle's dependence on Plato; also partly because it anticipates St. Augustine's later effective use of the theme; but mainly because it reminds us again of the connection between logic and ethics. The subjectivists, says Aristotle, who make all predications indiscriminately, should carry their theory into their conduct, and instead of actually walking to Megara should stay at home and merely think they are walking. Or, more pointedly, if all predications are equally true, why, when they are walking, should they avoid walking over a precipice? According to their theory the predicates good, pleasant, advantageous, attach to falling over a cliff as much as to keeping to the path. The skeptics' actual conduct, for skeptics do not jump off precipices any more than other people, shows that they do not really believe what they say.

Refutation of Protagoras

Logic is the organon or instrument that is needed for the study of all other subjects, and hence is systematically first in the development of Aristotle's philosophy. Of the various phases of logic the law of contradiction is being discussed first because it is the basis of all the rest and because its discussion gives Aristotle's relation to the Presocratic and especially the Sophistic movements. And this relation should be made as clear as possible because Aristotle does not accept the Platonic solution of these difficulties. Up to this point the account has centered on the logical defense of the law of contradiction, howbeit with some insistence that there are ontological implications. Aristotle completes his defense by coming to closer grips with the ontological and particularly the physical basis of Presocratic confusion and Sophistic skepticism.

He notes that the doctrine of Protagoras and the repudiation of the law of contradiction stand or fall together. The two mutually imply each other. If knowledge is perception and all opinions are true, then all statements are both true and false; for it is Protagoras' opinion that all opinions are true, and therefore this opinion is true; but it is

Plato's that Protagoras' statement is false; Protagoras' statement is therefore both true and false. But this means that the same thing is and is not: being is and is not. Since truth is a statement of reality as it really is, and since both contradictories are true, it follows that reality is and is not. Conversely, if reality is and is not, all opinions are true.

Now, how can Protagoras or any others have come to this opinion? The question is not without an intelligible answer. Aside from the frivolous arguments, the eristics of the *Euthydemus*, the serious Sophists base their views on observation of the sensible world. They think that contradictories or contraries are true at the same time because they see contrary qualities being generated out of the same thing. Water can become ice and it can become steam; wheat, when eaten, can become horse or man. Since, however, Parmenides has persuaded us that from nothing nothing comes, i.e., that which is not cannot come into being, the contraries so generated must have secretly coexisted in the thing, water or wheat, out of which they came: the water was really ice and steam at the same time and the wheat was both man and horse. This view was explicitly adopted by Anaxagoras, but implicitly it is Democritus' view as well; for Democritus says that all things are composed of atoms and void, and he identifies atoms with being and void with non-being. The Sophists merely made more explicit and put more emphasis on this line of reasoning that was imbedded in most of the thinking of the Presocratics. Now, these men were neither stupid nor were they rogues. There is an element of truth in what they say. But they failed to make a distinction. Water in a certain sense is ice and is steam: it is not actually ice and actually steam, but it is potentially the one and the other. The contrary qualities do not exist actually in the subject, but the subject is potentially both. This distinction between potentiality and actuality is a most important one for Aristotle, and while nothing more can be said about it at the moment, one should recognize that without this distinction Aristotle's philosophy would completely collapse. Another error of the Presocratics was their belief that all substances were subject to destruction, generation, or motion. It will be necessary later to defend the existence of another type of substance.

There is another though related line of argument by which thinkers have arrived at the skeptical position. Some of them have supposed that truth should not be determined by any democratic voting procedure: the fact that one hundred people believe a theory does not make it twice as true as another theory held by fifty. If a lesser number believe that olives taste bad and a greater number that they taste delicious, the greater number should not be accorded special privileges in truth. If they were, then insanity would be determined by vote, and in some society all those we now think sane would be institutionalized because they would be outvoted. Now, if two people receive different tastes from olives, or different colors from trees, there is no obvious way to determine which the real taste or real color is. In fact, the one quality is no more the true quality than the other. And thus all opinions are true. Even when the Presocratics did not explicitly say this, it is implied in their view that sensation is knowledge and is a physical alteration. These views are consistent with and depend on the notion that only physical or sensible things are real and that they are in constant motion. But in the first place physical things are not thoroughly or one hundred per cent actual; in sensible nature there is a large admixture of the indeterminate, i.e., potentiality. And in the second place, while it is true that no definite statement can be made about that which is always changing, it will be shown that change is not absolutely universal, even in the sensible world.

Change Is Not Universal

Aristotle has at least four reasons to advance, of which three will be here reproduced. First, change is not absolutely universal because when a thing is losing a quality, it still has some of the quality that is being lost. If liquid water is becoming steam, there must still be some liquid, for if there were no liquid and all were steam, it would not be in process of becoming: the process would have ended. At the same time the steam must have some of the new gaseous quality, for if this quality were not yet present, the change would not have begun. These two qualities therefore must exist: the liquid is liquid and the vapor is vapor. Hence in every case of qualitative change, one can distinguish at least in time and sometimes in space, a part which has changed and a part which has not changed. Both exist. In other words, the processes of generation and destruction can occur only against a background of being; and about this being true statements can be made.

Second, qualitative change is not the same as quantitative change. We may admit that every physical object is constantly changing in quantity; but we do not know things by their quantity. We know that Socrates is a man, not because he weighs one hundred and sixty pounds, but in virtue of the form man. This form remains; it does not change with the weight; and hence true and definite statements are possible. And in the next place, the mention of such a form indicates the existence of a nonphysical and unchanging reality: Socrates may change to be sure, but man is always man.

If it now be admitted that these arguments, and others also that are in Book Gamma, rather thoroughly dispose of relativism and subjectivism, it is still not clear that Aristotle can successfully build a system of philosophy without appeal to Platonic Ideas. This is the very beginning and already he has spoken of nonsensible reality: what can this be but a Platonic Idea? Just above he mentioned the form *man*. Would not Plato approve? Then too, this law of contradiction itself: what is it? Is it not some suprasensible, transcendent principle, independent of all flux, enjoying the same characteristics and privileges that Plato accorded to the realities of the Ideal world? To answer these questions it will be necessary to pursue logic further, beyond the law of contradiction, to Aristotle's explanation of the nature of the knowable and the process of learning.

LOGIC

The law of contradiction is of course logic, but because of its unique importance it was given special treatment. The remainder of logic for Aristotle contains not only the theory of demonstration, i.e., deductive logic proper, but also a vast array of details and distinctions, some of which appear to be merely grammatical, as well as a theory of learning or epistemology. Deductive logic, the construction of the syllogism, must be omitted. But some of the preparatory details are of use in the explanation of knowledge.

The Categories

In the section on the law of contradiction reference was made to the categories. It was said there that the categories are the types of possible predicates; approximately the same meaning is obtained by calling them the several meanings of the verb *is*. Presumably there are ten such, though Aristotle keeps neither the number nor the particular items constant in his various references to them. For elementary purposes only two or three need be considered.

All expressions that are not composite (Aristotle means nouns and verbs, each standing alone and not in a sentence) signify substance, quantity, quality, relation, place, time, position, state, action, or affection. Man and horse are substances; two feet long is a quantity; white is a quality; double is a relation; sitting is a term of position; shod or armed is a state; to cauterize is an action and to be cauterized is an affection. The most important of these is substance or reality.

Substance

Although these ten are called categories or predicates, substance in its primary sense is not a predicate at all. The primary and basic realities are individual things, such as Socrates or Mount Olympus, and these are always subjects and never predicates. Socrates is a man, but man is not a Socrates. Mt. Olympus is steep, but steep is not Mt. Olympus. For Aristotle therefore individual things such as these are the primary realities; and this is a viewpoint easily distinguishable from Platonism. If these individual things did not exist, says Aristotle, nothing else could exist. This assertion, however, even if its truth be fully granted, is not quite sufficient to prove that individual things are the primary realities; for a question to keep in mind as the account of the categories continues is, What would remain of an individual thing, if the other categories did not exist? It could not be white, two feet long, seated, shod, or cauterized. Could it be anything? Aristotle further asserts that every primary substance is just as real as every other. Mt. Olympus, this ox, and Socrates are equally real. And still further, no single substance admits of degrees of reality within itself. Not only is one man no more or less a man than another, but he is no more or less a man than himself at some other time. This is one distinguishing characteristic of substance as opposed to quality, for obviously one man can be more or less heavy than another and than himself at another time.

In a secondary sense, species and genera, and nothing else, are substances; for example, man and animal, or olive and plant for only these define a primary substance. Other statements, such as Socrates is white, are irrelevant to the definition. The species is more truly real than the genus because it is more closely related to individual things: in answer to the question, What? more information is conveyed by stating the species than by stating the genus. To be told that that thing growing out of the ground is an olive is more satisfying than to be told that it is a plant.[2]

The most distinctive mark of substance or reality is that it remains numerically one and the same while admitting contrary qualities. One color cannot be light and dark; one action cannot be good and bad; but one man at different times may be pale and ruddy, warm and cold, or good and bad.

There are great difficulties in the theory of substance, and perhaps one may be adverted to in passing. If one and the same man, Socrates, can be warm and cold, can he also be living and dead; did Socrates remain numerically the same substance after his execution? How could one tell? Is the numerical unity determined by knowing that the subject is a substance, or is it recognized as a substance because of its numerical unity? And again, if Socrates is no more or less a man than another; if, that is, the species or definition of man may be equally predicated of Socrates and Crito, what is it that distinguishes Crito from Socrates? What is it that makes an individual? These questions, all of which Aristotle at least tries to answer, take us far beyond the categories; but it is well to have them in mind as we proceed.

Relation

The second category was that of relation. Relatives are whatever is said to be of something else or otherwise referred to something. A cousin is always a cousin of someone. Above is always related to

---

[2] Cf. *Metaphysics*, 1042 a 21, 1053 b 21, where genus is removed from the category of substance.

underneath. But Socrates is never a Socrates of someone. The primary substances are never relatives. It is important also to ask whether secondary realities can be relatives. The answer is clearly negative, for man is not man of something: it is not defined by reference to anything external to it. Yet it might seem that hand and head, as secondary realities, are relatives because hand and head are defined with reference to a living body. A hand is the hand of someone.

And here some parenthetical criticism seems called for. The category of relation has been defined by the use of the preposition *of*, or the genitive case in Greek, plus the Greek preposition *pros* with the accusative. Later philosophers, especially in modern times, have complained that Aristotle thought the universe could be arranged according to the rules of grammar, and this seemed ridiculous to them. Must all nature obey the rules of Greek syntax? In answer, several things may be said. First, although nature cannot be supposed to be regulated by the peculiarities of Greek syntax as opposed to Latin or German, yet, if the universe can be explained at all, that is, if the universe is essentially rational, then it follows that there will be at least a close correspondence between nature and language on the assumption that language is itself rational. Language and nature may both be expressions of the same rationality, so that from the former we can derive valuable hints as to the latter. The converse would also be true, for if language and nature are both expressions of reason, an age in which grammar had not yet been formulated could discover hints for grammar in a study of nature. Then, second, it is a question of fact whether or to what extent Aristotle depended on the peculiarities of Greek syntax. Where he did so, we may not want to follow him; but where he merely seems to do so, we must do him justice.

Of course a hand is a hand of someone; but the previous grammatical definition of relation is not complete. It is not merely the use of the genitive case that makes a relative, but the reference to an external object. Now, head and hand are substances, and we can know them definitely without knowing that to which they are related; that is, it is not always possible to know whose head or hand is meant. Hence neither these nor any other reality is a relative. In this case at least Aristotle has not been deceived by grammar. He may of course be open to other criticisms; for example, although we do not know whose head lies there severed on the battle field, it may be denied that we can ever know the essential nature of head without knowing its relation to a living body. And there are some thinkers who have tried to resolve, not only heads and hands, but all substances into relatives.

Quality

The third category, and the last to be discussed here, will be quality. In Presocratic pluralism, and especially in Democritus, the difficulties attendant upon the concept of quality were heavily underscored. Not only does the inconceivability of origin make the appearance of new qualities paradoxical; not only is the relation between qualities and geometrical patterns an enigma; but those early men never said what the term *quality* means. Aristotle now begins by defining quality as that in virtue of which things are said to be such and such. For example, dispositions and habits are qualities; insanity is a quality; however, a mild irritation when vexed is not a quality but an affection; density also is not a quality but the relative position of the parts of the thing, and similarly smoothness. Some qualities, unlike substances, admit of degrees, for one thing can be more white than another and one man can be more just than another. Of course, justice itself can have no degrees, yet men are more and less just, though they cannot be more or less men. Other qualities, such as triangularity, obviously can have no degrees. The distinctive feature of quality, however, is the fact that likeness and unlikeness can be predicated with reference to quality only. And it is to be noted that some things may be classed as both quality and relation.

Because of modern suspicions about substance and because of the many difficulties that have clustered around quality, Aristotelian or nonaristotelian, the line of argument needs careful scrutiny. Is it true that likeness can be predicated only with reference to quality? Suppose two men are not merely qualitatively heavy, but exactly and therefore quantitatively two hundred pounds. Cannot they be said to be alike in this quantitative particular? Or, what is worse, perhaps two hundred pounds is not a quantity but a relation between a man and a unit of weight. In this case could the distinction between quantity and quality or relation be maintained? And surely, men can be alike in having cousins, a relation; and in being armed, which falls under the category of state. Can these other categories, then, preserve their distinctness? This suspicion is fostered by Aristotle himself when he says that some things can be both qualities and relatives; and still more so when, after choosing an example of a given category in one passage, he uses the same example for another category elsewhere. This might lead and did lead to an attempt to reduce the number of categories, for the Stoics admitted only four. Yet four is possibly too many, and there is the danger that all the categories will merge, so that not even substance will remain distinct. For example, if likeness can be predicated only with reference to quality, and if Socrates and Crito are alike in that they are both men, the substance *man* has been merged with quality. But it would be ruinous to Aristotelianism if substance should thus evaporate. Yet once more it is Aristotle himself who raises these suspicions. In the *Metaphysics* (1020 a 33) he says, "Quality means the differentia of the essence, e.g., man is an animal of a certain quality because he is two-footed . . . and a circle is a figure of particular quality because it is without angles." This very nearly equates quality with form or substance, especially because Aristotle frequently uses "two-footed" as the definition of man. To press this would imply that man is a quality. The frequent use of "two-footed" as the definition of man, presumably because Aristotle did not want to take the trouble to think out the exact definition, also raises the question whether it is actually possible to define a substance. If this should be impossible, then the most knowable of all objects in Aristotelian philosophy would turn out to be unknowable. But these problems are extremely intricate, and judgment must be reserved until the theory of epistemology is more fully explained.

Epistemology

The difficulties inherent in defining, distinguishing, and comparing the categories might possibly be overcome in one way or another, if a clear and unexceptionable statement could be made of the manner in which the mind learns them. The conditions of demonstration or science must also be explained. And these two desiderata are additional reasons motivating a theory of knowledge. The most important source of this epistemological material is the *Posterior Analytics*. All teaching and learning that is based on reasoning, says Aristotle, proceeds from pre-existing knowledge. It is to be noted that Aristotle does not claim that all learning without exception is based on pre-existing knowledge. Plato and Kant may say something like this, but for Aristotle there is no knowledge completely a priori. It is when a student comes to school for instruction that pre-existing knowledge is needed for reasoned teaching. The pre-existing knowledge may be the admission of a fact or the meaning of the term used, or both.

This principle helps us to surmount a preliminary obstacle. Plato in the *Meno* had taken note of sophistic objections to the possibility of knowledge. Learning is impossible, so it was said, for a double reason. If we already know some item, then obviously we cannot now learn it; but if we do not know a given item, we could not even begin to search for it — not knowing what to search for; and if we stumbled on it by accident we would not know that it was the item we wanted to learn. Learning is therefore impossible. Plato aimed to solve the problem by accepting the paradox that we learn what we already know. He assumed that all men are omniscient by virtue of a previous life, and that in the present life learning is reminiscence.

To Aristotle this solution is unacceptable. He approaches the problem through one of the tricks that Sophists used on their unsuspecting victims. Do you know, a Sophist would ask, that every pair is even? Upon receiving an affirmative answer, the Sophist would produce a pair of stones or coins or something whose existence had been unknown to the respondent; and since their existence was unknown, the fact that they, the stones or coins, were even had to be equally unknown. From which the Sophist concluded that the man had not known that every pair was even. Some Greeks, not Plato, tried to solve this problem by saying, Every pair I know is even. But Aristotle objects that no demonstration is limited to the cases one happens to know. Geometry does not conclude with the assertion, The triangles I have happened to see contain 180 degrees; it concludes that all triangles without exception have this property. The solution of the paradox lies in the fact that recognition of a truth sometimes contains both previous knowledge and knowledge acquired simultaneously with the recognition. In the sophistic example the previous knowledge is that every triangle contains 180 degrees; the Sophist's victim now learns, This is a triangle, or, This is a pair; and with this information he simultaneously knows that the universal property attaches in this case also. For, continues Aristotle, there is nothing to prevent a man from knowing what he is learning, in one sense, while in another sense he does not know what he is learning. That is, he may actually know the universal principle, and thus know, but only potentially know, the particular case. But obviously he cannot both know and not know in the same sense.

Cause and Demonstration

With this hurdle passed it is now possible to begin the description of knowledge. There are various types, but knowledge *simpliciter*, knowledge absolute or without qualification, scientific knowledge as distinguished from inferior forms of knowledge or awareness, is always a knowledge of the cause. Knowledge is explanation, and to explain a matter is to state its cause. If, for example, we wish to explain lunar eclipses, we must say what causes them; and when we are able to do so, we are satisfied and say that we know. The scientific form of such an explanation is demonstration. Not all syllogisms, not even all valid syllogisms, are productive of knowledge, for there are dialectic syllogisms with uncertain premises; but all knowledge in the strict sense comes through valid syllogisms. Modern scientists, repelled by the sterility of medieval physics, think that Aristotle overemphasized the syllogism; some rash souls, like Francis Bacon, talk as if there is no need for deductive logic; but one or two things may be said in Aristotle's favor. In the first place, valid reasoning is of the highest importance in any age and in any subject, physics included; and since Aristotle was the first to develop the theory of the syllogism, and since he did it so well that later ages could not change it very much, he may be pardoned if he stresses it a little. In the second place, the most highly developed science of his day was geometry; only here was there a semblance of reasoned explanation as opposed to the chaotic collection of facts in zoology. To take the syllogistic method of geometry as the model for all science was therefore quite natural. Surely this ideal of science is no more reprehensible than that of a large group of modern thinkers who have wished to reduce all knowledge to mathematical mechanics. Aristotle should not be judged too harshly under the historical conditions.

Demonstration then is the method of science, for it is the syllogism that can point out the cause. Consider the fact that the stars twinkle and the planets do not. Why do not the planets twinkle? Let C stand for the planets, B for proximity to the earth, and A for not twinkling. Then, B is an attribute of C, and A is an attribute of B; consequently A is predicable of C. The question, Why do not the planets twinkle? is represented by, Why is A predicable of C? The answer is B. B therefore is the cause and explanation. In general, the cause is the middle term of a demonstrative syllogism; the conclusion is the assertion of which we wish to know the reason; the middle is the reason. Stress should be laid on the notion of cause, reason, or explanation. It is not sufficient to show that a fact is so. A knowledge of facts alone, a mere collection of data, is strictly no knowledge or science at all, nor is it sufficient to refer an event to a prior event. What is needed is a statement of the reason, the why, the cause, and this implies that the conclusion not merely is so, but must be so. Necessity, not just truth, is the characteristic of demonstration. Truth obtained by demonstration is necessary, and the proper object of scientific knowledge cannot be otherwise than it is. Demonstrative knowledge must be knowledge of a necessary connection, for if there is no necessity, there is no cause.

Since the premises of demonstration in the strict sense are universal and necessary, the conclusion will be an eternal truth. No attribute can be demonstrated or known to inhere in a perishable thing. There is a sort of accidental knowledge of temporary and special cases, but it does not deserve the title of demonstrative. An eclipse of the moon on a given night cannot be the object of science, but the principle that lunar eclipses are always due to the interposition of the earth is an eternal truth and therefore a proper subject of demonstration. In biology not only are the individual events beyond the grasp of science, but the processes themselves do not always occur in the same manner, as lunar eclipses do. Though for the most part the processes are somewhat regular, there are frequent exceptions. Biology therefore is less scientific than astronomy. And the less regular the processes we investigate become, and the more particular the objects envisaged, the more they sink into an indeterminate and unintelligible manifold. It is the determinate that is intelligible. Universals therefore are the proper objects of knowledge.

Primary Premises

Now since it is the conclusion of a demonstration that we are trying to prove, and since it is proved by giving the premises, it follows that the premises of demonstrated knowledge are better known than the conclusion. If we did not know the premises, obviously we could not know the conclusion. The conclusion cannot be more certain than the premises on which it is based. The premises are the cause of the conclusion, and therefore they must be prior to it. And also, in demonstration, although not in every formally valid syllogism, the premises must be true. For demonstration is knowledge, and there can be no knowledge of the nonexistent. The premises therefore must be statements of what exists or what is so; i.e., they must be true.

Of course there may be a chain of syllogisms in a demonstration, as there is in geometry. But the chain must have a starting point, and such a starting point must be, not only prior, causal, and true, but in particular primary and indemonstrable. It must be an immediate, basic truth. Nothing can be more certain than these basic truths, for if the least doubt attached to them, doubt would likewise attach to all the conclusions; and this would mean that science would be tottery. But the conviction of pure science must be unshakable.

In the nineteenth century it was commonly believed that science was as unshakable as Aristotle could have wished; but the prevailing mood of the twentieth century is that science is tentative, and that laws stand in need of constant revision. Therefore the current objection to Aristotle is that the science which he describes is nonexistent. The formal validity of syllogisms may possibly be foolproof, but their applications to concrete material, and more especially the premises on which they are based, are not completely beyond all doubt. To Aristotle this would mean that there is no scientific knowledge, as he defined knowledge. There was a similar difference of opinion in his day. Some said there is no knowledge; others said all truths are demonstrable. But Aristotle agreed with neither the one nor the other.

Those who denied the existence of scientific knowledge argued that demonstration is the only method by which something can be known. But demonstrations depend on premises. And if the premises are to be known, they too must be demonstrated. This leads on back in an infinite regress, with the result that the demonstration is never finished, or more accurately, never begins. Accordingly, there is no scientific knowledge. The other group also held that demonstration is the only method by which anything can be known; yet they held that everything can be demonstrated because proof goes around in a circle: every premise is a conclusion, and there is a finite series in which the end and the beginning are identical. Aristotle replies that a proposition cannot be both prior and posterior as this view requires. Since the exact number of terms is irrelevant, they may be reduced to three and the absurdity becomes apparent. Circular demonstrations would be equivalent to saying that A is B; Why? — because B is C; Why? — because C is A; Why? — because A is B. With circular and infinite demonstrations both ruled out, it follows that not everything can be demonstrated and that there must be first, indemonstrable truths.

A philosopher of a different school, Hegel for instance, would no doubt admit that the three-term circle is an absurdity; but he might argue that the exact number of terms is not so irrelevant as Aristotle thought. A bad circle is a little circle; but if a circle can be drawn so as to include everything, it is a beautiful circle. In a rational universe everything is implicated in everything else; and precisely for this reason a three-term circle is absurd: it fails to show the other relationships of A, B, and C. Hegel might even attribute some very small and very bad circles to Aristotle himself: he might ask, Is Aristotle's reply anything more than a two-term circle, in which demonstration is possible because there are primary truths, and there are primary truths because there must be demonstration.

At any rate, against the two views, Aristotle asserts that not all knowledge is demonstrative. There must be primary basic truths because the regress in demonstration must end in these basic truths, and these are indemonstrable. Therefore, besides the scientific knowledge, which is demonstration, there is its originative source which enables us to recognize the basic indemonstrable propositions.

In case any one should think that these basic truths are the laws of logic and nothing else, a notion implying that all knowledge could be fitted into a single, comprehensive, demonstrative system, Aristotle insists that every separate science has its own peculiar premises. They may be neither too restricted so as to cover only a part of a science, nor too remote and inappropriate so as to combine two or more uncombinable subjects. One cannot demonstrate geometrical truths by arithmetic. It is true, of course, that geometry can be applied in mechanics and optics, and that arithmetic is used in harmonics. It is also true that besides the peculiar premises there are common principles, such as the laws of logic for all science, and principles applicable in all mathematics, such as, equals from equals result in equals. Such common principles are used "analogously" in the several sciences: they do not mean quite the same thing, so it seems, as they are shifted from one science to another. In the *Posterior Analytics* Aristotle's example of two distinct sciences is arithmetic versus geometry. Arithmetic, a science of properties *not as* inhering in a substratum, is not only superior to harmonics, a science of properties as inhering; but it is also superior to geometry because it has fewer basic elements. The unit of arithmetic is a reality without position, whereas the point in geometry has position.

This separation of sciences, one for each genus, each with its peculiar first truths, raises many questions about the relationships among them. Aristotle's denial of a single, supreme, and all-inclusive science endangers even the superiority of Aristotelian metaphysics to physics, zoology, and the other sciences. On a smaller scale, more easily grasped, there is the relation of arithmetic to geometry. Aristotle is quite clear that there is no separate science of isosceles triangles, no separate science of equilateral or scalene triangles. If one should use three separate demonstrations to prove that the three types contain 180 degrees, and even if one could prove that there were only three types, still there would be no truly demonstrative or scientific knowledge of the well-known theorem. For an isosceles triangle contains two rights, not because it is isosceles but because it is a triangle. Triangle therefore is the genus, and the basic truths are coextensive with the genus. But arithmetic belongs to another genus, and principles are not properly used if they bridge any two genera. One may wonder how Aristotle would explain analytic geometry, not to mention cybernetics. Or, what would he do with the contemporary reduction of chemistry, once thought independent, to physics? In one passage he naïvely gives himself away by saying, "It is hard to be sure whether one knows or not; for it is hard to be sure whether one's knowledge is based on the principles of each genus or not; and it is precisely this that constitutes knowledge." [3] But if this is so difficult, how can it be maintained that science is unshakable? This difficulty is both ancient and modern.

At any rate, there are for Aristotle more than a few basic truths. Each science or each genus has some of its own, which cannot be transferred: the unit cannot take the place of the point. Further, the laws of logic cannot serve as premises for all conclusions; they must be taken in conjunction with the generic truths. Now, since scientific conclusions are numerous, the primary and immediate truths are not much fewer than the conclusions themselves. How these indemonstrable propositions can with certainty be known must therefore be an essential part of Aristotle's theory.

Nonscientific Knowledge

It has been shown above that scientific knowledge or demonstration is impossible without immediate premises. However, since these principles are indemonstrable, a knowledge of them cannot be "scientific" knowledge. There must therefore be another kind of knowledge, a knowledge that is actually superior to scientific knowledge because conclusions cannot be more certain than the premises on which they depend. Plato might have called this knowledge innate. But it is incredible, says Aristotle, that we possess such accurate truths, more accurate than demonstration, and yet fail to notice them, not only in infancy, but at any time before we apply ourselves to scientific study. Such knowledge therefore cannot be innate, and must therefore be acquired.

[3] *Posterior Analytics*, I 9, 76 a 26. *The Works of Aristotle* edited by W. D. Ross (Oxford University Press).

Yet, if we acquire these basic truths, they too, like demonstrated knowledge, must depend on pre-existing knowledge and a capacity to develop them out of this pre-existing knowledge. This pre-existing knowledge and capacity, however, cannot be superior to its developed state. To be concrete: all animals are naturally endowed with the faculty of sensation by which they distinguish or discriminate one thing from another. In the lower animals sense impressions are evanescent and these animals seem to have no knowledge beyond their present sensations. In the higher animals sense impressions leave a trace that continues for a time. Among such animals some are not but others are able to order and arrange these persisting impressions into what we call memory. From many repeated memories of the same thing a universal concept is formed in the soul, the one beside the many, the common factor within them all. It is this possession of a universal that makes possible both the skill of the craftsman and the knowledge of the scientist. These states of knowledge are not innate, nor are they developed from any higher state; they come through sensation. It is like a rout in battle being stopped by first one man making a stand, and then another, and so on until order has been restored. The soul is so constituted as to be capable of this process.

As if the illustration failed to illustrate, and because the account is admittedly difficult, Aristotle thinks it best to repeat in interest of clarity.

When one of a number of logically indiscriminable particulars has made a stand, then for the first time there is a universal in the soul; for though the act of perception terminates on an individual the content grasped is a universal — i.e., we perceive man and not Callias. Again, another stand is made, and the process does not stop until the indivisible universals (the categories) are obtained; that is, first we grasp a certain species of animal, and then animal *simpliciter*, and then on to further generalizations.

This is the process of induction, and by it we are able to grasp the universals, such as species and genera, and the primary premises as well. The processes of opinion and calculation are sometimes mistaken; but both demonstrative knowledge and intuition are foolproof and unfailingly accurate. And as intuition or intellect gives the premises, intellect, possibly the Active Intellect to be mentioned later, must be regarded as the source of science. It is consoling to know that at least part of the time we cannot possibly be mistaken, if only we knew which part of the time it is.

FROM SCIENCE TO GOD

Aristotle looks on logic, not as a science itself, but as an organon or instrument of science. It sets the form and conditions of real knowledge. But important though logic is, the great body of Aristotle's writings is his system of science. Some of it, the celestial mechanics for example, is outmoded; the great amount of zoological detail does not meet even Aristotle's own requirements for science, though the work was invaluable as a first attempt at actual observation and description; of course there are factual errors, as when Aristotle makes light a nonpropagated force and denies its velocity — a very natural error at that; and on the whole it is possible for an unsympathetic modern to berate Aristotelian science quite severely. Yet, even aside from the strictly historical value of his work as determining the course of philosophical thought for over a thousand years, Aristotle, even Aristotelian science, retains some value of its own. The beginner sees the blunders; the scholar acknowledges the genius.

Although the great mass of zoological detail shows that this was one of Aristotle's favorite studies, it is a poor introduction to Aristotelian science precisely because it has more details than principles; and this is so because it studies only a limited portion of nature. For systematic presentation a more general, indeed the most general science must precede — the science of nature as a whole. The name of this science and of Aristotle's book on these basic principles is *Physics*, for *Ta Phusika* means *The Things of Nature* and is not restricted as our modern term *physics* is. In accord therefore with the logical conditions for scientific knowledge, the task is to discover the principles, causes, conditions, or elements of nature. We must start where we find ourselves, with nature in all its diversity as familiar to sense perception, and by analysis advance to the explanation, cause, and first principles.

Motion

If the subject is nature as a whole, and not just the peculiarities of zoology or some other limited science, the main object of inquiry must be the process of change or becoming, for change is common to all natural objects, while life is characteristic of some only. Not only is the importance of change or motion indicated by its universality, but the most troublesome problems of philosophy, the antithesis between Heraclitus and Parmenides, the Pluralistic compromise and the Sophistic outcome, all center around motion. Plato too may be said to have failed because his Ideas do not explain motion.

Sentence structure, because the phenomena of change are expressed in sentences, gives a clue to the solution. There are several modes of expression. One may describe a change by saying, the man becomes educated, or, the uneducated becomes educated, or, the uneducated man becomes an educated man. The first mode is concise and colloquial; the third is the most complete form. This third form shows that through the change there is something that remains the same, for the same man, equally man, is there both before and after. The man may have changed his state, or in other instances his quantity or quality, and there may also be generation and destruction, i.e., changes within the category of substance; but in all cases there is an underlying subject that does not change. In the example above the being of the man has not changed. What has happened is that one form, uneducated, has been replaced by another form, educated. As Plato taught, change goes between contraries; or if "uneducated" is not a form in the strict sense later to be explained, the change at least goes from the privation to the possession of a form. It follows that change always requires something composite — a subject and two contrary forms; something truly simple, a pure form for example, cannot change.

Change is the most universal of natural phenomena because change in a sense is nature. Some objects are artificial, e.g., beds and chairs; other objects exist by nature, and we call them natural objects. Why is it that these latter are natural? What is the property common to them all, yet not found in the artificial objects? The property is nature, and nature is a principle of motion and rest. Suppose someone tosses a stone out of a window and it falls through the air, into a lake, and comes to rest in the mud at the bottom. This is an instance of natural motion. The stone falls through air and water by nature. Nature is the cause of the motion. But it will be objected that a statue, chiseled out of stone, is an artificial object, and the statue too will fall through the air, the water, and come to rest in the mud. How then does this motion distinguish between natural and artificial objects? Aristotle replies that the statue falls, not because it is a statue, but because it is stone. The principle and cause of the motion is immanent in the stone *per se*; it is in the statue only *per accidens*. And the two objects come to rest at the bottom of the lake because they are both stone. The artificial object does not rest in virtue of its being artificial. Therefore nature is a principle or cause of rest and motion in that body in which it is immanent per se and not per accidens. Note too that nature is a principle of rest as well as of motion. Had the object been cork instead of stone, nature would have caused it to come to rest on the surface of the lake. But stone naturally sinks to the bottom.

Democritus had explained the motion of a stone, not by any inherent principle, but by the fact that someone had thrown it. Or, more generally, an atom moves because another atom has bumped it. And the second atom bumped the first because it too had been bumped by a preceding atom, and so on back to infinity. This scheme seems to explain every particular motion; it explains why each single thing moves; but, complains Aristotle, it does not explain motion. At best Democritus explains only why this stone moves now; he fails to give any reason or cause of motion in general. Now, Aristotle as well as Democritus is willing to admit that the series of particular motions goes back to infinity: there was always a motion preceding any given motion. His principle of nature is not to be understood as though an absolute initiation of motion were possible. If, per impossibile, the world had ever existed in a state of absolute rest, no motion would ever have started. A stone falls, perhaps when it is thrown, or perhaps when rain and wind remove an obstruction. In this connection the stone does not initiate the motion. But once the obstruction is removed, it is the nature of the stone that determines the type of motion and the point of rest. The growth of a plant, as much a change as the fall of a stone, requires antecedent motions, but the type of motion is determined by the nature of the plant. However, while Aristotle and Democritus agree that there was never a first motion, that the series goes back to infinity, Aristotle in opposition to Democritus holds that a series of explanations cannot go back to infinity. An explanation must be founded in an original principle, and it is nature that is the principle of motion.

But which philosopher is right? Can Aristotle prove the existence of this principle he calls nature? No, he cannot. He explained in the logic that not everything can be demonstrated; the conclusions of demonstration eventually rest on principles that are more evident and accurate than the conclusions themselves. These first premises are grasped not by demonstration but by intuition. Now the existence of nature is one of these principles. There is nothing more evident or certain than nature itself, from which the existence of nature could be deduced. The trouble is that Democritus' intuition failed to work; his mind was like an army in rout and unfortunately no soldier made a stand. Hence he arrived at a mechanistic system, when infallible intuition should have brought him to a different conclusion.

Since nature is defined as a principle of motion, it is necessary to understand the meaning of motion in order to understand nature. Eventually Aristotle classifies change into types: generation and corruption; qualitative, or, in modern terms, chemical change; quantitative change, as growth and decay; and motion through space. All these are discussed at greater length than can be afforded here. Then, too, it is necessary to discuss continuum, infinity, place, void, and time, for these terms must be used in the explanation. But, first, motion must be defined.

Potentiality and Actuality

In the section on Logic the solution of the paradox of learning as presented in the *Meno* depended on the distinction between actual knowledge and potential knowledge. Also, in the section on Contradiction, the problem of the coexistence of contraries was solved by the same distinction. These concepts of actuality and potentiality are basic in Aristotle's thought, and here they are necessary for the definition of motion. But potentiality and actuality cannot be defined. Just as conclusions depend eventually on indemonstrable premises, so various terms are at last defined by means of indefinable concepts. The mind must grasp them intuitively from experience. That a piece of marble can become a statue and that an ignorant boy can become a learned man are matters of common experience. Again, a scholar asleep can wake up and start to study. An induction from such cases gives the concepts of potentiality and actuality. These are not to be defined, but are to be grasped by analogy. As he who can build is to him who is building, and as he who, though not blind, has his eyes shut is to him who sees, so potentiality is to actuality. With these indefinable concepts it is possible to define change or motion in general.

The definition is: "the actualization of the potential as such is motion"; or, "the actuality of a potential being when it is actual and operative, not as itself, but as movable, is motion." Aristotle elucidates with examples. When the buildable, in so far as it is buildable, is in actuality, the change called *building* is going on. Or, when we say that bronze is potentially a statue, it is not the actuality of bronze as bronze which is motion, but the actualization of "potentially statue," the actualization of the bronze as changeable, which is motion.

Now, it may be quite true, as Aristotle goes on to argue, that all previous attempts to define motion were failures. This in itself, however, does not prove that Aristotle's attempt was a success. On the surface it seems that his definition of motion uses the very concept being defined. Motion, he said, is the actualization of an object in so far as it is movable. But if the meaning of motion has not yet been determined, the phrase "as movable" adds no information. Next, the term *actualization* — unless we translate it *actuality* — apparently refers to some sort of process and hence presupposes a definition of change. And, finally, not to press the problem of deriving the two terms by analogy, actuality and potentiality are hardly suitable for explanatory processes. No doubt bronze can be made into a statue — this is a matter of experience. But to explain why bronze can become a statue, the statement that bronze has such a potentiality does not increase our knowledge. To assert that a certain matter is potentially a certain form means only that similar matter in the past has become that form. This is a statement of fact; it is not an explanation of the fact. Perhaps Democritus was right and there is no explanation. Motion is just an inexplicable factor of experience, and only particular motions can be defined or explained. Or, perhaps, the Eleatic arguments against motion were just so much conceptual jargon, and to refute them all that Aristotle needs is more conceptual jargon. In modern times, too, Bergson has complained that his immediate predecessors failed to explain motion.

Be that as it may, the full explanation of motion, including the subsidiary problems of time, place, and infinity, goes on to culminate an argument to prove the existence of a first, unmoved mover — Aristotle's God.

No First Motion

As has been said, Aristotle insists that motion never began and will never end. That motion is thus everlasting can be understood by trying to analyze an alleged first motion. Now, obviously, there can be no motion unless there is some object that moves, a stone or an animal for example. Can a particular motion of one such thing be a first motion? No, for such things are either eternal or generated. If they were generated, this generation was a change preceding their alleged first motion. If, on the other hand, they are eternal, they could not have been motionless and then have started to move, because rest is the privation of motion, a sort of obstacle to motion; and the obstacle would have to have been removed before the alleged first motion took place. Any motion selected therefore requires a prior motion, and accordingly motion never began. Similarly motion will never end, for there will always be a motion subsequent to any alleged last motion. When a thing ceases to be in motion, it does not cease to be movable; but if it could never move again, it would not be movable. Or, if the thing in question is destroyed, so that it cannot move again, still the destroyer would have to be destroyed before motion would come to an end. The conclusion is that motion is eternal.

Movers

The next step in the argument for God's existence is the proposition that whatever is in motion is moved by something else. Since stones naturally fall downwards, it is a forced or unnatural motion when they are thrown upwards. In cases of unnatural motion the distinction between the thing in motion and the mover is evident. This distinction is also found, though not so evidently, in the case of an animal running. This is the natural motion of a self-moving subject. But though animals move themselves as organic wholes, they have parts, like ships: one part is in motion and another part causes the motion. It is sometimes difficult to identify these parts, but at least it is obvious that the ears and tail of a dog are moved but are not movers.

The distinction between mover and moved is least evident in the natural motion of inanimate things — a stone falling downwards. Being inanimate, these objects do not move themselves: if they did, they could stop falling at any moment, just as a dog can stop running — they might even be able to fall upwards. No, they do not move themselves. What happens is that an obstruction is removed, and the stone naturally rolls down the hillside. Whatever removes the obstruction is the cause of the motion as an accidental cause. The true cause of a stone's fall is the cause that made the stone a stone. There was a process of generation by which a body of weight came into being, and the cause of the weight is the cause of the fall. Or, to alter the illustration, a process of generation produced an amount of gas, i.e., something not heavy but light, as when smoke is produced by fire; and when its obstruction, if any, is removed, it naturally falls up. In both cases the generator is the mover. And this is sufficient to establish the conclusion that everything in motion is caused to move by something else.

A First Mover

The next step in the argument, which is to prove that there is a first mover, is one of the most difficult. A mover, Aristotle says, may cause its own motion, or it may be set in motion by something else. And of course, there may be several intermediates in a series. "If then everything that is in motion must be moved by something," as proved above, "and the mover must either itself be moved by something else or not, and in the former case there must be some first mover that is not itself moved by anything else, . . . for it is impossible that there should be an infinite series of movers, each of which is itself moved by something else, since in an infinite series there is no first term — if then everything that is in motion is moved by something else, and the first mover is moved, but not by anything else, it must be moved by itself." [4] This difficult passage may be paraphrased as follows: There may be several items in a series of connected motions (Aristotle mentions a stone moved by a stick, moved by a hand, moved by a man); any moved-mover, like the stick, implies an ultimate mover not moved by anything else; while intermediate moved-movers require this first mover, the first mover requires no intermediates, for if it did, an intermediate would have to be inserted between the first mover and the next item, and then another intermediate between the first mover and the previous intermediate, and so an infinite series would be generated.

In so far as this argument is supposed to prove the necessity of a first mover, it must be viewed with suspicion. Since Aristotle has already insisted that motion never began and will never end, there seems no good reason to object to an infinite series or to insist on a first mover. Even in the case of animals, which move themselves, there must have been a motion of generation prior to the animal's moving itself; and if the cause of a stone's fall is the cause which produced the stone, all the more the man who moves his hand to move the stick must be referred back to his parents. Or, if it be suggested that while the man's body was generated by his parents, his soul, which is the real and first mover, was not so generated, then it would be necessary to determine whether a soul so conceived agrees with Aristotle's definition of soul, in his *De anima*, as the form of the body. This point of psychology cannot be discussed here.

Another suggestion in defense of Aristotle might be that the stone, stick, hand, and man series is not a temporal series at all; it is an explanatory or logical series; and that therefore the fact that

[4] *Physics*, VIII 5, 256 a 13–20.

motion never began is irrelevant. We might, that is, disregard the fact that the man had to pick up the stick, move it to touch the stone, and then move the stone. We might begin the analysis at the moment when the hand, stick, and stone are in rigid contact; in which case they would all move simultaneously and there would be no temporal series. Maybe this is plausible, but Aristotle gives no hint of rigid connections and simultaneous motions. Further, all this seems to be restricted to living movers, and it is not plausible that all natural motions, including winds and rains, are to be referred to souls. If such criticism cannot be shown to be irrelevant, it will completely ruin the argument for God's existence. Whether or not the criticism is irrelevant will have to be judged in the light of the remainder of the passage, quoted to allow Aristotle to speak for himself.

"Every mover moves something and moves it with something, either with itself or with something else: e.g., a man moves a thing either himself or with a stick, and a thing is knocked down either by the wind itself or by a stone propelled by the wind. But it is impossible for that with which a thing is moved to move it without being moved by that which imparts motion by its own agency: on the other hand, if a thing imparts motion by its own agency, it is not necessary that there should be anything else with which it imparts motion, whereas if there is a different thing with which it imparts motion, there must be something that imparts motion not with something else but with itself, or else there will be an infinite series. If, then, anything is a mover while being itself moved, the series must stop somewhere and not be infinite. Thus if the stick moves something in virtue of being moved by the hand, the hand moves the stick: and if something else causes motion by the hand, the hand also is moved by something different from itself. So when motion by means of an instrument is at each stage caused by something different from the instrument, this must always be preceded by something else which imparts motion by itself. Therefore, if this last mover is in motion and there is nothing else that moves it, it must move itself." [5] Has Aristotle assumed the point at issue, or has he not?

[5] *Physics*, VIII 5, 256 a 22–54.

Motionless Movers

Even after the necessity of a first mover as opposed to an infinite series is admitted, the difficulties do not cease. Some of the passages are extremely puzzling. Now, obviously, a first mover must either move itself, if every mover is in motion, or there must be an immovable first mover. Aristotle aims to prove that not every mover is in motion. Consider the possibility that all movers are in motion, that the motion is accidental, and that the accidental motion is the cause of the motions the movers cause. But if all other motions depend on an accident, and an accident is not necessary, then it would be possible for all motion to cease. But this is impossible, as already demonstrated. However, consider the possibility that some movers are in motion and cause motion with an essential, not merely accidental, motion. In this case the motion of the mover either is or is not the same species of motion as the motion of the thing moved. But if it is the same species, a teacher teaching a lesson would be learning the lesson, and he who throws would be thrown; but this is contrary to fact. If the motion is another species, then a mover in locomotion would cause alteration, and a mover in alteration would cause growth. But since the species of motion are few in number, the same species would soon reappear; and since the earlier in any series is more truly the cause of the last motion than an intermediate is, it follows that the mover in locomotion causes locomotion, the teacher who causes learning learns, and he who throws is thrown.

Unfortunately Aristotle's argument seems to contain a confusion. If the series of species of motion is circular, then teaching produces learning which produces teaching, and the teacher is taught. But are not teachers taught? One teacher teaches his pupils, who become teachers, and these in turn teach other pupils. The species of motions, being finite in number, return upon themselves; but the individual movers and moveds, being infinite in number, need not do so; and hence the impossibility or absurdity that Aristotle relied upon, does not exist.

At any rate, the conclusion presumably is that not all movers are in motion; or, at least, since Aristotle betrays a little hesitation as to whether or not the argument has proved so much, if the first movers are in motion, it must be a self-motion. Some additional proof therefore must be given to show that a self-moving mover is not sufficient to solve the problem.

A self-mover cannot move itself as a whole, for if it did, it would then both cause and undergo the same change as a whole, specifically one and indivisible. But nothing can be both agent and patient in precisely the same relation. Motion or change, as was seen earlier, is the passage from one form to another, or from the privation to the possession of a form. But that which produces the form must already have it, as that which heats something must itself be already hot. Hence if a thing as a whole moved itself, it would as a whole both possess and not possess the form in question. Therefore all self-movers so-called must be divided into two parts, a mover and a moved. It is true that the part causing the change may be put in motion accidentally by the part that changes, as when the soul of a man causes the body to move from one place to another; here the soul in an accidental sense changes its place too. But since this is an accident and not necessary, such a situation need not arise, and where it does not arise, there is an unmoved mover. Accordingly, that which primarily imparts motion is immovable.

However, since the self-movers with which we are most familiar are corruptible, such as men and other living beings, Aristotle must show that there is an incorruptible and eternal first mover, neither accidentally in motion nor in motion per se. Souls, the soul of Socrates, for instance, exist at one time and not at another — though since they do not have parts they cannot be said to be generated or to perish. Yet, since they are and are not at different times, such souls cannot be the only unmoved movers because there must be some superior cause of their existence and nonexistence. The processes of generation and decay in the world, since they are continual, cannot be explained by any unmoved mover that at some time does not exist. Nor can the eternity and continuity of these processes be caused by any combination of such unmoved movers, for the causal relation required must be eternal and necessary. Hence there must be some supreme and all-inclusive unmoved mover — a single one, since it is better to assume one such, if adequate, rather than many. Furthermore, motion is eternal; anything eternal is not merely successive but continuous; a continuous motion is not many but single; and a motion can be one and single only if the mover is single.

A First Motion

Before Aristotle comes to his conclusion, he turns his attention for a time from the first mover to the first or primary motion. Locomotion is proved to be primary in the sense that growth, alteration, and all other forms of change cannot occur without it, though it may occur without any of them. Digestion, for example, requires the bringing of food to the stomach. Aristotle further asserts that locomotion is first in time also; although if the sublunar regions of growth and decay have always existed, it seems impossible that locomotion or any other type of motion could have been literally first in time. It may be admitted, however, that for eternal objects — the stars and planets are individually eternal, while the objects subject to growth and decay are not — locomotion is the only possible motion. Further, with reference to his theory of continuity, Aristotle holds that only locomotion can be continuous and eternal, and of locomotions, only rotary motion. Since the universe is finite in extent, as Aristotle had previously argued, any object moving in a straight line would, if it did not stop sooner, come to the end of the universe, be forced to stop its forward motion, and be turned backwards. This moment of rest and change of direction, as Aristotle shows at some length, breaks the continuity. Rotary motion, on the other hand, because it can continue without break forever, is the primary and eternal motion, as we can see with our eyes on any cloudless night.

The cause of this eternal rotation is the first, unmoved mover. It can have no magnitude, because, among several reasons, an infinite magnitude does not exist and a finite magnitude could not cause an infinite motion.

Accordingly, in conclusion, there exists a single, continuous motion of a single magnitude moved by a single mover. If this mover were in motion, it would require another mover, ad infinitum. Hence this is the unmoved mover. It causes motion eternally, for under these conditions no effort is needed. (If no effort is needed, why could not a mover of finite magnitude cause the eternal motion?) Since the motion is in a circle, the mover must be at the center or on the circumference. Since the circumference moves more rapidly than any inner sphere, and since the more rapid motions must be nearer the mover, the mover, having no magnitude, sits on the circumference.

God

A few pages back, where the explanation of motion merged into the proof of the unmoved mover, it was stated that the existence of God was in question. But *Physics* VIII as just outlined hardly palpitates with religious fervor, nor does the unmoved mover seem to have those divine characteristics historically attributed to the God of Hebrew-Christian tradition. It will be interesting therefore, when we arrive at the medieval thirteenth century, to see how St. Thomas Aquinas utilizes Aristotle for Christian purposes. Unpromising though Aristotle may seem to be in this regard and fundamentally irreligious as he obviously is, there are one or two phrases in the *Metaphysics* and *De anima* which are less so. In addition, the *Metaphysics* answers the very natural question, How can something not in motion cause motion? Though some of the argument is repetition, a short summary is not amiss.

Substances, says Aristotle, are the first of existing things, and if they are all destructible, the universe would be destructible. But motion cannot be destroyed; it must always exist. In fact, there is an eternal, continuous rotation. Therefore the cause of motion must be actual, for a mere potentiality need not be exercising its potency, and this would imply the possible cessation of motion. The cause must therefore be eternal, immaterial, unmoved actuality. An unmoved mover can cause motion by being the object of desire, as a beautiful picture in an art gallery causes many people to move toward it. This appeal to desire in such a speculative subject is not so inappropriate as it seems because the primary objects of desire and of thought are the same. The primary object of rational desire is the good, and the desire is consequent on opinion rather than vice versa; i.e., we desire what we think good, we do not think an object good because we desire it. Thought is moved by the objects of thought; among these objects is the good; and the first of these objects is substance; i.e., the supreme object of desire and the supreme object of thought coexist in or even are the same being. The unmoved mover therefore produces motion by being loved.

On such a principle the heavens and the world of nature depend. Its life is a waking, perceiving, thinking life, such as men are able to enjoy for short periods only. Thought and its object correspond: the best thought thinks the best objects. Thought also thinks itself because it shares the nature of the object of thought; for it becomes an object of thought in thinking its objects, so that thought and the object of thought are the same. Since actual possession is better than empty ability, the act of contemplation is perfect happiness. God always contemplates, and therefore life belongs to God, for the actuality of thought is life, and God is this actuality. Therefore life and duration, continuous and eternal, belong to God; for this is what God is.

Next, the nature of the divine thought needs some clarification. If the thinking of the unmoved mover depended on an external object, its substance would not be the act but the potency of thinking, and so it would not be the best substance. But it must think either itself or something else. It cannot think something else, for thought of evil objects would obviously detract from the value of its divine life, and even relatively good objects are still inferior to itself. Since the best life consists in thinking only the best objects, it itself must be the only object of its thought; and since its substance and essence is thinking, its thinking is a thinking on thinking. This seems unfamiliar and almost impossible because ordinarily in human life thinking first has something other than itself as an object, and itself only as a secondary object. But even in human thinking there are cases where the knowledge itself is the object: the objection occurs because so much of human experience deals with material objects, but not all does, for in the case of theoretical formulae or universal concepts, where all matter is excluded, the act of thinking is its own object. Since therefore the unmoved mover is a pure immaterial form, its thinking and its object will be identical.

These reflections on the nature of divine thought must be concluded with a reference to the *De anima.* In this most interesting tractate Aristotle studies the human soul in all its functions. He defines it as the form of the organic, human body, describes nutrition and growth, explains the process of sensation and imagination, and finally arrives at thought. Thinking is like sensation in that an object must act on the soul or intellect. Thus the intellect is receptive of form and potentially its objects. To have a form of its own would make knowledge impossible, for such a form would hinder the reception of other forms or distort them; hence the passive intellect is actually nothing before it thinks. However, this is not the whole story. As in nature generally, so here, the potential which becomes requires an agent or cause which produces. Therefore in addition to the passive intellect there must be an active intellect — an intellect agent to actualize the forms which the passive intellect becomes in its thinking. This actualization is like light shining on colors and making them visible; or, to go beyond a virtually meaningless analogy, it is the disentanglement of forms or concepts from the sensory images in which they first must come to the human mind. Thus the active intellect is similar to or even identical with the "intuition" of the *Posterior Analytics* by which concepts are formed in consciousness.

But it is not clear that Aristotle intended this active intellect to be a human function, strictly speaking. In medieval times the Arabs and St. Thomas opposed each other, the former asserting that there is but one active intellect for all men (making personal immortality impossible), the latter naturally dissenting and asserting that each person has one of his own. Aristotle himself is all too brief and vague; maybe he deliberately avoided the problem. At any rate he says, the active intellect is separate, impassive, and unmixed; it has no intermittence in its thought; it alone is immortal and eternal; and since purely immaterial, reason and reason alone enters man from without, for no bodily activity has any connection with it.[6] When examined closely it is by no means easy to harmonize the *Metaphysics* and the *De anima*; the latter brings God — if the active intellect is God — close to man and involves it in a great deal of human knowing; but this seems to be excluded in the *Metaphysics*. But if the Arabs, Zabarella, and the Greek commentator Alexander

[6] *De generatione animalium*, II 3, 736 b 27.

are correct, this obscure passage in the *De anima* is to be included in the theory of the unmoved mover, which, as a whole, is the culmination of the Aristotelian system.

FORM AND MATTER

In order to streamline the argument which proceeded from the definition of nature as the principle of motion and rest to the unmoved mover, some extremely important Aristotelian themes were submerged. In particular, no account was given of form and matter, although they were assumed and some references were made to them.

The Four Causes

Starting with the problem of explaining generation, decay, and every kind of physical change, Aristotle works out his theory of the four causes, of which form and matter are the chief. One is not said to know a thing or to be able to explain it until one has grasped the "why" or the cause of it. The difficulties in explaining generation are so great that some of the earlier philosophers came to deny its possibility: all becoming, they argued, must arise out of being or out of non-being; but being cannot arise out of being, for it already is and need not arise; nor can it arise out of non-being because something must be present as a substratum. What is, cannot come to be; what is not, cannot produce anything. Aristotle's solution to this paradox is that the being from which anything comes to be is both being and non-being, but in different senses. This that is both being and non-being is matter, and matter is one of the four causes. "That out of which a thing comes to be and which persists, is called a cause, e.g., the bronze of the statue, the silver of the bowl, and the genera of which the bronze and silver are species." The bronze exists or is being in so far as it is the substratum of generation; but it is non-being in so far as it is not the statue. On a lower level the earth or metals of which bronze is made are its matter, and in this relation it is their form. And on a still lower level the elements themselves are forms imposed on a prime matter, which, however, is not physically separable. Then by extending the meaning of material cause beyond gross physical objects, it may be said that letters are the matter of syllables, and premises are the matter of conclusions.

The second of the four causes is the form. To continue the first example above, the form would be whatever the statue was, Zeus for example, or a satyr. The other examples, however, show that form is not so much the physical shape of an object, as it is the essence or definition of the object. It is what the object really is. The form of the octave is the ratio of two to one. The form of a tree is the kind of tree it is — a form imposed on its matter. The soul is the form of the organic body. And as on the lowest level there is a prime matter, so on the highest level the unmoved mover is a pure form entirely apart from any matter. Form requires lengthy explanation, but first the other two of the four causes must be listed.

The third cause, called the efficient cause, is the primary source of the change; for example, the father is the cause of the child, the sculptor of the statue. And the fourth is the final cause, final in the sense of being that for the sake of which a thing is done; as health is the cause of physical exercise. Why is he exercising? we may ask; and the answer or explanation by which we understand his activity is that he wants to be healthy. Upon reflection it will be seen that the formal, efficient, and final causes are the same. The formal cause of the statue was Zeus; the efficient cause was said to be the sculptor, but, more exactly, it is the form of Zeus in the sculptor's mind; and the final cause or aim of his activity is also the form of Zeus. The same may be said of exercise too: for the end is health and health is the form of man. Therefore in a sense there are but two causes or two parts to the explanation of anything: form and matter. For an understanding of Aristotelianism these two causes and the relation between them must be studied with care, and the first point will be the significance of form as final cause. In this regard there was an omission in the chapter on Plato which must now be filled in, and a reference to Democritus is needed for contrast.

Teleology

In the *Phaedo* Socrates complained that Anaxagoras had promised but had failed to offer a teleological explanation of nature; and of

course Democritus did not even promise: on the contrary, he insisted
on a strictly mechanical analysis of all phenomena. Qualities such as
hot and cold were defined by the geometrical shape and arrangement
of atoms; class concepts such as plant and man would receive definitions similar in character; and natural events such as weather,
nutrition, sensation and so on would be explained in terms of
mechanics alone. Nature exhibits no purpose, and if men have
purposes, there are merely more complicated mechanisms.

For Plato this was unsatisfactory. If reality were entirely physical,
perhaps mechanism would be acceptable if it could escape sophistic
skepticism; but if Ideas constitute reality, not only is mechanism
out of place, but a much better possibility is provided. Mechanism
does not explain Socrates' sitting in jail conversing with his friends;
purpose does. Similarly, weather, sensation, and all class concepts
must be understood teleologically. The Ideas are purposes: purposes
are what we know when we know anything. Suppose the latest model
automobile has a new gadget and we ask what it is. If the salesman
or engineer should give us its mechanical description down to
the fraction of an inch, should reproduce its blueprint in words,
should enumerate its wheels, ball bearings, electrical circuit or whatever else it might have, we would still not know what the gadget
was. But if he should tell us that it is a new windshield wiper, a
better timer, or a stronger shock absorber, we would be satisfied. We
would know it when we know its purpose. What is it? It is its
purpose. The purpose defines it. The Idea is the purpose.

Aristotle's forms like Plato's Ideas are purposes, and all science is
teleological. Take rain, for instance. Democritus would have said
that warm moist air must of necessity arise — a strictly mechanical
action; that when it cools in the upper air, it must condense and
fall as rain. If it rains on a wheat field, the wheat grows by mechanical necessity; but the rain does not fall for the purpose of producing
wheat. Sometimes rain falls on a threshing floor and the wheat
there is spoiled. No one would say that the rain fell for the purpose
of spoiling the crop; it is just a matter of mechanical necessity.
Similarly, men and animals have teeth through a natural process of
growth; and having teeth men and animals chew; but the teeth did
not grow for the purpose of allowing men to chew. Or, the teleologi-

cal view can be ridiculed as Voltaire did by suggesting that noses were made for the purpose of holding spectacles.

Yet, says Aristotle, it is impossible that the mechanistic theory should be true. Why it is impossible involves a theory of nature in which form is the dominant factor. Mechanists, insisting on the necessity and inviolability of mathematical law deny the popular opinion that some things happen by chance. But Aristotle, more closely in accord with actual observation, distinguishes between those natural processes, such as the revolution of the stars, which occur always in the same manner, and others, equally natural, such as the growth of a plant, which are regular or usual, but not strictly invariable. In these latter processes, exceptions or irregularities occur, such as mutations in plants or freaks of nature like a two-headed calf. In matters of human deliberation all the more, there are irregularities, some of which are lucky, as the case of the man who went to the market place and accidentally found a debtor who paid him off. Irregularities occur when the normal process does not attain its natural end or when the end arrives without the normal process. Regularity, conversely, is the process actually producing its end. Nature is thus like art: it begins with matter and produces a form. If nature could grow a house, it would proceed on the architectural principles that a builder uses; and if architecture could build a tree, it would parallel the natural stages.

To return to an earlier example, the rains of spring, since they permit of exceptions, are not to be explained or understood in terms of inviolable mechanism; but since they are regular and are not themselves exceptional, they cannot be chance events; hence they are purposive. In the case of ants and spiders, the evidence of purposive action is too strong to deny; and if teleology be admitted in these cases, it cannot be denied on principle.

Or, take the case of life in general. A physico-chemical explanation of life would probably attempt to reduce it to some form of oxidation, and Aristotle, using ancient terms, asks whether life can be explained in terms of fire. The following reasons imply a negative answer. A fire can be made to take any shape. There are round bonfires. Once to burn a field of weeds, the writer sprinkled gasoline around its edges, and the fire was for a time a hollow rectangle.

Obviously there can be all sorts of shapes. There can also be all sorts of sizes, produced merely by adding more fuel. If the supply holds out, there is no limit to the size the fire may be. But in life there are limits. Even the fat woman in the circus, though she is not shapely, still retains a recognizable human shape. And long before her food supply runs out, she stops growing bigger. The difference between fire and life therefore is a form which controls the size and shape of the living being. And unless we understand the processes of nature as teleologically directed, we have missed the main point. Even fire itself is purposive and is directed by a form; but it is a form that controls the direction of its motion rather than its size and shape. And the supreme form, overarching all the subsidiary purposes, is the unmoved mover, the ultimate cause of all change.

Thus, in opposition to mechanism, the cause or explanation of any natural phenomenon is a purpose to be attained in the future rather than an event that has occurred in the past. While the mechanists claim that past events are causes because they necessitate their effects, the facts are otherwise. No past event or condition necessitates anything. So long as there is a distinction between the event called a cause and the event called an effect, so long as these two are separated by an interval of time, it is possible that the effect will not occur. The mechanist might say that eating food is the cause of nourishment and growth. But obviously in the case of seasickness or of death in battle, a good meal immediately prior will not cause the effect. Or, to use Aristotle's example, if bricks and wood and saws exist, it does not follow that a house must be built. But if a house is to be built, the bricks and wood and tools must of necessity pre-exist. Causality therefore works from the future to the present or past; it does not work from the past to the future. The cause occurs after the effect, not before it. This is the characteristic of purposive explanation as opposed to the mechanical theory, now shown untenable.

The foregoing account of form, emphasizing the antithesis between teleology and mechanism — a modern as well as an ancient subject of contention — has kept close to matters of scientific interest. At least it has not gone very far across the indistinct boundary between physics and metaphysics. A concluding section on matter might well push on a little farther into the subtle territory beyond.

Matter and Generation

Matter, it was said above, is the substratum of generation; without this concept an explanation of change would be impossible. For example, warm as such can neither affect nor produce cold as such; but a warm thing may become cold. Hence change requires a thing, a substratum, or a matter which possesses a given quality or form at one time and a contrary form at another time. If the matter did not remain identical throughout the change "no-thing" would change. In thus describing matter as a substratum, as a subject to which forms attach, and even once as a reality, Aristotle seems to be granting some independence to matter. However, enough qualifications are added to avoid this error. Because matter is as such indeterminate, or perhaps better indetermination, i.e., without a form of its own; because it cannot exist by itself but only in combination with some form or other; because it is the contrary of form and is potential rather than actual; matter should be regarded as falling under the category of relation, as indeed Aristotle indicates in *Physics* II 2. Yet even this classification makes it too real, for relative pairs are ordinarily on a line as it were — one is as real as the other; whereas matter is indubitably inferior to form, its contrary rather than its correlative.

The qualitative change from hot to cold, however, does not exemplify the problem as acutely as substantial change does. By substantial change is meant a change within the category of substance. When water becomes hot or when a plant becomes green, the change is qualitative; in such cases we say that something has become so and so; but there are other cases when something comes to be in an unqualified sense. Aristotle writes: In qualitative change "the bronze is now spherical and at another time angular, and yet remains the same bronze. But when nothing perceptible persists in its identity as a substratum, and the thing changes as a whole (when, e.g., the semen as a whole is converted into blood, or water into air, or air as a whole into water), such an occurrence is no longer 'alteration.' It is a coming to be of one substance and a passing away of another . . ." (*De generatione et corruptione*, I 4, 319 b 8–17). He had just previously written: "We must consider whether there is anything which comes to be and passes away in the unqualified sense; or whether nothing comes to be in this strict sense, but everything always comes to be something and out of something — I mean, e.g., comes to be healthy out of being ill. . . . For if there is to be coming to be without qualification, 'something' must without qualification 'come to be out of not-being,' so that it would be true to say that not-being is an attribute of some things. For qualified coming to be is a process out of qualified not-being (e.g., out of not-white or not-beautiful), but unqualified coming to be is a process out of unqualified not-being" (*De generatione et corruptione*, I 3, 317 a 32–b 6).

If these last words were taken at full face value, it would mean that a reality could spring into existence from absolute nothing. This is not Aristotle's intention, although the matter of substantial becoming is so close to absolute nothing that Aristotle has trouble in preventing it from passing away altogether. "I define matter," he says, "as that which is in itself neither a thing, nor a quantity, nor any other of the categories of being" (*Metaphysics*, VII 3, 1029 a 20–21). To prevent this tenuous nonreality from being a Parmenidean nothing, Aristotle calls it potentiality. In the other forms of change, the matter is an actual reality in some relation and is potential only with reference to the new attribute, as the potential statue is actual bronze; but the matter of substantial becoming is entirely potential and is in no way actual.

Undoubtedly Aristotle tries to mitigate the difficulties so evident in such a construction by insisting that the substantial becoming of one reality is always the destruction of another: "But about this absolute non-being one might ask whether it is one of the contraries — e.g., is earth, the heavy, a non-being, while fire, the light, is being? Or, on the contrary, does 'what is' include earth as well as fire, whereas 'what is not' is matter — the matter of earth and fire alike? And again, is the matter of each different? Or is it the same, since otherwise they would not come to be reciprocally out of one another, i.e., contraries out of contraries? For these things, earth, air, fire and water, are characterized by the contraries. Perhaps the solution is that their matter is in one sense the same, but in another sense different. For that which underlies them, whatever its nature may be qua underlying them, is the same; but its actual being is not the

same. So much then on these topics" (*De generatione et corruptione,*
I 3, 319 a 29–b 5). But so much is hardly enough.

Individuals and God

Since the four elements are the simplest bodies, their underlying
matter is clearly incorporeal and imperceptible. A body is sensible
and tangible; matter is not. To be tangible means to possess certain
qualities; matter is the opposite of form and therefore is in itself
devoid of quality. But worse than being imperceptible, its lack of
form makes matter unknowable. As pure potentiality it can be
grasped neither by sense nor by understanding, but only by analogy.
And this brings back a problem only touched on in passing. In the
section on Logic it was said that for Aristotle the primary realities
are individual things; not man, but Socrates. If such individual things
did not exist, nothing else could exist. At that point, in view of the
peculiar relationships among the categories, there was raised the
question whether individual things could exist if the other categories did not exist. This question, as the discussion of primary and
secondary substance proceeded, developed into the problem of
distinguishing two primary realities of the same species. For Plato,
the Idea Man was real and Socrates and Crito were only half real at
best; to distinguish between such semi-realities might not be too
important. But for Aristotle these men are primary realities, and
though they are both men, and equally men, Socrates is not Crito.
What then is the source of their individuality? Aristotle's unfortunate answer is that the source of individuality is matter. The form
man is in all cases the same; hence only matter can distinguish
Socrates from Crito. But since matter is a virtual non-being and is
unknowable, the primary realities, the independent and basic things
of the universe are beyond our understanding. And this is close
enough to skepticism to make any dogmatist shudder.

But there is still another complication. The things of experience,
the natural objects, are all composites of matter and form; below the
simplest natural objects, the elements, themselves composed of matter
and form, lies the pure matter just discussed; now to complete the
balance, above the primary realities Aristotle has placed his unmoved
mover, a pure form, without any matter whatsoever. It must be pure

form, for it is completely actual and contains no potentiality at all. But if this supreme being is pure form, it cannot be an individual, and cannot therefore be a primary reality. Then does it not have to be a secondary reality, a species, and hence inferior to Socrates and Crito? This is an inconsistency to remove which would require some major alteration in the Aristotelian system. Indeed it might require a retreat to the theory of Ideas that Aristotle has been anxious to escape. An individuality that is based on matter is a negative thing, almost a defect, rather than an excellence; an individuality that would be an excellence and hence attributable to God could not be referred to matter. Or perhaps it would be necessary to deny individuality to God and assert that the highest reality is the most universal class concept — from which it would follow that plants, animals, Socrates and Crito are species of God. Surely there is room here for more extensive study, both in Aristotle's own writings and all the more in subsequent history.

CHAPTER **4**

The Hellenistic Age

The history of Greek philosophy is divided into three fairly well-marked epochs. First, the Presocratic period extended from 585 B.C. to 399 B.C. It was characterized chiefly by an interest in cosmology and science, the difficulties of which turned attention to skepticism and epistemology, and therefore to ethics. The "therefore," i.e., the connection between skepticism and ethics, is important and becomes more obvious in the sequel. The second period (385–323 B.C.) produced the great systematic work of Plato and Aristotle. These two men, the greatest philosophic geniuses the world has ever seen, resolutely attacked the problem of knowledge and on their epistemologies built imposing systems of science, politics, and ethics.

The third epoch of Greek philosophy, though by far the longest (300 B.C.–A.D. 529), is often introduced with apologies. In these eight centuries there was no man of Plato's stature or Aristotle's comprehension, and there was only one who approximated those well-nigh unattainable ideals. The Hellenistic age therefore is often regarded as a period of decay; and for this reason it may, as here, be given a short exposition, or even omitted entirely. Yet to regard it as a dreary waste is an elementary misapprehension. For one thing, it was during this chronological period that Christianity took control of western civilization — an event of no minor importance. Still, from another point of view, the very fact that Christianity was such a world-shaking event results in subtracting rather than in adding importance to the philosophic history of the age as such. Two civilizations were struggling against each other: the paganism of

Greece with its awe-inspiring intellectual past, and the as yet un-known Hebraic revelation with its moral and religious fervor. Pedagogical reasons therefore indicate the wisdom of tracing out the purely pagan philosophy to its end before returning to take up new themes. This is more easily done than one might at first imagine because, although the struggle between the two worlds was violent, the Greek philosophical development continued with virtually no reference to the new ideas. Accordingly, while the Hellenistic age runs on to A.D. 529, the medieval period somewhat peculiarly may be said to have begun five centuries before the previous age ended.

Even with Christianity thus excluded, the Hellenistic age still is not a dreary waste. To stand comparison with Plato and Aristotle, and in such close proximity, is a severe test. It is all the more severe since the philosophic writings of the two centuries immediately following Aristotle are all lost, and our knowledge of them must be built on fragments as was the case with the Presocratics. What remains shows that there were men of force and brilliance, whose ideas are worth considering. Then, too, in the third century of our era Plotinus, a great man by any philosophic standards, worked out a system — a Platonic reinterpretation of the best ideas of all previous philosophies — that may well be called the culmination of Greek philosophy.

After Plotinus the Greek spirit quickly and visibly declined. Proclus alone (–485) deserves mention; and when Justinian closed the pagan schools in A.D. 529, it was not the book-burning, witch-hunting calamity that some antichristian historians have made it out to be, but rather a decent burial for a long dead tradition.

THE EPICUREANS

If the Presocratic era is characterized as scientific, and if Plato and Aristotle are predominantly though not exclusively epistemological, the chief interest among the philosophers of the Hellenistic age is ethical. This is not to say that the age was devoid of scientific and epistemological activity. In the first place there were scientists, excellent scientists, such as Aristarchus, Ptolemy, and Galen, who made vigorous advances in the details of astronomy and medicine;

but as special scientists they paid little attention to philosophy. In the second place, the philosophers perforce dealt with scientific or at least cosmological questions; but more clearly than Plato and Aristotle they emphasized the connection between science and the practical problems of everyday living. To be sure, Plato's view of the physical world is related to the doctrine of immortality with its ethical implications, and the study of physics for Aristotle is itself an intellectual virtue essential to the attainment of happiness; but the Hellenistic thinkers, and especially the Epicureans, were more conscious that their pursuit of science and epistemology was governed by the extent to which these subjects seemed to bear on ethics.

Religious Superstition

According to the Epicureans the great problem of humanity was the fear engendered by religious superstition. Religion consists mainly in the belief that the gods reward and punish, especially punish, mankind. Fear of punishment in a future life makes the present life unbearable. And to avoid the curses of the gods, men have resorted to human sacrifice, even to the extreme of a man's killing his own daughter so that his fleet might have a prosperous voyage. Religion is thus the greatest source of evil, and the task of a humane philosophy is to free men's minds from this fear. To do so, the basic assumption and first principle must be that "nothing is ever begotten of nothing by divine power"; and the implications to be drawn include an atomistic explanation of phenomena that rules out the theory of providence.

This anti-religious, ethical motivation of atomism is an interesting procedure.[1] Men of religious conviction might be tempted to argue that since the denial of providence results in atomism, atomism must be combatted in order to defend providence. Materialistic nineteenth-century scientists, on the other hand, while accepting atomism and rejecting providence, would spurn any ethical or personal motivation as being inconsistent with scientific objectivity. Both of these reactions, however, face unexpected complications. First, perhaps

[1] Cyril Bailey, *The Greek Atomists and Epicurus* (Oxford University Press, 1928), pp. 482–487, gives the impression that ethics depends on physics, or, more accurately, both on sensation. This impression is somewhat modified on p. 504. It would be difficult to defend the thesis that Epicurean ethics is an implication from an independent and purely objective physics.

atomism per se is not necessarily inconsistent with providence. Could not God have created the atoms and could he not control their motions? Or, at any rate, one might admit that the pagan religions were devilish and that Epicurus is to be commended for his attempt to undermine them. After all, the Roman populace lumped together atheists, Epicureans, and Christians in a common condemnation. Second, with respect to alleged objectivity, perhaps the Epicureans only admitted openly what is true of every system of philosophy: that there is an ethical motivation. Friedrich Nietzsche, who was not always insane, said, "To understand how the abstrusest metaphysical assertions of a philosopher have been arrived at, it is always well and wise first to ask oneself, What morality does he aim at?" If there must be undemonstrable assertions, as Aristotle admitted, can they be motivated by anything other than the conclusions to which they lead?

Chance and Free Will

At any rate, the Epicureans adopted atomism in order to be relieved of providence. Matter and the infinite void through which the particles move are the fundamental principles of nature, and there is no third reality, such as Ideas, Forms, or immaterial souls. The atoms move without purpose or wisdom. No mind has ordered their arrangement; but throughout all time their collisions have arranged them in every possible way, and the present world is but one of these infinite chance combinations. The world cannot be the work of a wise providence because it contains too many obvious defects.

To this point Epicurus has merely reproduced Democritus, and without some originality he would not be included in any short history of philosophy. But with great ingenuity he alters, though he hardly improves, the Democritean system. According to the earlier philosopher the atoms individually had no weight; Epicurus, on the other hand, believed that there is a downward direction in infinite space [2] and that the atoms first fell by their own weight. But if

---

[2] Diogenes Laertius, X, 60, quotes Epicurus as denying an up and down, i.e., a zenith and nadir, in infinite space. Cf. Cicero, De finibus, I, vi. From this and with a reference to Lucretius, De rerum natura, II, 184–215, L. Robin seems to deny a downward motion through infinite space. But cf. Lucretius, II, 216–218, and the pertinent continuation in D. L., X, 60. Robin himself continues with the usual interpretation.

atoms fall straight down, with equal speeds through the void, they could never collide and form a world. Therefore Epicurus asserts that at quite uncertain times and without any cause, an atom now and then swerves a little from its straight downward path. This uncaused declination is very slight, too slight to be seen; and because the eye cannot detect the difference between a perfectly straight fall and the slight swerving, no observation can disprove the theory.

The motivation behind this rejection of Democritean mechanism is not merely the need of collisions in the production of a world. The motivation is mainly ethical. Since man, like all else in nature, is a combination of atoms, it follows that if atoms were mechanically determined, man would have no free will; and without free will there could be no morality. Mechanism means fate. Indeterminism allows us to follow our pleasure. Therefore the world must be composed of particles that inexplicably swerve at no fixed time and in no fixed direction.

To progress more quickly to the ethical theory, the details of Epicurean science can be no more than briefly sampled. In fact, from the Epicurean point of view the details of science are unimportant. "There is nothing in the knowledge of risings and settings, of solstices and eclipses, and all kindred subjects that contributes to our happiness" (Diogenes Laertius, X, 79). And Epicurus' letter to Pythocles (D. L., X, 64–117), as well as Lucretius' De rerum natura, presents various rival explanations of each of many planetary and meteorological phenomena, all of which were regarded as possible: it was not essential to determine which explanation is actually true; any one is satisfactory if it rules out providence and gives peace of mind. When happiness is more immediately at stake, as it is in questions concerning life, the principle is the same, but more care is taken. Life originally resulted and still results from spontaneous generation. Soul and mind, as combinations of particularly fine atoms, begin with birth, for had they existed previously, as Plato claimed, we should be able to remember our earlier lives. As the soul began at birth, so at death the combination breaks up, its particles disperse hither and yon. Consciousness disappears; the soul, i.e., the combination, no longer exists; therefore it cannot be punished in a future life, and there is nothing to fear.

Sensation

Since atomism, in the light of the Presocratic development, might seem to involve skepticism, the Epicureans, when they came to the questions of life and soul, paid careful attention to sensation. How images detach themselves from things, travel through the air, and impinge on the eye; how these images are reversed and reflected by mirrors; their passage through glass; and the judgment of distance; all these and similar questions occupy an important section of Lucretius' *De rerum natura*. The motivation is always ethical. For if skepticism were to be admitted, there could be no ethical truth. Now, skepticism is self-contradictory: one who knows nothing cannot know that nothing can be known. The Epicureans therefore had to provide at least some rudimentary epistemology. Sensation is the basis. The senses give the first knowledge of reality and cannot be refuted. Reason cannot refute sensation because reason is merely an outgrowth of sensation: if the sense were false, reason would be more so. Nor can one sensation refute another. The ears cannot deny the eyes, nor touch disprove the data of smell. Nor can one visual sensation contradict another one: they are caused by different images and therefore they cannot conflict. This basing of knowledge on sensation is entirely consistent with ethics, is in fact demanded by Epicurean ethics, for the norm of life is pleasure, and pleasure is a sensation. Or, if pleasure is not positively a sensation, it is the absence of the sensation of pain; and pain is so real that Epicurus defends the validity of sight and hearing on the ground that they are just as real as pain (D. L., X, 32).

Pleasure

The aim of life then is the enjoyment of pleasure, for it is our first and natural good. Epicurus offers virtually no argument to support this fundamental proposition; assuredly he does not attempt in some speculative manner to erect a normative principle beyond the mere statement of fact. It is not so much that pleasure ought to be the aim of life as that observation shows that pleasure is the aim of life. All living beings, as soon as they are born, delight in pleasure and take offense at pain, naturally and without reasoning. Pleasure is the rule by which we judge every good thing and is the determinant of every choice and aversion (D.L., X, 34, 129, 137).

Pleasure, as was said above, is not so much a positive sensation as it is the absence of pain. In so defining it, the Epicureans attempted to avoid the difficulties that attached to the contemporary Cyrenaic position of indulgence in the sensual pleasures of the moment. There was verbal agreement between the two schools that pleasure was the good, but besides the fact that the Cyrenaics were even less interested in epistemology than the Epicureans were, the two groups disagreed as to the meaning of pleasure itself and therefore in actuality recommended two different types of life. For the Cyrenaics, pleasures were those more violent and intense sensations connected with wine, women, and song. In this they were perhaps closer to the connotations of colloquial language. These men praised and lived a roistering and even bestial life.

Now, Epicurus admitted that every pleasure, including the most licentious, is in itself a good. There is no qualitative difference among pleasures by which one sort would be honorable and noble and another sort wicked. Only quantity counts. All pleasures are good and all pains are evil. But from this admission it does not follow that we should seek every pleasure indiscriminately or avoid every pain. For it requires no great intelligence to see that a course of debauchery fails to achieve a life of pleasure: pleasures, no doubt, it has; but pleasurable it is not. On the contrary, the licentious life suffers from a preponderance of pain. As someone has parodied the Cyrenaic motto: Eat, drink, and be merry; for tomorrow we shall have gout, cirrhosis of the liver, and delirium tremens. These were results the Epicureans wanted to escape, and to do so they distinguished between two kinds of pleasure. When a thirsty man is drinking, he feels pleasure, assuredly; but when his thirst is fully quenched, he experiences a different type of pleasure. The first is a sort of motion; the second possesses a certain stability for which it is to be preferred. The Cyrenaics in their love of intense sense pleasures had to accept the motion, or emotion, and this involved pain. The stable and greater pleasure is not the mixture of pain and pleasure exemplified in the thirsty man drinking, but the pure, unmixed pleasure of thirst quenched, which is in fact neither more nor less than absence of pain.

Cicero complains that to define pleasure as the absence of pain is a violation of common speech and introduces confusion into the discussion. The Epicureans were indeed misunderstood, and while this definition was not the sole cause, it might have been wise to use the term *pleasure* less frequently, substituting for it the phrase absence of pain or the technical Epicurean term *ataraxia* — calmness, tranquillity, composure.

In distinction from the Cyrenaics, this view leads the Epicureans also to recommend the pleasures of the mind above those of the body. Of course, the mind itself is a body, a collection of very fine atoms situated around the heart; therefore there is no pleasure which is not basically sensuous or corporeal. "I know not," said Epicurus (D.L., X, 6), "how to conceive the good apart from the pleasures of taste, sex, sound, and form." Another fragment quotes him as saying, "The pleasure of the belly is the beginning and root of all good:" and the Epicurean Metrodorus praised eating and drinking as superior to Greek garlands bestowed for wisdom, and made the pleasures of the stomach not merely the beginning and root but also the measure of all good. If this latter idea is insisted upon, the pleasures of the mind might be little else than reminiscences and anticipations of good meals. Epicurus' more moderate statement could possibly mean that nourishment and health are prerequisite to other pleasures in themselves greater but not independent. At least he says, "Plain fare gives as much pleasure as a costly diet, when once the pain of want has been removed; bread and water confer the highest possible pleasure when they are brought to hungry lips. To habituate oneself therefore to simple and inexpensive diet supplies all that is needful to health, and enables a man to meet the necessary requirements of life without shrinking; and it places us in a better condition when we approach at intervals a costly fare and renders us fearless of fortune" (D.L., X, 131). Whatever be the verdict as to Epicurean consistency, and whatever be the charges, usually exaggerated and often false, of personal immorality and degradation, there can be no doubt of Epicurus' approval of the more valuable pleasures of the mind. Pleasure is not a succession of drinking bouts, of sexual love, of fish and delicacies; but rather it is sober reasoning, searching out the grounds of every choice and avoidance, and banishing beliefs that throw the soul into tumult. Prudence is the greatest good; we cannot live a life of pleasure which is not also a life of prudence, honor, and justice (D.L., X, 131–132).

By sober reasoning Epicurus, as has been pointed out, did not mean a disinterested investigation of scientific detail. General education also seems to be ruled out by the advice, "Young man, avoid all forms of culture" (D.L., X, 6). The sober reasoning therefore is a searching out of the grounds of choice and avoidance, a calculation of the amounts of pleasure to be derived from conflicting courses of action. This is the means by which honor and justice are found to be essential to the good life. To be sure, as licentious pleasures in themselves are not evil, so too injustice is not itself an evil. The distinction between justice and injustice, instead of being absolute or natural, as in Platonism, is merely conventional, the result of social compacts and reciprocal agreements. None the less, justice is essential to the good life because "it is impossible for the man who secretly violates any article of the social compact to feel confident that he will remain undiscovered, even if he has already escaped ten thousand times; for right on to the end of his life he is never sure he will not be detected" (D.L., X, 35, 151). Therefore injustice produces distress of mind which wise men avoid. Similar reasons of prudence support the cultivation of friendship. An egoist is often pictured as a surly, solitary schemer; but an intelligent schemer cannot fail to learn that surliness does not produce pleasure, that friends are needed in times of emergency, that the possession of friends removes the present fear of a possible future emergency, and that beyond this insurance friendship itself is very pleasant. The theory of course is egoistic: "friendship is prompted by our needs" (D.L., X, 120); and no one cares for another except for his own advantage. Yet in practice, however the theory may appear, Epicurus was personally distinguished for his friendly attitude toward his disciples, and by all reports the garden school in which he taught must have been thoroughly delightful.

But if prudence and calculation recommend justice and friendship, it is otherwise with a family and participation in politics. "Sexual intercourse has never done a man any good, and he is lucky if it has not harmed him. Nor will the wise man [except in unusual circumstances] marry and rear a family" (D.L., X, 118, 119). Children are a nuisance and the cares of the home are distracting. Yet Epicurus seems to have been kind to and even fond of the children he knew. Public life is still more disturbing. Even the successful politician, not to mention the frustrations of the disappointed aspirants spurred on by ambition and lust for more worlds to conquer, is far from tranquillity and happiness. Obscurity is much the better condition.

Death

But of all the distractions, fears, and pains to be avoided, the chief is the fear of death and divine punishment. The Epicureans, be it noted, were not literally or professedly atheistic. They were as polytheistic as any ordinary Greek or Roman. But they differed in that they ascribed to the gods in their interstellar domicile an Epicurean tranquillity that was not disturbed by any superintendence over human affairs. How to conceive of these gods, what kind of bodies they were — for they too must have been composed of atoms — and in particular how they could be immortal and eternal, are questions for which the extant sources do not supply sufficient answers and are points on which Epicurus himself was probably somewhat confused.[3] At any rate the gods did not fashion the world out of atoms; they certainly did not create the atoms; and with the exception of appearing to men sometimes in dreams, they do not interfere in human life or reward or punish men in any way.

Now, if there are no punishments after death, a future life need not be any more terrible than the present life. Indeed it could be much better, for if the gods are eternally happy, why could not man be so likewise? Logically therefore Epicurus is not compelled to deny immortality or to advocate atomism for this purpose. But perhaps there was a psychological compulsion. He may have been obsessed with the superstitions of his age, and to give himself double insurance he felt constrained to make death the termination of human existence. Man and all living beings (except the gods) are temporary aggregates of atoms; at death the finer atoms of the mind escape first from the aggregate, then the slightly larger soul-atoms disperse, and eventually the coarser atoms disengage themselves and the body crumbles to dust. Since sensation, memory, reasoning, and all the

[3] Cf. Bailey, *op. cit.*, pp. 441–467.

conscious and mental activities were functions of the aggregate, these cease too, and the ego or self vanishes. Even if, per impossibile, the same atoms could later be reassembled into a human body, it would not be the same person, for no memory would unite the two lives.

This view, if accepted, effectively disposes of divine punishment in a future life; but it raises another problem. Can a man be happy now, if he knows he has no future? Would not this knowledge make him miserable? Does this not make Epicureanism a form of pessimism?

These questions Epicurus attempted to answer in three steps. First, Epicurus rejected pessimism so far as the quality of the present life is concerned. If the world were controlled by inviolable mechanism, or by Fate as the Stoics said, nothing would be under our control and we could well be pessimistic. Or, on the other hand, if there were no regularity at all and all events happened by pure chance, then too our efforts would go for nought. But Epicurus avoids both of these forms of pessimism, the latter by asserting that the atoms are for the most part mechanically determined, and the former by positing the occasional and slight uncaused swerving on which our free will is based. Thus the future is not wholly ours nor wholly not ours, but it is enough ours so that we can make our lives pleasant. In the second place, the thought of death is no reasonable cause for depression. Death cannot hurt us, for when death comes, we go; and it is foolish to be disturbed now about an event that cannot disturb us when it happens.

But suppose all this is true; can a man be happy if he believes, not that he will suffer after death, but merely that he will no longer exist? Is not the hope of immortality necessary to a calm acceptance of our present lot? The third step in the argument is directed to this question. One of Epicurus' *Principle Doctrines* reads, "Unlimited time and limited time afford an equal amount of pleasure, if we measure the limits of that pleasure by reason" (D.L., 145). What is meant by the phrase, "if we measure the limits of that pleasure by reason"? There is one meaning to which relatively little objection can be made. If Epicurus is correct in saying that the absence of pain is the greatest pleasure, and that after this has been reached pleasures may be varied but not increased, then a later moment of tranquillity cannot be greater than an earlier moment: one has already experienced the maximum. But can Epicurus also mean that one moment of maximum pleasure, judged by reason, is as good as two such moments? This meaning, which does not so readily approve itself, seems to be required for an argument against immortality. Even if, as Epicurus says (D.L., 126), "men choose not merely the larger portion of food but the more pleasant," most men would regard two pleasant meals as better than one. Or, more exactly, there is not only a widespread belief in immortality, but there is a deep-seated repugnance to the thought of ceasing to exist. The best that Epicurus can offer is the promise that his philosophy will remove from our minds this yearning for immortality. But this promise is not so easily kept. Corliss Lamont, a contemporary humanist who has borrowed many Epicurean ideas, in his *Humanism as a Philosophy* has a chapter entitled *This Life is All and Enough*. But apparently it is not enough and Epicurus has failed his disciple, for Lamont confesses (p. 124), "Even I, disbeliever that I am, would frankly be more than glad to awaken some day to a worth-while eternal life."

THE STOICS

Zeno of Citium inaugurated Stoicism at about the same time (300 B.C.) that Epicurus founded his rival school; and the two philosophies continued in vigorous, corporate existence until eclipsed by Neoplatonism. Yet a summary does far less justice to Stoicism than to Epicureanism, for while the doctrines of Epicurus were propagated by catechetical instruction and suffered little modification at the hands of his students, the Stoic school was composed of original and independent thinkers who did not hesitate to make whatever changes they saw fit. To be sure, there was a common tendency and an area of agreement, without which there would have been no school to summarize; but the interesting variations, the historical development, and even much of the area of agreement must be omitted. Some of Zeno, less of Cleanthes (–232 B.C.), more of Chrysippus, president and able reformer from 232–206 B.C., and a slight reference to the Roman Stoics is all that can be attempted.

Like the Epicureans, the Stoics too were moralists, materialistic physicists, and empiricists in epistemology; but with this very general comparison the similarity ends, for theirs was not precisely the same sensationism, by no means the same atomism, and emphatically not the same morality.

Against Skepticism

First of all, as a prerequisite of moral theory, truth must be attainable. So far removed from skeptical suspicions was Zeno that he extravagantly claimed that the wise man never entertains a mere opinion, never regrets a decision, never is mistaken, and never changes his mind. Antiquity pointedly asked the Stoics whether such a man had ever existed. They usually answered that Socrates was a wise man, and perhaps a few others met the requirements. If, however, the Wise Man is only an ideal, never attained in history, as would seem to be more likely, then Zeno's words become unfortunately skeptical in another assertion that only the wise man can know anything. With respect to this and other extreme statements, the history of Stoicism is a procedure of smoothing the rough edges and making the whole more palatable to common sense. But they all agreed that truth is based on sensation.

Since the Stoics were materialists of a sort, a sensation, or, more accurately, a representation was for them a physical impression on a corporeal soul. Zeno used the words *stamp* and *seal*, thus suggesting an impression made by a signet in wax; Cleanthes took this illustration literally and spoke of depressions and elevations in the wax-like soul; but because such literalism raised problems about simultaneous impressions and about memory, Chrysippus said that the "impression" was a qualitative change, so that as the air can carry sounds and smells simultaneously, so the soul can have several "impressions" at once without confusion.

Among representations, some of which are deceptive and illusory, there is one type, the comprehensive representation, that guarantees its own truth. The comprehensive representation is one that has been stamped and sealed by an existing object just as it is, resembles the object itself, and could not have been produced by anything else. Just as light reveals to us, not only an object, but itself at the same time, so the comprehensive representation is self-authenticating.

When the skeptics complained that a criterion cannot be a criterion of itself, the Stoics replied that a straight line is the norm both of itself and of other lines, and a balance measures the equality of the weights in the pans and its own equality as well. Further, if the skeptic uses no criterion in his argument against the Stoics, his judgment cannot be trusted; but if he has a criterion, he contradicts himself by accepting a criterion in order to repudiate it. Thus, as necessary and self-authenticating, the comprehensive representation forces our assent and is the criterion of truth.

Unlike the Epicureans, who were satisfied with a bare refutation of skepticism and a naïve acceptance of sensation in general, the Stoics, not restricting themselves to what is immediately practical, developed their epistemology at length. They made an elaborate classification of judgments; they worked out a theory of validity; they pursued many purely grammatical distinctions; their theory of signs, things signified, meanings, semantics, ran counter to their materialism; their investigations were keen, varied, and detailed; but with the exception of that part of their logic which combines with physics to establish the doctrine of Fate, it must all be passed by in regretful silence.

Materialism

Above it was said that the Stoics as well as the Epicureans were materialists, but such a statement by itself is more misleading than informative. True, only body is real. Plato's immaterial Ideas and even Aristotle's Forms were abstract, ethereal, and therefore unreal. Reality is something solid, something that occupies space, something that you can knock your knuckles against. Of course, there are some bodies which you cannot literally knock your knuckles against, such as air and fire; but they occupy space and have been regarded as atomic. A magnetic field of force also occupies space, but it is not a collection of atoms, and someone might say that it is not a body. However, the corporeal reality that constitutes the universe, far from being atomic in structure, is, according to the Stoics, more like a field of force; it is a continuum, a fluid, a gas, or, to give the Stoic identification, an all-permeating fire. Therefore the world is strictly one body, not an aggregate of many bodies. This notion of a continuum implies another feature that distinguished Stoicism from Epicureanism. In a thoroughgoing atomism, living beings can be nothing other than particular arrangements of the discrete atoms. Individually the atoms are inanimate; only the group, the atomic structure, the machine can be alive. But in Stoicism the universal fire is itself alive; and therefore instead of speaking of materialism, it would be less misleading to call the Stoics hylozoists. Obviously they have not only passed over Aristotle and Plato; they have gone behind Democritus as well and have found their inspiration in Heraclitus.

Nevertheless, Aristotle was not without influence too. Although the Stoics might fundamentally be classed with the early corporeal monists, yet the puzzling relation between the one and the many, plus the strong insistence on the reliability of sensation and the reality of ordinary things, leads them to place great emphasis on the differences within the universal stuff. Thus the basic monism is made to accommodate a derivative dualism. Most important, and analogous to Aristotle's matter and form, potentiality and actuality, is the distinction between agent and patient. The patient is unqualified matter, inert, not of itself inclined to motion, but ready to become all things; the agent or cause is the informing reason inherent in the matter, the original fire in its pure state, and, in contrast with matter, the divine being or God. Monists are usually not too clear as to how such subsidiary dualisms arise from the pristine unity. To opponents it seems strange that a part of God should undeify itself.

But as this is a general criticism, applying to all forms of monism and not to Stoicism alone, and as Parmenides had already made the point, it may be well to consider a more specific objection raised by the great Aristotelian commentator, Alexander Aphrodisias. To him the particular Stoic construction seemed to imply that two bodies can occupy the same place at the same time, and this is an impossibility. He writes, "We might reasonably accuse them of saying that God is mixed with matter . . . for if God is a body, as they say, being an intelligible and eternal spirit, and if matter is a body, then in the first place there will be a body extending through a body. . . ." (von Arnim, II, 310).

The Stoics, however, were quite willing to admit that two bodies can coexist in one place. In fact this position is intimately bound up with the Stoic theory of ethics. Plato, in opposition to the materialists of his day, had argued: virtues are real, virtues are not bodies, therefore [at least some] realities are immaterial. But the Stoics replied: virtues are indeed real, all reality is corporeal, therefore virtues are bodies. But if virtues are bodies and if human beings are bodies, it follows that in a virtuous man two bodies coexist in the same space. This application to virtue is but one example of the general principle. Plutarch as well as Alexander found this phase of Stoicism perplexing. Referring to the thesis that all qualities, and not virtues only, are bodies, Plutarch (von Arnim, II, 380) argued that if qualities are bodies, they do not need any other reality to attach to as attributes, for they are real by themselves. Thus green or heavy or courage could exist alone, like a stone, a chair, or a cloud. Plutarch thus signaled a difficulty in Stoicism in that they called matter unqualified and yet, because of their materialism, were unwilling to call qualities immaterial. Clearly this "materialism" cannot be atomism, for two hard, impenetrable, discrete particles cannot occupy the same space. But two fields of force can interpenetrate; two fluids seem to do so; and the Stoics used the mixture of wine and water as a case in point.

Fatalism

The theory of an original fire, partly turning into the things of experience and at the same time permeating them all, is the basis for the Stoic doctrine of fate. The Fates were three mythological characters: Clotho who spins the thread of life, Lachesis who measures its length, and Atropos who cuts it off. But fatalism, even in the age of the Stoics, had long since dispensed with the Fates. In modern times some writers restrict the term *fatalism* to those deterministic views which deny divine foreknowledge and providence. St. Augustine, too, who lived not too long after the Stoics, defined fate as a necessary order, excluding the will of God and man; though later he says that one type of fatalism is more tolerable than an outright rejection of foreknowledge.[4] The Epicureans escaped fatalism by the uncaused swerving of the atoms, but Democritus and modern mechanists can be so called because they deny that nature has a purpose. The Stoics, however, called themselves and are regularly called fatalists, despite

---

[4] *De civitate Dei*, V, i & ix.

the fact that they vigorously asserted divine providence, because they held that all events are determined beforehand and contribute to the grand plan and purpose of nature.

God and Fate

This combination of determinism and purpose follows logically from their conception of God. Neither the inanimate atoms of Democritus and Epicurus, nor in all probability the water and air of the Ionians, could foresee the future, make a plan, or choose a purpose. But when the Stoics emphasized Heraclitus' suggestion that the original fire was a wisdom, a reason, an intelligence that steers the universe, providence and purpose could hardly be avoided. Nor can determinism be avoided. If this living fire were stupid, or if its presence and power were limited to certain times and places, then there might be as much freedom or indetermination as swerving atoms afford. But God permeates all things, and because he is reason, he does not change his mind. He is the universal Logos, and little sparks of the divine fire, the logoi, like seeds, control the development of each thing. Thus Epictetus, applying this physical theory to the problems of ethics, can say that there is a little bit of God in every man. Inasmuch as the notion of a spark of divinity in every man still finds frequent acceptance in this twentieth century, it is understandable that pantheism could call forth a popular response in Roman antiquity. The thesis that the universe is God and that men are parts of God (fish and worms also, for God is no respecter of persons) exhibits a perennial appeal.

Universal Causation

The Stoics did not base their fatalism on a bare inference from pantheism. Detailed reasons were given. In opposition to the Epicureans the Stoics argued that nothing happens without a cause and that the whole universe, past and future, is bound together in an infinite series of causes and effects. Chrysippus is supposed to have claimed that the misty atmosphere of Thebes made the Thebans sturdy and stupid, while the rarity of the air accounted for Athenian brilliance. But of course not even the Epicureans denied the existence of causes and effects. Pointing out instances of such does not prove

the infinite and inviolable series the Stoics wanted; and Cicero made
the obvious retort that Athenian atmosphere does not explain why
one Athenian becomes a Peripatetic and another a skeptic. But then
Chrysippus never meant that the climate was the only cause. There
are more particular considerations.

Logic and Fate

It is at this point that logic combines with physics, for determinism
seems to be an implication from a basic logical principle. Diodorus,
even if he was a Megaric rather than a Stoic, gives this good Stoic
argument. Every proposition is either true or false; therefore a true
proposition in the future tense states an unavoidable event, and a
false proposition in the future tense states an impossibility. With
respect to statements about the past, it is easily seen that their truth
value cannot be changed. That Alexander the Great died young is
true and cannot be made false. It is also obvious that some statements about the future cannot be made false, such as, Caesar will
die. But if some statements about the future are unchangeable, why
should it be thought strange that all are. Caesar will die must be true;
then why not that Caesar will die by the hand of his friend on the
Ides of March? This too must be inevitable and cannot be made
false. Thus pure logic supports the theory of fate.

Chrysippus gives a more detailed argument than Diodorus. If there
is a motion without a cause, he says, not every proposition is either
true or false; but since every proposition must be either true or false,
every motion must have a cause. This syllogism needs a little explaining. Aristotle in an unusual defiance of common opinion denied that
propositions relative to the future could be true. The prediction that
it will rain tomorrow or that Caesar will conquer Gaul is not true.
Even the proposition, Caesar will die, is not true. Nor are they false.
In Aristotle's opinion, truth is a statement of reality, and reality is all
past or present. The future is not real yet. Propositions in the future
tense become true or false as time passes, but in the present predictions cannot be true. Common opinion on the other hand accepts
predictions as either true or false and explains our inability to say
which on the basis of our common ignorance of what will happen.
Further, if a proposition in the future tense cannot be true, no

syllogism could contain one. To argue that two days hence will be Friday because tomorrow will be Thursday would be impossible. Indeed, a true statement is understandable and a false statement is understandable; but a statement neither true nor false seems like complete nonsense. Chrysippus therefore concluded that every meaningful statement is true or false.

The next point in the argument is the assertion that only through efficient causality can something be true or false. Suppose someone asks why there is a full moon tonight. The answer must be, *because* the moon rose directly opposite to the sun. And this statement is true *because* of other preceding motions. If there had been different motions from these, the statement would have been false. The motion therefore makes it true or false; but, note, if no cause had effected a motion, the statement would be neither true nor false; it would have been meaningless — there would be neither moon, nor sun, nor Chrysippus either.

The Objections

The logical force of the deterministic or fatalistic position and its further elucidation may be seen still more clearly in the Stoic replies to opponents' objections. Four will be discussed. One, if all events are predetermined, then there is no use of a man's exerting himself to accomplish an aim, for if the proposed event is predestined, it will happen anyway; and if it is not predestined, nothing the man does will bring it to pass. Two, it is simply untrue that external causes, like the atmosphere, account for human actions. Three, if Fate has decreed everything that happens, then Fate is blameworthy for all the evil in the world. And four, if the Universal Reason plans and executes all events, there could be no evil in the world; it would be impossible for man to disobey God's decree; and this would erase the distinction between moral and immoral actions.

The first objection is called the lazy argument because it suggests that there is no use of doing anything, since all events are inevitable. If a student is fated to receive A in a course, he need not study, for he will get A anyhow; and similarly there is no use to study if he is fated to receive F. Unfortunately for student complacency the contention is worthless. It assumes that the fated event occurs in isolation, outside a texture of causes and effects, just anyhow. But this is not the fatalistic theory. The student who has been fated to receive A has been fated to receive A by means of study. He does not receive his grade just anyway, but only in one particular way, for the studying is fated as much as the A. The objection misrepresents fatalism by supposing that ends are fixed apart from means, but the Stoics insisted that ends and means together form an inviolable system. Strange to say, even twentieth-century opponents of determinism sometimes use this objection — a fact which is probably significant for assessing human psychology.

The second objection is also a misrepresentation. If Stoic fatalism had explained human action on the sole basis of external causes, and like modern mechanism had tried to bring conscious phenomena within the scope of physico-chemical law, the opponents could have made a good showing. But even though the Stoics were materialists, they were far removed from atomistic mechanism. Perhaps some of their more unguarded illustrations gave a wrong impression. Chrysippus is reported to have used the following. Suppose a dog to be tied to a wagon. If he wishes to follow, the wagon pulls him and he follows willingly, so that his own power unites with the force of necessity; but if he does not wish to follow, the wagon will drag him along against his will. So too mankind may follow the decrees of fate willingly or be forced to do so unwillingly. Although the illustration is picturesque, it is not too enlightening. Obviously every man is dragged along by the wagon of history in directions he would rather not go; and even the Epicureans admitted that the future is not wholly in our power. More revealing is another of Chrysippus' illustrations. It occurs as he discusses the force of sensory stimuli. Assent to impressions, by which we determine our conduct, cannot occur without a sense stimulus; but the sensation is not the sole cause of our action. The situation is like a cylinder and a cone that someone pushes down an inclined plane. The two bodies cannot begin to roll unless someone pushes them, and we cannot make a decision to act without assenting to a sensory impression. But having been pushed, the cylinder's motion differs from that of the cone because of their different construction. Hence with the external cause there is an internal cause that determines the nature of the motion. Application of the cylinder and cone was made to two men, both of whom were stimulated by the sight of a beautiful woman.[5] One man's character is unstable, and even though he had previously resolved to be continent, he assents to the temptation. The other man, though the same sensory excitations and incitements occur, has a disciplined reason, is confirmed in his resolve, and drives back the desire. Thus as the free swerving atoms of the Epicureans did not bring all things under man's control, so Stoic fatalism does not remove all things from that control. Man is not at the mercy of external causes, though it might be said that he is at the mercy of himself because his actions spring from his own character. No doubt his character has been formed by previous causes; his actions are predetermined for he cannot violate his character, stable or unstable as the case may be; but the actions are still his, and he is continent or incontinent voluntarily.

The distinction between external and internal causes, in particular the Stoic insistence on the role of the will, introduces the reply to the third objection; and here too Stoicism escapes the accusation by its thoroughgoing consistency. Against an inconsistent determinism the objections might be devastating. The third objection was that Fate or God would be blameworthy if all events, some of which are evil, had been decreed from eternity. Or, to put it conversely, in order for man to be subject to moral blame, there can be no original plan or ultimate cause of the universe. Now, it must be noted that fate, determinism, or predestination does not deny the occurrence of voluntary actions. The proponents of free will, the Epicureans for instance, argue as if there could be no will unless it is free. But the point at issue is not the existence of will, but whether the will is free or determined. The previous illustration contrasted the voluntary act of an unstable character with the voluntary act of a man of good character. In each case the will was the cause of the act. Breathing and digestion, and being run over by a four-horse chariot, are not voluntary acts, and in such cases there is neither praise nor blame; but resisting temptation or succumbing to it is a voluntary act, and therefore praise or blame must attach to the immediate cause of the act, namely, the will, the character, the man himself.

If the third objection complained about the evil in the world, the

---

[5] Augustine, *De civitate Dei*, XII, vi, borrows this illustration to prove the freedom of the will! He supposes, however, that the two men are alike in mind or character.

fourth contradicts it by denying the existence of evil: since all events occur precisely as God has ordered them, nothing is inconsistent with his decree, and therefore everything is good. But again, this objection is based on a fallacy and a confusion. Consider insanity as an example. Every case of insanity occurs through natural laws and is in this sense rational. But insanity is not the natural condition of mankind, nor does it become desirable just because it occurs naturally. One must distinguish between the universal laws of nature and the nature of man. What is natural in the first context (and everything is), may be unnatural and evil in the second. In the first sense it is no doubt true that everything is good: God has planned, foresees, and does all things well. Even insanity contributes to the perfection of the whole. On this point the Stoics were very careful to reply to the Epicurean contention that the great amount of imperfection in nature disproves the doctrine of providence. But while immorality as well as insanity occurs by the plan of God, it does not follow that moral acts and immoral acts are indistinguishable. A horse and a lion both exist by the decree of fate, but this does not make the horse a lion. Nor, when the horse eats corn and the lion eats flesh, can it be said that God is eating. These acts are theirs, not his. Similarly a bad man exists as God has planned, but this does not make him any the less bad. He and not God commits evil acts; these are the opposites of good acts; and as he is their cause, they must be referred to him, i.e., he is to blame for them.

One might pause here critically to consider whether or not the Stoics were entirely consistent in their replies to these objections. Since there are several forms of determinism, the possibility must be faced that one form might, while another might not, provide satisfactory replies. If the objections had been squarely based on the pantheism of the Stoics, perhaps it would have been more difficult to maintain a real distinction between good and evil actions. Epictetus says that nature never gives us any but good inclinations and that we are fragments of God. On such a premise it might well follow that all our inclinations are good rather than evil, and that, since we are parts of God, our actions are immediately actions of part of God. Now if right is defined as that which God does, then on this pantheistic basis our actions would be *ipso facto* right, and there would be no evil in the universe. Pantheism like every form of substantial monism faces difficulties in maintaining the reality of distinct things. But however it may be with pantheism and monism, teleological determinism, if combined with some sort of pluralistic existences, more easily escapes these criticisms. It is also a curious and to the free-will Epicurean an inexplicable fact of history that determinism, at least teleological determinism, is regularly associated with a strict and vigorous morality, while the exponents of freedom have tended to a free and easy mode of life. Certain it is that this is the contrast in antiquity.[6]

The Rational Life

The general lines of Stoic ethics are seen in the above refutations of objections. The good life is a life according to nature — not the universal nature of earthquake, insanity, and immorality, but the nature of man, namely, reason. Reason in man, a purer fire than that found in plants and animals, is essentially the same as Reason in the universe. Everyone has, or even is a divine spark, a part of God. Contrary to the hedonistic theory, reason does not teach that pleasure is to be equated with good and pain with evil. Indeed, as a matter of descriptive fact, and the Epicureans made a point of descriptive fact, pleasure is not the sole nor even the basic human motive. As may be learned from observing infants who, before being spoiled with candy and soda pop, desire and enjoy wholesome food, there is no natural impulse to pleasure, but rather to self-preservation. Further, hedonism becomes plausible only through an ambiguous use of the term pleasure. Few people, not excluding the Epicureans, would be willing to identify the good life as one consisting of the intense sensory pleasure of licentiousness. Even a life

[6] For example, in the Judaism of Roman times the Pharisees, however hypocritical they may have been, made a profession of strict virtue, while the Sadducees surpassed the Epicureans in lax living. But it was the meticulous Pharisees, and even more so the strict Essenes, who were determinists, and the Sadducees who believed in free will. How close to Stoicism, at least on the points mentioned, the Pharisees were, can be seen in Josephus, *Antiquities of the Jews*, XVIII, i, 3: "The Pharisees . . . live meanly and despise delicacies in diet, and they follow the conduct of reason . . . and when they determine that all things are done by fate, they do not take away the freedom from men of acting as they think fit; since their notion is that it has pleased God to make a temperament whereby what he wills is done, but so that the will of man can act virtuously or viciously." Cf. also *Antiquities*, XIII, v, 9, and *Wars*, II, viii, 14.

of continuous good food is not altogether self-sufficient. But the pleasures of a contented mind, without which hedonism makes little appeal, are so dissimilar from the others that it is confusion to include both types in the same genus. Setting pleasure aside therefore, the Stoics assert that the only good is virtue and vice is the only evil. Pleasures and pains no doubt occur: pleasures tempt the virtuous and reward the vicious, pains torment them both; but virtue makes men superior to pleasure and pain alike.

The ideal of virtue differs in many particulars from the Epicurean ideal of ease. Whereas the school of pleasure found family life too much of a nuisance, the Stoics defended monogamy and the family with its reciprocal duties. They advocated education for women — even courses in philosophy. Whereas the Epicureans, too, withdrew from politics, the Stoics stressed patriotism and civic responsibilities. If a government should become extremely corrupt, the Stoics admitted that a wise man might permissibly retire, but normally virtue requires active participation in public life. Since, however, imperial Rome was usually corrupt, the Epicureans could charge the Stoics with some apparent inconsistency. Their accusation is given further plausibility by the Stoic cosmopolitanism. From a wider philosophic point of view, devotion to a small city state seems an illogical restriction of interest. All men are parts of God and one's loyalty should be centered in the human race as a whole. From a more strictly political point of view, as the Greek city states lost their independence, there was less and less opportunity for individuals to participate in government. The administration was now far away and the earlier intimate ties to the state were broken. Reduced legally from citizenship in Athens, or some other home town, to the status of conquered subjects of a foreign power, the Stoics claimed world citizenship. Not the *polis* Athens but the cosmo-polis was their home. With some show of reason therefore, but after all with not too much, the Epicureans could accuse the Stoics of the inconsistency between the latter and a recommendation of patriotism toward the actual government. At any rate, the Stoics held that man is naturally social and should therefore fulfil his social duties.

Yet the emphasis on social duties, Stoic though it is and exemplified both by the slave Epictetus and the emperor Marcus Aurelius, fails to locate the essence of virtue because virtue is not to be identified with such overt actions. Virtue is something more internal; it is the action of the will rather than of the hands; and if praise and blame are to attach, the action must be in one's power. But overt actions or the desired results of volition are not in one's power and therefore cannot be essential to virtue. For Aristotle it was necessary to be wealthy in order to exhibit the virtue of liberality; courage was impossible to the man lame or paralytic; and in general virtue occurred only in its exercise — a man asleep could not be actually virtuous. This theory removes virtue from our power because external factors control. The Stoics therefore centered virtue in a strength of will; for them it is the intention that counts rather than the external act and its effects; and this brings virtue within our power. Wealth and health depend on external forces, and if such possessions were necessary to a virtuous life, one could not be virtuous voluntarily — one might be immoral in spite of his deepest convictions and most earnest intentions. The secret of the good life therefore is a knowledge of what is and what is not under our control. Frustration is the mark of foolishness because it comes from desiring the impossible. The wise man restricts his desires to what he can do, and hence his desires are always satisfied. We cannot control circumstances, but we can control our reaction to them. Thus virtue is not an outward activity, but a disposition of the soul that makes us superior to all externalities.

It was said before that there are very few wise men; most of the human race is vicious. Nor are some less vicious than others. Just as a man can be drowned as dead in one foot of water as in water a mile deep, and just as a man one mile away from Athens is outside Athens as truly as a man a hundred miles away, so all who are not wise are equally vicious. The change from vice to virtue, like entering Athens, is instantaneous, a sudden conversion. But so few are converted; and these only late in life after a long struggle. The later Roman Stoics softened some of these rigidities, but the connotation of the term *Stoic* has remained true to the earlier rigor, virtue, and ascetic discipline.

NEOPLATONISM

Contemporaneous with the founding of Stoicism, a strong school of Skepticism, perhaps inheriting something from the Sophists, began its long history from Pyrrho, about 300 B.C., to Sextus Empiricus in A.D. 200. That skepticism should become strong in opposition to sensationism and materialism is what the Presocratic period would lead one to expect; but what may appear strange is that the Platonic Academy, originally dedicated to a vigorous dogmatism, shared the same attitude.

Now, it was the fate of the Stoics to flounder on two of their most important theses. Their sensory theory of knowledge was doomed from the start, and the Skeptics and Academicians had no difficulty in refuting the claims of comprehensive representation. But their materialism also suffered under a strain. It had been a peculiar materialism to begin with, and the more the Stoics struggled to justify their principles and manage their problem in its many details, the less solid, spatial, and inert their matter became, and the more it took on spiritual characteristics. Virtues and qualities, seminal reasons, interpenetration of bodies and complete mixtures, significance, meaning, and the expressible — none of these fit comfortably into a materialistic system. The time was ripe for a dogmatic reaction to skepticism and a spiritualistic reaction to materialism.

But Neoplatonism was more than just a reaction. Plato himself had left unsolved some questions about participation, space or magnitude, the Demiurge, and the origin of the world; Aristotle had brought to light many important considerations which demanded incorporation in a Platonic system; and the Stoics themselves, for all their loose ends, had made very valuable contributions; besides all of which it was necessary to do justice to the basic ethical motivation of the Hellenistic age. The history of Greek philosophy was calling for a systematic culmination, an integrated summation of all the wisdom acquired through eight centuries, a final burst of stellar brilliance to climax pagan antiquity. Plotinus (205–270), to be ranked not much lower than Plato and Aristotle, had the requisite gifts for this enormous task, and a pitifully inadequate account of his work will close this chapter.

Refutation of Materialism

One main point, and the point at which Plotinus began his literary career, is the refutation of materialism and the defense of the immortality of the soul. If the soul were material, argues Plotinus, both body and soul would decompose into the same elements. But since none of these is alive, it is hard to see how a combination of them could have been. Stoics and Epicureans no doubt assert that not every combination of elements is alive, but only combinations of particular determinate proportions. This overlooks the fact that there must first be a living agent, an intelligent soul, not a human soul of course, but a world soul, to determine the proportions. Inanimate compounds too, and even simple bodies could not exist without such a soul, for it is the imposition of a logos, a ratio, a reason, or a form on matter that makes a body. Matter, being inert, cannot inform itself, and without the soul there would be only chaos.

If materialism cannot explain the genesis of life and the phenomena of growth, nor even the orderly arrangement of the inanimate world, still less can it explain sensation, thought, or morality. To sense an object, the soul must be a unity of apperception, and the object must be perceived by the same being, even though several impressions enter through different sense organs. As both Plato and Aristotle pointed out, it would be impossible to know that a color is different from a sound unless both were presented to the same percipient. The soul therefore must be like a center on which sensations converge along different radii. All this would be impossible if the soul were a body, for in this case one end of the object seen would contact one end of the soul, and the other end of the object seen would impress the other end of the soul. Unless these two sensations arrived at an indivisible, immaterial point, they could no more be compared or combined than if Plato sensed one and Plotinus sensed the other. That is, if the soul were material and occupied space, a part of the soul might perceive a part of the object, but there would be no perception of the object as a whole. Neither could there be thought, for as sensation is perception by means of bodily instruments, thinking is perception without bodily instruments. If it were not, thinking and sensation would be identical. Sensation grasps sensible objects, but thinking grasps intelligibles. Even the Stoics admitted that there are thoughts of unextended objects. How then could an extended soul think an unextended object? If it should be said that thought relates to forms in matter, at least these thoughts arise by abstraction from the matter, and it is intelligence, not body, which abstracts a circle, a line, or a point. Beauty and justice are as unextended, eternal, and unchanging as the concepts of geometry, and a body could not grasp such objects. The soul therefore must be conceived as an immaterial, unextended, spiritual reality.

Against Aristotle

Not only does Plotinus attack the obvious materialism of the Stoics, he also rejects the inadequate Aristotelian theory of soul as the form or entelechy of the body. On this theory, he argues, an amputation would remove part of the soul; sleep would be inexplicable; reason could not oppose desire; there could be no thought independent of the body; nor could sensible images be preserved independently of the sensible thing; the desire for an incorporeal object would be inexplicable; the propagation of plants would be impossible; the soul would be divisible; and finally Aristotle's theory cannot explain how the soul of one animal can become the soul of another, either in propagation or when a worm is cut in half. The being of the soul therefore does not depend on its being the form of anything; it is a reality which does not owe its existence to the fact of having its seat in a body; on the contrary the soul exists before it becomes the soul of a particular living being. It is neither a body nor a state of body, but a true substance or reality. Corporeal objects are not true substances: they are a flux and process, they come and go, they never truly are, but derive their semi-reality by participation in the authentically existent.

Cosmology and Ethics

It will be noted that this discussion, entitled *On the Immortality of the Soul*, refers not so much to the destiny of individual persons, as if it were promising Socrates and Cicero a happy life in the Isles of the Blest; nor is its fundamental aim a clarification of the problems of scientific psychology, though here and more so elsewhere Plotinus examines sensation, imagination, memory, and thinking with great care and in great detail; but rather as a refutation of Stoicism and Aristotelianism the discussion primarily concerns the soul's cosmological functions. Reality is spiritual and the world depends on a principle of life. As Plato held, bodies are only semi-realities, but there is another nature, possessing its being in and of itself, a nature which can be neither generated nor destroyed. As the self-moving principle of motion, it causes other things to move. Holding its life from itself, not borrowing it from another, it animates living bodies. Not all things can have a derivative life, for this would entail an infinite regress; there must therefore be an original source of life, imperishable and eternal, to provide life for other living beings. The soul is not the substratum of life; it is life itself; and as life itself is a reality, it cannot die. Hence the soul is eternal and immortal.

But though Plotinus' theory of the soul is cosmological and the phrases above seem to refer to the world-soul, yet the individual souls of Socrates and Cicero are included. It is impossible that one soul should be immortal and another mortal. Both the world-soul and Socrates' soul are principles of motion; both are self-living; both grasp the same objects with the same faculty of intellection when they think the celestial and supercelestial realities; both seek to soar to the primal source of all. Knowledge, existing in the individual soul, is reminiscence, is eternal; and as the soul coexists with knowledge, Socrates is just as immortal as the world-soul. Even the souls of animals and plants are likewise immortal.

This type of immortality, however, the eternity and divinity of the soul rather than mere future existence, raises special problems connected not only with cosmology but with personal ethics as well. If the soul in eternity past lived in the celestial regions with the intelligible realities, how can it be explained that the soul has left its heavenly abode and has become incarcerated in the body as in a tomb? And if now incarcerated, an ethical theory must describe the way of escape. With respect to the cosmological problem Plato used the language of myth to describe the soul's losing its wings and falling to a lower sphere. In less figurative terms he held that the Demiurge imposed order on space by constructing in it imitations of the Ideas. This is Plato's final answer as to why there is a physical world in addition to the Ideal world. Plotinus alters this considerably as the remainder of the exposition will show. One subordinate point is that Plato's Demiurge is fused with the world-soul. But as the Ideas are superior to the Demiurge in Plato, so in Plotinus the Mind or Intelligence is superior to soul. Soul is a grade lower, characterized by desire, and, as pregnant and in birth pangs, is eager to bring forth an order similar to that of the intelligible realm.

With this cosmology the ethical motif is constantly interwoven. The *Phaedo* and the *Phaedrus* had pictured the soul's contact with the body as evil. By a sort of living death, shunning sensation and practicing rational contemplation, the philosopher was to strive for salvation from his bodily tomb. How can these sentiments be harmonized with a view that makes the formation of the world, and therefore the soul's indwelling the human body, a commendable action? As Plotinus continues with the explanation, the cosmological problem may become more and more of a puzzle, for his intention is not so much to explain the union of soul and body as it is to maintain the divinity of the soul in spite of this union. This divinity is defended on the ground that the human soul never really or completely separates from the world soul. In union with the perfect soul, our soul roams the heavens and administers the cosmos; it is not an evil for the soul to furnish the body with the power of existing so long as the soul's providence over the inferior body does not wrest the superior from its own high position. And yet, the human soul cannot be said without qualification to remain wholly in the heavens. The world-soul does so remain. It organizes the universe without coming into contact with it, by sending its lower powers to care for particular things. There is a sense therefore in which the human soul is sent and descends.

Yet Plotinus cannot completely escape the notion that the soul falls into evil, into suffering, experiencing troubles, fears, and desires in its corporeal tomb. The individual soul, he says, tires of being with the universal soul, it separates itself and becomes weak, and instead of remaining entirely rational it accepts the guidance of sensation. These admissions, however, Plotinus attempts to mitigate by asserting that the soul can regain its lost position, and that the fall is both free, necessary, and ordained of God. By its descent the soul is enabled, first, to learn of evil without being harmed, especially if it returns quickly, and, second, to actualize the potentialities of vegetative and sensitive life, which, having no place in the intelligible world, would have existed in vain. Without a lower world the soul would not even have known that it possessed these powers. There could be no world if only One existed; plurality is necessary; and the production of multiplicity must continue until all possible effects have been actualized. Though it would have been better for the soul to remain in the higher world, yet because it is a being not of highest rank but intermediate between two worlds, it is under compulsion to come into contact with the sensible realm. This experience of evil gives it a clear perception of the good. But no soul is totally or irretrievably engulfed in sensation. Salvation is always possible.

Adopting a theme from Plato's *Theaetetus*, Plotinus makes salvation consist in likeness to God. It is achieved by reascending the degrees through which the soul fell. The depths of this fall is hedonism. Men of this stamp, like the Epicureans, are immersed in sensation; they think that pleasure is the only good and pain the only evil. True, no man can live without sensation, and some men never rise above it. But others of a higher type, the Stoics, center attention on virtue and the practical duties of life.

The highest type of man, however, recognizes the soul's divine nature and works back to the purer states. Though this is done chiefly by leaving the realm of sense and entering into the realm of discursive reason, intelligence, and whatever may be higher, sense itself may provide a stimulus. One may ascend by loving visible beauty and seeking its first cause in Beauty itself. The beauty of the body is imposed on it by the soul, but the soul receives this beauty from the Divine Mind or world of Ideas.

That there is a Divine Mind is proved, not just by bodily beauty, but by the existence of the soul itself, which requires a higher principle. It is the Mind which has produced the soul, for the soul is an intermediate being between two worlds: on the lower side it touches the world of sense, but on the higher it is next to the Ideas.

The world of Ideas and the Mind are identical. One must not suppose that there is a Mind plus external, independent objects which it knows. Such a separation unfortunately seems to be found in the *Timaeus* where the Ideas and the Demiurge are separate existences. But Plato himself, even though only in one passage, explicitly said that the world of Ideas is a living Mind. Were this not so, the Mind would in itself be only potentially intellectual, instead of essentially actual. Mind is itself what it thinks, for if its objects were not its own reality, it could not know itself, and the Socratic injunction, *Know thyself*, would have become vain. Mind, therefore is the Ideas, and the Parmenidean phrase, To think and to be is the same, is justified. Along with this denial that independent objects actualize a potential Mind, it must also be denied that an independent Mind actualized or created Ideas by thinking them. Modern idealism is foreign to Plotinus' system. The Ideas and the Mind must be strictly identified: neither is prior to the other.

Platonic Themes

In his solution of the problem of the extent of the Ideal world, Plotinus' advance over Plato is seen still more clearly. One criticism of the Ideas, found in the *Parmenides* and often repeated since, is that class concepts are the essentially arbitrary productions of human minds and should not be illicitly transformed into independent self-subsistent natural objects. Not only may mathematical objects, like two and equality, be "purely formal," but justice and the other virtues are said to change with social custom, and the laws and classes of physics are interpreted as convenient shorthand signs invented as symbols for physical processes. Then, too, there could be no Idea of Athenian or Spartan, for these are patently man-made distinctions. And what of the artificial class ship or house?

To the nontechnical student the most plausible examples of natural classification are the species of plants and animals. Though the difference between an Athenian and a Spartan is man-made, and though perhaps mathematics is purely formal, the difference between an elephant and a lion is neither formal nor man-made. These types are obviously not arbitrary classifications; they really and truly exist in nature. A satisfactory theory would have to be consistent: either the arbitrary classes would have to be proved natural or the natural arbitrary. Therefore the dialogue *Parmenides* and those who studied it pressed the difficulty and questioned the existence of Ideas of hair and mud, of diseases and privations, of individuals like Socrates, and of artificial classes like ships and houses.

With respect to artificial objects Plotinus offered an ingenious explanation. The imitative arts, painting, sculpture, dance, and pantomime, and the productive arts such as architecture and carpentry, have no separate Ideas for themselves, but are implicated in the Idea man. Music stands in a higher position in that it is related to the perfect symmetry of the Ideal world. Geometry and philosophy are altogether in the higher realm. After a little hesitation Plotinus also affirms the existence of the Idea of Socrates — a profound modification of Platonism which deserves profound study.

One other point may well be mentioned in which Plotinus tried to improve on Plato. In order to explain the relation of things to Ideas, Plato described the Demiurge as forming the world by constructing copies of the Ideas in the independent space. But the admission of three ultimate and independent principles is so contrary to the genius of Plato and so disrespectful of the noble Parmenides that it must not be allowed to stand. There must therefore be a continuity of production without an independent matter. The soul, which has taken the place of the Demiurge, is itself a production of the Divine Mind, and the lower world is a production of the soul. But that the soul does not work on an independent space or matter is seen in the test case of magnitude.

This sensory world is as it were a set of reflections in a mirror. The real objects reflected are the Ideas. The reflections are of course the sensory objects. And the mirror takes the place of Plato's space. Obviously the mirror itself has none of the qualities it reflects. In itself it is not red, equal, or courageous; but note especially that it is not extended either. Magnitude or extension is an Idea reflected in it, but it is not extended. Therefore it is not an independent space. In fact, if the reflections should disappear, the mirror would disappear too. The mirror may be called matter, if anyone wish to do so, but it is an immaterial matter that exists only for the reflections. Since Plato had identified matter and space, this result is the equivalent of denying that space is extended. Things are extended; they participate in the Idea magnitude; magnitude appears in the mirror, or matter, but the matter is not itself extended.

The terms *mirror* and *matter*, however, have such substantial connotations that the account appears confused. Another figure of speech, Plotinus' favorite, that of light shining in the darkness, may dispel some of the obscurity. The light shines and its rays extend, becoming less bright and more dim until they are lost in darkness. The light represents existence — its source is the highest existent; the rays are lesser existences, such as the soul, and the still lesser visible things of the lower world. But since more dim is nothing less than less bright, the darkness into which the world has been projected is literally nothing at all. That is, there is no independent matter. All that exists or even half-exists is the light itself.

The One

The figure of the shining light leads to a final point. The Divine Mind is not the source of light. It is not the ultimate principle. Man's moral salvation begins with leaving sensation and ascending into the Mind by reason and intellection. But there is more. If a man conscientiously contemplates the Ideas, he may unexpectedly be granted a vision of the supreme principle. As it was necessary to reject the assumption of three independent principles, so for the same reason the Mind is not the highest. Multiplicity runs rampant in the sense world; but even in the Mind there is the duality of subject and predicate. Hence the Mind is not a true unity. There must therefore be a Parmenidean One superior to Mind. In the Mind there are distinctions. But since the Mind is the realm of knowledge, for knowledge requires distinctions, it follows that the One is strictly unknowable. Nothing can be predicated of it, no true statements can be made about it,[7] for all propositions require a

[7] There are more and still stronger statements of negative theology in Plotinus. But Paul Henry has recently called attention to a positive strand of Plotinus' thought. In V, iv, 2 and V, vi, 2 the One is called intelligible. Further, in some sixty cases masculine pronouns are used for the neuter One. This is obscured in the printed texts because modern editors have mis-corrected the language to conform to the usual rules of grammar. Then, third, in VI, viii, 13 and VI, viii, 16, the One is described as a rational, living soul. Although this passage is prefaced by the remark that the description is inaccurate, some of its terms occur in more technical sections. Father Henry concludes that negative theology must always be complemented by positive theology.

distinction between subject and predicate. Knowledge also requires the distinction, logical if not actual, between the person knowing and the object known. Hence salvation must consist, not in knowledge, but in a mystic trance, an unconscious absorption of the philosopher into the One. In this trance the soul no longer knows whether it has a body, cannot tell whether it is a man, or anything real at all. Even after one has recovered from the trance, one cannot say what the experience itself was. No doubt one can talk about it and say that it was wonderful or beatific, or attribute to the experience some other meaningless adjective. But only the person who has had the experience knows what it is; and he does not really know.

Mysticism has provoked extreme reactions: some hold the mystics to be the superhuman benefactors of the race, while others considered them deluded. Because of his mysticism, Plotinus has been called antirational;[8] but this appellation can be true only of his mysticism and not of his writings, for these are magnificent examples of discursive reasoning. Nor is Plotinus' mysticism itself divorced, as mysticism frequently is, from intelligent study. Only after great philosophic labor is this vision granted. Mysticism is also attacked on the ground that it is an incommunicable experience of only a few people. It is not open and public as is scientific experimentation or logical proof. In reply to this Plotinus claims that the experience is the exercise of a faculty all have; if only a few make use of it, the others have no just complaint. Still, modern writers who hold to a particular theory as to the nature of science argue that private experiences are illegitimate as bases for philosophy. But if this were literally true, color theory would be illegitimate because not everybody has the experience of distinguishing all the colors. If therefore the existence of color-blind persons does not invalidate color theory, the mere existence of nonmystical rationalists should not invalidate any truth founded on mystic visions. As the color-blind man must take another's word for it that distinctions in color exist, so the rationalist would have to accept the mystic's word. In aesthetics the critics and theorists scorn insensitive souls who see no value in and have no appreciation of great works of art. Perhaps the rationalistic scientist will have to repudiate art as an incommunicable mystic

[8] W. T. Jones, A *History of Western Philosophy* (Harcourt, Brace & Co., 1952), Vol. I, p. 298, col. 1; p. 300, col. 2; p. 301, col. 1.

experience. But even the taste of an olive is incommunicable. If then one wishes to argue against mysticism, let it be, not on the ground that few have the experience, or that it is incommunicable as the taste of an olive is, but on the ground that even with the experience the mystics can say nothing intelligible about it. The trance gave Plotinus no information by which his account of the Mind and Soul could be corrected. The philosophy was thought out apart from the vision, and the vision when added did not alter the philosophy. Mysticism then is apparently useless.

The descent from the One or the recovery from the trance, is again the production of the world. The One shines out as a light. It produces the duality of the Mind and the multiplicity of the Soul. There is no break in the continuity, no independent Demiurge, no space. Thus even the sense world is an "emanation" from the Parmenidean One. One and matter are extremities of a single continuous line. There are no breaks. The whole therefore is a monistic, pantheistic system. The One no doubt "transcends" sense objects; but this transcendence is merely a higher rank or position in a continuum. The significance of this will be better seen when contrasted with a very different transcendence found in Christian teaching, for the radical difference between Christianity and paganism centers in the nature of the supreme principle. The nature of God controls the explanation of the world, and one may wonder whether in fact Plotinus finally gave any better explanation of the world than Plato did, or even than Democritus. These had a world at the expense of pluralism. On the other hand, if the first principle is a pure One, how can the production of multiplicity be made intelligible? Illustrations of mirrors and shining lights do not suffice. If multiplicity and distinctions were in the One, even virtually, the One could not be pure Unity; but if there were no multiplicity in the One, how could it come out of the One?

Plotinus' answer reduces to the assertion that it does and it must. The issue or emanation of the many from the One, he says, is the most sublime instance of the law that all reality necessarily gives birth to something inferior, as the sun produces its light and warmth. And given the Greek presuppositions and the history of Greek philosophy, it is difficult to see how the culmination could have been otherwise.

PART TWO

The Middle Ages

CHAPTER **5**

The Patristic Period

PAGANISM AND CHRISTIANITY

The source of all contrasts between paganism and Christianity is the difference in their concepts of God. In any system the ultimate principle determines the form of the whole and shows its implications in the details of ethics, physics, and epistemology. Sometimes it is said that whereas Greek philosophy had known only immanent principles, the Hebrew-Christian religion introduced the idea of transcendence. Although this statement is substantially correct, the two terms are not used in the same senses by all authors, and the several meanings must be distinguished in order to avoid misapprehension. Immanence and transcendence are always opposed to each other in ordinary speech; but technical language can specify different types of opposition. When immanence and transcendence are taken as contradictory or contrary terms, the former is applied to systems in which God is the essence of the universe and the universe is the essence of God. In such a sense no principle can be both immanent and transcendent. At the same time Christian theologians, though retaining the colloquial opposition between the two words, have used them not as contraries but as subcontraries. Thus they can say that God is both immanent and transcendent. However, with certain clarifications, the first or divine principles of the Greek philosophers may be called immanent in the stricter sense so that all notion of the transcendence is precluded, and thus the pagan systems are throughout radically different from Christianity.

Greek Immanentism

To be specific, let us go back to Thales. In the absence of adequate information, no theological importance can be assigned to his statement that all things are full of gods. On the face of it, it is evidence of a polytheism in which the gods, far from being first principles, are products of natural forces. Water, on the other hand, is his first principle, and as the things of the universe are modifications of water, this first principle is fairly called an immanent principle. It is in no sense supernatural: it is nature itself. Were it not for the fact that Thales left no evidence of any particular interest in religion, his views might have been called pantheistic, but in the actual situation the term *naturalism* has more appropriate connotations. Parmenides cannot be called a naturalist in any sense of the word, although his acosmism might be considered a form of pantheism. If one hesitates to apply the term *immanence*, it is because other systems of immanency allow for some plurality through and in which God is immanent. But it is clear enough that since only one Being exists, there is no transcendence in Parmenides' philosophy.

Thales and Parmenides do not fit so well into a religious catalogue because of their general indifference to religion. But Heraclitus and especially his later descendants, the Stoics, used a more religious terminology, so that it does not seem peculiar to call their thought an immanentistic pantheism. Fire is God and God is the universe; besides this one substance, and its modifications, there is nothing.

Plato is the hardest to classify accurately, mainly because the usual terms are too rigid to fit Plato's more elastic language. The Greek authors, nurtured in a polytheistic culture, used the term God in a much looser sense than those who are strongly influenced by Christianity. Then too the Hebrew-Christian concept of God unites elements that are kept separate in Plato, with the result that it is difficult to say what Plato's God was. If God is the cause and maker of the physical world, then Plato's God is the Demiurge of the *Timaeus*. But if God is the first, highest, and ultimate principle, Plato's God is the Idea of the Good. In the first case God is confronted with two equally eternal and equally independent principles. He uses the Ideas as blueprints to impose order on chaotic space. In this arrangement God is neither immanent nor transcendent. On the one hand, while the Demiurge enjoys a rank higher than space, he is not the cause of everything in the physical world: if appeal is made to the *Republic* God can be the cause of only a few things because evil is more extensive than good. On the other hand, since the Demiurge occupies a rank lower than the Ideas, he cannot be transcendent, for he is not the highest principle. Now, in the second case, if the term God is to be restricted to the supreme principle of any philosophy, then the Demiurge is not Plato's God, and attempts to classify Plato on this basis are beside the point. The Ideas are Plato's true reality and the physical world is only half real. In the world of Ideas, the Good is supreme. Lower Ideas are known only through the Good and only through the Good do they exist. This seems to make the Good transcendent, and no one can deny that it is the supreme Idea. But supremacy is not precisely transcendency. The Good is not the creator or even the maker of the Ideas, but rather a supreme genus of which the inferior Ideas are species. If anyone should hesitate to qualify this relationship as one of immanence, it might be argued that Plotinus removed the confusion and indicated Plato's essential meaning. In any case, neither the Demiurge nor the Good corresponds to the Hebrew-Christian concept of Deity: the Demiurge makes the world but is not supreme, the Good is supreme but does not make the world.

Aristotle's God is the least pantheistic and least obviously immanent of all the Greek first principles. If a critic outside the system should wish to make a point, he might argue that since Aristotle correctly refused to admit the existence of prime matter, except as an unreal limit of abstraction, on the other end of reality he should not have admitted the real and separate existence of a Form apart from matter. The unmoved mover ought to have been the Form of the World, and thus an immanent principle. But historically although Aristotle denied separate existence to matter, he broke the symmetry of his system and asserted it of God. In this sense therefore Aristotle's God is not altogether an immanent principle. But this unmoved mover is not transcendent either. Of course, it is barely possible to define transcendence so as to exclude omniscience; but the quasi-transcendence of a God who is ignorant of past evils and of all future events, is not the transcendence of the Biblical view.

The Epicureans do not need to be considered on this point, and the last section of the previous chapter sufficiently showed the pantheism and emanationism of the Neoplatonic system. In this connection a specific example may be pressed of how the nature of the first principle controls the subordinate parts of a philosophy. Because the One and the Divine Mind are what they are, a salvation in Neoplatonism becomes an escape from sensation into a mystic trance. With a different first principle, Christianity is not interested in salvation from sensation but from sin; and if the Apostle Paul had any visions, they were not the mystic trances of Plotinus.

Hebrew Transcendence

To complete this summary contrast between Greek theology as an immanentism, with the qualifications and varieties indicated, and the Hebrew-Christian view of a transcendent Deity, it will be necessary to give a preliminary statement of the Biblical concept of God. When this concept is clarified, the radical difference between the two world views can hardly be missed even in subsidiary details.

Since immanence and transcendence are used as contradictory, contrary, or subcontrary terms, depending on the author's choice, the Biblical meaning can be more vividly conveyed by specifying two instances in which this view diverges fundamentally from paganism. The first of these is the doctrine of creation. That God is transcendent in the sense of being the Creator of the world contrasts with every form of Greek philosophy. The first sentence of the Bible is: "In the beginning God created the heavens and the earth." The Hebrew verb to create, in the form or "voice" used in Genesis 1:1, never denotes human productions. Even the other "voices" in which a human subject cuts down a tree or kills an enemy are extremely rare. Verbs of doing or making occur hundreds of times in the Bible, but this verb, when it has a human subject, occurs less than five times. Its characteristic use is to express divine production. This production, this creation, is by divine fiat. The words are: "Let there be light, and there was light"; "By the word of the Lord were the heavens made"; "He spake and it was done." Thus the Scriptures describe a Deity who creates the world out of nothing by divine fiat. That this creation was ex nihilo is shown negatively by the absence of any mention of a pre-existing matter to be molded or fashioned. Positively, what God created is so extensively expressed that there is no room for an uncreated matter. God is said to have created all things. A few of the passages are the following: "Thou hast made heaven, the heaven of heavens, with all their host, the earth, and all things that are therein, the seas, and all that is therein" (Neh. 9:6); "For by him were all things created, that are in heaven, and that are in earth, visible and invisible . . . all things were created by him and for him" (Col. 1:16); "Thou has created all things, and for thy pleasure they are and were created" (Rev. 4:11). Supporting these passages which assert that God created all things, are others in which God's sovereignty over all things is expressed; as well as those which state that the world had a beginning: e.g., "Before the mountains were brought forth or ever thou hadst formed the earth and the world, even from everlasting thou art God" (Ps. 90:2); "O Father, glorify thou me with thine own self with the glory which I had with thee before the world was" (John 17:5). It may be left to theologians and philosophers to construct an appropriate theory of time, and on this they may differ, but it cannot be denied that the Bible represents the world as having a first moment. It is also to be noted in the passages quoted, and others not quoted, that the New Testament does not alter the Old Testament view. The two Testaments are identical on this point, so that creation can fairly be called a Hebrew-Christian view. Admittedly, undoubtedly, God is immanent in the sense of knowing and controlling all history; but the Hebrew-Christian position is radically opposed to any immanentism in which the world is supposed to be a modification of the divine being. It is equally opposed to a plurality of independent, eternal principles, as in Plato, and to the ignorant God of Aristotle. And, finally, since a fiat is a voluntary act and not a necessary emanation, Christianity has no sympathy with Neoplatonism. For the Bible God is transcendent.

If the doctrine of creation obviously has implications for ontology and cosmology, there is a second instance of the Christian meaning of transcendence which controls epistemology. That God necessarily knows everything about the world he planned and created, as opposed to the unmoved mover who knows only a part of the past and none of the future, is not the phase of epistemology intended at the moment. The point here relates to human learning. The Greeks may have differed as to the precise roles of sensation and reason, and Christian theologians differ too, but in Christianity there is a source of knowledge not admitted by the Greek philosophers, namely, revelation. God not only creates the world, but he also speaks and communicates information to men. In the first place he told Adam what he required of him and what the penalty of disobedience would be. Then after Adam sinned against God, God gave him a promise of redemption. Likewise God spoke to Noah, Abraham, Moses, and the prophets. These messages were written down as the words of God for posterity and in time the canon of the Old Testament grew until Malachi wrote the last book. Therefore, by the time of Christ, who constantly appealed to the Hebrew Bible and insisted that "the Scripture cannot be broken," the idea of a canon was not a novelty. The Christians did not gradually invent, they inherited the notion of a canonical set of writings. True, the canon of the New Testament did not exist from the first. The books were written over a period of fifty years to widely separated recipients. Another fifty years or more were needed to make copies of them for distribution, to gather, by the slow and difficult methods of transportation, a set of these copies in the several cities, and in each city to make sure that the books or letters had been written by apostolic authority. For this reason some of the earliest lists compiled omit this or that book. But there is no evidence that the letters or books were not immediately accepted as revelation by the churches to which they were first sent; nor is there evidence that they were not immediately accepted by the other churches as soon as their apostolic imposition was established. The recognized canon of the New Testament may have developed over a century; but the idea of a canon did not develop. The idea of an authoritative canon was familiar from the beginning, and a book known to be approved by an apostle was immediately received as such. Obviously nothing like this existed in pagan philosophy, and the opposition of modern paganism to Christianity is more vigorous on this point than even on the doctrine of creation. The heirs of Greek thought find it repugnant to accept information revealed by God; they insist on discovering truth by their own resources; and if this cannot be done in any case, they would rather go without the truth than to receive it as a gift from God.

Functions of Revelation

In the intellectual contest with paganism, as distinguished from common evangelistic activity and from efforts at self-preservation in the face of organized persecution by emperors such as Nero, Domitian, Trajan, and the Stoic Marcus Aurelius, the Biblical revelation served a double function. In the first place it determines what Christianity is. Just as Platonism or the theory of Ideas is what Plato wrote, so Christianity is what the prophets and apostles wrote. Just as, also, the Platonic Academy, with its apostolic succession of presidents regularly inaugurated, diverged from the theory of Ideas, became skeptics, and ceased to be Platonists, so, too, many people who have some historic connection with the primitive Christian community have ceased to teach Christianity because their theories are not Biblical. In ancient times, when great numbers of pagans were converted and accepted Christ as their Lord, the need for a fixed, written statement of Christianity was imperative. Having been reared in a heathen, polytheistic environment, these converts could not always distinguish a Christian idea from a pagan idea. Their minds were a confusion of two antagonistic philosophies. Undoubtedly they trusted Jesus Christ for salvation; but did this imply creation *ex nihilo* or was there a preexisting matter which God formed? Such questions, and there were many, could be answered only by an appeal to written revelation. In addition to Christian converts who still felt the effects of paganism, there were also groups of pagans who felt the influence of Christianity. Their minds also were a confusion, though to a less extent. To identify these groups, chiefly the Gnostics, as heathen rather than Christian, a written revelation, authoritatively stating what Christianity is, was necessary. Otherwise the disputes would have resembled a quarrel among a motley group of boys trying to play ball without a rule book. One boy claims another is unfair because he is using a spherical ball three inches in diameter when the ball ought to be a foot-long oval. A third boy mediates this quarrel by agreeing with the first that the ball should be spherical and agreeing with the second that it should be a foot in diameter; but he claims the others are unfair because they have nine or eleven on their teams, when five is the proper number. And then a truly ecumenical spirit argues that such differences are trivial and to discuss them is unsportsmanlike — the important thing is that they should all play ball together.

The second aspect of this double function is in fact nothing but an extension of the first. The determination of what Christianity is serves not only to separate pagan groups from Christian groups, but by the same method enables Christians to progress in understanding Christianity. Has God created? If Aristotle's arguments in the *Physics* VIII are valid, the world was never created. If, however, they are invalid — and after all it is not too difficult to find flaws in them — then antiquity is left in ignorance on the matter. Perhaps no proof is possible pro or con. But if God speaks and says that he has created the world, the question is answered. This is not to say that the Scriptures answer all questions and that we need be ignorant on no point; none the less there are many points, the most important points, on cosmology, psychology, philosophy of history, epistemology — not to mention morality and religion — on which the Bible protects the Christian against plausible but false theories.

Superficial Similarities

Failure to notice the radical difference between Greek immanence and Biblical transcendence, between sensation or reason and revelation, results in the discovery of apparent similarities and of alleged borrowing by the latter from the former. But in reality these similarities are superficial and the borrowing never took place. The only Greek school which in the New Testament receives anything like a word of commendation is Stoicism. Speaking before a group of Stoics and Epicureans on Mars Hill, the apostle Paul quoted a Stoic poet who said, "In him we live and move and have our being." But it takes an insensitivity to the forms of politeness and a lack of historical imagination to suppose that Paul meant the words in their original sense and was now preaching pantheism. Had this been so, Paul would not have mentioned the resurrection, and the audience would not have walked out on him. Stoic influence may also be suspected in II Peter 3:7, 10, where the apostle says that as once the world was destroyed by water at the time of Noah, so also by the word of God the earth and heavens are treasured up for fire. And in the day of the Lord the elements shall be dissolved with great heat and the earth shall be [burned up] discovered. Not only is this suggestive of Stoicism, but further it is not characteristically Hebrew.

The notion of a final conflagration is not a frequent one in Jewish literature. The Sibylline Oracles *ca.* 140 B.C. mention it several times; it occurs two or three times in other early works; and there are several references to it in the rabbinical literature. But while so infrequent in Hebrew thought, it is a relatively prominent part of Stoic theory. However, Stoic influence on Peter is an untenable hypothesis because of the radical difference between the two systems — a difference appearing in the nature of the conflagration as well as in the first principles.

First, the Stoic theory of conflagration depends on a system of physics completely absent from II Peter and from the New Testament as a whole.

Second, and more conclusively, the conflagration in II Peter is a sudden catastrophe like the flood. But the Stoic conflagration is a slow process that is going on now: it takes a long time, during which the elements change into fire bit by bit. The Stoic process is a natural process in the most ordinary sense of the word; but Peter speaks of it as the result of the word or fiat of the Lord.

Third, the Stoic conflagration is a sort of deification of all things, but Peter's is a judgment on sin. This fact may explain why the verb "shall be discovered" in verse 10 is a better reading than "shall be burned up." It is by the fire of judgment that the true value of the works in the earth shall be revealed.

Fourth, the Stoic conflagration occurs an infinite number of times in the infinite universal cycles. Peter's occurs just once, like the flood. The new heavens and new earth are not a repetition of past history point by point as in Stoicism, but the final state of everlasting felicity with our Creator and Redeemer.

Only by a misinterpretation of the New Testament can one talk of "The Stoic Strain in Christianity."[1] and only by a misinterpreta-

---

[1] E. Vernon Arnold, *Roman Stoicism* (Cambridge University Press, 1911), Chapter XVII.

tion of Plato can one write a volume entitled, *The Christian Element in Plato*.[2]

Alleged Sources of Pauline Theology

More recently the theology of Paul has been traced to some Eastern Cults, to the Hermetic literature, or to the Greek mystery religions.

The first of these possibilities depends on interpreting Paul's account of the struggle between the flesh and the spirit in terms of a dualism of matter and spirit. This dualism may be ultimate as in the case of Zoroastrianism where two eternal principles account for the universe, or the dualism may be derived from some earlier unitary state as was usual in Gnosticism. The idea that matter or body is inherently evil and the spirit inherently good led to two contrasting types of conduct: since the body is evil, one must live an ascetic life and mortify the deeds of the body; or since an inherently evil body cannot be sanctified, and since an inherently good spirit cannot become impure, one need not worry what his body does. Paul has never been accused of licentiousness, but he has often been misunderstood as teaching asceticism. That this is not Paul's theory and that his theology was not so derived can be shown by several evidences. Obviously there is no ultimate dualism in Paul. One triune God is the sovereign principle of all. The Gnostic form of a derived dualism of body and spirit is also foreign to Paul's thought. Undoubtedly he describes a moral struggle: nearly every ethical writer does. The essential point is to identify the two antagonists. Plato said desire and reason; the dualist body and spirit; Paul flesh and spirit. By careless reading, the word *flesh*, which Paul uses in a derogatory sense, can be mistaken for body, but a little attention to Paul's remarks makes it clear that he means, not body, but the sinful human nature inherited from Adam. Note that in the beginning God created man, male and female, and pronounced his creation very good. He commanded our first parents to be fruitful and multiply and replenish the earth. This is inconsistent with the theory that matter or body is inherently evil. When Adam fell, it was the result of a rebellious will, and not because he had a body. Secondly, the existence of evil

[2] C. Ackermann (T. & T. Clark, 1861).

spirits shows that spirits are not necessarily good; and the resurrection of the body, particularly of believers, is inconsistent with the theory that matter is inherently evil. Thirdly, when Paul lists the evil works of the flesh, adultery and lasciviousness might possibly be taken as sins of the body, but idolatry, hatred, wrath, heresies, and envy are surely psychical rather than corporeal. Note too that Paul attributes to some heretics at Colossae a "fleshly mind" (Col. 2:18). Surely no one could see in this phrase an Epicurean theory of a material or corporeal spirit; and even if this perverse idea were accepted, it would ruin dualism. Nor is the fleshly mind to be understood in terms of sensuality and lasciviousness. These heretics, on the contrary, were ascetics. They were guilty, not of fornication or gluttony, but of voluntary humility, of worshipping angels, of neglecting or punishing the body, and of living by the evil maxim "Touch not, taste not, handle not." Paul was no ascetic. He knew how to be abased and how to abound. The stringency of his example and precepts is not motivated by a desire to free a divine soul from a bodily tomb, much less by the idea that pain is good and pleasure evil. Rather, Paul was engaged in a race, to win which required him to lay aside every weight as well as the sin which so easily besets. Willing to suffer stonings and stripes for the name of Christ, he never practiced self-flagellation, and a Simeon Stylites would have provoked his hearty condemnation.

A second attempt to explain the origin of Paul's religion finds his ideas in the Hermetic literature — a set of tractates purporting to be a revelation by the Egyptian god Tot. But in the first place these tractates were most probably written after Paul had been executed, so that if they contained Christian elements, they and not Paul would have done the borrowing. In the second place it requires some imagination to see Christian elements in them. The salvation they talk about is a deification and is more closely allied with the dualism mentioned above than with the Pauline doctrine of redemption from sin. The method as well as the nature of salvation is different. In the New Testament the death of Christ saves; in Hermes one is saved by learning cosmology.[3]

[3] For further details, cf. J. Gresham Machen, *The Origin of Paul's Religion* (The Macmillan Company, 1921). A translation of four of the tractates and some notes are found in *Selections from Hellenistic Philosophy*, by the present writer, (F. S. Crofts & Co., 1940).

A third attempt to derive Pauline theology from paganism refers it to the Greek mysteries. One author, in the absence of all evidence, supplies the deficiency with his personal courage and asserts that Paul was an initiate.[4] A literary flourish suffices to remove Paul's intense Pharisaic adherence to Old Testament monotheism and turn him into a cultured polytheist. Such surmises are not so much bad scholarship as prejudiced irresponsibility.

If these attempts to find Pauline theology in paganism fail to dissipate the uniqueness of Christianity, Paul is then made out to be a mystic or an epileptic, depending on what one wishes to make of his visions. A study of the visions, however, leaves little but a fertile imagination to support these views. True, Paul claimed to have had visions, and if having visions makes one a mystic, then Paul was a mystic. But the visions he had, possessed characteristics incompatible with Plotinus' mystic experiences. Plotinus' trances neither contained nor produced knowledge. Paul's visions were full of subjects and predicates. On the road to Damascus Paul saw a heavenly figure who spoke to him: "Why persecutest thou me?" Paul was puzzled. He recognized this heavenly figure as the Lord and yet he was not conscious of having persecuted the Lord. When he asks, "Who art thou, Lord," the word *Lord* does not mean *Sir*. Had Paul meant, "Who art thou, Sir," the reply "I am Jesus" would have only aroused his greater anger, and as he was intent on persecuting Christians, he would have ordered his soldiers to arrest this man. But the person speaking to him was no ordinary Sir; he was the Lord. *Lord* here must be taken in the sense, as was usual when Jews spoke Greek, of Adonai—the Jehovah of the Old Testament. Accordingly Paul submitted, and asked "What wilt thou have me to do?" Then Jesus gave him certain instructions to follow. Such was his vision, but neither Plotinus nor an epileptic remembers what happens in a trance. Paul never forgot. Paul also had another vision, and though he would not tell whether or not he was in the body, he heard words. What they were, he refused to disclose; but they were words and his experience was not an unconscious state in which nothing is known. And the things known, the doctrines revealed, are not echoes of Greek philosophy or mystery religions.

Two Cautions

For such reasons as these it may be concluded that paganism and Christianity are radically distinct. Any points of similarity are superficial and trivial. To speak of them as alike is no better than identifying Epicureanism and Platonism on the ground that both were founded by men. This conclusion is not weakened by two cautions that should be observed. First, since the New Testament was written in Greek, it uses words found in pagan writings. John even used the term *Logos*. But the point in question is not the use of words but the occurrence of ideas. Logos in John and hypostasis in Hebrews are not evidences of pagan ideas. Nor should one find Aristotle in the Nicene Creed because it says God is a substance or reality. One cannot forbid Christian writers to use common words on pain of becoming pagans. The second caution is that while Christianity and the Greek philosophies, as systems, have no element in common, the Christians, as people, often held pagan ideas. They had been converted from paganism and could not divest themselves of familiar modes of thought all at once. Therefore when they came to expound and defend Christianity, they inconsistently made use of Platonism or Stoicism. By a long and arduous struggle these inconsistent elements were gradually removed from a few fundamental areas, and thus a purely Christian Nicene Creed came into being. But on other topics, and especially in cases of individual authorship, the struggle was not so successful. Then, too, as time went on, the attempts to escape pagan ideas and to preserve the purity of New Testament thought grew weaker, and, one might say, almost ceased. It is an intricate story and only a simplified account can be given.

PHILO

The first medieval philosopher — or, since he lived during the lifetime of Christ, it is better to say, the first philosopher to make use of divine revelation — was Philo, a devout Jewish scholar of Alexandria. For nearly three centuries a Jewish community had prospered in Alexandria because Alexander the Great had founded the city on principles of religious liberty; and in this cosmopolitan city with its free exchange of ideas the Jews had learned of Greek philosophy. A few apparent traces of this knowledge appear in certain words used to translate the Hebrew Scriptures into the Greek Septuagint; more of the influence is found in other Jewish writings of the second and first centuries before Christ; and Philo shows himself to be well acquainted with the Greek schools. But though Philo knew this history and spoke respectfully of the philosophers, it does not follow that he accepted their views. Certainly he did not accept them un-modified. The Presocratics he condemned for their irreligious mate-rialism; with respect to Aristotle he rejected more than he adopted; from the Stoics his borrowing was greater, though of course he dis-dained their materialism; Neopythagoreanism, resuscitating the earlier school's mathematics and adding some metamathematics of its own, Philo flatly contradicted; Plato influenced him most, and yet here too Philo was not uncritical. If Moses is superior to Plato, some type of Ideal theory may be sound philosophy, but there must be extensive alterations from the Platonic original.

The possibility of Philo's combining Hebrew revelation with pagan philosophy depends on a complex of factors, which, if they seem strange today, were taken as normal good sense then. First, the Bible presumably does not contain all truth, and therefore it is possible that Plato and Aristotle may have discovered some. Second, so admirable is Plato's general viewpoint and so often in accord with Scripture that one should not rule out the possibility that somehow or other he had received information from Moses. Then, third, Philo believed that the Scriptures should be interpreted allegorically, with the result that an indefinite latitude was permitted within which many philosophic themes might be found. Inasmuch also as the early church fathers accepted the method of allegorical interpretation directly from Philo, some examples of how it works are in order.

Allegory

Concerning Genesis 2:5 Philo writes: "What is the meaning of the words, 'And God made every green thing of the field before it came into being on the earth, and every grass before it grew'? In these words he alludes to the incorporeal ideas. For the expression, 'before it came into being' points to the perfection of every green thing and grass, of plants and trees. And as Scripture says that before they grew on the earth he made plants and grass and the other things, it is evident that he made incorporeal and intelligible ideas in accordance with the intelligible nature which these sense-perceptible things on earth were meant to imitate." Again on Genesis 2:7 Philo writes similarly: "Who is the 'molded' man? And how does he differ from him who is made 'in accordance with the image of God'? The molded man is the sense-perceptible man and a likeness of the intelligible type. But the man made in accordance with God's form is intelligible and incorporeal and a likeness of the archetype, so far as this is visible. And he is a copy of the original seal. And this is the Logos of God, the first principle, the archetypal idea, the pre-measurer of all things." One or two examples may be added of allegorism on points of less philosophic importance. Paradise is symbolical of wisdom and in it the Ideas are planted as trees. God planted Paradise toward the east because the motion of the world is from east to west. The four rivers are four virtues: prudence is Pishon, moderation is Gihon, the Tigris is courage, and the Euphrates is justice. Or, more mysteriously, on Genesis 16:16 Philo writes: "Why is Abraham said to be eighty-six years old when Hagar bore him Ishmael? Because that which follows the eighty, namely the number six, is the first perfect number. It is equal to its parts and is the first even-odd number. . . . And the number eighty is the most harmonious of numbers, consisting of two most excellent scales, namely, of that which is by doubles and that which is by triples in the scheme of fourths. . . ." Then when Abram's name is changed to Abraham, Philo explains it to mean that Abram had advanced beyond the level of a natural philosopher and had become the wise lover of God. Sara also was changed from specific virtue to Sarrha, generic virtue. Hagar means encyclical education and her son Ishmael is sophism. One of the better known examples is the interpretation of the account of the Israelites, who, as they were about to escape from slavery in Egypt, borrowed jewels from their former masters. Egyptians means Greeks, and since jewels are precious possessions, they mean philosophy; from which it follows that Philo or any child of God may borrow Greek philosophy.

One reason Philo submits for using the allegorical method is that the Scriptures speak of God in anthropomorphic terms. Mention is made of the arm of the Lord or of his eyes. But since it is clearly revealed that God is not corporeal — this is the fact that underlies the strong prohibitions against making images — these expressions, though useful for pedagogical purposes, cannot be taken literally. And if not literally, must not one interpret them allegorically? It seemed so to Philo. It might not seem so today because the recognition of figures of speech does not logically require the allegorical method. In figures of speech the intent of the author is not too obscure. If God is said to have eyes which run to and fro throughout the whole earth, it is obvious that the writer is picturing God's omniscience. There is a natural connection between seeing and knowing, and in all languages a puzzled student of geometry for instance may at last exclaim, "I see it," when literally he does not see but understands. With the allegorical method, on the other hand, there is no natural connection between the literal and the allegorical meaning. The four rivers of Eden could be asserted to mean anything anyone wished with equal reason. Abram could mean "utilitarian" as easily as "natural philosopher," and Abraham could mean "Kantian." Or, vice versa. Sara might mean "daily labor" and Sarrha "Sabbath rest." Differences of opinion can indeed arise over figures of speech; it may not even be clear whether a given phrase is a figure of speech or not; but with the allegorical method there is no control whatever, linguistic, historical, or logical. Each allegorist has unrestrained freedom to make anything mean anything. The final result is that the text being interpreted becomes superfluous: one can get Plato or Aristotle out of the *Arabian Nights* as easily as out of Moses. This method of interpretation plagued the Christian church down to the time of the Protestant reformers, who insisted on a grammatico-historical method for determining the intent of the authors.

Yet, while the allegorical method puts no limits on what may be made out of the Scriptures, Philo's Jewish sober-mindedness did. He accepted the Old Testament as the authoritative revelation from God. As much of it as could be understood literally he took as literally true. Abraham, Hagar, the Egyptians and their jewels bear allegorical meanings for the learned interpreters, but the literal events actually took place in history and may be read with edification by the common people. Philo's attitude toward the Scriptures contrasts with that of

Plato's toward the Greek poets. For the Greek philosophers, the poets exhibit a primitive and popular wisdom far inferior to the rational discoveries of the philosophers themselves. The poets by a kind of mad inspiration may have had dim premonitions of truth, but they had no accurate information from God. For Philo the Scripture was precisely information from God, and no human wisdom could even equal it. Although it was to be understood allegorically, as well as literally, and in spite of the fact that allegory is inherently uncontrolled, Philo accepted certain fundamental doctrines to which allegory and philosophy must submit. "It is best to have faith in God," he says, "and not in our dim reasonings and insecure conjectures." Such faith certifies the belief in one God and his providence over the world he has created. Philo also believed that revelation requires acceptance of a theory of incorporeal ideas. Hence it may be stated that for Philo allegorism is limited by the doctrines of monotheism, creation, providence, Ideas, and, of course, revelation.

Platonic Ideas in Moses

Of these fundamental beliefs by far the most important is the doctrine of God, for it is here that Philo's radical alteration of pagan views is most clearly seen. But perhaps the most interesting approach to this theology is through his theory of Ideas. This for several reasons. Here if anywhere we have more of Plato and less of Moses; therefore we suspect a greater dependence on the allegorical method. Beyond method there is also the result of combining two divergent worldviews. Can Moses and Plato be harmonized? What is the effect of the attempt to do so on the Scriptural concepts of God and creation? Then, too, it is in connection with the theory of Ideas that Philo speaks about a Logos whom he calls the Son of God. Can it be that at the very expiration of the Old Testament age, during the lifetime of Christ himself, this great Jewish philosopher, unaware that the Son of God had come to earth, and with no help besides Plato and Moses, anticipated the Gospel of John and the doctrine of the Trinity? If this should be so, or even if his contemporaries merely thought so, it would explain why the Christian fathers received Philo with enthusiasm while the Jews neglected him for fifteen hundred years.

The Old Testament support for the doctrine of Ideas, found in the first two examples of allegorical interpretation above, may be dismissed with a brief mention. Because Moses had been ordered to construct the tabernacle according to "the pattern which was showed thee on the mount," Jews before Philo's time supposed that there was in heaven a model tabernacle with models of all the vessels. Not only the tabernacle, but tradition also asserted the pre-existence of Abraham and a number of other things. These might well help to constitute an Ideal world. But to establish his Ideal theory Philo relied more on speculation than on revelation. "For God, being God, foreknew that a beautiful copy could not be produced without a good model and that nothing perceptible to the senses could be faultless unless fashioned with reference to an archetypal Idea conceived by the intellect. When therefore he determined to create this visible world, he first formed the intelligible world in order to have a divine, incorporeal pattern for the production of a material world as a later creation, the image of the earlier, containing as many species of sensible things as there were intelligible species in the Ideal world." [5]

That God used a model in order to produce a beautiful copy sounds very much like Plato's *Timaeus*. But when we see the relation between God and the model, the illusion that Philo depends entirely on Plato for his philosophy vanishes. The quotation above and other passages teach that God formed or created the Ideal world, somewhat as we may suppose God created a heavenly model of the tabernacle for Moses to copy. As creator therefore God is superior to the Ideas. In the *Timaeus* on the contrary neither the Demiurge nor the world of Ideas owes its existence to the other, and in fact the Demiurge occupies a subordinate position. Another indication that Philo is repudiating rather than reproducing Plato is his use of the sun as an illustration. By the sun Plato had symbolized the Good as the cause of knowledge and existence. This function and this illustration Philo refers to God. More explicitly he asserts that God is "superior even to the Good itself and Beauty itself" (*De opificio*, II, 8). If this type of thought can in any sense be called Platonism, it is such a fundamentally altered Platonism that Plato would not have acknowledged it.

Still not all is clear, for Philo's figures of speech and changing illustrations, often inconsistent among themselves, make accurate

[5] *De opificio*, IV, 16.

interpretation difficult. In sharp contrast with the argument in the *Parmenides* to the effect that the Ideas must exist independently of and prior to God's knowledge of them, Philo not only makes God's subjective mental activity prior to the Ideas, but also in one passage seems to do away with all necessity for objectively created Ideas. In discussing the creation of this visible world he remarks that a beautiful copy requires a beautiful pattern. Then to explain the formation of this intelligible pattern he uses the illustration of an architect who conceives plans for founding a city. Philo is very careful not to allow the architect a blueprint: all the details of all the building to be built are carried in the architect's mind. Explicitly he says, "the world discerned by the intellect is nothing else than the Word of God when he was already engaged in the act of creation; for the city discernible to the intellect is nothing else than the reasoning faculty of the architect in the act of planning to found the city." [6] These words would seem to equate the World of Ideas with the mind of God and render an external blueprint unnecessary. From an independent philosophical point of view also, epistemological and cosmological requirements seem to be satisfied if the Ideas are eternally subjective in God's mind. Yet historically it must be reported that Philo also asserted the objective existence of the Ideas, and even in the context of the passage just quoted there are indications to this effect.

The Logos

Since the Logos or Word of God is the highest Idea, the Idea of Ideas, or the totality of Ideas, second only to God himself, these seemingly contradictory passages complicate the exposition of Philo's Logos doctrine. The quotation above makes the Word nothing else than the faculty of reason in God; that is, the Word is God himself. Philo calls the Logos eternal and ungenerated. On the other hand Philo also asserts that the Logos was generated and that the Ideas were created. In some passages where the Logos is called eternal, the intention may be only that the Logos is everlasting; and in other passages there is a contrast between the eternal God and the incorruptible Logos, which may mean that God was originally alone but that now after he has generated the Logos, he will not annihilate it. Then, too, Philo says that God is superior to the Logos, and that the

[6] *De opificio*, VI, 24.

Logos is the Son of God, second to God, and a second God. One explanation of this confusion would be that Philo was an unmethodical eclectic. Obviously interested chiefly in edifying his coreligionists, he gathered materials wherever he could find them without troubling himself about consistency and the problems of systematic philosophy. On the other hand it is not implausible that such a well educated gentleman, even if he left the minor details in confusion, would have been fairly consistent in his main positions. Therefore a measure of harmony may be obtained by supposing [7] that the Logos passes from a stage internal in the mind of God to a stage external as a really existing world of Ideas, and even to a third stage in which it becomes immanent in the sensible world.

Undoubtedly it was the title Son of God which brought Philo's theory of the Logos to the sympathetic attention of the early Christian thinkers. Inasmuch as John's Gospel teaches that Jesus the Logos made all things and without him was not anything made that was made, Philo's theory that God used the Logos or Wisdom in creation seemed to be an anticipation of the Trinitarian position. However, such a Christian interpretation of Philo cannot be successfully maintained. It depends too greatly on Philo's highly figurative language. Obviously Philo personifies the Logos, but this personification is entirely metaphorical. Philo also says that Laughter is a Son of God, God is the husband of Wisdom, Wisdom is the daughter of God, Wisdom is the mother of the Logos, and, even, Wisdom is the father of instruction. Such metaphors cancel each other out. Philo's sober position is that for epistemological and cosmological reasons there must exist a world of Ideas, but contrary to Plato God must be supreme.

In the history of Philonic studies another reason has been advanced for giving the Logos a greater degree of independence or substantial personality. Because of the righteousness of God it has been argued that he could not even by an act of creation come into contact with a world that was to exhibit sin; or more generally it was held that the supreme Deity, infinitely superior to all finitude including finite

---

[7] This is the interpretation of H. A. Wolfson, *Philo* (Harvard University Press, 1947). Cf. also James Drummond, *Philo Judaeus*, 1888; and Emile Bréhier, *Les Idées philosophiques et religieuses de Philon d'Alexandrie* (Paris, 1925).

human knowledge, would compromise his unique position, if he should have contact with the world. Therefore it would be necessary for God to use intermediate beings in producing this lower world. The first form of the argument, in so far as it involves the problem of evil, might well occur to any thoughtful Jew or Christian; though it is not so evident that intermediate personal beings would solve the problem. The second form of the argument is so incompatible with the contents of revelation, and with the very possibility of revelation, that it would be most surprising to find it in orthodox or even in heretical authors. Philo was not puzzled as to how an immaterial and supreme Deity could create a material world. It was done by an act of almighty will according to a wise plan. And after the world had been created, God could and did deal with it both directly and by means of intermediates as he deemed appropriate.

There is, however, one troublesome difficulty in connection with the creation of the visible world. Sometimes Philo speaks of God not as creating this world *ex nihilo*, but as forming it out of matter or out of reality. Then when he says that God is not only a Demiurge but also a Creator, it is argued that God is the creator of the Ideas but only the Demiurge of the visible world. On the other hand, even though God created this world out of matter, it remains possible that God had also created the matter previously. Evidence for this may be found in certain expressions which seem to indicate that Philo, again contrary to Plato's *Timaeus*, thought space to have been created. If Philo has altered Platonism in one major respect, nothing prevents the conjecture that he altered it in another. The desire for consistency would be a motive. Although the phraseology may not be decisive, yet an uncreated matter and a basic dualism seem so manifestly incompatible with the Old Testament that an admirer of Moses can hardly be supposed to have adopted such a view. However, as philosophers have often done strange things, and as the ancients often surprise the modern mind, perhaps this matter should be left an open question.

Transcendence and Knowledge

More rewarding will be a closer study of Philo's view of the nature of God. Some indications of God's transcendence have already been given. God is not merely eternal and independent, but he alone is: there are no other independent principles. He is not merely the highest term of a series of gradations, but between him and all else is the chasm that separates Creator from creature. In addition to the few quotations already made, there is another on transcendence which seems to be directed against the Neopythagoreans. Philo writes, "God has been ranked according to the one and the unit; or rather, even the unit has been ranked according to the one God, for all number, like time, is younger than the cosmos" (*Allegorical Interpretations*, II, 1).

Since any author who makes such statements claims *ipso facto* that he knows something about God, the doctrine of God may be approached by considering whether human knowledge of God is possible, and if so, how. This problem not only echoes down through the Middle Ages and reverberates in Protestant theology, but it is also a problem, sometimes under a disguise, that secular philosophy cannot escape. The immediate question is whether or not Philo's theory of God permits men to know him. The uninstructed are tempted to make short work of the matter: if God is unknowable, then we can make no justifiable statements about him and should cease talking; if on the contrary Philo makes such statements, obviously he believes that God can be known. However, there are complications. For although Philo's notion of transcendence did not separate God from the world to the extent of requiring personal mediators, none the less there are such strong statements of God's superiority and man's finitude that the possibility of human knowledge of God becomes problematical. In one frequently quoted passage Philo says, "Who can assert of the first Cause either that it is without body or that it is a body, that it is with quality or without quality; in a word who can make any positive assertion concerning his substance, or quality, or state, or motion?" Such a denial of the possibility of making positive assertions about God, limiting human knowledge of God to what God is not, was later called negative theology. But taken out of its context this quotation is entirely too extreme to represent Philo's normal position; even with certain qualifications from the context and with the recognition that the key terms are Stoic, it is still too skeptical. For, if anything is clear, Philo was quite willing to assert not only negatively that God is not a body, but positively that he is righteous, that he is creator, and so on. However, such an extreme statement, though not characteristic of Philo, could be made only by a thinker for whom man's ability to know God was definitely limited.

A knowledge of God's existence and some impression of his wisdom and power may be gained by observing his wonderful creation.

That Philo intends to assert the formal validity of the cosmological argument is very doubtful; and in any case knowledge of God derived from the world is only an apprehension "by means of a shadow cast, discerning the Artificer by means of his works." In contrast with this indirect knowledge, Philo seems more impressed with the possibility of knowing God through our own minds. By seeking solitude and shutting out sense impressions, by introspection and abstraction, one may attain a self-knowledge that leads to God. There is an analogy between the relation of the mind to the body and that of God to the world. In this way a better understanding of God is obtained than by studying cosmology. Indeed, forgetting momentarily the skepticism of the previous quotation, Philo with what is surely excessive enthusiasm asserts that it is possible for the person whose mind is "thoroughly cleansed . . . to lift his eyes above and beyond the creation and obtain a clear vision of the uncreated One." Thus Moses knew God, not by his reflection in any created thing, but by "a clear vision of God directly from the First Cause himself" (*Allegorical Interpretations*, III, xxxiii, 100–102).

And yet the skepticism returns, for the analogy does not furnish a perfect parallel. "Do not, however, suppose that the Existent which truly exists is apprehended by any man; for we have in us no organ by which we can envisage it, neither in sense . . . nor yet in mind. . . . And why should we wonder that the Existent cannot be apprehended by men when even the mind in each of us is unknown to us? . . . It is a logical consequence that no personal name even can be properly assigned to the truly Existent. Note that when the prophet desires to know what he must answer to those who ask about his name, he says, 'I am He that Is,' which is equivalent to 'My nature is to be, not to be spoken'" (*De mutatione nominum*, II, 7–11).

That God is inapprehensible, that his nature is not to be spoken, that indeed he has no name — this latter, based on Leviticus 24:16

interpreted as prohibiting the naming of God — is supported by further considerations. Since God transcends the Good and the One, there is in him no distinction of genus and species or form and matter. God is not a supreme genus (in spite of Philo's words that God is the most generic of all beings) of which other things are species, nor is he a species of some higher genus. This means that God cannot be classified. But if so, then God is unknowable, for all knowledge is expressed by classifying the subject term under the wider predicate term. We can know what a lion or camel is by classifying it with other mammals or other vertebrate animals. Without such classification we would not know what a lion is. Or, in different words, what a lion is, is the definition of lion; and according to Aristotle a definition is framed by identifying the genus and adding the specific difference. Now, unless a nonaristotelian theory of definition be worked out, which Philo did not do, the conclusion will be that God cannot be defined and we cannot know what God is. Rather one must speak of God as the Israelites spoke of the manna: they did not know what it was, and so they called it, *what is it*. More generally, all human knowledge is a matter of discerning likenesses. To call a lion a mammal is to assert its likeness to many other species. Whenever we learn anything about a hitherto unknown object, it is by being told what it is like. But for Philo God is unlike everything else. In explanation of the Lord's declaration never again to destroy the world by flood, a declaration which indicates regret, repentance, or a change of mind, Philo writes: "Now it should be said that all such forms of words are generally used in the Law rather for learning and aid in teaching than for the nature of truth. For as there are two texts which are found in the Legislation, one in which it is said, 'God is not like man,' and another in which the Eternal is said to chastise as a man chastises his son, the former is the truth. For in reality God is not like man nor yet like the sun nor like the world perceptible to the senses, but only like God, if it is right to say even this. For that blessed and most happy One does not admit any likeness or comparison or parable; nay, rather he is beyond blessedness itself and happiness and whatever is more excellent and better than these." [8]

Note again how foreign to Greek thought this theme is. Even

[8] *Quaestiones in Genesin*, II, 54.

Plotinus' ineffable One provides only a superficial resemblance, and, besides, Plotinus was still two hundred years in the future. Undoubtedly Philo was extensively influenced by the Greek philosophers, but it is an influence mainly in terminology and minor details. If one wishes to determine the source of his first principles, instead of going far afield and searching the Greek texts, it would be better to read the Hebrew Isaiah. "To whom then will ye liken God. . . . I am the first and the last, and beside me there is no God. . . . To whom will ye liken me and make me equal, and compare me, that we may be like? . . . I am God, and there is none like me." [9]

Of course, this is not to say that Philo's interpretation of Isaiah is any more correct than his interpretation of Leviticus 24:16.

Revelation and Skepticism

Yet a revealed religion, a religion in which God gives men information about himself and about their salvation, cannot be basically skeptical. If Philo inconsistently affirmed and denied the possibility of knowing God, he has not been the only one to stumble at this point. And although it will not advance the exposition of Philo's thought, yet because the difficulties reappear through the centuries in several guises, a brief survey of them may well end this subsection. On the assumption that God created man in his own image, it cannot further be asserted that God is totally other and unlike. Though God's thoughts are far above our thoughts, though God is infinite and man finite, and even in spite of the intellectual blindness due to sin, a revealed religion must assert that man can know God. The extent of this knowledge, however, has been a matter of dispute. Every so often an individual or a group has espoused some form of irrational mysticism, has replaced knowledge with a trance, has reduced religion to an emotion, and has limited speech to confusing illustrations and analogies. More learned than this in appearance perhaps, but not greatly superior is negative theology, which asserts that we can know that God is but not what God is — i.e., we can know the existence of God but not his essence. Knowledge of God's existence is to know *that* God is; knowledge of God's essence is to know *what* God is. But if we do not know what God is, we do not

[9] Isa. 40:18, 25; 44:7; 46:5, 9.

know what we are asserting the existence of. God becomes merely an
unknown object. And why anyone should worship an unknown object, or how anyone could adjust his conduct to such, is hard to
explain. Apparently allowing for greater positive knowledge is the
position that the attributes of God can be known, but not God himself. That God is righteous and merciful is no doubt true; other
attributes may similarly be asserted; but the God or essence that has
these attributes, i.e., the substance to which these attributes attach,
is said to remain in impenetrable darkness.

Essence and Attribute

The discussion of these and other solutions has been attended with
considerable confusion, arising both from the difficulties of the problem itself and perhaps even more from ambiguities in terminology.
If the existence or Being of God is considered apart from and prior
to the essence and the attributes of God, these latter, after a chemical
analogy, take on the aspect of added elements, and this seems to compromise the alleged simplicity of the divine Being. But even if simplicity should not require the identification of existence and essence,
such an identification is necessary to avoid reducing the existing God
to an unknown object, for the *what* must exist and the *that* must be
known. The distinction between substance and attribute is also difficult. Substance is a synonym for essence, is it not? But what are
attributes? And what is their relation to essence? Are not attributes
predicates which are distinct from the subject or substance to which
they attach? Yet, if the attributes are not the essence, are they unessential? Would the essence of God remain unchanged in itself, if one
of the attributes were taken from it? Would God be *what* God is, if
omnipotence or omniscience could not be predicated of him? In fact,
what is essence or what is essential other than the attributes?

In addition to the distinction or the denial of a distinction between
essence and attribute, the status of the attributes themselves has also
been a matter of dispute. It has been asked, Do the several attributes
have different definitions when applied to God, as they have when
applied to men? Wisdom and power, righteousness and love do not
mean the same thing in human affairs, but is there a real difference
between them in the case of God? Or, are the attributes merely

human ways of apprehending the manifestations of God's activity? If the attributes are merely subjective, and perhaps arbitrary human representations, and the distinctions do not exist in God, then it would seem that knowledge of them would not constitute knowledge of God. Words ought to have definite meanings; and when righteousness, power, and love are made synonymous, they convey no definite thought. Such seems to be the result of removing objective or real distinctions from God's being. Yet perhaps this skeptical conclusion does not strictly follow. God's essence, to be equated with one attribute, could be omnipotence. Being omnipotent, God promulgates and enforces laws of morality. It is a function of omnipotence, but men may call it righteousness. Being omnipotent, God plans and executes the course of history so as to produce a chosen culmination. This too is omnipotence, but men may call it wisdom. Thus though righteousness and wisdom are not distinct in God, they have points of reference in experience, are therefore distinguishable, and hence can be known. It cannot be objected that in this case God is not "really" righteous, but merely inflicts a penalty for sin; to inflict a penalty for sin is to be "really" righteous. Also, the one attribute of omnipotence is not an empty, indeterminate concept, and God is not reduced, as mystics sometimes reduce him, to a divine Nothing or celestial Void.

Some of the difficulty in this problem is real and some is only verbal. Contemplation of the majesty and sublimity of God, of whom our knowledge is admittedly inadequate, often leads religious minds to a mystical and skeptical view of transcendence. But, as has been said, this is inconsistent with a revealed religion. Related to sublimity, though more a philosophic than a distinctly religious motif, is the simplicity of God's essence. For Christians, however, the doctrine of the Trinity precludes a simplicity that would reduce God to an Eleatic or Neoplatonic One. And for Philo, who of course knew nothing of the Trinity, as well as for Christians, the Ideas in God's mind rules out an utter unity. When God is conceived of as a mind, he may be the one and only God beside whom there is no other; but his mind need not be an immense blank or a homogeneous confusion. On the other hand, much of the difficulty is verbal because of an incomplete theory of logic. Some theologians seem to have no precise definition of the terms *essence* and *attribute*, and therefore the relation between them is nebulous. Aristotle made substance or reality his first category and attempted to define property, attribute, and accident. He was not altogether successful, as a preceding chapter briefly indicated, but the Christian theologians, it must be said, did no better. When, as in the later Middle Ages, they consciously followed Aristotle, the original difficulties reappeared. When they did not follow Aristotle, as in the Patristic and Protestant periods, it is hard to guess what they meant by these terms. Even the listing of the attributes falls into confusion. Are knowing and willing attributes? Are the Ideas in God's mind attributes? How could one be able to answer these questions without knowing the meaning of the term attribute, without a developed theory of logic? And this is what has frequently been missing.

THE EARLY PATRISTICS

As a Jew living before the New Testament was written Philo recognized only the Old Testament as divine revelation. With the life and death of Jesus Christ and the writing of the New Testament, the fundamental Hebrew themes were freed from their Pharisaic interpretation, were developed into a much richer theology, and were effectively proclaimed to the Gentile world. It was of course this more ample revelation that dominated the Middle Ages.

The Theology of Jesus

Jesus himself is sometimes pictured as a naïve, nontheological teacher of simple morality. The historical evidence, however, does not support this unflattering delineation. To be sure, he earnestly urged his audiences to repent, forsake their sins, and follow the paths of righteousness. But in this he hardly advanced beyond the Law and the Prophets, or even beyond some of the better rabbis. For example, his famous summary of the Law, reducing the Commandments to the love of God and the love of neighbor, is taken word for word from Deuteronomy and Leviticus. Had Jesus been the simple teacher of morality that this liberal reconstruction of history makes him, he would today be more obscure than the rabbi Hillel.

That Jesus' pre-eminent position in history does not depend on a successful teaching career, especially not on a teaching of prosaic morality, is evident from two considerations. First, his purpose in life was not to teach but to die. Unlike the Stoics who thought that all men were children of God, Jesus viewed mankind as born in sin, as children of the devil, who therefore needed to be born again. Jesus came therefore so that men who were not, could become children of God. The foundation for this possibility was to be laid by his death, not by his moral teaching. In the second place, his lack of success as a teacher is seen in the fact that even his most intimate disciples misunderstood his message. This is not altogether surprising, first, because, so far as the general public was concerned, "these things are done in parables, that seeing they may see and not perceive, and hearing they may hear and not understand"; and second, because his person and the future events he was darkly hinting at were contrary to the disciples' expectations.

But though his audiences failed to perceive the theology of his message, he himself was not without a well developed theology. On this point his bitterest enemies saw more clearly than the disciples. In this theology Jesus naturally accepted the Old Testament revelation, appealed to it, and emphasized it. But he also expanded it. That God enjoins righteousness and will punish sin is clearly taught in the Old Testament. Jesus not only stressed righteousness, but he also made the details of the punishment more vivid than they had been. In the well known Sermon on the Mount he threatens hell fire, and in other passages he speaks of the fire that shall not be quenched and the worm that dieth not. By making these additions to the Old Testament teaching, he in effect claims authority equal to Moses and the prophets; or, rather, he claims an authority equal to the authority that gave Moses and the prophets their message. In the Sermon on the Mount again he claims to be the Judge of every individual's final destiny. "Many will say to me in that day, Lord, Lord, ... and then will I profess unto them, I never knew you: depart from me, ye that work iniquity."

After seventy of his disciples had returned from a preaching tour and reported that some people had believed and some had not, Jesus offered a prayer (Matt. 11:25–27 and Luke 10:21–22) thanking the Father that he had hidden the significance of the message from the wise and prudent and had revealed it unto babes. So it seemed good in God's sight. Then Jesus continued, "All things are delivered unto me of my Father; and no man knoweth the Son but the Father, neither knoweth any man the Father save the Son and he to whomsoever the Son will reveal him." The last phrase of this prayer shows that Christ claims power equal with God's to choose which persons shall understand the revelation and from which persons it shall be hidden, for all revelation had been delivered into the Son's hands. Even more, the Father's knowledge of the Son, which is of course a divine, eternal, and complete knowledge, and the Son's knowledge of the Father are equated. Nothing less is involved here than a claim by Jesus that he is God. This claim was made in various forms on many occasions; and finally when repeated under oath at his trial, it became the ground for his condemnation to death. His rising from the dead, leaving the tomb empty, and his appearance to over five hundred witnesses, justified the claim.

When the apostle Paul preached this good news to the Gentiles, explaining its significance more fully than the historical conditions made it wise for Christ himself to do, two interlocking results soon became evident. First, the accepted Jewish monotheism had to be adjusted so that the one God should consist of three Persons. But second, the converts to Christianity, unlike Philo, were mainly Gentiles imbued with heathen religions and philosophies; naturally therefore their first attempts to assimilate the New Testament revelation showed a larger admixture of Greek ideas than Philo did. And from a theological as distinct from a political point of view, the first three centuries, culminating in the Nicene Council, were taken up with efforts to extrude pagan ideas from the formulation of the basic doctrine of Christianity.

Historical Divisions

Medieval philosophy is divided into two well marked epochs. The second or Scholastic period begins with John Scotus Eriugena after the reign of Charlemagne. The prior Patristic period must be subdivided. First, the early Patristic period includes: the subapostolic writers, of more importance to church history than to philosophy; the Gnostics, heretical or pagan groups which invented mixtures of Christian and Greek ideas marvellous to relate; Justin Martyr (died 166); Tertullian (*ca.* 200); Origen (*ca.* 250); and Athanasius (293–373). In this early Patristic period theology, and what philosophy there was, were closely interwoven; and the main effort was to formulate the doctrine of the Trinity. After Athanasius, further doctrinal studies were undertaken and philosophical themes began to emerge from their theological background. This later Patristic period must itself be subdivided, chiefly because of the disintegration of the Roman Empire. Gregory of Nyssa (335–394) may best be regarded as a not too important forerunner of the one really great philosophical writer of this millenium. St. Augustine (354–430) is outstanding by any method of measurement, and easily forms a subdivision of the Patristic period by himself. Then with the fall of Rome, which occurred in Augustine's lifetime, and continued barbarian invasions, the Dark Ages engulfed the world for three hundred and fifty or four hundred years.

Minor Patristics

After the destruction of Jerusalem (A.D. 70), which broke Christianity's last visible ties with organized Judaism, the Roman world recognized that there was a new religion to contend with. Though the majority of converts came from the lower classes, as must always be the case with a religion, Christianity even in New Testament times had penetrated Caesar's household. And as educated pagans were from time to time brought to accept Christ, they could not help trying to answer the philosophic questions which their new religion raised. Such attempts moreover were necessary to appeal to other educated pagans. Some of the subapostolic writers reflected unsystematically on the implications of the faith, but Justin, not to mention the Gnostics whose spiritistic fairy tales cannot here be repeated, was the first to address himself conscientiously to the task. In the face of persecution through which at last he earned the title of Martyr, he pleaded for toleration of Christianity on the ground that it too was a philosophy. Justin could speak as a philosopher because he had studied the best thought of his day and had been converted to Christianity from his previous Platonic position by the arguments against the natural immortality of the soul. What the *Phaedo* aimed to prove was not so much the immortality of the soul in the Christian and etymological sense of the word, but the eternity of the soul. Not only will the soul survive death, it existed before birth. And this eternity is a natural and inherent quality. Justin Martyr, and many other Greeks too, came to regard the Platonic arguments as fallacious. The New Testament says that "God only hath immortality" in his own natural right, and that human immortality is a divine gift. Converted in this way, but in keeping with the prevailing intellectual tendencies, Justin as a Christian remained an eclectic. He respected the Pythagoreans, admired the Stoics in certain particulars, and continued to hold to a form of Platonism, believing that many of Plato's teachings had been derived from Moses. This type of mentality, typical of the age, was not capable of avoiding confusion. Although Justin represented God as a living God in opposition to the abstractions of the philosophers, he seemed not to grasp creation *ex nihilo*. The Logos he identified with Christ, but as might be expected he had difficulty with the relation of the Father to the Son. The Father begat Christ by an act of will so that Christ is not personally eternal but came into being at a point in time. The substance of the Logos, however, is eternal and is one with the Father, but the numerical and personal distinction is a later addition. The Logos, being the reason of God, is found wherever there is reason. In Socrates, for example, the Logos condemned the errors of Greek religion. But if all men share at least to an extent in the Logos, why do they fail to recognize Christ? Justin explains that man has free will; he has the ability to choose the good; there is little or no flaw in human nature; Adam's sin was the first sin, but it was not the cause of later sins; were it not for the demons who originated polytheism, the Logos would have restrained men from doing evil. What is now needed is reason and teaching; the Logos became incarnate in Jesus Christ; although he also conquered death and cleanses from sin by his blood, his main purpose was teaching and the correction of errors. Baptism remits prior sins, and we gain reward for subsequent good works. Thus two inconsistent lines of thought are intertwined.

A different type of personality was Tertullian. Not only did he advocate righteousness, he went further and adopted an ascetic position. It was only grudgingly that he admitted the permissibility of marriage; celibacy is best; and a second marriage is sin. Heathen culture is evil and philosophy is the mother of heresies. Whereas Justin had spoken appreciatively of the pagan literature, Tertullian is best known for his harsh condemnation of it. Skilled in the rhetoric of the law schools, he declaims, What has the Christian in common with the philosopher? Jerusalem with Athens? The Church with the Academy? Revelation with reason? And to illustrate his contempt for all heathen rationality, modern authors sometimes quote him as accepting the Gospel in the words, *Credo quia absurdum*. There is no evidence that Tertullian used this particular phrase, although he did say, *Sepultus resurrexit; certum est quia impossible est*. However, those who deprecate philosophy are often the ones who philosophize with the least restraint. And for all his repudiation of paganism, Tertullian seems to have absorbed quite a little Stoicism. He was in fact a materialist, holding that nothing exists except bodies and that all substance is corporeal. God himself is a body, as well as the soul of man. Though materialism is an anomaly in Christian history, Tertullian was able to make it serve a view of human nature more in accord with the New Testament than Justin's view had been. Man is not born innocent; a depraved nature is transmitted by bodily inheritance from Adam so that from birth the thought and will of each person is corrupted by sin. Therefore what vitiated intellects think impossible or even absurd, such as the resurrection of Christ, may very well be the truth. Still the human race is not utterly evil, for some of Adam's original goodness is also inherited, at least enough to preserve free will and the ability to choose the good. Tertullian also occupied himself with the relation of the Father to the Son. Although like Justin he did not say clearly that the Son as Son is eternal, but rather that there was a time when the Son was not, and in accordance with the Logos doctrine of the age represented the Son as produced by the Father for the purpose of creating the world, yet on the other hand his conscious adherence to the statements of the New Testament, including the hitherto unnoticed or baffling statements about the Holy Ghost, led him to strain this type of subordinationism to the point of speaking of one substance in three persons. In these passages he almost reached the Nicene position.[10]

[10] Cf. B. B. Warfield, *Studies in Tertullian and Augustine* (Oxford University Press, 1930).

At this point it is convenient to break strict historical continuity in order to pay our respects to Athanasius. A parenthetical paragraph will suffice because the very success which made him of supreme importance in the history of doctrine removes him from philosophic consideration. His arguments, as may be seen in the De decretis, rely entirely on Biblical exegesis and are completely purged of pagan elements. His opponent, Arius, intensifying the subordinationism of the Logos speculation, not only asserted that there was a time when the Son was not, but concluded plausibly that therefore the Son had been created out of nothing. Athanasius, against imperial hostility by which he was falsely accused of crime and exiled several times, and in spite of the inertia of a house of bishops, caused the Christian church to recognize that the doctrine of the Trinity is the foundation of the faith.[11]

Other Christian thinkers, however, particularly on subjects other than the Trinity, were not so successful in escaping pagan influence. To return to the century before Athanasius, Origen of Alexandria (185–254) was even more of an ascetic than Tertullian, though like Justin he was more inclined to accept Greek philosophy. Aside from his subordinationism, which was not so extreme as Justin's, Origen discussed the created universe. The question that troubled him was whether or not the world was eternal. On the one hand eternity involves incomprehensibility; and as God comprehends the world, it cannot be eternal. This too is in accord with the Genesis account. On the other hand creation would imply a change in the immutable God. God creates because he is good, and if ages had passed before Creation, it would seem that during such a period of inactivity God had not been good. Origen offers a solution to the antinomy by suggesting that the present world was created at a point of time as Genesis says, but that there is an infinite series of worlds — not identical in every respect as the Stoics taught — so that the good God has been eternally creating. (Unfortunately, if an eternal series is also ipso facto incomprehensible, the original problem of God's knowledge reappears.) Since there is no variety in God, the spirits whom he first created were all alike. This unity was destroyed by the exercise

11 For the doctrine and its significance, cf. Athanasius, De decretis, and Wm. G. T. Shedd, A History of Christian Doctrine (Charles Scribner, 1864).

of free will, and a hierarchy of beings resulted because some sinned less and others more. Although God had not intended to create a material world, he did so as a punishment for sin; and human souls, somewhat degenerate descendants of the fallen spirits, are forced to enter bodies and be born. However, what free will has done, free will can undo. Even the devil will choose to be saved (though just how a *free* will must eventually choose the good is difficult to understand), and in accordance with I Corinthians 15:25–28 the end state will be like the beginning. At the same time and in spite of his immense erudition and ability, Origen seems also to draw a parallel between the fixed goodness of the elect in heaven and the fixed evil of the reprobate in hell.

Between Athanasius and St. Augustine, Gregory of Nyssa alone will be mentioned. His chief claim to distinction is an attempt to explain the Trinity on Platonic principles. Let it be assumed that the Father is God, the Son is God, and the Holy Ghost is God, three persons in one substance: how can this be? What is the relation between the substance and the personal distinctions? Platonism solves the problem. Just as Peter, James, and John are three persons and yet participate equally in the Idea man, so the Father, Son, and Spirit are three persons in one substance. The essence of God is like a Platonic Idea under which there are, in this case just three, particulars. This ingenious attempt to "rationalize" the Trinity was never well received by the Christian church. But it raised the question whether or not the doctrines of the Bible can be rationally deduced; that is, whether demonstrations of the doctrines can be completed independently of revealed information. And on this question many of the later writers had something to say. Gregory also thought that Platonism could similarly explain the doctrine of creation. If God is pure spirit, how can there be a corporeal creation? The answer is: If from a tree we abstract color, hardness, magnitude, and so on, there is no tree left; in reverse God can put together the spiritual Ideas of color, hardness, and so on and produce a corporeal existence. Origen and Gregory were outstanding men in their time, more worthy of renown than this abbreviated report indicates; but they cannot compare with St. Augustine. Few men can.

ST. AUGUSTINE

St. Augustine (354–430) was born of a heathen father and a Christian mother in Tagaste, Numidia; he attended school at Carthage, accepted the Manichaean religion, became a professor of rhetoric, turned skeptic, visited Rome and Milan, enjoyed the polished style of St. Ambrose's sermons, studied Neoplatonism, read the Bible, and was converted; he became a priest in 391, was elected bishop of Hippo in 395, and had a distinguished ecclesiastical and literary career.

Augustine's intellectual activity began and long continued with the problem of evil. During his twenties he found it impossible to believe that a good God could be the sole ultimate cause of a world in which misery was so widely experienced, or, for that matter, experienced at all. The dilemma, formulated perhaps first by Lactantius (ca. 300) and repeated by Voltaire and many others, is this: God either wants to rid the world of evil or he does not want to; in the latter case he is not good and in in the former he is not omnipotent. The Manichaeans, rejecting omnipotence, concluded that there are two original and independent principles, Light and Darkness, a mixture of which constitutes this world. In the third century Mani, the founder, combined some Babylonian, Parsee, and Buddhist themes to replace Zoroastrianism in Persia. A little Christian terminology was included, which probably grew in proportions as the religion spread to northern Africa. Here it won Augustine's acceptance. But after eight or nine years its inherent defects made themselves felt. Although Augustine was not particularly interested in physical science, he saw that the Manichaean astrology compared unfavorably with the exactitude of mathematical astronomy. Then too their moral theory was deficient, for in spite of their asceticism, taboos, and scruples — the stricter Manichaeans were celibates — the underlying dualism destroyed personal responsibility. The real I belongs to the Light and it is the Dark nature that sins; therefore whatever evil my nature does is not to be charged against me. And in particular the dualistic implication that evil is a substance or reality is one which Augustine came to combat most vigorously for the remainder of his career. At the moment, with further perplexities about materialism, Augustine passed into a period of skepticism. Through the study of Neoplatonism, helped by Christian influences, Augustine wrote against the skeptics; and with these arguments Augustine's system of philosophy may be said to begin. Perhaps one should not say that Augustine had a philosophical system. Although he was not so desultory a writer as Philo, yet his books are more rich, variegated, and stimulating than they are systematic.

Skepticism and Happiness

It is the peculiar merit of Augustine to defend the possibility of knowledge, not alone on purely logical grounds, but mainly on moral grounds. He does not set out to frame a genetic account of knowledge, but he approaches the matter from the broadest teleological point of view. In the previous chapters, e.g., the opening paragraph of the Hellenistic age, mention was made of the connection between ethics and epistemology. On this point Augustine leaves little additional to be said.

The skeptics, including the Academicians, had argued that one cannot with certainty know anything: one cannot even know that one cannot know with certainty. By etymology the skeptic is one who searches for the truth; the search itself, without the discovery, is wisdom; by suspending judgment on all matters a man frees himself from snares and delusions; he will govern his actions not by truth but by probability; and thus by the end of his life he will be worthy of happiness.

To this Augustine replies first that a search without any possibility of discovery cannot be accepted as the definition of wisdom. It is rather a description of foolishness. Certainly no one can be happy if he does not have what he wants. The seeker for truth professes to want truth. The skeptic therefore cannot be happy, he cannot accomplish the aim of his life. Nor can his useless search provide any guidance for day-to-day living. The skeptics wish to act on what is probable; but if "probable" means only what seems good to a person at the moment, a man might commit the worst crime without blame, provided he thought it was probably good. But probability

may mean something more. It may mean "approximating the truth."
The skeptics call propositions false, doubtful, probable, and plausible. Their basic principle, however, does not in consistency permit
them to use any of these terms. A false proposition is one opposite
to the truth. How then can one say that a proposition is false,
unless one knows the truth? A doubtful proposition is one that
might possibly be true; a probable or plausible proposition resembles
or approximates the truth. But it is impossible to apply these terms
without knowing the truth by which they are determined. One might
well ask, Is it true that a foredoomed search for truth is wisdom?
The skeptic would have to reply that he did not know. Is it probable
that such a search is wisdom? Or with respect to everyday living, is
it probable or doubtful that eating lunch today is wise? Again the
skeptic could not know. A theory of probability must itself be based
on truth, for if the method of determining the probable wisdom of
eating lunch is false, the conclusion that it is safe to eat lunch could
not be known to be probable. Without the possession of the·truth
therefore it is impossible to act rationally even in the most ordinary
situations.

Now, fortunately, truth is not only possible to attain, it is impossible to miss. There are some truths indubitably certain. Even
sensation is not uniformly deceptive, and, more to the point, thought
is not altogether dependent on sensation. For example, complete
disjunctions, such as, either you are awake or asleep, and implications
based on them, such as, if there are only four elements, there are
not five, are unquestionably true. Similarly, the law of contradiction,
which underlies all logical forms, cannot be disputed; and at this
point it might be well to review Aristotle's pertinent remarks.
Furthermore the propositions of mathematics cannot be doubted;
nor is this science any more than logic based on sensory experience.
Even if it were possible to sense a given number, such as three,
ratios, divisions, and the other operations cannot be perceived.
Things perceived by sense, rivers and trees, do not long endure; but
that the sum of three and seven is ten endures forever. There never
was a time when three and seven did not add up to ten, nor will
there ever be a time. Such inviolable, eternal truths cannot be
abstracted from a mutable matrix. Nor can the given numbers
themselves be so abstracted. Three — or, better, one, since the

number series depends on one — cannot be perceived by sense, for every object of sensation is many, not one. Bodies have parts innumerable; at least they have three dimensions, a center and a surface, a right and left side; and therefore no body can be one. If therefore unity pure and simple is not an attribute of body, unity cannot be abstracted from body; for we cannot abstract what is not there. The truths of mathematics, accordingly, are grasped, not by sense, but by reason or intellectual intuition. And these truths are indubitable. But the most crushing refutation of skepticism comes when Augustine asks his opponent, Do you know that you exist? If he so much as hears the question, there can be no doubt about the answer. No one can be in doubt as to his own existence. "We both have a being, know it, and love both our being and knowledge. And in these three no false appearance can ever deceive us. For we do not discern them as things visible, by sense. . . . I fear not the Academic arguments on these truths that say, 'What if you err?' If I err, I am. For he that has no being cannot err, and therefore my error proves my being" (*De civitate Dei*, XI, 26; cf. *De libero arbitrio*, II, 3). Thus in the immediate certainty of self-consciousness a thinker has contact with being, life, mind, and truth.

Twelve hundred years later Descartes repeated the argument, *Cogito ergo sum*; only, Descartes in order to appear original altered its form and spoiled its force. Further Descartes made this proposition the premise from which all other truths were to be derived. Augustine indeed derived many other truths, possibly too many, from this original certainty; but it was not the only original certainty. It is one case, a particularly obvious case, of intellectual intuition. The skeptics had enjoyed considerable success in their contest with the Stoics because both schools limited themselves to sensory intuition. Augustine's aim was to force the admission of at least one case of intellectual intuition; and if one case be admitted, the possibility of others is opened. Another modern philosopher, Immanuel Kant in the eighteenth century, never tired of denying the possibility of an intellectual intuition; with him, though not exactly like the Stoics, all intuition was sensory. The opposition between these two types of philosophy is fundamental.

The ethical motive in the defense of truth deserves a little more emphasis. Philosophers and scientists have often been characterized as engaged in a disinterested search for truth. Speculation is the passive position of a spectator, one who sees the show but is not an actor in it. Such a one observes mathematical relations, observes them keenly, and perchance invents calculus, but not for the purpose of building bridges; he may be interested in the pressure of gases, but not in a steam engine. The goal of his observation or experimentation is knowledge for its own sake, which he enjoys in an "ivory tower." The picture may of course be a distortion, for Plato was deeply concerned with the relation of scientific knowledge to ethics and with the application of ethical principles to concrete situations. Even Aristotle, who made contemplation the highest activity, wrote carefully about moral virtues. But though the picture of the ivory tower be exaggerated, it is an excellent antithesis to Augustine's view of philosophy. Of course the Hellenistic age, particularly the Stoics and Epicureans, had put greater stress on ethics than had Aristotle, but Augustine puts still more. This is in keeping with what might be called his personalism. The previous philosophers had started from physical nature and for them man was but one item among a number of curiosities. But Augustine with his appeal to the immediate certainty of self-consciousness was the first philosopher to use psychological categories exclusively. Even Plotinus, for all his spiritualism, still retained the five Platonic categories of which two were the physical categories of rest and motion. Augustine's key terms on the other hand are thought, doubt, memory, will, and blessedness. Although he compared astrology unfavorably with the exact predictions of astronomers, he was not greatly interested in physical science. In so far as the visible world shows us the glory of God, well and good; but "O Lord, God of truth, does it suffice to know those things [astronomy] to please Thee? Unhappy is the man who, though he knew them all, does not know Thee; and happy is he who knows Thee, even if ignorant of them. As to him who knows Thee and knows them also, it is not those things which make him happy; he owes all his happiness to Thee" (*Confessions*, V, iv, 7). Some modern scientific minds are appalled by this view. Perfectly certain that no God miraculously interferes with the course of nature now, and that hereafter there can be no dreams to give us pause when we have shuffled off this mortal coil, they center their affections on refrigerators, autos, and atomic bombs, infallibly convinced that because of science the human race is now far happier than it was in Augustine's day. But what can these modern minds mean by happiness? The first condition of happiness, reasons Augustine, is that it be permanent. To love what can be lost is to live in fear. Freedom from fear thererore can be found only in the immutable possession of an unchanging object, and the only object independent of flux is God. To know and love God and to know oneself is the aim of philosophy. Nothing more is needed. These two knowledges, as John Calvin later repeated in the opening chapter of his *Institutes*, cannot be separated. I cannot know myself unless I recognize my relation to God; I must place myself below God but above the body and its passions. And the chief obstacle to this knowledge is the sin of pride. Man is unwilling to submit to a superior. He intends to be alone the captain of his soul. Thus philosophizing is fundamentally a moral activity, and knowledge has a practical puιpose rather than being speculative purely. There is involved, basically involved, the question of *my* destiny. This is not to say that Augustine was a forerunner of modern pragmatism any more than he was a disciple of Protagoras. Man does not make and remake truth; truth is fixed and eternal; and there must be speculation in the sense of discovering and seeing the truth; but we want the truth because it alone brings personal happiness. That is, it will bring happiness if knowledge of God is possible.

Truth and God

Doubtless Augustine thought that the existence of God could be proved. A brief statement about "existence" is required, and a little longer explanation of proof. As to the previously mentioned distinction between existence and essence, Augustine sometimes shows the influence of negative theology. In one place he wonders "if indeed anything can be spoken of him [God] properly by the mouth of man." This remark comes in the course of an argument to the effect that the Ideas are not superior to God, as if God participated in a higher Idea of greatness or goodness, but that the Ideas are in God and as attributes are identical with each other in God. "He

is great with that greatness by which he himself is that same greatness . . . for it is the same thing for God to be and to be great. . . .
Let the same be said also for his goodness. . . ." (De Trinitate, V,
10, 11). This seems to say that greatness, being, and goodness are
the same thing in God. Also, "his greatness is the same as his
wisdom" (ibid., VI, 7, 8). And by inference knowledge, will, and
action are identical, for in God quality and substance are the same.
"He is without doubt a substance. . . . God is the only unchangeable
substance or essence, to whom Being itself, whence comes the name
essence, most especially and most truly belongs" (ibid., V, 2, 3).
But there is a difficulty. God should not be called a substance.
"If, I say, God subsists so that he can be properly called a substance,
then there is something in him as it were in a subject and he is
not simple. . . . But it is an impiety to say that God subsists and is a
subject in relation to his own goodness, and that this goodness is
not a substance or rather essence and that God himself is not his
own goodness, but that it is in him as in a substance. And hence it
is clear that God is improperly called substance, in order that he
may be understood to be, by the more usual name essence, which
he is truly and properly called; so that perhaps it is right that God
alone should be called essence. . . ." (ibid., VII, 5, 10). The quotation is confusing, particularly the distinction, alluded to but not
explained, between substance and essence. It would be tempting
to say that Augustine refused to put God under any category; and
in a sense this is true, although he uses the category of relation in
speaking of the three Persons and of their relation to the world.
Two other passages contain stronger statements of the negative
theology. One is, "Who is better known by knowing what He is
not," and the other, "Of Whom the soul has no knowledge save to
know how it has known Him not" (De ordine, II, 16, 44 and 18,
47). But these two statements cannot bear too weighty a conclusion. First, Augustine introduces them incidentally and hesitat-
ingly — they do not form a part of the main argument; second,
the treatise is a very early one, written immediately after his conversion when the influence of Neoplatonism was stronger than it was
later, for the writings of Augustine are not entirely consistent
throughout — as time went on he modified his opinions, dropping

out various pagan elements, e.g., Plato's reminiscence and the eternity of the soul, and finally writing a series of Retractions; then third, the extremity of negative theology, that no positive statement about God is possible, cannot be Augustine's position, for his writings are full of positive assertions, and the proof *that* God is has a great deal to do with *what* God is.

What "proof" is, is another matter. Augustine certainly does not begin with physical motion and laboriously argue to an unmoved mover, though he does offer what probably seemed to him not only a convincing but a conclusive demonstration. But it is not the difficult series of syllogisms that Aristotle offered, for Augustine thinks it so easy to prove God's existence that he does not use extreme care to produce formal validity. Nor does he place the same weight on rational demonstration that Aristotle has done. There is a more natural way to begin. It is natural because all men know there is a God; such knowledge is inseparable from the human spirit. And if some fools say in their heart there is no God, theirs is a willful ignorance; God is still present to their minds, if they would but pay attention. Rather than beginning with rational proof, Augustine chose the way of faith, and in doing so he raised the problem of the relation of faith to reason.

To the secular mind reason and faith are antithetical, the former good and the latter intellectually dishonest. How dishonest then must all secular minds be! Faith is not something strange or irrational, used only in accepting divine revelation; it is an indispensable mental activity. Faith is the acceptance of a proposition as true on the testimony of witnesses. If one has seen and measured the walls of Carthage, one may be said to know their height; but if a Carthaginian tells a Roman how tall they are, the Roman does not strictly "know"; he accepts the statement on faith and "believes" it. Nearly all the contents of even the most secular mind are matters of faith. Augustine uses this illustration. A young man believes that a certain older man is his father on the testimony of his mother; and even the identity of the mother is a matter of faith. Faith is the basis of family life and of society. Granted that faith is not direct knowledge, still it is not irrational. It is not blind. There are reasons for believing a witness. If a man had never seen the walls of Carthage, it might be irrational to take his word as to their height. But if he is an eyewitness and if he is trustworthy, faith in him is neither unnatural nor unreasonable. In fact, not only is most so-called knowledge faith, but also there can be no knowledge in the strict sense without faith. All knowledge begins in faith. Our parents and teachers tell us things, and we believe them. Later in life we may reason out some of this information for ourselves. But we could not have obtained the later understanding without the prior faith; and Augustine formulates a sort of motto, which St. Anselm afterward borrowed: *credo ut intelligam* — I believe in order to understand. Understanding as the goal is superior to faith as the starting point; but the start must be made. Only in writers who otherwise define faith, and who therefore are not talking about the same thing, or who do not take the trouble to define faith and who therefore do not know what they are talking about, can an incompatibility between faith and reason be found. For Augustine the two are intimately connected, and philosophy becomes the rational exploration of the content of faith. The application of this view to the existence of God is that the apostles were eyewitnesses of Christ; both they and he attested their divine message by miracles; and the message informs us that God exists.

Once a person has divested himself of pride so as to believe this message, he can advance to a rational proof of God's existence. In fact, although faith of some sort is prior to all reasoned knowledge, faith in the Bible is not a necessary prerequisite for avoiding skepticism, learning mathematics, or even proving God's existence. Though not a necessary prerequisite, it is the easiest way, none the less; and we must remember that the eternal destiny of individuals, most of whom are not philosophers, is too important to hang on the accidents of formal education. There is a proof, however, and it leads from the possession of truth to the necessity of God.

Skepticism, as indicated above, was refuted because the human mind as such necessarily possesses a number of indubitable truths. One cannot doubt that seven and three are ten. Intellectual intuition also reveals the moral truth that one ought to seek wisdom. Then there are the laws of contradiction and disjunction. And above all, I think therefore I exist. None of these truths, it will be noted, depends on sensation. The bodily eye frequently deceives us, but the eye of the soul, reason itself, does not. No one can be mistaken as to his existence. Hallucinations and doubts do not occur unless one is, lives, and thinks. These truths are therefore necessary. But if necessity, universality, and normative obligation cannot be based on sensory experience, neither can they be based on the subjective reason of an individual person. Were that the case, truth would change from person to person. But these truths are common to all men: they are universal. These truths are unchangeable: human minds waver. While they exist in our reason, they are superior to it. If truth were inferior to reason, we would sit in judgment over it; we would say seven and three ought to be ten, and then we would make it so. But actually we judge that seven and three must be ten. We do not make these truths, we discover them and judge other things by them. Since these truths or this body of truth is the norm to which reason submits in judging, truth is superior to human reason and reason is inferior to truth. Yet reason is a very excellent thing; by it man is superior to the animals; and its abilities are awe-inspiring. If therefore truth is superior to reason, truth must be God. And therefore it is proved that God exists. If truth is not God, and there is something superior to truth, then this higher something would be God. So once again it is proved that God exists. However, since truth has been shown to be immutable and eternal, and since God alone is immutable and eternal, we may say that God is truth. The conclusion therefore is that in grasping truth, the mind knows God. In making all knowledge a knowledge of God, in saying that Christ is the Light that lighteth every man, Augustine is not trespassing on the sphere of redemptive grace. All men are illumined by God's light, but not all are saved. The present problem lies entirely within the limits of epistemology, and Augustine is far from denying that the heathen can have knowledge. The Scriptures say, "In him we live and move and have our being," and this applies to the pagan as well as to the believer. God is the universal light for all men, and all see truth in this light. Obviously the skeptic is not a believer, yet it is he who is forced to admit the certainty of his existence. This is epistemology, not grace.

The thesis that all men in their knowledge have contact with God, or that God is the universal light, enabled Augustine to solve a problem which the previous philosophers had largely neglected. Gorgias, a Sophist and a contemporary of Protagoras, in addition to denying the existence of Being and arguing that even if Being existed it could not be known, went further and claimed that even if Being could be known, two people could not talk about it; for, aside from the Presocratic materialistic impossibility of the same thought existing in two places at once, it would be impossible for sounds in the air to produce a recognition of Being, when the assumption is that recognition of Being is the cause of the sounds. Augustine set himself to this problem in a brilliant treatise, *De magistro.*

Communication

Speech or communication, he argued, is a matter of words, and words are signs — they signify something. The relation between a sign and the thing signified, the theory of semantics, forces the difficulties in the problem of communication, though Augustine went into more detail than is necessary for the present purpose. Ordinarily when we attempt to indicate what a word signifies, we use other words; for example, a *city* is a densely populated area. Thus one sign is explained by other signs, and if we are ignorant of the latter, the thing signified escapes. Of course, in the case of concrete nouns, like city or wall, it would be possible to indicate the things signified by pointing the finger at them. At least this is true for visible objects, though we cannot point a finger at a sound, odor, or taste; and to indicate what is signified by prepositions is still farther outside the range of pointing. Then too it must be noted that while the wall itself is not a sign but is the thing signified, pointing the finger at it is as much a sign as a word would be, and as before we have used a sign to show the thing. It appears, however, that there are certain actions which can be shown without a sign. If one wishes to know what walking is, the teacher may indicate the action signified by walking, i.e., by the thing itself and not by a sign. And if the learner were still in some doubt, the teacher might walk a little faster. But just here is the difficulty. How could the pupil distinguish walking from hurrying? Or how could he distinguish between "walking" and "walking ten paces." The matter is further complicated if we wish to explain, not walking, but speaking; not wall, but word, gesture, letter, and in particular the words noun and verb; for in all these cases the sign is a sign of a sign; and incidentally a written word is the sign of a spoken word. Thus "noun" when spoken, is an audible sign of audible signs; whereas "wall" or "city" is a sign of a thing.

Neglect of these semantic distinctions provided humor for an old sophist who asked his victim whether what is expressed proceeds from the mouth. Upon receiving an affirmative answer, the sophist turned the conversation so that the man pronounced the word *lion*; this permitted the sophist to heckle him about lions proceeding from his mouth when he spoke. Yet nouns proceed from our mouths when we speak. What is lion? One answer is that lion is a noun; another is that lion is an animal. The distinction that the sophist missed is that when lion is called a noun, lion is construed as a sign; but when lion is classed as an animal, it is construed as the thing signified.

Returning now to the signifying of walking and speaking, Augustine concludes that nothing can be shown except by signs. Nothing can be taught or communicated by itself alone. But here arises the paradox. For it is equally evident that nothing can be taught by signs. When signs are used, the pupil either knows the thing signified or he does not. If he does not, the sign teaches him nothing. It is as if the teacher said *caput* to someone ignorant of Latin. But if the pupil already knows the thing signified, the pronunciation of the sign does not teach him what it is. Quite the reverse: because the pupil already knows what "head" is, the repeated pronunciation of the word leads him to associate the sign with the thing signified that he already knows; and he learns that the word is a sign only through knowing the thing. Otherwise it might be merely a noise without significance. The thing therefore must be known first; the sign is learned later. Communication is of course possible only by means of words or some other signs; but the words instead of teaching anything new, rather stir up our memories of things we had previously understood. Thus when a speaker says something, unless he is referring to sensory objects present at the moment, we consult the Truth within our minds to see whether or not he is telling the truth.

In the Platonic dialogues a series of questions stimulates reflection, and the learning or assent comes from within. It is not the words of Socrates that effect the teaching, for had Socrates said, Do you not agree that two equals three? the pupil would have instantly replied, No, not at all. The pupils in the dialogues usually reply in the affirmative because they see the truth in their own minds. Instead of the pupils learning from Socrates, they sit in judgment over him. This is possible only through an understanding of the truth; and if the pupils do not understand, Socrates' words are to no purpose. Peculiar situations can arise. Suppose an Epicurean, who does not believe in an immortal and incorporeal soul, should give an account of the arguments designed to prove it; the pupil might judge that the arguments are sound though the teacher believes them fallacious. Is it to be said that the Epicurean teaches what he himself does not know? The peculiarity only enforces the solution that communication and teaching, although making use of words or signs, is possible only because the mind possesses Truth. Socrates or Augustine is not really the teacher or master: the true master is Christ, who is the Truth and who enlightens every man.

Although the problem of communication and the refutation of skepticism that lies behind it presuppose the existence of individual persons, and some slight reference has been made even to sensory perception, the preceding material concerned chiefly the existence of God. It is now time to consider more directly the existence of the world and God's relation to it. This is the more urgent inasmuch as Augustine began his famous career by breaking away from Manichaean dualism, passing beyond Neoplatonic emanationism, and accepting the Christian doctrine of creation.

Creation

The precise issue of dualism or pluralism must be supposed to have been settled by the rational necessity of some kind of unity. It is interesting to note, however, that few of the Greeks consistently maintained a monism. Plato had three independent principles. Aristotle failed to end up with a unified world because each individual substance was a composite of matter and form, and these two were irreducible: for even if matter did not actually exist

separately, pure form does. Possibly the Stoics were more successful. But the Neoplatonists, who are ordinarily regarded as most
insistent on unity, hide a dualism as basic as that of the Manichaeans. For aside from the difficulty of understanding how the
One could produce multiplicity, there is the existence of that unreal
Darkness in which the light of the One shines forth and is finally
extinguished. If reason demands unity, then, it seems, only the noble
Parmenides was rational. But now the problem of the world must
be considered from another angle.

The Christian view of things also seems to resemble a dualism:
at least the world and God may be called two "substances"; neither
one is the substance of the other. But actually Christianity is more
successfully monistic than Neoplatonism was. God alone is the
eternal substance, the independent principle; apart from the creation
of the world nothing exists besides him. This underlines the essential and controversial elements of the Hebrew Christian doctrine.
First, as Creator God is viewed, not as an undifferentiated One that
produces a world by necessity, but as a living mind who with foreknowledge creates voluntarily. Plotinus explicitly denied will to
his One; but will is one of the most prominent aspects of the Biblical
Deity. Second, precisely because God is Creator, the world is called
into being by divine fiat alone: there is no pre-existing matter to
be formed or organized; there is not even a Darkness or Void out
of which or into which the universe is created. And third, this implies that the world had a first moment and that its past history is
finite.

It was this last point that Augustine thought needed special
defense against the previous philosophies, for whatever their differences were, they all agreed that the world has always existed. If
Plato's Demiurge formed the world-soul and organized chaotic space,
it is none the less an eternal activity; Aristotle explicitly maintained
that motion never began and will never end; the Stoics indeed gave
the present world a finite history, but they made it one of an infinite
series of worlds, a view strangely adopted by Origen also; and of
course the emanation of the world from the Neoplatonic One is
a necessary and eternal process. The view that the world began has
its only source in Biblical revelation.

A standard objection to the Christian view is that creation implies a change in God, who has already been declared immutable. The objection may be expressed in more graphic terms, such as, Why did not God create the world sooner, or later? How could God take it into his head to create the world when this notion had not occurred to him previously? Behind this objection, however expressed, is the Parmenidean assumption that rationality excludes change, or to put it in a form more immediately relevant to Christian terminology, rationality can take no account of an event that happens once for all. Science, knowledge, or reason explains what is common or universal. Even in physics, where pendulums and levers are changing things, the knowledge does not grasp an individual pendulum as such; the object of scientific knowledge is the law of the pendulum, i.e., a relationship uniformly exhibited. Any unique factor, such as the color of the pendulum or the fact that it swung on a certain day is an irrelevant accident and lies outside the scope of science or philosophy. Now, Christianity abounds in unique events, the death of Christ, the end of the world, and, the present perplexity, the beginning of the world.

Augustine gave a double reply to his opponents. The first part is somewhat of an *ad hominem* argument or perhaps a dilemma; either they themselves must admit a unique event inconsistent with their boasted rationalism or they must deny the most precious part of their system. And it is to be noted again that this reply, consistently with Augustine's basic ethical motivation, depends on the view that philosophy is a means to happiness and wisdom. The Neoplatonists had offered as the culmination of philosophic reflection a beatific trance to which they assigned supreme value. Plato too wanted to escape the prison house of sense and let his soul soar to the world of Ideas. But if these are states of blessedness for which philosophy prepares us during our present miserable condition, and if the soul with the rest of the world is eternal, then, since the soul soars and falls again, blessedness and misery must have alternated eternally. Or, better, blessedness never has occurred and never will. For if there is such an alternation, the soul cannot be happy even in the Isles of the Blest because it will foresee its coming fall and misery. Or, if, in the Isles of the Blest or in Plotinus' trance, the soul does not foresee its returning misery, it is ignorant and deceived; and surely true blessedness is not a state of being deceived. On the other hand, if a philosopher asserts that the soul attains to a state of permanent happiness, as indeed Porphyry maintained in opposition to the common principles of his school, then there is a unique event, and one might ask, Why did it not occur sooner? If Porphyry sees the need of one unique event, he cannot on principle deny the possibility of another, such as the creation of the world and of man. For if the world or the course of history had no beginning, it could not have an end, goal, or culmination. And if these remarks apply to Neoplatonism, they are all the more evidently relevant to the Stoic theory of eternal recurrence.

History

Before the second part of Augustine's defense of the doctrine of creation is given, one consequence of assigning significance to unique events deserves more than a footnote. Because the Greeks thought that reason demanded the exclusion of unique events (if unlike Parmenides they were forced uncomfortably to admit changes, accidents, and individuals, they put them beyond the pale of science), it never occurred to them to produce a philosophy of history. History for them was unimportant; but for Christianity, which teaches that the second Person of the Godhead became man in the town of Bethlehem and died on the cross precisely on the fourteenth of Nisan, history is all-important. Finally, however, there occurred an event which disturbed even the pagan mind. When the city of Rome was sacked by barbarians in A.D. 410, the pagans attributed the catastrophe to the people's forsaking the Roman gods in favor of Christ. To answer this charge Augustine wrote a gigantic work, *The City of God*, in which for the first time in all literature (except the Bible) a philosophy of history was formulated. That history exhibits a rational plan is an idea Thucydides never dreamed of; and outside of Christianity no one attempted a study of history until Hegel and Karl Marx prepared the way for Spengler, Toynbee, and Sorokin. It is unlikely that this notion would have occurred to these recent writers without the stimulus of Christianity, yet had not Alaric sacked Rome during Augustine's lifetime, it is still probable that his fertile mind under the stimulus of Old Testament prophecies, the incarnation, life, and death of Christ, and his predictions of the end of the world, would have elaborated essentially the same ideas.

Time

The second part of Augustine's reply to objections against the creation of the world, particularly in reference to the questions why the world was not created sooner, whether time had run infinitely before there was a world, and whether God was idle before he created anything, is a discussion of the nature of time. The problem is treated at length in the *Confessions*, Book XI, which it is wise to follow.

Augustine opens with a prayer that God might grant him an understanding of creation: the world is evidently a creation because it changes. But how could God have created it? Not with any instruments or pre-existing material, for these are part of the created universe. Or, where could God have created? An artist might produce his work in Athens or Rome, but God could not have created the earth on the earth or in the heavens; God could not have created the universe in the universe; for all these themselves were created. God simply spoke and things were. But some people ask, What was God doing before he spoke? Was he idle? And if so, why did he not stay that way? Was the creation a new act of will, not an eternal act? and if this is inconceivable, if, that is, God's will is eternal, why is not the world eternal also?

These questions rest upon a misunderstanding of God's Being. God is eternal, and eternity is not perpetual motion. Eternity is motionless; it permits of no succession; everything is present at once; there is no past or future. The literal and precise answer to the question, What was God doing before he did the heavens and earth? is, he was doing nothing. For if he had done anything, that thing would have been a creature. Obviously God could not have made any thing before he made anything.[12] It is not true that

---

[12] In Latin *facio* carries the senses of both *do* and *make*, which English cannot reproduce in one word. The argument sounds much better in Latin: *Antequam faceret deus caelum et terram, non faciebat aliquid. Si enim faciebat, quid nisi creaturum faciebat? Confessions*, XI, xii, 14.

untold centures passed before God created, for centuries could not exist before God created them. The doctrine of creation *ex nihilo* has as one consequence that time was created. Time is not an independent principle, or a Neoplatonic Darkness into which God projected the universe. What time is, we must soon see; but time like every other creature began.[13] Hence it is absurd to ask what God was doing *before* he created; there was no before, for there was no time.

What then is time? At this point (*Confessions*, XI, xiv, 17) Augustine gives his famous answer, "If no one asks me, I know; but if I wish to explain it to someone who asks, I do not know." But this much is clear: if nothing had ever happened, there would have been no past time; and if nothing should ever happen, there would be no future time; and if there were nothing now, there would be no present time. Yet again, since past time no longer is, past time is not, does not exist; and since future time does not yet exist, future time does not exist. And if the present were always present, it would not be time at all, but eternity; therefore, since present time in order to exist at all must lose itself immediately in the past, how can we say that present time exists? Further, we speak of the past or the future as being long, although the present cannot be long; but how can anything that does not exist be long? If we should say that the past was long, do we mean that it was long after it had passed or when it was present? But the present cannot be long and the past does not exist. The present cannot be long because the present century, the present hour, the present minute, are half past and half future. What is present, the now, is but a point in time, without duration, and therefore cannot be long; it cannot even be time, for it has no duration — if it had any duration whatever, half would be past and half future. And yet we compare these nonexistent times and say that the past century was longer than next year will be. Stranger still, we compare or measure past times, not in the past when they were, but now in the present after they have ceased to exist; similarly we measure future times or compare them with past times, not in the future, but only in the present now. How can we measure what does not exist? How can we measure yesterday today? It is not here and now for us to measure it. Worse, if the

[13] *De civitate Dei*, XI, 6; XII, 15.

future does not exist, how could the prophets foresee the nonexistent, and if the past does not exist, how can historians talk about it? Now, really, past and future must exist somehow, somewhere; and if they do not exist in the past or in the future, they must exist now in the present. The historian talks about past events because the past remains present in his memory; and the prophet who predicts the end of the world, the astronomer who predicts an eclipse, or even you and I who plan for tomorrow, have these future times in the present imagination or consciousness. Time therefore exists; it exists in all three modes; but it exists only in the mind.

Of one thing Augustine is quite certain: time cannot be explained by physical categories. Time cannot be identified with the motion of the sun or of a planet, for even if a given motion ceased, time would go on. Nor can time be identified with motion in general, for motion takes place *in* time. The motion is measured by the time, not, as Aristotle claimed, the time by the motion. To identify a motion, one must specify two points in space, its beginning and its end. But this same motion between these same two points can be completed in varying lengths of time. The motion therefore does not determine or measure the time. Furthermore, a body sometimes moves from one point to another at unequal speeds, and sometimes remains at rest. Even its rest is measured by time. Time therefore is not the motion of bodies.

What then is time? It is the activity of our minds, memory and expectation, in which past and future exist. Time passes in the mind. And for this reason the original objections as to what God was doing before he created anything have no sense. There was no time before God created. Time as the activity of a created mind begins only with the creation of such minds. Similarly with space. If the opponents ask, Why did not God make the world sooner, they may as legitimately ask, Why did he make the world here rather than there? This question also has no sense. God did not create the world in space any more than he created it in time. Space is a characteristic of the world and was created with it. The doctrine of creation posits God alone as the sole original principle. He created out of and into nothing. Any attempt to make space and time independent of God's creation is inconsistent with the assumption of a single first principle. It would be a pluralism, like Plato's, except that instead of Ideas, Demiurge, and Space, it would have Space, Time, and Deity.

Evil

However, the more monism is stressed, the more acute becomes the problem which motivated so much of Augustine's writing: the problem of evil. For if God alone is eternal and independent, if he has created the world out of nothing, and if the only motive of creation is goodness, how can the evident evil in the world be explained? Had there only been some Darkness, chaos, or space, just a wee bit of dualism, God could have been preserved blameless. Evil is a problem which all thinkers must face. Even a purely mechanistic philosophy, like that of Democritus, must account for evil, or in this case perhaps it should be called the problem of good and evil. Theistic systems have no problem, i.e., no perplexity, about good; but mechanism finds it just as hard to explain good as evil, or, if you wish, just as easy to explain evil as good; at any rate good and evil must both be mysteriously generated out of inanimate atoms. Neoplatonism also attempted to explain evil, and from it Augustine borrowed one half of his solution. It is just here perhaps that Augustine was least successful in purging his mind of current pagan ideas.

Above it was said that for Augustine God is not a substance but an essence, and the reason Augustine insists on essence is that *essence* is derived from *esse*, to be. God is the reality that truly *is*; God is Being in the highest and strictest sense. Augustine believes he has Scriptural support for this notion in God's words to Moses, "I am that I am. . . . I am hath sent thee." If, further, God alone truly is, it follows that other things are not. Augustine virtually says as much, for after quoting the words above, he continues, "As if in comparison with that which truly is, being immutable, the things that are mutable are not — a truth which Plato held strongly" (*De civitate Dei*, VIII, xi). The nonexistence of mutable things, however, is not to be taken too literally or absolutely. "For God, being the highest essence, that is, eternal and unchangeable, gave essence to his creatures, but not such as his own: to some more and to some less, ordering nature's existence by degrees" (*ibid.*, XII, ii). Mutable things therefore exist, but exist to lesser degrees than God. These things God made and they are good. Existence itself is good. Just as a living being is better than a nonliving being, so even an inorganic corporeal element is more excellent than pure nothing. Therefore everything that exists, in so far as it exists, is good. Nonexistence is evil, and per contra evil is nonexistence. Or, a little more fully, evil can be defined as the privation of good, the extreme degree of which is absolute nonbeing. "If things are deprived of all good, they absolutely do not exist; therefore so long as they are, they are good; therefore whatever is, is good; and evil . . . is not a substance because if it were substance, it would be good" (*Confessions*, VII, xii, 18). By this theory God is absolved of all blame in creating the universe. He created each thing with certain perfections, some with more, some with less. This was an act of goodness, and since no created being had or has any claim on God, even the least degree of perfection is to be received with thanks. For the same reason no being can justly complain that God has not given it more perfections. In fact there could be no world at all if God was under compulsion to treat all beings alike or to give the supreme perfection to each. To treat all being alike would mean a world, say, of all dogs and no cats — all dogs and no sun, moon, or stars, no trees, fields, or rivers: obviously an impossible state of affairs. On the other hand, if God were under compulsion to give supreme being to everything he created, the absurdity would be still greater. For the Uncreated and the Eternal is more perfect than the created; a world in which all beings possessed all possible perfections would be a world of eternal Gods, and such would be neither a world nor a logical possibility. Thus half of the problem of evil is solved.

But this may be thought to be such a small half that though it is a good solution to something, it has little to do with evil. Existence and goodness have been made synonymous — an identification which probably means only that all existences have some purpose, and a defense has been made for differences and variety; but what has this to do with evil, with badness, unrighteousness, and sin? Maybe the devil is good (for something) as Augustine says, but still he is wicked. Men are also good for something, but they are sinners. And while God can easily be absolved of blame in creating differences, how can it be explained that he created a world in which he knew wickedness would appear? This is not so much the second half of the problem of evil as it is the whole problem.

As the doctrine of the living God and his creative fiat distinguishes Christianity from paganism on a macrocosmic scale, so too on a microcosmic scale the relation between the living God and man, particularly man as a rebellious sinner, is a strictly Christian theme. The Greeks, the Stoics more than any others, had some sense of right and wrong; they commended what they thought was virtue and despised unmanliness. But the seriousness of deliberate rebellion against the living God had at most a faint analogy in their thought. The absence of a recognition of sin is all the more complete in modern humanism, and it leads to a strange blindness in some historians of philosophy. One of them refers to Augustine's "neurotic exaggeration of guilt and sin, an unhealthy otherworldliness." Now, it is not necessary to claim that Augustine attained perfection in his later Christian life, nor to say that his analyses and his scale of particular values were always the exact and perfectly balanced truth. But to suppose that such an energetic and successful bishop was neurotic stimulates the prayer that God might bless us with more neurotics. The author refers to the words by which Augustine introduces his confession of sin and says, "This opening seems to prepare us for revelations of hideous crimes, but what actually did Augustine's sins amount to?" They were "pranks and escapades which are the normal products of youthful exuberance" such as stealing a few pears.[14] Quite definitely the prank of stealing the pears was "normal" in the sense that all boys do similar things. But does that make stealing innocent? Or does it show that all boys are sinful? Augustine was well aware that stealing those pears was not a "hideous crime" on the level with a brutal murder, and it was because the boyish escapade seemed so trivial that he chose it for analysis. What was involved? In Augustine's neighborhood there was a pear tree whose pears were neither beautiful nor juicy. One night with a group of boys he stole the pears. They were not worth eating, so the boys threw them to the pigs. Now, how can this theft be explained? If a man commits a murder in order to enjoy the riches or the wife of the victim, we believe we have found an understandable motive. Most murderers do not kill for the pure pleasure of killing. Even the monstrous tyrant who practices barbar-

[14] W. T. Jones, A History of Western Philosophy, Vol. I, p. 390, col. 1; p. 346, cols. 1, 2.

ity "without any motive" as it is said, does so in order to retain his throne by intimidation. And a throne is an understandable motive. But what was Augustine's motive in the theft of the pears? It was not hunger, for he had good meals at home; nor was it an extra dessert, for the pears were not worth eating. The only motive for the theft was the theft itself. He loved evil for its own sake, just for the fun of it. Even worse, the boy Augustine would not have gone out that night to steal pears by himself: there would have been no fun in that, unless he had been motivated by hatred of the owner, but this was no more his motive than was hunger. It was the fun of stealing with the gang. The motive then was the pure love of evil enhanced by complicity in crime. When Augustine later wrote his *Confessions*, he knew quite well that the theft of the pears did relatively little damage to the owner. In this sense it was trivial and leads those who lack penetration to call him a neurotic. But however externally trivial that theft might have been, what can be worse than a pure love of evil for its own sake?

Those who have little sense of sin, because they have little sense of God, have also little recognition of the problem of evil. Augustine with his thoroughly Christian emphasis on the extreme wickedness of rebellion against God escapes any charge of minimizing the problem. He may not have satisfactorily solved it, but he surely did not shirk it. At least two questions are involved. In addition to the perplexity as to how God would be, shall we say, so foolish as to create man when he foreknew how depraved the human heart would become, there is also the psychological difficulty of explaining how Adam, created with a good will, could have chosen evil.

Free Will

Augustine answers both these perplexities by asserting the freedom of the will. Virtuous action is possible, says Augustine in contradiction to the Stoics, only if the will is free, and therefore God, since he wanted man to live righteously, had to give him a free will. Now, if man uses his freedom wrongly, God is not to blame. We do not object to wine just because some people use it wrongly, so why should we blame God if some misuse their freedom? Hands too may be misused, but no one complains that God gave men hands; (although one might still wonder why God permits the wrong use of hands, wine, and freedom). What is the cause of these evil choices? What makes a will evil? Augustine replies that there is no cause of an evil will, for the will is the sole cause of all evil. Evil wills cause evil acts, but if the will had a cause, either this cause would be a good will or an evil will; now, a good will would not cause an evil will, and to say that an evil will is the cause of an evil will only pushes the problem back to the unexplained first evil will. This original evil will obviously cannot have been caused by a previous evil will. It were better to say that the first evil will was made by something that is not a will. But such a thing could not be superior to the will it affected, for if it were, it too would be a will. For the same reason, this thing could not be the equal of the will in question. Therefore it must be inferior to the will that becomes evil. Yet such an inferior thing must be good because everything that is is good. How then can a good thing be the cause of an evil will? Strictly it cannot be the cause of an evil will; what happens is that the will turns from a superior good and desires an inferior good. It is the turning of the will and not the desired thing that is evil. The inferior good thing does not deprave the will, but the will depraves itself by desiring it. Here Augustine borrows the Stoic illustration of the two men who see a beautiful woman.[15] Since by supposition the two men are alike in body and mind, there was no cause of the evil will of the one in the face of temptation. The man's nature is good, for all natures are good; therefore an evil will has no efficient cause. It has, however, a deficient cause. The case is similar to seeing darkness and hearing silence. We do in a sense perceive darkness by the eyes and silence by the ears, but this perception has no existent form as its real or efficient cause; we perceive because of the privation of form; we perceive that we do not perceive.

But the complications are not yet at an end. Let it be granted that the will has no efficient cause; and though Augustine gives no argument in favor of the assumption, let it also be granted that moral action presupposes a free will; still, if God foresaw that men would sin, how could they do otherwise? Does not foreknowledge make sin inevitable? Could not God have prevented sin? Although Augustine strongly suggests the contrary, could there not have been a world with

15 Cf. *The Hellenistic Age*, p. 165.

sufficient variety without degrees of sinning? God therefore must have wanted a sinful world or he would not have made it this way. The problem has been felt in all ages; some Christians try to avoid discussing it or even thinking about it, to the delight of their enemies; others like Augustine face it squarely and do their best with it; but few or none have written so satisfactorily as John Calvin and Jonathan Edwards, not even Augustine.

One element in Augustine's theory is that being is better than non-being, and that it is better to exist unhappy, presumably even in hell, than not to exist at all. To defend this he argues that a horse astray is better than a stone not astray, that unhappy men prefer to live rather than to die, and that even a soul that perseveres in sin is better than an inanimate object which cannot sin through lack of will. But since an unhappy man who prefers to live has hope of better days, it would seem that this consideration does not apply to the hopeless unhappiness of hell, nor does it agree with the Scriptural statement, "It had been good for that man if he had not been born."

In the next place Augustine denies the assertion that I *must* will as God foreknows. To say *must* means that the act is necessitated, and by necessity Augustine probably has in mind something like mechanical causation or at least external compulsion; and this is equivalent to denying that the action is willed. If a man is knocked down by a blow, he must fall; but since he must, it is not done voluntarily. Hence it is not true that I must do as God foreknows. God foreknows that the elect will be happy in heaven; but this is not to say that they will be happy unwillingly. God's foreknowledge does not do away with our power. For example, if one man knows that another will sin, this knowledge does not make the second man sin. Foreknowledge applies no force. Just as memory of past events does not cause the past, so foreknowledge does not force the future. An illustration is sometimes given of a man standing high in a tower or on a cliff. Below on the right he sees an auto speeding south; below on the left he sees another speeding west; he foresees that they will crash at the intersection; but obviously his foreknowledge does not cause the crash. This line of argument, however, makes God a mere observer who causes nothing and who learns by observing independent agents; and in any case the crash is supposed to be inevitable, for otherwise there would be no foreknowledge. Foreknowledge and inevitability are correlatives, for if the crash had not happened, there would have been only fore-ignorance.

But finally in spite of all his insistence on free will, Augustine reverses himself, in part at least, and denies that men now have free will.

Pelagius

There was a British monk, Pelagius by name, who came to Rome preaching and emphasizing free will and man's ability to do good works. One thing particularly disgusted him. When he preached righteousness and rebuked the people for their sins, they would excuse themselves on the ground that they had an evil nature and could not help it. David the Psalmist in contrition confessed to the Lord, "I have committed a great sin, but what is worse I have an evil nature with which I was born: purge me thoroughly in the inward parts, create in me a clean heart." Contrary to David's contrition those who heard Pelagius were saying, "My will chose evil but I am not to blame because I was born that way." With such self-excusings Pelagius was disgusted. Therefore he told the people that they had free will, sinning was not inevitable, there is no inborn depravity, and that they could choose the right. It seemed absurd to Pelagius to command men to do what they could not do. To order a soldier to jump fifty feet may be the device of a brutal martinet, but it could not be the requirement of a reasonable master, much less of a good God. Obligation therefore is limited by ability. From which it follows that if God commands men not to sin, they are able not to sin; if God commands men to be holy and to be perfect as their Father in heaven is perfect, men are completely able to fulfil this requirement. Pelagius even went further and asserted that it is possible to do more than God requires; and in order that this should be no empty or hypothetical possibility, he asserted that some men have lived without sin. It further follows that actual sins do not impair the will. If the will is free, if it is not caused or determined, then no matter how many times one commits sin, the will still retains its original freedom and innocence. There can be no such thing as an evil character or a depraved nature, for this would be a denial of freedom. Sin consists solely of specific acts, and after the act is finished no trace of sin remains.

This Pelagian view entails certain consequences inconsistent with the common understanding of the Gospel. Two relatively minor points are these: Paul asserted, "All have sinned and come short of the glory of God"; but Pelagius held that some had not sinned and have even surpassed God's requirements. Second, if there is no inherited depraved nature, and if sin consists solely in voluntary acts, why should infants be baptized? When Pelagius asserted that some unknown persons centuries ago in far lands had been sinless, it was impossible to check up on his statement; but since infants were being baptized every day from Great Britain to Persia, Pelagius in order to avoid an obvious repudiation of Christianity had to misconstrue the significance of the rite and declare that baptism was not a sign of the washing away of sin but was performed in order to attain a higher state of salvation.

There was another obvious and far more important element of Christianity with which Pelagius came into conflict. Christianity if it is anything at all is the offer of divine grace for the salvation of sinners. The name Jesus means Savior. But if some men exceeded God's requirements, they had no Savior; and if all men can meet God's requirements, they need no Savior. In other words Pelagius denied the need of grace. True, Pelagius might refer to the giving ot the Law and the example of Christ's life as grace. These were divine gifts which men can use as aids. But in the sense of an inward power or ability to keep the Law or to imitate Christ, an ability given before the good works could be done, Pelagius denied grace. Grace is inconsistent with free will. With the doctrine of grace Augustine was able to answer the otherwise plausible theory of Pelagius that ability limits responsibility. God undoubtedly commands the impossible. His requirements are totally beyond our resources. Since, however, they are not beyond God's resources, Augustine can pray, "Give what thou commandest, and command what thou wilt."

The ecclesiastical struggle against Pelagianism and the episcopal activity of Augustine are more matters of church history than of theology or philosophy. Nor can time be given to Augustine's sermons on baptism and grace. Although Pelagius and his followers twisted, squirmed, and made large use of ambiguous language, Augustine's appeal to the Scripture was overwhelming. But it led Augustine almost to an outright denial of free will. He soon saw that men today with their sin have no free will. Without faith, which is a gift of God, it is impossible to please him; the carnal mind is enmity against God, for it is not subject to the law of God, neither indeed can be; we are dead in sins and by nature the children of wrath. On this point he would no doubt have approved of a book written by a later Augustinian monk, Martin Luther, on *The Bondage of the Will*. But he was not willing absolutely to renounce free will. If men today are not free, at least Adam before the fall was. Or, in reality, the situation is a little more complicated. When the saints shall finally have arrived in heaven, it is obvious that they will not sin nor will they desire to. Their wills will be immutably determined to good. Yet this complete determination of the will may be called free will in the highest sense, for the will will be free from sinning. Not even Adam had a free will in this sense. Adam's will before the fall was free in the sense that it was possible for him not to sin; the freedom of the saints in heaven is that it is impossible for them to sin. But for men on earth it is not possible not to sin. Augustine with his constant flair for oratory gets off three Latin phrases: for Adam, *posse non peccare*; for us, *non posse non peccare*; for those in heaven, *non posse peccare*.

It is no surprise, then — in fact it was stated at the start — that heaven is our goal, for the good is the final end of all desires, and life eternal is the supreme good. Certainly this earthly life does not contain the good. Here we are subject to manifold miseries. Crimes, tortures, and wars; even foreign languages, an obstacle to communication, are miseries; friendship is indeed a good, but it can cause sadness too and is therefore not an absolute or unmixed good. The pure and supreme good can be found only in the perfect peace of heaven. Earthly peace, that imperfect peace between man and man, is like friendship a great good; but peace between man and God, a peace that cannot be broken, is alone the supreme good. The deep sadness, the frustration, the unfilled longing of the human heart is essentially a lack of this peace; it is the absence of peace; it is war with God. And nothing can cure the horrors of war, only thinly disguised by the diversions of the world and the wiles of the devil, except peace. *"Magna es, domine, et laudabilis valde . . . quia fecisti nos ad te et inquietum est cor nostrum donec requiescat in te.* Great art thou, O

Lord, and greatly to be praised . . . for thou hast made us for thyself, and our heart is restless until it rests in thee" (*Confessions*, I, i, 1).

THE DARK AGES

The imperial government had earlier abandoned Rome for Constantinople, and the once proud city became a provincial town. It was sacked in A.D. 410, its bishops were insignificant in comparison with the brilliance of Hippo, and when Augustine died, leaving behind him no intellectual ability among either Christians or pagans, a darkness of centuries descended first on the West and later on the East.

The one pagan worthy of mention is Proclus (410–485), the last of the Neoplatonists. By a strange providence he exerted an immense influence on the subsequent history of Christianity. Before the end of the century a professed Christian attempted a combination of Neoplatonism and Christianity in which there was far more of the former than ever Augustine had admitted. In particular his discussion of evil is nearly a verbatim reproduction of sections of Proclus. The author adopted the name of Dionysius the Areopagite whose conversion by the apostle Paul is recorded in Acts 17:34, and inasmuch as the darkness was already so deep that the forgery was undetected, the writings were accepted as having almost apostolic authority. Thus the tendency of the Church, so vigorous in Tertullian and Athanasius, to purge itself of pagan ideas was checked and the direction reversed. Even Thomas Aquinas, brilliant as he was, accepted these writings as genuine and allowed himself to absorb some though not all of their Neoplatonic teachings.

Dionysius' theory of evil is similar to that of Augustine's; the language, however, is more strongly Neoplatonic. Evil is a turning from a higher good to a lower good and has no efficient cause; it is privation, nonbeing, or even something worse, lower, and less real than nonbeing. In addition to the theory of evil, Dionysius stressed the unity and goodness of God in such a way that mysticism and a fully developed negative theology resulted. As evil is below nonbeing, so God is superior to Being. He is pre-being and super-being. No name properly applies to him because he is above all. Only negative statements are permissible. God is not mind, not soul, not spirit, and not being. If any positive statement is true, it would be that God is cause. Therefore since God is ineffable, i.e., since man cannot speak of God, mysticism is our only resource, and the language we must use, the language Dionysius used, becomes unintelligible. "Triad supernal, both super-God and super-good, Guardian of the theosophy of Christian men, direct us aright to the super-unknown and super-brilliant and highest summit of the mystic oracles, where the simple and absolute and changeless mysteries of theology lie hidden within the superluminous gloom of the silence, revealing hidden things, which in its deepest darkness shines above the most super-brilliant, and in the altogether impalpable and invisible fills to overflowing the eyeless minds with glories of surpassing beauty" (*Mystic Theology*, 1:1). And, "Deity of our Lord Jesus, the cause and completing of all, which preserves the parts concordant with the whole, and is neither part nor whole, and whole and part, as embracing in itself everything both whole and part and being above and before, perfect indeed in the imperfect as source of perfection, but imperfect in the perfect as super-perfect and pre-perfect, form producing form in things without form as source of form, formless in the forms as above form, essence penetrating without stain the essences throughout, and super-essential, exalted above every essence, setting bounds to all principalities and orders and established in every principality and order" (*Divine Names*, 2:10). Undoubtedly a fitting introduction to dark ages.

As the darkness deepened, there lived in Rome, where he was eventually appointed consul, a certain Boethius of scientific, political, and philosophical bent. He tinkered with chronometers and attempted to systematize the coinage system. Imprisoned on a charge of treason, he wrote his last work, *The Consolation of Philosophy*. Putting his story in the form of a vision, Boethius describes Philosophy as a majestic woman come to console him in the face of impending death. She argues that virtue is its own reward and the wicked are never happy. There are also arguments designed to show that divine foreknowledge is not inconsistent with freedom. Although Boethius was presumably a Christian, his *Consolation* contains no mention of Christ. So soon after Augustine has Christianity faded from men's minds. The *Consolation* would never have brought Boethius fame, but his name is preserved chiefly because he translated Aristotle into Latin; and as the knowledge of Greek died out in the West, it so happened that the medieval schoolmen studied Aristotle in Boethius' translation.

During the lifetime of Boethius Italy was ruled by the Ostrogoths: Boethius was consul for their chieftain Theodoric. Justinian later defeated the Ostrogoths and reunited Italy to the Empire. The Visigoths held Spain, and the Burgundians clashed with the Franks in Gaul. Under Clovis the Franks were successful, not only in subduing the Burgundians, but also in destroying forever all imperial power in — shall we now call it France? North Africa, the scene of Augustine's glory, became a Vandal kingdom. Justinian also reconquered this territory. But he was able to hold Italy for barely ten years. Then the Lombards devastated the already ravished land and divided it into the petty duchies such as plagued Italy down to the nineteenth century.

In times of war, poverty, famine, and anarchy, philosophy does not flourish. Cassiodorus (480–575) is just a name. Isidore of Seville (560–636) knew Greek and Hebrew, introduced Aristotle into Spain, and established seminaries. But he is more important for the early history of the developing Spanish language than for any philosophical work. The venerable Bede (672–735), a saintly Englishman, also knew Greek and Hebrew; but whatever influence he might have had was largely destroyed by the invasion of the Danes. More important than these was Alcuin (735–804), who labored patiently and even heroically both to defend the orthodox faith against the heresy of Adoptionism and to bring success to Charlemagne's endeavors to rekindle the light of learning. Rabanus Maurus (776–856), a German pupil of Alcuin, continued to press for greater scholarship.

CHAPTER **6**

The Scholastic Period

Customarily the Dark Ages and the Patristic period are said to end with the beginning of the ninth century. There is a political and an intellectual reason for this division, both centered in the person of Charlemagne. After a period of cruel anarchy Charles Martel (690–741) managed to impose some unified authority in the Frankish domain. His most notable exploit was to save Europe, at the battle of Poitiers in 732, from Islam, which had already conquered North Africa and had advanced through Spain. Charles' son, Pepin, was also a vigorous ruler. The grandson was Charles the Great. Although there had been no Roman emperor in the west for three centuries, Charlemagne tried to revive the old tradition and had himself crowned Emperor on Christmas Day 800. Even though the unity of Europe did not outlast Charlemagne's life, the period of extreme anarchy and invasion was over. Politically therefore the Dark Ages had ended. Charlemagne also had intellectual ambitions for his empire, and, though he himself could neither read nor write, established schools in Paris, Fulda, and especially at Tours, encouraged the gathering and preservation of manuscripts, and instituted courses in the seven liberal arts. All this was done with vigor; but it can hardly be said that learning revived. Fully two hundred years of darkness had yet to be endured before some spontaneous and continuing illumination appeared. Therefore although the Patristic period had ended — possibly one could say it ended with Augustine — what is called the prescholastic period of the ninth century, even if not the early scholastic period from 1050–1200, can also be included in the Dark Ages.

The high scholastic period runs from 1200 to 1340, and late scholasticism continues to the Reformation and Renaissance.

Philosophically the period ending with 1200 was characterized by its restricted knowledge of Aristotle. Some but not all of his logical writings were known; Porphyry's *Introduction to the Categories* and the *Commentaries* of Boethius were used; and that was about all. Although knowledge of Plato also was restricted to a translation of the *Timaeus*, the general tenor of philosophic thinking was Platonic and Neoplatonic because of the influence of Augustine with a large admixture of Dionysius. About 1200 the other works of Aristotle were discovered and a new viewpoint soon became supreme; but while the solutions were different, on both sides of this dividing line the chief problems were the same: the relation of faith to reason (with respect to which the tendency developed to separate theology and philosophy), the everlasting enigma of universals and individuals, and, later, the primacy of the will or intellect.

JOHN SCOTUS ERIUGENA

After the death of Charlemagne his schools deteriorated, and Charles the Bald, attempting a reorganization, called John Scotus Eriugena (810–877?) to Paris. As his name indicates, he was a Scot born in Eriu or Erin, for Ireland was called Scotia Major until A.D. 1100. He seems to have achieved fame mainly by default, for his system is not so much original as it is modeled on Dionysius the Areopagite, whom he translated into Latin and whose viewpoint he completely absorbed. By this translation he was a large factor in imposing a Neoplatonic and mystical cast on the next six centuries.

Aside from this translation, his first work was written at the request of Hincmar, Bishop of Reims, who wished to refute an Augustinian monk, Godescalcs or Gottshalk, on predestination. In the section on Augustine it was not mentioned that as his views matured he ascribed to God not only foreknowledge but a predestinating causality. This thought is stronger in the later works, but Augustine never fully developed it nor consistently applied it to the question of free will. Gottshalk, probably reading more of Paul into Augustine's words, like a lonely Presbyterian born out of due time, anticipated John Calvin in a clear notion of predestination. In this view the precise number and identities of the saved and the lost are definitely and unalterably predetermined. This evangelical doctrine, which became so prominent in the Reformed churches, was given a cool or should one say a hot reception in these later Dark Ages. Gottshalk was imprisoned and scourged, and as he did not recant, his tortures were prolonged for twenty-one years until he died in prison. But John's refutation of predestination did not prove acceptable either. It has been described as a thorough and self-conscious pantheistic philosophy which combines rationalistic pelagian elements with Neoplatonic speculation. Though this judgment may be extreme, particularly the term "self-conscious," it is not without some evidence.

John's greatest work was his *De divisione naturae*, published about 867 and condemned at least three times by ecclesiastical authorities. He begins with the Augustinian view that philosophy and religion are identical, a view that was to pass away later. All our inquiries must start with revealed wisdom; we must not place our experience above God, but rather trust the revealed word. If in this John is not hypocritical, and there is no reason to believe he is, it is impossible to judge him a rationalist in the theological sense of the term, or at least a self-conscious rationalist. In order to understand the Scriptures, however, one must study the Church fathers, and unfortunately they disagree in various particulars. We must therefore choose what is reasonable in them, for authorities are such only in so far as they are reasonable. Thus in any conflict between reason and the authority of the fathers, reason is supreme. There is no indication that John made reason superior to the authority of the Scriptures, but rather he would say that they are on the same level, for true reason and true authority cannot conflict.

John's doctrine of God follows the negative theology of Dionysius. God's essence is incomprehensible or unknowable to man; in fact God as No-thing does not even know himself. "God does not know *what* he himself is because he is not a *what*." The highest cause cannot be truly designated by any name; all our expressions are only symbolic. Metaphorically God can be called Truth, Good, Essence, Light, Sun, Star, Breath, Water, and an infinite number of other things. But God

is actually above all these predicates, for each of these has a contradictory — truth and falsehood, good and evil, light and darkness —
but God has no contradictory. He is super-essential, super-good, and
so on, as Dionysius said. Creation is likewise a Neoplatonic emanation depending on the independent existence of the Platonic Ideas.
The appearance and perhaps the reality of pantheism derives from
the representation of God as the supreme genus of which finite
classes, such as man and animal, are species. As things have developed out of God, so too there is a reverse process of salvation or
deification, connected with a form of the Logos doctrine, by which all
things return to their source. This reabsorption of all men and things
into God is easily taken for a mystical pantheism. Man, he says, becomes penetrated with God as air is penetrated with light, and God
will be all in all when there is nothing but God alone. The mysticism
can hardly be denied, but whether it is pantheism or not depends on
what John intended by certain words of caution. For though air is
penetrated with light, it still is air; and the reabsorption into God is
an *adunatio sine confusione vel mixtura vel compositione*. Whether
by such phrases John wished consciously to deny or consciously to
conceal pantheism is doubtless an unanswerable question.

ANSELM

After death had extinguished the feeble light of John Scotus
Eriugena, darkness continued for another century and a half. All the
political efforts to stimulate learning had failed. But with Anselm
(1033–1109), who became Archbishop of Canterbury, and without
the political stability that had marked the life of Charlemagne, scholarship began spontaneously, developed, and has not ceased to this day.

In his general philosophic position Anselm followed Augustine, not
slavishly nor sterilely, but pushed on with surprising originality to new
fields of inquiry. Adopting from Augustine the motto *Credo ut
intelligam,* he accepted the essential identity of religion and philosophy and the competence of reason to rationalize faith. Faith supplies
the propositions with which one must start, propositions relating to
the existence of God, the Trinity, the Atonement and so forth; reason

is able to elaborate rational proofs of these doctrines. In one sense the work of reason is superior to faith and in another it is not. It is superior in that a developed understanding is an advance, a growth in grace, a goal for which faith is designed. On the other hand, understanding of the doctrines is not to lead to their repudiation or reinterpretation into something else; if that were the case, it would not be the doctrines of faith that had been proved and understood. No, the content of faith is inviolable and cannot be made more certain through ratiocination. In religion faith plays the part which experience has in science. As a blind man cannot see and hence cannot understand light and color, similarly an unbeliever does not perceive, does not have the experience, and hence cannot understand the doctrine. The terms *proof* and *understanding*, however, are susceptible of two meanings. Apparently Anselm meant that the doctrines of the Bible and of the Church could be demonstrated apart from Scripture on independent grounds. Reason therefore is in itself a source of information, and not simply the syllogistic process of deducing a system of consistent theology from the statements of Scripture. This latter sense is also possible and is particularly important when anyone claims, as Luther later did, that the Bible and the Church do not agree. It is not clear that Anselm distinguished the authority of the Bible from that of the Church, for in the trial of Roscellinus he advised the court not to engage in discussion with the accused but to demand an immediate recantation. Such a demand leaves the alleged heretic unconvinced and gives him the choice of becoming a martyr or a hypocrite. Unlike Gottshalk, Roscellinus by his own later admission preferred hypocrisy.

The question now comes, Can all the doctrines of Christianity be demonstrated without appeal to Scriptural premises? Whereas Augustine had defined philosophy as the rational exploration of the faith and had defended the plurality of intellectual intuitions, he did not answer this question too explicitly and of course he could not attempt the proofs of all doctrines. Anselm seems to take it for granted and attempts to prove not only the existence of God and the Trinity (which Augustine to a degree attempted also), but the Incarnation as well and particularly the Atonement. In his work *Cur Deus homo,* a masterpiece of theology, Anselm is the first in church history to have grasped the precise significance of Christ's death. It is not the purpose here to explain the Atonement, or as it was more properly called the Satisfaction, but to consider the relation between faith and reason. In the Preface Anselm says of his book that "leaving Christ out of view, as if nothing had ever been known of him, it proves by absolute reasons the impossibility that any man should be saved without him . . . it is moreover shown by plain reasoning and fact that human nature was ordained for this purpose." This proof is written out not only to gladden the hearts of believers but also to answer unbelievers who think that Christianity is contrary to reason. Anselm denies that his proof will consist of aesthetic appreciation of the beauty and harmony of God's plan; he aims at rational proof and necessity. The question is, What necessity was there of God's becoming man when he could have saved us by some less painful method? The death of the God-Man must be proved "reasonable and necessary," so as to convince one "unwilling to believe anything not previously proved by reason." And at the end of the work Anselm's pupil gives this conclusion: "By this solution . . . I see the truth of all that is contained in the Old and New Testaments, for in proving that God became man by necessity, leaving out what was taken from the Bible, viz., the remarks on the persons of the Trinity and on Adam, you convince both Jew and pagan by the mere force of reason." Similarly in the *Monologium* he says, "in order that nothing in Scripture should be urged upon the authority of Scripture itself, but that whatever the conclusion of independent investigation should declare to be true, should, in an unadorned style, with common proofs and with a simple argument, be briefly enforced by the cogency of reason and plainly expounded in the light of truth."

Of course Anselm's proof is a failure. In addition to remarks on the Trinity and on Adam, Anselm smuggled in many premises taken from Scripture without rational and necessary proof. His understanding of the Bible was far better than his understanding of the force of pure reason. And in the remaining history of medieval philosophy, the force of pure reason, i.e., reason as a source of information independent of the Scriptures, became less and less, while at the same time reason as a method of valid argumentation was more widely, consistently, and strictly applied.

This emphasis on reason, however, perhaps in both senses and surely in Anselm's sense, though it has a certain historical affiliation with the view of John Scotus Eriugena, is a curb on and a reversal of negative theology. The mystic view is that the doctrines are really false, colloquial accommodations to human limitations. But Anselm believed that God has revealed the truth and that this truth itself, not some ethereal negation of it, could be demonstrated. This must not be taken to imply that certain attributes cannot be denied of God. John Scotus had called God Sun, Star, Breath, and Water, only to empty them of all significance. Anselm keeps the significance and denies that these are attributes of God. But other attributes which are better than these belong to God. He is living, just, wise, powerful, and eternal. At the same time Anselm is careful to point out that God is not wise or just by participation in a superior Idea. God himself is justice. That is what he *is*. As this line of reasoning applies to all attributes, so by them we know not merely *what sort* of being God is, but *what* God is. And is this not to know his essence, which the negative theologians said was unknowable? However, this concession, if it be a concession, must be made to negativism. Since God is one, without any composition, it follows that Justice is Life, Power is Eternity, and all attributes are the same. Obviously if Justice is God's essence, and if God's essence is Power, Justice and Power are identical. Each attribute exhausts every other "because whatever God is essentially in any way, this is all of what he is" (*Monologium* XVII).

The *Monologium* is an attempt to prove God's existence by the Platonic method of hypostatizing goodness, justice, existence, and so on. Anselm thought the proof sound enough, but he longed for a less complicated and more convincing demonstration. By a stroke of genius, after long unsuccessful meditation, the proof came to him. The proof proper [1] is not more than two pages long, but the discussion it has engendered since that day must fill more than two thousand volumes. It is on the Ontological Argument that Anselm's fame chiefly rests. Since it is so short, it may be quoted in full, even the first paragraph which is more of a meditation than an argument.

"And so, Lord, do thou, who dost give understanding to faith, give

[1] *Proslogium* (Open Court Publishing Co., 1926) Chapter II.

me, so far as thou knowest it to be profitable, to understand that thou art as we believe, and that thou art that which we believe. And indeed we believe that thou art a being than which nothing greater can be conceived. Or is there no such nature, since the fool hath said in his heart, there is no God? (Ps. 14:1). But at any rate this very fool, when he hears of this being of which I speak — a being than which nothing greater can be conceived — understands what he hears, and what he understands is in his understanding; although he does not understand it to exist.

"For it is one thing for an object to be in the understanding, and another to understand that the object exists. When a painter first conceives of what he will afterward perform he has it in his understanding, but he does not yet understand it to be, because he has not yet performed it. But after he has made the painting, he both has it in his understanding, and he understands that it exists, because he has made it.

"Hence even the fool is convinced that something exists in the understanding at least than which nothing greater can be conceived. For when he hears of this, he understands it. And whatever is understood, exists in the understanding. And assuredly that than which nothing greater can be conceived cannot exist in the understanding alone. For suppose it exists in the understanding alone: then it can be conceived to exist in reality, which is greater.

"Therefore if that than which nothing greater can be conceived exists in the understanding alone, the very being than which nothing greater can be conceived is one than which a greater can be conceived. But obviously this is impossible. Hence there is no doubt that there exists a being than which nothing greater can be conceived, and it exists both in the understanding and in reality.

"And it assuredly exists so truly that it cannot be conceived not to exist. For it is possible to conceive of a being which cannot be conceived not to exist; and this is greater than one which can be conceived not to exist. Hence if that than which nothing greater can be conceived, can be conceived not to exist, it is not that than which nothing greater can be conceived. But this is an irreconcilable contradiction. There is then so truly a being than which nothing greater can be conceived to exist, that it cannot even be conceived not to exist; and this being thou art, O Lord, our God.

"So truly therefore dost thou exist, O Lord, my God, that thou canst not be conceived not to exist; and rightly. For if a mind could conceive of a being better than thee, the creature would rise above the Creator; and this is most absurd. And indeed whatever else there is, except thee alone, can be conceived not to exist. To thee alone therefore it belongs to exist more truly than all other beings, and hence in a higher degree than all others. For whatever else exists does not exist so truly, and hence in a less degree it belongs to it to exist. Why then has the fool said in his heart, there is no God, since it is so evident, to a rational mind, that thou dost exist in the highest degree of all? Why? except that he is dull and a fool!"

Is this argument valid? It is not a question whether or not God exists. Thomas Aquinas and Bishop Berkeley both believed in God, but neither of them believed that this argument proved the existence of God. The seventeenth-century rationalists thought that the argument was sound, and a few Protestant theologians have treated it with respect. Kant analyzed it with extreme care and decided it was a fallacy. But Hegel, though not sharing Anselm's faith in the Atonement and the other Christian doctrines, had a system that is nothing but a transformed and expanded ontological argument. In Anselm's own day his argument provoked an immediate attack by the monk Gaunilo.

Gaunilo's refutation is not too clearly expressed, and whether or not he put his finger on the argument's weak point has been questioned even by those who reject the argument. He begins by attempting to show that Anselm's illustration of the painter and his work of art is deceptive. Not only is the idea of God in my understanding, he says, but there are ideas of many unreal objects. To prove the existence of God therefore, it would be necessary to show that we cannot have him in the understanding in the manner in which we have the unreal objects. But if we cannot have God in this manner, then there will be no distinction between what has precedence in time, namely, the having of this object in the understanding, and what is subsequent in time, namely, understanding that this object exists. In the illustration of the painter this distinction in time was prominent. He was first supposed to have in his understanding an unreal object, and later, after he painted the picture, he had a real object in his understanding. To speak more accurately, the painter did not at first have the picture in his understanding. What he first had, namely, the plan of the picture, is strictly a part of the painter's soul; when the painter knows this plan, he is knowing his own soul, not some external object. If therefore Anselm wishes to use the illustration of the painter, he should show the necessary connection between the first state of knowledge and the second: the connection in the case of the picture is that the painter in the meantime painted it; but what is the connection in the case of God? On the other hand, if God cannot be conceived not to exist (although the painting may be), what is the purpose of the argument? For in that case, no one could possibly think that God does not exist.

Gaunilo proceeds. It is not possible to have God in the understanding or to conceive him. The human mind does not know that reality itself which God is. Man cannot intuit God. Nor can man conjecture what God is from other things, for no other thing is like God. It is quite easy to conjecture what a man unknown to us is like, because we all have had experience of many men. From these experiences the concept of man has been derived. But nothing of the sort happens in the case of God, therefore the concept of God is impossible for the human mind. Anselm's phrase about the greatest of all beings is too vague to produce a concept; it is just a series of words; and an object can hardly or never be conceived from words alone. There is virtually no chance that a man on hearing a verbal definition of an unknown object could form a correct image of the thing. Anselm's argument requires the verbal formula to be the greatest of all beings; but this Gaunilo denies: the formula is not the greatest of all beings; its existence is only the existence of a verbal formula; therefore there is nothing absurd in asserting the existence of a being greater than the verbal formula "the greatest of all beings." Any real stone is greater than "the greatest of all beings."

Then follows Gaunilo's famous illustration of the lost island. This island is the best of all islands. Its wealth and delicacies are inestimable. Now therefore, if the ontological argument were valid, we could conclude, "You can no longer doubt of the existence of this unknown island which is more excellent than all islands, since you have no doubt that it is in your understanding. And since it is more excellent not to be in the understanding alone, but to exist both in the understanding and in reality, for this reason it must exist. For if it does not exist, any land which really exists will be more excellent than it; and so the island already understood by you to be more excellent will not be more excellent."

Fortunately Anselm wrote a reply to Gaunilo, but as Gaunilo was a Catholic speaking on behalf of the fool, Anselm thought it was sufficient to reply to the Catholic who was not a fool. Now, if the greatest conceivable being cannot be conceived, as Gaunilo claimed, then either God is not such a being or else God is not conceived. The first alternative is false by definition, and the second is inconsistent with our faith and conscience. As for the lost island, the illustration is deceptive. The lost island can be conceived not to exist, but God cannot be conceived not to exist. Gaunilo has seriously misunderstood the original argument, for he constantly speaks of the greatest of existing things. Now, obviously if two or three things exist, there must be one that is greatest. And in this sense there is a greatest island. But the ontological argument concerns not the greatest of existing things: its validity depends on the fact that it concerns the greatest conceivable reality. If three things existed, a stone, a star, and a stump, none of them would be God for the greatest of the three would not be the greatest conceivable being. Because Gaunilo confused the greatest being with the greatest conceivable being, he was able to talk about his lost island. Furthermore, it is not true that God is so unlike other things that we can have no conception of him. A lesser good, in so far as it is good, resembles a greater good. If we can conceive of a good that begins and ends, we can next conceive of a similar good that does not end; and finally we can conceive of a good that neither begins nor ends. Hence from lesser goods it is quite possible to form a considerable notion of a being than which a greater is inconceivable. And this observation applies to the fool as well as to the Catholic.

CONCEPTUALISM

To what extent either Anselm or Gaunilo saw the presuppositions of their arguments is debatable; but these presuppositions immediately became the chief topic of controversy and continued as such to the end of the Middle Ages. The moot point is the nature of concepts; and whether the concept under discussion is the concept of God or the concept of man, the issue is the same. Porphyry in his *Introduction to Aristotle's Categories* had asked the question, Do genera and species, such as man and lion, justice and equality, really exist in nature or are they only thoughts of one's mind? And if they really exist, are they separate from things or do they exist in things? Boethius also asked the question whether categories, substance, quantity, relation and the others, are things or mere words, *res* or *voces*. Those who said that the categories were *res* came to be called realists, a word that bears a different sense in modern English; and those who said that the categories were mere words were called nominalists, from the term *nomen*. These questions are the equivalent of asking what the science of Logic treats of. Does Logic deal with things, or is it a science of words? And the answer one gives to these questions has such far reaching implications that it controls every detail of the resulting system of philosophy.

Under the influence of Augustine the early scholastic period was realistic. Words designate realities, and hence the word *man* refers to an existing object. It is the common quality of men, and the philosophy of this time accepted this common quality as the essential nature of the men. The more common, that is, the more universal the concept is, the more real it is; and as God is the most real of all beings, he is the most universal. This of course seems to entail negative theology in that God would have the fewest determinations or none at all; it also seems to entail pantheism in that God is the supreme genus. But on the other hand realism seems to give a good ground for the Trinity, since three persons can be one substance, reality, or genus; and it also fits in with the unity of the human race which sinned in its entirety in Adam. It was the orthodox elements in realism that attracted attention in Anselm's day, rather than the pantheistic tendencies.

Roscellinus (1050–1120), of whose writings only one letter remains, was the first or at least the chief of the early nominalists. He held that individuals are the primary realities and that categories or species are mere words, *flatus vocis*, the breathing of the voice. Although he discussed such matters of logic and dialectic as the status of wholes and parts and the composition of the syllogism, his fame arose from his application of the theory to the Trinity. Having defined a person as a rational substance, he had to conclude that the three Persons of the Godhead are three substances, in fact, three Gods, and that the "Trinity" is but a name. Anselm, who used the Platonic thesis that several men are one Man to maintain that the three Persons are one God, located the source of Roscellinus' heresy in his sensory epistemology. Like Gaunilo he was limited by too lively an imagination.

The most famous pupil of Roscellinus was Abelard (1079–1142), who also studied under the extreme realist William of Champeaux. Against the latter Abelard directed the timeworn objection that if Man were in Plato and Plato were in Rome, then since Man is in Socrates, Socrates must also be in Rome. The treatment is so cavalier that Abelard seems to have been emotionally unable to consider realism seriously. His undoubted ability was turned in another direction. At first he accepted the position of Roscellinus that a universal is a mere word, but with one eye on the Trinity and with an acute mind on logic, he produced a compromise between nominalism and realism which was in effect a rediscovery of Aristotelianism. What can a predicate be, he asks. When one says that Plato is a man or is tall or old, what is the status of man, tall, and old? Since things, like stars and stones, cannot be predicates (for we do not say "the heavy is stone" or "the old is Plato"), realism which claims that the predicates are things or *res* must be rejected. But for precisely the same reason nominalism must also be rejected. The predicate cannot be a mere word, for a word or sound is a thing just as much as a stone is. The predicate therefore is not a *vox*, but, to invent a new term, it is a *sermo*. Abelard's alteration of Roscellinus' formula is for the purpose of indicating that a word, in addition to being a sound in the air, carries a significance; and this significance or meaning is the predicate.

The process by which the mind produces the significance more fully determines the nature of universals. If we think of Plato, we have in mind a singular substance, an individual thing, Plato as Plato. But if we think that Plato is old or is a man, we have limited our attention to this or that aspect of Plato. We no longer think of Plato as Plato, but as a man; that is, we think of his rationality by which he belongs to a certain species; or we may think of his being old, or of some other quality which he has in common with other things. This process of selection or abstraction results in a concept. The common quality therefore becomes a predicate when it is abstracted and attended to. It is not a thing in nature like an individual, though it has its basis in the individual and is not an empty sound. Thus the predicate is in one sense in the thing, and in another sense it is in our mind. But in addition to the phrase, *universalia post rem*, which might be applied to nominalism, Abelard is also willing to assert *universalia ante rem*, the formula of the realists. For these universals also exist eternally in the mind of God. Conceptualism therefore is intended to salvage the elements of truth that were in the other theories without their indefensible flaws.

Whether conceptualism with its sensory epistemology can escape Roscellinus' difficulties with the Trinity need not now be examined; but from the more restricted view of logic and dialectic one may question the existence of a common quality. That there was such a common quality was assumed by both Abelard and by Aristotle. But if it is not implausible to suppose that every red rose displays a different shade of red, and that hence red instead of being a common quality is merely a name for a series of qualities in the spectrum, it is less implausible that men, who are more complicated than roses, have different "shades" of humanity and a wide variety of physical, mental, and moral qualities, and are therefore without a common quality. If someone should argue in favor of the existence of common qualities on the ground that we cannot perceive any difference in the red of these three roses, the reply could be given that a color blind person would be less able to distinguish differences and would therefore find many more common qualities. But this would suspend the fate of the common quality upon defective vision; and it is hardly likely that Aristotle or Abelard would have approved of such a basis. At any rate no defect can be attributed to God's knowledge. If therefore God from all eternity planned to create Socrates and Plato, would he not have distinct ideas of these two men, and not confuse them in an undifferentiated concept of man? Perhaps therefore a common identical quality nowhere exists.

Abelard made another great contribution also. In his *Sic et non*, Yes and No, he collected the opinions of the fathers on a large number of points and arranged the passages on each point in opposite columns so as to bring out the discrepancies. Then he attempted to reason out the issues thus defined. This procedure, which is in fact an imitation of Aristotle's method of stating difficulties to set a problem, had a great influence on Abelard's successors. The theological *Summae* of the thirteenth century, including those of Thomas Aquinas, were written on this model. For this reason those modern historians must be mistaken who hold that Abelard because he was a freethinker adopted this method as the only safe method of casting doubt on Christianity.

If we are to trust his own statement, his aim was to harmonize the fathers and solve the puzzles of Christian doctrine. In the result there undoubtedly are unorthodox sentiments on occasion as well as a profession of faith in Christ and the Church.

There is also some confusion as to the relation of faith to reason. Anselm had already distinguished between the rational knowledge that is based on necessary axioms independent of Scripture and the faith which is satisfied with revelation. This distinction without alteration was adopted by Thomas Aquinas and has become standard in Roman Catholicism. Anselm, however, probably did not understand the full significance of his distinction, and certainly he did not apply it consistently. He also held that all the truths of faith could be demonstrated by reason, so that while philosophy and theology might differ in method, they do not differ in content. When therefore Abelard expressed dissatisfaction with the prevailing views on faith and reason and anticipated later developments, he was not so original, at least in principle, as sometimes he is pictured. His advance was more by way of insisting on rigorous reasoning, of deprecating metaphor and oratory, of making dialectic the great instrument for defending the faith. It is true that he questioned the possibility of establishing the faith by reason, on the ground that God is incomprehensible. Yet he has the well deserved reputation of being more of a rationalist than a fideist. Dialectic is indispensable for theology; it is competent to determine the truth or falsity of any thesis; and it could have been successfully used even to prove the Trinity to the satisfaction of the ancient heathen philosophers. In fact, they virtually arrived at the Christian doctrine because their One or Good is the Father, the Logos and the Ideas are the Son, and the World-Soul is the Holy Ghost.

Not inconsistently with this, in his effort to avoid the tritheism of Roscellinus, Abelard so stressed the unity of the Godhead that the personal diversity was almost reduced to a unitarian modalism. Coupled with an arrogant pride in his dialectical ability, which led him to quarrel with his superiors and his equals, his several unorthodox positions brought on him the enmity and condemnation of the great twelfth-century mystic, Bernard of Clairvaux. Even had Abelard been completely orthodox, the mystics would not have been satisfied with him, for they were not interested in a clear apprehension of the meaning of the doctrines they believed, but in emotional experiences and ecstatic visions. And if their absorption into the divine being was as pantheistic as Abelard was unitarian, it seemed to entail no danger so long as it was not clearly reasoned out.

That the scholarly activity of the twelfth century was spontaneous and would not disappear as it did after the death of Charlemagne is evidenced by the work of a dozen lesser thinkers in the school of Chartres. Though these men were realists, the school has the credit of publishing some hitherto unknown logical works of Aristotle, and it was the continuing rediscovery of Aristotelian texts and their study that was soon to revolutionize the medieval outlook. Another, though perhaps lesser, evidence of the life of scholarship was the school of St. Victor, to be mentioned only in passing as an attempt to mediate between dialectic and mysticism. Then there were also a number of attempts, stimulated by the work of Abelard, to systematize theology. The most famous of these was the *Sentences* of Peter Lombard. At the same time there was philosophic activity among the Jews. The greatest name is Maimonides (1135-1204). But though the Jews contributed to the introduction of Aristotle into Western Europe, the most influential group was the Mohammedans.

THE MOHAMMEDANS

The diffusion of Christianity in Syria and in Mesopotamia, in which the Nestorians took a prominent part, brought to those Eastern lands the New Testament in Greek, the Church fathers, and some Greek philosophy, especially Aristotle's logic. When Islam replaced Christianity, it took over some of the philosophy, and as it marched westward, for example into Egypt, it came into possession of the other works of Aristotle. Accepted as Aristotelian were two Neoplatonic writings: *The Theology of Aristotle*, which is an excerpt from Plotinus; and the *Liber de causis*, by Proclus. This mixture of Aristotelianism and Neoplatonism, in many respects similar to the twelfth-century developments in Europe, produced a Mohammedan scholasticism not favored by the strictly orthodox. These scholastics affirmed free will, denied predestination, and merged the divine attributes which the Koran had separated. Under the circumstances, for the Mohammedans met Christian Europe in Spain, there could not fail to be philosophic interaction.

Mohammedan philosophy began with a veritable genius, Avicenna (980–1037), who had memorized Aristotle's *Metaphysics* by the time he was eighteen and who published more than a hundred books before he died. He worked out a conceptualism very similar to that of Abelard. The concept, the *universalium post rem*, is the grasp of our intellect as it abstracts a form and relates it to many individual things. The universality lies in this act of relating. Abstracting therefore produces something in the mind that was never external to it, and this subjective production can itself be an object of thought. When under the term *man* we consider Plato, the term *man* is taken in its "first intention," but when we consider man as our subjective concept, it is a "second intention." The field of logic lies with second intentions. A similar distinction between intentions later arose among the Christian philosophers. Avicenna also held that matter, the principle of individuation, is eternal and that the world is a timeless emanation from the divine being. These views determined the course of Mohammedan philosophy.

Al Gazali (1059–1111) attempted to prevent the general acceptance of Aristotelianism. Although reason in the sense of logical argumentation is useful in systematizing theology, as an independent source of information reason is a failure. In other words, Al Gazali was a philosophical skeptic. He attacked the validity of the arguments used to prove the eternity of matter, the timeless emanation of the world, the confusion of the divine attributes, and other heresies. Most interestingly, in defense of the almighty power of God, he anticipates the Scottish philosopher David Hume in an attack on the concept of causality. The only ground that philosophers have for asserting a causal relation between two events is the observation of their succession in time. But there is no valid argument that can pass from temporal succession to necessary connection. Unlike Hume however, Al Gazali concludes that the only agent in the world is God and that miracles are possible. At this juncture Mohammedan philosophy came to Spain where a large degree of religious toleration contributed to its vigorous development.

The greatest of the Mohammedan philosophers was Averroes (1126–1198). For the greater part of his life he was favored by the authorities and was loaded with honors, but later under a resurgence of orthodoxy he was condemned for undermining religion and teaching that truth could be obtained by reason alone. The frequent strife between religion and philosophy Averroes explains as resulting from the inability of the common people to understand rational argument and profound truth. Such people should be taught the literal sense of the Koran or even be limited to receiving moral exhortation. Above the masses are the theologians. These are more capable and have made use of dialectic to systematize their theology. But they are content with probable arguments and do not require exact demonstrative knowledge. This latter the philosophers alone can handle. Trouble arises when a lower class tries to sit in judgment over a higher class. The sacred Koran, to be sure, is addressed to all three types, but each person should study it in the sense of which he is capable; and it is foolhardy to try to teach a higher sense to a lower class. When the philosopher discovers that the literal sense of the Koran is inconsistent with philosophic truth, he must reinterpret the Koran. The three interpretations or senses are all the same truth, or they are approximations in different degrees of the absolute truth. The truth is the same, but the expressions differ.

This view of the different senses of Scripture and the relation of philosophy to religion either is itself or it leads to the theory of twofold truth — the theory that what is true in philosophy may be false in theology and conversely. In theology it is true to say that there is a hell, but in philosophy it is true that there is no hell. Both these expressions are the same truth. The picture of rewards and punishments motivate the common people to good works, but the theological picture when turned into philosophical language becomes (to use more modern terms) the a priori autonomous demand of the pure practical reason. Thus the assertion, there is a hell, is both true and false; true in religion and false in philosophy. By this device a philosopher when questioned by the hostile orthodox could reply, with whatever sincerity the theory allowed him, that he did indeed hold it true that there is a hell. Whether Averroes used this theory of the twofold truth is subject to a little doubt, partly because of discrepancies between the Latin and the Arabic texts, but it is supposed that he said, "By reason I conclude of necessity that the (active) intellect is one in number (for all men), but I firmly hold the opposite by faith." Similarly his remarks on the immortality of the soul give the impression of being cautiously ambiguous.

Averroes' philosophy is an Aristotelian Neoplatonism. In antiquity two interpretations of Aristotle had been proposed. The one was more favorable to religion, whether Christianity or Mohammedanism; the other was the brilliant naturalistic interpretation of Alexander Aphrodisias. It was this latter that Averroes in general adopted. In his view the Aristotelian matter becomes metaphysically self-subsistent, bearing in itself as seeds or living germs the forms that actualize individual things. Although higher forms actualize the lower, so that the highest form, God, is the first mover, it is not clear that God is transcendent or separated *realiter* from matter. Rather the theory tends to be a naturalistic immanentism. The world is produced by God or from God in an eternal emanation. The details of the progression follow a Neoplatonic model. With respect to human beings and their wonderful power of knowledge, Averroes identifies the mysterious active intellect of Aristotle with God. This was the meaning of the quotation above that there is but one active intellect for all men. Since the passive intellect is strictly united with bodily functions, and only the active intellect can be immortal, the assertion of a single active intellect is in effect a denial of personal immortality.

Averroes was perfectly sincere, not only in believing that these conclusions are necessitated by reason, but also that this is the correct interpretation of Aristotle's texts. Since he died before Thomas Aquinas was born, and was thus the most authoritative Aristotelian scholar in Europe, it was natural that the Augustinians, who had for centuries dominated Christian thinking without competition, should regard Aristotelian influence as dangerous to the faith. In 1210 the teaching of Aristotle was forbidden at Paris, except the *Organon* which had long been in use; in 1245 the prohibition was put into effect at Toulouse; and in 1263 the prohibition was renewed. But Aristotle was being studied none the less, even by Augustinians. St. Bonaventura (1221–1274) produced a thoroughly Augustinian synthesis, in which however he had introduced Aristotelian elements. And it was he who was the outstanding contemporary opponent of Thomas Aquinas. Albertus Magnus (1206–1280) reversed the proportion and allowed some Augustinianism to color his Aristotelianism. He saw that Aristotle had to be modified to conform with Christianity, but he also believed that when modified Aristotle could be of great service. He seems also to have been the first to hold that the Trinity could not be made a matter of philosophic demonstration. Bonaventura and those before him, even Abelard, who held that the Trinity was a profound requirement of reason, betrayed thereby an ignorance of what a rational and rigid demonstration is. Scientific knowledge is possible of those things only whose principles can be found in experience; since self-examination gives us a unity and not a trinity of persons, the doctrine of the Trinity can be accepted only on the basis of revelation. Thomas Aquinas, of course, was the culmination of the Aristotelian movement, and what was prohibited during his lifetime, became a required course in the next century.

THOMAS AQUINAS

Thomas Aquinas (1225–1274) was in the words of the German historian Geyer "der klärste Kopf und der grösste Systematiker des Mittelalters." Although this unexaggerated statement dispenses with any need for further praise, the importance of building a system may well be stressed. The intellectual labors of the preceding two centuries, often brilliant, were largely spent on special problems. Anselm's *Cur Deus homo* is an instance, and for that matter so was his *Proslogium*. But even though Augustinianism furnished a unity of approach, no one, not even Bonaventura who came closest to doing so, succeeded in placing the multitudinous details in their mutual logical relationships. Without an integrated system it is easy to "solve" two special problems from two incompatible principles without noticing the inconsistency; with an integrated system it is easy to demolish less skillful constructions. This is what Thomas did.

Born near the village of Aquino in Italy, Thomas received his early education under the Benedictines in the abbey of Montecassino, and then attended the University of Naples. In 1244 against his family's wishes he entered the Dominican order, which was a teaching order. Then to Paris; then to Cologne where he absorbed a great deal of Aristotle under the inspiration of Albertus Magnus. From 1259 to 1268 he taught in Italy. Then he was sent to Paris to teach theology and to engage in a bitter struggle against the Augustinian Franciscans. The opposition between the traditional views and the Aristotelian innovations was more than philosophical; it had become a matter of ecclesiastical politics in the rivalry between orders; and the Dominicans shrewdly chose their best man for the most prominent post. Thomas' strategy, well developed in his mind from his days with Albertus Magnus, was first to produce an interpretation of Aristotle less hostile to religion that that of Averroes. He also disguised his break with St. Augustine by claiming that Augustine had cited but had not adopted various Platonic or Neoplatonic views; the same purpose was served by clever reinterpretations of Augustine's words, and, if necessary, by silence. *Der klärste Kopf* won the battle. In 1272 he returned to Naples and two years later he died as he set out to attend a Council in Lyons. He was canonized in 1323.

Faith and Reason

As for his system, the distinction between faith and reason which Anselm had formulated but had not thoroughly applied was adopted by Thomas and worked out in great detail. Theology is founded on revelation; philosophy is based exclusively on reason. Here the only difference between Anselm and Aquinas is one of clarity; whereas Anselm introduces it somewhat parenthetically, Aquinas makes it a definite point in his exposition. He stresses the fact that philosophy is demonstrative and that theology is not. For example, he says: "By the very act of relating the principles to the conclusions one assents to the conclusions by reducing them to the principles . . . for in scientific knowledge the movement of reason begins from the understanding of principles and ends after it has gone through the process of reduction. . . . But in faith the assent . . . is not caused by the thought but by the will."[2] This wording reflects the strict Aristotelian interest in logic. Aquinas continues by quoting Hebrews 11:1, that faith is the evidence or conviction of things that appear not. Faith therefore grasps objects that are not evident; what is evident is grasped by reason. Faith is "less than scientific knowledge because faith does not have vision as science does, although it has the same firm adherence. And yet it is said to be more than opinion because of the firmness of the assent." Later on he uses the word *necessary* and the phrase *forced by necessity*, both of which show that he has formally valid arguments in mind. "Anything which can be proved by a necessary argument can be known as a scientific con-

[2] Quotations from St. Thomas by permission from Anton C. Pegis, *Basic Writings of St. Thomas Aquinas* (Random House, 1945).

clusion. . . . Whenever the understanding is forced of necessity to assent to something, it has scientific knowledge. . . . Whatever things we know with scientific knowledge properly so-called, we know by reducing them to first principles which are naturally present to the understanding. . . . Hence it is impossible to have faith and scientific knowledge about the same thing" (*De veritate*, Qu. 14, Art. 1, 2, and 9). And he immediately adds that we can know scientifically the existence of God.

Aside from the Aristotelian epistemology by which Thomas wished to establish the first principles, Anselm would have agreed with all this. But because Aquinas has a stricter sense of demonstration and insists as the above quotations show on formal validity, the disagreement begins to appear in that Aquinas does not regard all revealed truths as susceptible of philosophic proof, at least not by men. No doubt for every dogma there exists a thoroughly rational demonstration; and ideally in God's mind philosophy and theology are identical. But for us it is not so. There are some truths that our reason can see; there are others that it cannot. In the latter cases, when a Mohammedan or a heretic, or we ourselves, argue to a conclusion inconsistent with Scripture, reason has the obligation and the ability to retrace its steps and detect the fallacy. Since all truth forms one system in God's mind, it is impossible for reason and faith to contradict; and furthermore it is always possible for us to show the absence of contradiction; but it is not always possible to prove the truths of faith. For example, the doctrine of the Trinity, in spite of Augustine, Anselm, and Abelard, is no part of philosophy. The process of rational demonstration starts from sense perception of this world. Now, granted that this world is a creation, the creative power of God is common to all three Persons and thus belongs to the unity of the Godhead and not to the personal distinctions; therefore no argument from human experience, i.e., no philosophical argument can have the Trinity as a conclusion. Similarly Thomas excludes from philosophy the doctrines of the temporal creation, original sin, the incarnation, purgatory, the resurrection of the body, the judgment, heaven and hell. No doubt the church fathers showed how plausible, how beautiful, or how appropriate these doctrines are; but philosophy requires valid demonstration from first principles, and the principles of these doctrines are not accessible to natural reason.

Some propositions, however, are to be found both in theology and in philosophy. The reason is that the Scriptures are given for the salvation of all types of men, morons as well as geniuses; hence God included in his revelation information which indeed philosophers could obtain naturally, but which the duller and by far the more numerous part of humanity could never have figured out. This is not to say that any one man can believe and know the same truth. Understanding completes and puts an end to faith. Wherever the former is possible, one should not be content with the latter. Faith adheres to truth that is not evident; philosophy is clear vision; and the two are therefore incompatible by definition. But though no person can believe and know a given truth, the truth itself may exist both in theology because it was revealed, and in philosophy because someone has understood its demonstration. Such is the case with the existence of God.

Natural Theology

Thus natural theology, by which is meant the logical demonstration of the existence of God from first principles, is the boundary between theology proper and philosophy. Beyond this boundary is theology, on which of course Thomas wrote voluminously; but up to this point everything is preparatory. The existence of God is the last truth philosophy proves and the first truth that God reveals. This makes natural theology the center of Thomas' system and with it his fame is indissolubly bound. Thomas faced two other contrasting views. One is that the existence of God is self-evident and neither needs nor is susceptible of proof from prior first principles. Those who hold this view argue that God has implanted in all men an elemental knowledge of himself. The idea of God is innate. On this showing any argument or so-called proof could be nothing more than a clarification of already present ideas; and such in effect was the nature of Augustine's, Anselm's and Bonaventura's attempts. Now, in one sense Thomas is willing to admit that God's existence is self-evident: it is self-evident in itself, it is self-evident to God; but it is not self-evident to us. God has not implanted ideas in the human mind, and all knowledge must be based on sensory experience. The Augustinian position implies that man can grasp what is purely intelligible and that therefore every intelligible object must be intelligible to us. This is what Bonaventura meant when he argued that if the mountains gave us the strength to carry them, the heavier mountains could be carried the most easily. But all this is refuted because man is corporeal, not purely spiritual, and his knowledge must be developed through sense and imagination. There is also a second view which Thomas rejects. "Some have said, as Rabbi Moses relates, that the fact that God exists is not self-evident, nor reached through demonstration, but only accepted on faith. . . . [This] opinion is obviously false, for we find that the existence of God has been proved by the philosophers with unimpeachable proofs" (De veritate, Qu. 10, Art. 12). We can also be assured that the proof is possible by the words of the apostle Paul, "The invisible things of him are clearly seen, being understood by the things that are made" (Rom. 1:20). This verse could not be true, says Thomas, unless the cosmological argument were valid. That the demonstration proceeds "from the things that are made" is in accordance with Aristotle's theory of demonstration. There are two methods of demonstration: one is from cause to effect, the other from effect to cause. "From every effect the existence of its proper cause can be demonstrated, so long as its effects are better known to us; because, since every effect depends on a cause, if the effect exists, the cause must pre-exist. . . . When the existence of a cause is demonstrated from an effect, this effect takes the place of the definition of the cause in proving the cause's existence. This is especially the case in regard to God, because in order to prove the existence of anything, it is necessary to accept as a middle term the meaning of the name, and not its essence, for the question of its essence follows on the question of its existence. Now, the names given to God are derived from his effects. . . . Consequently in demonstrating the existence of God from his effects, we may take for the middle term the meaning of the name God. . . . From every effect the existence of the cause can be clearly demonstrated" (Summa theologica, Part I, Qu. 2, Art. 2). Obviously therefore with this Aristotelian background Thomas presents his proofs as formally valid demonstrations.

In the *Summa theologica* Thomas claims to prove the existence of God in five ways. Aside from the fact that the fifth includes teleological considerations absent from the others, they are all essentially similar. The first, however, Thomas says is the clearest, and it will be sufficient to reproduce this one only.

"The first and more manifest way is the argument from motion. It is certain and evident to our senses that in the world some things are in motion. Now, whatever is moved is moved by another, for nothing can be moved except it is in potentiality to that towards which it is moved; whereas a thing moves inasmuch as it is in act. For motion is nothing else than the reduction of something from potentiality to actuality. But nothing can be reduced from potentiality to actuality, except by something in a state of actuality. Thus that which is actually hot, as fire, makes wood, which is potentially hot, to be actually hot, and thereby moves and changes it. Now it is not possible that the same thing should be at once in actuality and potentiality in the same respect, but only in different respects. For what is actually hot cannot simultaneously be potentially hot; but it is simultaneously potentially cold. It is therefore impossible that in the same respect and in the same way a thing should be both mover and moved, i.e., that it should move itself. Therefore whatever is moved must be moved by another. If that by which it is moved be itself moved, then this also must needs be moved by another, and that by another again. But this cannot go on to infinity, because then there would be no first mover, and consequently no other mover, seeing that subsequent movers move only inasmuch as they are moved by the first mover; as the staff moves only because it is moved by the hand. Therefore it is necessary to arrive at the first mover, moved by no other; and this everyone understands to be God."[3]

This quotation, however, is more realistically understood not as a complete demonstration, but as a summary of a demonstration. Obviously its premises need to have been established elsewhere. Potentiality and actuality, the definition of motion, the necessity of a mover, the repudiation of infinite regress, all are conclusions from a long series of prior arguments and involve discussions not only

[3] *Summa theologica*, Part I, Qu. 2, Art. 3.

on physics, but chiefly on epistemology. If there is a break anywhere in this long chain of reasoning, the culminating proof quoted above will depend on a fallacy. For example, an important link is the denial of infinite regress. If the series of movers and things moved regressed to infinity, argues Thomas, an infinite number of bodies would have to exist. Each of these would necessarily be causing motion and would be in motion at the same time. But, concludes Aquinas, it is impossible for an infinite number of bodies to be in motion in a finite time; for Aristotle discovered by scientific observation that when one body moves another, they must be in contact; and this would require the alleged infinite number of bodies to be one single body; and this single body would have to move in a finite time, which is impossible. Thomas has other arguments against infinite regress, but they are certainly not more conclusive than this one; so if there is any flaw in this chain of reasoning, the proof for the existence of God is invalid.

Any discussion of Thomas' philosophy is criticism of the proof of God's existence, for this proof is the culmination of the philosophy; and it is difficult or rather impossible to remain within the limits of the quoted proof; yet so far as can be done, one more criticism will be made before losing sight of Thomas' summary formulation. An intricate criticism, it questions whether the meaning of the verb *is* or *exist* in the conclusion, God exists, is identical with the meaning of *exist* in the several premises which speak of the existence of bodies in motion. If the meaning of a term changes between the premises and the conclusion of a syllogism, obviously the syllogism is invalid. In Thomas' proof as quoted, there are three possibilities. First, the term *exist* is univocal throughout. If this is the case, then God exists in the same sense in which things exist; but Thomas explicitly denies this, for with God existence is identical with essence, and with things the two are not identical. For this reason the second possibility is that the term *exist* has changed its meaning, and that therefore the proof, even if it contained no other flaws, is a fallacy on this account. The third possibility is that although the term *exist* is used in two senses, there is some connection between them by which the fallacy is avoided. It is this last construction that Thomas defends. The connection between the two senses depends on a theory of analogy, which should be preceded by a short account of the negative knowledge of God.

In mundane matters knowledge of what a thing is, i.e., the definition of the thing, is expressed by giving its genus and specific difference; but as God is not a genus and as he exceeds all that the human mind can grasp, we cannot know what God is — we cannot know his essence. However, it is possible to know what God is not. Such a knowledge, though admittedly imperfect, is none the less true as far as it goes. Thus it is true that God is not changeable, therefore not temporal, therefore eternal. Similarly God is not passive, for potency involves contingency, and God is not contingent; therefore God is pure act. Therefore he is not matter, and hence without parts and simple. Simplicity entails the identity of essence and existence. Yet, when we say that God is eternal or simple, we have no concept of eternity or simplicity. Though the words seem positive, the knowledge, because it refers to nothing in experience, is negative, imperfect but true.

In addition to negative knowledge Thomas allows one other and a higher variety: analogical knowledge. Because essence and existence are the same in God, it follows that predicates or attributes referring to God cannot bear the same sense which they bear when referred to man. In the assertions, God is wise, and man is wise, the term wise is not used univocally. Univocal predication is impossible between God and creatures for the reason that the creatures are not effects proportionate to the infinite power of God, and hence they fall short of similitude to their efficient cause. The relation is exemplified also in the case of the sun which causes heat in things on the earth but which itself is not hot in the same sense of the word hot. When therefore it is said that a man is wise, the term *wise* signifies a quality distinct from the man's essence, distinct from his power, and from his being. But when we say that God is wise, we do not signify anything distinct from his essence, power, or being. The term *wise* applied to man circumscribes and comprehends the thing, the man, signified; whereas in the case of God the term leaves the object, God, uncomprehended. Hence no name or predicate can be applied to God and things univocally. Not only is this true of names and predicates, it is also true of the verb *to be*. When we say that God exists and that man exists, the verb does not bear the same meaning in the two cases. In God existence and essence are identical; in all other things they are not. Hence God *is* not in the sense that a man *is*. Yet if these predications were actually equivocal, it would be impossible to learn anything about God from a study of nature; whereas the apostle Paul has assured us that we can. And besides, this would contradict Aristotle too. Therefore these predications, neither univocal nor equivocal, must be analogical. Just as we predicate *healthy* of medicine and of an animal, because medicine is the cause of health in an animal body, so various predicates can be attached to God and to things. For in analogous predications the meaning is not one and the same, as in univocal predications, nor is the term used equivocally so that the two meanings are utterly diverse, but the term in the two cases signifies different proportions to some one thing, which makes analogy a mean between univocity and equivocation.

Whether or not this explanation exonerates the cosmological argument from the charge of fallacy depends on certain considerations of which one or two may be mentioned. In Thomas' explanation he referred to the sun as being the cause of heat, and drew a parallel with God's being the cause of wisdom in man. Perhaps this suffices to preserve intelligibility for the predication of wisdom to men and to God; but does it not assume that the predicate *cause* is used in the same sense for God and for the sun? If the assertions, God is a cause, and the sun is a cause, do not use "cause" in a univocal sense, then what can be meant by saying that God is the cause of wisdom as the sun is the cause of heat? Thomas explicitly declared that univocal predication is impossible between God and creatures, and that no name is predicated univocally of God and of creatures. Since this applies to the term cause as well as to the terms hot or wise, the parallel fails. Our knowledge of causality comes entirely from things; of divine causality it must be said that we have no true concept; from which it would follow that the theory of analogy does not advance us beyond negative knowledge. Or, more generally, it would seem that any useful theory of analogy must be based on some univocal element. Take the case of the medicine and the animal which are both said to be healthy. Of course in elegant English one might refer to the medicine as *healthful* and thus indicate a slightly different meaning from that of the adjective *healthy*. But in more ordinary language the latter is often used in both senses. And the senses can well be called analogous. But it is possible so to define healthy that it means exactly the same thing whether applied to medicine or to an animal. To be sure this single sense will be wider and vaguer than the ordinary two senses. It may be merely "having some positive relation to health." But though vague, this single meaning can be univocally predicated of both the medicine and the animal. And more to the point, if there were no such single univocal meaning, it would be impossible to have the two analogous meanings. There would be only equivocation. Analogy, as Thomas himself admits, must depend on some sort of similarity; but if so, that similarity can be designated by a single term, however broad in meaning; and unless this broad term has one meaning equally applicable to the two things in question, the similarity does not exist and there is no analogy at all. Hence if the term *exist* bears a temporal meaning in the premises of the cosmological argument, but in the conclusion bears the meaning of eternity of which we have only a negative knowledge (i.e., we know only that it does not mean what it means in the premises); if thus there is no univocal meaning in this term or in any other; then the proof of God's existence turns out to be not a demonstration but a fallacy.

Sensation, Imagination, and Intellect

These criticisms leave no doubt that the cosmological argument assumes the truth of a particular theory of knowledge. With certain adjustments of detail Thomas takes over the Aristotelian position that all knowledge arises out of sensation. The perception of green or red is an abstraction from a leaf or an apple; this abstraction remains, after sensation has ceased, as an image in the imagination; out of a complex of images the active intellect abstracts and produces concepts in the passive intellect; and the combining of concepts is thinking, which combinations or propositions may be true or false. Of course, such an extremely abbreviated statement as this, a reminder rather than a summary, is equally unjust to friend and foe. It may be more unjust to friend than to foe to select one or two points for criticisms, but limitations of space make it most convenient. And if it be remembered that Thomas has argued at length on a hundred such points, even adverse criticism will produce admiration of his systematic thoroughness.

Now, it seems clear that if knowledge is to be obtained by abstraction from sensory material, the first step of the process, the sensation itself, must correctly represent the physical object. Aristotle therefore asserted that sensation cannot be mistaken; and Augustine had said "if all bodily senses report as they are affected, I do not know what more we can require of them." But these two statements do not mean exactly the same thing, and in this case Thomas modifies Aristotle to conform more closely with Augustine. There are three types of sensation, as Aristotle had said. The least accurate of these is called accidental perception. Such perception occurs when we see a man or a tree. Speaking with strict accuracy, we cannot see a man or a tree; the proper object of sight is color alone; and when we see a color of a certain size and shape, we infer that it is a man. Perception *per accidens* therefore is not pure sensation, but is rather an intellectual construction which both Aristotle and Aquinas admit may be mistaken. The second type of sensation is the grasp of common sensibles. These are certain qualities, like shape, magnitude, motion, and number, which can be perceived by touch and sight; they are not proper to any one sense but are common, at least to these two senses. For Aquinas this type of sensation too may be mistaken. The third type of sensation is the perception of the proper sensibles; namely, color for the eye, sound for the ears, odor for the nose, and so on. According to Aristotle it is impossible to be mistaken with respect to these. But Aquinas adds a qualification. He says that we cannot be mistaken, except accidentally and rarely because of an indisposition of the organ. For example, sweet may seem bitter to a sick person. Of course the sick person is not deceived as to the fact that he tastes bitter, but his sense has reported the physical object to him otherwise than as it truly is. In cases of such inaccurate reports it would seem obvious that the higher intellectual activities, depending as they do on the sense material, would be vitiated from the start. This in itself might not be fatal to Thomas' theory, for he must and does admit that error is possible. A theory which made error impossible would be an impossible theory. However, one can question whether these inaccuracies of sensation are as accidental and rare as Thomas seems to think. While human beings rarely have a fever of 104°, it is strange what different colors several healthy artists can see in the same object at one time, and what different colors anyone can see in the same object at different times. We say that the observed color depends on the light. But is the true color of the object the color we abstract when the object is in the sunlight, when it is in candlelight, or when under a daylight bulb? And is the real taste of a rollmop pleasant or disagreeable? That sense sometimes reports its proper sensibles accurately does not absolve us from answering these questions before we can credit the cosmological argument for God's existence. Then when Thomas immediately proceeds (*Summa theologica,* Part I, Qu. 17, Art. 3) to add that as sense is not mistaken about its proper sensibles, so the intellect is not deceived about the essence of a thing, the same type of difficulty is aggravated on the higher level.

The stage above sensation in the learning process is imagination, for on the assumption that knowledge is not innate, unless something is preserved in the imagination after sensation has ceased, the process could go no further. Hence Aquinas insists on the necessity of images, or, as he calls them, phantasms, from the Greek for appearances. It is from these images that the active intellect abstracts concepts. That images must be used in the intellectual process, Thomas deduces from two facts. Since the intellect itself is not and has not a corporeal organ, its activity could not be hindered by any defect in a corporeal organ unless the intellect depended in some way on such an organ. But intellectual activity is hindered by frenzy, by anesthetics, or even by fatigue, so that a man fails to understand things which he previously knew quite well. Obviously then knowledge in some way depends on the body. Second, anyone can see for himself that when he tries to understand something, he calls up images: if he wishes to think of trees, he reproduces the image of a tree he saw last week and examines in this image the precise point he wishes to understand. These two facts or alleged facts show that images must be used because the universal nature, e.g., the common quality in all trees, exists in the individual things, and we apprehend individuals through sense and imagination. Even in the case of God and other incorporeal beings, of whom there can be no image, we know by comparison with sensible bodies: we know God as cause by way of excess and remotion, i.e., by augmenting our concept of physical causation and by way of eliminating inappropriate factors.

Of these arguments about imagination the first is undoubtedly strong; perhaps it is the strongest reason Thomas can urge in defense of his whole system; for no one can deny that bodily disturbances affect or in some way are related to the conscious thinking process. The relation of body to mind has to be faced by every systematic philosopher and it will reappear in seventeenth-century rationalism. But even if Thomas' first fact is admitted without qualification, and if it is granted that the body causally produces mental phenomena, the second alleged fact neither follows as a conclusion nor is established by experience. Is it true that when we think of something, we must call up images? Apparently Thomas had a lively visual imagery. When he thought of a tree he could see it in his "mind's eye" and from its shape recognize it as an elm rather than as an oak. He then assumed that all other people were like him in this respect. But this assumption must be called in question. If a large number of people are asked whether they can now see an oak tree, their breakfast table, or the face of an absent friend, although most will answer yes, some will say no. If it be further asked whether the image of the breakfast table is in color and whether they have technicolored dreams, many more will say no. If further questions be asked, such as, can you hear a tune now, can you smell a.rose, can you feel the texture of paper, cotton, or silk, the negative answers will increase. Only after a number of people have denied having such images, will a person with a lively visual imagery perplexedly and reluctantly admit the possibility that images are not necessary to thought. Sometimes such a perplexed person asks, "But how do you recognize your friend when you meet him unless you have an image of him in your mind?"

Yet suppose this person in turn is asked, "Do you recognize your friend, as he approaches you, by comparing the sensation with an image remaining from a previous sensation, as if you took a photo out of your pocket and compared it with your approaching friend?"

The person usually with the same perplexity and reluctance admits that he does not. And when it is not a matter of friends, breakfast tables, or trees, but of justice and courage, of logarithms and the square root of minus one, the need for images is hardly plausible. Then third, whether we understand God by comparing him with sensible things, and his causality by means of excess and remotion, raises the question as to the value of purely negative knowledge. If we do not know what God is, how would we know what to eliminate from the knowledge of sensible causes? In fact, if we do not know what God is, is it even possible to know what he is not? So much then for imagination.

Above imagination comes the intellect, both passive and active. This subject, however, is so intricate that a brief mention of it is no indication of the volumes of discussion it has caused. Aristotle had said that the passive intellect is actually nothing before it thinks; Thomas speaks of it as a clean tablet on which nothing is written. When something is written on this tablet, i.e., when something is understood, we say that the potentiality has been raised to actuality. The interesting question is how or by what the potentiality is actualized. Thomas in his usual manner first states an objection. It would seem, he says, that there is no active intellect needed to actualize the passive intellect for the same reason that there is no active or agent sense to actualize sensibility. Sensible things actualize the senses; so why should not the intelligible objects themselves actualize the intellect? This objection, however, assumes that intelligible objects actually exist. In other words, this objection is based on the existence of Ideas apart from sensible things. If such Ideas existed, then no active intellect would be needed. But Aristotle showed that Ideas do not exist; and since forms embedded in matter are not actually intelligible, i.e., immaterial, these forms must be raised from their potential intelligibility to actual intelligibility. But nothing can be raised from potentiality to actuality except by the causal efficacy of something already actual. Accordingly there must exist an active intellect.

If now this active intellect were numerically one for all men, then as Averroes showed, personal immortality would be impossible. Thomas therefore is required by faith at least to expose the fallacy of Averroes, and to prove if he can that each person has his own active intellect. This latter he attempts to do by showing that the active intellect is something in the soul. The objections, however, are weighty. Thomas first notes that the Apostle John said, "He is the true light that enlighteneth every man." Since the purpose of the active intellect is often described as that of illumining the objects of knowledge, it would seem that the active intellect is God. Second, Aristotle said that the active intellect never ceases to understand: there is no intermittence in its thought. But this is not true of human beings, and hence the active intellect cannot be in our soul. Third, conversely, since agent and patient suffice for action, the existence of both a passive and an active intellect in the soul would result in uninterrupted understanding, or at least we should be able to understand whenever we wished to. In the face of these objections and others Thomas answers that there exists above the intellectual soul of man a superior intellect, such as the Apostle referred to; men participate in this higher intellect and derive from it an imperfect copy. The existence of the divine light, however, does not remove the need for this derived power in each man's soul, for without this power the soul could not raise the potentially intelligible to the actually intelligible. This is but one case of the general principle that particular causes as well as universal causes are necessary for an effect: for example, the sun alone does not generate men, but in man himself there is a particular generative power. Therefore the soul itself possesses a power to illumine images, and this power is the active intellect. This consideration carries with it the existence of an active intellect for each soul, and thus personal immortality is provided for.

It was said at the outset that Thomas was a system builder. He integrated multitudinous details into a tolerably coherent whole. These details include not only a great deal of theology proper, but within the sphere of philosophy they take in the problem of creation, the existence of angels, a small amount of natural science, enough psychology to substantiate his epistemology, and all the intricacies of ethics and politics. It must all be omitted here. But the more he wrote, the more the Franciscans were convinced that they had nothing in common with him but the fundamental dogmas, and

they even came to believe that he had reintroduced paganism into
Christianity. But Thomas and Aristotle gained the day.

DUNS SCOTUS

The victory of Thomas over Augustine was neither immediate nor
complete. Twentieth-century Catholicism is far more Thomistic
than the fourteenth and fifteenth centuries were. At the beginning
of the fourteenth century Duns Scotus (1270–1308) attacked
Aquinas on several important points. Some historians picture him
as essentially an Augustinian who accepted a fair amount of Thom-
ism, while others, particularly the harmonizing Romish scholars,
with considerable textual evidence make him a Thomist who reintroduced a small amount of Augustinianism. In any case, he
prepared the way for William of Occam, who was still less Thomistic. Biographically it may be noted that if Thomas' life was short,
Duns' was much shorter. In view of this, their accomplishments
are amazing.

How fluid the tides of philosophy are may be seen in Duns'
development of Thomas' separation between philosophy and theology. Thomas had judged the Augustinians to be too lax in their
sense of demonstrative validity; therefore he concluded that the
Trinity and several other doctrines have no place in philosophy, but
that the existence of God and the immortality of the soul can be
proved on Aristotelian principles. But Duns Scotus had a stricter
notion of logical rigor than had Thomas, a strictness induced at least
in part by the scientific and mathematical studies of the Franciscans
at Oxford. The principle by which philosophy is distinguished from
theology, Duns accepted from Anselm and Aquinas, but he still
further restricted the area of philosophy. For example, he held that
the doctrine of immortality cannot be demonstrated. Three arguments had been tried. The first was based on the proposition that
the soul is a self-subsistent form; but Duns declared that this
proposition cannot be proved. The second argued that the in-
justices of this world must be balanced by rewards and punishments
in the next; but it cannot be proved that God is just. The third

argument held that the constitution of the universe provides for the satisfaction of all natural desires; hence our desire for immortality must be satisfied. However, this begs the question because a desire cannot be known to be natural until after its satisfaction has been observed.

The area to which Duns was willing to extend philosophy has been subject to some doubt because of several spurious treatises associated with his name. These give long lists of propositions said to be indemonstrable; e.g., that God is living, that he is wise, that he has volition, that he is now active, that he is one, immutable, simple, and eternal. The fact that these treatises were collected with Duns' genuine writings may indicate that they issued from his circle of disciples. Certainly they are evidence of a growing tendency to restrict philosophy and enlarge theology; but it is also certain that Duns himself did not go so far.

There is no doubt that Duns believed it possible to prove the existence of God. His arguments, however, sometimes have appeared to return to the Augustinian and ontological view. Thomas' emphasis on motion is nowhere found, and there is a great reliance on the concepts of essence and infinite being. He also speaks of the superiority of demonstrations *quid, a priori,* or from cause to effect over demonstrations *quia, a posteriori,* or from effect to cause. And the proposition, God exists, is said to be a self-evident truth. Despite phrases of this type, Duns has not returned to the ontological argument. Demonstrations *quid,* from cause to effect, however superior they may be and however possible in heaven, are beyond man's present capabilities. The ontological argument requires a direct intuition of God, and this will be vouchsafed to us only in the beatific vision. Duns' arguments therefore start from sensible experience and are as *a posteriori* as Thomas'; but they seem to be more conceptual because they do not start from the same phenomena that Thomas had used. Thomas was interested in motion; Duns in being. The properties of experienced being must be referred to a cause, a cause as real and as existent as the beings from which the argument starts. Since these properties include plurality, dependence, and composition, the cause must be one, independent, and simple.

The difference between this argument and that of Thomas,

while not so great as the difference between a demonstration *quid*
and a demonstration *quia*, is still considerable, for along with the
points mentioned, there goes also a different notion of being, of
existence, of essence, and of their mutual relations. Being with
Duns designates both the essence and the existence of that which
is. In so far as essences are the essences of actual things, essences
exist. Since a thing is defined by what it is, its essence is a part of
its being. And, it may be noted, these remarks have a certain
Augustinian sound. It is interesting therefore to wonder whether
Duns believed he had really demonstrated God's existence *a posteriori*. Does the existence of God find a place in philosophy, or in
theology only? It would appear that Duns hedged on this question.
Or, perhaps he was so subtle that we fail to follow the reasoning.
He was indeed subtle and earned the title of Doctor Subtilis. He
also provides the etymology of our derogatory term *dunce*; but this
is probably accounted for by the fact that his terminology is as
technical as a modern symbolic logician's. At any rate, a truth
belongs *simpliciter* to the science which can demonstrate it *a
priori*; but the same truth may belong secondarily to the science
quia, i.e., the science which shows that it is so but not why it is so.
Therefore God's existence belongs *simpliciter* to theology, but
secondarily to metaphysics. Yet, however formally valid the arguments are, the necessary being of metaphysics is not the God of
theology. In particular, science or philosophy has the general or
universal for its object, while God is a singular, unique being; and
besides, the infinite and absolute power of God, which Duns stresses
for other reasons, is indemonstrable. Therefore the existence of
God is not a link or a common area between philosophy and theology, as it was with Thomas.

Omnipotence and Freedom

The absolute power of God is a theme for which Duns is well
known. The fact that no philosopher has ever demonstrated such
a power is sufficient evidence that it is indemonstrable and is strictly
a Christian notion. There is a sense in which the God of the
philosophers can be called all-powerful: they believe that God causes
all effects; the unmoved mover is a universal cause whose efficacy

is everywhere present. But for the philosophers this efficacy is un-exceptionally mediated by natural means. God causes the birth of a child somewhat as the sun does; without God and sun there would be no child, but still a father is indispensable. In a world thus conceived the actions of God are necessary: God is all-powerful, but he is not free, he does not act voluntarily, secondary causes cannot be dispensed with. Duns, on the contrary, no doubt with miracles in mind, defines omnipotence as the ability to produce any possible effect without the use of one or more of the usual secondary causes. With the Greeks secondary causes were needed, not only to main-tain the uniformity of nature, but also to account for the finitude, limitations, or imperfections of nature. They had argued that whatever God might produce immediately would be perfect, and hence mediators are required for finite effects. The Christian view, according to Duns, is that God can restrict his causality; it is not necessary that God exercise all his power in every case; that is, God acts freely.

This is not to say that God is free to do the absurd or impossible. He cannot "cause" an "effect" that has no cause. He cannot create a four-sided triangle. But this is no limitation on his power or freedom, for the tasks indicated are in fact no tasks at all: they are self-contradictory combinations of words, and as meaningless they set no real problem. By the same token also the intertrinitarian activity of the Godhead is necessary. The general principle is that natural motion, even though the term *motion* is not properly ap-plicable to God, precedes voluntary motion. Therefore God's first act is to know himself, naturally or necessarily, and this knowing is the eternal begetting of the Son. Thus an intellectual act precedes all volition; from which it follows that God is not to be defined simply as omnipotent will. Whether God's simplicity is violated by attributing to him both intellect and will is another question; at least Duns agrees with Thomas in making nature and intellect supreme in God. The first voluntary act is God's love by which the Holy Ghost proceeds from the Father and the Son. This voluntary love is also necessary, but though necessary it may be called free because of the absence of external constraint. The free-dom of God, therefore, — freedom in the sense that a different

choice might have been made — is found only in God's activity
ad extra, and not in all of that. The point that attracts attention
is the relation of God's freedom to the moral law.

Admittedly God could have created a world very different from
this one. There might have been a planetary system of only five
planets. Perhaps God could not have created water, i.e., the nature
or essence with which we are familiar, so as to freeze at zero instead
of at thirty-two, for this would be self-contradictory; but he could
have created a world with an analogous fluid that would freeze at
zero. God was free to create anything not logically impossible. And
when he had created man, he could have imposed various types of
obligation upon him. Obviously there is nothing necessary about
the Mosaic ritual: it did not exist before the time of Moses and it
has been abolished with Christ. But what about the Decalogue?
First of all, one must remember that as a matter of fact God has
imposed the Decalogue and no human authority can dispense with it.
The problem does not concern man's actual duties in this world; and
if it can be concluded that God could have required the contrary
of the Ten Commandments, these still remain binding on us now.
In the next place, God was not free to command the opposite of the
first two (Protestants would say first three) commandments. It is
the nature of man to desire the supreme good; in fact it is the nature
of any created object to tend toward the good; but since this good
is God, there would be a contradiction between the nature of man
and a command not to worship God. God therefore is not free to
make such a command. But there is no contradiction between the
nature of man and a command to kill or to commit adultery. Hence
God was free to impose either the present requirements or their
opposites. In fact God did command the Israelites to kill their
enemies on certain occasions; hence the command not to kill is
obviously not necessary. Most moral laws therefore depend solely
on the free will of God.

Considerable criticism has been directed against the notion of
an arbitrary Deity. He is castigated as an oriental, irrational despot.
Though the term *oriental* might be a symptom of race prejudice, the
accusation of irrationality is evil in any language. It is universally
recognized that a man who acts arbitrarily or irrationally is ignorant,

stupid, or irresponsible. In the case of man, however, there are entities and conditions which he does not control. Knowledge of these is required for rational action for the very reason that an action is rational because the conditions have been taken into account. But in the case of the Christian God there are no independent conditions; there are no superior Ideas to which he must conform. In fact, the characteristics of infinity, omnipotence, and liberty, which Duns stressed, should have led him to deny the distinction between intellect and will in God and to come closer to the position that God is will. Intellect and rationality are clearly subordinate to things known, and there can be no things to know unless God wills to create them. Only one apparent exception can be mentioned. It might be said that God first knows himself, and this is what Duns actually maintained; and knowing himself he *ipso facto* knows the range of infinite possibility; then secondarily he wills to create several but not all of these possibilities. At the same time, however, God wills himself, wills to exist, eternally wills to beget the Son and send forth the Holy Ghost; with the result that self-knowledge and self-will become indistinguishable. Like Plotinus who denied that the One acted voluntarily, all critics of arbitrary Deity reject the concept of a living, personal God; and on the basis of an impersonal, blind, mechanical, involuntary world force, they understandably take issue with Christianity.

Not only do they reject the notion of a living God, but all the more they reject the notion of a loving God. Duns stresses the love of God; and love, a volition, is clearly arbitrary. Even in human affairs, it is often a mystery why one person loves another; we often say that there is no reason at all; or perhaps we say that Peter loves Heloise because of her pleasant qualities, failing to recognize that other persons have the same or even better pleasant qualities without attracting Peter's love. This is more profoundly true in the case of God's love for some men above others. All men are sinners and rebels before God; none have any merit before him or any claim to his grace; he has no respect for their persons; yet he elects, chooses, or loves some and not others. Of all things, love is the most arbitrary. The term *arbitrary* which these critics apply to God is of course loaded. A Christian in more honorific language would speak of the sovereignty of God. In working out his plan, God shows wisdom and reason, in the sense that the means are perfectly proportioned to the end. But the end, as end, cannot be a means to anything further; and as Aristotle said that one can deliberate about means but never about ends, so the Christian would say that God's end is a matter of sovereign choice or will. Otherwise there would be no universal teleology and, to skip several steps in the argument, the absence of moral principles for man would make the choice between life and suicide irrational.

One might suppose that emphasis on the omnipotent freedom of God would have led Duns to some form of determinism for man. The old Augustinian doctrine of original sin would also support the same conclusion. But Duns seems to have considered the effect of sin to be rather superficial. One reason why God imposed the Ten Commandments, rather than a million commandments which he could have required, is that though the Ten Commandments are difficult to observe, they are not impossible or even very difficult. With reasonable effort any man can amass merits with God. The will is perfectly free to obey, and of course free to disobey. As there is no cause of God's will, so there is no cause of man's will. Here Duns repeats the illustration Augustine had borrowed and altered from the Stoics: all things being equal two men who see a beautiful woman will act differently. Otherwise there could be no praise or blame; in fact, otherwise there would be no will. A will that could have a cause would not be a will at all. On this point Duns takes issue with other theologians including Thomas Aquinas. Although Thomas had various things to say about free will, his theory, perhaps unintentionally, is or at least resembles a psychological determinism. First, man is so created that to desire the general good is an absolute necessity. To be sure he does not always know what the true or final good is; but if and when his intellect comes to know the good, he naturally (should we say automatically?) wills it. This occurs in heaven: the blessed, confirmed in grace, necessarily will God because they see his essence. This first point, so Augustinian, fairly represents St. Thomas. About a second point there may be some dispute. In this life we do not see clearly the final good, but various objects appear to us as goods. It would seem therefore that the images in our mind, or more simply the apparent good, would move our wills, in which case the determinism would extend to this life also. After all, if a necessitated will is not a contradiction of terms in heaven, and if God can both freely and necessarily cause the procession of the Holy Ghost by love, why could not the apparent good exercise a causal efficacy on the will here and now? Duns avoids saying that Thomas intended to teach a psychological determinism, and in all likelihood Thomas did not so intend, but Duns seems to think that some of his words imply it. Since Duns wishes to assert the complete indetermination of the will, he takes pains to argue that the image or the apparent good does not cause the will. Of course, one cannot will an unknown object; knowledge has a role to play; but the will is completely free to choose or not to choose. Even in the beatific vision, the object, God himself, does not necessarily cause the will. But if such perfect freedom exists in heaven, is it not possible for the blessed to choose to sin?

Individuation

Duns was deeply interested also in another problem, one which forms a convenient connecting link with his successors. It is the problem in individuation. Aristotle had held that the difference between two things of the same species, two men for example, is in the matter. Since they are alike in form, in common quality, in species, it is only by the matter that each is one thing. But matter is pure unknowable potentiality; and therefore it seems that individual things, which Aristotle admitted are the primary realities, would be unknowable. Thomas Aquinas had essentially the same view. True, he altered it somewhat. For him the principle of individuation was not matter in general, but *materia signata*: in the definition of the species of man there is matter in general, but in Socrates and Plato there is *materia signata*. Whether this is an evasion or whether it approaches Duns' later position are questions that need not be answered here. At any rate Duns was dissatisfied with the prevalent teaching. It seemed to deny individuality to the active intellect, which has no matter, and therefore to undermine immortality. It also seemed to tend toward pantheism in that God, being immaterial, cannot be an individual, but must be regarded

only as a supreme genus. Of course, Thomas denied these conclusions; but at least he admitted that angels are species and not
individuals. For these theological reasons therefore Duns felt compelled to work out a better theory of individuation; and perhaps his
more lively sense of the individual may also be connected with his
emphasis on free will.

Duns' theory of individuation is one of his most subtle and
intricate. To begin with it includes a reworking of the notion of
matter. If individuals are the primary realities, if too they are composites of matter and form, it follows that matter cannot be pure
nothing. A composite of form and nothing is not a composite; nor
would a reality that owes its reality to nothing be a reality. Matter
therefore must be positively something. Then too if God created
matter as Augustine taught, matter must be something. It is
not a form to be sure; but it is not nothing. It is so much something
that it is knowable; in fact, since God created it, there must be an
Idea of matter in God's mind; and for other complicated reasons it
can exist apart from form. Now, if matter is something, it is one
something, it is an individual; but since matter cannot be the
principle of individuation for itself, there must be a principle of
individuation other than matter.

To emphasize the problem let it be asked why a stone cannot be
so divided that each part is the same stone as the original one. Perhaps a better example would have been the division of a one-celled
animal into two animals. Why is neither of the two the same as
the first? Is an in-dividual simply an un-divided? Duns believed
that this explanation was unsatisfactory because it would base
individuality on privation, negation, and defect; and individuals
as primary realities are too real to be the result of negation. For
Duns the individual is not only undivided, but indivisible. Of
course, a stone can be divided into two others; but insofar as it
is a singular thing, it is indivisible—its singularity cannot be divided.
Hence, thought Duns, there must be some positive intrinsic factor.
Privation is insufficient.

It is a general principle that the more particular possesses a determination not found in the universal; e.g., to the genus animal
one must add the difference rational to have the species man.

Similarly something positive must be added to the species man to get Socrates. As the specific form *rational* constitutes the species man, so the principle of individuation makes Socrates what he himself is. The comparison between species and individual can be taken one step further. As the species is specifically indivisible, so the individual, as was said above, is individually indivisible. But here the comparison ends because the species can be divided into individuals, but the individual cannot be further subdivided. Therefore individual unity is the strictest of all unity. Now, further, although added determinations usually give rise to lower species, this is not true in the case of God. When infinite being is predicated of God, the result is not a species of God. Rather, God is thereby individualized. Similarly the principle of individuation is not an added form, but is the ultimate reality of the given form. There is a gap between the species and the individual. Individuality and form belong to different orders. Although one may abstract forms from individuals, one starts this process from the nature of the individuals and not from their individuality. In other words, individuality is a metaphysical factor for which there is no concept. It is neither form nor matter. It is the ultimate reality of being. Modern existentialism also holds that conceptual thought fails to grasp the ultimate realities, and it might be argued that Duns only inconsistently avoided their skeptical, irrational, paradoxical conclusions. Maybe so, but Duns actually concluded that although this ultimate reality is unintelligible to us now, although we cannot define it, although there is no knowledge or science of it, still God has Ideas of the singulars and we too shall know them in heaven. Individuals are not in themselves unintelligible as modern existentialism holds; the trouble lies with us, who are like owls blinded by the sunlight. What then is the principle of individuation? It can only be named: *haecceity*, or *thisness* — a term which Duns used little, but which became frequent later on.

It is fair to say that Duns emphasized individuals more than Thomas had done. It is also true, with technical qualifications, that Duns was more realistic and gave a larger role to the Ideas. And in the assertion that there are Ideas of individuals, one suspects a mixture of realism and nominalism that was far from Plotinus' thought;

at any rate, after Duns the most important development was in the direction of nominalism.

WILLIAM OF OCCAM

William of Occam, or Ockham (*ca.* 1300–1349), was, like Duns Scotus, a Franciscan, educated at Oxford. His fame rests largely on his revival of nominalism, not perhaps in the simple or crude form of Roscellinus, but in a more intricate and complete theory. For him as for all critics of Platonism, the attribution of reality to universals entailed many absurdities. If a universal is a real independent being *ante rem*, and not merely a mental construct, it must be as individual as any thing; but if individual, how could it also be universal? Then too, if the Idea is an individual, there must be as many Ideas of man as there are men; and this is too many for comfort. But of course Thomas had repudiated ideas *ante rem* in this sense. However, if with Thomas it be said that universals exist *in re*, not in actuality but requiring to be actualized by the active intellect, then universals do not exist *in re* as universals; for clearly our intellect does not make the external object, it only produces the concept in our mind; hence universals cannot exist *in re*. There cannot be a common quality, a common red or a common man; there exist only the singular instances of reds and men. The principle operating in this criticism, though derived from Aristotle, was given the picturesque name of Occam's razor. Aristotle had claimed that the Ideas were an unnecessary duplication of sensible things; Occam expressed it by saying that entities should not be multiplied beyond necessity. His conclusion was that *universalia in re* are as unnecessary as *universalia ante rem*. Therefore shave them off. Everything can be explained with the individual things alone and our concepts of them.

Universals are of two types. First there is the natural universal, a mental concept that exists only in the mind; and second there is the conventional universal, a word which we use as a sign of the concept. In one sense, in their second intentions as Occam called it, words, and concepts too, are singular real entities. A word is a sound in the air or marks on paper, and a concept is an individual temporal concrete act of the mind. But these concrete things in another sense, in their first intentions, become universals in virtue of their predicability. What is predicability? A word is predicable because it can stand for or be a sign of many things. Man is the predicate of Socrates, Plato, and Aristotle because the word man can be put in place of these three men. Now, if there is no common quality, no universal really in the three men, a realist would raise the following objection. Could we not, he would say, collect a man, a tree, and a stone and let the term *snark* stand for this collection? In other words, classification is not so arbitrary as the predicability of terms seems to imply; there must be a real common quality in the things in virtue of which we bring them together and apply the same term to them. Because of this absence of a common quality in man, tree, and stone, no language has a specific term to stand for them. Occam has an ingenious answer for this objection. It has to do with the role of natural universals. The mental concept or natural universal is a sign in the sense in which smoke is a sign of fire and sobbing a sign of grief. This beginning of an answer is not too clear, and one wonders how smoke can be a sign of fire. Is it that fire causes smoke, grief causes sobbing, while Plato and Aristotle cause the concept man? If so, smoke could be a universal; yet Occam asserts that no external object can be predicated of many things, and the parallels seem to diverge. However, the answer to the objection above is that the universals, though they are figments of the mind, i.e., something made by the mind, are not purely figmentary as if nothing in the real world corresponded to them. They are copies or images of the individual sensory realities. (Note that smoke is not a copy or image of fire.) But they are not perfect copies; for if they were, the image of Plato could not stand for Aristotle. Such an image as is needed must be something like a composite photograph of various individuals that agree with one another. "It can be called a universal because it is an exemplar and indifferently looks back upon all the external individuals; and because of that similitude in its mental existence (*in esse obiective*), it can stand for the external thing."

Several interesting and important conclusions follow. If universals are merely pictures in the mind, and if things are not composites of matter and form, the problem of individuation disappears. Each real thing is an individual in its own right, and no unnecessary principle need be sought to explain its individuality. Another conclusion is that no active intellect or even will is presupposed by abstraction. The concept follows of itself upon sensation; or if not upon sensation, then upon internal intuition, for introspection gives us even surer knowledge than sensation does.

More interesting are the conclusions that bear directly on matters of theology. Ideas in God's mind can only be considered according to the analogy of the pictures in human minds: they are not a part of God's eternal essence, but are only his knowledge of individual things. Unfortunately this seems to imply that God was ignorant until after he had created the individual things, and then first looked around to discover truth. Occam surely did not intend this absurdity, for he did not minimize the prerogatives of God: in line with Duns' view that God can act independently of second causes, Occam said that God may produce a picture in our mind without the presence of the external object. If this happens very frequently, half of the things we see do not exist. What if all our pictures are immediately produced by God? But first, can Occam prove that there is a God. Obviously he cannot use the ontological proof, for in this system all proofs must be inductive or *a posteriori*. But the *a posteriori* argument is invalid as well. The principle of causality on which it is based cannot be substantiated; the impossibility of an infinite series cannot be proved; there is no demonstration of the unity or infinitude of God; and a plurality of worlds, each with its own cause, is conceivable.

In Augustine and Anselm the areas of philosophy and theology were mutually inclusive. In Thomas there was some overlapping, but a number of truths had been withdrawn from philosophy and assigned to theology alone. With Duns the overlapping became less, philosophy was further restricted, and theology enlarged. Now with Occam even the existence of God was made totally a matter of theology. But what of philosophy? Had it been so restricted that its area was now zero? If so, the nominalist Occam and the realistic Augustinians had come to essential agreement: there is but one area of knowledge, and whether it is called philosophy or theology makes no difference. But this agreement would have required of Occam the admission that no truth can be discovered by reason apart from revelation. By those who do not recognize divine revelation, such an admission is called skepticism. If there is no revelation and if reason can prove nothing, then knowledge is impossible.

Now, Occam was hesitant to draw the skeptical conclusion in philosophy. Perhaps logic demands this conclusion, but Occam was interested in the mathematics and science at Oxford, and was one of many who in a small way prepared for the modern scientific outlook. In this he was an early forerunner of the Renaissance; but he was also in a way the forerunnner of the Reformation. The civilization of modern times — "modern" meaning from 1500 to the mid-twentieth century — has been a mixture of Renaissance and Reformation views. A Christian spiritualism and a scientific materialism have been strangely combined. Occam's splitting of philosophy and theology resulted in the choice of scientific philosophy by the Renaissance and of divine revelation purged of Neoplatonic and Aristotelian elements by the Reformers. The immediate successors of Occam were more skeptical and less scholastic than he. John Huss and John Wycliffe were both Oxford men, and like Occam opposed the totalitarian system of the papacy. Huss had a combination of Scotism and nominalism. Wycliffe followed the logic of Duns' views of omnipotence to its deterministic conclusion. An obscure German nominalist, Biel, and his better known pupil, Staupitz, were the instructors of Martin Luther. Luther also declared that he belonged to Occam's school, and argued, but more on Scriptural than on scholastic grounds, in favor of The Bondage of the Will. Similarly Calvin based all his arguments on Scripture alone. Protestantism therefore was not philosophical in the scholastic or in the modern scientific sense of the term. Its efforts were expended in reforming religion and renewing Biblical Christianity. Therefore the history of modern philosophy, although some Christians took part in it, is predominantly secular. It was tacitly assumed that even if there be a God and a future life, men are not sinners, need no redemption, and should concern themselves more with the physics and politics of this world than with the blessedness of heaven. The questions were: How is truth obtainable? Can it be found in science? What is science? Or, has the area of philosophy been permanently reduced to zero?

PART THREE

Modern Philosophy

CHAPTER 7

Seventeenth-Century Rationalism

The New Civilization

The Renaissance, marking the end of the Middle Ages and the beginning of modern times, was not merely or even chiefly a philosophical development, for this came a little later; but it was, rather, the birth of a new civilization in all its phases. Between a major philosophical advance and its immediately preceding political, religious and literary conditions there is an intricate relationship. Philosophy, as others have said, is not written in a vacuum, and every author gathers up the currents of his day; but in so far as the author is great and proposes new ideas, to that extent his work is less the effect of the past than it is the cause of the future. For this reason a history of philosophy might well omit the Renaissance proper, for its influence on the main development of philosophy was not determinative; yet because it contributed certain elements and because the Renaissance is so inherently interesting, it should not be passed by in complete silence.

Frequently the literary and scientific advances of this epoch are called the Renaissance so as to distinguish these from the religious awakening called the Reformation. With respect to this latter, something has already been said.

The peoples of Western Europe became disgusted with the idolatry, corruption, and immorality of the Roman church and under leaders like Luther, Zwingli, Calvin, and Knox sought to re-establish the doctrine and life of the New Testament revelation. In place of the previous superficial view of sin, they taught total depravity; for free will they substituted God's grace in predestination; and therefore instead of earning heaven by human works, they were justified by faith alone. But though the Reformation had very widespread effects on civilization, it did not have as much influence on the history of modern philosophy as might be expected. The genius of the Reformation was to avoid the skepticism that results from dependence on unaided reason and to accept truth as a revelation from God; whereas the philosophical development is an attempt to show that knowledge is possible without recourse to any special or supernatural revelation. Perhaps the chief influence of the Reformation on the philosophers was to lead them into inconsistencies. In the account of the Presocratic period mention was made of the cultural isolation of the Greeks that prevented them from being confused by Hebrew-Christian concepts. Now, as the Middle Ages had diluted its Christianity with pagan ideas, so the modern philosophers (although Leibniz and Berkeley were personally Christians) put varying thicknesses of Christian veneer over their basic secularism. It would be wiser therefore to ignore the Reformation in a history of what is commonly accepted as the main line of philosophic development.

Perhaps the least important, though possibly the most spectacular phase of the Renaissance as distinguished from the Reformation, was the purely political. From the ruins of the loose and complicated structure of European feudalism there arose the nationalistic and despotic states of Spain, France, and England. These three were able to dominate the scene because Italy and Germany remained a congeries of petty kingdoms, while Hungary defended Europe from the Turks on the east. Aside from political action, political literature is represented in Campanella's *City of the Sun*, Machiavelli's *Prince*, and Sir Thomas More's *Utopia*. Machiavelli has acquired an unpleasant reputation, but nothing could be more revoltingly totalitarian than More's Utopia. Absolutism was the fashion, and the Protestants could not permanently dislodge it in England until 1688, nor the atheists in France until 1789. With politics, one may associate geographical discovery and expansion. From the year 1100 on, the Crusades and their results widened the geographical horizons of Europe; but it is not evident that this had much to do with the Renaissance. During the fourteenth century, trade with India and China began, which toward the end of the following century led to the discovery of America; and it was by massacring the Incas and plundering their gold that Spain became the dominant power in Europe, until William of Orange drove their cruel regime from Holland and England defeated their Armada.

These political developments, however, stretch over so many years that perhaps they should not be included in the Renaissance itself; surely they are not its cause. If an immediate cause is to be identified, the most plausible is the capture of Constantinople by the Turks in 1453. Until this time the Roman Empire had continued a moribund existence in the East. There the scholars preserved a great mass of ancient manuscripts. Occasionally an Eastern scholar would travel to Italy; then, as the danger of the Turks increased they came in numbers, bringing their treasures with them. Although some of Plato had always been known in the West, and Aristotle had been discovered in the twelfth century, the full glory of Greece and Rome was now for the first time made known in Italy. But without another event of quite a different order, the introduction of these manuscripts into the West could only have slightly accelerated the previous rate of change. It so happened that just before the capture of Constantinople, a German invented the printing press; and while a printing press is useless if there is nothing to print, a manuscript is nearly useless if it cannot be printed. The laborious process of copying by hand was now at an end, and Plato, Homer, and Cicero became best sellers. This does not justify characterizing the Renaissance as a "rediscovery, exercise and enjoyment of the powers of the mind." The scholastics of the thirteenth and fourteenth centuries had exercised their minds no end, and undoubtedly enjoyed doing so. What had happened was the discovery of a brilliant literature with which the mind could exercise and enjoy itself. And the Italians rose to the occasion.

Or, did they sink below it? Roman Catholicism had become for them merely a matter of social form. They loved luxury rather than God. With Cellini's beautiful silver and gold they could serve a superb dinner and poison their honored guest most politely.

Earthly pleasures rather than heavenly bliss was the goal of the popes and priests as well as of the Borgias. When Savonarola condemned their sins, the Church condemned him and had him burned in 1498. It was a time of licentiousness, violence and deceit. The more scholarly, whom we fondly hope were not so base, studied the classics, edited, translated and commented on the texts, becoming in the process enthusiastic Neoplatonists or Neopythagoreans. Some of the more superstitious resurrected the Greek mystery religions and pursued numerics.

Among all the factors which characterized the Renaissance, art occupied a unique position. Much earlier than the literary revival, the change in painting is seen in Giotto (1276–1336). Then too, while other aspects of the Renaissance took some time to spread from Italy northward, art seemed to move more rapidly and a new style is seen in the Flemish Van Eyck (1385–1441). Also the artistic development can be said to have been fairly well completed — at least more so than the scientific development — within the Renaissance period itself, for the greatest Italian painters finished their work in the sixteenth century: Leonardo da Vinci (1452–1519), Raphael (1483–1520), Titian (1477–1576). The change in form is of most importance to the history of art, while philosophy is more concerned with the change in content. The gilt backgrounds signifying heaven were replaced with landscapes; Biblical history and medieval religious legends gave way to classical or contemporary themes; and in the pictures of Christian content sometimes John the Baptist was indistinguishable from Bacchus and the artist's favorite prostitute served as a model for the Virgin Mary.

The mention of Leonardo da Vinci brings us closer to that scientific development which more than the previous factors contributed to the dominant philosophic views of modern times. That amazing genius read Archimedes, insisted on mathematical demonstration in connection with experiment and verification, investigated the principles of mechanics, and anticipated Galileo by more than a century. Yet Leonardo was not the first scientist. One must not suppose that the night before the Renaissance there had been no science and then suddenly the next morning Miss Scientia burst forth from the head of Jupiter. If the change from one culture to another should be plotted as a curve, it might be represented by a hyperbola or parabola. The Middle Ages had been going in a certain direction, almost in a straight line; then one perceives that the line has already curved a little; just where it began no one can say; the degree of curvature rapidly increases and then decreases, but the change of the change is too smooth for fixed limits. Scientific experiments had been conducted by Roger Bacon (1210–1290), who in order to peer more deeply into chemistry and biology invented the microscope.[1] Several minor figures between Occam and Leonardo studied the laws of motion; and astronomy was a perennial subject of investigation.

It is astronomy too that has caught hold of the historian's imagination and has led to somewhat exaggerated statements about the role of Copernicus (1474–1543). As in connection with Christopher Columbus, it is inaccurate to say that the new age began with "the discovery that the world was round instead of flat," for it had been known throughout the Middle Ages that the earth is spherical; so too it stretches the truth to say that Copernicus' heliocentric theory "destroyed all outer evidence of man's focal and privileged situation in the universe." Historians ought to note that the focal and privileged position which Christianity assigned to man was neither motivated by nor did it depend on geocentric astronomy. The position is spiritual, not spatial; it relates to God's plan for saving sinners by the death and resurrection of Christ; and the planetary motions are at most stage scenery for the divine comedy. Conversely also if proximity to the center conferred a privileged status on man, the fish of the ocean depths ought to have greater privileges, and the greatest would belong to the mineral or metal core of the planet. In any case, the geocentric theory does not put the earth at the center of the system; and though the later Greek philosophers generally, with Plotinus as a good example, accepted the Ptolemaic theory, it never suggested to them a Christian view of man. No, the significance of Copernicus lies within astronomy, and even here, he has sometimes been regarded too optimistically.

This is the background. Plato in his extreme old age "repented of having given the earth the central position" in the planetary system

[1] W. R. Newbold and R. G. Kent, *The Cipher of Roger Bacon* (University of Pennsylvania Press, 1928).

and worked out a rudimentary heliocentric theory, which Aristarchus (*ca.* 275 B.C.) brought to considerable perfection. But common sense and the authority of Aristotle convinced the majority that the sun circles around the earth. Although Aristotle's form of geocentrism, the concentric spheres of Eudoxus, was rather inept, the system of cycles, epicycles and excentrics, which Ptolemy (*ca.* A.D. 150), an Egyptian astronomer, formulated with a great precision based on many accurate observations, remained dominant in all essential points throughout the Middle Ages. A diagram will give a tolerably clear picture of the scheme. Point C is the center of the system. To one side of it is the earth; diametrically opposite the earth and equidistant from the center is E'. Point X moves around circle C so that the line E'X has a uniform angular velocity, and the planet P circles X.

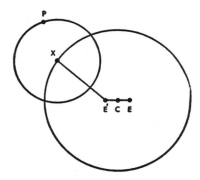

Given the correct distances and velocities for any planet, this arrangement describes the observed motions.

In addition to an interest in comets, the medieval astronomers were occasionally puzzled by the peculiarities of Mercury and Venus, and a Spanish astronomer suggested that these two planets could be regarded as satellites of the sun. As the fourteenth and fifteenth centuries wore on, interest in astronomy seems to have increased. Now, Copernicus was struck with the fact that the Ptolemaic system was extremely complex, and he set about to discover a simpler method of description. That he discovered it in his own mind rather than in the ancient literatures recently brought from the East is more than doubtful. In the final revision of his book he deleted his references to Aristarchus; for what motive we cannot say. At any rate Copernicus was the first in modern times to propound a heliocentric theory. So far as scientific detail is concerned, a great deal remained to be done. Tycho Brahe argued that if the earth moved around the sun, there should be an apparent shift in the position of stars. No shift could be observed. Therefore he concluded that the earth must be at rest. As a matter of fact this parallax was not discovered and the heliocentric theory "proved" until 1838. The reason for this, aside from the need for powerful telescopes, is that the stellar distances are so much more vast than Copernicus and Tycho imagined. Even their ideas of the solar system were too restricted. Ptolemy had established the sun's distance from the earth as 1,210 times the earth's radius. Copernicus' estimate was even smaller: 1,142. The present figure is about 23,000. Then too the Copernican construction could not predict or describe so accurately as the Ptolemaic system. Scientific observation was definitely more favorable to the old than to the new. But science is not all observation.

There was one other factor that weighed heavily, indeed conclusively, for Copernicus. The Ptolemaic scheme was mathematically cumbersome; the heliocentric theory is mathematically simple. And in science mathematical simplicity counts more than accurate observations. There is this interesting sidelight, however. Copernicus had discarded Ptolemy because of aesthetic considerations; the beauty of mathematical simplicity appealed to him. But what is the truth? Does the earth really and truly revolve around the sun? If the aim of science is mathematical simplicity, then all scientific laws are ingenious attempts at simple description; and a later, more ingenious scientist can invent a simpler description. But while Copernicus rejected Ptolemy on aesthetic grounds, and not because of any failure to account for the observed facts, yet, when he arrived at his own conclusions, he took the position that now at last the real truth had been found. Since his day, the majority of scientists, and certainly the majority of the overawed populace, though the theories are being constantly replaced, have entertained a firm and dogmatic belief that science achieves truth. Many philosophers also have hoped to achieve truth; but even the most dogmatic of them have been more sensitive to the difficulties. In spite of the astounding achievements of Galileo (1564–1642), and of Kepler (1571–1630), who discarded circles for ellipses, and the continued rapid advance through the seventeenth century, the philosophic hope for truth was not based on empirical discovery.

RENÉ DESCARTES (1596—1650)

Descartes, upon graduating from "one of the most celebrated schools in Europe" in which he had expected to acquire "a clear and certain knowledge of all that is useful in life," found himself so involved in doubts and errors that he was convinced he had learned nothing but the depth of his ignorance. Languages are of course very important, but they do not guarantee the truthfulness of the books written in them. History is inspiring, but one cannot trust its accuracy. Mathematics, because of the certitude of its reasoning, was his favorite study, and he was astonished that on such solid foundations no loftier superstructure had been erected. Theology, a matter of divine revelation, is not subject to the impotency of reason. And philosophy, "cultivated for many ages by the most distinguished men," contained "not a single matter within its sphere which is not still in dispute"; and considering "the number of conflicting opinions touching a single matter that may be upheld by learned men, while there can be but one true," Descartes "reckoned as well-nigh false all that was only probable. As to the other sciences, inasmuch as these borrow their principles from philosophy" he "judged that no solid superstructure could be reared on foundations so infirm." [2]

Descartes had a horror of being deceived. Although his education had not furnished him with any truth, he could mitigate his plight by avoiding error; and his reason convinced him that he ought not the less carefully to withhold belief from what is not entirely certain and indubitable, than from what is manifestly false. But is this principle itself indubitably certain? William James later affirmed that it is better to believe many truths and some error than to escape all error

[2] These phrases come from Descartes' *Discourse on Method*, but the exposition in the main follows *The Meditations*.

at the risk of having little or no truth. Perhaps this antithesis be-tween Descartes and James is not too pertinent at the moment, for Descartes insisted on trying to doubt everything for the purpose of discovering something that could not be doubted. The ancient skep-tics and his own experience sufficed to show that all the results of sense perception were extremely doubtful. A naïve person might reply that to doubt I am a man, seated in this chair, holding a book in my hands, is a mark of insanity. Perhaps it is; but where is the proof that I am not insane? Or on a lesser scale, where is the proof that I am not asleep, dreaming that I am a man when I am really a woman, dream-ing that I am seated with a book in my hands, when as a matter of fact I am lying in bed with my hands amputated. With such consid-erations as these the prudence of doubting sensation, and all the sciences based on observation, is evident. Mathematics, however, seems to escape this skeptical criticism, "for whether I am awake or dreaming, it remains true that two and three make five." Here Descartes seems to imply that we cannot dream that two and three are four, though he does not explicitly say so. Nevertheless, there is one condition under which even the truths of mathematics would be doubtful. It may be thought that this condition is an absurdity; but if we have not yet discovered any indubitable truth, we have no norm by which to distinguish what is absurd from what is most probable. In the absence of truth, nothing is absurd. Let us suppose, therefore, that the world is controlled, not by a good God, but by an omnip-otent demon whose chief delight it is to make us believe that two and three are five, when in reality they are four. How he chuckles over our mistaken mathematics! Granted, we do not know that such an omnipotent demon exists; with good fortune we may later be able to prove there is no such demon; but at the moment we do not know that this demon does not exist; and until we can dispose of him, mathematics is as suspect as empirical science. Therefore, if knowl-edge is to be possible, we must find a truth about which not even an omnipotent demon could deceive us.

Descartes was acutely conscious that the Middle Ages had expired and that he was the first philosopher of modern times. He frequently claims that he has erased all the supposed learning of the past and is starting afresh on new foundations. In a sense this claim is justified, for seventeenth-century rationalism is not found either in the Middle Ages or in antiquity; but the first truth, about which it is impossible to doubt, sounds very much like St. Augustine, and the subsequent truths based upon it usually have their antecedents too. No philosopher can break entirely with the past.

The Cogito and Logic

What is this first of all truths, a truth about which it is impossible to be deceived? It can have nothing to do with body, shape, extension, or motion. It cannot be a truth of science or mathematics. But though I have doubted about earth and sky, and have cast suspicion on mathematics, though even a demon constantly deceives me, it still remains indubitably certain that I doubt, I think, and therefore I am. I must exist if I am deceived. *Cogito ergo sum.* And if Archimedes needed only one fixed point in order to move the earth, the one truth of my existence is a sufficient base for all philosophy.

Here one must pause to consider what is going on and in which direction philosophy will advance. The examination is complicated by the fact that Descartes did not express himself with perfect clarity and that he may be suspected of some inconsistency. But if he is regarded as the founder of seventeenth-century rationalism, his main intentions may be judged by the outcome in Spinoza and Leibniz. The test of a true idea, Descartes constantly repeats, is its clarity and distinctness. This does not mean its vividness as a picture or image in the mind. Unlike St. Thomas, the rationalists show no dependence on visual imagery. The clarity Descartes intends is a logical clarity. Consider a college class in Logic. The professor explains that all men are mortal and that Socrates is a man. Does it not follow that Socrates is mortal? At this point the football star whose I.Q. is not half his weight protests, "I agree that all men are mortal and that Socrates is a man; but I don't see that that has anything to do with Socrates' being mortal. Explain to me please why the third proposition follows from the first two." The challenge is too difficult to meet. Anyone but a moron can see clearly and distinctly that the conclusion must follow from these premises. Nothing else can be seen more clearly. This is logical clarity, and it is with this clarity that I see I think. Why for example is it so clear I think? It is not because thinking is such an intense psychological experience that introspection cannot fail to notice it; rather the reason is that the proposition *I think* is one whose very denial proves it true. I do not have to walk in order to deny that I am walking, but I cannot deny or doubt that I think without thinking. *Ambulo ergo sum* cannot be substituted for *Cogito ergo sum*. Accordingly rationalism is a system of philosophy which holds that all knowledge is based on reason alone. In this connection reason is not contrasted with revelation as it was in the Middle Ages, but with sensation. Less ambiguously one might say that all knowledge is based on logic alone. Only by logic can one escape the deceptions of sense and malevolence of a demon. And if all knowledge is based on logic alone, the first truth must of necessity be a self-proving truth, a truth to deny which proves it true: and all other truths have to be deduced from it.

If Descartes had produced a system that perfectly corresponded to this definition of rationalism, there would have been no need of later philosophers to correct him. But unfortunately he was not altogether consistent in the application of his rationalistic principle. A flaw appears immediately in the *Cogito ergo sum*. By what logic is the *sum* deduced from the *cogito*? If one should say, "I am a thinking being, all thinking beings are existing beings, therefore I am an existing being," one would undoubtedly have a logical syllogism that is beyond reproach. But where could the premise, that all thinking beings are existing beings, have come from? Descartes was accused of having smuggled in a proposition that had not yet been demonstrated. To this charge he makes a curious reply. He denies that he has smuggled in such a premise, and he also denies that *Cogito ergo sum* is a logical syllogism. The force of the *ergo* in this case is not that of ordinary demonstration. On the contrary we see that the conclusion follows, not by logic, but by natural light.

The difficulty in such an appeal to a non-logical or at least non-demonstrative principle is easily seen when we compare this instance with another. Later Descartes considers the reasons which lead most people to believe in the existence of sensible bodies. One of these is that we are so taught by nature. This natural teaching, however, is only a certain spontaneous impetus that impels one to believe in a resemblance between ideas and their objects; it is not a natural light that affords knowledge of the truth. Natural light and this spontaneous impetus are very different; "for what the natural light shows to be true can in no degree be doubtful, as for example that I am because I doubt, and other truths of the like kind but with respect to natural impulses I have observed . . . that they frequently led me to take the worse part." This is highly unsatisfactory, as may be seen by applying the phraseology to demonstration. Suppose it were said that demonstration is very different from fallacies because in demonstration the conclusion follows, while in fallacies it does not. Such a statement is of no help in distinguishing a demonstration from a fallacy. And even if natural light led to truth while natural impulse did not, we would still be unable to distinguish one from the other; for as we must know the form of valid demonstration before we can say that the conclusion follows in this particular case, so we would have to identify natural light before we could know that the result is true.

Descartes also uses the term *intuition*. He says that there are two "operations" by which we are able, "wholly without fear of illusion, to arrive at the knowledge of things . . . *viz.*, intuition and deduction." One of his descriptions of intuition is this: "By intuition I understand, not the fluctuating testimony of the senses, nor the misleading judgment that proceeds from the blundering constructions of imagination, but the conception which an unclouded and attentive mind gives us so readily and distinctly that we are wholly freed from doubt about that which we understand. Or, what comes to the same thing, intuition is the undoubting conception of an unclouded and attentive mind, and springs from the light of reason alone; it is more certain than deduction itself, in that it is simpler, though deduction, as we have noted above, cannot by us be erroneously conducted. Thus each individual can mentally have intuition of the fact that he exists and that he thinks; that the triangle is bounded by three lines only, the sphere by a single superficies, and so on."

Since this paragraph specifies that there are just two operations for attaining truth, we may conclude that intuition and natural light are the same thing. But the various phrases purporting to describe

intuition do not relieve the difficulties. The trouble is not chiefly
that Descartes admits two methods of obtaining truth when philosophic simplicity would require but one; nor is it that he does not fit
the historian's convenient definition of rationalism, or that he falls
short of the perfection of Spinoza; the main flaw is that Descartes gives
no reason for saying that intuition is more trustworthy than sensation. It is interesting to note that one of Descartes' examples of
intuition is the knowledge that a triangle is bounded by three lines.
Is this an undoubting conception of an unclouded and attentive
mind? It sounds very much like a definition; and in Spinoza definitions will play an important role.

But to continue the exposition: after proving the existence of the
ego, Descartes carefully reminds himself that he has not proved the
existence of a human body. Indeed he began by doubting all sensory
experience, and if in the face of this doubt it still remains certain
that I exist, it is clear that this I is not or at least need not be a body.
There was no good evidence that sensation existed, for we might be
dreaming. The existence of the ego is based not on sensation but on
thinking. Of course, thinking includes what is often called sensation: thinking includes doubting, understanding, affirming, denying,
imagining and willing. Thought for Descartes includes all mental
phenomena and may be equated with what in later English was
called consciousness. To doubt is to be conscious; but although this
doubter may believe he has sense organs and sees the mountains and
the sky, the only proposition of which he can be certain at the start
is that he is a thinking thing. It may, and it does, turn out that
bodies and the human body exist; but the existence of thought or
of the soul is more certain than the existence of bodies.

Such is the pervasiveness of our old prejudices, such the force
of natural impulse, that we automatically believe that bodies can
be more clearly known than the soul. Of this error our minds
can be disabused by the examination of a commodity, sealing wax,
more commonly used in Descartes' day than at present. If the senses
could teach us what body is, we should surely be able to know what
wax is because it is perceived by all five senses. It is red — we see
it; since it is very fresh, it still has the odor of the flowers — we smell
it; and for the same reason it is still sweet with the honey of the

hive — we taste it; it is cold and hard — we touch it; and if we strike it against the table, it makes a distinct sound — we hear it. What greater amount of information could we desire about a body? But place this piece of wax near the fire. The taste exhales, the odor evaporates, the color changes, the shape is altered, the size increases, it becomes sticky or liquid, and when struck it emits no sound. All the original sensory qualities have been replaced by others. Is it the same piece of wax? If it was the senses that informed us about the wax, can it be the same wax? Now, not to break with common opinion, let us maintain that it is the same piece of wax; but then we did not learn of the wax by sensation. The wax was not the sweetness of the honey or of the flowers; it was not the red or the sound; it was nothing that I sensed. At most we can only say that the wax is a body which appears under some forms at one time and under quite different forms at other times. The only thing that remains the same under all this diversity is that the wax has extension. Not that it always has the same extension, for the wax is larger when hot. All the more is it impossible to identify the wax with shape, for it can take on an infinite variety of shapes. The conclusion is that we cannot see, smell, touch, or even imagine the wax. The perception of it was never an act of sensation, though such was our old belief, but it is an intuition of the mind — an intuition that may have been confused, but which can become clearer as we learn to know what extension is. We have therefore, a more original and clearer knowledge of the soul than of the body. I see the wax and may be mistaken; but I cannot be mistaken on the fact that I am a thinking being.

God and Mathematics

One might suppose that Descartes in view of his repudiation of sensory-based information would be out of sympathy with the lively development of science that was taking place all around him. Such is not the case. Descartes kept abreast of and took part in the scientific advances of his century, for he believed that experimentation could "suggest" many truths that logic might later prove. Then too, both because mathematics is the most powerful instrument which science needs and because it best exemplifies the rationalistic method, Descartes was sufficiently interested in it to invent analytic geometry. But before one can rely on mathematics, one must get rid of the omnipotent demon. It may be indubitably certain that I exist; but if two and three are really four, it would appear that I shall not be able to learn very much. Mathematics, therefore, must be based on a sound theology, for it is only by proving the existence of God, who of course is good and will not deceive, that the demon's spell over the mathematics can be broken.

That I think means that I have thoughts. I have ideas of sky and mountains, of demons and hippogryphs, and of God. Perhaps none of these exist in external reality; even if they did, the objects might not be at all similar to my ideas, but, regardless, I have these ideas. "Now, it is manifest by the natural light that there must be as much reality in the efficient and total cause as in its effect; for whence can the effect draw its reality if not from its cause? . . . And hence it follows, not only that what is cannot be produced by what is not, but likewise that the more perfect . . . cannot be the effect of the less perfect." And furthermore (note how medieval the argument has become) although one idea can cause another idea, this regress cannot be infinite; we must in the end reach a first idea, the cause of which is the archetype in which all the mental reality that is found in the idea is contained actually or objectively. In other words, no idea could occur unless there is a really existent object.

What object, then, can be the cause of my ideas? In the case of sky and mountains, i.e., in the case of all finite objects, there is no more mental reality than the soul itself possesses objectively. Therefore, I myself could be the sufficient cause for the idea of any finite being. It is not necessary to suppose that the sky exists any more than that a hippogryph exists. But can it be maintained that I am a sufficient cause for the idea of God? Descartes gives several reasons for denying that a finite reality can cause the idea of an infinite being. First of all, the idea of infinity is not an idea of negation. In this Descartes repudiates negative theology. We may apprehend darkness only as the absence of light, but we clearly perceive that there is more reality in an infinite substance than in a finite one. In fact, if there is a negative knowledge, it would be the knowledge of the finite, not of the infinite, for the finite is the limitation of the infinite rather than vice versa. For example (Descartes does not use this illustration at this point, but in the light of later developments it is apposite), in order to know what a cubic foot of space is, it is first necessary to know what space is of which this is a cubic foot. The knowledge of infinite space must precede the knowledge of a limited space. And although Descartes had made the *Cogito* the first truth of his system, here he seems to say that before we can know ourselves, we must first know God, at least "in some way I possess the notion of the infinite before that of the finite, that is, the perception of God before that of myself, for how could I know that I doubt, desire, or that something is wanting to me, and that I am not wholly perfect, if I possessed no idea of a being more perfect than myself, by comparison of which I knew the deficiencies of my nature" (Meditation III).

If an opponent should deny that a knowledge of God must precede the knowledge of self, it would be necessary for him to show that the idea of God can be constructed out of one's own powers. David Hume later made such an assertion, but he seems to have ignored the argument by which Descartes anticipated him. The construction of the idea of God would have to begin with the progress we have made from universal doubt and ignorance to the knowledge of our existence. We were ignorant; now we know something. On this basis, we may suppose that it is possible for us to learn some other truths also. Now, by projecting this increasing knowledge to infinity, we arrive at the idea of omniscience, and this may be equated with the idea of God. This construction fails, Descartes argues, because the idea of omniscience is not the idea of an ideal limit of our progress. The idea of omniscience is the idea of a perfect knowledge that was never preceded by ignorance or doubt, a knowledge that never came into being by learning, and a knowledge that will never increase. Obviously, therefore, the ego cannot be the cause of this idea, and we are forced to say that there is a being, actually omniscient, who is the cause. To this consideration Descartes adds that I am a dependent being, for otherwise I would have conferred all knowledge on myself; even if I should be an eternally existing being, I am still dependent, because a force which I do not have is required to preserve my being. To say that I depend for my being

upon my parents misses the point, for they do not preserve my
existence, nor can they preserve their own. There remains, therefore,
only the conclusion to which we have just come: God exists, and he
has so made me that I have an innate idea of him. Since God is
the being who possesses all perfections, he is not a demon; and,
therefore, mathematics is reliable.

It would be possible to dissect and discuss this argument at great
length. It contains the defect, previously mentioned, of depending
on natural light for the principle of causation. Then again, Hobbes,
a contemporary English philosopher, denied that we have an idea
of God on the ground that an idea is a picture. For Descartes an
idea is not a picture or image. And if these two points do not allow
for interminable discussion, there are no doubt others also. In order
to avoid all this, let us restrict our attention to the question whether
this argument for God's existence is consistent with the general
rationalistic procedure. Is the whole of it deduced by logic alone?
The answer is clearly negative, though most readers fail to find the
break, and when it is pointed out to them, they often dismiss it as
trivial. As is the case with so many arguments, the weak point is
the very start. Descartes had said, I have an idea of God. Un-
objectionable as this at first seems to be, it is a proposition that has
not been deduced by logic alone. No doubt, I think; but by what
argument do I deduce the further conclusion that I think God?
Common opinion would say that this does not need proof; I think
any ideas I think, and all that is necessary is to observe the various
ideas, mountains, hippogryphs, and God that pass through my mind.
This common opinion is so plausible that it may lead to the rejection
of the ideal of rationalism of proving everything by logic alone; but
in the history of philosophy it first led to discarding this argument, to
discarding the *Cogito*, and replacing it with the ontological argument as the basis of the system.

Not only did Spinoza follow this method explicitly, Descartes himself seemed to be dissatisfied with the causal argument. A second
time he asserts that God is the object we know best. And then he
works into the ontological argument. Since this has already been discussed at length and will reappear as Kant criticizes it, it need only
be mentioned that Descartes somewhat simplifies Anselm's pres-

entation; and it can be still further simplified into a single syllogism: God by definition is the being who possesses all attributes; existence is an attribute; therefore, God exists. Why this displaces the *Cogito* in Spinoza may be guessed, though it will be explained a little more fully a few pages below.

Error and Free Will

But whether this be the first truth or the second, the existence of God is necessary in order to prove the existence of a material world. And as study of the material world will lead to many truths, where the range of possible blunders will automatically increase, a preliminary statement relative to God's veracity and our errors must be made. For if God's goodness is the guarantee of mathematics, why should not his goodness extend to all subjects to such an extent that we should never make a mistake. Mere ignorance, the absence of knowledge, is not too hard to explain; there are many plausible reasons consistent with the goodness of God why we begin life in ignorance and must put forth effort to learn; and even with all the effort of which we are capable, the goodness of God does not require him to divulge information he prefers to keep for himself. In particular, God has not provided us with any method of discovering his purposes, at least in the field of science as distinguished from theology. No doubt a good God has a purpose in creating the world, and even in putting this tree right here and that mountain over there. The qualities of opium, fire, and everything else were given for a purpose; but no amount of study will enable us to discover it. For one thing, if we should try to find the purpose of this tree, or of the substance opium, we should be led to view it as contributing to the purpose of something else, and so on until we had connected our first object with the whole universe. In other words, a teleological explanation of one object could not be completed until the entire universe was thoroughly understood. Obviously this is not for us. Plato and Aristotle with their final causes had unwittingly subjected philosophy to an impossible infinite regress. And it was the teleological point of view that had made medieval science so sterile. Physics must be approached mathematically, that is, mechanically. We must remain ignorant of purposes.

However, error is not the same as ignorance; and while a good God might keep us in ignorance about some things, it is more difficult to see why he should allow us to believe falsehoods. Still, it is not too difficult. Note that God has given us an intellect; it is a finite intellect, but as man has no claim on God, he cannot complain that his intellect is not more ample. A world must have a great variety of things, and as dogs cannot complain that God did not make them elephants, so too man has no ground for demanding that God give him the gifts of angels. In addition to the intellect God has also given man a will; but whereas the intellect is finite, the will is so ample and perfect, so superior to all limits, that a greater is inconceivable; it is thus chiefly the will which constitutes man's similarity with God. God's will, of course, is greater than man's in respect of the knowledge and power that are conjoined with it; it is more efficacious and extends to a greater number of things; but per se or definitionally God's will and man's are the same, for the power of the will consists only in being able to do or not to do the same thing, i.e., to affirm or deny, to pursue or shun. These phrases seem to describe a will as free as Duns Scotus could have desired.

But Descartes immediately adds certain qualifications which Spinoza used toward another end. The freedom of the will, says Descartes, consists in the fact that when we pursue or shun a proposal, we are not conscious of being determined to the action by any external force. Aside from the question of whether unconsciousness of an external force proves there is none, there is the equally important question of the existence of internal forces. These latter Descartes admits. Freedom is not to be equated with the liberty of indifference, and we may be inclined to choose an action either by natural knowledge or by divine grace. But these internal determinants, far from diminishing our liberty, rather augment and fortify it. In another place (*Principia philosophiae,* 1, xli), however, he seems inconsistently to accept the liberty of indifference; but what the principles of rationalism logically demand will be made clear later. At the moment, the question is how God can be good and permit man to err.

The answer lies in the relation between the finite intellect and the infinite will. As we have no ground to complain about our finite intellect, so we have even less ground to complain that God has given us an infinite will. Yet because of this infinity the will is always outstripping the intellect. God in his goodness has given us sufficient equipment so that we need never be deceived. It is our fault, not his, if we rush ahead and give assent to propositions before they are logically demonstrated. We should resolutely refuse to judge of obscure matters, and if we keep our minds fixed on this warning and impress it deeply on our memories, we can acquire the habit of never making a mistake. But why do so many of us neglect Descartes' advice and foolishly refrain from developing such a valuable habit? Why do we assent to the obscure proposition that an extra slice of apple pie contains very few calories? Is it humanly possible to refrain from judging obscure matters?

The Material World

But does apple pie or the trees from which the apples came exist? Can the veracity of God guarantee the existence of a physical world? The argument begins with a concession. Imagination differs from cognition; we can conceive of a triangle or even of a chiliogon, and we can conceive of them with perfect clarity, being able to deduce from the conception a series of theorems. But we cannot imagine a chiliogon. If we should try to do so, the resulting picture would be so blurred that it would be indistinguishable from a myriogon or any other figure with many sides; and besides, the image would be of no use whatever for the discovery of any of their properties. Imagination, therefore, is no part of the essence of man; thinking can well be carried on, in fact better carried on without images. Imagination, therefore, must depend on something different from the mind, and because of this makes probable the existence of bodies. To the same end, it is noted that some images, particularly sensory perceptions, are involuntary. Since I cannot construct them, nor prevent their occurrence, there must be some cause of them outside myself; and this cause has to be either God or bodies. But if God should cause the perception of bodies, he could not avoid the charge of deception. Therefore, bodies must exist. Let it be insisted upon that this does not guarantee the accuracy of our perceptions. The bodies may be, and are, quite different from their appearance to us, for our sensations are confused; but God has given us sufficient equipment to avoid deception and arrive at the truth; the limitations of sense do not reflect on his goodness. Only if there were no bodies at all, could it be said that God had used deceit.

If, then, bodies are not as they appear, if the real physical world is not red, blue, bitter, wet, sweet, and so on, what is the nature of body, the nature of that wax whose qualities were altered? It must be something that can be clearly and distinctly apprehended, and the illustration of the wax anticipated the answer. "The nature of body consists not in weight, hardness, color, and the like, but in extension alone" (*Principia*, II, iv). "The same extension in length, breadth, and depth, which constitutes space, constitutes body" (*ibid.*, x). Thus Descartes' conclusion that matter is space seems to recall Plato. But the motives and the results of the two philosophers are not the same. Plato had chosen space to be the receptacle of Ideas; Descartes identifies matter as space because geometry can be deduced by logic alone. Geometry is the science of space; therefore, geometry is the science of physics. Or, more accurately, the study of physics is mechanics. In view of Galileo's *Two New Sciences*, in which he made such remarkable deductions, the distinction between geometry and mechanics could easily be minimized, and the rationalistic program of deducing all science by logic alone was not so implausible in the seventeenth century as it may seem in the twentieth.

The first and most universal law of nature is that the quantity of motion is a constant. Since space is matter, there is no empty space; bodies are everywhere. If one body begins to move more quickly, another must slow down; there is no way to increase or to decrease the amount of motion in the universe. This fundamental law of physics is presumably deduced by logic alone from the nature of God. God, being good, wants the world to be as much like himself as a world can be. Obviously a world cannot be a world and also have the same simplicity and immutability that God has. A world must exhibit motion. But the immutability of God can be imitated in the world by assigning it a constant quantity of motion. There must be change to make it a world, but a good world will have, and therefore this world does have an immutable amount of change.

From this point on the pretense of deducing the laws of nature by logic alone grows thin. What is worse, there are points at which not even a pretense remains. Descartes was interested in all science, from astronomy to medicine. He attempted a derivation of the solar system by means of a vortex theory. The details must be omitted, but it is clear that if God had set up vortices of other magnitudes, a world different from ours could have resulted. It is also true that the present world could have resulted from an arrangement different from that which Descartes describes. And even if the fundamental law of physics comes inexorably from being of God, the subsidiary laws of motion do not follow with the same rigor. As it is, every particular event within Descartes' system of mechanics follows the preceding event necessarily; but the system itself is not necessary. It depends on God's choice. This is an irrationalism which will demand a Spinoza.

Soul and Body

But even in the physical system itself, Descartes admits an exception to the law that every event follows its predecessor by mechanical necessity. Note where the argument has led. The characteristics of bodies are size and shape, the modes of extension; and laws of physical nature are the laws of motion. But before we even came to know that matter existed, we knew that mind existed. The characteristic of mind is thought, not motion or extension. Thus the world consists of two types of substance, the one thinking but unextended, the other extended but unthinking. However, since they are both parts of the same world, and especially since in human beings they are intimately connected, the relation between these two substances must be examined. Can a mental event, an act of will, produce a result in bodily motion? Can the mind produce a motion that violates the laws of mechanics?

It is clear that Descartes had a high regard for mechanical law. Not only did he explain levers, pulleys, the motions of stones and planets mechanically, he also viewed animals as machines. Acquainted both with ingenious toys that could go through their tricks when the proper button was pushed, and with the still more marvellous system of nerves, muscles, and veins which he discovered in his dissections, he was convinced that animal mechanisms were intricate enough to explain the behavior of a dog, cat, or horse. Stick a pin into a dog, and it howls; just as striking a drum head with a stick makes a note. If Descartes could have known the electric eyes that open doors for us, he would have been the more convinced that when a dog sees us and comes, the action is entirely mechanical. There is no thought, consciousness, idea, or feeling in animals. They are literally machines.

But man is different. That man thinks is more certain than that bodies exist. It is human conduct that must be related to mechanical motion. First of all there is the question of the location of the soul in the body. If thought, feeling, and volition are connected with the motions of the human body, the soul must surely be somewhere in the body. But how can an unextended entity like the soul be in a place? Geometry provides an easy answer for this question. An unextended element in geometry is a point, and although a point does not occupy space, it has a location. Hence there is nothing irrational in saying that an unextended soul can be inside the body. But where? It is plausible, even if not demonstrable by logic alone, that the soul would be at the focus of the nervous system. In dissecting the brain, Descartes observed that it consisted of two hemispheres and that its parts came in pairs. The pineal gland, however, was an exception. This part was single, situated between the two hemispheres directly above the duct through which the animal spirits must pass from the anterior to the posterior of the brain, or vice versa. The slightest motion of this gland can alter very greatly the path of these spirits, and conversely the most minute change in the flow of the spirits can greatly affect the gland. For Descartes animal spirits were subtle fluids coursing through the nerves and controlling the muscles. Left to itself, the human body, like that of an animal, would function mechanically; and with but one exception, it does function mechanically. The muscles and bones are like so many levers and pulleys; the animal spirits are a sort of hydraulic system. But in the pineal gland the soul is able to exert a force by which it changes the direction of the flow and so controls the body. In conformity with the fundamental law of physics, the soul is denied the power to increase or decrease the amount of motion, but it can alter the direction. To put it a little crudely, and yet rather accurately at that: if an atom bumps into the surface of the pineal gland when the soul is not interested in moving the body, it will, like a billiard ball, bounce off the cushion at the same angle with which it hit it; but on desire the soul can put some English on the atom so that although it hits the surface of the gland at an angle of thirty degrees, it bounces off at an angle of fifty-one. This explains why with the feeling of disgust our hand shuts the philosophy book and lays it on the desk.

Or perhaps we will otherwise. It is hard to conceive of an immaterial point's altering the laws of mechanics. It is hard to conceive that mechanical law can be altered. If a ball does not bounce at the right angle, there simply must be some physical factor to account for the alteration. It must have been the cue and not the soul that put on the English. And yet who can deny that the sequence of thoughts and feelings are indissolubly tied in with the series of physical motions? Descartes has already made a mistake or two in working out rationalism; perhaps this is another one. And yet, mistake and all, he is to be credited with seeing a problem that had never occurred to the medieval thinkers, because they had not had the same view of mechanism. Its roots must be sought, if at all, in ancient Greece, where the antithesis of mechanism and teleology was first encountered. Accordingly, instead of laying the book down in disgust, a curious mind might will to read on and see whether Spinoza handles this problem more satisfactorily and more in accord with rationalistic principles.

SPINOZA (1632—1677)

To a large extent Spinoza agreed with Descartes. Mathematics, mechanism, and rationalism were common watchwords. Then too, many of the phrases in Descartes' *Principia* are also found in Spinoza, but with a difference. The difference is in the direction of a stricter rationalism, and therefore Spinoza will here be portrayed as one who "corrected the mistakes" of Descartes. This portrayal may do neither man full justice, but justice is never done in a history of philosophy.

Definition and Existence

In the first place, as was stated above, Spinoza discards the *Cogito* and builds on the ontological argument. There is a very good reason for this, which must be understood if the main thrust of rationalism is to be grasped. It is not that "I think" cannot be proved by logic alone; it is more closely connected with the difficulty of proving that I exist; but the point can be more accurately stated as having to do with the existence of something, not necessarily of myself. The rationalistic method has been pictured as demonstration. When Descartes added a word about intuition, he either became confusing or he gave an example instead of a definition. Now, in geometry there are definitions and axioms, and then demonstrations give the theorems. So, too, Spinoza, who characteristically entitled his main work, *Ethica ordine geometrico demonstrata*, began with definitions and axioms and worked out a series of theorems. But it would seem — and because of developments in geometry since the time of Spinoza it now all the more seems — that some other philosopher could choose a different set of axioms and deduce a different set of theorems. In the case of competing philosophies, therefore, how can one distinguish the true philosophy, the philosophy which describes the real world, from a philosophy that is merely a *tour de force*, a consistent system no doubt, but one which applies to nothing at all? Rationalism cannot here appeal to sensation. We cannot look and see if there are things which correspond to the definitions. Therefore it is absolutely essential that rationalism depend on a definition, or a set of definitions, that prove the existence of the thing defined. The definition of a triangle, of a tree, as well as of a snark, does not guarantee the existence of the object; but unless existence and essence coincide somewhere, unless the *that* and the *what* are identical in at least one object, there is no hope of passing from definitions to a real, existing world. And in all the history of philosophy, only one object has ever been thought to satisfy this specification. Therefore, the ontological argument is essential and basic to rationalism.

Whereas Descartes had simplified Anselm's argument, Spinoza sees fit to complicate it. The conclusion that God necessarily exists takes the form of the eleventh theorem deduced from a set of definitions and axioms. By summarizing somewhat and working backwards, the argument can be stated as follows: God necessarily exists, that is, his essence involves his existence, because substance cannot be produced by anything external — it must be its own cause; substance must be its own cause because there is nothing beside substance and attribute, and one substance cannot produce another substance; this is true because there cannot be two substances with an identical attribute, since an attribute by definition constitutes the essence of substance; further, things which have nothing in common cannot be one the cause of the other, for if they have nothing in common, one cannot be apprehended by means of the other; and this last is clear from Axiom V which states that things which have nothing in common cannot be understood, the one by means of the other — the conception of one does not involve the conception of the other. And for the rest, any loose ends in this summary depend on the other definitions and axioms.

There are eight definitions and seven axioms for Part 1 of the *Ethics*. A few are given here as samples.

1. By that which is self-caused, I mean that of which the essence involves existence, or that of which the nature is only conceivable as existent.

3. By substance I mean that which is in itself, and is conceived through itself; in other words that of which a conception can be formed independently of any other conception.

7. That thing is called free, which exists solely by the necessity of its own nature, and of which the action is determined by itself alone.

These definitions and axioms, although they appear on the first page of Spinoza's book, must have been nearly the last formulations he settled upon. In consonance with a deductive system, all the theorems are implicitly contained in the beginning. Inasmuch as this start replaces Descartes' *Cogito*, immediate attention should be directed to the process whereby Spinoza derives the world from God. Descartes had claimed to derive the existence of bodies from the veracity of God; the fundamental law of physics followed plausibly from God's immutability; but the number of planets, the precise acceleration of gravity, and in general, the particularities of the world depended on the choices of positions and velocities that God made when he created things. From a rationalistic viewpoint, however, a divine choice that could have been otherwise is caprice; there is no necessary connection between the nature of God and the positions and velocities in question; there is no logic or mathematics involved.

The Best of All Possible Worlds

Then there is also another consideration which has not as yet been mentioned. Descartes had assumed that the goodness of God led him to impose a constant quantity of motion on the world; and it may in general be taken for granted that the world is a good world. But this does not quite answer the question whether God could have created a better world; for example, is a solar system with ten planets better than one with five? On this point and its explanations Descartes, Spinoza, and Leibniz disagreed. On Leibniz' showing, God was acquainted with an infinite number of plans for worlds. It was as if God looked over a great mass of blueprints. Some of these plans were relatively poor, some were very good, and there was one that was best of all. It was in fact so good that it could in no way be improved upon. Since God is good, his choice of a world would naturally be motivated by what is excellent; and hence he chose to create this best of all possible worlds. This is the theme which Voltaire with broad burlesque rather than keen wit ridiculed in his *Candide*. Little brilliance is required to write a story in which the hero undergoes the most extraordinary misfortunes, each of which is explained as a blessing in disguise in this best of all possible worlds. As a piece of satire *Candide* can be judged by each reader according to his literary taste; as a rational argument against Leibniz its superficiality contrasts with the penetrating analysis of Spinoza. To portray God as choosing a plan which in itself is better than all others, Spinoza argues, implies that there is a principle of goodness external and superior to God. In such a scheme the goodness of the blueprint does not depend on God, but God's choice depends on the goodness of the blueprint. Leibniz has in effect set up a Platonic Idea of Good and has reduced God to the inferior status of a Demiurge.

Not so for Descartes. The world is no doubt good, but instead of God's choosing the world because it is good, the world is good because God chose it. Caprice or not, it is God's will, somewhat as in Duns Scotus and Occam, that determines what goodness is; and if God had chosen a different world, a world with fewer planets and more mosquitoes, it would have been good. This view at least maintains the supremacy of God. Voltaire might have ridiculed it as much as he ridiculed Leibniz' view, with even less reason; but Spinoza confesses that the theory which subjects all things to the will of an indifferent deity and asserts that they are all dependent on his fiat is less far from the truth than the theory of those who maintain that God acts in all things with a view of promoting what is good. But neither view satisfies him, and he wishes to show what rationalism requires.

Common to Descartes and Leibniz is the failure to remain consistent with the rationalistic concept of causality. All three philosophers say that God is the cause of the world; but the other two represent this causality as a choice. A reversion to teleology, whether Greek or Christian, this representation is inconsistent with mathematics and logic. If all truths are to be deduced by logic alone from the being of God, this world cannot be the best of all possible worlds because there are no other possible worlds. Are the theorems of geometry the best of all possible theorems? The question is meaningless, for there are no other theorems. God therefore exercised no choice in causing the world; he is its cause in precisely the same sense in which the axioms of geometry are the cause of the theorems.

Rational Causality

This is what underlies one of the steps in the ontological argument that may have seemed more obscure than some of the others. Proposition III is: Things which have nothing in common cannot be one the cause of the other. To the unphilosophical this is puzzling. A hammer struck against steel causes a noise; what do the hammer and the noise have in common? The poisons sodium and chlorine cause nonpoisonous table salt. The sun causes the grass to grow. What can be meant by the statement that things which have nothing in common cannot be one the cause of the other? The proof that Spinoza offers for this proposition is this: If they have nothing in common, it follows that one cannot be apprehended by means of the other, because Axiom V states that things which have nothing in common cannot be understood the one by means of the other; the conception of the one does not involve the conception of the other. Therefore the one cannot be the cause of the other because Axiom IV states that the knowledge of an effect depends on and involves the knowledge of a cause.

The initial perplexity upon reading this early theorem of Spinoza's system results from preoccupation with efficient causes. When logical causation is considered, these axioms, propositions, and proofs become clear. As was pointed out in the exposition of Descartes' criteria of clarity and distinctness, nothing can be clearer than the necessary connection between premises and conclusion. Explanation consists in giving a reason. If it be asked why something is true, the answer is that the premises require it. Understanding comes only through reasons which show, not just that a thing is so, but that it must be so. The premises are the cause.

Consistent rationalism therefore cannot admit that any other world is possible. This is the only world because it is necessary, and it is necessary because of the nature of God. Since God is perfect, he causes a perfect world. A different world would presuppose a different God, an imperfect God, which of course is logically absurd. The reason people think other worlds are possible is that they assign to God a type of freedom inconsistent with Definition VII: That thing is called free which exists solely by the necessity of its own nature, and of which the action is determined by itself alone. Instead of this freedom, those who believe other worlds are possible assign to God an absolute free will. Yet these people admit that each thing is what it is because of the decree of God, for otherwise God would not be the cause of all things; they also admit that the decrees of God are eternal, for otherwise God would be mutable. And as further there are no temporal distinctions in eternity, it follows that a different set of divine decrees is an impossibility. It is also admitted on all hands that God's intellect is entirely actual: there is nothing potential, undeveloped, or imperfect in God. Since then God's intellect, will, and essence are identical, it follows that if his will or intellect were different, his essence would be different too. But to suppose that God's essence could be different from what it is; to suppose, that is, that God could be other than God, is obviously absurd.

To speak more accurately, neither intellect nor will belongs to God's nature. Those who accept the common view face an insuperable objection. Although they conceive of God as supremely intelligent, they deny that he can create everything he understands; for if God created everything that is in his intellect, he could create nothing more, and in this case he would not be omnipotent. Spinoza, on the contrary, holds that God's infinite nature never ceases to imply an infinite number of theorems, and that thus God's omnipotence is constantly displayed. The oddity of denying that God can create everything he understands depends on attributing to God an intellect and a will as these terms are ordinarily meant. However, if God has an intellect and will they are as far apart as the poles from human intellect and will. Between them there would be nothing in common but the name; there would be about as much correspondence between the two as there is between the Dog, the heavenly constellation, and a dog, an animal that barks. Consider: the divine intellect could not be, as ours must be, posterior to the things understood, for God is prior to all things by reason of his causality. And God is the cause, not only of the existence of things, but of their essence as well. Man is one of the things. Since therefore that which is the cause of existence and of essence must differ from its effects both in essence and in existence, it follows that the essence or definition of a divine intellect or will must differ from the essence or definition of a human intellect or will. But if the definitions differ, the two objects have nothing in common but the name.

One Substance

The nature of God and the implications of the ontological argument require further exposition. In the *Principia* (Part I, li) Descartes had written: "By substance we can conceive nothing else than a thing which exists in such a way as to stand in need of nothing beyond itself in order to its existence. And in truth there can be conceived but one substance which is absolutely independent, and that is God. . . . And accordingly the term *substance* does not apply to God and the creatures univocally." To simplify this, Spinoza denies that there are any finite substances. A finite substance would be one limited by some other substance; but if both are substances they would have to have an attribute in common, and this was previously proved impossible. Accordingly there is only one substance, the infinite God. Since now the ontological argument defines God as the being who possesses all attributes, God must be conceived as an extended as well as a thinking substance. Individual things are nothing but modifications of the attributes of God, or modes by which the attributes of God are expressed in a fixed and determinate manner. Body is one such mode. It should not be said that God is a body, for a body has a definite quantity, a given size and shape. But God is infinitely extended and altogether indivisible. It is not less absurd to assert that extended substance is made up of bodies or parts than it would be to say that a surface is made up of lines, or a line of points. If substance could be so divided that its parts were really separate, why could not one part be destroyed while the others remained joined as before? But this would create a vacuum, and a vacuum cannot exist in nature. The reason people commonly divide substance into parts is that they depend on imagination. But if instead of imagining quantities, we conceive extension intellectually, it will clearly appear one and indivisible. Matter is everywhere the same and its parts are indistinguishable. The distinctions we imagine are modal, not substantial. For example, water as water is divisible, its parts can be separated, it can be produced and destroyed; but in so far as it is extended substance it is neither divisible, producible, nor destructible. The parts of space are indistinguishable. Thus God is an extended being as well as a thinking being.

Criticism at this point is difficult. Either it must be so specific as to become highly technical or so general as to attack all points at once. One example of the former would be an examination of the validity of Spinoza's syllogisms. Are his theorems deduced with Euclidean rigor? Some critics give the impression that this type of analysis is a little unfair; yet what test could be more appropriate for a philosophy which claims to base all truth on logic alone? It would be unfair only if the fallacies discovered were trivial, leaving the system largely undamaged. But this would have to be shown in detail. Undoubtedly such an examination would be tedious, and for this reason it will, as is customary, be omitted. Another example of a highly technical criticism is that directed against the distinction between attributes and modes. Attributes constitute the essence of substance, and extension and thought are attributes of God. Modes are modifications of substance, or more specifically modes are referred to attributes (II, vi), and love and desire are modes of thought. Individual things are modes. Are singular events, such as the discovery of America, modes also? And what are the particular laws of physics, such as the equality of the angles of incidence and reflection? This raises a question that could stand lengthy criticism, viz., is the relation between an axiom or theorem and the system of which it is a part the same as the relation between a substance and an attribute or mode? How this apparently technical difficulty underlies many of the larger questions will soon be seen.

The more general criticisms attack all points at once and therefore run the risk of being repetitious; but even so, they can be defended pedagogically as a way of turning over the matter for better understanding. Not the most unmanageable subject relates to the necessity of all the definitions and axioms. Even if the ontological argument, assumed to be valid, justifies the premises on which it is based because it demonstrates the existence of its object, Spinoza adds other axioms that do not have this *raison d'être*. For example, the law of physics that the angles of incidence and reflection are equal is given as one of the axioms in Part II. Would Kepler's three laws of planetary motion also be axioms? A scientist might possibly be willing to forgive the rationalistic rejection of experiment, or at least regard it worth a try, if the laws of physics were ostensibly deduced from plausible axioms; but to assume as axiomatic the particular laws themselves leaves inexplicable the choice of these laws rather than others. Why not assume that the angle of reflection is twice that of incidence?

No doubt the most unmanageable and therefore the most interesting issue is that of Spinoza's pantheism. He has defined God as a being absolutely infinite: "I say absolutely infinite; not infinite after its kind; for of a thing infinite only after its kind, infinite attributes may be denied; but that which is absolutely infinite contains in its essence whatever expresses reality and involves no negation." For this reason Spinoza concludes that God must have the attribute of extension.

For this reason also it is incorrect to say that the God revealed in the Bible is absolutely infinite. Therefore critics of Christianity sometimes charge that the Bible presents a finite God, while orthodox theologians vehemently deny the charge. The confusion arises from the two types of infinity. Aside from the persistent question of what attributes are and what are attributes, Christianity clearly denies to God the attribute of space or materiality as well as the attributes of sensitivity, stupidity, and evil, if these be attributes. The God of Spinoza's ancestors is infinite in power, wisdom, and justice, or, if Spinoza's terms must be used, he is infinite after his kind. More particularly the God of the Bible is personal. To some thinkers personality is a limitation which makes this God finite. Admittedly Christianity teaches that God is definite and would argue that any being devoid of all limitations in the sense of definite attributes would be the unknowable nothing of negative theology.

Now, Spinoza, far from denying that God has attributes, asserts that God has an infinite number of attributes. Yet one may wonder whether Spinoza's substance with all its attributes is not after all much the same as an unknowable nothing. For two reasons. In the first place the two known attributes of God seem to be so incompatible that they could not both attach to any conceivable substance. The reason Descartes had admitted two created substances was that thought and extension are so disparate that they are mutually exclusive. A universe exhibiting diversity may contain some extended things or modes and some thinking things; but the more the unity of substance is stressed, the less we can conceive of the same thing being both extended and conscious. A body can be heavy and can fall with an acceleration of thirty-two feet per second per second, but a thought cannot. A thought can be witty and one thought can imply another, but bodies have no such potentiality. When these disparate attributes are said to inhere in the same substance, substance comes close to being an empty name.

Then in the second place Spinoza mystifies us by claiming that of the infinite number of divine attributes only these (incompatible)

two can be known. Would this justify the criticism that what may
be known of God is equal in amount to the fraction two over infinity? If it is useless to speculate about the unknowable, Spinoza's
pantheism can be considered from the standpoint of the known attributes of personality and justice which he refuses to ascribe to his
God. It is fair to say that Spinoza does not count such attributes as
among the unknown, but definitely denies them to God. Personality
may be a mode of God's attribute of thought in so far as there are
human beings in the world, and justice in so far as some of these
persons are just; but as God was not a body, so too he is not a person. The God of Spinoza is the world itself. One of his favorite
phrases is *Deus sive natura*, God or nature. In English, the word *or*
is ambiguous, for we may say "red or blue," meaning that they are
mutually exclusive, and we may say "even or divisible by two"
meaning the same thing. Ordinarily in Latin the first *or* is *aut*; the
second is *sive*. God or nature means that God is nature. In I xiv
Spinoza says, "Besides God no substance can be granted or conceived," and then in the proof of I xv he adds, "but substances and
modes form the sum total of existence."

At this point the criticism becomes more intricate than ever. Two
courses are open. First the matter may be viewed from the standpoint
of the ontological argument. This argument was supposed to prove
the existence of God. Now, suppose that the term substance is restricted to God on the ground that it denotes absolute independence
and can therefore never be applied to things. Let it also be granted
that God or substance has many attributes and modes. Still this does
not seem to demand the definition that body is a mode of God's
existence (Part II, Def. 1); therefore it does not prove that bodies
exist. That is, Spinoza has not proved the existence of the type of
body he desires, nor conversely has he disproved the existence of a
type of body — a body which is neither a Spinozistic substance nor a
Spinozistic mode — he does not desire. In other words, one may
wonder whether Spinoza has shown any absurdity in the conception
of God's creating things which, although they are not independent of
him, and cannot be conceived without him, are yet not modes of his
essence. Does Spinoza avoid a serious argument by combining and
confusing two dissimilar ideas in his definition of mode?

Or in the second place, we may view the matter, not from the standpoint of the ontological argument traditionally conceived, but from the standpoint of nature. Supposedly we have proved the existence of God, but now it appears that we have proved only the existence of the world, for Spinoza's God is nature. Acknowledging that rationalism must demonstrate the existence of the world, for it cannot rely on sensation, one asks what necessity there is for considering it as one substance. Presumably a universe must have some kind of unity, but why should it be the unity of a substance and its attributes? And why cannot there be, as Anselm and Descartes said there must be, a transcendent God independent of this universe? But these questions return us to the rationalistic conception of causality. Theological connotations and voluntary choices are regarded as irrational; the world to be rational therefore must be a closed system of implications; and thus Spinoza's theory follows.

Mechanism and Thought

However there is a further complication. It has been sufficiently emphasized that Spinoza rejected the teleological conception of efficient causation in favor of the logical relationship between premise and conclusion, which is then identified with the relation of substance to attribute and mode. At the same time, as the reference to the law of equal angles shows, Spinoza also wanted to maintain a mechanical causation. Different as those two types of cause appear to be, Spinoza thought himself justified in merging them, or, better, he saw no difference between them because he had already assimilated mechanics to geometry. Now, to put criticism aside, the most interesting aspect of Spinoza's mechanism is its greater consistency over the theory of Descartes.

Descartes had been willing to maintain mechanism except in the case of interference by a human mind or soul. Upon the act of volition the laws of physics break down at the pineal gland. If however the laws of physics can be deduced by logic alone, as Spinoza thought, it follows that a violation of them is unthinkable. The human body as well as the body of an animal must be a machine. "A body in motion or at rest must be determined to motion or rest by another body . . . and so on to infinity" (II xiii, Lemma 3); and "Body cannot determine mind to think, neither can mind determine body to motion or rest" (III ii). For Spinoza as well as for Descartes thought and extension are mutually exclusive, but for Spinoza the incompatibility is logical, not adjectival: that is, although thought and extension are attributes of the same substance, a thought cannot cause or imply a motion and a motion cannot imply or cause a thought. What then is the relation between the mind and the body, between physics and psychology, between God as an extended being and God as a thinking being?

If all the previous criticisms are dropped from view, the first formulation of the answer to this question is not hard to understand. Body is an attribute with an appropriate set of axioms. These imply a series of theorems which by obvious necessity are theorems of extension. Since the axioms contain no statement concerning ideas or thoughts, neither can the theorems. Similarly thought is an attribute of God, and it too has a set of appropriate axioms which imply a series of theorems among which no statement concerning motion can be found. Since logical implication is causation, obviously no thought can cause a motion and no motion can cause a thought. But since thought and extension are both attributes of the same substance, the two sets of theorems describe the same object and form as it were parallel columns.

To quote from the note that follows *Ethics* III ii: "Mind and body are one and the same thing, conceived first under the attribute of thought, secondly under the attribute of extension. Thus it follows that the order of concatenation of things is identical, whether nature be conceived under the one attribute or the other; consequently the order of states of activity and passivity in our body is simultaneous in nature with the order of states of activity and passivity in the mind. Nevertheless . . . I can scarcely believe . . . that men can be induced to consider the question calmly and fairly, so firmly do they conceive that it is merely at the bidding of the mind that the body is set in motion or at rest, or performs a variety of actions depending solely on the mind's will or the exercise of thought. However, no one has hitherto laid down the limits to the powers of the body . . . no one hitherto has gained such an accurate knowledge of the bodily mechanism, that he can explain all its functions; . . . the fact that many actions are observed in the lower animals, which far transcend human sagacity, and that somnambulists do many things in their sleep, which they would not venture to do when awake . . . are enough to show that the body can by the sole laws of its nature do many things which the mind wonders at."

Thus our ignorance of the powers of the body rules out volition as a cause of our actions. At the same time, strangely, our ignorance of the powers of the mind leaves us no ground for supposing that volition produces action. It may be true that the body remains inert unless the mind is in a fit state to think; but it is equally true, says Spinoza, that the mind remains inert unless the body is in a fit state to act. Consider sleep and anaesthesia. If it be objected that by volition we speak or keep silence, Spinoza replies somewhat irrelevantly, "The world would be much happier, if men were as fully able to keep silence as they are to speak. Experience abundantly shows that men can govern anything more easily than their tongues, and restrain anything more easily than their appetites."

But there is more. Descartes had other followers besides Spinoza who were exercised by the relation of soul to body. Malebranche and Geulincx agreed that extension and thought were too dissimilar to attribute to one substance; but if so, extension and thought are too dissimilar to interact. Their solution, which is called Occasionalism, is that the two substances act according to their own laws, neither affecting the other, and yet so adjusted by the Creator that when the will acts the body moves and when the body is injured a pain occurs. The one event is the occasion but not the cause of the other. It is tempting to suppose that Spinoza merely dropped the idea of a Creator, spoke of two attributes instead of two substances, and kept the parallelism or occasionalism; but this interpretation is too simple and easy to do justice to all that Spinoza wrote. The Occasionalists were concerned with the relation between the human mind and the human body, or at most included in their purview the consciousness of animals, if animals are conscious. Of course, Spinoza was also interested in this, but his thought went beyond these limits. Naturally he did not believe that his substance was a mere name: he took the unity of substance very seriously. "Substance thinking and substance extended are one and the same substance, comprehended now through one attribute, now through the other. So also a mode of extension and the idea of that mode [the body and the mind] are one and the same thing, though expressed in two ways . . . so that, so long as we consider things as modes of thinking, we must explain the order of the whole of nature, or the whole chain of causes, through the attribute of thought only. And insofar as we consider things as modes of extension, we must explain the order of the whole of nature through the attribute of extension only" (II vii, note).

These words seem to indicate not merely that the human mind and the human body are the same thing, but that the whole of nature is both extended and thinking. More specifically Spinoza says, "The propositions we have advanced hitherto have been entirely general, applying not more to men than to other individual things, all of which, though in different degrees, are animated" (II xiii, note). Although his definition of the term *idea* as a mental conception which is formed by the mind as a thinking thing may sound Cartesian, as if the mind as a substance produced the idea as an act, Spinoza later speaks of the idea as constituting the mind. The idea is the mind. And in the case of the human being, the idea which constitutes the mind is the idea of the human body and nothing else. Now, as there is an idea of the human body, so there is an idea of every body; and if we do not call these other ideas minds, the only reason is they exhibit a lesser degree of perfection.

Is this a theory of panpsychism? If panpsychism means, as with Leibniz, that minds are the fundamental realities, Spinoza is not a panpsychist even though he says all things are animate. Is this theory on the contrary a form of behaviorism? It could be made to look so by taking the term *idea* to mean a truth or a proposition. The various theorems are truths about the one substance. Some of them are expressed in one language, the language of thought which we may call Greek; and others are expressed in the language of extension which we may call Latin. But both sets of truths say the same thing; that is, they are describing the same reality, and the one language can be easily translated into the other. This analogy of two languages is not a bad one, but Spinoza would have doubtless denied that the theory is behavioristic. Behaviorism would hold that Latin alone makes sense, and that Greek does not exist. Spinoza on the contrary put extension and thought on the same level as attributes of God, substance, or nature. Therefore he should not be called a behaviorist nor a panpsychist; since clearly he is not an interactionist, the difficulties remain the fundamental ones previously mentioned; chiefly, whether substance is a name without meaning.

Ethics and Freedom

The title of Spinoza's book is *Ethica ordine geometrico demonstrata*. The *demonstrata* has been well exemplified, but the reader may wonder about the ethics. In a system of pure logic, in an order of inevitable modes, in a nature that has no purpose, can ethics have any place? Common opinion connects ethics with free will, therefore with indeterminism, and less explicitly with teleology.

Although Spinoza denied that nature has a purpose, he was willing to admit that there are purposes in nature. Those particular modes of the attribute of thought, called human beings, have purposes, and the problem of ethics can be viewed as the avoidance of frustration. But can frustration and defeat be avoided if there is no freedom? Well, of course there is freedom. In the first place, God is free, for by Part I, Def. 7, "that thing is called free, which exists solely by the necessity of its own nature, and of which the action is determined by itself alone; on the other hand, that thing is necessary or rather constrained which is determined by something external to itself to a fixed and definite method of existence or action." But this can have little to do with ethics because obviously not man but God alone can enjoy this freedom. It is also clear that man cannot enjoy free will, for if everything is determined by logic alone by the process of deduction from original definitions and axioms, it follows that everything is logically necessitated, and the actions of an individual man can no more be otherwise than the theorems that follow the definition of a triangle. Logic guarantees inevitability.

The exponents of free will often assert that they are intimately conscious of their freedom and that nothing could be more certain. Sensation may deceive them, but their sense of freedom cannot. Although this is an appeal to experience and is therefore outside the pale of rationalism, Spinoza takes the trouble to show that this consciousness of freedom does not imply free will. Suppose little Tommy, age two, has missed his afternoon nap. About four o'clock he becomes very fussy and stamps his foot and wants what he wants when he wants it. The dear little angel thinks he is free, he is conscious that he can stamp his foot, and he knows what he wants at each successive instant. But a wise parent knows that far from being free he is not his sweet little self because the poisons of fatigue are controlling his actions and his desires. And a wise man knows that there are causes which control the desires of adults as well as of small children. And a wiser man knows that his own actions are controlled. "I assume . . . that all men are born ignorant of the causes of things, that all have the desire to seek for what is useful to them, and that they are conscious of such desire. Herefrom it follows first that men think themselves free, inasmuch as they are conscious of their volitions and desires, and never even dream, in their ignorance, of the causes which have disposed them to wish and desire" (Part I, Appendix). Thus what is called the consciousness of freedom is nothing but the unconsciousness of causation. Only an omniscient mind could know it was free, for so long as any ignorance remains, it is possible that within the sphere of that ignorance a cause of the desire might be hidden.

Yet, though neither God nor man has free will, and though only God can be free, Spinoza entitles one section of the Ethics, *Of Human Freedom*. If with all the mechanism of bodily motion and all the necessitarianism of logic it seems that man can have neither purposes nor freedom of any kind, Spinoza's meaning may be indicated by an illustration. At the seashore, if one sits out a little way on a pier, one can observe the waves moving in toward the shore. But when a piece of wood is thrown out a distance, instead of being brought in to the shore by the waves, it simply rises and falls. Then one can see that although the waves move to the shore, the water itself does not: it moves up and down. In the physics laboratories of many colleges also there is a demonstration piece that shows how a horizontal wave motion can be produced by particles that move only vertically. Thus we may picture an ocean of mechanism with its waves of purpose and freedom. For there is a sense in which Spinoza's system permits of freedom. The common view of freedom is that the will is uncaused or inexplicable and therefore that it has equal ability to choose either of two mutually exclusive actions under the same conditions. For Spinoza freedom is not the ability to choose different actions under the same conditions, but the ability to choose the same action under varying conditions. For example, if you toss a grain of wheat out the window, it may fall into some good, loose earth, where it will have the freedom to grow. No doubt this is not much freedom, for had the grain of wheat landed on the sidewalk, it would not have had the freedom to grow; a bird would soon have eaten it. Unlike the grain of wheat, the bird may alight on the sidewalk, and when there is no wheat there, it can fly off to find food elsewhere. The bird is freer than the grain of wheat because it can live under a greater variety of conditions. Similarly a man is freer than a bird. Under conditions of drought or in great storms, which would destroy the bird, a man with knowledge can survive. And if numbers of men cooperate in the conquest of nature, the range of freedom is greatly extended. Ignorance is bondage, but knowledge makes a man his own master.

But what about death? Since self-preservation is the basic virtue, and since Spinoza died of tuberculosis at an early age, is not defeat as inevitable as anything else and is not frustration our common end? In the answer to this question lies the core of Spinoza's philosophy and the motivation of the title *Ethics*. Here is to be found the value of deducing all truth by logic alone. In a preliminary way, requiring further elucidation, it may be said that things in themselves are neither good nor bad; for instance, "music is good for him who is melancholy, bad for him who mourns, and for him who is deaf, it is neither good nor bad" (IV Preface). The goodness of anything relates to its usefulness to us; and "we know nothing to be certainly good . . . save such things as really conduce to understanding" (IV xxvii). Hence if a man can come to know things as they really are, deducing them from the nature of God, he will no longer regard them as evil, horrible, unjust, or base (IV lxxiii, note). This principle must apply to death as well as to other things, but some of the lesser events may well be explained first.

Frustration results from wanting what cannot be had. A baby in its crib will reach for the moon and cry when it cannot play with the pretty sphere; an unprepared student may wish that the facts of history or chemistry were conformed to his erroneous answers on the examination; a parachuter hopes that the force of gravity is less and the air's resistance greater; we all pity the unfortunate and regret our foolish actions. But the unprepared student shows his immaturity as truly as the baby in its crib; the parachuter is in bondage to fear; and the rest of us who pity or regret do so through ignorance. "He who rightly realizes that all things follow from the necessity of the divine nature and come to pass in accordance with the eternal laws and rules of nature, will not find anything worthy of hatred, derision, or contempt, nor will he bestow pity on anything, but to the utmost extent of human virtue he will endeavor to do well, as the saying is, and to rejoice. We may add that he who is easily touched with compassion and is moved by another's sorrow or tears, often does something which he afterwards regrets; partly because we can never be sure that an action caused by emotion is good, partly because we are easily deceived by false tears" (IV 1, note). "The more this knowledge, that things are necessary, is applied to particular things, which we conceive more distinctly and vividly, the greater is the power of the mind over the emotions, as experience also testifies. For we see that the pain arising from the loss of any good is mitigated as soon as the man who has lost it perceives that it could not by any means have been preserved. So also we see that no one pities an infant because it cannot speak, walk, or reason, or lastly because it passes so many years, as it were, in unconsciousness. Whereas if most people were born full-grown, and only one here and there as an infant, everyone would pity the infants; because infancy would not then be looked on as a state natural and necessary, but as a fault or delinquency in nature" (V vi, note).

No reasonable person hopes that a theorem of geometry may be different or regrets that it is what it is. It is not rational to hate an eclipse of the moon or to be frustrated by such an occurrence. No one can worry about what he knows to be inevitable. Unhappiness is caused by the saddest, but most mistaken, words of tongue or pen — "it might have been." Frustration, by daily disappointments, by tuberculosis, by war, and by death itself comes through desiring the impossible. But when a contemplated event is known to be impossible, we cease to desire it as we have ceased wishing for the moon. The secret of a happy life therefore lies in knowledge. With knowledge, not only does the desire for the impossible vanish, but for the same reason fear of the inevitable also disappears. Our death, heretofore regarded with aversion as the defeat of all hopes, is now seen to be a theorem as necessarily deduced from God's nature as the Euclidean theorems are deduced from their axioms. Thus death will be viewed *sub specie aeternitatis*, as Spinoza expresses it, and man will live a blessed life.

At this point a paragraph of criticism may well be inserted. That a knowledge of inevitability will banish frustration is an ingenious idea, and Spinoza made it all the more plausible by his personal conduct. True, Spinoza was not the most tragic figure in history: although he was cast out of the synagogue and although the Christians resented his attacks on the Bible, his residence in Protestant Holland spared him the persecution that had been the lot of minorities in France and Spain. If he was ostracized, it was due as much to voluntary retirement as to social pressure, for he could have had a professorship for the acceptance. At the same time, although he escaped most external misfortunes, his health was poor and he clearly saw his approaching death. Tuberculosis made it inevitable, and inevitability was supposed to make it rational and palatable. However, one must not conclude from Spinoza's equanimity that the argument is sound. Personal conduct, no matter how laudable, is not the equivalent of logical validity. Nor do geometrical examples suffice. The fact that we do not hate a geometrical theorem may not depend on its inevitability; hate is reserved for human beings, and even if a theorem were not inevitable, it is hard to think that we would hate it. The illustration of not pitying an infant appears more to the point. Yet if infants were inevitably and naturally born so as to suffer until they could walk, it is not so certain that we would not pity them.

Perhaps Spinoza's mistake, for such it seems to be, is not his insistence on inevitability but his omission of another factor. In times of great distress the thought of inevitable final happiness, if one can entertain it, is comforting; but who could be comforted by the thought of inevitable and final misery? An indeterminate outcome offers more comfort than the latter, just as it would offer less comfort than the former. But in Spinoza's system no place is found for a satisfying culmination of the universal process. Teleology is denied.

The world keeps on going, but it goes nowhere in particular. Nor is a satisfying culmination guaranteed to any individual life. Only the misery of death is guaranteed. Everything must be viewed *sub specie aeternitatis*, and individualism is a delusion. But, finally, aside from these objections, which are based on non-spinozistic principles, Spinoza on his own showing did not have full right to comfort and blessedness because he could not attain to his own ideal of knowledge. He might have faith that all things are deducible by logic alone; and if all things, then his own existence and miseries were included. But he never actually deduced them from his original axioms. Even if it be granted that tuberculosis is a necessary consequence of the universe, the knowledge that Spinoza's case was inevitable cannot be had; and without that knowledge there was a cloud on his title to blessedness. The underlying problem is the problem of knowledge, and here it appears with respect to individual persons and particular events.

Sub Specie Aeternitatis

So much must suffice for the fundamentals of Spinoza's ethics; but his remarks on death lead to a further and somewhat unexpected development. He continues: "Things are conceived by us as actual in two ways: either as existing in relation to a given time and place," which is an inferior type of knowledge, "or as contained in God and following from the necessity of the divine nature. Whatsoever we conceive in this second way as true or real, we conceive under the form of eternity" (V xxix, note; cf. II, xlv, note). "Our mind, insofar as it knows itself and the body under the form of eternity, has to that extent necessarily a knowledge of God and that it is in God and is conceived through God. . . . In proportion therefore as a man is more potent in this kind of knowledge, he will be more completely conscious of himself and of God; in other words, he will be more perfect and blessed" (V xxx and xxxi, note).

In this quotation temporal forms of knowledge have been subordinated and we have been told to take the viewpoint of eternity by which our mind knows that it is in God. Spinoza even said: "Now I have finished with all that concerns this present life. . . . Therefore it is now time to pass on to those matters which appertain to the duration of the mind without relation to the body" (V xx, note); and

"The human mind cannot be absolutely destroyed with the body, but there remains of it something which is eternal" (V xxiii). What can these phrases mean in Spinoza? Has he deceived himself by the ambiguity of the words *eternity* and *God*, and subconsciously salvaged some orthodox salvation? If such be the case, obviously this part of Spinoza's theory would have to be counted as a gross inconsistency. Or, on the other hand, did Spinoza choose these traditional terms to mask his atheism and deceive the public? Why should a man say God when he means the world? Why should he say eternity when he means logic? Well, since axioms, implication, and theorems are timeless, perhaps it is permissible to call them eternal. And although some historians attribute a doctrine of immortality to him, Spinoza himself seems to avoid that word, contenting himself with the term *eternity*. At all events one should try to make an author as self-consistent as possible and not invent discrepancies where none are.

That Spinoza has nothing in mind similar to the Platonic immortality of the individual soul, much less the Christian resurrection of the body, can admit of no doubt. St. Augustine well made memory the test of individual personality, and Leibniz considers memory essential to immortality, but Spinoza says, "the mind can only imagine anything, or remember what is past, while the body endures" (V xxi). "Nevertheless," he continues (V xxii), "in God there is necessarily an idea which expresses the essence of this or that human body under the form of eternity. Proof: God is the cause, not only of the existence of this or that human body, but also of its essence. This essence therefore must necessarily be conceived through the very essence of God, and be thus conceived by a certain eternal necessity, and this conception must necessarily exist in God. Prop. XXIII: The human mind cannot be absolutely destroyed with the body, but there remains of it something which is eternal. . . . Note: This idea, which expresses the essence of the body under the form of eternity, is, as we have said, a certain mode of thinking, which belongs to the essence of the mind, and is necessarily eternal. Yet it is not possible that we should remember that we existed before our body, for our body can bear no trace of such existence, neither can eternity be defined in terms of time, or have any relation to time. But, notwithstanding, we feel and know that we are eternal. For the mind feels those things that it conceives by understanding, no less than those things that it remembers. For the eyes of the mind, whereby it sees and observes things, are none other than proofs. Thus, although we do not remember that we existed before the body, yet we feel that our mind, insofar as it involves the essence of the body, under the form of eternity, is eternal, and that thus its existence cannot be defined in terms of time or explained through duration. Thus our mind can only be said to endure, and its existence can only be defined by a fixed time, insofar as it involves the actual existence of the body. Thus far only has it the power of determining the existence of things in time and conceiving them under the category of duration."

The rationalistic dependence on deduction, the most perfect example being geometry, should be the guide to the understanding of this section. The idea of the human body, which Spinoza has already equated with the human mind, is eternally in God as the Pythagorean theorem is eternally in its axioms. To say that this or that is in God means that the thing in question is implied by the original definitions and axioms. When one knows the deduction, the thing is viewed under the form of eternity. Hence Spinoza said that God is the cause of the essence of the body as well as of its existence. And since implication is eternal, something of the mind or idea of the body remains after the body is temporally destroyed. Accordingly the mind is eternal.

This consistent interpretation of Spinoza, divested of misleading religious connotations, shows that the mind's eternity is no more an immortality than it is a pre-existence. Or, rather, neither of these two terms is appropriate, for if anything continues *after* the body decays, eternity has been confused with infinite time; but as Spinoza said in the last quotation, eternity can have no relation to time. Certainly we do not speak of the immortality or pre-existence of the Pythagorean theorem, though occasionally it is called eternal. Further, by hinting that the body is destroyed while the mind survives, Spinoza seems to break the parallelism he had so carefully constructed. The only eternity Spinoza's basic thought allows is an eternity in which everything shares alike. Not merely the human mind, but also the human body, and dogs, and stars, and every other theorem exist necessarily and eternally in God. But perhaps the real difficulty with Spinoza's system is not so much the justification of an eternal existence for temporal things as it is the deduction of temporal things in the first place. How can abstract, general, universal axioms imply that Spinoza, an individual, was born in 1632 in the city of Amsterdam? The Spinoza of the system, or perhaps man in general, is as eternal as any theorem of geometry; but was there ever a spatio-temporal individual who died of tuberculosis on February 21, 1677 at 3:00 P.M.? Can it be maintained that individual persons and historical events are deducible from the ontological argument? The fate of rationalism depends on the answer.

LEIBNIZ (1646—1716)

Spinoza had lived the life of a private citizen, grinding lenses for a living, and working on his philosophy when he could. Leibniz was into everything. He took his academic degree in law; he served as a diplomat for the Elector-Archbishop of Mainz, and later entered the service of the Duke of Brunswick; he met or corresponded with all the leading scientists and philosophers in Europe and pursued investigations on nearly every known subject; independently of Newton he invented calculus; he tried to reconcile the Roman and Protestant churches; but he died in obscurity. The quiet life of Spinoza allowed him to write systematically, and although his thought is difficult, one can follow it step by step. Leibniz, however, distracted by numerous interests, was never able to write out his thought in systematic form, with the exception of a relatively brief compendium, the *Monadology*. He discussed separate topics in papers, letters, and short monographs. The result is that it is difficult to put it all together. For the present purpose only a few items will be discussed.

Leibniz was a rationalist: theoretically all knowledge is based on logic alone, and in one place he boasts that he has demonstrated that the earth moves and that the vacuum does not exist, "not through experiments, for they do nothing, but by geometrical demonstrations." Nevertheless his rationalism is quite different from that of Spinoza both in form and content. Spinoza, attached to his *ordine*

geometrico, may have made some little use of experience unconsciously or reluctantly, for after all the theory permitted observation
to suggest theorems that might later be proved; Descartes had deliberately experimented; but Leibniz with an intense interest in specific
scientific problems found little time for formal deduction. He busied
himself with the invention of adding machines, water pumps, and
microscopes. Not only did his scientific, religious, and historical
labors detract from the geometrical form of his writing, but the content differed both from Spinoza and from Descartes in that he paid
more attention to the derivation of contingent, temporal truths from
eternal and necessary truth. Experiments with inertia led him to
substitute a law of conservation of momentum for Descartes' constant
quantity of motion; and with the notion of force involved he rejected
Descartes' concept of matter as extension, reinterpreted the nature of
physical bodies, and developed a metaphysics, summarized in his
Monadology, which is neither Cartesian nor Spinozistic.

The Monads

According to Descartes the created world consisted of a great number of unextended, thinking souls and a great number of extended,
unthinking bodies. Though God alone should be regarded as substance in the strictest sense, Descartes was still willing to call souls
and bodies substances. On the other hand, Spinoza reduced thought
and extension to the rank of attributes of a single substance. Now,
Leibniz disagreed with both these views. First, in opposition to
Spinoza, Leibniz believed that the existence of many substances is a
conclusion from the obvious fact that there are composites in the
world. Who can deny that the things of ordinary experience are
composed of parts? These parts may themselves be composed of
smaller parts, but in the end every composite or aggregate must be
therefore a plurality of simple substances. But in the second place, if
Leibniz' reason for asserting many substances can this easily be stated,
his explanation of the nature of these elements and his rejection of
the Cartesian type of extended, bodily substances are much more
complicated. Spinoza's view of substance had been controlled by the
idea of complete independence; and since only one being could be
completely independent, Spinoza admitted but one substance. For

Leibniz, however, independence, at least complete independence, was not essential to the concept of substance. He did, indeed, hold that the elements are independent of each other, but he did not deny that they have been created and are dependent on God. The essential characteristic of substance in Leibniz' opinion is unity and simplicity; and this leads him, as we shall see, to deny that bodies are substances.

The elements out of which the world is composed Leibniz calls monads, a Greek term for unit. Since these substances are simple and unitary, they can have no parts; and therefore they can have no extension; and therefore they cannot be divided. That is to say, the fundamental elements of the world cannot be bodies, for all bodies are both extended and composite. That bodies are extended is obvious; since they have parts, for they have a top and a bottom, a right and a left, it is also obvious that they are composites. Hence they are not substances. Furthermore, since extension is infinitely divisible, there is no such thing as a smallest atom. Therefore a substance can have no size or shape whatever. Then, too, because the elements are unities, they can neither be produced nor destroyed through natural means; for that which has no parts cannot be taken apart. Monads therefore can begin and end only all at once; that is, they can begin only through creation and end only by annihilation. Nothing but composites can begin and end gradually.

Although the monads have no size or shape, they must have some sort of quality or they would be nothing at all. And their qualities must differ, for otherwise perceptual changes could not take place. In a Democritean world with its empty space, a collection of atoms could be differently arranged from another collection of the same number. The design of the one group could be perceived against a background of empty space and thus distinguished from another design perceived in the same way. But the rationalists did not admit empty space. Now, in a *plenum*, or completely filled space, it would be impossible to perceive differences or changes if all the elements were qualitatively identical. It would be like the design of molecules in a glass of clear water, only more so. No matter how they were rearranged, one state of things would be indistinguishable from another. Motions and replacements would make no difference, for no design could emerge. Therefore in a plenum the elements must be qualitatively different. In fact, for the best of all possible worlds, the greatest possible difference should be asserted; that is, each monad must be different from every other monad, and this will make the world beautiful.

Beauty consists of unity in diversity; the greatest beauty is the maximum unity in the maximum diversity. A simple still life or even an abstract painting may be beautiful because it unifies several colors, planes, and lines. On the other hand that remarkable canvas of a swan eating a marshmallow on a snowy day has a maximum unity, but diversity is lacking. The paintings of the great masters, in comparison with good still lifes, have great unity and great diversity also. The world therefore, as the most beautiful of all objects, contains no two things exactly alike. No two leaves of the forest, no two finger prints, are identical. And if the thumb print of an alleged murderer is found at the scene of the crime, a rationalistic jury will conclude that he has been identified or individuated. The man accused, however, with a different philosophy, protests that he was a thousand miles away at the time of the murder and that the thumb print must be that of his double. Here the ancient and medieval problem of individuation begins its modern course. In the discussion of Abelard's conceptualism considerations were advanced against the existence of a common quality. Leibniz would have agreed with the conclusion at least; and so criminology seems to be strangely related to aesthetics and epistemology.

Each monad then must have its own quality; and more, Leibniz assumes it as admitted that each monad is subject to continuous change. Since no monad can affect another, the change must be due to an internal principle. Then, too, change implies variety, and yet the monad is simple and unitary. What type of quality and of change satisfies these conditions? The answer is not hard to guess — thought, or, better, perception, for it is not precisely the Cartesian thinking. In conformity with the principle of maximum variety and not without a basis in experience, Leibniz asserts an infinite and continuous gradation of perception. There are vivid perceptions like thunder or the roar of the ocean; there are clear and distinct rational and logical processes; but there are also vague, dream-like perceptions, fading off into what is ordinarily called unconsciousness.

These *petites perceptions* Descartes had not acknowledged. In addition to the principle of maximum variety, which implies infinite gradations, another reason for asserting unconscious perceptions relates to one of the paradoxes of Zeno the Eleatic. Arguing against atomism, Zeno inferred that if an ocean wave, as it dashed against the rocks, is composed of atoms of spray, the roar of the ocean would have to be composed of atoms of roar; but since a single atom of spray causes no perception of sound, the roar cannot be explained by atomism. Leibniz not only rejects atomism as Zeno did, but unlike Zeno he asserts the existence of infinitesimals of perception. Because Descartes had restricted his attention to the greater perceptions, those we call conscious thinking, he came to the erroneous conclusion that animals have no sensation. For Leibniz even stones and clods of earth are composed of substances that perceive; they do not have the higher ranges of perception characteristic of human beings, and for this reason Leibniz doubts whether the terms *soul* and *spirit* are strictly applicable; but every substance is a monad and every monad perceives.

That the basic elements of the world are minds or souls is completely opposed to every form of materialism. Between the time of the Epicureans and the rationalists there had been few defenders of materialism. There was now an English philosopher, Thomas Hobbes, who was the first of several modern thinkers to advocate this theory. Representatives of atomism either deny the existence of consciousness, as in contemporary behaviorism, or more often attempt to explain thought as a complicated physico-chemical epiphenomenon. Leibniz believed that such an explanation is impossible. Since the brain is a physical body, we can imagine one to be built the size of a large building. Walking through its hallways and corridors and examining its rooms and closets, we could see the machinery in motion. We could see its cam shafts and belts; we could see its magnets and circuit breakers; we could see its ball bearings and lubrication system. But in all this mechanical motion of pieces, we could not see any perception. Materialism therefore is a failure.

But Leibniz' theory is also to be contrasted with the views of Descartes and Spinoza, even though these two were not materialists.

For Descartes, thinking and mechanism were so disparate that it was necessary to attribute them to two different substances, even though he allowed the two to interact. Spinoza, while he admitted but one substance, made thought and motion so independent of each other that interaction was impossible. With respect to interaction and the inviolability of mechanical law, Leibniz agreed with Spinoza; and no one could assert more emphatically that mind is independent of mechanism and that motion can in no way produce or explain thought. But his general construction and in particular his analysis of the concepts of body and substance are different. "He who will meditate upon the nature of substance . . . will find that the whole nature of bodies is not exhausted in their extension, that is to say, their size, figure, and motion, but that we must recognize something that corresponds to soul. . . . It is even possible to demonstrate that the ideas of size, figure, and motion are not so distinctive as is imagined, and that they stand for something imaginary relative to our perceptions, as do . . . the ideas of color, heat, and the other similar qualities in regard to which we may doubt whether they are actually to be found in the nature of things outside of us. This is why these latter qualities are unable to constitute substance" (*Discourse on Metaphysics*, XII). Also in a letter to Arnauld, Leibniz says: "It may be surprising perhaps that I deny the action of one corporeal substance upon another, when this seems so evident; but besides the fact that others have already done this, we must also consider that it is rather a play of the imagination than a distinct conception. If the body is a substance and not a mere phenomenon, like a rainbow, nor a being brought together by accident or by accumulation, like a pile of stones, its essence cannot consist in extension, and we must necessarily conceive of something which is called substantial form and which corresponds in some sort to the soul." In other places he argues from inertia, as briefly alluded to above. If the essence of body, he contends, consists in extension; if there were no more body than what geometry teaches plus the notion of change; then when a small body rolled against a very large one, the two would continue in motion together with undiminished velocity, for pure extension could not offer any resistance. This result, says Leibniz, rationalist though he was, is entirely irreconcilable with experiments. Hence there is something in matter beyond what is purely geometrical, beyond extension and motion. This something is substance or force. In various places, e.g., in a letter to a certain Wagner, Leibniz identifies this force as a vital principle, i.e., a principle of life, endowed with the faculty of perception, which in brutes is their soul. Matter or body, on the other hand, with its attribute of extension, is not a substance; it is a plurality of substances. Bodies are multitudes. A substance is a unity. And thus Leibniz arrived at his theory of monads.

Teleology and Mechanism

Because the universe is composed of souls, it can be explained teleologically. Not only do human souls have purposes, as even Spinoza admitted, but God also acts purposefully in creation. Some pages back the three rationalists were compared with respect to their views on the relation between God and the world, and it was explained that for Leibniz God chose this world because its arrangements were the best. True, we may entertain erroneous opinions as to what God's purposes are; but whereas Descartes had denied the possibility of knowing the final causes in nature, the error Leibniz acknowledges is mainly one of incompleteness. We are likely to accept one part of God's purpose as the whole. For example, Spinoza ridicules Christianity for believing that God made the world for the sake of man; now, replies Leibniz, it would be a great blunder to think that God made the world only for man, though it is quite true that he made it entirely for man and that there is nothing in the universe that does not affect us. Not only may we have a general knowledge of God's purposes, but even in the details of physics a knowledge of purpose is possible and useful. It is even more easily obtained than a knowledge of mechanical causation. The laws of the refraction of light, so Leibniz affirms (*Discourse on Metaphysics*, XXII), were discovered through a knowledge of final causes. And the account given by the two men, Snellius and Fermat, who made use of teleology, is much more satisfactory than the demonstration of Descartes, who did not.

Nevertheless Leibniz, unlike Descartes, does not conclude that souls and their teleology violate the laws of mechanism. In this respect he is closer to Spinoza's position. Even though "everything takes place in souls as if there were no body," still "everything takes place in bodies as if there were no soul." "The physicist can explain his experiments, now using simpler experiments already made, now employing geometrical and mechanical demonstrations without any need of the general considerations which belong to another sphere, and if he employs the cooperation of God, or perhaps of some soul or animating force, or something else of a similar nature, he goes out of his path quite as much as that man who, when facing an important practical question, would wish to enter into profound argumentations regarding the nature of destiny and of our liberty" (*Discourse on Metaphysics*, X). Repeatedly Leibniz asserts that every motion has its origin in another motion according to the laws of mechanics, and these laws are never violated in natural motions. Not only does mechanism hold for bodies commonly called inanimate, but Leibniz also does not hesitate to designate the bodies of plants, animals, and human beings as all alike automata.

But if the human body is an automaton, what is the relation between motion and perception, between mind and matter, between mechanism and teleology? It cannot be interaction, for a monad cannot be affected by anything external and a body can only be affected mechanically. Nor can it be a Spinozistic parallelism, for each monad is a substance. But it might be a different type of parallelism, although Leibniz had another name for it.

Then too the problem involved is more than the body-mind problem as Descartes had envisaged it. It is rather the relation of monad to monad that must be considered. Every body, for Leibniz, is a collection of monads, not a substance but an aggregate of substances, an army, a herd, or a pond full of fish. The illustration of the pond of fish occurs several times. If we were canoeing on a lake, we might see something like a water-soaked log floating in a given direction just under the surface. Coming closer we would discover that it was not a log, but a school of fish. Similarly when we see a stone, a clod of earth, a chair, or any thing, it appears inanimate to us because of the obscurity of our sensory perception. Coming closer to it by reason, we understand that it is composed of an infinite number of living monads. The problem Leibniz faces therefore is not just the relation of body to mind, but of every monad to every other.

The dominant monad in the human body, which is one's mind or soul, may in some sense be superior to the others that are grouped around it; but its relation to them, the body, is to be explained on the general principle that applies to all. For the apparent interaction of soul and body is no less a problem than the coherence of other monads in a stone or chair. The name of the principle that explains all cases and therefore the relationship among all created monads, Leibniz calls pre-established harmony.

A modern illustration may help. Suppose that every room of a large building contains a single musician with his instrument and his own score. Seated before a microphone each musician begins to play at a given signal. Under these conditions it is evident that the note from the bass drum in the boiler room has no causal efficacy on the piccolo in the penthouse, nor does the violin in the lobby affect the cornet on the mezzanine. Yet when all the sounds are gathered together through their respective microphones to a center and broadcast, the totality is a symphony. That all the notes of all the instruments fit together can be explained only on the assumption that a single composer has written all the scores. The symphony is a pre-established harmony.

So it is with all the monads that compose the universe. God wrote the definition or life history of each so that they would all work in perfect conjunction to produce the world we know. The definition of Alexander the Great includes the predicate that he will conquer Darius, and conversely a predicate of the concept of Darius is that he will be defeated by Alexander. Leibniz also gives Julius Caesar as an example. The events leading up to Caesar's dictatorship are all contained in the concept of Caesar, and the corresponding acts of his enemies and friends are contained in theirs. Leibniz does not here follow the strict rationalist model and say that the opposites of these events involve logical contradictions. This is not the only possible world, and the predicates of Alexander and Caesar do not attach to them with the necessity by which a geometrical predicate attaches to its subject. Contrary events are always logically possible, for these predicates attach to Caesar only by the decree of God's free will. Yet so attaching, the events are certain and their opposites will never occur. Each monad therefore plays the score, and nothing else but the score, that God has written for it. Hence it is that thoughts and motions harmonize, and that when we pick up one end of the pencil the other end follows along. The course of all nature is a pre-established harmony.

Because Leibniz did not systematize his philosophy in one comprehensive volume, an account of his views tends to be a sort of appendix to rationalism, in which some of the special problems are given interesting alternative solutions. However suggestive his ideas may be, and it cannot be denied that they are exceptionally brilliant, rationalism as a system is not greatly advanced thereby. It might even be said that Leibniz' attention to contingent truths, the details of physics and the events of history, underlined the difficulty of deducing individual events from the being of God. As this is no little matter, it is hardly surprising that rationalism fell into disfavor and that the eighteenth century attempted a new method.

CHAPTER 8

British Empiricism

Rationalism, the theory that all knowledge is based on logic alone, owed something to the science of the Renaissance. It was the mathematical ideal of Galileo that had inspired Descartes and Spinoza. The empirical or experimental side of science, however, had proved embarrassing to rationalism. Too wide a chasm separated the axioms of the philosophers from the particular conclusions of the scientists. One might therefore expect that a failure to justify physics on the sole basis of logic would be followed by an attempt to establish mathematics by the methods of experimental physics. The statement should doubtless be made more general. Experimental physics is a very complicated affair, and a scientist must bring to it a great deal of prior experience. Not only must he have a certain amount of formal education, but through this education and still earlier in life he must have the common experiences and sensations of mankind. Wheat and weeds, dogs and birds, sun and stars must be seen as common objects before one can study botany, zoology, and astronomy. The future scientist must learn to count marbles before he can invent calculus. But these common prerequisites to scientific study are matters of experience. Cannot all knowledge then be based on experience alone? An affirmative answer indicates the theory of empiricism.

Although rationalism dominated the continent during the seventeenth century, it never captured the British Isles. From the time of Roger Bacon onward, philosophy in Great Britain had been mainly empirical. Thomas Hobbes, a contemporary of Descartes, was so little rationalistic that he advocated materialism. And just before the beginning of the eighteenth century empiricism received powerful support from the amazing success of Sir Isaac Newton. The theory of gravitation, which combined and completed the work of Galileo and Kepler, with all the mathematics it involved, depended entirely, according to Newton's claims, on accurate experimentation. Only four years later (1690) Locke published his *Essay Concerning the Human Understanding*. This and the works of Berkeley and Hume make the eighteenth century the century of empiricism.

JOHN LOCKE (1632—1704)

Innate Ideas

When Locke decided to attack rationalism, he did not begin, as the previous account might seem to suggest, with an attempt to show the invalidity of the ontological argument; neither did he emphasize the failure to deduce the minor laws of physics and the particular events of history from the being of God. Instead of centering his attention on these obvious and basic factors, he chose a point that has so little needed mention in the foregoing exposition that one may at first wonder whether it is really essential to rationalism at all. Yet it proves to have been presupposed throughout. The point concerns innate ideas. Descartes indeed used the term *innate* very little, and Spinoza less. But if knowledge is not received through sensation, the mind at birth must possess something in the way of intellectual equipment — the concepts of logic at least. In fact, since the theorems are deduced from the original axioms, there is a sense in which all ideas are innate. Plato in his own way would have agreed. On the other hand, various intuitionists, some of whom Locke evidently had in mind, because of their somewhat different viewpoint, limited the range of innate ideas to a few basic principles, including with the laws of logic the concepts of number, of God, and of elementary moral distinctions. But whatever the extent of this ideal world, a theory in which knowledge is not altogether based on experience requires some innate ideas, just as a theory which finds knowledge in experience alone cannot admit even one.

Therefore Locke's introduction to empiricism, Book I of his *Essay*, attempts the refutation.

The alleged fact that all men without exception have certain ideas is sometimes used as evidence to prove that these ideas are innate. Everyone, so it is said, has the idea of God, of number, of morality, of logical contradiction. To this Locke replies that even if these ideas were universally present, it would not prove them innate. They could have been derived by all men from the common factors of experience. For example, the mountains of Tibet and the Amazon jungle are sufficiently different geographically to explain the differences in the economic and agricultural ideas of their respective populations, but the physical conditions of motion and the impossibility that one body is another are the same the world over. Ideas based on such identical conditions could therefore be universal without being innate. Furthermore, Locke insists, in point of fact none of these ideas is universally accepted. That there are no universally accepted ideas of morality, Locke thinks he easily shows by a survey of various cultures. The Greeks thought it was right to murder infants and the Eskimos to kill their grandparents. There are cannibals and there are vegetarians. Whether or not Locke deals fairly with the bare idea of a distinction between right and wrong, for all tribes make some distinction, at any rate he has no difficulty in showing its contradictory applications.

Locke has other arguments which bear on speculative ideas as well as on moral ideas. He finds that the term innate is ambiguous. If *innate* or *inborn* refers literally to physical birth, then obviously the laws of logic are not innate because imbeciles never learn them, and normal children must have some years of experience before they can assent to them. If, however, *inborn* refers figuratively to a birth of reason, such a birth can only designate that acceptance or assent which is given when the ideas are understood. Such an interpretation of innateness is doubly impossible. First, it would imply that all ideas, understood and accepted, are innate; and Locke cannot believe that anyone would admit millions of innate ideas. Second, the understanding and acceptance of these ideas is itself the result of learning by experience. There is another possible meaning of the term *innate*, viz., "proved by logic alone." On this meaning, however, the most difficult theorem of geometry would be an innate idea — a ridiculous conclusion.

Such are some of the arguments in the first Book of Locke's *Essay*. They may be fallacious. Leibniz read them, thought them to be based on a misunderstanding of rationalism — as seems to be the case — and proceeded to reply under the title, *New Essays on the Human Understanding*. But the value of empiricism is not to be tied too closely to Locke's introduction. It is the constructive theory that counts. If Locke can show in detail how all ideas, including the most abstract and speculative, are derived from common experience; if he can avoid skepticism and make knowledge possible for a mind unfurnished with prior ideas; if, in other words, he can justify empiricism, then the minor points about innate ideas are automatically disposed of.

Simple Ideas

Empiricism is the theory that all knowledge is based on experience alone. "Every man is conscious to himself that he thinks" (II, i, 1), and the objects he thinks are ideas. The term *idea* is that which "serves best to stand for whatsoever is the object of the understanding when a man thinks, [therefore Locke has] used it to express what is meant by phantasm, notion, species, or whatever it is which the mind can be employed about in thinking" (I, i, 8). Examples of ideas are: whiteness, hardness, motion, elephant, army, drunkenness. "Let us then suppose the mind to be, as we say, white paper, void of all characters, without any ideas; how comes it by that vast store which the busy and boundless fancy of man has painted on it with an almost endless variety? Whence has it all the materials of reason and knowledge? To this I answer in one word, from experience; in that all our knowledge is founded, and from that it ultimately derives itself" (II, i, 2). Empiricism therefore is the theory that all knowledge is based on experience alone.

Now, experience is of two kinds. First, there is sensation by which one receives the ideas of yellow, white, heat, cold, soft, hard, bitter, sweet, and all those which we call sensible qualities. Second, the mind, although it has no innate ideas and is purely receptive in sensation, operates on the sensory ideas it receives. These operations we can perceive by introspection, and thus we are furnished with a second set of ideas, called ideas of reflection, such as perception, thinking, doubting, believing, reasoning, knowing, willing, and all the different actings of our own minds. Besides these two sources of ideas, sensation and reflection, there is no other. Nor can the mind invent any new simple idea. A man born blind can have no idea of color, nor a man born deaf, of sound. Suppose I should ask you to imagine the taste of roast buffalo or fried rattlesnake. Buffalo of course tastes like meat, but not like beef, lamb, or pork. Fried rattlesnake looks like chicken neck, but does this give you any idea of its taste? Obviously one who has never experienced these tastes cannot possibly imagine or invent the sensation. All ideas come from experience, and even the most complex knowledge, be it the theory of gravitation or the divine moral government of the human race, must be derived from these two classes of simple ideas and from nothing else. If the music of Beethoven and Bach has for its elements only a hundred notes, why should it be thought impossible to construct physics and theology out of simple ideas? For although sensation and reflection are the only sources of ideas, the ideas themselves are extremely numerous. The colors, with their several degrees or shades and mixtures and the variety of smells are each a distinct idea. Because of their great number there are most frequently no names for them, for though we apply the name *sweet* to the smell of a rose and the smell of a violet, they are certainly very distinct ideas. Solidity, rest, motion, pleasure and pain, unity, existence, and even space and darkness, are all simple ideas of sensation, though some of these, unlike colors and smells, are received through more than one sense. Thus the elementary units of knowledge exist in sufficient number.

Before describing the operations by which the mind constructs all complex knowledge out of these simple units, it is necessary to note an important distinction between two sorts of sensory ideas. Knowledge, of course, relates to a real external world; and one of the difficulties with rationalism was the suspicion that a definition could not imply objective existence. Empiricism proceeds on the assumption that experience, in particular sensation, puts the mind in contact with reality. But because uneducated common sense

accepts this notion so wholeheartedly, Locke, instead of emphasizing it as a point of superiority over rationalism, takes pains to add
strictures and reduce its scope. It is true and it is essential that some
ideas of sensation faithfully reveal the external world. The ideas of
solidity, extension, figure, motion or rest, and number are produced
in our minds by the qualities of extension, figure, and so on in
physical bodies. These qualities are utterly inseparable from a body,
in what state soever it be. In all the alteration it suffers, it constantly
keeps them. Grind a grain of wheat to the finest flour, and each
particle, even though so small as to be invisible, retains the afore-
mentioned qualities.

Parenthetically it might be asked how, if all knowledge is based on
experience, one can know what qualities an invisible particle has?

In addition to these primary qualities, Locke calls attention to the
far greater number of secondary qualities. One must not think, as
perhaps usually is done, that all ideas are exact images or resemblances
of something inherent in the object known. In fact, the majority of
sensory ideas are no more the likeness of anything external, than
their names are the likeness of our ideas (II, viii, 7). For example,
flame is called hot and light, snow white and cold, and pastry is
called sweet. Yet the same fire which at one distance produces the
idea of warmth in us, at a closer distance produces the far different
sensation of pain. Pastry can produce pain too, and so can snow. As
few people would be inclined to assert that the quality pain really
exists in the external object, they should be willing to consider
whether there is any reason to suppose that hot, cold, and sweet
really exist in bodies. An invisible body may yet possess solidity
and figure, but in the absence of the sensation of pain, pain simply
does not exist. Similarly, let the eyes not see light and the tongue
not taste, nor the nose smell, and all colors, tastes, and odors cease
to exist. A color is a sensation: it follows then that if there is no
sensation, there is no color. In the external world these secondary
qualities are nothing but the powers which primary qualities have of
producing such sensations in us. We say colloquially that the
radiator or the sun is hot. But neither of them ever wipes the per-
spiration from its brow. Strictly speaking it is not they but we that
are hot. The radiator or the steam in the radiator is in motion, in
such rapid motion that it produces the sensation of heat in us. Sim-

ilarly, a smooth surface, and smooth is a kind of shape or figure, looks shiny to us; roughen it, that is, change its shape, and it will look dull. It is the shape that really exists in the world; the color exists only in our minds. In the same way the primary quality of motion in the air produces the sensation of sound. But sound is a sensation and exists only in a perceiving ear. The real world, therefore, the world of Newtonian science, the world that rationalism failed to know, is a world devoid of color, odor, sound, and, it might be said, of all human interest: a consideration that has caused some contemporary philosophers to pause and ponder.

Compound Ideas

The formation of complex ideas out of all these simple ones depends on three activities of the mind: compounding, abstracting, and relating. One might at first suppose that the simplest of compound ideas would be the things of everyday experience, such as a book, a tree, or a stone. These seem to be formed by combining several simple ideas of color, solidity, figure, and possibly odor or some other simple idea. However, Locke believes that there are still simpler examples of compound ideas. A book and a stone require the addition of several different qualities, such as gray, hard, and heavy; but the more elementary compound ideas are combinations of one simple idea repeated a number of times. The simple idea of space comes through sight and touch, for it is obvious that we see the distance between two bodies. From many observations of such distances, that is, from the one idea of space repeated many times, we can build up the idea of immense space. Similarly a time is perceived to elapse between two successive ideas in the mind, and by repeating this simple idea we can build up the idea of eternity. Then too there is no idea more simple than unity, and by repeating this idea we get the ideas of one, two, three, four, and so on. More generally the idea of infinity, whether in space, time, or number, is obtained by repeating a finite measure without stopping. But as this repetition in experience never reaches an actually infinite number, we can have no idea of infinite space or infinite time. Arguments in which infinite space is a factor have always been confused because the idea itself is an impossible one.

Space and time may indeed be simpler than other compound

ideas, but, as Locke points out, they have been sources of great confusion. Even on Locke's showing, one must see, and have the ideas of, two bodies, a stone and a book, before one can see the distance between them. This might indicate that the idea of space is not a simple idea of sensation but rather an idea produced by the later activity of relating. Then too, when Locke argues that the repetition of this idea of space never brings us to a positive idea of infinity (which Descartes claimed must precede any idea of the finite), it seems that he must have such a positive idea or he could not know that the repetition was not bringing us nearer to it. Certainly when we travel, if we know we are not approaching New York, we must know what New York is and that it lies behind us. The riddle of space and time will bear watching, particularly as Kant later will make it a cornerstone of his philosophy.

Abstract Ideas

The ideas of things, the book and the stone, are also compound ideas, produced by combining the several simple ideas that occur together. A book, for example, is a combination of the idea of brown, the dusty smell of leather, and the tangible sensation of its crumbling, plus the idea of its size, shape, and other qualities. But there is an ambiguity in the word *book* that points to the second of the three mental operations, namely, abstraction. It was previously stated that language does not afford enough names for every idea, even every simple idea, to have one of its own. If we look at snow, we have the simple idea of white; but usually when we use the word *white*, we do not intend to refer to that single sensation. We have received similar ideas from chalk, milk, paper, and other snowfalls. From these several sensations of whites we abstract the common quality of white, so that usually our idea of white is not a simple but an abstract idea. This is still more evident in the case of book. We have many compound ideas of books, long shelves of them. But by abstracting their common qualities, and discarding their individual peculiarities, e.g., the circumstances of time and place, the exact size of each, and so on, we frame for ourselves the abstract idea of *book*. This abstract idea of *book* can then be used as the representative for all the compound ideas of books. And the same holds for all other examples of what are ordinarily called *things*.

But there is a still further step in abstraction before the idea of book, or even the idea of this book, is completed. It is a matter of curiosity and one requiring explanation that several simple ideas can frequently occur together. How is it possible that the idea of brown, the smell of dry leather, and the idea of a particular shape should accompany each other? There is nothing in the color brown to require one smell rather than another, or any smell at all. It is evident therefore that no one of these ideas depends on or inheres in any other. Brown cannot inhere in a dusty odor. Nor can the two of them exist "out there" by themselves. Brown cannot sit on a shelf all by itself, nor can brown and odor together do so. The white of the snow cannot fall from the clouds by itself, nor can the idea of cold. These simple qualities cannot walk around unchaperoned. They could not meet and form groups all by themselves. Accordingly "we accustom ourselves to suppose some substratum wherein" the qualities "subsist and from which they result; which therefore we call substance" (II, xxiii, 1). Substance thus serves the important function of uniting qualities so that a thing can be said to exist.

Substance also serves to individuate things. Leibniz, for the rationalists, had explained individuation on the theory that every thing or monad was qualitatively distinct from every other one. From Locke we gain the impression that the same set of qualities may possibly exist in two numerically distinct substances. Two books or two stones could have precisely the same color, shape, odor, and so on; they would be two things because there were two substances. When Locke comes to discuss the idea of identity, however, instead of referring to substance, he says that the principle of individuation is existence itself; for example, an atom at any instant is the same as itself because it is what it is. This existence, he further says, determines a being to a particular time and place, and these two determinations figure prominently in our recognizing a body as the same body through various changes of position. Thus Locke does not explicitly state that substance is the principle of individuation; in fact, his use of time and space in this connection might be taken to imply that it is not. Yet, if qualities need a support and could not occur together in one thing unless they inhered in a single substance, it would follow that substance exercised the function even if it did not receive the name. Whether or not there is some confusion here in Locke's mind, it is indubitable that the abstract idea of substance is essential to his system because without it the simple ideas could not regularly occur together.

Unfortunately, the idea of substance brings difficulty with it. "If anyone will examine himself concerning his notion of pure substance in general, he will find he has no other idea of it at all, but only a supposition of he knows not what support of such qualities which are capable of producing simple ideas in us. . . . If anyone should be asked, what is the subject wherein color or weight inheres, he would have nothing to say, but the solid extended parts; and if he were demanded what it is that solidity and extension adhere in, he would not be in a much better case than the Indian who, saying that the world was supported by a great elephant, was asked what the elephant rested on; to which his answer was, a great tortoise. But being again pressed to know what gave support to the broad-backed tortoise, replied, something he knew not what" (II, xxiii, 2).

This means that the cause of the existence of things is unknown. Our knowledge of a lump of gold or a piece of iron is limited to the qualities we observe; the substance which unites them so as to make one thing is never a part of our experience. A curious advantage to religion accrues from this ignorance. It must be noted that the simple ideas of reflection, i.e., thinking, doubting, willing, and so on, can no more subsist of themselves than the sensory qualities can. Therefore a spiritual substance or soul is just as necessary as a material substance or body. And without soul or spirit religion would be as badly off as physics would be without matter. The materialist, who will have neither soul nor God — and Locke believes that the existence of God is demonstrably certain — assumes that he has a clear knowledge of matter, though he believes that the idea of spirit is confused nonsense. But on this point materialism is certainly mistaken, for we know as much about the one as the other, even though we know nothing of either. Locke goes so far as to say, "By the complex idea of extended, figured, colored, and all other sensible qualities, which is all that we know of it, we are as far from the idea of the substance of body, as if we knew nothing at all" (II, xxiii, 16). Needless to say, this conclusion is a disappointment, and later philosophers may be expected to re-examine the reasoning behind it.

Ideas of Relation

The third and last activity of the mind by which simple ideas are made into more complex knowledge is the operation of comparison. It is thus that ideas of relation are produced; for example, husband, wife, father, son. The ideas of old and great, although one may not suppose them to be so at first, are also relative terms, for a dog is old at seven years and a man at seventy. In fact, the idea of seven years and a date such as 1066 are ideas of relation because they require comparison with a number of the earth's revolutions around the sun. The same holds for space — or at least a space like a mile.

The most important ideas of relation are doubtless the ideas of cause and effect. One cannot fail to notice that qualities and substances begin to exist and later pass away. Trees grow and chairs are made. A tree begins to grow and the chair is produced by the due application and operation of some other being, either sun and rain or carpenter and tools. By comparing the producer and the product the mind forms the ideas of cause and effect.

But Do We Know Reality?

Locke in company with many English writers of the seventeenth and eighteenth centuries tends to be prolix. He inserts amounts of unimportant detail and explores various side issues. There is, however, one further point that needs mention before passing on to his successor.

At the beginning of Book IV Locke repeats his initial thesis that the only immediate objects of knowledge are our own ideas. (Previously he had not used the word *immediate*.) The theory as it has now been developed makes knowledge the perception of the agreement or disagreement between two ideas; e.g., white is not black. But there is the possibility that our ideas are bare visions, mere fancies, corresponding to nothing real. Cannot a visionary or fanatic perceive the agreement or disagreement between two of his ideas? "That a harpy is not a centaur is by this way as certain knowledge and as much a truth as that a square is not a circle" (IV, iv, 1).

Since part of the force of this objection lies in the supposition that human knowledge is very extensive, Locke goes to some length in showing how little one can know. The indubitable experience we have of bodies never rises to the level of science; that is, there are no general and unquestionable truths concerning bodies, nothing certain or demonstrative. Of spirits, God or angels or other spirits if such there be, we have still less knowledge. And the connection between spirit and body is completely opaque. By experience we know that primary qualities produce secondary ideas in us; by experience we know also that a thought or volition can produce a bodily motion; but far from knowing how mind and body can affect each other, we do not even know how primary qualities can produce secondary qualities. Human knowledge then is confined to narrow limits.

The original objection, however, is not met by restricting the scope of our knowledge. Empiricism may be satisfied with very little. But one wishes to know whether even one idea conforms to a real external object, or whether our supposed knowledge is all visionary. So far as the real existence of self is concerned, Locke depends on intuition by giving a psychological interpretation to *Cogito ergo sum*. The existence of God, as was said before, he believes to be demonstrably certain. But if the existence of bodies can be known only through sensation, what is the criterion distinguishing an idea that conforms from one that does not? Locke's answer comes in several stages (IV, iv, 4–12).

First, since all simple ideas are involuntary and are produced in a natural way, the goodness of God guarantees their conformity with things, or at least a degree of conformity sufficient for human needs. Second, as complex ideas, with the exception of ideas of substances, do not profess to represent anything outside the mind, the problem does not arise. For example, the knowledge of mathematics, though and because it consists only of the agreement of ideas, is real knowledge and not a fancy. If there exist triangles in external nature, the theorems will apply also to them; but whether or not there are physical triangles, the theorems are true and certain. In the third place it must be admitted that ideas of substances often fail to correspond to real things. But, says Locke, "so far as they agree with those, so far our knowledge concerning them is real" (IV, iv, 12). The paragraph is not an easy one. It seems to say that ideas of substances must correspond to real archetypes, though few of them do, and these do not conform very exactly. Thus we have real knowledge, but not much. If the student thinks that this summary fails to do justice to Locke's handling of the main objection, he is invited to puzzle through the paragraph for himself. Undoubtedly there is a difficulty. Perhaps the next philosopher can dispose of it.

GEORGE BERKELEY (1685–1753)

Scarcely twenty years of age, George Berkeley, a student in Dublin, was attracted by the philosophy of Locke; and before he was twenty-five he had published two works, *A New Theory of Vision* and *Principles of Human Knowledge*, which brought him lasting fame. In these he wholeheartedly accepted the basic principle of empiricism. Experience is the source, foundation, and touchstone of all knowledge. But, as the previous pages have shown, Locke had left some rough passages that needed smoothing; he got into difficulties he could not overcome; and this occurred because he had not followed out his empirical principles consistently. These inconsistencies Berkeley promises to remove.

Abstract Ideas

The Introduction to his *Principles of Human Knowledge* is mainly a criticism of Locke's theory of abstract ideas; and in view of the fact that the operation of abstracting eventuated in that most troublesome notion of substance, it would seem that Berkeley could hardly have chosen a better starting point. He describes the process of abstraction (para. 9) so as to bring out its absurdity: "For example, the mind having observed that Peter, James, and John resemble each other, in certain common agreements of shape and other qualities, leaves out of the complex or compounded idea it has of Peter, James, and any other particular man, that which is peculiar to each, retaining only what is common to all; and so makes an abstract idea wherein all the particulars equally partake, abstracting entirely from and cutting off all those circumstances and differences, which might determine it to any particular existence. And after this manner it is said we come by the abstract idea of man, or, if you please, humanity or human nature; wherein it is true there is included colour, because there is no man but has some colour, but then it can be neither white, nor black, nor any particular colour; because there is no one particular colour wherein all men partake. So likewise there is included stature, but then it is neither tall stature nor low stature, nor yet middle stature, but something abstracted from all these. And so of the rest."

Now, continues Berkeley modestly, since abstract ideas are admittedly not attained without great pains and much study, it may be that some very learned persons have them; but for himself and all ordinary people, there is no such thing. "The idea of man that I frame to myself must be either of a white or a black or a tawny, a straight or a crooked, a tall or a low or a middle sized man" (para. x). No argument is required to prove the point: one need only observe the contents of one's own mind. "If any man has the faculty of framing in his mind such an idea of a triangle as is here described, it is in vain to pretend to dispute him out of it, nor would I go about it. All I desire is, that the reader would fully and certainly inform himself whether he has such an idea or no. And this, methinks, can be no hard task for any one to perform. What more easy than for any one to look a little into his own thoughts, and there try whether he has, or can attain to have, an idea that shall correspond with the description that is here given of the general idea of a triangle, which is, neither oblique, nor rectangle, equilateral, equicrural, nor scalenon, but all and none of these at once?" (para. xiii).

It is true that we make use of what may be called general ideas. But such an idea is in itself a particular idea that has been put to specific use. "Suppose a geometrician is demonstrating the method of cutting a line in two equal parts. He draws, for instance, a black line of an inch in length; this, which in itself is a particular line, is nevertheless with regard to its signification general, since, as it is there used, it represents all particular lines whatsoever" (para. xii).

It is also true that words may be called abstract. The word triangle applies indiscriminately to all triangles; it does not signify any one idea, but signifies indifferently a great number of ideas. Frequently a word does not signify any idea. In the early stages of learning the word *good* or the word *danger* may at first have occasioned the particular idea of a definite good or dangerous thing. But when these words have grown familiar, a father may promise his son something good or warn him of danger and so produce the appropriate emotion or reaction, without the son's having any idea of what the good or the danger may be. The use of words without accompanying ideas occurs still more frequently in learned discussions; and because of this many philosophic controversies are purely verbal. Error, especially philosophical error, comes chiefly from the careless use of words. "So long as I confine my thoughts to my own ideas divested of words, I do not see how I can be easily mistaken. . . . I cannot be deceived in thinking I have an idea which I have not. It is not possible for me to imagine that any of my own ideas are like or unlike, that are not truly so" (para. xxii). Who can mistake the smell of a rose for the smell of turpentine, or the image of a square for the image of a circle? "He that knows he has no other than particular ideas will not puzzle himself in vain to find out and conceive the abstract idea annexed to any name. And he that knows names do not always stand for ideas will spare himself the labor of looking for ideas where there are none to be had. . . . In vain do we extend our view into the heavens and pry into the entrails of the earth; in vain do we consult the writings of the learned and trace the dark footsteps of antiquity; we need only draw the curtain of words to behold the fairest tree of knowledge, whose fruit is excellent and within the reach of our hand" (para. xxiv).

For a better understanding of the issues involved in the discussion of abstract ideas and to indicate that no system of philosophy can escape a decision on this point, a reference back to the medieval controversies can be made. Roscellinus, it will be remembered, reduced universals to mere sounds in the air. Abelard and Aquinas defended a theory of abstraction. Occam, improving on the nominalism of Roscellinus, claimed to have disposed of the problem of individuation. Of course, the modern framework differs somewhat from the medieval: there is a different focus, as it were; and the British empiricists draw conclusions that probably would have shocked the scholastics. Yet, one can hardly fail to see that the difficulties are the same.

Can Two Senses Perceive the Same Idea?

Abstract ideas are not the only point at which Berkeley in the name of experience parted company with Locke. The older man's account of distance, figure, motion, and some others was also defective. Therefore some of the arguments in Berkeley's *New Theory of Vision* will be summarized before passing to his main constructive effort in the *Principles*. It was stated but not emphasized above that the ideas of space, distance, and motion are, in Locke's view, perceived both by sight and by touch. Berkeley objects. The main point, that no simple idea is received through two senses, is supported first by the observation that space or distance is not a simple idea. We cannot see distance. In World War II when aviators had to bail out over the North Sea, they would of course float down in their parachutes, hit the water, sink a few yards into the ocean, and then rise to the surface. But too often upon rising they would find their parachute over them; and if unable to tear through it, they would drown. To avoid this, the high brass ordered them to cut themselves loose from the parachute about fifteen feet above the surface of the ocean. Then by the time they had plunged and risen to the surface, the parachute would have blown away. Obeying this command, the men broke their necks. Since the surface of the ocean is relatively smooth and lacks such familiar objects as houses and trees, it was impossible to judge one's distance from the surface. The ocean at five hundred feet produces the same impression that it does at fifteen. That is, distance is not a simple idea. It cannot be seen. It must be judged. One must judge distance by comparing present impressions with past experiences. Berkeley puts it as follows.

Distance cannot be directly perceived because an object at any distance in a straight line projects itself to one point only in the eye;

and a man born blind, upon receiving his sight, could not at that first instant know the distance to what he saw. He would have to learn to judge distances. This learning consists of several parts: sensations of muscular activity in the eye, variation in the size and clarity of the image, and comparison of these with other sensations of touch. That is to say, after having the visual sensations the man born blind would walk forward and touch the object in question. By repeated experiences of the amount of walking necessary before the sensations of touch follow the sensations of sight, he comes to judge or anticipate the distance by sight alone. But strictly speaking color only, not space, figure, or motion, is the object of sight. These details of how distance is to be learned are perhaps not so important for Berkeley's claim to be more empirical than Locke as his sharp distinction between ideas of sight and ideas of touch. In Locke's theory the ideas of motion, shape, position and others come through both senses. But Berkeley is surely correct in pointing out that no idea can come through two senses. The visual sensation of a colored shape is perfectly distinct from the tactual sensation of a hard shape. In both cases the one word *shape* is used; but the ideas or images are totally different. Because space is a key concept in philosophy, these considerations profoundly influence Berkeley's advance over Locke, and later provide material for Kant. Locke had made space a simple idea. It is immediately impressed on the mind by sensation and is not the result of a later operation. But the identical idea is impressed both by sight and touch. Because it is common to two sensations, Locke can easily think that space is something objective, existing independently of the perception. Such an objective space, if it does not positively require the existence of material substance, at least makes such an assumption possible, and thus contributes to the explanation of the otherwise mysterious fact that disparate qualities can regularly occur together as things. This Lockean construction is now seen to be doubly impossible. Since there is no idea common to two senses, Locke's space has proved to be nonexistent, and whatever space remains is deprived of all appearance of objectivity. It becomes something like Locke's secondary qualities which, like pain, exist only while one perceives them. Then, further, if this visual space which Berkeley allows, is not itself a simple idea but is learned only after considerable experience of eye strain, sharply focused images, and so on, and is thus subsequent to rather than prior to the perception of compound ideas; and if material substance, as will become clear in the next few paragraphs, is as unreal as any other abstract idea, a new explanation is imperative for the regular coexistence of different qualities in the same place. With this demand Berkeley's constructive work in the *Principles* can no longer be postponed.

Esse is Percipi

This he begins by accepting the main outline of Locke's scheme: the objects of knowledge are simple ideas of sensation and reflection, and complex ideas formed by mental operations. In the continuation Berkeley's own language cannot be improved upon. "As several of these ideas are frequently observed to accompany each other, they come to be marked by one name, and so to be reputed as one thing. Thus for example a certain color, taste, smell, figure, and consistence having been observed to go together, are accounted one distinct thing, signified by the name apple. Other collections of ideas constitute a stone, a tree, a book, and the like sensible things. . . .

"But besides all that endless variety of ideas or objects of knowledge, there is something which knows or perceives them, and exercises divers operations, such as willing, imagining, remembering, about them. This perceiving active being is what I call mind, spirit, soul, or myself. By which words I do not denote any one of my ideas, but a thing entirely distinct from them, wherein they exist, or, which is the same thing, whereby they are perceived; for the existence of an idea consists in being perceived.

"That neither our thoughts, nor passions, nor ideas formed by the imagination, exist without the mind, is what every body will allow. And (to me) it seems no less evident that the various sensations or ideas imprinted on the sense, however blended or combined together (that is, whatever objects they compose), cannot exist otherwise than in a mind perceiving them. I think an intuitive knowledge may be obtained of this, by any one that shall attend to what is meant by the term exist, when applied to sensible things. The table I write on, I say, exists, that is, I see and feel it; and if I were out of my study

I should say it existed, meaning thereby that if I was in my study I might perceive it, or that some other spirit actually does perceive it. There was an odour, that is, it was smelled; there was a sound, that is to say, it was heard; a colour or figure, and it was perceived by sight or touch. This is all that I can understand by these and the like expressions. For as to what is said of the absolute existence of unthinking things without any relation to their being perceived, that seems perfectly unintelligible. Their esse is percipi, nor is it possible they should have any existence out of the minds or thinking things which perceive them.

"It is indeed an opinion strangely prevailing amongst men, that houses, mountains, rivers, and in a word all sensible objects have an existence natural or real, distinct from their being perceived by the understanding. But with how great an assurance and acquiescence soever this principle may be entertained in the world; yet whoever shall find in his heart to call it in question, may, if I mistake not, perceive it to involve a manifest contradiction. For what are the forementioned objects but the things we perceive by sense, and what do we perceive besides our own ideas or sensations; and is it not plainly repugnant that any one of these or any combination of them should exist unperceived?" (*Principles*, i–iv).

Berkeley was aware that nearly all men, and not Locke only, believed in the real external existence of material substances. But he thought that only a little reflection was needed to convince anyone of the absurdity of the common view. Matter is an abstract idea, and abstract ideas do not exist. Even if they did, they would exist in the mind, the only place in which an idea can exist. And because colors and tastes are perceptions, like pain, it is only in the mind that apples, mountains, and rivers exist, because these are ideas too, complex ideas, but nonetheless ideas. Locke of course admitted that the secondary qualities of color, taste, and smell, exist only in the mind. But Berkeley in consequence of his analysis of the ideas of space, position, and magnitude, now shows that all qualities are "secondary." The tangible quality of solidity is as much a sensation as the color red. The shape perceived by touch is as much a perception as the shape seen. And perceptions exist only in a perceiving mind.

If it be objected that although the perceptions exist only in the mind, there are real things outside the mind of which the perceptions are effects and copies, Berkeley replies that an idea can only be like or be a copy of an idea: a color can only be like a color. And further, are these alleged external things, of which the ideas are supposed to be copies, perceptible or not? If they are perceptible, they are ideas in the mind. If they are not perceptible, then a color would have to be a copy of something invisible, and solidity a copy of something intangible. Can anything be greater nonsense?

A philosopher who wishes to defend the existence of matter ought to have reasons for believing it to exist, and he ought to be able to show its usefulness. But although these two requirements remain unfulfilled, Berkeley is willing to surrender if someone can merely conceive it possible for an extended substance, or any idea, or anything like an idea, to exist otherwise than in a mind perceiving it. The appeal is to experience. "I do not argue against the existence of any one thing that we can apprehend, either by sense or reflection. That the things I see with mine eyes and touch with my hands do exist, really exist, I make not the least question. The only thing whose existence we deny, is that which philosophers call matter or corporeal substance. And in doing of this, there is no damage done to the rest of mankind, who, I dare say, will never miss it. The atheist indeed will want the colour of an empty name to support his impiety; and the philosophers may possibly find they have lost a great handle for trifling and disputation. . . .

"But, say what we can, some one perhaps may be apt to reply, he will still believe his senses, and never suffer any arguments, how plausible soever, to prevail over the certainty of them. Be it so, assert the evidence of sense as high as you please, we are willing to do the same. That what I see, hear, and feel doth exist, that is to say, is perceived by me, I no more doubt than I do of my own being. But I do not see how the testimony of sense can be alleged as a proof for existence of any thing which is not perceived by sense" (*Principles*, xxxv, xl).

Do You and I Exist?

At the start Berkeley had distinguished between ideas, which are purely passive, and the active spirit or mind that perceives them. If the existence of an idea consists in its being perceived, there must obviously be a perceiving spirit. The discussion of spirit, however, is attended with some difficulty. Because ideas are passive, without any power or agency in them, and spirit is active, the two must be radically different — so different that an idea cannot possibly represent a spirit. Spirit or mind is characterized by the activities of understanding and willing, but no idea has such characteristics. That is to say, we have no idea or image of a spirit. On the face of it, this makes the mind unknowable, for the first sentence of the *Principles* identifies the objects of knowledge as ideas. But if it is unknowable, how could Berkeley have written about it? How could he have admitted even the ideas of reflection, since willing is active and ideas are passive? To avoid such a devastating conclusion, he writes, "It must be owned at the same time that we have some notion of soul, spirit, and the operations of the mind, such as willing, loving, hating, inasmuch as we know or understand the meaning of these words" (*Principles,* xxvii). This expedient can scarcely be thought satisfactory, particularly in the case of Berkeley, who earlier had referred the large majority of philosophic stupidities to the use of words apart from ideas. Ideas remain the objects of knowledge, and if "notions" are different from ideas, Berkeley makes no effort to explain their status. In fact, paragraph v used *ideas, impressions,* and *notions* as synonyms. When later (chap. cxl) this precarious knowledge of one's own mind is made the basis for the knowledge of other minds, the danger of solipsism becomes clear. Perhaps I am the only person in the world. Or, better, the only world is the one in my mind.

Of course Berkeley tries to defend the existence of other human beings (cxlv, cxlvi), but he says we have better reason to believe in the existence of God. Our knowledge, or at least our supposition that human beings exist comes by way of the ideas they excite in us by their bodily motions. That there must be other human spirits is not immediate knowledge, but an inference to account for some of my ideas. But whereas these ideas are few in number, those from which we infer God's existence are extremely numerous. And if from our visual images of heads, arms, legs, and torsos we say we see men, we can say we likewise see God in virtue of our sensations of trees, rivers, and mountains. Scripture declares: "The Lord, he causeth the vapors to ascend; he maketh lightenings with rain; he bringeth forth the wind out of his treasures (Jer. 10:13)" (*Principles*, cl).

It is of interest to note that of the three rationalists Leibniz was a devout and active Christian. He believed that his type of philosophy agreed with and furnished support to his religion. Descartes was perhaps a nominal Christian, and Spinoza attacked Christianity. In empiricism Locke was at best a nominal Christian, and Hume was an enemy. But Berkeley's personal devotion is seen not so much in his being chosen Bishop as in his strenuous but disappointing missionary activity. For him this empiricism, which made the existence of God more evident than the existence of other men, and which deprived atheistic materialism of its material substance, was the bulwark of Christianity. Yet Leibniz and Berkeley could not both have been right. Since rationalism and empiricism are incompatible, they cannot both be the foundation of Christianity. At the same time, Berkeley and Hume could not both be right, nor could Leibniz and Spinoza. Neither empiricism nor rationalism can both defend and destroy Christianity. What is the trouble? Has something dropped out of view since the medieval period?

Science and Causality

Aside from the question of religion Berkeley had to square his theory with science. For this purpose too the existence of God is necessary. Common sense and science both assume that the trees, the waterfall, and the mountain do not cease to exist when one returns to the cabin and goes to bed. Otherwise, how is it that when we wake up the next morning the trees and mountain are in the same place? The common assumption is that they stayed there all the time. But Berkeley has shown that, because they are ideas, they could not have existed there all the time. "There" means in my mind, and it is plainly true that the sensation ceased through the night. But it regularly reappears in the morning when I look out the window. Even if the sensation is in my mind, there must be some external cause of it. The idea was involuntary. When I look in the proper direction I cannot help seeing trees and mountains, and when I look away I cannot see them no matter how hard I try. Now, Berkeley admits that there must be an external cause of involuntary ideas, a cause too of their regularity of appearance; but this external cause, instead of being an abstract idea of material substance, is God. And the regularity with which God produces ideas in our minds furnishes to science its field of investigation and distinguishes real objects from dreams and subjective illusions.

Regularity in the sequence of ideas permits us to designate certain collections of ideas as things, and when one or two of their qualities appear, such as the visual sensation of a given size and shape of red, we expect that the other qualities of an apple, its taste, will or may soon occur. But of course science goes far beyond this ordinary experience. What the nature of science is, should be clearly stated, for there is some confusion about it; but the denial of matter no more makes science impossible than it makes the sight and taste of an apple impossible.

The materialists claim that man is invincibly ignorant of the true and inner nature of things because it is only their outward appearances that the senses can grasp. There is something in every drop of water and every grain of sand that is beyond the power of the human mind to comprehend. If such skepticism is permitted in science, says Berkeley, religion too will eventually suffer. But it is unwarranted even in science, for it depends partly, as has been explained, on the supposition of the abstract idea of unknowable matter. In part also it depends on a mistaken notion of causality. Not to belabor the medieval physicists for their belief in essences and occult powers, the modern scientific explanation of qualities in terms of weight, figure, and motion, that is, the theory of mechanical causes, is equally far from the truth. Perceptible qualities, such as weight and motion, are causes of nothing, for ideas are purely passive. Only spirit is active. Newton's theory of gravitation, at least as popularly understood, is an appropriate example. Since the publication of his *Principia*, the great mechanical principle in vogue has been attraction. That a stone falls to earth or that the sea swells toward the moon is supposed to be explained by attraction. Every two particles of matter, it is said, attract each other as the product of their masses and inversely as the square of the distance. But does the word *attraction* enlarge our knowledge? Are we to suppose that one atom puts on lipstick and attracts another as they come closer together? Or that if two atoms both use lipstick, they repel each other? The term *attraction* simply disguises our ignorance and depends on a mistaken notion of causality.

Science in fact has nothing to do with causality; its aim is the discovery of similarities. When Galileo observed the acceleration of freely falling bodies, he did not discover the cause of their fall: he discovered the rate of their fall. More than this, he discovered that all freely falling bodies fall at the same rate. His success consisted, not in observing a cause, but in noticing a similarity. Again, Kepler discovered that the motions of the planets are similar. Each orbit is an ellipse; each radius vector sweeps out equal areas in equal times; and the squares of the periodic times are proportional to the mean distances from the sun. Thus Kepler did not discover the cause of planetary motion, but he described how the planets move. Newton, although he may have been no more brilliant than Kepler, achieved greater scientific results because he discovered wider similarities. He saw that Galileo's freely falling bodies and Kepler's planets move in precisely the same way. The moon falls to the earth and the earth falls to the sun in the same path that a marble falls to the earth. One equation describes all three motions. But why does anything move? Science has no answer: it has no concern with causality.

The only cause is a mind or spirit, working for a purpose. "Considering the whole creation is the workmanship of a wise and good agent, it should seem to become philosophers to employ their thoughts, contrary to what some hold, about the final causes of things. And I must confess I see no reason why pointing out the various ends to which natural things are adapted and for which they were originally with unspeakable wisdom contrived, should not be thought one good way of accounting for them and altogether worthy a philosopher" (*Principles*, cvii).

Do Two and Three Equal Five?

One more point must be alluded to, even if briefly, before going on with Berkeley's successor, David Hume. As the rationalists had chosen the method of mathematics for their ideal, so it is mathematics which seems most impervious to empirical procedure. Berkeley has several things to say, after the manner of Locke, about the infinite divisibility of lines and space, and even about infinitesimal calculus; but the empirical basis of mathematics is best seen in the nature of the unit. Leibniz might have considerable success in reducing arithmetic to a deductive system, but the empiricist asks about the origin of unity. Two and three are five, but what is one? Naturally Berkeley cannot admit that the number one is an abstract idea. The idea in our minds is the idea of one grain of sand or of one pile of sand. Whether the pile is one or one million depends on how the percipient views it. There are no numbers in the abstract, but only collections of things. The science of numbers is therefore entirely subordinate to practice, and experimentation will be the test of its truth. Berkeley's insistence that mathematics is a practical science might be illustrated by some elementary chemistry. The rationalist asserts that two and three are always five; and the most careful experiment shows that two pounds and three pounds make five pounds. It is not necessary that the pounds be pounds of the same stuff. Two pounds of lead and three pounds of feathers make five pounds. But two and three do not always make five. Experimentation shows that two pints of water and three pints of sulfuric acid do not make five pints. Still further, according to rationalism two and three give the same result as three and two; but woe to the student who thinks that two pints of water added to three pints of sulfuric acid give the same result as three pints of sulfuric acid added to two pints of water. Such nonempirical arithmetic may blow him through the roof. Mathematics therefore is as much a useful experimental science as physics is; and Berkeley believes that he has succeeded in basing his whole system on experience alone. But Hume thought that one correction was still needed.

DAVID HUME (1711—1776)

In the writings of Locke and Berkeley there are phrases that describe human intellectual achievements with optimism. The former speaks of the busy and boundless fancy of man, and the latter refers to the choir of heaven and furniture of the earth. This is as it should be, for empiricism in the wake of rationalism's shipwreck aims to show that knowledge is possible. But as one begins to read Hume, a fear arises that not all is well. "Man is a reasonable being," he says in his *Enquiry Concerning Human Understanding* (Section I), "and as such receives from science his proper food and nourishment: but so narrow are the bounds of human understanding that little satisfaction can be hoped for in this particular, either from the extent or security of his acquisitions." Can it be that empiricism also will fail to provide a basis for knowledge?

Do We Think in Images?

Hume, of course, is an empiricist. All objects of knowledge, or as Hume says, "all the perceptions of the human mind resolve themselves . . . into impressions and ideas" (A *Treatise of Human Nature*, p. 1). These two may be distinguished by introspection, the impressions being lively and vivid, the ideas being fainter images of them. Thought may range the heavens and fancy may picture monsters and incongruous shapes, but "all this creative power of the mind amounts to no more than the faculty of compounding, transposing, augmenting, or diminishing the materials afforded us by the senses and experience. . . . When we analyze our thoughts or ideas, however compounded or sublime, we always find that they resolve themselves into such simple ideas as were copied from a precedent feeling or sentiment. . . . We may prosecute this enquiry to what length we please, where we shall always find that every idea we examine is copied from a similar impression" (*Enquiry*, Sec. II).

When Hume uses the term *impression*, he "would not be understood to express the manner in which our lively perceptions are produced in the soul, but merely the perceptions themselves" (*Treatise*, footnote 1). He specifically denies that impressions are impressed by the action of any external body. Accepting Berkeley's correction of Locke, he says that although men have a natural instinct to believe in an external universe which would exist even in the absence of every sensitive creature, the slightest philosophy teaches that nothing can be present to the mind but an image or perception. The table which we see seems to diminish as we move away from it; could we see it from the other end of a long hall, it would appear very little; but the alleged real or external table is supposed to remain the same size regardless of our distance from it. Evidently therefore what we saw was an image and not an external table.

On this point Hume simply repeats Berkeley. It is therefore appropriate, before continuing with Hume's advances in the theory, to examine this area of agreement. Even Locke, for all his material substance, had also defined the objects of knowledge as ideas, phantasms, or images. Since this is common and basic to empiricism, a decision here is of fundamental importance. In the chapter on the Middle Ages the section on Thomas Aquinas suggested that empiricists are handicapped by too lively an imagination. In particular, Berkeley and Hume urge their readers to look into their own minds and see what ideas are there, never doubting but that all men will find the same imagery. Consider this quotation from the *Treatise* I, i, 1: "That idea of red, which we form in the dark, and that impression which strikes our eye in sunshine, differ only in degree, not in nature. That the case is the same with all our simple impressions . . . everyone may satisfy himself . . . by running over as many as he pleases. I know of no way of convincing him but by desiring him to show a simple impression that has not a correspondent idea. . . . If he does not answer this challenge, as 'tis certain he cannot. . . ." But this is not certain at all, for there are persons who deny that the impression of red in the sunshine has a correspondent copy in the dark. Hume is still more explicit: "When I shut my eyes and think of my chamber, the ideas I form are exact representations of the impressions I felt." But others than Hume not only lack representations that are exact, they do not have even inexact images. Many persons will admit that they have no images of odors and sounds; and if they have visual images none the less, their deficiency (if it is a deficiency) in the other types of sensation may lead them to credit the assertions of those who say that they have no visual images either. Hume's theory would imply that people devoid of images cannot think — a conclusion resentment to which proves that they do. Even if imagery were universal, it would by no means follow that all objects of thought are such representations. Vividness of imagery and clarity of thought do not always vary in direct proportion, as they should on this empiricist definition. The difficulty here is not merely a chance mistake in observation, as if Hume had merely not happened to meet such people; nor is it merely a faulty argument that one author has blundered into. Superficial errors can easily be corrected without detriment to the system as a whole. But Hume's misstatement of fact when he said, "as 'tis certain he cannot," involving the assumption that all minds are in this respect alike, is an error for whose correction empiricism provides no method. Not to mention the difficulty of knowing the minds of all people, past and future, empiricism makes it impossible to know any other person's mind. Just as you cannot feel my toothache, so no two empiricists can have the same idea of red, of apple, or of anything. Each one has his own images only, and cannot possibly perceive what is in his neighbor's mind. It is the method of empiricism itself that prevents Hume from being certain of what another man can or cannot do. Hume could of course take refuge in solipsism. If he is the only mind, then all thinking is imagery, for all thinking would be Hume's thinking. Berkeley, too, it will be remembered, had some difficulty with solipsistic implications. Now, solipsism is usually regarded as a *reductio ad absurdum* of any system, and there is no evidence that Hume desired to avail himself of such an anti-social expedient. Therefore the difficulty concerning images remains.

Who Does the Thinking?

There is, however, another difficult point in Berkeley that Hume definitely seeks to avoid in his theory of his own mind. Berkeley had argued, "Besides all that endless variety of ideas or objects of knowledge, there is likewise something which knows or perceives them, and exercises divers operations, as willing, imagining, remembering, about them. This perceiving active being is what I call mind, spirit, soul, or myself." Yet Berkeley experienced some embarrassment when he tried to account for the possibility of knowing our own minds. Since the mind is active and the ideas are passive, and since the ideas exist in a mind which is their substratum, it follows that there can be no idea of mind or spirit. And if ideas are the objects of knowledge, the mind cannot be known; or, in other words, there is no evidence in experience that a mind, soul, or spirit exists. Hume draws this latter conclusion by using the same method Berkeley had applied to Locke. If the impossibility of abstract ideas rules out an unknowable material substance, an unknowable spiritual substance fares no better. Impressions and ideas exist, i.e., they are perceived, but they are impressed on nothing and nothing perceives them.[1]

It is the resolve to base all knowledge on experience that leads to this paradoxical conclusion. Some philosophers, and Hume must have had Berkeley in mind—if he had a mind—assert that we are intimately conscious of what we call our Self; no proof is needed because it is an immediate experience. But, continues Hume, all experience is opposed to such an assertion. There is no impression from which the idea of self can be derived. The impressions red, sour, heavy, and so on are neither singly nor collectively the originals of the alleged idea of self, for these impressions and their derivative ideas are constantly changing—we see red one moment, blue the next, and then we hear a sound—while the self is supposed to remain constant. If, however, a few metaphysicians think they have such an idea, Hume himself and the rest of mankind "are nothing but a bundle or collection of different perceptions. . . . The mind is a kind of theatre where several perceptions successively make their appearance. . . . There is properly no simplicity in it at one time nor identity in different. . . . The comparison of the theatre must not mislead us. They are the successive perceptions only that constitute the mind; nor have we the most distant notion of the place where these scenes are represented, or of the materials of which it is composed" (*Treatise*, I, iv, 6).

The propensity to ascribe to oneself an invariable and uninter-

---

[1] In the Author's Advertisement to his *Enquiry*, Hume seemingly retracts his earlier work, A *Treatise of Human Nature*: he sent it to press too early, it contained some negligences in reasoning and more in expression, it was a juvenile work which the author never acknowledged, and "henceforth the author desires that the following pieces may alone be regarded as containing his philosophical principles." Now, since the argument against spiritual substance is found only in the *Treatise*, Hume gives the appearance of having repudiated it. On the other hand, the Author's Advertisement speaks of some, not many, negligences, and admits that most of the reasonings in the *Enquiry* are found in the *Treatise*. The substantial agreement between the two works, and especially the cogency with which the denial of spirit is derived from their common principles, make it unlikely that Hume consciously ceased to hold the point in question. Certainly he never came to assert the existence of spirit, nor did he substitute any other view for the one omitted. And even in the unlikely case that he gave up his earlier position, the arguments against the existence of spirit have played their role in the history of philosophy and should be so noted.

rupted existence is the result of confusing two distinct ideas. From a perception that remains invariable for a space of time, we derive the idea of sameness or identity. The idea of diversity, while it may come from a succession of unrelated objects, also arises from a succession of objects closely related. But though these two ideas are perfectly distinct and even contrary, yet they are generally confounded with each other. Thus we substitute the notion of identity for that of successive related objects, and suppose the continued existence of a soul, self, and substance. A ship provides a good illustration. On its first voyage a few of its minor parts prove defective and are replaced when it reaches its home port. Its next voyage is stormy and a mast is broken. On a later occasion it strikes some rocks and its keel must be repaired. This process continues until every part of the original ship has been replaced. Now, if the new parts had been put together all at once, we should have called it a new and different ship; but because they were replaced gradually, no one of them bearing a large proportion to the whole, and especially because the ship preserves the same size and functions in the same manner for the same purpose, we do not scruple to call it the same ship. Similarly, if a bundle of ideas were completely replaced by another set all at once, or even if a small number — identified as the body — should remain over, while the memory, education, and habits be lost, we should say that a new person had appeared; but if the change be gradual, if the mutual relation of the parts continues, and the whole preserves the same general functions, we recognize it as the same person and mistakenly ascribe to it an uninterrupted existence.

Causality Again

To pass to another topic, Hume's theory of causality, perhaps even more than his view of personal identity, was a stimulus and provocation to Kant and later philosophers. That this influence on the future should be Hume's rather than Berkeley's is somewhat strange because Hume adds little to Berkeley's theory of causation except clarity and emphasis. Perhaps Kant never had read Berkeley; or, more likely, he was asleep when he read him, for Kant reports that it was Hume who awakened him from his dogmatic, rationalistic slumbers.

The question is how one can be assured of any real existence and matter of fact beyond the present testimony of the senses or the records of memory. If a man be asked why he believes his friend is in France, he would put in evidence a letter just received. What is presupposed in this reply is a connection between the present fact of the letter and the friend's being in France, which is inferred from it. All evidence intended to establish an absent fact depends on a causal connection between what is absent and what is present. The question then becomes how we arrive at the knowledge of cause and effect.

An empirical philosophy must assert that this knowledge is wholly based on experience and cannot be had a priori, prior to experience. One warm afternoon shortly after his creation, Adam was sitting on the bank of the river Euphrates, dangling his feet in its waters. He could see the fish dozing comfortably in the cooling stream and concluded that the best place to take a nap that hot day would be at the bottom of the river. Although his rational faculties were perfect, he could not have inferred from the fluidity and transparency of the water that it would suffocate him. No a priori knowledge warned him that he could not do what the fish were doing. Only by experience could he learn the connection between the sensations of cool fluidity and those of drowning. Hume gives other examples also. Present two smooth pieces of marble to a man who knows no physics; he will never discover by the most careful examination of their qualities that they will adhere together in such a manner as to require great force to separate them in a direct line, while they make so small a resistance to a lateral pressure. Again, what is there in the appearance of gunpowder that would lead one to expect an explosion, or in the looks of a lodestone that would indicate magnetism?

Great familiarity sometimes deceives us into supposing that we could have guessed effects from their causes; we fancy that without experience we could have inferred that the impact of one billiard ball would communicate motion to a second. Or that a stone raised into the air and left without support would fall. But were it not for experience, we could as well suppose that the second billiard ball would stop the first and that the stone would stay put or even fall upwards.

Since every effect is a distinct event or sensation from its cause, any a priori connection between them must be purely arbitrary. And even after experiencing the succession of cause and effect, the connection must still appear arbitrary. Science can never show the action of that power which produces any single effect in the universe. The ultimate springs and principles of nature are totally shut up from human curiosity and enquiry. The most perfect philosophy of the natural kind only staves off our ignorance a little longer, as perhaps the most perfect philosophy of the moral or metaphysical kind serves only to discover larger portions of it.

Hume insists that our conclusions relative to causes and effects are not founded on reasoning or any process of the understanding. "Our senses inform us," he says, "of the color, weight, and consistence of bread; but neither sense nor reason can ever inform us of those qualities which fit it for the nourishment and support of the human body. . . . But notwithstanding this ignorance of natural powers and principles, we always presume, when we see like sensible qualities, that they have like secret powers, and expect that effects similar to those which we have experienced, will follow from them" (*Enquiry*, Sec. IV, ii). This expectation compounds the difficulty. First we could not know why the sensations of sight and smell which we call bread were in a past instance followed by nourishment; now second the inference that nourishment will follow similar sensations in the future is completely without logical justification. This inference is not demonstrative because there is no contradiction in supposing that brown could be followed by poisoning as well as by nourishment. Of course, as a matter of fact, people expect the future to be like the past, and so we eat our lunch; but "if there be any suspicion that the course of nature may change, and that the past may be no rule for the future, all experience becomes useless and can give rise to no inference or conclusion." Is this suspicion absurd? Can the resemblance of the future to the past be proved? Obviously not, if all knowledge is based on experience, for nothing is more certain than that we have not experienced the future. "It is impossible therefore that any arguments from experience can prove this resemblance of the past to the future, since all these arguments are founded on the supposition of that resemblance." "We have said that all arguments concerning existence are founded on the relation of cause and effect; that our knowledge of that relation is derived entirely from experience; and that all our experimental conclusions proceed upon the supposition that the future will be conformable to the past. To endeavor therefore the proof of this last supposition by probable arguments, or arguments regarding existence, must be evidently going in a circle, and taking that for granted which is the very point in question" (*ibid.*).

How is it then that men take a casual and arbitrary succession and make of it a causal and necessary connection? Experience shows only that one impression follows another; why do we say that one produces the other? To this question Hume gives a remarkable answer. "The principle" by which men are determined to draw a causal conclusion "is custom or habit. For wherever the repetition of any particular act or operation produces a propensity to renew the same act or operation, without being impelled by any reasoning or process of the understanding, we always say that this propensity is the effect of custom. By employing that word we pretend not to have given the ultimate reason of such a propensity" (*Enquiry*, Sec. V, 1.). This statement is remarkable in that the term *custom*, by which Hume wishes to explain the causal inference, is itself defined in terms of causality: the repetition of an act *produces* or causes a propensity to repeat the act, and this propensity is the *effect* of custom. However, the circular nature of the statement need cause no disturbing effect because Hume admits that he has not given the ultimate reason or cause of such a propensity. Here is something, surely, that a future philosopher must examine.

Why Believe in God?

Another point of importance is empiricism's final word on the existence of God. Although Locke and Berkeley condemned the ontological argument along with all the rationalistic method, yet they believed that the proposition itself could be proved by the order, beauty, and wisdom observable in the universe. It is understandable therefore that Hume should consider the matter. In effect the outcome has already been decided: if there is no spiritual substance, there can be no God; and if causality is custom, arguments that the world is an effect which must have a cause are invalid. But Hume is not content to let the matter rest there. For the present purpose he is willing to ignore the question of spiritual substance and to grant validity to causal arguments; but even with these concessions the existence of God cannot be proved.

"When we infer any particular cause from an effect, we must proportion the one to the other, and can never be allowed to ascribe to the cause any qualities but what are exactly sufficient to produce the effect. A body of ten ounces raised in any scale may serve as a proof that the counterbalancing weight exceeds ten ounces; but can never afford a reason that it exceeds a hundred. . . . Nor can we by any rules of just reasoning return back from the cause and infer other effects from it beyond those by which alone it is known to us. No one merely from the sight of Zeuxis's pictures could know that he was also a statuary or architect, and was an artist no less skillful in stone and marble than in colours" (*Enquiry*, Sec. XI).

Accordingly, if our knowledge of God is derived from the universe considered as an effect, we can ascribe to him only that precise degree of power, intelligence, and goodness necessary to account for our experience. And as in the case of Zeuxis, so with God, we cannot conclude that in the future he will give a more magnificent display of his attributes and produce a better world than this. That is, there is no reason to believe in heaven. In all causal arguments the knowledge of the cause is derived from the effect, and no further inferences can be drawn. This evidently correct estimate of the force of the argument leaves future punishment as well as future reward without a basis of proof, and in a manner removes the problem of evil. There is nothing that experience teaches about God that would require good to triumph and evil to be punished. If there are marks of distributive justice in the present world, God may be assigned that degree of justice; and justice is satisfied. If there are no marks of justice present, there is no reason to suppose that God is just.

To all this a believer in God might reply that anyone who saw a half-finished building could legitimately infer, not only that it was the effect of a designer, but further that the builder would soon return and finish it. Likewise the world is imperfect; yet as it shows order, we may infer a completion at a later date.

The believer's reply, however, is without merit. One may indeed infer that a building has an architect or builder because experience has provided many examples of the connection between a builder and a house. Experience has also included many half-finished houses and builders who later completed them. But the case is not the same with our reasonings from the works of nature. Experience has not provided many examples of the connection between a God and a universe. Nor have we seen several half-finished worlds which God later completed. But an inference, in order to have any show of plausibility, must be based on more than a single observation. There is therefore no reason to suppose that God, if he has made the world incomplete, will return to perfect it; in fact, there is no reason to think that the world is incomplete. Experience is a blank on these points, and one must remain a skeptic.

Skepticism

To conclude Hume's philosophy, to summarize the results of empiricism, and to prepare for the next chapter, a certain amount of criticism must be subjoined. Hume had no intention of giving aid and comfort to Christianity; and many orthodox believers, knowing him to be an enemy, are tempted to attack his refutation and to put the argument for God's existence in valid form. But contrary to both Hume's intentions and the fears of these particular believers, it could be that Hume injured himself more than Christianity. If arguments from experience do not prove the existence of God, the trouble might lie in experience rather than in the existence of God. The important point is not whether Hume can come to a knowledge of God, but rather whether Hume can come to a knowledge of anything. It is empiricism that is on trial. Can any knowledge be based on experience alone?

The criticism will begin with what is more superficial and proceed to basic issues. To continue with the religious themes for just a moment longer, Hume in addition to refuting the cosmological argument wrote a chapter against miracles. Though the religious implications are peripheral for the most part, Hume's definition of a miracle as a violation of natural law invites comparison with the common view of science, with Berkeley's view, and with a medieval Mohammedan's. The common view leans heavily on the notion of cause and effect: one event is supposed to produce a subsequent event; and if there should be no necessary connection between them, their conjunction would seem to be merely a coincidence and would not exemplify any scientific law. Hume, obviously, cannot object to miracles on this basis. In the medieval chapter there was mentioned the Arab philosopher, Al Gazali, whose view of causality coincided with that of Hume. But where Hume denies miracles, the Mohammedan, more understandably to common people, concluded in their favor. With the repudiation of causal efficacy not only do miracles seem possible on rare occasions, but every event appears to be miraculous. Nonetheless Hume's denial of necessary causation still allows for natural law of a sort. In one respect Hume's view of science is quite similar to that of Berkeley. Although ideas are passive and devoid of all force, there is a regularity in their sequence, and the task of science is nothing more than to describe this regularity. Berkeley, however, based the regularity of ideas on their control by the divine Spirit; for Hume on the other hand it is a brute, inexplicable fact that impressions always occur in the same series. Since therefore natural laws of this sort may exist, Hume can consistently define a miracle as "a transgression of a law of nature." But whether or not the remainder of his argument is consistent depends on rather fundamental factors in empiricism. Hume continues to the effect that "there must be a uniform experience against every miraculous event, otherwise the event would not merit that appellation"; for "a firm and unalterable experience has established these laws" of nature; and a miracle "has never been observed in any age or country." In this, which is the center of his argument, Hume begs the question. Miracles cannot have happened, he says, because no one has ever experienced one. Such a statement offers for proof the very proposition which it is supposed to prove. This *petitio principii* has wider implications than the religious issue of miracles. The question becomes whether empiricism is entitled to even that sort of law which a denial of causality seems to allow. Obviously no one has experienced every age and country. It is impossible to discover a firm and unalterable sequence of ideas. The law of nature that Hume requires against miracles is a universal law; and no one can have a universal experience. As Hume himself said in opposing the proof of God's existence, the conclusion must contain no more than the premises. If we cannot ascribe to God more justice than we actually see, neither can we suppose that nature continues to be regular beyond the limits of our observation. The phrase "beyond the limits of our observation" is not geographical and temporal only. Of course it includes the experiences of men in other places and other ages who report that they have seen miraculous events. But it also includes the elemental structure of nature that lies below the threshold of our observation. Since our gross experience does not give us perfect regularity, there is no empirical reason for assigning perfect regularity to the hypothetical atoms that (do not) cause it.

So far this critical conclusion has attacked points found in the middle or toward the end of Hume's philosophy. But the most serious difficulty with empiricism occurs at the very beginning. When Locke furnished his blank mind with a variety of simple impressions, he had to combine some of them before he could have the perception of a thing. As Berkeley also said, an apple is the combination of sensations of sight, taste, and touch. But why should a mind totally unfurnished with preconceived notions make one combination rather than another? Let Berkeley on one occasion combine the ruddy color and the juicy taste to make an apple, if he wishes; but may he not on another occasion combine that color with the smell of hydrogen sulfide and the sound of B flat to make a boogum? Locke's easy answer to this question is that some ideas occur together and others do not. He further provides a material substance to account for a set of qualities being together. However, with the disappearance of matter, Berkeley can rely only on spirit, and in fact God's spirit, to account for togetherness; and with the disappearance of spirit and God, Hume can rely on nothing. Now, perhaps this is not so fatal as it seems. Why can it not be a matter of experience alone that some ideas come in groups? To be sure, such a brute fact would lack explanation and leave the universe unintelligible or irrational, but Hume never claimed to be a rationalist, and empiricists would not be dismayed at brute facts. They might be dismayed, however, if they were forced to explain precisely how they knew that groups of ideas or impressions occurred together. The question, in other words, is, Can empiricism show that a knowledge of togetherness is possible?

Once again, Locke tried the easiest answer in making space a simple idea. But it is so obvious that space cannot be seen, touched, or smelled, that apparently even Locke had misgivings. At least in Berkeley and Hume, space became an idea of relation, and as relations are derivative and later ideas, a knowledge of them cannot exist in the beginning. Yet it is at the beginning that a knowledge of togetherness is needed. Unless the mind is free to combine sensations into boogums, the initial sensations must be recognized as occurring together before the mind combines them into things; though the empirical theory makes this idea of togetherness the result of comparing things subsequent to the act of combining.

The empiricist cannot escape this embarrassment by an appeal to the experience of brute fact. It does no good to point to the regularity in the perceptions of things. Let the regularity of things be granted: there is no regularity among the simple impressions of an infant, nor of an adult, either. The sensation of red does not regularly accompany a juicy taste, the smell of hydrogen sulfide, or any other sensation. Sometimes we see red and a moment later enjoy a taste; other times a loud noise follows. Empiricism therefore fails at the beginning: it surreptitiously furnishes its unfurnished mind with the use of time and space, while it professes to manufacture these ideas at a later stage of the learning process. Insist on a blank mind, and learning never begins. No wonder Hume called his philosophy Skepticism: it is even more skeptical than he thought. Thus the second modern attempt to establish knowledge leaves the subject in worse confusion than either rationalism or late scholasticism left it.

CHAPTER **9**

Immanuel Kant

There must be something like national styles in philosophy, for, as rationalism never gained a foothold in Great Britain, so Germany never went through a period of empiricism. Voltaire and others introduced Locke's philosophy into France where the English outlook was widely adopted; but east of the Rhine from the time of Leibniz to the publication of Kant's *Critique of Pure Reason*, rationalism had lumbered slowly along in the person of Christian Wolff. Kant (1724–1804), though educated in this tradition, came to recognize a positive value in experience that made rationalism obsolete, but at the same time with Hume's help he saw the defect in empiricism that made it untenable. Thus by a single leap German thought was spared eighty or ninety years of British experience and passed directly from rationalism to Kant's reconstruction of philosophy, called Criticism.

Rationalism was the theory that all knowledge is based on logic alone. Its ideal was the deductive method of mathematics, and physics was tortured to fit the scheme. The empirical school went on the principle that all knowledge is based on experience alone, and mathematics was made an experimental science. Although these two systems are otherwise so different, Kant found in them a profound similarity which he believed to be the cause of their failure. His efforts to replace them he characterizes as a Copernican revolution.

Copernicus, instead of assuming with his predecessors that the heavenly bodies revolve around the spectator, made his great advance by turning the universe inside out and assuming that the spectator revolves while the stars remain at rest. Similarly, preceding philosophy had always assumed that human cognition revolves around or must conform to the objects of knowledge; but now Kant proposes to try the assumption that objects must conform to the conditions of cognition. Since the first assumption has resulted in constant failure, the second is worth the attempt.

THE A PRIORI

It might occur to anyone who has followed modern philosophy to this point that if logic alone and experience alone fail to provide knowledge, a combination of logic and experience might succeed. But since experience alone gives nothing at all, the combination cannot be such that logic gives mathematics and experience gives physics. It cannot be a combination in the sense that each method has its own exclusive area. On the contrary, logic and experience must cooperate in all fields of learning. How they cooperate required the genius of Kant to discover.

"That all our knowledge begins with experience there can be no doubt." Such is the first clause of Kant's introduction to his *Critique of Pure Reason*, for he is convinced as much as any empiricist that the understanding is raised to activity only by the stimulation of sensation. However, although all knowledge begins with experience, it does not all arise out of experience. Empirical knowledge is a compound of sensory impressions and something which the mind supplies from itself. The task of philosophy therefore is to identify the elements of this compound; that is, we must separate the a priori factors, the knowledge that is independent of all sensuous impressions, from the a posteriori contributions of sense.

Because universality and necessity cannot be derived from experience, they are the infallible criteria of the a priori. Experience may teach that philosophers are impractical and that politicians are thieves; but such judgments are true only for the most part. No absolute necessity inheres in them. We have not met all philosophers and all politicians; and even if our experience could be complete, which the remote past makes difficult and the proximate future makes impossible, still it could give us no knowledge of any necessary connection. Universal and necessary judgments exist, however. Take the simplest mathematical proposition, such as two and two are four. We do not say that it is true for the most part, true sometimes, true in the past, but who knows what it will be tomorrow? Rather we say, it has always been true, it always will be true, because it must be true. Or, in physics, we do not say that most changes have a cause; rather we say every change must have a cause. Such principles do not have experience for their basis; on the contrary they are the basis of experience. There could be no knowledge without them.

The a priori is exemplified in individual notions as well as in judgments. For example, an economist, noting the decrease in the supply of good lumber, might hope for the invention of a sturdy but thin door. To save the greatest amount of lumber, the door should be very thin; in fact, the problem is to invent a door so thin that it has but one side. Although many people would dismiss this notion as foolish, it must be remembered that color television, ordinary radio, and even the telegraph were considered impossible and absurd a hundred years ago. It is not too soon therefore to begin considering doors with only one side. Yet a suspicion remains that there is a difference between these two cases. Television may be miraculous; but is not a one-sided door an impossibility? Experimentation might be needed to see whether television works; but do we not know ahead of time, before any experimentation, a priori, that a one-sided door can never exist. Unlike the problems which our inventive geniuses have solved, this one seems to conflict with the necessary conditions of space itself. Space cannot be tampered with, rearranged, or altered. Space is something necessary. We must necessarily think it as it is. This is not true of other parts of our experience. We can fancy that there is no red or blue; we can suppose that there is no body; we may remove from our conception of a body first its color, then its hardness, and each of its sensible qualities in turn, so that the conception of the body will vanish. But the space which it occupied still remains and cannot be annihilated in thought. Space therefore is an a priori factor.

Since one of the chief causes of empiricism's failure was the attempt to base a knowledge of space on experience, for a recognition of the togetherness of ideas was surreptitiously utilized at the start though the explicit theory did not provide for it until later, Kant's description of space as an a priori factor must be an initial and crucial component of his philosophy. Kant had long studied the subject. When he was promoted to the position of a full professor, he delivered, as was the custom, an *Inaugural Dissertation*, which analyzed space and time. His great work, *The Critique of Pure Reason*, which was published ten years later (1780), in its section on space and time, does little more than condense the earlier statement. He had also written a short article on space in 1768.

SPACE AND MATHEMATICS

Kant's first point is that space is not a conception which has been derived from outward experiences. The recognition that a sensation relates to something external to me, i.e., to something that occupies a different part of space from that in which I am, presupposes a prior knowledge of space as its foundation. Similarly, in order to recognize several sensations as being together, near to each other, or in different places, I must already have the representation of space. Consequently, the first stage of the Copernican revolution is this: my knowledge of space cannot be derived from the relations of external phenomena through experience, but on the contrary external experience becomes possible only through an antecedent knowledge of space. That is to say, space is an a priori notion. It has the characteristic of necessity, for we cannot imagine the nonexistence of space, though we may easily think that no objects are found in it. To repeat: space is an a priori representation that provides the basis for external experience and is by no means an empirical concept.

An Intuition

In fact, space is not a concept at all, but a pure intuition. A discursive concept is an abstract notion of a common quality found in many things. It is a genus or a species with many instances under it. For example, the instances under the concept of philosopher are Aristotle, Descartes, Hume, and others. But although there are many philosophers, there is only one space. We do, of course, talk about many spaces: there are sixty-four spaces on a chess board and many cubic feet in a storage room. But the parts of space are not related to the one all-embracing space in the same way that the instances of a concept are related to the species or genus. Note that Aristotle could have existed even if Descartes had never been born. In the case of empirically derived concepts, such as that of philosopher, there is no difficulty in preserving the concept while annihilating one or more of the instances. Space, however, is quite different. Each of its parts is necessarily conceived as inseparable from all the others. Try for example to think of a cubic foot of space here, another over there, and several others scattered around, but with no space between them. It was Locke's notion that one could take these separate spaces, bring them together like building blocks, and construct from them a notion of immense space. This implies that one cubic foot of space, like Aristotle, could exist even though another cubic foot of space did not exist. But the attempt to think of several spaces as independent of each other founders when one asks through what does one of these cubic feet move in order to be placed next to another. Or, for that matter, what is immediately adjacent to a certain cubic foot supposed to be lying by itself? If nothing lies between two cubic feet, that is, if there is no space between the two, are they not already continuous with each other? Space therefore is essentially one; it is not built by the addition of spaces, but spaces are made by dividing space.

For these reasons space is not a concept but a pure intuition. And this is the answer to the empirical account of mathematics. The truths that space has only three dimensions, that two sides of a triangle are greater than the third, that there is but one straight line between two points, are never deduced from general conceptions of line and triangle, but are intuited in the single concrete space. It is impossible to describe discursively the distinction between two equal and similar but incongruent triangles. A description of the right hand, so far as it is conceived solely with reference to extension, applies word for word to the left hand; and yet though the intelligible terms are identical, the boundaries of the two extensions cannot coincide. Incongruence therefore can be apprehended only in a pure intuition.

Synthetic and Analytic Judgments

These considerations are inconsistent with empiricism and rationalism alike. For the empiricists analytic judgments, i.e., judgments whose predicate merely repeats the contents of the subject, are tautological, trivial, and do not constitute real knowledge. To save geometry from this fate they made its propositions a posteriori and synthetic, i.e., the proposition's predicate, when discovered in experience, enlarged the subject concept. The result is, as Berkeley explained, that the propositions of mathematics are neither universal nor necessary. Rationalism, on the other hand, had held that all real knowledge, because deduced by logic alone, consisted of analytic propositions. But neither the one school nor the other had even imagined a type of proposition other than a priori analytic and a posteriori synthetic. Kant's reflections on space and epistemology now led him to assert the existence of the hitherto undreamed of synthetic judgment a priori: a judgment whose predicate enlarges the subject concept but which does not depend on experience.

Kant does not deny the obvious fact that the theorems of geometry are deduced from the axioms. In this sense the theorems are obtained analytically. Nonetheless they are synthetic propositions because the axioms themselves are synthetic. This is what was meant when it was said that one cannot deduce from the general conception of line and triangle the truth that two sides of a triangle are greater than the third. But unlike the synthetic propositions of experience, geometrical judgments are a priori because they are necessary and universal.

Yet here is a difficult problem: how are a priori synthetic propositions possible? To both the empiricists and the rationalists the combination of synthetic with a priori would have seemed as absurd as a square circle. Kant must also render intelligible the existence of an external intuition that is anterior to the perception of sensory objects. These two related difficulties are removed by considering space as the formal capacity of the mind's being affected by an object of sense. Space is the form of the external sense.

An Illustration

Once upon a time a housewife made a batch of jelly and stored it on the pantry shelves for the winter. One jelly glass, brighter than the others, sat through the months reflecting on its experience. It noted that one winter its contents had been bright red in color, soupy in consistence, and had the taste of cherry. Another winter its experience was dark blue, rubbery, and tasted like grape. Its object on another occasion had been orange and bitter. Then a most remarkable discovery jolted this Kantian jelly glass out of its dogmatic slumber and empirical dreams. Although the red, blue, yellow, sweet, and bitter came and went, the objects were always the same shape. How could this be? The change in experience could be accounted for by foreign material being poured into it; but the only permanent factor to account for the identity of shape must be the jelly glass itself.

Kant's language, however, is that of a German professor, and one can sympathize with the student who wrote in his translation of the *Critique*, "I can't read German, no matter what language it is written in." Yet the thought is as clear as a jelly glass, even if jelly glasses are not always clear.

Things in Themselves

Space then is not a property of things in themselves, nor is it their relation to each other. Space is the form of appearances, the subjective condition of sensibility. Since receptivity or the capacity of the mind to be affected by objects necessarily antecedes all intuitions of these objects, it is clear how the form of phenomena can be given in the mind prior to all empirical perceptions. Space is applicable to things only in so far as they appear to us; therefore it is clear that we cannot make the special conditions of sensibility into conditions of the possibility of things, but only of the possibility of their existence as appearances. Space therefore contains all which can appear to us externally, but it does not contain things considered in themselves. The proposition, "All objects are beside each other in space," is true only under the limitation that these objects are phenomena, i.e., objects of sensory intuition. To make the proposition universally true, one should say, "All external appearances are beside each other in space." In other words, space is empirically real, but transcendentally ideal.

Obviously this does not mean that space is subjective in the same sense that colors and tastes are subjective. It is possible to have experience without experiencing a particular color or taste. Many people have never experienced the taste of fried rattlesnake. But it is not possible to have experience without experiencing space. That is to say, space belongs necessarily to an intuition, but red does not. With the exception of space, no representation, subjective and referring to something external to us, can be called a priori. Colors and tastes furnish predicates for a posteriori judgments; space gives synthetic judgments a priori, and is therefore empirically real and objective as those are not. Colors and tastes are not properties of things, but only changes in the perceiving subject, changes which may be different in different men. If color were on the same plane as space, the phenomenal rose would pass for a thing in itself, appearing differently to each person. But the transcendental conception of phenomena in space is a warning that nothing appearing in space is a thing in itself; nor is space a form which belongs as a property to things. What we call objects are nothing else than mere representations of our sensibility, and space is the form of our sensibility. But the independent correlate, the thing in itself, cannot be known by sensation and is forever beyond empirical investigation.

The distinction between the known object of experience and the unknown and unknowable thing in itself may be illustrated, but only illustrated, by ordinary perspective. As one stands on a straight stretch of railroad tracks and looks a mile down the tracks, they converge and vanish at a point. It is commonly said that they only appear to converge, whereas in reality they are always the same distance apart. This appearance is then referred to the subjective conditions of our perceiving. It is we who make really parallel tracks meet at a point. Similarly for Kant the conditions of our perceiving make really nonspatial things in themselves appear in space as appearances or phenomena. It is we who make appearances spatial. But if railroad tracks always appear to converge when we look at them, what do they do when we do not look at them? Can we say they remain parallel when we have never seen them so? Certainly no experience can inform us of the nature of unexperienced objects. Thus, while phenomena appear to us in the "perspective" of space, things in themselves, things as they do not appear, must remain unknowable.

PHYSICS AND LOGIC

Corresponding to space as the form of external sense and the basis of geometry, time is the form of internal sense and is the basis of arithmetic. This completes the first section of Kant's task: he has shown how mathematics, with its universal and necessary propositions, is possible, and at the same time he has shown the possibility of recognizing the togetherness of perceptions. The second part of Kant's task is to show how physics is possible. In the previous chapter two difficulties with empiricism were emphasized. With the first disposed of, Kant must now turn to Hume's explanation of causality. If causality is inexplicable custom, and if universal and necessary judgments, such as every change must have a cause, are logically indefensible, then physics and all the other sciences are impossible. Thus, after mathematics and sensation, Kant must discuss physics and logic. This turns out to be more complicated than one might at first imagine. The reason for the difficulty is that physics of course requires far more than the bare perception of objects.

There are in fact two sources of knowledge in the mind: receptivity for impressions and spontaneity in the production of conceptions. Both are necessary. Without sensuous intuition — and Kant repeats a dozen times that all intuition is sensuous, he denies over and over that there can be intellectual intuition — without sensuous intuition no object can be given in experience; but without understanding and conception, no given object could be thought. Thoughts without content are empty; intuitions without concepts are blind. That is to say, sensation alone might present us with a star or a tree, but without concepts we could not think that stars are suns or trees are plants; conversely without sensation we might think that "all a is b" or "no a is b," but we would have no real knowledge. Sensation and understanding are both necessary, though their roles are different. The previous section on sensation, because of etymology, was called

Aesthetic: since physics requires conception and thinking, this
section is called Logic.

A Priori Concepts

As Kant in the Aesthetic answered the empirical theory of sensation by discovering the a priori forms of sensibility, forms which of
necessity apply to every possible object of experience, so in the Logic
he attacks the problems of causality by searching for the a priori
forms of the understanding. These a priori forms of conception,
these categories, are as necessary in thought as space and time are
in sensation. A person may fail to have the concept of plant or of
gymnosperm, just as he may fail to have the sensation of red or of
buffalo; but no one who thinks at all can fail to have these a priori
concepts. Empirical concepts have a sensory content, but the categories, because a priori, are *ipso facto* pure. They must be something
like the concept of unity or of cause, rather than like the concept of
plant. But which are these a priori concepts? How are they obtained?
Can we be sure we have discovered all of them? The answer to
these three questions depends on deducing the categories as a system
from the idea of understanding itself. Unless deduced as a system,
a list of concepts can be only a haphazard aggregate. This explains
the difference between Kantian analysis and Socratic analysis. The
concepts Socrates analyzed were empirical, and he proceeded from
one to the next in no determinate order and toward no determinate
end. After he had analyzed courage, he might turn indifferently to
temperance or to piety. But the Kantian analysis of conception is
not an analysis of this or that empirical concept; it is an analysis
of the faculty of conception, the faculty of understanding itself.
The Kantian analysis seeks its concepts by a rule so that the results
will form a system and be known to be complete.

Unification of Experience

The understanding or faculty of conception is a nonsensuous
faculty of cognition. Since the mode of receiving knowledge by
sensibility is intuition, the understanding's mode of cognition must
be discursive, that is, through conceptions. For there is no other
mode of knowing. Now intuitions depend on receptivity; the mind is

passive, is affected, receives what is given; but conceiving or understanding through conceptions is an active function. When a person frames a concept, he arranges diverse representations under one common representation; for example, he intuits, if not the choir of heaven, at least some of the furniture of the earth, such as oak trees, wisteria vines, and common grass; all these he collects or classifies under the concept plant. He unifies the multiple intuitions by arranging them under a concept. Concepts therefore are based on the spontaneity of thought and are forms of unity imposed by the mind on sensory multiplicity. This implies that a conception does not relate immediately to any object of sense; it relates immediately to an intuition, a sensory representation, which in turn relates immediately to the object.

Though conceptions are thus one step removed from reality, they are indispensable to knowledge, for it is by concepts that judgments are possible. A judgment is a mediate cognition of an object, a representation of a representation of it. The concept gathers into a unity the representations under it. All judgments therefore are functions of unity; and the unification of experience is the purpose of the understanding, for it is the faculty of judging. Now, the significance of all this is as follows: since the understanding unifies experience, and since this unity is expressed in judgments, it is possible to discover all the functions of the understanding, all the basic forms of unity, all the a priori concepts, by an examination of the several types of judgment.

Synthesis

Prior to listing these a priori concepts or categories, Kant inserts a further preliminary paragraph on synthesis. His terminology is undoubtedly awkward, but it will not prove too unintelligible if the motivation is not forgotten.

In opposition to the blank mind of empiricism, Kant wants to specify the a priori equipment for thinking. This equipment will include the category of causality so as to make physics possible. And the list of categories is to be deduced by an analysis of the understanding itself.

Such an analysis is possible because the mind's functions of unity are expressed in judgments. Nearly all judgments, as in the examples above, are empirical. General logic abstracts from their empirical content and identifies their forms — the universal or particular, the affirmative or negative form of a judgment. Transcendental logic has all the forms of general logic and a few others in addition because, unlike general logic, it has lying before it the manifold content of a priori sensibility. The spontaneity of thought requires that this manifold, the diversities of space and time, be received into the mind and connected synthetically.

Synthesis is the process of joining different representations together and of comprehending their diversity in one cognition. Synthesis may be pure or empirical. In an empirical situation a synthesis must always precede, not merely a judgment, but even the intuition of a sense object. Though this is always the case, it is more easily recognized in the perception of very large objects. When we see a building or a mountain, our eyes run up one corner, then across the roof or ridge, then crisscross back and forth across the face of the building. It is impossible to sense the complete object instantaneously. We focus on one part after another in great rapidity. The many sensations thus received are held in memory or imagination and then put together or synthesized into one object. Even with smaller objects, the eyes move from one side to the other. This gives the percipient a variety of sensations, a variety of colors, shapes, textures. These then are synthesized into the perception of one object; but the process is so common and so speedy that we are seldom conscious of it.

Distinct from this empirical synthesis which results in the perception of sense objects, there is also a pure a priori synthesis. As the material synthesized is space and time, the result is found in arithmetic and geometry. Our cognition of a number, and once more large numbers are clearer examples, is a synthesis by conceptions, taking place according to a common basis of unity, for example by tens or hundreds. Now, then, transcendental logic reduces to concepts, not the representations of buildings and mountains nor even of numbers, but it reduces to concepts the pure synthesis of representations.

The language may be awkward and the thought abstruse, but

moderate attention will remove the difficulties. Transcendental logic reduces to concepts the pure synthesis of representations: that is, the process of synthesis above exemplified is analyzed into factors; these factors are concepts by which one or another form of unity is necessarily and universally imposed on all the content of thought. There are three stages in the a priori cognition of any object: first, the diversity of space and time; second, the synthesis of this diversity in imagination; but a third factor is also required for any cognition, viz., the concepts which give unity to this synthesis, concepts which consist solely in the representation of this necessary synthetical unity. The same function that gives unity to the different representations in a judgment also gives unity to the synthesis in an intuition. Thus the understanding, by the same process it uses in producing the logical forms of judgment, introduces a transcendental content into its representations. Therefore these representations are called pure conceptions of the understanding, and as pure they apply a priori to all objects.

THE CATEGORIES

It is now time to name the categories and show their derivation from the logical forms of judgment. Fortunately this result is more easily understood than the preliminary paragraphs. There are twelve categories, the first of which is unity. In logic, either general or transcendental, the form of judgment usually put first is the universal form. Often we unify experience by collecting all trees under the concept plant and say, All trees are plants; or in the a priori area we say, All triangles are plane figures. This all-are relationship, which distinguishes the universal judgment from the others, is the work or result of the a priori category of unity.

Contrast this with Berkeley's view. In his effort to base mathematics on experience Berkeley proposed to discover the unit in experience; he would make a single grain of sand the unit or a large pile of sand, as it suited his empirical purpose. For Kant, however, Berkeley's treatment is superficial. Let it be granted that we can choose anything as an empirical unit; the underlying question concerns the origin of the idea of unity. If anything at all in experience can be chosen as a unit, it is particularly impossible to discover unity in the things themselves. They may be made into units, but the idea of unity must precede this making. Quite the reverse of empiricism's attempt to base unity on experience, Kant's position is that experience, or, rather, the possibility of meaningful experience is based on the idea of unity. If the mind had no a priori category of unity, it could never recognize anything as one thing. And apart from such elemental recognition, experience could be nothing better than complete chaos. The same general principle holds of the other categories also: they do not depend on experience, but experience depends on them.

Causality

In addition to the universal form of judgment, there is the particular form: Some plants are trees, or, some plane figures are triangles. The category at the basis of this form is the category of plurality. Most of the others, totality, reality, negation, limitation, substance, reciprocity, possibility, existence, and necessity, can safely be omitted from this account.

But the category of causality cannot be omitted. As Aristotle had selected the middle term of the syllogism to indicate the cause of the conclusion, Kant in roughly similar fashion finds that implication in logic depends on the category of causality. Implication is one way of unifying the multiplicity of experience. When we say, "If this be true, then such and such must also be true," we join a number of experiences in one judgment. Though it is a more complicated judgment than the simple universal or particular forms, it is still a synthesis and unification. This judgment of implication preeminently characterizes the laws of science. If certain conditions are set, then determinate results will follow. If the sun, moon, and earth are at given positions, moving at definite speeds, along defined curves, then an eclipse will occur at a fixed time. Such an implication, such a scientific statement, is possible only because the mind is equipped with the a priori concept of cause. Of course causality is found in experience, but our knowledge of causality is not based on experience. Causality is found in experience because the mind puts it there; it is the form or jelly glass into which experience is poured. This is the Copernican revolution: previous philosophy had always assumed that cognition revolves around and must conform to the objects of knowledge; but now Kant has made the objects of knowledge conform to the conditions of cognition.

There remains something to be said about science and causality, but first a caution must be introduced that applies to all the categories. It must be understood that cognition is possible only when the categories are applied to objects of experience. Thinking and knowing are not the same thing. We can think or make judgments about snarks and hippogryphs: all hippogryphs are snarks, but some snarks are not hippogryphs. But in cognition there must be, not only the category by which an object is thought, but also an intuition by which an object is given. Intuition is always sensuous; consequently our thought of an object by means of a category can become a cognition only if the object is given in sensation. Even the propositions of mathematics, which combine categories and the a priori intuitions of space and time, are not strictly knowledge; mathematics becomes knowledge only on the supposition that there exist sensory objects to which the mathematical forms can be applied. Therefore the categories, even by means of pure intuition, do not afford any cognition of things. Sensation is indispensable. That is to say, the categories serve only to render empirical cognition possible; their application to sensory objects is their only legitimate function. Since the objects of sensation are appearances, phenomena and not noumena, nothing can be known of things in themselves. Beyond the limits of sensory experience neither space and time nor the categories have any valid application. If one could suppose an object of intellectual or nonsensuous intuition to be given, the knowledge of it would be entirely negative: it would not be extended in space, it would have no duration in time, it would not be a unit, a plurality, a substance, a cause, or an effect. Even on the assumption that there were an intellectual intuition, an assumption which of course Kant does not seriously grant, such negatives are ignorance, not knowledge. How this restriction of the forms of the mind to sensory material will affect the question of God's existence may easily be anticipated.

A Theistic View

In the final paragraph of Kant's long deduction or justification of the categories, before he turns to a closer view of the principles of science, he pays his short respects to every other possible epistemology, and particularly to any theistic attempt to avoid skepticism. His initial disjunction is that either experience makes the categories possible or the categories make experience possible. Since the former view, under the analysis of Hume, resulted in skepticism, the second alternative alone remains. Still "it is quite possible that someone might suppose a species of preformation system of pure reason, a middle way between the two alternatives just mentioned, to wit, that the categories are neither innate and a priori nor derived from experience, but are merely subjective aptitudes for thought implanted in us contemporaneously with our existence, which were so ordered by our Creator that their exercise perfectly harmonizes with the laws of nature which regulate experience" (B. 167).

Perhaps Kant's objections to this type of theistic epistemology do not depend on a certain confusion inherent in the quotation; but it ought to be noticed that if our Creator has implanted in us certain categories or aptitudes for thought contemporaneously with our existence, Kant is hardly justified in denying that they are a priori. Instead of saying that God-given categories would be neither a priori nor derived from experience, it might have been more nearly accurate, howbeit paradoxical, to describe the categories of a theistic epistemology as both a priori and derived from experience. In any case there is no justification for denying that they would be a priori.

Kant's first objection to divinely implanted concepts is that one could never determine the point at which the employment of such predetermined aptitudes should cease. This objection is ambiguous. If it means that the use of categories will be extended beyond experience so that judgments about God become possible, theism would admit it. If, on the other hand, the objection means that the precise application of a given category in a concrete empirical situation is not automatically determined by the general theistic view; if, that is, we do not know what is the cause of what, or whether we should now apply the concept of reciprocity instead of causality; the obvious reply is that Kant's theory itself faces the same difficulty.

The second objection to divinely implanted concepts, and an objection which Kant asserts as conclusive, is that the categories in this case would entirely lose that character of necessity which is essentially involved in the very conception of them. He explains this objection by an example. "The concept of cause," he says, "which expresses the necessity of an effect under a presupposed condition, would be false, if it rested only upon such an arbitrary subjective necessity of uniting certain empirical representations according to such a rule of relation. I could not then say, 'The effect is connected with its cause in the object (that is, necessarily),' but only, 'I am so constituted that I can think this representation as so connected, and not otherwise.' Now this is just what the skeptic wants."

But must the theistic position deprive the categories of necessity and invalidate the concept of causality? (Theism, and certain non-theistic theories too, may of course reject Kant's view of mechanistic causation, but this is another issue.) Certainly on the assumption that God has implanted aptitudes for knowing and has so ordered them as to harmonize with the laws of nature, Kant is patently mistaken in saying that the conception of a causal relation under presupposed conditions would be false. When immediately he refers to this causal relation as arbitrary and subjective, it seems that he is depending on his previous assertion that a concept implanted at our creation cannot be a priori and innate. But such an assertion is without reason and implausible.

And finally, Kant should be the last one to deplore the statement, "I am so constituted that I can think . . . not otherwise"; for whatever value the objection may have, it applies with greater force to Kant than to theism. Is not the jelly glass so constituted as to shape its contents "not otherwise"?

THE LAWS OF SCIENCE

The table of categories is not sufficient of itself and without further elaboration to provide for the possibility of physics. The categories are concepts; what is needed further is a set of a priori judgments. These judgments, as the basic laws of science, are to be discovered in the relation between the categories and sensibility. Although they are called, and properly called, the basic laws of science, they are not the principles of mathematics or physics which one finds in the ordinary scientific textbook. Even the law of gravitation, as universal as it is, is not one of these judgments, but like the other laws of nature is itself merely a particular application of the pure, a priori principles of the understanding. These are the principles which make the law of gravitation possible.

Extensive Quantities

The first principle, called the axiom of intuition, is, "All intuitions are extensive quantities." In other words, magnitude must be illustrated in experience. This is an a priori judgment, and as a priori can be known prior to experience. That there are magnitudes is not an inductive, empirical discovery. Phenomena can be apprehended only under the forms of space and time, and since these involve extensive quantity, every phenomenon exhibits extension in space or time.

Intensive Quantities

The second principle, the anticipation of perception, is, "In all phenomena the Real, that which is an object of sensation, has intensive quantity, that is, has a degree." Kant justifies this principle by supposing that apprehension does not need a series of sensations. It may be true that our perception of a building or any thing requires a synthesis of many sensations, but a single sensation can be apprehended without a synthesis and may therefore take place in a moment. Therefore a single sensation, as distinguished from the perception of an object, has no extensive quantity. (If a sensation can occur instantaneously and thus avoid extension in time, does it follow that it also has no extension in space?) The lack of a sensation at a given instant can be thought of as zero — the instant is empty; between zero and a complete reality there is an infinite series of intermediate gradations. Sensation therefore is a continuum, and as a quantity apprehended instantaneously in which plurality can be represented only by an approximation to zero, it is an intensive quantity, or is measured by a degree.

As the first of these two principles contributes to the justification of arithmetic and geometry, so the second, here streamlined by the omission of several difficulties, justifies calculus. But as geometry and even calculus antedated Kant, his profundity can better be judged by his influence on his successors, for it is the implications of this section that stimulated those psycho-physical measurements of the intensity of sensation for which Fechner later became famous.

Necessary Connection

The third of these principles turns out to be a set of three, called the Analogies of Experience, subsumed under the general statement, "Experience is possible only through the representation of a neces-sary connection of perceptions." Now, Kant agrees with Hume that in experience no necessary connection appears from the perceptions themselves. On a strictly empiricist philosophy Adam could not have anticipated suffocation in the water of the Euphrates nor can the most discerning of scientists see why the motion of one billiard ball should necessitate the motion of a second. However, Kant was far more troubled than Hume by the consequences of such a theory. A series of unconnected perceptions would be purely rhapsodic, chaotic, and meaningless: so chaotic in fact that Hume could have written neither philosophy nor his History of England. Skepticism, as Plato and St. Augustine well knew, demands silence, or at most noise.

Then too, Kant also saw, or thought he saw, a means of escaping Hume's predicament. The general principle of the three analogies, stated just above, i.e., the assertion of a necessary connection of perceptions, results from the synthetic unity imposed on the manifold of sensation. Kant is here trying to say that the universe cannot appear chaotic. Apart from the full skeptical implications of empiricism, not only would a particular law of physics be at best an unexpected discovery, but even the fact that some law or other might be discovered could not be known prior to the discovery of a particular law. On the empirical scheme the scientist runs the risk of finding the universe completely lawless.

Kant denies that there is such a risk. Could the atoms which compose the world be in lawless motion as we might suppose a swarm of gnats to be? Could we experience or perceive a completely lawless universe? No, Kant insists; all perception presupposes a law. The atoms, supposed to be swarming like gnats, have mass or they would not be atoms; and the concept of mass presupposes the law of gravitation. Only by the law of gravitation is it possible to recognize atoms. Well, then, if mass was an invention of Sir Isaac Newton, and if this makes it improper to use the modern concept of an atom, what about mere bodies? Could not lawless extended bodies be observed? Again the answer is No, because extension involves measurement, and measurement requires a law. Therefore anything we can say about a body implies that it is an element in a law abiding system. One cannot observe complete lawlessness. Kant's view here contrasts with both rationalism and empiricism. If empiricism held that it is possible to think away anything, not only this law, but also lawfulness, rationalism held the extreme opposite, that nothing could be thought away, for this is the only thinkable world. Kant rejects both extremes and contends that though any particular law of science can be thought away, there must be Law, for experience, meaningful experience, presupposes Law.

Permanent Substance

The first analogy under this general principle is, "In all changes of phenomena, substance is permanent, and its quantum in nature is neither increased nor diminished." Kant's defense of this analogy is beset with considerable difficulty. All phenomena, he begins, exist in time, and only in time can coexistence and succession be represented. Now time itself cannot be an object of perception. From this fact Kant professes to deduce the conclusion that in objects of perception there must be found a substratum which represents time in general, and in which all change and coexistence can be perceived by means of the relation of phenomena to it. This substratum is substance. Were there no substance, no permanent foundation, we could never distinguish between what is coexistent from what is successive. The argument, in effect, defines change in a manner that recalls Aristotle. Change can take place only in relation to an unchanging substance. Absolute origin, something coming from nothing, cannot be perceived, because the previous nothing, the void time, cannot be perceived. Only the permanent makes perception of change possible. On one's first reading of Kant, it is doubtless wise to postpone an investigation of the difficulties contained in this argument. That change requires a permanent may be granted as plausible; but it is a question whether Kant has argued sufficiently well to show that the permanent exists as a substance in the physical world. Possibly time itself could be the necessary permanent; or, if not, perhaps the requirements could more plausibly be satisfied by the mind, the self, the "transcendental unity of apperception," of which time is the form. Unfortunately, criticisms such as this require extremely delicate reasoning.

Cause and Effect

The second analogy, which may be considered the focus of the Critique, is, "All changes take place according to the law of the connection of cause and effect." Although Hume had raised only the question of causality and had failed to see the generalized problem of all the categories, still even for Kant it was causality that remained the crucial point. This lengthy section justifying the principle of causality contains at least six arguments, most of them substantially the same. But because there are minor inconsistencies, it is concluded that Kant did not write the chapter at one sitting. Presumably, both in this case and in several other sections of the Critique, he had tried a half dozen times to formulate a proper argument, and when he decided to publish, he hurriedly pasted them all together and sent them off to the printer. The general line of thought is the same that Kant has followed throughout. For the empiricists the uncertainty of a causal connection between a particular event x and another event y, casts doubt on causality in general. The rationalists, as is so clear in Spinoza, make causality a logical connection inherent in the meaning of x and y. Kant, however, allowing for doubt in particular cases, makes the general principle of causality inherent in the meaning of experience.

But the proofs of the principle are disappointing and confusing; what is worse they become the more so as they are the more carefully studied; until it seems that Kant, who had so courageously attacked the unsolved problems of empiricism, is in danger of failing. I perceive that phenomena succeed one another, he begins. This perception of change is possible only because I have connected two perceptions in time. Now, connection is not an operation of mere sense. On this point Hume is unassailable: connections are not given in sensory experience. But as connections in fact exist, they must be the products of a synthetical faculty of imagination. Imagination, however, can connect two perceptions in two ways, so that either the one or the other may antecede in time; for time itself cannot be perceived, and what in an object precedes and what follows cannot be empirically determined in relation to it. The succession therefore is in my imagination, not in the object. This is true of my perception of a building. My sensations may begin with the roof and end with the foundation or vice versa; they may proceed from right to left or from left to right. But there is neither succession nor causal relationship in the building. On the contrary, to cognize the relation of succession as determined, the order must be made necessary and irreversible. Now, necessity can come only from a pure conception of the understanding, and in this case the concept is that of cause and effect. It follows (at least Kant says it follows) that it is only because we subject the sequence of phenomena, and consequently all change, to the law of causation, that experience itself, that is, empirical cognition of phenomena, becomes possible. Consequently, phenomena themselves, as objects of experience, are possible only by virtue of this law.

This conclusion shows clearly what Kant is driving at, even if it does not follow from what has been said. There are, however, a number of later paragraphs, some of which may lead in the desired direction. That a change takes place or that something happens cannot be perceived unless there was a previous phenomenon. An event or a reality which should follow upon a void time, as for example God's creating the world out of nothing, can no more be apprehended than the void time itself. Therefore every apprehension of an event must follow a previous perception. Now, I note, as a ship floats downstream, that my perception of its later position follows my perception of its earlier position, and that it is impossible to perceive the two positions in reversed order. The order is determined. Thus the perception of the ship's change of position is different from the perception of the building because in the second illustration the connection is made according to a rule and the sequence is necessary. This subjective sequence of perceptions must be based on the objective sequence of phenomena; otherwise the contents of my mind would be arranged only arbitrarily and there would be no knowledge.

The common opinion is that the concept of causality comes from experience like the concept of ship, but in this case causality would be as contingent as the things in experience. Seeing a ship is not a necessary element in experience; inhabitants of the interior may never have seen one; and thus the law of causality would be neither universal nor necessary. But causality, unlike the ship, is necessarily found in experience; it is found in experience because we put it there, and our putting it there makes experience possible.

Now finally, there is one objection that should be examined; and the difficulty applies to space and time as well as to cause and the categories. It may be said that Kant's theory makes all these purely subjective. Space and time were called empirically real but transcendentally ideal. But how can space or cause be real if it is the mind that imposes them on experience? How is it possible to refer our conscious states to objects? Has Kant any better than Berkeley or Hume escaped from his subjective states to make contact with a real world? It will be remembered that rationalism faced the same difficulty. The ontological argument was supposed to bridge the gap between definition and actual existence; but aside from doubts as to its validity, it seemed to be insufficient for the derivation of individual existences. Now, sensation has encountered a similar impasse. The question is obviously of primary importance, but the series of failures points up the Herculean task it proves to be. How is it possible to refer our conscious states to objects? Or to phrase the question as Kant wished to answer it, What sort of new property does 'relation to an object' give to our subjective representations? Kant explains that the difference between purely subjective representations in arbitrary succession and representations that refer to an object is that the latter have been conformed to a necessary rule of connection. It is only because a certain temporal order among our representations is necessary that objective significance can be ascribed to them. Space, time, and causality may be said to be objectively real because of necessity they apply to all objects of experience. Did not Berkeley's theological construction provide as much?

THE EXISTENCE OF GOD

Now, by the omission of the third Analogy, the three Postulates of Empirical Thought, and some other intensely interesting material, it will be possible to consider Kant's views on the proofs of God's existence. By this time Kant claims to have shown that mathematics and physics are possible; but since the categories cannot validly be applied beyond the range of sense perception it is clear that metaphysics and theology are impossible. To support this conclusion, which is inherent in his exposition of the categories, he analyzes the traditional arguments and uncovers the fallacies they contain.

There are three and only three possible types of argument purporting to prove God's existence. One type, the physico-theological or teleological argument, is that which makes use of all possible experiential data. The world presents to our view so magnificent a spectacle of order, variety, and beauty that we are led to attribute all possible perfection to a primal, self-subsistent, and supreme cause. This argument, says Kant, always deserves to be mentioned with respect; it is the oldest, the clearest, and that most in conformity with the common reason of humanity. But in order for it to be valid, the second type of argument, the cosmological argument, must be valid.

The cosmological argument is that one which derives God's existence from the least possible experience. In outline it runs: If anything exists, an absolutely necessary being exists; but I myself at least exist; therefore God exists. Unless this argument is valid, the teleological argument will lack its necessary foundation. Kant is aware of Hume's objections to these arguments, and he is willing to admit that they are conclusive. In fact he says, "in this cosmological argument are assembled so many sophistical propositions that speculative reason seems to have exerted in it all her dialectical skill to produce a transcendental illusion of the most extreme character" (B. 634). But the chief flaw, more serious than any of Hume's objections or even than Kant's restriction of the principle of causality to sensory phenomena, is its dependence on the ontological argument. Experience, on which the cosmological argument professes to rest, gives us no information as to the properties and attributes of the supreme being whose existence the argument seeks to prove. The identification of this supreme being as an absolutely necessary being requires the third and only other type of argument, an argument that depends on no experience whatever. "Thus arose that unfortunate ontological argument, which neither satisfies the healthy common sense of humanity nor sustains the scientific examination of the philosopher." Then with Kant's destructive analysis of this basic argument, all hope of proving God's existence is lost.

Philosophers have talked about an absolutely necessary being; they have defined it verbally as something the nonexistence of which is impossible; but neither their verbal definition nor their explanations throw any light on the conditions which render it impossible to cogitate the nonexistence of an object. As an illustration of absolute necessity they point to geometrical propositions, such as, a triangle necessarily has three angles. But all such examples are examples of necessary judgments, not of necessary things. The conditions of these two necessities are surely different. Far from asserting that three angles necessarily exist, the geometrical proposition above says merely that upon the condition of a triangle's existence, three angles necessarily exist in it. This explains nothing as to the necessary existence of an object. If in any analytical or identical judgment the predicate be denied while the subject is asserted, a contradiction results. But a contradiction cannot result if both the subject and the predicate be denied; for, since nothing is left, there is no means of forming one. It is contradictory to assert triangle and deny three angles; but it is entirely admissible to suppose the nonexistence of triangle and angle together. Similarly, "God is omnipotent" is a necessary judgment, and to assert God while denying omnipotence is contradictory; but if it be said that God does not exist, omnipotence and all other predicates disappear with the subject, and no contradiction is possible.

This analysis forces the reply that, apart from all predicates, there is a subject that necessarily exists. But this returns us to the beginning, for it was to explain the meaning of the necessary existence of a thing that the geometrical proposition was introduced.

Consider the matter again. Is the judgment, "God exists," an analytic or a synthetic judgment? If it be analytic and the idea of existence be logically contained in the subject, then the predicate existence adds nothing to the concept of the subject. But in this case, the conception in the mind is identical with the thing itself; and it is merely the existence of the concept that has been proved. Therefore the judgment "God exists" must be, as every existential judgment is, a synthetic judgment. But if synthetic, no logical contradiction arises from denying the predicate of the subject.[1]

To apply this analysis to Descartes' form of the ontological argument, Kant denies the minor premise, "Existence is a perfection." Being is not a real predicate: it is merely the positing of the thing with its several predicates. To affirm that God exists is not to add another predicate to the list of omnipotence, omniscience, and so forth. The affirmation of God's existence is nothing but the positing of an object in relation to the mental concept. The content of the object and of the concept are identical. The real contains no more than the possible. A hundred real dollars contain no more than a hundred possible dollars. If the content of the real dollars were more than the content of the concept, the concept would not be a representation of the entire one hundred dollars. Of course, so far as one's bank account goes, a hundred real dollars is more, is one hundred dollars more, than a hundred possible, conceptual dollars. For the real dollars are not contained analytically in one's conception, but they form a synthetical addition, although this objective reality, this existence, does not increase the number or the predicates of the dollars in the least. Therefore the minor premise of Descartes' argument ruins it. A knowledge of mathematics and physics may be possible, but there can be no knowledge of metaphysics and theology.

MECHANICS AND MORALITY

For the sake of argument, let us accept these conclusions at face value. Let there be no knowledge of God and let causality, mechan-

---

[1] An interesting, though minor, point arises here. Kant says that a contradiction can occur only in connection with analytic judgments, never with synthetic judgments (B. 626). But since a priori synthetic judgments are universal and necessary, would there not be a contradiction in asserting their subjects while denying their predicates? Of course, the rationalists did not say that "God exists" is a synthetic a priori judgment.

ical causality, control all experienced change. Then what about human life, human desires, plans, and volitions; in short, what about morality?

In some stretches of a history of philosophy it is possible to ignore moral problems. If Locke and Berkeley could have established knowledge, a knowledge of ethics would have caused them little additional trouble; and if Hume destroyed all knowledge, it hardly needs to be mentioned that moral knowledge vanishes too. But at other times when the epistemological theories have not so obviously failed, the moral problem can become the crucial one. Even with skepticism, it was necessary once, in the case of Sophism, to point out that there are moral, or immoral, results. If knowledge is impossible, a man can only choose an irrational end and try to be successful by fair means or foul. But St. Augustine turned this view upside down and used the practical choices of human living to disprove skepticism. If thus skepticism cannot dodge the question of morality, a positive philosophy cannot want to. Whatever the epistemology or the metaphysics may be, it has a bearing on the issues of life. In modern times Spinoza, as we have seen, tried to harmonize morality with inviolable mechanism. Common opinion regards this as an impossible task. Now Kant too must face the same paradox. If God cannot be known and if all observable objects, motions, appearances, sensations, are subject to the law of causation, can there be such a thing as moral obligation? Kant, much more than Spinoza, was convinced that there is. Two things never ceased to excite his wonder and awe: the starry heavens above and the moral law within. But how can the mechanism of the one permit the freedom of the other?

The Ethics of Calculation

The starting point, however, is not freedom, but the moral law; and the nature of this law, which is to determine the will, is approached by considering whether it is a priori or dependent on experience. Now, if moral law is derived from experience, it must depend on pleasure and self-love. An empirical ethics would have to be a hedonism, gross or refined. But this point of view faces certain objections. In the first place, if pleasure is the end of action, the means are indifferent, except as to efficiency; that is, the end justifies the means; and this is commonly and correctly thought to be immoral because means, as much as or even more than ends, are subject to moral praise and blame. In the second place, if pleasure is the end, there can be no significant qualitative distinction among pleasures: the pleasures of a hog, an aesthete, and a sadist would be on a level. And this too offends common sense. Third, if nature had meant to provide simply for man's happiness, it could have done better than to equip man with the powers of reason. In fact, the very worst way of securing enjoyment, especially in the case of a man of refinement, is to make use of reason. Cruder men following their natural impulses and animals of instinct seem to be more successful in achieving happiness; and this implies that morality is irrational. In the next place and conclusively, since people get pleasure from very different sources, no objective moral law can be derived on a hedonistic position. Precepts of skill or efficiency cannot be universal, as a law must be, because people do not seek the same objects. That is to say, a hedonistic moral law is not a law at all.

That a moral law cannot be based on experience is enforced by two other commonly accepted opinions. Whenever a man is known to calculate the consequences of his acts, he may be regarded as sly and tricky, he may even be regarded as wise and prudent; but he is never thought of as outstandingly moral. Moral actions are done without fear of consequences, or hope of consequences, either. Calculation is not a moral characteristic. The second commonly accepted opinion that conflicts with an empirical ethics is an implication of the first: viz., a man is never regarded as moral on the ground that he has been successful, nor is he branded as immoral because his plans fail. Whether the failure is due to his poor practical decisions or to disasters beyond his control, people generally credit his intentions in judging his character. Calculation and success are the privileges of the highly intelligent or the unusually fortunate; but morality is surely within the reach of the lowly and humble. Moral law therefore cannot be based on experience.

The Categorical Imperative

As might be expected, Kant sees the mark of the a priori in the law's necessity, objectivity, and universality. Empirical precepts of prudence cannot be universalized. An individual man may decide for himself to increase his fortune by every safe means; but this subjective maxim cannot apply universally. Suppose an elderly widow secretly gave this man a sum of money for the purpose of taking care of her in her remaining days, with the verbal instruction that after her death he should give the balance to such and such a church or charity. At her death he could safely keep the money for himself because no one knew of the trust. But if this maxim of prudence were made universal so that all men regularly appropriated their trust funds, such deposits would cease to exist. Thus the universalizing of the maxim abolishes it. It is self-destructive, self-contradictory, and therefore neither true nor moral.

To avoid self-contradiction, any particular moral law must fall under the general moral law, "Act in conformity with that maxim and that maxim only which you can at the same time will to be a universal law." In doing wrong we will the opposite of our subjective maxim to be a universal law. We decide to appropriate a deposit or to tell a lie, but we hope that all other men will be honest and tell the truth; that is, we hope to be an exception. There is thus a contradiction in our will, for a principle is recognized as universal and yet is held to admit of an exception. In doing what is right, however, no such contradiction arises. Or, perhaps, one should say, when no such contradiction arises, the act contemplated is right. The voice of duty therefore is a categorical imperative. Hypothetical imperatives command an action upon the supposition of a desired end; for example, if you wish to bisect a line, you ought to draw certain arcs. But this is not the *ought* of morality. Duty has no *ifs*. It is no categorical imperative to say, If you want a good reputation, be honest and tell the truth. In fact, a person who was honest in order to enjoy a good reputation would be somewhat less than moral. The categorical imperative commands, Tell the truth! — regardless of consequences. The act must be done out of pure reverence for duty, and not for any ulterior motive. Moral acts, then, are those whose maxims can be universalized.

Freedom

The details of Kant's ethical theory and their criticism would diverge too greatly from the main line of the present argument. They must be omitted in order to examine the relation between mechanical law and the possibility of ethical conduct. The latter requires freedom and the former seems to exclude it. The attempt to manage this dilemma begins with the recognition of duty, with our knowledge of the moral law. The categorical imperative is an undeniable a priori fact. And from this fact freedom can be deduced. Ask a man if he could refuse to bear false witness when his King ordered him to lie in court. The man might doubt that he would refuse, but he would not doubt that he could refuse. Therefore he recognizes his freedom and judges that he could because he ought. The categorical imperative is the *ratio cognoscendi* of freedom as freedom is the *ratio essendi* of the moral law.

But if freedom must be admitted and if mechanism must be admitted, is there not here such a deep-rooted contradiction that either morality has no meaning or mechanism and the whole theory of knowledge behind it is false? Kant did not refuse to face this dilemma.

In human beings, argues Kant, there is a type of causality other than mechanical. It is a rational causality and it is called the will. In so far as the will is not determined to activity by any cause other than itself, this rational causality is freedom. In contrast, natural necessity is the property of all nonrational beings to be determined to activity by a cause external to themselves. Now, causality of any type involves determination by law, for the effect is conceived as determined by the cause. Hence, freedom does not mean lawlessness; freedom means independence of the laws of nature. In nature there are no self-causes; everything is determined to activity by something external to it. But the will is a law to itself; that is, its principle is to act from no other than a universal maxim. Hence a free will is a will that conforms to moral laws.

One must not suppose that freedom is the ability to indulge one's desires and natural impulses. These are external to a rational will, and actions done under their influence are governed by mechanical causation. A will is free only when self-caused; it is rational only when unbiased; and these conditions are violated when natural impulses control. Reason therefore must be the author of its own principles of action; it must be independent of external influences. In other words, the will of a rational being can be his own will only if he acts under the idea of freedom and morality.

However — and Kant himself sees it and says it — while the argument has indissolubly connected freedom with morality, it has furnished no speculative proof that man is actually free. Kant has assumed that the moral will is a type of causality other than natural causality; but he has not produced any evidence that such causality exists. The only justifiable conclusion so far is that without presupposing freedom we cannot conceive ourselves as rational beings as Kant defines rationality. "It looks as if we had, strictly speaking, shown merely that in the idea of freedom the moral law must be presupposed in order to explain the principle of the autonomy of the will, without being able to prove the reality and objectivity of the moral law itself. It must be frankly admitted, that there is here a sort of circle from which it seems impossible to escape."

The Two Worlds

Kant does not leave the matter here; he has something further to say; but whether he decreases the difficulty or on the contrary augments it, must remain an open question until his argument is completed. The argument depends on Kant's assumption that there are two worlds, an intelligible world as well as this world of phenomena. Man as a rational being is a member of the former, but as a natural being, of the latter. Freedom is then to be connected with the intelligible world while the phenomenal world is subject to mechanical necessity. To show that there is an intelligible world, and to explain its nature and its relationship to the visible world, it is necessary, before the discussion of freedom and morality can be completed, to return to the *Critique of Pure Reason* and examine certain points that were not previously emphasized.

In the Aesthetic space and time were described as the forms of sensation. The mind imposes these forms on experience. It would seem therefore that there is something independent of the mind. Whether this something is soupy, like the jelly poured into the glass, or whether it is rigid like the railroad tracks that are made to converge by perspective, at any rate Kant talks about things in themselves as distinct from things as they appear. Unfortunately these things in

themselves remain forever unknown, because, first, they are by definition outside space and time and *ipso facto* invisible; and, second,
since the categories apply only to sense objects, the things in themselves cannot be thought. But Kant throughout takes it for granted
that such things exist, and so we have the first set of objects with
which to populate the intelligible world.

There is also a second set, which more directly concerns morality.
Indispensable to the whole of Kant's epistemology is the ego or self
that imposes forms and unifies the manfold of experience. This is not
the empirical self. The self that appears to us in experience is essentially Hume's collection of ideas. Introspection reveals sensations of
red and blue, bitter and sweet, and thoughts of causes, substances,
and laws. These elements of experience change with a rapidity that
would satisfy the skeptical Scot. But in addition to this collection of
ideas, there must be something that has collected them. If all these
experiences have been unified, there must have been a transcendental
unity of apperception. But this transcendental Self cannot appear
as a phenomenon, and is therefore a member solely of the intelligible
world.

In addition to things in themselves and selves in themselves, it is
possible that there is one other member of this higher world. Possible; but not certain, as we shall see. This other member would be
God. Although Kant has taken great pains to show that God's existence cannot be proved, he also remarks that God's existence cannot
be disproved. Perhaps then there is a God. Particularly in his ethical
writings Kant seems to believe that God exists. This impression, however, must be modified by a section in the earlier Critique. A distinction is drawn between constitutive principles and regulative principles. The former actually exist as parts of the known world; but the
latter exist simply as rules for the guidance of scientific investigation.
For example, the remarkable connections and adaptations of parts to
parts in the world may be regarded as if they had been arranged by a
divine intelligence. Not only may the world be so regarded, but one
might almost say that it must be. The speculative interest of reason
forces us to think of the world as if it were designed by a Supreme
Intelligence. But only as if. To think of God as a constitutive principle would lead to a relaxing of scientific effort through an indolent

reference of details immediately to the will of God. If, however, God is recognized as a regulative principle, we are thereby invited to investigate experience and to unify its details by teleological laws. This way of looking at the matter, when applied to the field of ethics, as distinct from science, results in the paradoxical principle that although we cannot know there is a God, we ought to live as if there were one. Perhaps then God is not a member even of the intelligible world, but at least Kant believed that rational human beings are.

Because of the distinction between the intelligible and the phenomenal worlds, Kant can deny that he inconsistently attributes freedom to rational beings. As phenomena men are subject to mechanism; but as rational or as selves in themselves, they are subject to the supersensible causality of freedom. However, the removal of such an inconsistency is not of itself sufficient to make the intelligible world intelligible to us. The theory of the categories strictly limited their application to the phenomenal world. Not only is causality denied to things in themselves, which therefore cannot be regarded as the causes of sensory experience, but all knowledge of a world beyond sensation becomes impossible. Kant answers, perhaps lamely, that the objective reality of causation can be entertained with respect to noumena — the realities behind appearances — not for the purpose of having knowledge, but merely for practical purposes. The notion of a being with a free will is the notion of a noumenal cause; and although this constitutes no enlargement of our theoretical knowledge, it is justified practically.

Whether this appeal to practical purposes beyond the limits of knowledge is lame or not can better be judged by noting how Kant treats a particular voluntary event that occurs in time. There can be no freedom, he says, for things or events in time; all temporal factors are physically determined. But, he adds, these events are appearances, and freedom can be attributed to noumena. How the latter freedom and the former determination may be combined in a single act may be illustrated by a case of theft. The particular act of theft, the visible, physical motions are mechanically necessitated. Some moralists have tried to preserve freedom by denying that the motions of theft are mechanically determined, while asserting that they are produced by some sort of psychological causation; thus the thief is said to be free because the causes of his action are internal rather than external. This is but a wretched subterfuge, says Kant, and petty word-juggling. A freedom which is merely a freedom from external compulsion is still necessitated in time, and leaves no room for transcendental freedom. Kant on the other hand wants what he believes to be a real freedom without in the least minimizing the determinism of events in time. All physical motions, and all series of psychological states likewise, are necessitated. Therefore the motions and thoughts of a man committing theft are necessitated. But the man, though he is partly in time, is also partly beyond time. It is in this latter respect that he is free. Hence, concludes Kant — and the conclusion must certainly give us pause — hence the theft in itself could have been avoided, although the appearance of the theft could not have been avoided.[2]

More easily understood is a conclusion in Kant's *Fundamental Principles of the Metaphysics of Morality.* "Reason would, therefore, completely transcend its proper limits, if it should undertake to explain how pure reason can be practical, or, what is the same thing, to explain how freedom is possible.

"We can explain nothing but that which we can reduce to laws, the object of which can be presented in a possible experience. Freedom, however, is a mere idea, the objective reality of which can in no way be presented in accordance with laws of nature, and, therefore, not in any possible experience. It has merely the necessity of a presupposition of reason, made by a being who believes himself to be conscious of a will, that is, of a faculty distinct from mere desire. The most that we can do is to defend freedom by removing the objections of those who claim to have a deeper insight into the nature of things than we can pretend to have, and who, therefore, declare that freedom is impossible. It would no doubt be a contradiction to say that in its causality the will is entirely separated from all the laws of the sensible world. But the contradiction disappears, if we say, that behind phenomena there are things in themselves, which, though they are hidden from us, are the condition of phenomena; and that the laws of action of things in themselves naturally are not the same as the laws under which their phenomenal manifestations stand.

[2] *Critique of Practical Reason,* T. K. Abbott's translation (Longmans, Green & Co., 1909), pp. 189–191.

"While, therefore, it is true that we cannot comprehend the practical unconditioned necessity of the moral imperative, it is also true that we can comprehend its incomprehensibility; and this is all that can fairly be demanded of a philosophy which seeks to reach the principles which determine the limits of human reason." [3]

TELEOLOGY AND ORGANISM

This appeal to ignorance, feebly disguised by the assertion that we comprehend its incomprehensibility, is so unsatisfactory that one naturally asks whether a great thinker like Kant had nothing further to say. It seems incredible that he should have left the matter in such a confusion, not to say in such a contradiction. One's amazement may be partially diminished by three considerations. First, Kant's wonder at the starry heavens and his intense awe of the moral law necessitate the conclusion. If morality is assumed to presuppose free will, and if "I ought implies I can," what else but contradiction can result from a mechanistic system? Second, it must be admitted that even great thinkers have blind spots. What is obvious to one man is not necessarily obvious to another. Then in the third place, Kant did not leave the matter exactly as has been indicated. He still had something further to say. But whether or not it radically changes the total picture is somewhat doubtful.

In a third Critique, the *Critique of Judgment*,[4] Kant examined teleology in nature. One of the motives of this work was Kant's belief that the mechanical world and the moral world can somehow be harmonized if nature may be viewed as purposeful. Now, organisms are the most obvious instances of natural teleology, and to them Kant directs his penetrating gaze. To be a natural end a thing must be its own cause and its own effect, and in a double sense. For example, a tree produces another tree. Since the two are specifically the same, the tree is its own effect and its own cause. But in addition to this specific relationship, a tree is self-productive even as an individual. It grows; it grows itself. As Aristotle had long before argued, growth is quite different from any merely mechanical increase in size. The

[3] *Fundamental Principles of the Metaphysic of Morality*, Chap. III (end).
[4] The following summary covers paragraphs 62–76.

water which the tree incorporates into its mass, it first works up into a specifically peculiar quality. This is a type of change that does not occur in machines. Thus the tree produces itself by use of a material which, as assimilated, is its own product. Furthermore, each part of the tree is self-productive, in that the preservation of one part is dependent on the preservation of all the rest: while the leaves are the product of the tree, the tree in turn depends on the leaves, for if tne tree is repeatedly denuded of its leaves, it dies. How different these common characteristics of an organism are from those of a machine may be forcefully presented by an attempt to substitute in the illustration a machine and its parts for the tree and its leaves. For a thing to be a natural end, explicable in terms of purpose, its parts must be possible only in relation to the whole; and also, in order to distinguish a natural end from an artificial, human contrivance, it must be possible irrespective of any intelligent cause external to it. Accordingly its parts must be reciprocally cause and effect of each other. A body is therefore a natural end only if all its parts mutually depend on each other both as to their form and their combination, and are thus themselves the cause of the whole; while conversely the whole may also be regarded as the cause of the body. Under such conditions the conjunction of efficient causes is at the same time regarded as an effect through final causes.

This interesting analysis of the nature of organisms, so valuable in itself, can solve the dilemma of mechanism and morality only if natural purpose renders freedom intelligible. Now, up to this point the discussion of teleology has thrown no light on how a theft in itself could be avoided while the appearance of the motions of the theft are mechanically necessitated. Be it noted that purposive organisms in no way conflict with mechanism. When Kant says, "the conjunction of efficient causes is at the same time regarded as an effect through final causes," he is asserting, not denying mechanism. And while a watch or an auto is an artificial machine, and not a natural end, such machines are perfect examples of the compatibility of purpose and mechanism. In fact, the more inviolable the mechanism, the better it serves its purpose. Similarly organic bodies are both purposive and mechanical. We have here something not too dissimilar to Spinoza's viewpoint. For him the theorems of extension were one description of nature and the theorems of thought were another, equally possible and equally true, description of the same nature — as if the same object were being described first in Greek and then in Latin. Or, better, one of Van Gogh's paintings could be described by its peculiar technique and also by its subject matter or aesthetic impression. The same painting is entirely strokes of paint; it is also entirely an aesthetic presentation of stars or cypresses. But if Kant has done nothing but reproduce Spinoza, he ought to drop free will and the categorical imperative, and reproduce Spinoza's ethics too.

Regulative and Constitutive Principles

To avoid this, Kant turns from the purposiveness of particular organisms to investigate the possibility of a universal purpose. Could the universe as a whole be an organism? Or could there be a Supreme Intelligence who directs it to an ultimate end? If so, mechanism must in some sense be made subordinate. As the discussion proceeds, however, Kant several times remarks that such a conception can be only regulative, not constitutive. Whatever the subordination of mechanism may mean, the principle of purpose in no way interferes with the principle of mechanism, nor does it entitle us to regard anything whatever as a purposive end of nature.

In dealing with nature as a totality of sensible objects, reason may first proceed from the a priori laws prescribed to nature by the understanding. In this case the maxim of judgment is: All production of material things must be judged to be possible according to purely mechanical laws. Second, reason may proceed upon laws which are capable of indefinite addition as experience is extended. But so multifarious are the particular laws to be learned by experience that the a priori principles, i.e., the axioms of intuition, the anticipations of perception, etc., are insufficient to conduct the investigation in an orderly way. Something further is needed so that empirical knowledge may form a connected and orderly system. In this case, as reason starts from some particular principle and seeks to form a judgment on corporeal nature, the maxim is: Some products of material nature cannot be judged to be possible according to purely mechanical laws, but require a different law of causation, namely, that of final cause.

Insoluble difficulties arise if these two regulative principles of investigation are converted into constitutive principles of nature, for they would then be: All production of material things is possible by mechanical law, and some production of material things is not possible by mechanical law; and these two are patently contradictory.

However, the first two maxims, stated purely as regulative principles, are not really contradictory. To say that all events in the material world (including the theft that has driven us to this lengthy explanation) must be *judged* to be possible on purely mechanical laws is not to say that they *are* possible in this way alone, or apart from some other sort of causality. All that is implied is that a scientist must use mechanism in all his investigations and apply it as far as he can, since without it there can be no knowledge of nature at all. But this does not prevent a zoologist or a moralist, if the occasion arises, from using the second maxim in explaining either organisms or nature as a whole. Teleological explanation does not deny the value of mechanism, nor does it imply that organisms cannot be mechanically produced. Teleology merely means that human reason by following mechanism will never be able to discover any ground for the specific character of natural ends. Since human reason does not know and cannot know the inner ground of nature, our ignorance allows us to believe that mechanism and teleology may somehow be connected in nature itself. But we are not able to connect them; for us they are principles which simply regulate our thought.

The human mind has an irrepressible tendency to suppose some unconditionally necessary existence or original ground of nature; and therefore the concept of God is an indispensable idea of reason; but it is an idea which remains an insoluble problem for human intelligence. It arises from the peculiar nature of our cognitive faculties and therefore does not hold true objectively, but merely subjectively. Now, just as theoretical reason must assume as an idea this unconditioned necessity of the original ground of nature, so practical reason presupposes its own freedom. Thus a morally necessary act is regarded as physically contingent; since that which ought to occur, frequently does not. Evidently then moral laws are represented as commands owing to the subjective constitution of the practical reason. However, freedom, which is the formal condition of an intelligible world, is for us a transcendental conception, and is therefore incapable of

serving as a constitutive principle. But as a merely regulative principle it commands everyone to act in accordance with the idea of freedom as absolutely as if it were a constitutive principle.

Beyond this, there is little further argument pertinent to the
dilemma of mechanism and freedom. There are some phrases which
seem to confuse the impossibility of deducing the details of physics
from universal formal principles with an objective contingency that
would leave such particulars mechanically undetermined. That these
details are logical accidents of the principles seems to be transmuted
into the assertion that they are mechanically accidental, i.e., purely
chance events. But although freedom may be preserved if moral
choices are purely chance events, undetermined by either external or
internal causes, it is impossible to believe that Kant so intended; for
then the dilemma and the intricate argument to solve it would not
have come into being. Yet if we examine the main course of his
argument, as we have here done, are we not forced to judge that the
confusion is no less a wretched subterfuge than the view Kant thus
characterized. And maybe more so. At any rate the brave attempt to
avoid the skepticism of Hume and to show that knowledge is possible
has not been an altogether unqualified success.

CHAPTER 10

G. W. F. Hegel

MINOR POSTKANTIANS

Two or three otherwise obscure philosophers soon diagnosed Kant's basic defect. A thinker by the name of Schulze complained that the *Critique* set an impossible problem: it sought the pre-conditions of experience while it denied that these conditions are objects of experience. Kant had in effect argued that before we investigate the world and God, we must investigate whether the mind is capable of investigating the world and God. But does it not follow with at least equal evidence that before we investigate whether the mind is capable of knowing the world, we must investigate whether we can investigate whether the mind is capable of knowing the world? And so there must be prior and still prior Critiques.

More popular and a little less obscure than Schulze was the criticism of F. H. Jacobi. He coined the clever phrase: without the *Ding an sich* one cannot get into Kant's system, and with it one cannot stay in. As the brief criticisms inserted in the foregoing exposition have shown, Kant failed to avoid the skepticism of Hume. Neither a real thing nor a real self nor a real God is found in consciousness. Obviously therefore this is something that his successors had to deal with immediately. Jacobi's reinstatement of a sort of pre-Kantian realism, in which things are neither mere appearances nor representations joined by categories, but are real objects guaranteed by sensation, is not too important. However, the remainder of his constructive work was more influential because he anticipated an irrationalism that developed into literary romanticism and religious mysticism.

Jacobi

Jacobi, taking his cue from the primacy which Kant assigned to the practical reason, sought to validate the immediacy of faith as opposed to the reasoned understanding of a Spinozistic system. In fact, it was at this time rather than earlier that Spinoza exercised his greatest influence. Now, Jacobi admitted that Spinozistic mechanism is not only logical, but it is the only logical system. All demonstration leads, not to an extramundane personal God, but merely to the totality of the universe. Reason works with conditioned things and cannot rise to a sovereign, unconditioned Being. To prove the existence of God would require a ground of proof superior to God himself; so that a God who could be known, rationally, would be no God at all. However, although Spinozism is logically unassailable, it must be rejected because, cold and merciless, it violates the undeniable demands of the heart. Kant had admitted that while we cannot prove God's existence, neither can we prove his nonexistence. Therefore, Jacobi concludes, where the understanding is silent, we may believe by faith.

Faith also improves Kant's ethical theories. His arguments for the postulates of morality, i.e., God, freedom, and immortality, were weak; and it is better, thought Jacobi, to base morality on an immediate ethical feeling. This faith Jacobi also calls *Reason* in opposition to the *Understanding* that characterizes Spinozism. Of course this faith is not what Augustine and Aquinas, much less Luther and Calvin, had in mind when they used the same word. And quite likely the word *Christian* has not the same meaning when Jacobi claims to be a heathen in his understanding but a Christian in his heart. He whose heart is content with Spinozism cannot be argued out of it; his punishment is to be denied the noblest content of spiritual life.

Less interested in faith than Jacobi, Salomon Maimon added a worthwhile comment on the *Ding an sich*. Although the thing in itself is a self-contradictory conception, there was a motive for inventing it; and this motive must be satisfied. Kant had distinguished between the content and the form of experience. There was the jelly and the glass into which it was poured. Since the form alone depends on our minds, something else must explain the *given* in consciousness. Space, time, and cause may depend on us; but where do red, bitter,

and hard come from? It was to answer this question that Kant
assumed things in themselves. The fact that Kant's answer was a
blunder merely returns us to the original question. But again, Maimon's construction — an attempt, somewhat similar to Leibniz'
theory of the *petites perceptions* of monads, to account for the given
in terms of consciousness — is not too important; but the need of
relating thought to a real world can hardly be exaggerated.

Fichte

Johann Gottlieb Fichte (1762–1814) was the most important
thinker between Kant and Hegel. Like Jacobi, Fichte admitted that
Spinozism was perfectly logical: I am an object in the world of
nature, and since nature is a connected whole, I am as physically
determined as any other object; my sense of freedom is but the sense
of nature's power within me; accordingly everything is necessitated.
But, argues Fichte, however intellectually satisfying this may be, it is
morally and emotionally unacceptable. Mechanism indeed cannot
be disproved, nor does Fichte claim that he can prove his own view.
The reason is that here we are faced with a choice between ultimate
principles. The starting point of a philosophy cannot itself be the
consequence of a prior argument. Therefore what sort of principles a
man chooses, depends on what sort of man he is. Fichte, being the
sort of man who was profoundly influenced by Kantian morality,
rejected mechanism and chose freedom. Thus it is not science that
gives access to reality, but faith — the immediate consciousness of
myself in moral relations with other selves.

Dependence on faith, this type of faith, was not a peculiarity of the
philosophers of this period, but was the common factor in the romanticism that was writing a new literature, discovering Greek art anew,
building a new culture, developing a sense of new values. It was a
revolt against established decadence. The political action of the
French Revolution was supported by the intellectual efforts of the
Enlightenment or Age of Reason. Seeing that the Church favored
oppressive autocracy, the agitators cried, *Ecrasez l'infâme*, and aimed
to suppress all Christianity. Consciousness of sin, humility, and a
sense of worthlessness were replaced by the feeling of self-confidence.
Human nature was considered to be fundamentally good. In German

literature Goethe was the great romanticist. Writing a letter to Herder he complained that even Kant, who late in life had enquired into the radical evil of human nature, was too friendly toward orthodox Christianity: "Kant's philosophic garment . . . needs to be cleaned of bungling prejudice, as it is criminally besplattered with the stains of radical evil, with which even Christians are decoyed to kiss its hem." In the same vein, Faust, in lewd league with the devil and the perpetrator of dastardly crimes, is pictured by Goethe as a good man who will comfortably earn heaven and win an indulgent God's approval by making a few minor mistakes.

Goethe's immoralism and Fichte's emphasis on obligation do not at first sight seem to belong to the same system of ideas. Now, it is true that the several romantic writers differ in their preferences for particular values; but for them all the fundamental fact about the universe is that it contains values. These values are grasped, perceived, or appreciated by an immediate faith. Science, scorning faith and claiming to be the only approach to reality, may broaden the area but it does not increase the depth of our understanding. Reality isn't atoms; it is life. Doubtless the positive sciences and even the narrow epistemological themes of Hume and Kant are not to be prohibited; nature is worthy of study; but the more penetrating view assigns greater importance to the human values of emotion, art, morality, religion, and culture.

For Fichte, as has been indicated, it is the value of morality that removes from philosophy the absurdity of the *Ding an sich* and gives a consistent idealism. The type of self disclosed in the consciousness of obligation is quite superior to Kant's empirical self. Since this latter was hardly different from Hume's bundle of images, sensory experience seemed to need things in themselves as its basis. But Fichte's self, more nearly similar to Kant's transcendental unity of apperception, though not unknowably outside of experience, is sufficient to account for the content as well as the form of perception. The objects of nature therefore are constructions of my consciousness. Materialists without exception, whether Democritus of antiquity and some of the modern exponents of the French Enlightenment who in denying fundamental reality to consciousness make it at best a derivative epiphenomenon, or Spinoza who puts matter and mind on the same level, or, we might add, twentieth-century behaviorists who deny even the existence of consciousness, are all guilty of a great absurdity. Knowledge can begin only with some sort of *Cogito*. Philosophy and experience both start with the self, and the objects of nature are inferences therefrom. Having so deduced them, a philosopher cannot then reverse himself and profess to explain the self as a result of nature.

If this disposes of the troublesome *Ding an sich,* the same factors enable Fichte to avoid Berkeley's solipsism. Faith in or consciousness of moral obligation is the indisputable fact. Neither Humean images nor Kantian phenomena can have obligations. Even if the perceptions of red, bitter, and hard could as causes have effects, still it is meaningless to say that images *ought* to do something. Obviously therefore I am not a phenomenon. But further, if images have no obligations, it is equally true that no one has obligations to them. Obligations can exist only among persons. Therefore there must be a real supersensuous world of free spirits, of which I am a member. And the physical universe is but the material of duty made sensible.

There is one slight difficulty, the removal of which will complete Fichte's system. If both the form and the content of experience are the constructions of an active ego, a plurality of selves would produce a plurality of universes. Each transcendent person would be the supreme and solitary sovereign of his own world. But because this would permit of no contact among selves, solipsism is reintroduced and obligation is denied. Obviously something is wrong.

It may be remembered that in the Middle Ages Averroes and Aquinas differed in their interpretations of Aristotle's theory of the active intellect. The Mohammedan taught that there is but one active intellect for all men, thus denying individual immortality; on the other hand the Christian philosopher provided for personal immortality by defending a plurality of active intellects. Now, Kant had left the impression that to every empirical self there corresponded a transcendental unity of apperception; but since this, an individual's deepest self, was unknowable, the impression may very well be mistaken. Our ignorance would allow the possibility that one "active intellect" is sufficient. And since a plurality leads to a denial of obligation, we are forced, not indeed to deny a plurality of finite selves, but to conclude that beyond this plurality there is a single Absolute Self. Without this Absolute Self there could be no obligation. Even if it were possible for totally independent selves to inhabit one world, such an aggregate would be anarchical; temporary peace and order would be only a breathing space between wars; morality could not exist. Neither could such a world exist: no individual self, only the universal self can form a world out of itself by the productive imagination. Therefore the individual person has an external world that determines him both in thought and action. Thus the relation of selves in a common world requires them to be parts of a single all-inclusive absolute.

Fichte's Absolute Self is not to be considered as a personal God, at least not in any theistic or Christian sense. Although his denial of the *Ding an sich* and his immediate faith in himself reinstated the metaphysics excluded by Kant, Fichte did not mean to reinstate theology and the theistic proofs. When he was accused of atheism — and from a theistic point of view Fichte was as atheistic as Spinoza — he framed a reply by changing the meaning of the accusation. Atheism he equated with irreligion, and then on the basis of his faith he claimed to be very religious. As this too obviously evades the issue, he diverted attention by charging Christians with worshipping the devil. Theists are hedonists, he claims, since they desire the enjoyment of heaven. What is worse, in asserting that God created the world for his own glory or pleasure, they make God a hedonist too. Such opinions are the result of a radical blindness in spiritual things and a complete alienation from the life of God. Such a God is in fact the devil, the prince of this world, an idol. Fichte was not the sort of man to choose this view. On the contrary, Fichte identified God, or, better, the divine, with the impersonal moral world order. This order, which is the most certain of all facts, has no superior cause. "It is not doubtful . . . that there is a moral world order, that to each individual his determinate place in this order is assigned . . . that every part of his fate, insofar as it is not caused by his own conduct, is the result of this design . . . that every good action succeeds and every evil fails, that for those who rightly love only the good, all things must work for the best. . . .

It can just as little remain uncertain . . . that the concept of God as a particular substance is impossible and contradictory. . . . "

HEGEL: THE PHENOMENOLOGY OF MIND

Without exception G. W. F. Hegel (1770–1831) was the dominating genius of the nineteenth century. This is partly explained by the breadth of his interests. Whereas Fichte stressed morality, Jacobi and Schleiermacher religion, Schelling nature, and lesser romanticists their taste, Hegel combined all these and added to them an appreciation of their historical development which the romanticists and especially the exponents of Enlightenment lacked. But more than the breadth of his interests, it was Hegel's detailed and intricate profundity that made him the ruling prince of philosophy for a full century, not only in Germany, but in Britain and America as well. Unfortunately, these factors of his genius are precisely those that make any elementary account fragmentary, therefore misleading, and in a peculiarly Hegelian sense, false. The plan adopted here is to show how the *Phänomenologie des Geistes* begins, to show how the *Logik* begins, and to hope that some student may be fortunate enough to take another step or two in a more advanced course. One advantage, however, attaches to a summary of the *Preface* of the Phenomenology; viz., Hegel wrote it after completing the remainder of the volume and in it gives somewhat of a survey of his position.

This *Preface* begins with a consideration of what prefaces to philosophy books ought to be. The usual procedure, in which the author compares several earlier systems, relates the circumstances that gave rise to his efforts, and anticipates his conclusions, is to be condemned because such a string of desultory assertions is not a proper manner of expounding philosophical truth. Moreover, such a preface encourages the common notion that truth is fixed and that one system contradicts another. At this early point Hegel indicates what he means by truth, contradiction, and philosophic method; and his notion of these must be fairly well understood before much further progress is possible. But because the *Preface* relies on the brief though appropriate metaphor of bud, blossom, and fruit, instead of giving a full explanation, it seems best to combine with the *Preface* certain additional material taken from other places.

Dialectical Evolution of Truth

Truth, instead of being fixed and immutable, as Plato, Aristotle, and nearly all philosophers had believed, evolves and grows. As the bud disappears in the blossom, and the blossom in the fruit, so the truth of one age or system disappears and becomes the different truth of a later time. No doubt the Stoics contradict Aristotle and the empiricists contradict the rationalists: of course there is such a relationship as contradiction, but it is not what ordinary logic thinks it is. Instead of the opposition's being fixed and everlasting, the one part becomes the other. The bud and the blossom are contradictories; they are mutually incompatible; and the bud is a false form of the blossom as the blossom is a false form of the fruit. Thus the rationalism of Spinoza is a false form of Hume's empiricism; the two are contradictory, but the former grows into the latter. Extend this image so as to include the complete history of philosophy, and the result will be that the theories of Heraclitus, Parmenides, St. Augustine, Descartes, and Kant are not disjointed, externally and arbitrarily juxtaposed systems in temporal sequence, but they are all essentially phases, aspects, or *momenta* in an organic unity. That is to say, there really is such a thing as history; it is one thing, not a mere aggregate of independent events; it is an organic whole in which the earlier grows to become the later. This process of organic evolution in history is mirrored in the proper method of philosophy, the dialectical method which was anticipated by Kant, used self-consciously by Fichte, but popularly connected with the name of Hegel because Hegel developed it to an extraordinary degree of perfection.

The essence of the dialectical method consists in choosing what seems to be an appropriate and plausible starting point, called the *thesis*, which upon analysis is seen to imply a contradictory proposition or concept called the *antithesis*; this internal contradiction is removed and the true significance of the original concept is preserved by finding a higher unifying concept, the *synthesis*. This synthesis then becomes a second thesis, giving rise to its antithesis, and producing a higher synthesis; and so on until the highest and all-inclusive synthesis is obtained, a synthesis which no longer contains a contradiction. This method is supposed to proceed with a logical rigor equal to that of mathematics and rationalism; and by it every category, every concept, i.e, all reality, is derived.

The Law of Contradiction

The traditional Aristotelian law of contradiction is unexceptionable so far as it goes. Thought always implies a distinction. Insisting against Protagoras that a thing must be itself, Aristotle needed to mark off one thing against another. But Aristotelian contradiction is too restricted, for thought is not only a matter of distinction. It is also a matter of relating: it connects one thing with another. And even Aristotle admitted that the knowledge of opposites is one. If a thing without distinctions is unthinkable, a thing without relations is also unthinkable. While every object must be differentiated from everything else, no object can be so differentiated as to exclude an identity that transcends the difference. That is to say, an absolute distinction cannot exist: all antagonisms can ultimately be reconciled. Every definite thought excludes the opposite thought; but it also has a necessary relation to its negative and cannot be separated from it without losing its meaning. Therefore every definite thought includes its opposite. It is and it is not itself, for it contains in itself its own negation. If we pass from the first thought to the second as we necessarily must by this method, and then wish to return to the first thought again, we can do so only by combining it with its negative in a higher third thought, in which it is partly denied and partly affirmed. Thus the bud both disappears and is preserved in the bloom. But contradiction between philosophical propositions has usually been conceived as fixed and insurmountable. Relief from conflict and the resulting onesidedness has not been attained, because the mind perceiving the contradiction has failed to recognize in what seems to be inherently antagonistic the presence of mutually necessary momenta. (In these last sentences we have returned to the *Preface* itself.)

Results and Methods

When the opposition between truth and falsity is taken as fixed, or even if truth is considered to have evolved to a given point, there is a tendency to see the significance of philosophy in the results so laboriously achieved. And in ordinary prefaces, perhaps in ordinary systems, these results are contrasted with the results of other authors. College students in particular think they have learned philosophy when they can state these results: such as, Aristotle said the world was finite; Plotinus put a One above the Intelligible World; Descartes argued, *Cogito ergo sum.* If they write them down correctly, they think they should get a good grade. That these propositions should be supported by reasoning hardly occurs to them. What is worse, instructors sometimes obscure the reasoning by using the twentieth-century pedagogical stupidity of so-called objective examinations. In reality all this sort of thing is an attempt to combine the appearance of being in earnest with an actual neglect of the subject matter. These results by themselves are not philosophy. Common unreflective opinion usually distinguishes between the method and content of the positive sciences; but in philosophy no such separation is possible. The conclusions arrived at are meaningless apart from a knowledge of the process by which they were obtained. Disjointed propositions can hardly be called true: truth can truly exist only in systematic form.

Romanticism

In consonance with this, the only medium of truth is conceptions. The romanticists of Hegel's day, Jacobi, Schelling, Schleiermacher, claimed that contact with reality is not made conceptually or intellectually, but intuitively, mystically, immediately. Thus reality, God, or the Absolute would not be conceived, but merely felt; and the writings of such men turn out to be expressions, not of the real object, but of their own subjective feelings. For example, Schleiermacher, who originated Protestant liberalism and exercised tremendous influence down to World War I, abandoned theology and substituted the psychology of religious experience. Instead of writing about God, he wrote about himself. As Schleiermacher was interested in the value of religion, and Fichte in morality, so Schelling adopted a mystic approach to nature. Men in this state of mind are like the prodigal son. They have left home; that is, they have left the satisfaction and security arising from the sense of certainty that life can be reconciled with ultimate reality. Quickly spending their capital in unsubstantial reflection, they become conscious of their loss. Then turning away from the rationalistic husks of the pigsty, they seek not a lost knowledge but a lost comfort. Philosophy is not expected to open up the compact solidity of substantial existence and to restore orderly ways of thought. This mentality does not seek distinct concepts to remove its chaos: it wants more chaos, fewer distinctions, less order and system; it wants ecstasy, not argument. Well, if this is what a man wants, he will soon find something to rave about. But the force of mind, asserts Hegel, is only as great as its conceptual expression. Those who place obscurantism and apocalyptic utterance above precision of meaning and who hold accurate statements in contempt are not so much devoted to God as to the fortuitous content of their own minds. They think they receive wisdom from God in sleep: we grant them that their productions are dreams.

These Romanticists, and here Hegel is probably thinking of Schelling more than of anyone else, dazzle their readers and give the impression of having vast knowledge by sweeping references to familiar scientific material. With this they couple an emphasis on curious, unusual, and extraordinary phenomena. To the whole they apply their formula that in the Absolute, all is one. But if we examine their grandiose system more closely, we find that, instead of showing how a single principle takes shape in diverse ways, it is but a shapeless repetition in which the one idea is applied externally to various items. This is no substitute for scientific detail. A monotonous formalism, a bare idea without concrete realization, does not have the substantive value of actual knowledge. They will tell us that while a specific fact is doubtless something specific here and now yet in the Absolute no such single thing exists, for there everything is all one. But to pit this empty formula against the organized whole of determinate knowledge is the very naïveté of vacuity. Such an Absolute is a night in which all cows are black.

Substance and Subject

Much of Hegel's difficult language can be understood as a protest against the disappearance of essential differences in the simplicity of an empty universal. On this point Spinoza was as much to blame as Schelling. Not only is there the difficulty, previously discussed, of attributing space and thought to the same substance, but, Hegel more particularly urges, Spinoza's substance is devoid of self-consciousness. One might say that this concept of substance leaves Spinoza himself outside, looking on reality as a spectator, when, of course, he is himself a part of reality. Therefore, Hegel insists, everything depends on grasping and expressing the ultimate truth, not merely as substance but as subject as well.

On the other hand, this subject cannot be precisely Spinoza or Fichte as individuals. If thinking is taken as purely subjective, the same loss of differences, the same abstract empty uniformity results again. Kant and Fichte were too individualistic. They had shared too largely in the ideas of Rousseau and the French Enlightenment, in which freedom was attributed to men as individuals. But in attempting to make the individual a god, the revolution revealed that he was a beast. Anarchy and its obverse, the terror of dictatorship, are the results of individualism. Ethics and religion, however, presuppose definite relations of man to man and of man to God. In rejecting these definite relations and obligations as inconsistent with freedom, the eighteenth century ended in disaster.

Now, for Hegel, the recognition of organic unity is needed to correct the abstract idea of freedom. The universe is an all-inclusive organism. Mind and object, subject and substance, and the several self-conscious subjects as well form a unity. No one is outside or independent. As particulars or parts of this unitary organism, men are free in their limiting conditions. Man is free because he is determined by his own nature, which in turn is determined by its relation to the whole of nature; nor is nature to be considered alien to man, for ultimately the two are identical. The identity, however, is not abstract or empty, but is one that preserves all differences, without which the truth would be falsified.

The Truth Is the Whole

The truth therefore is the whole, and the whole is nothing but being completing itself through its own development. The Absolute is essentially a result; only at the end is it what it is in very truth. At the beginning, or expressed immediately, the Absolute is only the universal. To suppose that this is what the Absolute truly is, would be the equivalent of mistaking the simple phrase *all animals* for the science of zoology. Neither the word *animal* nor the word *absolute* expresses what it implies. Yet only mere words like these express intuition as immediate. Zoology, however, requires concepts combined into propositions; but the very first proposition is already a process and a form of mediation, and as such has passed beyond immediate intuition. The Romanticists have a horror of mediation because they are unaware that reality is a process. Contrary to their opinion, and contrary to common opinion, there is no distinction between truth and the process of arriving at truth. We misconceive the nature of reason if we exclude reflection or mediation from ultimate truth; this it is that constitutes truth the final result and at the same time does away with the contrast between the result and the process of arriving at it. That is to say, reason is purposive activity, and the result is the same as the beginning because it is the purpose of the beginning. The previous philosophers with geometry as a model attempted to base their systems on a first and fundamental principle. This basic truth, so-called, even if true, is also false. Its refutation consists, not in some external attack upon it, but in developing its own inherent defects. Defective it is, because it is merely a principle, i.e., a beginning.

Accordingly knowledge is only real when set forth in conceptual, systematic form. That truth can be realized only in a system and that substance is essentially subject, Hegel expresses by representing the Absolute as Spirit. Spirit is the only reality, the inner being of the world. It assumes determinate form and enters into relations with itself; for it is externality or otherness and exists for itself. Yet in this otherness it is still one with itself, self-contained and self-complete. At first in the historical process it is we who know this self-containedness. The Absolute is self-contained for us. Later the

Absolute must become self-contained for itself. It must become self-conscious, conscious of itself as its own object. Mind, thus developed, knows itself to be mind; and this is science. Science (not to be limited to the twentieth-century American connotation of the term) is the realization of the Absolute.

Science flourishes in a mind that knows itself. But self-knowledge attains its meaning only through the long process of developing it. Naïve self-consciousness looks on science as concerned with external objects, separated from mind. The objects are out there; the knowledge is in here. Emphasize the objects, and materialism results; emphasize knowledge, and a Berkeleyan subjectivism results. The former makes the mind seem unreal, and the latter, depending on a self-certainty that is external to science, makes science seem unreal. In opposition to this naïve opinion, science itself considers such a separation as the very opposite of science. The two parts, each of which regards the other as a perversion of the truth, must be combined. The combining, a long process which cannot occur all at once, is the development of science and the theme of the *Phenomenology of Mind*. The first chapter considers mind in its naïve state of sense-consciousness; then a laborious dialectic journey, leading through many unexpected stages (perception, understanding, self-certainty, reason, spirit, morality, religion), brings us to the portals of absolute knowledge.

Universal Mind

Since the mind whose phenomenology Hegel describes is not so much an individual mind as it is the universal mind or absolute spirit, a digression here may be made for the purpose of clarifying the concept by noting some of its historical motivation. In prior philosophy with but a few doubtful exceptions, thinking was always the activity of an individual person. But for Hegel, whom Fichte somewhat anticipated in this respect, there is a thinking subject which is neither an individual human being nor the personal God of theism. This mysterious Absolute, neither man nor God, is the conclusion to which Hegel was driven by the unfortunate implication of common opinion. If thinking is essentially and exclusively an individual capacity, there seems to be no fair escape from solipsism. As with Berkeley a given object, such as this tree, miraculously becomes real time and time again in the separate, casual acts of perception of an individual subject. On the other hand, if we wish to credit Berkeley's illogical denial of solipsism, the result is no more acceptable, for in this case the objects usually supposed to be common to many persons are actualized or become real in the countless perceptive acts of a plurality of individuals. This latter form of the problem, complicated by the difficulties of causality, Kant himself did not solve too well, or at least too explicitly. In his view the new property which "relation to an object" confers upon a perception consists merely in being connected with other perceptions according to a rule; but this a priori category of causality can easily be taken as a pompous German expression for Hume's straightforward admission of an inexplicable subjective habitude. Of course, this was not Kant's intention. When anyone asserts a proposition, he assumes that its truth is not dependent simply on himself. Remarks that such and such is merely one man's opinion, or that Mohammedanism is true for the Arab and Christianity true for Western civilization, are polite ways of saying that these are not true. Therefore Kant intended the categories to be the same in all persons and to apply to a world that was common to them all. But how can an individual recognize that there is a unitary world common to all percipients? Surely not in virtue of any essentially individual experience. There must be some sort of universality in which all objects and all persons participate. In some sense all experience must be one. For these and further reasons Hegel posits an absolute spirit, a concrete universal, of which both things and persons are modifications. Since these further reasons would extend this digression unwarrantably, it is best to break off at this point and return to the *Preface*.

The History of Philosophy

The phenomenology of mind is of course the history of any individual mind as it progresses from common opinion to absolute knowledge. However, since few or none complete the journey, the progress must be viewed in the general mind or the history of philosophy. Progress is evident because the topics which in former days engaged the energy of men of mature mental ability have now sunk to the level of information for children. The children of the later age, that is, the individual minds, become educated or cultured by acquiring or absorbing this ready-made information. Culture, however, when viewed from the standpoint of the universal mind, means nothing else than that this information gives itself its own self-consciousness and brings about its own inherent process and its own reflection into self.

The history of philosophy exhibits the development of culture, not only in its detail, but more importantly in its necessity. The goal to be reached is the mind's insight into what knowing is. Impatience wants to reach the goal without going through the process. But the long journey must be endured, for every step is necessary. Because the world-soul has had the patience to go through the various stages and to take upon itself the prodigious labor of the world's history, and because by nothing less could that all-pervading mind become conscious of what it itself is, the individual mind cannot expect by much less toil to grasp what its own substance (or knowledge) contains. Fortunately, the task is a little lighter, for some of the process has now taken place. A number of philosophic concepts have already been elaborated; we are no longer confronted with mere immediate existence; reflection has accomplished the reduction of various forms and shapes to their intellectual abbreviations, to determinations of thought pure and simple. What remains to be done is to transcend the notions now made familiar. For what is familiar is not intelligently known. Therefore subject, object, God, nature, and so on retain the character of uncomprehended immediacy; and since they are uncritically presupposed as fixed points of reference, argument based on them is superficial.

Analysis of these concepts does away with their familiarity. We break them up into their ultimate elements by returning upon their momenta — the stages by which they were first formed. These early stages do not have the form of the resulting concept, but are the immediate property of the self. In antiquity the aim of philosophy was to raise the individual above the sensuous level to that of an idea. The Greeks, testing life at all points, sometimes by rather casual reflections on objects here and there, created an experience permeated through and through with universals. But in modern times the process must be retraced. The abstract forms are now ready made and the temptation is to take them as immediately given. Therefore the present method of study is to actualize the universal and to give it spiritual vitality by breaking it down and superseding it as a fixed and determinate thought. But it is a more difficult task to make fixed thoughts fuse with one another and form a continuous whole than it was to rise above sensuous existence. The reason is this: determinations of thought get their substance and existence from the ego in so far as the mind makes a negative judgment, a judgment that something is not something else; but determinations of sense find their existence in impotent, abstract immediacy. Thoughts become fluid and interfuse when thinking pure and simple knows itself as a moment in the process when the fixity both of the ego and of the concepts is surrendered. In virtue of this process pure thoughts become what in truth they are, what their substance consists in, namely, spiritual entities.

Scientific Procedure

This process constitutes the nature of scientific procedure in general. It is the necessitated expansion and concatenation of the content of these spiritual entities into an organic systematic whole. Thus even the early casual and desultory reflections cease to be such, for the road to science compasses the entire objective world of conscious life in its rational necessity. Therefore a systematic exposition must include the moment of immediate sense consciousness, for the immediate aspect of mind, if it is nothing more, is at least the necessary beginning.

At every stage in the evolution of mind the opposition between cognition and objectivity is present. Since these stages are modes or forms of consciousness, the scientific statement of the course of this development is a science of experience. The substance and its process are considered as the object of consciousness. That is, since mind consists of this process and since the process may be an object of science, mind becomes an object for itself. It is both subject and object. It is its own other. The dissimilarity between the ego and its object is their inner distinction, or the factor of negativity. One is not the other. Though this negativity may be thought of as a defect in each of the opposing terms, it is actually their very soul and moving spirit. Democritus vaguely anticipated this by taking the void, the not-atom, as the principle of motion, though of course, he had not yet thought of it as self. This negative factor, while at first it appears as an inequality between the ego and the object, is just as much an inequality within the substance itself. What seems to take place outside the object, the activity of knowing directed against it, and what seems to take place outside the ego, the activity of the object impressing itself on the mind, are their own doing; and substance shows that in reality it is subject. When this identity is completely evidenced, mind has made its existence adequate to and one with its essential nature, and the separation between subjectivity and objectivity, between knowing and the truth known, is overcome. With this attainment the argument of the *Phenomenology of Mind* will conclude, and the further development of an organic system of categories will remain for the *Logic*.

History and Mathematics

This general point of view, with its new concepts of contradiction and of evolving truth, must answer two objections which Dogmatism presents as examples of fixed truth. Does it not seem that the propositions of history and of mathematics are unchangeable? Can the date of Caesar's birth or the Pythagorean theorem be altered?

As regards truth in matters of history, even the purely historical element, the bare fact, such as the date of Caesar's birth (which perhaps with some inconsistency Hegel characterizes as belonging to a sphere of contingent and arbitrary particularity), is impossible without the activity of self-consciousness. To get this fact, one must consult books and manuscripts; and a great deal of intellectual construction, usually unnoticed, goes on in historical investigation. Even when we witness an event, we can know it only as we know the reasons behind it: a naked fact all by itself without explanation or context is never a truth of history.

As for mathematics, we would never consider a boy to have geometrical knowledge, if he had merely memorized the theorem without understanding the proof. And a three-four-five rule of thumb, learned by experience, is equally unsatisfactory. Yet, though a knowledge of the proof is essential, it is not a moment in the result itself. The proof is over and has disappeared when we get the result; it does not belong to the theorem but to the knower. The entire process of producing the result is an affair of knowledge which takes its own way of going about it; and the nature of a triangle does not break up into factors in the manner set forth in the proof. In mathematics the insight required is external to the subject matter. Doubtless the construction or proof contains true propositions; but their content is false. The triangle is taken to pieces and its parts are made into other figures. Only at the end of the proof do we find our original triangle again. In the course of the construction it was lost sight of and was present merely in fragments that belonged to other wholes. This is a negativity that must be called falsity. Furthermore, the necessary steps of the proof do not come from the theorem. We choose to draw certain lines, though any others are equally possible, in the fond hope that they will serve our purpose. This purpose, which controls the process, is external because it is only after the proof is completed that it comes to be known. Besides all this, the pride of mathematics rests on the poverty of its purpose and the defectiveness of its material. Philosophy must scorn to have anything to do with it. Quantity is nonessential and superficial. Space, on which the concrete notion inscribes the diversity it contains, is (like Plato's receptacle) an empty, lifeless element whose differences subsist in passive, lifeless form. What is concretely actual is not something spatial. The material of mathematics is unreal, and with it neither concrete sensuous perception nor philosophy has anything to do. Therefore the fixity of mathematical propositions is the fixity of unreal truths.

Philosophy, on the contrary, deals with what is real and essential. This real, not abstract but living, creates its own momenta as it develops; and the whole of this process constitutes the positive content and truth of the real. Negativity which if it were considered in abstraction would be called falsity, is also included in the process. But though this element disappears, it is essential. Appearance and disappearance are both parts of the process, but the process itself neither comes into being nor passes away. Since this is the case, scientific method cannot be geometrical, as Spinoza thought. The popularity of mathematics, of axioms, principles, proofs, and theorems, with the equally rigorous refutation of opposing positions, belongs to a past age. Even those who do not clearly understand why mathematics is unsuitable consider it out of date. And if it had been as excellent as Spinoza thought it to be, it would have made itself acceptable. The rejection of such fixed proof, however, does not mean the approval of romantic surmise and inspiration, for this latter contemns scientific procedure altogether. The proper philosophic method is that of dialectic triplicity, which Kant rediscovered instinctively but which unfortunately he left lifeless and uncomprehended. The resulting formalism takes the shape of teaching that thought is electricity, that animals are nitrogen, or that some determination of a schema is the predicate of a given subject. Although this procedure can be made impressive to one who has no experience, it merely confers the semblance of unity on its material and fails to express the meaning that underlies sense-ideas. Eventually one becomes disgusted with such schematic labels, drops the purely verbal distinctions, and lets all science fall into the formless identity of a blank Absolute. Such is the result of lifeless understanding and an external process of knowing.

Being Is Thought

Science can become an organic system only by the inherent life of the notion. Determinations are needed which are the self-directing inner soul of the concrete content. The schematizing process of understanding is a pigeon-holing process which furnishes nothing more than a table of contents; the contents themselves it does not furnish at all. For example, understanding may predicate magnetism of an iron bar. But as a predicate magnetism is an inert entity, not known as the living principle of the existing bar. Nor can understanding comprehend how in this bar its intrinsic and peculiar way of expressing and producing itself takes effect. Science, on the contrary, must grasp the inner necessity controlling the object; sinking itself into its material, true knowledge returns back into itself, yet not before the content is taken in its fullness, is reduced to a determinate characteristic, drops to the level of a single aspect of an existing entity, and passes over into its higher truth. By this process the whole as such emerges out of the wealth where bare reflection seemed to get lost.

One can hardly refrain from wondering whether understanding and predication, even the schematic understanding of affixing labels, can be quite so lost as Hegel seems to be at this particular point. Who can escape attaching predicates to subjects? And who can do more than this? It is a predication to say that Being is Thought, and Hegel's books are full of sentences. Is it not paradoxical to construct propositions for the purpose of denying that the subject-predicate relation fails to grasp the truth? What is there in the concept or notion that makes it more fit for science than propositions are? Four paragraphs below Hegel faces these questions and tries to distinguish his method from the common procedure of his predecessors; but one must try to decide whether he recommends his own only by failing to specify the defects in the other. But let us continue now with the notion or predication that Being is Thought.

Being is Thought and Substance is Subject. The substance of anything is its self-identity. But self-identity is pure abstraction, and this is thinking. Quality, a simple determinateness, distinguishes one entity from another. Because of its quality, an existence exists. But it is therefore essentially Thought. Existence is quality, self-identical determinateness, determinate simplicity, or determinate thought. But as self-identity is also negativity, for this is not that, fixed and stable existence carries the process of its own dissolution within itself. Having its own otherness within itself, and not externally forced upon it as might first appear to be the case, is implied in the very simplicity of thought. Therefore understanding is a process, and being a process it is Rationality.

The process and rhythm of the organic whole is rationality. The concrete shape of the content is resolved by its own inherent process into simple determinate quality. Thereby it is raised to logical form and (shades of the ontological argument!) its being and its essence coincide. The concrete existence is merely the process that takes place. No formal scheme needs to be applied in an external fashion to the concrete content, for while the content is in its very nature a transition to a formal shape, this form, far from being external, is the indwelling process of the concrete content itself.

Hence the student of science is obligated to undertake the strenuous toil of conceptual reflection. Attention must be focused on simple and ultimate determinations, such as being-in-itself, self-identity, and so on. These concepts are self-determined functions of a kind that might be called souls, were it not that their conceptual nature denotes something higher than soul. Conceptual thought interrupts and is therefore annoying to both the habit of thinking in figurative ideas (empiricism) and the rambling process of formal intelligence (rationalism). Thinking in images, materialized thinking one may call it, is a fortuitous mental state absorbed in what is material; and hence this habit finds it distasteful to lift itself clear of its matter and be confined to itself alone. Rationalism, on the other hand, detaches itself from all content with an air of conceited superiority. This arbitrary freedom should be abandoned; it should sink into and pervade the content. We must abstain from interrupting the immanent rhythm of the movement of conceptual thought; we must refrain from arbitrarily interfering with it. Only by such restraint can we get at the real nature of the notion. The process of formal reasoning adopts a negative attitude toward the content and reduces it to nothing. After seeing what the content is not, the ratiocinative process comes to a dead halt. It does not have even its own negativity for content. Further content can be obtained only from outside (as Spinoza gave an axiomatic status to a particular law of physics). But in conceptual thinking the negative aspect falls within the content itself and is the positive substance of that content because it is the entirety of its inherent character and moving principle.

Propositions and Concepts

Hegel writes at considerable length in an effort to differentiate his method of thinking from that of his predecessors. The rationalistic, or for that matter the empirical, propositions with their distinction between subject and predicate, are subverted by the dialectical method. For example, take the proposition, God is Being. Since the predicate Being has substantive significance, it absorbs the meaning of the subject within itself. Being is not meant to be a predicate but the essential nature of the subject. Therefore God seems to cease to be what he was when the proposition was first stated, viz., a fixed subject. Ordinary reflection is hereby blocked because, instead of progressing from subject to predicate, it has found the two to be identical, and no progress has been made. Since the predicate is meant to express the esssential nature of the subject, thinking loses the fixed objective basis which it had in the subject, just as much as in the predicate it is thrown back on the subject.

Complaints about the unintelligibility of philosophical writings are the result chiefly of the fact that propositions are not what they seem to be. The objection is made that so many passages must be read several times over before they can be understood. And if it be granted that rereading is objectionable, philosophy can offer nothing in its defense. Since the philosophical proposition is still a proposition, it suggests the usual relationship of subject to predicate and seems to imply that the customary procedure is knowledge. Then it is discovered that the statement was intended in a different sense, and the whole must be reread.

Speculative thinking, in abolishing the form of the proposition, must not do so in an immediate manner, merely through the bare content of the proposition; on the contrary, we must give explicit expression to this cancelling process. Not only must thought be confined within its own substance, but also this turning of the conception back into itself has to be expressly stated. This process, which constitutes what formerly had to be accomplished by proof, is the internal dialectical movement of the proposition itself. Instead of a systematic statement of this dialectical movement, previous philosophy often has been content to rely on an inner intuition. Of course, the dialectical exposition consists of propositions, and so it might seem that we have not escaped the old ways of thinking. However, this recurrent objection is cancelled by a similar difficulty in the ordinary process of proof: the premises it makes use of must themselves be demonstrated by prior premises, and so on back *ad infinitum*. Furthermore, the element of the dialectical method is not strictly a proposition but a bare concept. This furnishes a content which is through and through subject per se. There is no content standing in a relation to an underlying subject, getting its significance by being attached to this as a predicate. The proposition as it appears is a mere form.

A concept should be distinguished from a mere name. For example, "God" is a name, and for this reason should be avoided. On the other hand, Being, the One, and Subject are concepts. Philosophic exposition of speculative truth must faithfully retain the dialectical form and exclude everything which is not grasped conceptually and is a conception.

The study of philosophy finds obstruction also in the unreasoning conceit that builds itself on well established truths which the possessor believes to need no examination. In the spheres of art and handicraft it is never doubted that, in order to master them, a considerable amount of trouble must be spent in being trained. As regards philosophy, on the contrary, the assumption is prevalent that, although everyone with eyes and fingers is not on that account able to make shoes if only he gets some leather, yet everybody understands how to philosophize simply because he possesses the criterion for doing so in his natural reason — as if he did not in the same way possess the standard of shoemaking in his own foot. Thus the possession of philosophy is equated with the lack of knowledge as a form devoid of substantial content. A direct divine revelation or the healthy common sense of mankind, untroubled and undisciplined by study and reflection, is held to be a good substitute for real philosophy as chicory is accepted as a substitute for coffee. Uncultivated ignorance and barbarity of mind proclaims itself to be intellectual freedom and the inspiration of genius!

There is no royal road to science. True thoughts and scientific insight can be won only by the labor of the notion. Conceptions alone can produce universality in the knowing process.

Hegel concludes his *Preface* by doubting that such a difficult system as his will find much acceptance. Yet, it is the nature of truth to force its way to recognition when its time comes; and such is the rationality of the historical process that truth never appears too soon, never finds a public not ripe to receive it. So far as this principle applies to his own system, Hegel was far from disappointed.

Sense Certainty

Since the intellectual labor of working through Hegel's philosophy is all that he said it is, there is little use in touching upon the high points of the *Phenomenology of Mind*. Nor can a chapter from the middle of the book be selected for more careful exposition because the dialectic produces each later step out of the preceding. The result has no meaning apart from the method of arriving at it. Therefore, beyond a summary of the *Preface*, nothing else can be done but to start with the first chapter on *Sense Certainty*. The difficulties begin immediately with the alternate title: *Das Dieses und das Meinen*. Despite Hegel's literary ponderosity he was a witty man; in fact he could descend to the level of a pun. *Das Dieses and das Meinen* can be translated, The This and the Meaning, or Individuality and Significance. But *Meinen* is also the personal possessive adjective *mine*. How meaning is mine is the point of the chapter.

The phenomenology of mind starts with the most ordinary and naïve view that in knowledge one should stick to the facts. Interpretations are embellishments; the truth is the thing itself. Our immediate object of knowledge must be knowledge of the immediate, the existent; we must take it as it is and change nothing. Sensory certainty seems to be the richest knowledge. It has no limits either in the far reaches of space and time or in the minutest portion of the present. It also seems to be the truest knowledge, for it does not alter its object. However, this turns out to be the poorest knowledge, for it can say of its object only that it is. The truth of sensory certainty contains only the existence of the object. Consciousness, on its part, under these conditions, takes the shape merely of pure Ego. I am, merely as a pure this; and the object likewise exists merely as a pure this. I, *this* particular conscious I, am certain of *this* fact before me, not because I have developed myself in connection with it and in manifold ways set thought to work about it; and not, again, because this thing of which I am certain, in virtue of its having a multitude of qualities, was replete with possible modes of relation and a variety of connections with other things. Neither the I nor the thing comports manifold relations. The I does not think; nor does the thing mean what has a multiplicity of qualities. The thing is, merely because it is. The essential point for sensory knowledge is the bare fact of being. That alone constitutes its truth. In the same way, the certainty, as a relation, the certainty "of" something, is an immediate pure relation. Consciousness is I, nothing more, a pure this. The individual consciousness knows what is individual.

However, there is a great deal more implied in that pure bare being, which constitutes the kernel of this form of certainty and is given out by it as its truth. For one thing, in sense experience the pure being breaks into two parts, the I and the object, each a this. Reflection upon this distinction shows that neither the one nor the other is immediate; neither merely *is* in sense certainty, but each is mediated. I have certainty through the object, and the object is certain through me.

Will it prove possible to save immediacy by discovering that one of these two is unessential and that the certainty belongs immediately to the other?

In sense certainty, i.e., in the naïve mind taken as it is in itself rather than as we philosophize about it, the object seems to be the essential factor. The ego is unessential to the certainty because the ego as knowing or as knowledge exists only through the object. The object remains as it is whether I know it or not; but the ego does not so remain, for if the object be suppressed, the knowledge or the ego vanishes. Therefore the object seems to be the essential reality and the real truth.

We must ask, however, whether the object in fact exists in sense certainty itself as the essential reality that this certainty gives it out to be. It is not a question of what the object might be in truth, but merely whether its meaning and notion, essential reality, corresponds to the way in which the object is present in sense certainty. In effect, we are asking sense certainty, What is This? The clearest answer is that the object is Here and Now. To the question, What is the Now?, we reply that Now is night-time. To test the truth of this certainty, we may write it down. A truth surely cannot be lost by writing it down and preserving it. (In German there is a sort of pun, in that the verb *preserve* sounds like putting the truth down, on paper.) If now we preserve the truth on paper for twelve hours, and examine it Now, at noon, we shall have to say that our preserving the truth has made it false. The Now that was night was kept fixed; it was treated as sense certainty gave it out to be, as something that is. But it has turned out to be something that is not. The Now as Now continues to exist; but it exists as not-night. Soon it will exist as not-day again. It is always not-something. As a general negative, however, it is not anything immediate; it is mediated, i.e., it is determined by means of something else. In being simply Now, it is neither day nor night, and it is both day and night; that is to say, the Now in itself is not affected by this otherness. A simple entity of this sort, which exists through negation, which is neither this nor that, which is a not-this, and with equal indifference is this as well as that — such a thing is called a universal. In point of fact therefore the truth of sense certainty, the content of sense experience, is the universal.

Although we do not imagine the universal, it is the universal that we express. If we say, It is, we express only being in general. But since being in general is not what sense certainty meant, we have not expressed what we mean. Our speech therefore directly refutes our meaning. Since truth is universal, and expression also, it is impossible to express in words any sensuous existence that we may "mean."

The same dialectic applies to the Here. Here is a tree, and Here is a house. Negation and mediation are essential to the pure Being of sensuous certainty. Hence this pure Being is not what we mean. The conclusion is that the object is no longer essential. It has become a universal and its certainty exists in the knowledge, the ego, which was previously set aside as unessential. Its truth is in the object as *meinem* (mine); that is to say, as *Meinen* (meaning). It exists because I know it. I am the permanent and essential factor. The Now is day because I see it; Here is a house because I am pointing to it.

Unfortunately, another I has another Now and instead of a house this other I sees a river Here. It is this I that has this Now and this Here. But thisness is universality. It is useless to try to point out this This. Point at this Now, and it is already other. The Now which was pointed out is a has-been (*gewesenes*), not an is, or Being (*Wesen*). What was, is not. Similarly, the Here, which was pointed out, is not here. It is before, behind, over, and under; it is a negative this.

Those who assert the immediate certainty of This do not and cannot say what they mean, for language can express only universals.

And This is the most universal of all words. Everything is this thing. To designate the individual I must pick it up as in truth (*Wahrheit*) it is; and instead of knowing an immediate, I pick it up true (*nehme ich wahr*), that is, I perceive. Sense certainty has therefore become perception. Perception will in turn become understanding. And the phenomenology of mind will go its merry dialectical way.

THE LOGIC

Hegel's *Logic* is as closely reasoned as, and even more technical than his *Phenomenology of Mind*. Therefore the present limitations can allow nothing beyond a partial table of contents and a little explanation in conclusion. Although the *Logic* may well be called Hegel's analogue of Kant's theory of categories, instead of an even dozen Hegel deduces a hundred or so. It is all the more necessary therefore to show that these are not a haphazard aggregate. The list has a necessary beginning, a rational completion, and the dialectical progression from one end to the other is as rigorous as even Spinoza could have wished.

The Categories

Obviously the first category must be the simplest, the emptiest, and the most abstract: pure Being. But though it is the emptiest explicitly, it contains all the others implicitly; so that the dialectical analysis will discover its antithesis in it and prepare for the synthesis. At the other end, the last, the ultimate, or the logically first category, the Absolute Idea, gives rise to no further antithesis, but contains all the preceding categories explicitly.

Pure Being, as mere existence, is not green or heavy, living or conscious, qualified or quantified, or in any way determined. Pure Being therefore is the equivalent of Nothing. It has turned into its antithesis. But since Being becomes Nothing, it has given rise to the category of Becoming, which is the synthesis of Being and Nothing. The dialectical method proceeds by triads, and this is the first, Being, Nothing, and Becoming. This triad turns into Determinate Being, that is, quality, whose sub-categories are reality and negation. Quality produces limit with its sub-categories, and then comes the true infinite. The list continues as is indicated in part below, but no further attempt will be made to reproduce the dialectical procedure from one to the next.

1. Quality
    1. Being
        1. Being
        2. Nothing
        3. Becoming
    2. Determinate Being
        1. Quality
        2. Limit
        3. The True Infinite
    3. Being for Self
        1. The One
        2. The Many
        3. Repulsion and Attraction
2. Quantity ⎫
            ⎬ (sub-categories omitted)
3. Measure ⎭

. . . .

7. The Subjective Notion
    1. The Notion as Notion
        1. The Universal
        2. The Particular
        3. The Singular
    2. The Judgment
        (four (!) sub-categories)
    3. The Syllogism
8. The Objective Notion
    1. Mechanism
    2. Chemism
    3. Teleology
9. The Idea
    1. Life

2. Cognition
3. The Absolute Idea

At this point the categories, technically defined as the predicates that necessarily attach to everything without exception, reach their end, but Hegel continues the deduction of other universals, universals that apply in restricted areas and not to everything without exception. As with the categories a few from the larger list are selected as examples.

X. Art
    1. Beauty in General
    2. The Types of Art
        1. Symbolic Art
        2. Classical Art
        3. Romantic Art
    3. The Particular Arts
Y. Religion
    1. Religion in General
    2. Definite Religion
    3. The Absolute Religion
Z. Philosophy

Comparison with Kant

The significance of Hegel's theory of categories can best be understood in relation to the problems Kant left unsolved.[1] The Kantian category to which most attention was paid was the concept of cause. In Kant's view this concept is not only the predicate of an object, when for example the current of a river is called the cause of a ship's floating down stream; but it is also the predicate of the mind which makes this judgment, in that causality is a method of thinking. Unfortunately Kant left this union of subjective and objective in some confusion. On the objective side the categories apply to each thing individually and to their aggregate, the phenomenal world as a whole. Yet the phenomenal world is only a quasi-whole,

---

[1] This comparison of Hegel and Kant follows G. R. G. Mure, *Introduction to Hegel* (Oxford University Press, 1940), chap. IX.

not a true whole, because the chain of causes and effects, as temporal events, gives an indefinite regress. Kant, it will be remembered, had argued that nothing could succeed upon a blank time. Causality is mechanical and a first cause is unintelligible. Therefore the world we know is a quasi-whole, defined partially by the categories. On the subjective side the categories are necessary because we must think objects as causally connected. Causality is a form of thought as well as a form of phenomena. Since therefore the same predicate, cause, attaches both to objects and to the mind, there appears to be some sort of identity between subject and object. This object is of course phenomenal; Kant's categories do not apply to things-in-themselves, but are merely empty forms of possible experience. Content can be poured into these empty forms only by sensation. Therefore Kant's phenomenal world, the world of objects, is not actual and concrete except as this or that individual person knows this or that individual instance of cause and effect.

It has been pointed out that this is not so very different from the skeptical position of Hume that causality is an inexplicable habit of an individual mind. Kant, however, intended it to be different; he did not want truth to depend on the judgment of an individual; he wanted the categories to be structural elements of a world that is the same for all experiencing subjects. But what Kant overlooked, if we may trust Hegel's insight at this point, was that a finite subject can recognize the world of experience as the same world that other people experience only insofar as he recognizes himself as a more-than-finite, a universal, mind. That is to say, Hegel asserts that awareness of a common world can belong to finite minds only if they are differentiations of a universal mind. In this way Hegel believes that a theory of the Absolute, which Kant did not have, is required to escape the skepticism of Hume.

Now, to return to the point that it is sensation which provides the content for the empty categorical forms, Kant held that sensory intuitions require a synthesis that precedes analysis. The analysis is a matter of abstracting or eliciting universal concepts from the particular intuitions; and for Locke this process exhausts the nature of judgment. What Locke failed to see, and what Kant insists upon, is that the process of abstraction uses data other than the simple ideas of white, yellow, bitter, and so on; abstraction makes use of data which are themselves products of a synthesis. This is not to say that the synthesis comes first in time and is then followed by the process of analysis. The priority of synthesis is logical, not temporal, for in Kant's view time itself is a formal factor of experience, and not the presupposition of critical reflection itself. Analysis and synthesis are therefore inseparable factors in all judgment. But if so, the given, the data, are not Locke's simple ideas; the only datum is the sensuous manifold of which we are not conscious, for this manifold is only the formless residue after judgment, concepts, and even space and time are abstracted from our conscious experience.

Nebulous as this residue is, Kant will not get along without it. Otherwise the spontaneity of thought would not be based on the receptivity of sense, concepts would not be empty, and an intellectual intuition would have to be admitted. But for Kant understanding does not create the object; there is a sensory immediacy, and it is this sensation that is the test of reality. Conversely, the material of sensation, the real world, cannot be reconstituted in thought without residue. An essential part of reality therefore remains unknowable.

The refusal to admit an intellectual intuition causes difficulty at other points also. What about Kant's regulative principles? There is no more reason to believe that these regulate experience than that they yield knowledge of the *Ding an sich*. Not only may they be merely subjective aptitudes, but also, for this very reason, there may be minds without them. To be truly regulative, such principles would have to be constitutive. It was the same difficulty also, aggravated by Kant's restriction of knowledge of the self to the empirical self as object so that the transcendental subject remains unknowable, that wrecked his theory of morality. Finally and in general, all knowledge relates to intuitions, and philosophy is limited to knowing phenomena; but the cooperation of understanding and sense in the knowing is not a sensory intuition or phenomenal object; and hence this cooperation, which is Kant's philosophy itself, cannot be known. Here one must recognize that Kant has asked but has not answered the question, What is experience? What is that whole complex of mind-cognizing-object? Knowledge of this complex, i.e., knowledge of what experience is, must contain a non-sensuous intuition; for if experience exists, it does not exist as a phenomenal object exists. And the conclusion of all this criticism of Kant is that the more modestly we try to limit the scope of human knowledge, the more impossible it becomes to justify even the modest knowledge we claim.

No Unknowable

Hegel therefore denies that there is any limit to knowledge; there is no unknowable, whether *Ding an sich* or transcendental self. To know the limited or the conditioned is impossible without knowing the limit. And to know that something is a limit is to know that beyond the limit the previous material does not continue. But if we thus know the beyond, it is neither a limit nor unknowable. Not only are mathematics and science possible, but metaphysics is also possible. For if we know the phenomenal world as conditioned, we must know the unconditioned or Absolute. As this is true of the object, so is it true of the subject. In the commonest of conscious experiences Hegel finds a revelation of self-transcendence, from which he infers that a universal mind is immanent in the finite mind. Therefore thought is intuitive, with its own content. Hegel's categories, then, are not empty forms of possible experience; it is not our imposing them that makes them valid. Our minds constitute the object because they themselves are constituted by the activity of the universal mind within them.

Herr Krug's Pen

But, alas, it is easier to see the faults of Kant than it is to accept the corrections of Hegel. Undoubtedly his criticisms are keen and many of his arguments are profound. Those who, later in the nineteenth century, chose as their slogan, Back to Kant, were certainly headed in the wrong direction. But though one cannot withhold immense admiration of his genius, it does not follow that Hegel satisfactorily disposed of the Kantian inconsistencies. Let us consider: if there is no residue from sensation that cannot be reconstituted in thought, if there is no unknowable, if all things can be explained— and explanation means, not the indicating of a mechanical cause that merely is, but the giving of a reason why it must be—if all this is so, then a certain Herr Krug demands that Hegel deduce, explain, and thus know the pen in his hand. If Hegel cannot do so, has he escaped the nemesis of the given? It would seem that in the relation between the categories and the pen, Hegel has fallen back into the Platonic difficulty of sensory objects' participating in the Ideas. To say that there is something in the individual thing besides the universals is to assert an unknowable *Ding*. Hegel seems forced therefore to consider each individual as a congeries of universals. But if this is so, he ought to accept the challenge to deduce Herr Krug's pen. As a matter of fact, he crushed the obscure professor by the pomp of his position. Did he not occupy the chair in the University of Berlin? Was he not the official philosopher of the Prussian state? To be sure, he did more than throw his weight around. He could refer to the first chapter of the *Phänomenologie*, written years before Krug asked his question. The argument showed that it is impossible to speak of an individual that we mean. The sensuous immediacy of the pen is an inexpressible "mine" that turns into perception, then into understanding, and so on through the system again. And if Krug cannot talk about his pen, Hegel need not deduce it.

But does this entirely meet the difficulty? The suspicion that some unknowable *Ding* is still lurking in the shadows increases when Hegel elsewhere speaks of individuals as contingent and irrational. In his philosophy of nature he even refers to some minor species of plants and animals as being incapable of deduction, on the ground that nature is so irrational that she cannot stay within the bounds of reason but runs riot in productivity. Is not this the inexplicable given? If so, Hegel has succeeded no better than Kant. And his failure is the more glaring by contrast with his claims. If furthermore the Absolute Spirit is realizing itself dialectically in the whole historical process, then every minor event as well as every minor species ought to be rigorously deduced. But once again, although Hegel managed to force the general course of history into something of a logical development, the irrational productivity of innumerable events was too much for him. Or, are we being too severe? Perhaps we can judge more justly after tracing the sequel for another hundred years.

CHAPTER **11**

Contemporary
Irrationalism

With the death of Hegel the history of philosophy rapidly approaches our own lifetime. This proximity, instead of easing the task of the historian, augments the difficulty. For historians are notoriously far-sighted, and when they try to focus on what is recent, the image becomes blurred. For example in the middle and late nineteenth century there were two philosophers, the German Lotze and the British Spencer, who outranked all their contemporaries. To question their permanent importance in philosophy was a sign of ignorance or prejudice. Yet in the mid-twentieth century, only fifty years after the death of the latter one, they have sunk into obscurity and their influence is virtually nil. Far from nil is the influence of a young Hegelian who was obscure to that generation, Karl Marx. If then, historians of 1850 paid no attention to Marx, is it probable that an author of today can select the most important of contemporary figures? Recently in America John Dewey has enjoyed the popularity once accorded to Lotze and Spencer. To question his omniscience is still a sign of perversity, at least in New York. If his disciples were even mildly theistic, it could be said that they deify him. But within the next fifty years it is entirely possible that he may drop from sight and become a small paragraph in Uberweg's *Geschichte der Philosophie*. But an author must bring his story down to date in some way. Therefore this concluding chapter will omit Lotze and Spencer; will select, even in one or two obscure thinkers, what seems to be the distinctive viewpoint of the post-

Hegelian era; omit a great deal else; and await some distant century's judgment as to what has occurred in the recent past. In pursuance of this aim of simplification the chapter will be divided into a section on the German development and a section on Pragmatism, chiefly American.

POST—HEGELIAN THOUGHT IN GERMANY

At the moment the distinctive advance, or retreat, during the last hundred years has been the repudiation of Hegelian rationalism. In fact anti-hegelianism has gone to such lengths that this period may well be called the epoch of irrationalism. Hegel had been made the champion of reason. The real is the rational and the rational is the real. But no sooner had a real though irrational case of cholera removed him from the scene than suspicions that his system had failed began to breed a revolution in thought surpassing Kant's Copernican claims. Kant as well as Descartes had held reason in high regard, however much they differed in its elaboration. But if Hegel could not deduce Krug's pen, the trouble cannot be merely whether the object revolves around the subject or the subject around the object, but whether real existence can at all be an object for the mind. Kant had asked, Is reason capable of knowing reality? Rephrasing his question gives another connotation: Is reality capable of being known? Perhaps the universe is irrational. This bold conclusion took some time to develop into its most virulent forms. Even if it appears rather clearly in one mid-nineteenth-century writer, Soren Kierkegaard, this strange man, like Karl Marx, remained obscure until the present century. But though the hints and anticipations were at first slight and popularly ignored, the direction that thought was taking seems clear now. No attempt will be made to expound any one of these writers in detail; most of them are still considered obscure; but the first, a contemporary of Hegel, achieved considerable popularity.

Schopenhauer

Arthur Schopenhauer (1788–1860) is one whose irrationalism is fairly well pronounced, although he does not perfectly fit in here for the reason that he is more a representative of the post-kantian romanticism which Hegel himself took note of, than he is a post-hegelian bent on destroying the "System." By romanticism, of course, is not meant a knight in shining armor fighting tournaments for his lady-love or a troubadour singing lighthearted lyrics. Schopenhauer hated women and as a pessimist taught that this was the worst of all possible worlds. Rather, romanticism may be considered the secular successor of mysticism. As the mystics had no hope of knowing God and tried to experience him irrationally, so the romanticists consider the intellect as superficial and take refuge in some deeper form of life. For Schopenhauer this deeper activity is not sensual indulgence, as it usually was with literary and artistic romanticists, but the activity of the will. In Schopenhauer's view the will is the Kantian *Ding an sich*; and as such the understanding, which operates by the categories, cannot grasp it. Science is superficial; it merely describes phenomena and never penetrates to the inner nature of things. The content which fills the empty categorical forms contains something that is not completely knowable, something that cannot be explained by or deduced from other factors, something that is groundless. This something is the *Ding an sich*. It is not an object of knowledge and essentially the categorical form is foreign to it. Therefore the understanding cannot penetrate to the inner nature of things. When science is accorded privileges beyond its rights, it attempts to reduce life to physico-chemical motion. Motion in turn is the subject matter of mechanics, and mechanics is mathematics. Such were the pretensions of Democritus in antiquity and of La Place at the end of the eighteenth century. The crude materialism of the nineteenth century has similarly denied vital force. Thus light is supposed to be a mechanical vibration in an imaginary ether. A vibration of 483 billion beats per second is red and 727 billion is violet. This makes color blindness an inability to count! But however much science can describe the *how*, it can say nothing of the *what*. For the *what* is the will, and the will is subject neither to the categories nor to space and time. Since it is not in space and time, it is not individual, for space and time are the principles of individuation. The universe therefore is the manifestation of a universal but incomprehensible will.

Fichte too had given the will a decisive role, but his irrationalism was less pronounced than Schopenhauer's inasmuch as for Fichte the world process was both rational and moral. But in Schopenhauer's view the will was neither, and nature is a blind and purposeless struggle. Human life has no goal, or at best nothing more of a goal than a Buddhist Nirvana. It is unnecessary, however, to pursue Schopenhauer's pessimism, by which he became the idol of the dilettante women he hated, for the main point is that post-kantian romanticism transmitted a strong irrationalism into the post-hegelian period.

During the last thirty years of Schopenhauer's life, while he was sinking from the level of post-kantian philosophy to that of shallow literature, there was a group of thinkers, stimulated directly by Hegel, who, though they represented diverse interests, agreed to oppose their great master and initiated the anti-hegelian tone that still characterizes contemporary philosophy. Their diverse interests were political, religious, and scientific, of which the two latter were more definitely metaphysical, or, to avoid misunderstanding, more violently antimetaphysical. It might also be said that the religious interest is better called anti-religious.

To an orthodox Christian Hegel could hardly appear as a staunch defender of German Lutheranism. Not only is his Absolute more akin to Spinoza's pantheistic substance than to a transcendent Creator, but also — and this was more obvious to nonphilosophical believers — he denied the particular contents of the creeds. On the other hand his radical followers complained that though he denied the contents he retained the form, for a quirk of his theory put him in the peculiar position of seeming to champion the status quo, both in religion and in politics. When the course of history is considered as the rational development of the Absolute Spirit, each stage must be regarded as right, proper, and timely. At the conclusion of the Preface to the *Phenomenology*, it may be remembered, Hegel modestly doubted whether such a difficult system as his could find any widespread acceptance; he comforts himself, not so modestly, with the remark that it is the nature of truth to force its way to recognition when its time comes, and that the rationality of the historical process is such that truth never appears too soon and never finds a public not ripe to receive it. This that he said of his own system applies equally to all political and religious developments. The result is that Hegel always justifies the status quo. And if the Lutheranism of his day happened to be lifeless and formal, and if Prussia was a rising power, these conditions were as right and proper as they were real and rational. Of course, Hegel's system also implies that the Absolute Spirit would continue to develop rationally as long as time allowed, so that Lutheranism and Prussianism will inevitably disappear; but Hegel, basking in the favor of a state-controlled educational system was willing to conceal this mild radicalism from public view and to pose as the justifier of the actual. Inasmuch as the church as well as the university was controlled by the state, reaction against this hypocritical distortion had to be both political and religious. Since the principals in this anti-hegelian reaction were contemporaries, and since, with perhaps the one exception of Kierkegaard, politics, science, and religion occur in varying proportions in all of them, the order of exposition must be arbitrary.

Strauss

Unlike that of Schopenhauer, the thought of David Friedrich Strauss (1808–1874) issues directly from the Hegelian philosophy. He was the first and the least important of the radicals here to be mentioned; for his writings are almost exclusively religious in content, with a minimum of scientific philosophy appended. At the same time his religious radicalism is part of the more general political and philosophical revolution of the mid-nineteenth century. Strauss' choice of New Testament criticism may possibly be explained as the easiest and safest method of initiating an attack on Prussian politics. In 1835 by the publication of his *Leben Jesu* he aimed to complete Christianity's destruction, which Schleiermacher and Hegel had so timidly begun. These two had indeed impugned the foundations of Christianity. Those who took the Biblical accounts at their face value, as Luther had done, had been reduced in number and divested of influence. In the universities the scholars gave naturalistic explanations of supernatural texts. The fall of man in Eden was interpreted to mean that Adam ate some poisoned food which permanently injured the human digestive system; and Christ multiplied the boy's loaves and fishes by inducing everybody to un-pack their lunches. Thus something called Christianity that had but a superficial connection with the Bible, supported and was sup-ported by the Prussian authorities.

Strauss tore away the frock coat of this intellectual dishonesty and revealed its naked hypocrisy. He was willing to begin with Hegel's thesis that there are deep and important truths, not only in Christianity, but in all religions. These truths, however, occur in historical or pictorial form; and it is the task of philosophy to elevate these in-adequate expressions to the strict philosophical form of the truth. But while Strauss agreed with this Hegelian thesis, he thought that much more remained to be done. It seemed useless to him to raise the Gospel narratives to the level of philosophic concepts, merely to sink back again to the original level. Hegel did not really so sink back; he was not averse to criticizing the accuracy of the Gos-pels; he had definitely abandoned their asserted historicity. But Strauss was not so much interested in preserving the conceptual truth of religion as he was in proving that the alleged historical facts were the products of mythologizing. Boasting that he was free from all presuppositions and prejudices (a self-delusion wherever it occurs), he claimed that although there might have been a man Jesus, the figure of Christ as described in the Gospels was the result of centu-ries of legendary accretions. Instead of Christ's founding the church, the church invented Christ.[1]

Although Christianity must therefore be repudiated — and Strauss explicitly denies being a Christian himself — religion can remain in the form of a feeling of dependence on a naturalistic universe: there is no future heaven, and the treasures of a divine life are to be realized in earthly society. Strauss, though for a time an idealist, finally accepted a form of materialism. At least he denied that there is any difference between a consistent idealism and a consistent materialism. The important point is to maintain a monism as against the Christian dualism of spirit and matter. Unlike his radical theory of mythologizing, however, the materialistic tendency

---

[1] Bruno Bauer, on the contrary, argued that the figure of Christ is the self-conscious fabrication of the Gospel authors. Neither succeeded in tracing the connection from "the historical Jesus" to "the theological Christ."

was not original with him. Its source, or one of its sources, and a clarification of the idea of heaven on earth must be sought in a more important man.

Feuerbach

Ludwig Feuerbach (1804–1872) started his philosophic career as an idealistic Hegelian. In an early treatise he argued against the theory that thought is a function of the brain. He noted the epistemological difficulty that materialism cannot maintain a distinction between true and false statements; nor can sensation pure and simple, limited as it is to the immediate present, give propositions about the future. However, he finally came to accept a purely physiological explanation of thought. The reason for this reversal, by which he discarded all the contents of Hegel's *Logic* and retained only the dialectical method, was, pictorially and mythologically, Herr Krug's pen. That is to say, Feuerbach held that reality was individual; he adopted a nominalism in which universals are simply names. When Hegel argued about the Here and the Now, he may have succeeded in dissolving or sublimating the concept of here; but This-Here sensory pen still confronts us. In allowing no place for immediate sensory intuition, Hegel cut himself off from real existence. The deduction of existence from essence is a dream; it achieves an appearance of credibility only because Hegel distorted sensation and smuggled empirical information into his concepts. But only sensation can disclose real existence — not some abstract Self-Consciousness. Hegel therefore was a failure in the field of natural science, and it is only the sensory-based positive sciences that give an understanding of the universe. Hegel's Absolute Spirit is simply the ghost of a discredited theology: in reality the Absolute Spirit is nothing else than the Absolute Professor.

Natural science, however much it must take account of pens and things, finds a much more important object in human beings. They too are real and individual. Here again Hegelianism was deficient. First, it did not overcome solipsism; and, second, it considered the essential nature of man to be intellectual and cognitive. But there are men who never philosophize, and there is an aspect of every man, even of Professor Hegel, which does not philosophize. Human nature is fundamentally emotional and passionate, not intellectual. What Hegel and all traditional philosophy had overlooked is the active, limited, temporal, needy, suffering man — the individual, who is born, who senses, and who must die. Although overlooked, these are the realities. The bodies of these men may be determined to activity by some mind or spirit — no doubt we consciously choose to eat or to walk; but first the conscious activity of choice has itself been unconsciously determined by the body. We choose to eat because the body is hungry; and eating material food is more important than idealistic fancies. In consonance with his materialism Feuerbach out-puns Hegel in his famous statement, *Der Mensch ist was er isst*. Since this might imply that Hegel suffered from a deficient diet, Feuerbach, now descending into the abyss of anti-intellectual, anti-metaphysical, and uncritical passion, laments the potato diet of the peasants. Instead of Berkeley's *esse est percipi*, he writes, "Being is one with eating. . . . Only in eating does the empty concept of being acquire content. . . . Food is the beginning of wisdom." The revolution of 1848 failed because the peasants ate only potatoes; for the same reason the Irish can never drive out the English. "Do you want to improve the people? Then instead of preaching against sin, give them better food. Man is what he eats."

If Feuerbach denies that his physiological explanation of thought is materialism, it is only because the term *matter* has been taken to designate an unknowable substratum of sensation. Instead of materialism, sensationism might be a more appropriate term, though humanism is the term that came to be accepted. Feuerbach commences or recommences a humanism in which man is the measure of all things. He refuses to argue about solipsism and an external world because the existence of mankind is a primary fact of life. The actual ego is not a neuter *Das*, but is either a man or woman; and I have been generated naturally in another human being. By this insistence on a human community, he hopes to avoid the purely individualistic theory of truth as defended by Protagoras. The distinction between subjective and objective may be maintained because objective truth is social. Whatever appears to me at the moment, whatever I sense, must be checked by what appears to or is sensed by other persons. Truth consists in agreement; mankind is the ultimate standard. Although he had previously spoken so highly of the immediate and underived truth of sensation, now he says that the sensations of individuals, distorted by their uncritical imaginations, are somewhat capricious. They must be reworked. Science does not begin with real sensible objects and work toward thoughts and concepts; the real things stand at the end of the scientific procedure because science makes objective or visible to common eyes what was previously invisible. Here we have the germ of the social theory of truth, later to be developed by F. C. S. Schiller and John Dewey.

Feuerbach naturally continued the attack on Christianity. His method was not that of historical criticism, such as Strauss had used, but rather a psychological examination of *The Nature of Christianity* — a volume praised by Marx and Engels. Religion is an expression of the immediate nature of man; and of course its essence, as with Schleiermacher, is feeling. Religious beliefs are disguised wishes reflecting man's inability to control nature. In his frustration man comforts himself by inventing stories of miracles. Thus the resurrection of Christ objectifies the desire to survive death. When a man says that he has a knowledge of God, what he really has is a knowledge, but a confused and indirect knowledge, of himself or human nature. Progress in religion consists in clarifying this knowledge by attributing less and less to God and more to man. For this reason Protestantism is an advance over Catholicism. Protestantism is not interested in what God is in himself; it is not speculative or contemplative as Catholicism is; it has no theology, but only a Christology. To complete this advance from Christianity to religious anthropology, Deity must be completely replaced by Humanity. As a matter of fact, this has been accomplished. At most Christianity exists only on Sundays; the other days of the week it is contradicted by insurance companies, industries, railroads, steamships, theaters, and the more effective implements of war. Instead of prayer, we have work; instead of religion and faith, we have politics. Since the state is human nature writ large, its strength depends on a practical atheism. Religion is a divisive force; it never unites a nation. The ecclesiastical establishment is a form of politics that is inimical to the happiness of man on earth. Religion and the church therefore must be destroyed if we are to inaugurate a democratic republic. To accomplish this end, we shall strive to increase all political controls until a strong leader can make the state supreme. Thus Feuerbach prepares the way for Karl Marx.

MARX

After Feuerbach the next development centers in Karl Marx (1818–1883) and his assistant Friedrich Engels (1820–1895), the founders of communism. Although today information about communism is widespread, it surprises many people to learn that Marx was an Hegelian philosopher. It would surprise them still more if they had a better knowledge of Hegel. For what two systems of thought could be more antagonistic than the highly academic, conservative idealism of Hegel and the brutally practical, radical materialism of Marx and Engels? Engels wrote that life originates from nonliving matter, that man is a product of nature, and that thought is a product of the brain. He predicted that the cooling of the sun will finally extinguish life on earth, and that eventually all the stars will flicker out, leaving the total universe cold, dark, and dead. And his suggestion that collisions between dead orbs may afterwards produce new stars with the attendant possibility of life hardly seems optimistic enough to remind one of the Absolute Spirit unfolding itself with perfect rationality. Yet, antithetical as absolute idealism and communistic materialism may be, Feuerbach had already shown how Hegelianism could produce unexpected results, and other elements in Marx will indicate the bridge by which he crossed this chasm.

Dialectical Materialism

Most important of the connecting links between Hegel and Marx is the dialectical method, for Marx prided himself on his dialectical materialism as distinguished from the previous metaphysical materialism. If a man, untutored though of fair intellectual ability, begins to reflect on nature, he will be struck with its all pervading flux. He will immediately become a Heraclitean. Everything changes; it is and it is not; nothing remains fixed. This view of nature is essentially correct, but in its first form it furnishes no account of the particular phenomena. No less than Schelling's night in which all cows are black, this too is but a shapeless repetition. To understand the details of nature, one must detach them from the flux, isolate them, stop their motion, and turn them into fixed metaphysical things. Then the thinker says: It is this and not that; a thing cannot be itself and something else; positive and negative, cause and effect are rigid contradictories. This abstract, metaphysical thinking, useful as it is for certain limited purposes, distorts nature and eventually flounders in insoluble paradoxes. One must then return to the truly scientific and dialectical method: cause and effect, for example, are not fixed concepts; their validity is limited to their application to individual instances; and when an instance is seen in its continuity with the Heraclitean flux, cause and effect merge and dissolve into the matrix of universal action and reaction. While this stress on dialectic and process shows Hegel's influence, it should be noted both here and later that the Marxist dialectic is not a logical activity as with Hegel but a natural or material process.

Marx does not abandon dialectics even in his economic arguments. Obviously imitating Hegel's deduction of the categories, Marx makes the proletariat and wealth opposites which form a whole; private property as wealth is forced to maintain its own existence and thereby the existence of its opposite the proletariat. Then by the law of dialectics the proletariat abolishes itself and therefore abolishes its opposite which made it what it was . . . and so on.

Collectivism

Another connection between Marx and Hegel, a consequence of the dialectical method, is their common opposition to individualism. Whether the All is Heraclitean flux or the unfolding of an original Absolute Spirit, there can be neither a Leibnizian monad nor a true individual who forms governments by social contracts. Individualism, so Hegel believed, splinters the unity of society; it atomizes the human race; it denies the Absolute or all-inclusive Whole. Such a view is irreconcilable with a rationally planned society where the choices of each person are beneficently controlled by the state. Individualism is selfish: it subordinates the collective good of the whole to the particular goods of individual persons. With this collectivism Hegel and Marx unite in opposition to Protestantism. Luther had defied organized society; he had said, *Ich kann nicht anders*; he put his own conscience above social authority. Hegel explicitly attacks Christ and his disciples for their divisive, anti-social morality. An appeal to conscience, or to natural rights, may at times be a protest against injustice; but in its denial of the priority of the group over the individual it is anarchical. Social ties exist before moral standards, and these latter have as their purpose the enforcement of the former. Christianity therefore is obviously inconsistent with an all-powerful state. Marx, to be sure, rejected Hegel's idealism and gave his theory a naturalistic basis; but his socialism as well as his dialecticism was originally Hegelian.

Too Religious

The Marxian criticisms of Hegel followed and advanced beyond those of Feuerbach. According to Engels, Hegel's system was fundamentally self-contradictory. His insistence on process and flux was highly meritorious; but he vitiated his whole contribution to philosophy by ending the flux in a fixed Absolute. The two cannot coexist. If the universe is in process, as it certainly is, an Absolute is impossible, and an Absolute Spirit doubly so. There is no need of any mysterious metaphysics beyond the separate materialistic sciences. These give all the knowledge obtainable. Pure logical schemata, such as Hegel enjoyed, can relate only to the forms of thought, not to forms of being. These latter can be derived from the external world alone; for unless these forms came from being, it would be extremely remarkable that the laws of thought and the laws of being should so closely correspond.

Although Hegel and Marx unite in opposition to Protestant individualism, the materialistic denial of Spirit leads Marx to regard Hegel and even Feuerbach as themselves too religious. He berates Hegel as the speculative expression of the Christian Germanic dogma of the opposition between matter and spirit. The Absolute is just "God" all over again. So vigorous was Marx's attack on Hegel that some of the conservatives, in spite of Hegel's anti-christian declaration "without the world there is no God," and in spite of his opposition to the morality of Christ and the disciples, began to think of

Hegel as a defender of the faith. Such mistaken acceptance of Hegelianism was more plausible a century ago because of the then common opinion that Hegel was an exponent of the status quo. And so Marx also regarded him. But Marx considered even Feuerbach to be too Christian. Though Feuerbach's influence on Marx was so great, he did not hesitate to call him a sheep in wolves' clothing. The conservative Hegelians claimed to comprehend everything as soon as it was reduced to a category; the young Hegelians criticized everything by pronouncing it a theological matter. Both groups, however, think that religion rules the existing world, even though the latter consider its rule a usurpation. But comprehension and criticism are equally at fault. Hegelian comprehension takes the fact that a cat eats a mouse; then by reflection cat is equated with nature and mouse is equated with nature; cat eating mouse is therefore the consumption of nature by nature or the self-consumption of nature. Therefore the fact of a cat eating a mouse is philosophically comprehended in the self-consumption of nature. On the other hand, criticism acts as if people could be saved from drowning if they can be persuaded to renounce the idea of gravity as a religious superstition. Both procedures are too abstract. Philosophy has been a retrospective evaluation when it ought to be a forward-looking social activity. The existing world may need to be understood or comprehended, if not rationalized; but its greater need is to be changed.

Human Activity

The older metaphysical materialism, even that of Feuerbach, and the British empiricism which goes with it, were seriously at fault in regarding man as essentially passive; and the idealists, for all their fancies, are to be credited for recognizing man as active. For if man is a part of nature in flux, how could he be less active than anything else? Man is not simply pushed this way and that by external forces. Neither thinking nor even the simplest perception can be explained mechanically. Sensation, instead of being an impression passively received, is an interaction between the percipient and the thing perceived. This is not to assert that the mind is idealistically independent of material conditions; the interaction is an interaction between two bodies, in which the man's body is as active as the other. This action is such that sensation may be said to be a matter of voluntary attention. *How* a man sees *what*, depends as much on him as on the object. Men from different cultures, brought together in a strange environment, will see things differently. What one person sees as food, another looks on with disgust. Thus the given — *das Gegebenes* — involves the person to whom it is given. John Dewey seems to have borrowed this viewpoint from Marx, but he has improved the language by substituting for "the given" the expression "the taken." One person takes snails as food, while another does not. Thus human activity, socially conditioned, makes a thing what it is by taking it as such.

Unfortunately, the idealists, though they took man as active, did not make him active enough. Actions are concrete events; and not only was Hegel's concrete universal too abstract, Feuerbach's humanism was also too abstract. Instead of starting with real human individuals in their actual economic and social conditions, he had started with "man," i.e., with abstract human nature. Disinclined to revolution, content with his picture of an ideal society, worshiping unhistorical abstractions, Feuerbach was too religious. His materialism, for which sensible reality consisted of objects ready to hand, failed to see that objects are the products of human activity. Hegel of course acknowledged objects to be the product of human activity, but his was a merely abstract mental activity. The basis of their complementary errors — the one asserting materialism but denying activity, the other asserting activity but denying materialism — is bourgeois society, a society of rugged individualists who enjoy their food without realizing that all they consume must first be produced. An apple is the result of cultivating an orchard; a cherry is an importation of commerce. Feuerbach, in accepting the apple without the labor, shows his affinity for the Christian doctrine of divine creation. When a consistent atheism removes all traces of religion, then men will believe in themselves, and instead of merely *interpreting* the world as human, as Feuerbach did, they will *make* the world human by revolutionary activity.

Making Man Human

Not only is the world to be made human, but, what is more important, man is to be made human. Feuerbach considered man as chiefly a biological product. If this were so, there would be little use for revolutions. However, the nature of man is determined by history, that is, by the economic forces which mold society. What man thinks, the ideological reflex formed in his brain, is the echo of his material life process. Life is not determined by consciousness, but consciousness by life. "The fundamental proposition which forms the nucleus" of the Communist Manifesto "is, that in every epoch, the prevailing mode of economic production and exchange, and the social organization necessarily following from it, form the basis upon which is built up, and from which alone can be explained, the political and intellectual history of that epoch." That political developments are determined by economic factors, anyone may admit, is a plausible hypothesis; but when Marx and Engels in their *German Ideology* account for the Napoleonie continental system on the basis of the scarcity of coffee and sugar, they have pinpointed a detail that may be open to question.

Communism, however, does not limit its principle of economic determinism to kings, captains, and conquest. It is inclusive of all human thought and effort. The type of morality and religion that a nation accepts depends on its social structure. The institution of the family is a correlate of private property and the abolition of individual economy is self-evidently inseparable from the abolition of the family. Society makes man what he is; or better, society makes men what they are. Like material goods a man in civil society has a natural value and an exchange value. The one is independent of the other. All men are the same in natural value (which is very little), but in civil society one man is a General and another is a Banker. A man is only what he is particularly, and this is determined economically. By ignoring the workers, a bourgeois considers himself to be Man, when he is only a Bourgeois. Man must be freed from these class distinctions; man must be made man, i.e., he must be made human. To be human is quite the opposite of being an atomistic individualist. To be human means to live in and be formed by a human world. Only so long as an individual is not a "political animal" and is therefore not the property of the state, can a private man appear as the true man. To sublimate the private person or mere citizen, it will be necessary to revolutionize private and public life from the ground up. Men must be made to recognize that they are products of society.

Men will become human in a socialized society where every human institution is collectively controlled. In a society that acknowledges private rights, i.e., in a capitalistic society, each man is forced into a division of labor from which he cannot escape if he does not want to lose his means of livelihood; but under communism, where each person can become expert in any sphere of activity he wishes, society regulates the general production so that I can hunt in the morning, fish in the afternoon, rear cattle in the evening, and criticize literature or music after dinner — all without becoming a hunter, fisherman, or critic. (*The German Ideology*, edited by R. Pascal, p. 22.)

The Abandonment of Reason

With the delights of communism or the evils of class struggles in a capitalistic society, the present account has little to do. More to the purpose is Marx's position in the history of philosophy. And it would seem that he can be cited as an example of the rise of contemporary irrationalism. A minor evidence of his abandonment of reason, argument, or logical consistency is his invention, along with Engels, of the technique of abusive language which has been faithfully followed as a permanent communistic procedure. The distortion of history to the disadvantage of religious leaders, capitalists, and even of less revolutionary socialists is an extension of the principle of abuse. For example, in his *Dialectics of Nature* Engels wrote, "Protestants outdid Catholics in persecuting the free investigation of nature. Calvin had Servetus burnt at the stake when the latter was on the point of discovering the circulation of the blood." Now, aside from the probability that Calvin didn't care a hoot whether the blood circulates or not, the story that he had Servetus burnt at the stake is an invention of Calvin's enemies. At least twice in his writings Calvin calls on Servetus' judges as witnesses that he urged them not to burn Servetus. But the calumny is so good that even today it remains a favorite with those who dislike the all too logical reformer.

Logic as well as history suffers at Engel's hands. In order to crush a socialist professor who might have challenged their leadership, he just quotes him as saying, "The person who can only think by means of language has never yet learned what is meant by abstract and pure thought"; and then retorts with this gem of illogicality, viz., "On this basis animals are the most abstract and pure thinkers because their thought is never obscured by the officious intrusions of language."

More important than these incidental matters, it is soon noted that although Feuerbach early mentioned and then later forgot the epistemological difficulties of materialism, Marx and Engels never bothered themselves with them. Or, at best, solipsism is rejected, not because of any philosophical argument, but because it is a mockery of the efforts of the working class to liberate itself. The trouble with empiricism is not any epistemological difficulty in explaining our knowledge of a thing in which simple ideas are conjoined, but it is the abstract collection of dead facts when we should start with real men in their economic development. Disregarding the analyses of mathematical knowledge made by Berkeley and Kant, Engels assures us that the idea of number arises from counting our fingers; at the same time it requires the ability to exclude from consideration all properties of the objects counted except their number — an ability which is the product of a long historical evolution based on experience. By so pushing a problem back in time and calling it solved thereby, Johnny in high school could argue that his proof of the theorem must be correct, for he took so long to do it.

The relativism of such a viewpoint is to be noted. Marx and Engels were definitely and consciously relativistic in their ethical theory. It was previously stated that ideas of morality and religion are the products of economic conditions. They have no independent status of their own. There is no absolute morality. Rights are class demands that are to be enforced, rather than proved by rational argument. The claim of one class must give way to the other; and only force decides which. All theories of absolute rights are only disguises of the hidden class interests. Marx does not dogmatize; he predicts. The test of truth is pragmatic: Will the proposed line of action produce the desired results? If the proletariat can so arrange things that I can fish in the morning and hunt in the afternoon, then communism will be true.

However, a great many passages in Marx and Engels seem to present materialism as a fixed truth independent of economic conditions and class claims. In this case Marxism would provide its ethical relativism with a dogmatic naturalism. And perhaps Marx often thought of it in this manner. But if truth changes for Hegel, how much more must all truth change in a dialectical materialism that has no absolute. If thought is simply the product of the brain, no doubt it cannot contradict nature; but then on this basis no thought can contradict nature, and insanity is as natural as any other state of mind. If all thought is thus natural, there is no logical reason to believe that some thoughts, ideas of dialectical materialism rather than of absolute idealism, are more natural, more true, or more valuable, than others. Marx himself seemed to have had some faint appreciation of this, in that he acknowledged that even pure science is given its aim through trade and industry. It seems to follow that science would be as little fixed as industry. Accordingly, while Marx may not be as self-consciously irrationalistic and as consistently inconsistent as some of those who came later, yet he rather clearly avoids a coherent explanation of the hitherto prominent problems of philosophy.

KIERKEGAARD

Soren Kierkegaard (1813–1855), although he would not be classed with Karl Marx by the superficial reader, and though even a more careful reader may think that he defies all classification, is nonetheless in certain basic respects a typical representative of the mid-nineteenth century. In his revolt against the systematic rationalism of Hegel, in his attack on official Christianity, and in the anti-intellectualism that permeated the Romantic movement, this melancholy Dane expressed the widely held opinion that there was something rotten in the state of Denmark, i.e., Europe or Christendom. He also largely agreed with Feuerbach and Marx as to the symptoms of rottenness; but with respect to the cause and the cure, he diverges from them radically. It is in this, together with his peculiar literary style, that he seems to defy classification.

The Individual

Marx had diagnosed the sickness of society as an economic malady; and in this judgment the socialists of France and England concurred.

But, asserts Kierkegaard, the social reform which the time demands is the opposite of what it needs. The malady is not economic; it is spiritual and religious. The Spirit of the age has been substituted for the Holy Spirit, man has taken the place of God, and time has swallowed up eternity. If Marx, in his erroneous diagnosis, had criticized Hegel for being too Christian and too abstract, Kierkegaard attacks them both: Hegel for not being Christian enough and Marx (or at least socialism, for it is not clear how definitely S.K. had Marx in mind) for being too Hegelian.

Their common flaw, for after all Hegel was a socialist in fact if not in name, was their disregard of the individual. Herr Krug's pen was doubtless enough to confront abstract thinking with the problem of individual existence; but individual persons are more important than pens and cannot so easily be brushed aside. Persons are important; in particular I am extremely important to me, and my problem, i.e., the problem of the person in his individuality, is basically religious. Now, Hegel had lost the person as well as the pen in the universality of the world process, for systematic rationalism cannot give an account of real individual existence. It is not true that the real is the rational. Reality, asserts Kierkegaard, cannot be grasped by reason. In spite of the argument in the *Phenomenology*, the immediate, the now, the this, and especially the mine, cannot be *aufgehoben* or suppressed. Hegel tried to explain the world by the movement of the idea; but there is no motion in logic, nor is there logic in motion. Motion is illogical; becoming is open, not closed; reality is chance, and chance cannot be put into logic. By his identification of essence and existence, Hegel got conceptual existence only, while real existence eluded him. His inability to see the difference between thought and being was a result of his thinking as a professional thinker rather than as a man. Perhaps for philosophy existence and nonexistence are of equal worth; the System (and the Proletariat as well) is not concerned with a single person. But for the existing individual, e.g., for me, I and my existence are of greatest value. Contrary to all abstractionism, whether of Plato, for he was a communist too, or of Hegel, or of Marx, the *what* is unimportant and the *that* is essential. Therefore the duty of man is not exemplified in the studious activity of Professor Hegel. Reality cannot be taught or communicated rationally and academically; it must be grasped personally, passionately, anti-intellectually. It is not conclusions that are needed, but decisions.

The same criticism applies to Marx and Feuerbach also. They are scarcely less abstract than Hegel. In Humanity as well as in the Absolute Spirit the individual cannot be found. Mass movements of faceless men undoubtedly have the strength of numbers, but such leveling and amalgamation weakens the individual ethically. The mass man has lost responsibility and the power of making decisions. To face the confusion of the times and to stand before eternity requires, not human similarity, but Christian individuality.

The State Church

Yet if Hegel and Marx are to be criticized, the Christianity of the times is to be criticized still more. Hegel's reconciliation of Christianity and the State has produced the mediocrity of citizen-Christians. The common opinion is that one is a Christian simply in virtue of having been born in Denmark. The State itself is Christian, and hence citizenship confers a Christian status. How different, how opposite to original Christianity! If a Roman statesman had been asked whether he thought Christianity was a good state-religion, he would have considered the idea ridiculous. Christians were those who had resolutely and passionately renounced the world, and the *world* is concentrated in the State. The Roman State appointed, let us say, a thousand officials to persecute Christianity: this was not nearly so dangerous as the practice of modern states which appoint a thousand officials to protect Christianity, for pay, who see to it that people call themselves Christians while remaining in ignorance of what Christianity is. Mediocre, faceless, mass-men without passion or decision! In nature, the individual is merely an instance of the species; anyone who improves a breed of sheep changes every individual. But religion is not a matter of the species and it is foolish to suppose that Christian parents automatically produce Christian children. Spiritual development is radically individual; and the cure for society is the cure of individuals. Because society is afraid of individualists, this cure will not be easy. There will be bloodshed: not the bloodshed of communistic revolution and battle, but the bloodshed of individual martyrs.

Anyone but an Hegelian or a socialist must feel a measure of sympathy for this rugged individualism; and they can applaud the sarcasm that S. K. directed against an empty and insincere religious formalism. But when one turns from the negative to the positive, from the destructive to the constructive, can one seriously conclude or decide that Kierkegaard's statements are true? No doubt he is right in recognizing that Feuerbach's dissolution of theology into anthropology was a necessary consequence of Hegel's integrating Christianity with world history. No doubt his judgment is just when he shows more respect to a man who openly prefers heathenism to Christianity than to a man who says they are essentially the same and that the one is the fulfilment of the other. Then too, no one can demur when both Feuerbach and Kierkegaard acknowledge that Christianity is a religion of affliction. For the Christian as well as for Christ, suffering is the natural condition, just as health is the natural condition of the sensual person. And finally, even though the antithesis is not quite fair either to the Romanists or to the Protestants, Feuerbach and Kierkegaard have a point in contrasting the externality and "objectivity" of Romanism with Luther's intense experience of subjective appropriation by faith. This led Feuerbach to favor Protestantism as an advance toward the humanization of God; S. K. admitted that Protestantism was in danger of becoming a religion in the interest of man and then of turning into a reaction of men against Christianity. To avoid this danger Kierkegaard offers a theory of paradox, subjectivity, and inward appropriation. And of this theory one must ask, is it true?

Subjectivity of Truth

For Kierkegaard, God is truth; but truth exists only for a believer who inwardly experiences the tension between himself and God. If an actually existing person is an unbeliever, then for him God does not exist. God exists only in subjectivity. This emphasis on subjectivity and the corresponding disparagement of objectivity results in the destruction of Christianity's objective historicity. The historical is not the religious and the religious is not historical. If Christ were an historical figure who lived a long time ago, he would have no religious significance now. Conversely, if Christ is a religious figure, the historical interval must be cancelled by an inner contemporaneity. Real religion does not consist in understanding anything; it is a matter of feeling, of an anti-intellectual passionateness. The acceptance of any objective historical truth depends on historical methods; and the objective student of history is too modest to put his own feelings into his conclusions. Speculative thinkers are not personally interested in suffering; they do not study the subjective truth of appropriation.

But Christianity has always been regarded as an historical religion, not merely in the sense that it has had a history of nineteen hundred years, but specifically in the sense that it is based on historical events that happened that long ago. For Hegel these events and their significance are integral parts of universal history regarded as the developing expression of the Absolute Spirit. But for Kierkegaard the relation between the process of history and eternal truth is a paradox. In the language of Kierkegaard and his twentieth-century followers the term *paradox* indicates something more embarrassing than those queer puzzles which after some difficulty can be solved and understood intellectually. An elementary student of physics is puzzled when he is told that the water pressure at the bottom of one container is twice that of another even though the former container has but half the weight of water. This is a paradox. It is solved by learning the relation of height to pressure. But an existentialist paradox is insoluble. It is a contradiction to suppose that eternal blessedness can be based on historical information. Therefore the subjectivity of appropriation is not continuous with, but stands in opposition to an historical dissemination of Christian teaching. Passionate appropriation, the moment of decision, does away with the interval of history and makes one inwardly contemporaneous with Christ. The method is not intellectual; it is an experience of suffering and despair. The detached objective truth of Christianity is not to be had. Beginning with the preaching of the Apostles, all the centuries of history are worthless as a proof of it. The objective truth of Christianity is equivalent to its subjective indifference, its indifference to the subject, i.e., to me.

This type of thought provokes an obvious question. If there is no objective truth, if the How supersedes the What, then can truth be distinguished from fancy? Would not a suffering Satan be just as true as a suffering Savior? Would not an inner, infinite, decisive appropriation of the devil be as praiseworthy as a decision for God? The philosophy of William James will later raise the same question though James does not seem to be aware of the question; S.K. notices the dilemma, but can hardly be said to solve it. There is a half-hearted effort to distinguish between the inwardness of infinity and the inwardness of the finite; and he seems to say that the infinity of Christian inwardness is based on God; whereas the inwardness of finitude relates to some other object. Now, if there were objective knowledge of God and of other objects, an individual could judge the quality of his passion on the basis of its objective reference; but if God and perchance the devil also are hidden, and if one is limited to a subjective, passionate appropriation, there would seem to be no distinguishable difference between the truth of God and the truth of Satan. Objectively it is indifferent whether one worships God or an idol. Whether God exists or not is immaterial. What counts is the individual's relation to an unknown Something.

In his vivid style Kierkegaard describes two men in prayer. The one is in a Lutheran church and he entertains a true conception of God; but because he prays in a false spirit, he is in truth praying to an idol. The other is actually in a heathen temple praying to idols; but since he prays with an infinite passion, he is in truth praying to God. For the truth lies in the inward How, not in the external What. Or, again, Kierkegaard says, "An objective uncertainty held fast in an appropriation process of the most passionate inwardness is the truth, the highest truth attainable for an existing individual."

Finally, another statement, also found in his *Concluding Unscientific Postscript*, a statement just as definite as the preceding, expresses Kierkegaard's subjectivity. After remarking that a search for objective truth takes no account of the relation of the individual to that truth, S. K. continues, "If one asks subjectively about the truth, one is reflecting subjectively about the relation of the individual; if only the How of this relation is in truth, then the individual is in truth, even though he is thus related to untruth."

Suppose now that there are serious flaws in Hegel's "System"; suppose too that the communistic mass-man violates the prerogatives of the moral individual; suppose in the third place that the Danish

Lutheran church was formal, hypocritical, and dead; suppose there-fore that S. K. has made some telling criticisms of his contemporaries. Does this then imply that the cure can be effected by a suffering or passion, a subjective feeling, to which objective truth and untruth are equally indifferent? If this were true, not only would an idol be as satisfactory as God, but Hegel or Marx would be as satisfactory as Kierkegaard.

Recent Developments

This irrationalism, though it calls forth a passionate reaction from those who honor logical consistency, eventually received a wide acceptance. The deadness of European Protestantism continued through the last half of the nineteenth century, and American Protes-tantism gradually conformed. A type of thought called Modernism came to control the churches, with its evolutionary emphasis on the automatic and natural progress of the human race. According to Herbert Spencer, who though not an ecclesiastical leader voiced the prevailing sentiments of his day, evil was about to vanish from the face of the earth. But World War I showed Europe, and World War II showed America, that modernistic thought was based on an illusion. And between the two wars Kierkegaard, who had remained in Danish obscurity, was discovered. The mid-twentieth century was ripe for irrationalism. Karl Barth first attracted attention in Europe, and a little later Emil Brunner won the leaders of American Protes-tantism.

Although this volume on principle excludes living philosophers from its purview, a minor exception may perhaps be allowed for the purpose of adducing a slight bit of evidence to show the continuing irrationalism of this present-day movement. In his *Divine Human Encounter* Brunner assigns words a merely instrumental significance, and even their conceptual content is not the thing itself, but just its framework. The words, the sentences, the conceptual contents need not be objectively true, and in fact, "God can . . . speak his Word to a man even through false doctrine." The existentialists, e.g., Heideg-ger and Sartre, have developed this irrationalism in an atheistic form. But if God may lie and if concepts are false, there seems to be little difference remaining between atheism and pious phraseology.

Kierkegaard had to wait seventy-five years before winning a popular hearing in Protestantism. Outside of Protestantism, the anti-christian movement, even before World War I, continued the spread of irrationalism.

NIETZSCHE

Friedrich Nietzsche (1844–1900), so far as German philosophy is concerned, was the culmination of the nineteenth century. Its second half had brought great advances in science. Physicists considered that they had completely demonstrated the truth of mechanism. Fechner, although he attempted to found an empirical psychology, rejected mechanism under the inspiration of grand romantic ideas and peopled his universe with souls, angels, and gods. Lotze made the intellect, not an instrument for representing things, but for transforming them. Being is in flux, and reality is richer than thought. Granted, Lotze nonetheless remained a monist. Wundt abandoned monism and pictured the universe as a plurality of wills. And Darwin, though not a German, revolutionized, not only biology, but all phases of philosophic thought. From these sources Nietzsche took what appealed to him and completed the nineteenth century's atheistic, materialistic, anti-hegelian world view.

Evolution

In a very profound sense Nietzsche can be called the philosopher of evolution; not only has the physical constitution of animals and men evolved, but religion, society, philosophy, and even logic are evolutionary products. This does not mean, however, that Nietzsche agreed with Darwin. Darwin made some enormous blunders. For example, the notion that slight changes are useful for survival and are therefore passed on to succeeding generations, in which these changes continue to develop in a fixed direction, is entirely without justification. During the greater part of the time occupied in the formation of a new quality or organ, argues Nietzsche, the change is of no use and even impedes survival. Furthermore, every species has its limitations beyond which evolution cannot carry it. Man as a species is not progressing; nor is man an advance in comparison with any other animal. There is no development from the lower to the higher, but all forms develop simultaneously and haphazardly. In fact, the term *higher* merely designates those forms which perish more easily. Only the lowest forms are apparently imperishable. Evolution does not favor the better or superior individuals; it suppresses the lucky variations; the mediocre win out; the superior are weak when confronted by the organized gregarious instincts of the majority. The flaws of Darwin's theory can perhaps be reduced to two, one a scientific mistake, the other a perverse evaluation. The scientific mistake is the idea that the world process is explained by the concept of self-preservation. Such a concept, however, is a superfluous teleology — a remnant of the idea of God. The wrong evaluation, a fundamental error of biologists, is that the species are important.

Against these two Darwinian errors Nietzsche proclaims the Will to Power. Self-preservation, mere survival, does not do justice to natural phenomena. What should be abundantly evident to all but the blind is the tremendous inner power of nature to create forms. That it is not a matter of survival is clear from the many instances in which the discharge of this power brings death. Darwin put too much stress on passive adaptation; life is active, it is a matter of growth and expansion. While life always lives at the expense of other life, the struggle is not merely for survival; it is for power, it struggles to produce more, faster, oftener. The urge to self-preservation is a restriction on the fundamental instinct; it is the result of a distressed condition. But it is not distress, it is extravagant abundance that characterizes nature. Kant and previous thinkers with their theological prejudices considered nature as neat and tidy, as awe-inspiringly efficient, as doing nothing in vain; on the contrary nature is incredibly wasteful and prodigal.

The Superman

Not only does the Will to Power correct Darwin's scientific mistake, it also points to the proper evaluation. That which makes nature worth-while is the occurrence of especially fortunate individuals, geniuses, supermen. The species is of no value, except as a means to produce these gifted persons. (Incidentally, Nietzsche often attacks romanticism, as he attacked Schopenhauer, Wagner, and nearly every source with which he had previously sympathized, yet his attachment to the superman, on which all the values of his philosophy depend, is thoroughly romantic and anti-intellectual.) It must be emphasized that the Superman, in spite of the comparison of ape to. man to superman, is not a future evolutionary species; the supermen are superior individuals, such as Caesar and Napoleon. The idea of individuality carries with it the connotation of variety. Unlike the monotonous similarity of a species the superior individuals are all different. Monotheism is evil because the idea of one God implies a single standard for all men; Christianity therefore destroys individuality by trying to make all men alike. Polytheism, on the other hand, recognizes many standards and hence gives the individual his proper value. Supermen repudiate conformity to any norm, except the norm, Be yourself: each realizes his own unique self. To understand this as an evolutionary development rather than as an individual achievement is an interpretation possible only to "scholarly oxen." The goal of humanity therefore and the justification of life are found in the highest specimens; these are not found at the end of the evolutionary process but are scattered and accidental occurrences. The value of these superior individuals does not depend on any good they do to society; they are valuable in themselves as the supreme manifestation of the Will to Power. Napoleon is not appreciated because he rescued France from revolutionary anarchy, but conversely the revolution was good because it made Napoleon possible. The existence of Napoleon justifies the revolution. For a similar great man to occur again, European civilization in its entirety will have to collapse.

Eternal Recurrence

The value of these superior individuals, and therefore the value of all evolution and history, is so great that none of them can be thought to have occurred only once. Since Caesar and Napoleon are supremely valuable, they must have occurred an infinite number of times. The theory of eternal recurrence, according to Nietzsche, is the most scientific of all hypotheses. If evolution had a goal, that goal would have been reached by now, for time has been infinite. Therefore evolution has no goal. Further, if space were infinite, a goal in the form of equilibrium, the even distribution of energy according to the second law of thermodynamics, would have been reached. Since this state has not been reached, though time is infinite, it follows that space is finite. Under these conditions, any given state of the world must recur; that is to say, every state of the world must recur again and again for ever. "If the universe may be conceived as a definite quantity of energy . . . it follows therefrom that the universe must go through a calculable number of combinations in the great game of chance which constitutes its existence. In infinity, at some moment or other, every possible combination must have once been realized; not only this, but it must have been realized an infinite number of times."

This view in the ancient Stoics St. Augustine considered pessimistic. Nietzsche calls it optimism. "Everything," he said, "seems to me much too important for it to be fleeting; I seek an eternity for everything." Accordingly the French Revolution will occur again and again and be justified always by the emergence of Napoleon. "The universe is a monster of energy, without beginning or end; a fixed and brazen quantity of energy which grows neither bigger nor smaller, . . . but only alters its face. . . . It does not stretch into infinity, but is a definite quantum of energy in limited space . . . with an ebb and flow of its forms . . . saying yea unto itself . . . forever blessing itself as something which recurs for all eternity, a becoming which knows not satiety or disgust or weariness — this, my Dionysian world of eternal self creation, of self destruction . . . without aim, unless there is an aim in the bliss of a circle, without will. . . . This world is the Will to Power — and nothing else!"

The Forms of Reason

Such is Nietzsche's world view. But is it true? Or, rather, can it possibly be true? What is the logic, the evolutionary logic, to support these conclusions? Has Nietzsche used a tenable epistemology? Or has he contradicted himself? And what effect would evolution have on self-contradiction?

Kant, after denying that God had implanted in man's mind a set of original notions which were preformed adequately to fit the external world, allowed a set of a priori forms that we impose on experience. In doing so, however, Kant did not remain so far away from theology as he thought. His transcendental unity of apperception, a subject, a Cartesian *Cogito,* a substance, is nothing but a fictional or metaphysical image of God. In Nietzsche's view there is no such thing as a mind; the proper starting place is the body as it has evolved. Belief in the body is much more firmly established than belief in spirit. What Kant and Descartes mistook for an ego, instead of being a single simple subject, is a multiplicity of conflicting desires or urges. (Freud often parallels Nietzsche.) Therefore the notion that the world proceeds so that human reason must be true is downright simple-minded. Not less so is the Kantian assumption that the intellect can criticize itself and fix the limits of its validity. On the contrary, everything that reaches our consciousness is simplified, adjusted, and interpreted. We never find a fact of nature; we never grasp things as they are. The whole apparatus of knowing is a simplifying device, directed not at truth but at the appropriation and utilization of our world. Consciousness extends only so far as it is useful; all our perceptions are permeated by our evaluations. Philosophers have believed that in the forms of reason a criterion of reality has been found; whereas the only purpose of these forms is to master reality by misunderstanding it intelligently. Originally there was chaos among our ideas; then some ideas perished and others survived. Thus logic grew out of the more powerful desires.

Logic began by comparing things, that is, by equalizing them: this is like that, this is the same as that, these two are identical instances of one class. The coarser the perceptive organ, the more likeness it sees. But, clearly, no two things are really identical. However, after the long evolutionary process, logic now assumes that identical cases exist; and this means that the will to logical truth presupposes a fundamental falsification of all phenomena. What we now call truth therefore is that kind of error without which a species cannot live. The object of mental activity is not to know, in any scholastic sense, but to schematize and to impose as much regularity on chaos as practical needs require. Reason and Euclid's space are but idiosyncrasies of one species of animal. After all, why should we be so greatly interested in truth? Falsity is no objection against an opinion; the important question is, Does this opinion sustain life? The cult of objectivity, assiduously followed by philosophers, is hypocrisy. Mystics openly claim inspiration; but philosophers, not so honest, are advocates who do not wish to be recognized as advocates. "Indeed, to understand how the abstrusest metaphysical assertions of a philosopher have been arrived at, it is always well and wise to first ask oneself, What morality does he aim at?" [2] Behind all logic there are physiological demands for a mode of life.

Logic depends on the law of contradiction, but instead of this law's being necessary it is only a sign of inability — our inability to affirm and deny one and the same thing. Aristotle of course was right in saying that the law of contradiction is the basis of all reason. We cannot talk without using it. But for this very reason it should be examined more carefully. The law of contradiction — as was explained at tedious length in the chapter on Aristotle — claims to be ontological as well as logical. It assumes something about Being.[3] But to suppose that logic is adequate to reality requires a knowledge of reality prior to and independent of the law. Obviously then the law of contradiction holds good only of assumed existences that we have created.

Granted, again, that Aristotle was right in saying that we cannot think otherwise. Our inability to think otherwise is also at the basis of Kant's a priori categories. We believe in causality because we cannot avoid interpreting a phenomenon as the result of design. But this does not save causality from being an illusion or subject reality to the law of contradiction. These ways of thinking have been bred in us through the long evolutionary process, and they are now so ingrained that no amount of experience can change them. They are indeed a priori for the individual, but for the human race they are evolutionary end-products. Belief in causality and contradiction may be and is useful; but this does not make them true. In fact, they must be false, for knowledge and evolution are mutually exclusive. The character of the world in process of becoming is not susceptible of intellectual formulation. Parmenides said, One can form no concept of the non-existent. We are now at the other extreme and say, That of which a concept can be formed is certainly fictional.

2 Cf. page 148 above.
3 Cf. page 98 ff. above.

Since now Parmenides was certainly a rationalist, can Nietzsche logically object if we call him an irrationalist? And further, if Nietzsche could not avoid using the law of contradiction, until of course his final insanity ended his literary career, how can we believe that his "rational" productions correctly describe the irrational world? Or conversely, if the world is such an evolutionary irrationalism, what hope is there of saying anything reasonable about it? If Nietzsche's theory is true, it must be false.

PRAGMATISM

The preceding German development was not the only source from which pragmatism accepted some of its leading ideas; especially in the case of William James, pragmatism borrowed from French philosophy also.

Comte

One of the most vigorous anti-hegelians was Auguste Comte (1798–1857). Like Strauss and Feuerbach he welcomed Hegel's insistence on history, but purged it of all metaphysical overtones. The history of the human mind begins with a theological motivation by which events are referred to the immediate action of supernatural beings. Untenable as theology is, it is nonetheless the necessary point of departure for human understanding. Then the mind rises to a metaphysical stage and gives abstract explanations of phenomena, such as were typical of scholasticism. In this type of thought abstract forces have been substituted for personal wills. The third and final stage of intellectual evolution, never to be surpassed, is that of scientific or positive law. The scientific mind has given over the vain search for absolute notions; it is no longer interested in the origin and destiny of the universe, nor in the causes of phenomena; it studies only laws, i.e., the invariable relations of succession and resemblance. For example, the law of gravitation is not a cause of motion but a description of how things move. Each of our leading conceptions passes through these three stages. Astronomy and physics, because of their generality, simplicity, and independence, were the first to arrive at the positive stage. Social phenomena, because they are the most complicated and most dependent on other sciences, will be the last to arrive; but their time has now come, and we shall soon be rid of the theological and metaphysical notions of divine right, sovereignty of the people, and the other catchwords of adolescent thinking.

Durkheim

Comte's invention of the science of sociology, his oversimplified classification of the sciences, his curious religion with its catechism and all its saints' days, that is to say, most of his philosophy of positivism, must be omitted. But his genetic method of explaining concepts, with perhaps some aid from Nietzsche, results in the irrationalism of Emile Durkheim, a French positivist of the early twentieth century.

Our judgments, Durkheim holds, depend on the categories of time, space, genus, number, cause, substance, and so on. Thought cannot escape from them. Now, these categories are born in and of religion; that is, they are social products, products of rites that had the purpose of modifying the mental states of the worshippers. Take time for instance. Time relates not only to the subjective mental changes of an individual, but it relates to other people. Time is not my time; it is the time of my civilization. It grows out of ritual periodicity and public ceremonies. Time therefore is a social product. Similarly, space: the Australians and North American Indians conceive space as circular because their camps were circular. The law of contradiction is also social, for it varies from tribe to tribe. What one nation thinks is contradictory, as modern men think of mythology, another people does not. This view of the categories solves the dilemma between the empiricists and Kant. The former could not explain why all men have the same categories though their other ideas differ; nor could empiricism explain why we cannot think without them. But the apriorists with their innate ideas, since they refuse to make the categories and sensations homogeneous, are forced to void the categories of all content and to reduce them to empty names. Others try to solve the problem by an appeal to a Supreme Reason. But there is no scientific technique to prove the existence of any God. Now the dilemma is this: if reason is but a form of individual experience, there is no reason; but if it is more than individual, it is beyond science. The solution is to make the categories social. They are collective representations, resulting from an experience wide in space and immense in time. To explain the categories by a long gradual process removes all the difficulties. The categories are necessary because otherwise society would be impossible; therefore when an individual disputed the categories with his tribe, they treated him as insane. At the present date the custom of long generations prevents us from thinking otherwise.

Renouvier and Boutroux

Besides positivism there is another current of French philosophy that contributed to pragmatism, especially to the pragmatism of William James. In consonance with the physical scientists and their mechanistic theory derived from Spinoza, Hume, and Kant, Comte had spoken of invariable or inviolable laws of nature. This "scientific" viewpoint, however, had never been universally accepted. Fichte, for one, had defended morality and human freedom. Now in France Renouvier and Boutroux argued that the regularity of mechanism is a superficial illusion; even in physics rigorous necessity is inconceivable; and in the richer and more complicated forms of experience, contingency and freedom are easily apparent. Like Nietzsche, though presumably in complete independence, Boutroux held that identical cases do not exist; and therefore no general formula is adequate to the ever-changing spontaneity of reality. Renouvier, to whom James acknowledges a great debt, also emphasized plurality and differences. Unfortunately the details of their arguments cannot be reproduced here. Similarly subject to the maximum of curtailment is the work of the American philosopher C. S. Peirce. Peirce supplied James with the term *pragmatism* and confirmed his inclination to indeterminism though he did not althogether approve of the manner in which James worked out his ideas.

JAMES

William James (1842–1910), Professor at Harvard, was a most interesting and energetic man. He had a large share in importing laboratory psychology from Germany; his *Varieties of Religious Experience* gives some of the amazing results of his psychical research; and then there are his several volumes of philosophy, written in such a lively style that pedantic Spinoza, Kant, and Hegel, if they could have read them, would have been thoroughly scandalized.

The Serpent of Rationalism

James continues the general attack on Hegel. Over the domain of theism and of absolutism, writes James, "You find the trail of the serpent of rationalism, or intellectualism" (*Pragmatism*, p. 19). Intellectualism is a serpent because its transcendental principles are useless. The Absolute, says James, might have thought out and thereby "made any one of a million other universes just as well as this." Spinoza, of course, who was a sort of absolutist and who was certainly an intellectualist, had taken pains to argue that this is the only thinkable and only possible world; and Hegel, for all the embarrassment of the now familiar pen, would also have found some inaccuracy in James' remarks. The pen, however, enables James to continue, "You can deduce no single actual particular from the notion of it. . . . And the theistic God is almost as sterile a principle. . . . Theism is more insipid, but both are equally remote and vacuous."

James also repeats the accusation that Hegel confuses conceptual flux with physical flux, for which reason the conceptual treatment of the flow of reality is inadequate. Inadequate, that is, to the reality itself. Knowledge must come through experience: not experience consisting of discrete, atomic simple ideas, but experience as an ever flowing stream of consciousness. There are no discrete data; nothing is separate or distinct; things are constantly merging into each other; there are no distinctions such as matter and form, substance and relation. To be sure, concepts have a practical value; we select portions of experience and arbitrarily set them off; this process serves our purposes well, but such concepts are far from satisfying the demands of rationalistic speculation; they are purely practical.

James also finds the existence of evil to be an insuperable difficulty to absolutism. Evil and pain would have to be part of the experience of the Absolute, but in such a way that the Absolute knows the pain without suffering it. Now, if this were the case, it would result in a lack of sympathy between man and the Absolute; man would stand in fear of the universe, or, at best, he would lack the intimacy that a different philosophy affords. But the view itself is untenable. If the world is the rational unfolding of the Absolute Spirit, the evil that is so painfully present simply could not have occurred.

Then too, another evidence of James' irrationalism is his adoption, along with Nietzsche and Durkheim, of the evolutionary explanation of the intellect. Our fundamental ways of thinking, the categories and the law of contradiction, are discoveries of exceedingly remote ancestors. Lobsters and bees no doubt have other modes of apprehending experience. Children and dogs do not use our adult categories; their experience is virtually chaotic. Space and time are not Kantian intuitions but patently artificial constructions, for the majority of the human race uses several times and several spaces. Although our categories are very useful, we cannot dogmatically deny that other categories, unimaginable by us today, might have proved just as serviceable as those we now use. In this case, if we may apply James' principles in the selection of an example, the primary form of the syllogism, called Barbara in the Logic books, might have become a fallacy, and asserting the consequent could have formed a valid argument. This suggestion should not be dismissed on the ground that it is illogical, for the present forms of logic are not foolproof. Whatever other categories there might have been, given a different evolutionary process, our familiar modes of thinking quickly flounder in insoluble paradoxes. The infinite divisibility of a line, the continuity of motion, and all the delights of Zeno the Eleatic are beyond intellectual understanding. When the rationalists came to recognize that the real world escapes their neat formulas, they invented unreal worlds from which these stubborn facts were barred. Kant's rational will emigrated to the world of noumena; Bradley escaped all contradictions somehow in the Absolute; and Green relied on a transcendent Mind. But this is only to say that human concepts falsify reality.

Truth and Falsity

Spurning the escapist inventions of intellectualism and saying yes, as wholeheartedly as Nietzsche, to the real world with its continuities and discontinuities, its ones and its manys, its wholes and its parts, James offers a theory of knowledge or truth that is at least a step in advance of Nietzsche's. There are passages in Nietzsche, perhaps inconsistent with his evolutionary derivation of the categories, which seem to presuppose the old-fashioned distinction between truth and falsehood. Not that Nietzsche is particularly friendly toward the truth. On the contrary he says, "The falsity of an opinion is not for us any objection to it. . . . The question is, how far an opinion is life-furthering. . . . the falsest opinions . . . are the most indispensable to us. . . . To recognize untruth as a condition of life: this is certainly to impugn the traditional ideas of value" (*Beyond Good and Evil*, I, 4). If, however, one does not wish to interpret these lines as a semi-conscious admission of the traditional distinction, at least Nietzsche does not explicitly assign the title of truth to those falsehoods which further life. James does; and he calls his theory pragmatism.

The pragmatic method, says James, is primarily a method of settling metaphysical disputes that otherwise might be interminable. Every notion — monism, free will, materialism — is to be interpreted by tracing its practical consequences. If no practical differences can be found between, say, idealism and materialism, then these two concepts have the same meaning, and disputes between their proponents are purely verbal. C. S. Peirce, from whom James took his cue, had said that a belief is a rule for action; to develop the meaning of an opinion, one need only determine what conduct it is fitted to produce; this conduct is its whole significance. Take for example the concept of pragmatism itself. What does it mean? What conduct does it lead to? One of the practical differences that pragmatism would make is that rationalistic teachers would not be appointed to university positions. Young Kantians and Hegelians would be frozen out. This is of course not the whole significance of pragmatism, but it is a part of the resulting conduct and therefore a part of the meaning of the term. Pragmatism, like every other theory, is not an answer to an enigma; it is an instrument for guiding action. The theory is true if the action is successful. Ideas become true in so far as they help us to get into satisfactory relation with other parts of our experience. Any idea that carries us prosperously on is true to that extent, is true instrumentally. A theory is true in proportion to its success; but success in solving a problem is eminently a matter of approximation. One theory is more satisfactory than another, i.e., more satisfactory to ourselves; and individuals will emphasize their points of satisfaction differently. What is true to one person may be false, or at least not quite so true to another. Even theism can be true to people of a certain temperament. So too absolutism. Belief in the Absolute means that finite evil is already sublimated or overruled, and that therefore we can trust that the universe will turn out all right; this means, further, that we can dismiss our fears and worries, relax our responsibility, and take a moral holiday, knowing that the universe is in better hands than ours. Now, moral holidays occasionally are good; therefore Absolutism is true — in this sense and so far forth. To deny the Absolute would be to insist that men should never relax.

Incidentally and parenthetically, could an absolutist relax, could he even be an absolutist, if he believed that the whole significance of the concept of the Absolute was exhausted in his own actions of relaxing? In the hour of adversity can a man trust God, if "God" is simply his own conduct?

Religious Empiricism

One of James' boasts is that empiricism is tough-minded; rationalism on the other hand is the choice of tender-minded individuals, for a man's philosophy depends more on choice and temperament than on objective reasons. Rationalism is usually optimistic and religious; it assumes free will (Spinoza?); it is dogmatic; it is monistic and explains the parts by the whole. Empiricism is the choice of those who are not afraid to face the facts; it is materialistic and not very optimistic; it is irreligious, fatalistic, skeptical, and pluralistic, starting with the parts and building up what wholes it can.

Yet not all of these characteristics of empiricism are essential to it. In particular, it need not be irreligious, for contrary to the opinion of many scientists, there is a good defense for adopting a believing attitude in religious matters without logical coercion. Huxley and Clifford, as James quotes them in his famous essay on the *Will to Believe,* represent the prevailing scientific philosophy. Huxley considers it the lowest depth of immorality to pretend to believe what one has no reason for believing; and Clifford asserts, "It is wrong always, everywhere, and for everybody to believe anything upon insufficient evidence." But, replies James, all of us, scientists too, believe a great deal without evidence, from the Monroe Doctrine to the possibility of truth. We choose to believe what we need. Huxley and Clifford did not need Christianity, while Newman needed pope and bishops. Scientists choose to ignore the evidence for telepathy, or extrasensory perceptions, because, even if true, they want it suppressed and concealed. Their scientific viewpoint itself is a voluntary choice. Clifford himself does not attack Christianity on the basis of insufficient evidence: he is infallibly sure that Christianity is wrong.

The profession to rely on conclusive evidence is a delusion because objective evidence does not really exist. All concrete truths have been doubted; look at the contradictory theories held by philosophers; list their various criteria of truth; why, Hegel even doubted Aristotelian logic. Nevertheless, the empiricist still believes he can have some truth, or at least get nearer to it; and whether the truth comes to him by passionate choice or by intellectual coercion makes no difference.

With reference to the motivation of Clifford and Descartes, James asks whether one should seek truth or shun error. Descartes had such a fear of error that he would content himself with very little truth, if only he could avoid ever being mistaken. Believe nothing, he might have said, rather than risk believing a lie. But why not act on the advice, Accept truth, even if some error comes with it? Now, notice: whichever advice one chooses, it is a volitional choice without coercive logical reasons. The scientists believe that they should not believe without sufficient evidence, and they believe this without sufficient evidence.

Such volitional belief is not just an unfortunate inconsistency that a scientist can correct; it is an inescapable necessity. On some scientific trivialities it is safe to suspend judgment and avoid error; but the important speculative and moral questions cannot await coercive evidence. To wait is to deny, to make a negative choice. For example, shall we engage in scientific investigation? Science has no proof that science is good; at best science claims to produce other goods which cannot be proved good. Or, again, do you like me? The answer usually depends on whether I am willing to believe that you like me. If I refuse to unbend until there is objective evidence that you like me, you will never like me. Here the desire that something be true, makes it true. Faith makes fact. Is Huxley right in calling this the lowest form of immorality?

Now religion says, (1) the best things are eternal, and (2) we are better *now* if we believe proposition (1). Suppose (1) and (2) are both true: then religion is a momentous, living option; and it is also a forced option. We cannot avoid the choice. Skepticism may avoid error if (1) and (2) are false, but it loses the good if they are true. In fact, skepticism or suspension of judgment has the same practical effects, i.e., means the same thing, as dogmatic denial. The skeptic says, Better risk loss of truth than chance of error. He is wagering on one side as much as the believer wagers on the other; he believes it is better to yield to fear of error than to hope of truth. But why is dupery through hope worse than dupery through fear? Just as we must be friendly to make a friend, so too a man who tries to extort God's recognition willy-nilly forfeits his only opportunity of making God's acquaintance.

The objective, scientific view of Clifford and Huxley may sound empirical and plausible at first, but a rule that prevents us from acknowledging certain truths, even when those truths are really there, is an irrational rule.

The *Will to Believe* may in spots sound like a defense of orthodox theism. The God we may believe in seems to be more objective and absolute than "changes in one's behavior." However, such an understanding would conflict with the main principle of pragmatism that the full "cash value" of any concept is exhausted in the changes it makes in my experience. Now, it may be, and almost certainly is the case, that James himself was confused and inconsistent at this point. He oscillates between the idea that the independently real will prove useful and the idea that the subjectively useful is the only real. Then, again, though the *Will to Believe* seems to allow us to believe in the orthodox Almighty God, it must be recognized that James repeatedly denounced theism as an untenable position. Therefore, to put this essay in proper perspective, one must compare it with other material, such as the last chapter of the volume on *Pragmatism*.

Uncertainty and Risk

In arguing against monism and rationalism, James denies their claim that unity and good exist *ante rem* as a necessary principle; these ideals are only a possible *terminus ad quem*. The significance of such intellectualistic concepts lies in the moral difference they make. The concept of the Absolute means, even though the absolutist doesn't mean it, that all good things are certain and all bad things are impossible. The concept is a limitation placed on possibilities and a guarantee of a pleasant outcome. That is to say, absolutism and pragmatism signify two different religious attitudes. One man insists that the world must be and shall be saved; the other believes that it may be. There is also another view; namely, the world cannot be saved. Pragmatism therefore is an attitude midway between pessimism and optimism; it may be called meliorism. The world may become better because we can make it better. But can we make it enough better to be worth our trouble?

James then offers this choice. Suppose the world's author came to you before creation and said, I am going to make a world not certain of being saved; it can be saved only if every agent does his level best; [if any eases up on the job, the result will be unfortunate]; now, then, do you want the chance of taking part in this world, with its real dangers, with no guarantee of safety, or would you prefer to relapse into the slumber of nonentity from which I have just aroused you?

Note that God or James does not offer us a choice between this dangerous world and one in which the good is absolutely guaranteed. Absolutism seems here to have been forgotten. The choice is between danger and Nirvana. And James is ready to make the choice for us. Any "normally constituted" person with his "healthy-minded buoyancy" would find such a universe exactly to his liking. Only a few "morbid minds," "Buddhists" who are "afraid of life," would refuse the opportunity. These latter may be religious in a sense, but they are not moral. "In the end it is our faith and not our logic that decides such questions." It is a faith in our fellow men, that they will all do their level best. It is also a faith in superhuman forces, for there is a God, not an Almighty God who controls the outcome, but a limited and finite god who helps along; in fact he is such a help that the danger is considerably reduced. Belief in this type of a god is true because it works. Of course we do not know certainly that this god exists, "for we do not yet know certainly which type of religion is going to work best in the long run." It is a matter for personal decision. "If radically tough, the hurly-burly of the sensible facts of nature will be enough for you, and you will need no religion at all. . . . But if you are neither tough nor tender . . . the type of pluralistic and moralistic religion that I have offered you is as good a religious synthesis as you are likely to find."

In the section on Soren Kierkegaard the question of personal decision was also acute — a decision apart from any objective knowledge. Kierkegaard personally made a choice that is not too different from James'; although S. K.'s Christianity is not what James would have preferred, still both of them, along with Nietzsche, say Yes to the universe. But when James calls his choice moral and other choices morbid, he seems to imply that it is more than a personal choice. How can James distinguish between a moral and an immoral choice? If he says that truth is that which works, and that which works is that which gives personal satisfaction, then the man who chooses Nirvana to danger seems to have achieved more satisfaction than a pragmatist is likely to. Is it likely that all men will do their level best? Faith in mankind is an inspiring slogan, but the tough facts suggest that one or two men in history have not worked full time to make the world better. Assuredly James is consistent in choosing danger for himself, since his theory depends on his personal decision; but precisely for this irrational reason he cannot conclude that anyone else ought to make the same choice.

Unfortunately these objections are allegedly based on the law of contradiction, and there is still a little more to be said on this point.

SCHILLER

F. C. S. Schiller (1846–1937) is as interesting a writer as William James. Sometimes this interest derives from the shock of his slightly too vigorous condemnation of those who disagree with him: indolent spectator, monstrous, officious formalism, sheer calumny, pallid fungus, grotesque impertinence, sterilizing pedantry, a gigantic bluff. Fortunately the interest usually depends on clever argument. And sometimes it is a matter of vivid writing and good literary style.

Practical Consequences

In opposition to the absolutists, who begin with truth and delay as long as possible all consideration of error, Schiller opens his volume, *Studies in Humanism,* with the problem of distinguishing truth from error. The absolutists are wise in avoiding this question because rationalistic intellectualism has no real answer. The only solution is the one intellectualists disallow, viz., the practical consequences of the proposition to be tested.

It must be said again that the significance of pragmatism, or of humanism as Schiller prefers to call it, does not lie in the fact that truths have practical consequences. An intellectualist would be willing to admit this much. For example, a Christian would say that a belief in a transcendent God brings the practical consequences of God's blessing; and he might not be averse to admitting that the heavenly consequences are the test of truth of this belief. But this is not what pragmatism means. Even though James sometimes relapses inconsistently into an intellectualistic expression, and perhaps Schiller too makes one or two slips, Dewey very pointedly shows that for pragmatism truths consist in their consequences. If a belief in God results in an integrated personality, the integrated personality is God. In order not to repeat this point again, Dewey's position may be anticipated: "Is it meant that when we take the intellectualistic notion and employ it, it gets value in the way of results, and hence has some value of its own; or is it meant that the intellectual concept itself must be determined in terms of the changes effected in the ordering of life's thicket?" In this latter sense humanism has no room for a transcendent God, but only for the term *God* as applied to certain changes in experience.

Usually, of course, Schiller is clear enough. There is no super-celestial world of a priori, immutable truth. Neither is there any "pure intellect." Truths must be made; they must be made true by the production, not merely of some consequence or other, but of some good consequence. If the concepts of pure intellect and immutable truth produce the consequence of entertaining a rationalist, they will of course be true to that limited and trivial extent. But amusement is not intrinsically venerable. Then too we must exclude morbid concepts, even if these can produce results that satisfy some. Truth will be the successful concepts or plans of serious work.

The Man-Measure Theory

Schiller does not say exactly how the venerable and serious is distinguished from the morbid and trivial, but he indicates clearly enough what or who makes the determination. If it were all a matter of individual preference, as pragmatic expressions usually suggest, each person would have a private truth and the result would be subjectivism. Such was Plato's misunderstanding of Protagoras' Man-Measure theory. Schiller is rather hard on Plato. Offhand one would think that the great Plato could have understood just about any theory any philosopher should propose. But Schiller complains that Plato had not "the faintest idea of the scope and significance of the argument" (*Studies in Humanism*, pp. 37–38). Protagoras, although he made clumsy use of the term *truth*, based his theory on judgments of value. He should have said that valuable judgments are true; but his technical insufficiency on this point cannot disguise the significance of his repeated assertions that some opinions are good, are better than others. Then when it is said that man is the measure, it undoubtedly means that each man is the measure, each man is the judge of his own condition. If this were all it meant, it still would not be so individualistically subjective as Plato makes it; for Schiller, like James and Dewey, assumes that there is at least broad agreement on what is good. Of course there are some individuals who disagree; and this leads to a fuller understanding of the Man-Measure theory. It is not only men who are measures — even Plato understood that much; the further significance is that Man is the measure. Objective truth is manufactured by men in cooperation. Truth is not merely subjective; it is collectively social. The individuals who disagree are mad or sick; society must coerce or cajole them; brainwash them; or in recalcitrant cases put them in concentration camps. Plato's anti-empiricist attack on Protagoras is paralleled by the modern intellectualistic attack on pragmatism; but the attack will fail precisely because it cannot command the services of an executioner (*ibid.*, p. 38); today it is the pragmatists who wield the power to coerce.

Pessimism and Disagreement

Perhaps Schiller is just describing actual human nature and society; not only tyrants and dictators but democratic majorities also are often intolerant; Kierkegaard and others have protested against the leveling forces of socialism; but though Schiller may thus be describing human nature, he himself may not completely approve, for, at least in an earlier work, he was not so brutally totalitarian. Humanism is tolerant, he had said, while barbarism, though it is human too, is intolerant and shows itself in sectarianism. This, however, is ludicrous—to insist that everybody must accept the same absolute creed (*Humanism*, p. xxvi). Even though this Preface contains an amount of vituperation, the sentiment seems to admit that the pragmatic creed is not unquestionable and cannot demand universal sway. Schiller seems very serious in his consideration of the pessimistic view of life that opposes both rationalistic optimism and pragmatic meliorism. Pessimism is a view that cannot be refuted rationally. It must be simply accepted or rejected. "It is one of those ultimate alternatives the choice between which rests essentially on an act of will" (*ibid.*, p. 157). To be a pessimist it is not necessary to assert that there is more pain than pleasure in life; pleasure might predominate and yet, since it seems petty, there might be too few other good ends, too little virtue and knowledge. That is, life just isn't worth the nuisance of living. This pessimistic view, Schiller admits (p. 164), is theoretically tenable and is a question of really paramount importance. Such an admission makes pragmatism also an irrational choice without at the same time making it theoretically tenable.

Irrationalism, since it does not labor under the limitations of consistency, may be both tolerant and intolerant. In another tolerant passage Schiller discusses solipsism. To those who entangle themselves in epistemological puzzles the temptation to beat a retreat into solipsism is overwhelming. But humanists escape solipsism by simply choosing to believe in the existence of other selves. The theory that there are other selves works very well, and it will be true, i.e., useful, as long as it works. Besides, it helps one to escape too great a responsibility. But solipsism is not theoretically absurd; it suffers a worse fate. Since the solipsist, who denies the real existence of other persons, can learn to understand and manage his dreams only by empirical methods, solipsism is pragmatically indistinguishable from pragmatism.

Pragmatic Logic

If it is true, as Schiller implies, that intellectualism cannot prove the existence of other selves, it will be still more devastating if logic itself, the citadel of rationalism, proves to be worthless. For Nietzsche, James, and Durkheim it was evolution that exploded the pretensions of logic; but Schiller uses a different approach, more analytic than genetic. There is no need to push the problem of the categories back into long past ages; the present applications of logic show how feeble it is.

Traditional logic, he says, has collapsed into a state of impotent skepticism, for its intellectualistic presuppositions force the conclusion that the actual processes of human learning are inherently irrational and logically invalid. Although men are constantly predicating, inferring, proving, discovering, and knowing, all these activities are impossible paradoxes and insoluble puzzles. After thus making havoc of the ordinary cognitive procedures, logic retires into an ideal world of its own invention, a world out of space, out of time, and almost out of mind.

Such a desperate plight ought to suggest that the trouble is largely of the logician's own making. It is not the actual world that is at fault, but it is the unfortunate concept of logic that needs to be amended. Originally the logician undertook to provide a reasoned theory of actual knowing. Actual knowing is an empirical fact. It is the datum for and the touchstone of the logician's theories. If he fails to understand it, his failure does not abolish the fact. And if his failure is the result of the ideals of thought which he sets up, then so much worse for the ideals. A theory of knowing must begin with psychology; that is, the first step is a description of the mental processes of individual minds. All knowledge is first a psychical process, and this process appertains to the science of psychology. These common cognitive processes must be described as they are, without arbitrary attempts at reserving some of their aspects for the exclusive consideration of another science. The cognitive process is naturally productive of knowledge and is valuable as such; mental life is packed with values; and it is for psychology to record this fact and to describe these values.

The difference between other values and cognitive processes is that the latter make a claim to be true. It is this distinction that makes cognitive processes the objects of logic after they have first been objects of psychology.

Logic, then, developing continuously out of psychology, is the systematic evaluation of actual knowing. Its normative function arises quite naturally out of our actual procedures when we observe that some cognitive processes are more valuable than others. The two sciences are continuous; nothing psychological can be affirmed a priori to be irrelevant to logic. Although a logician, from motives of practical convenience, often ignores trivial characteristics of the actual psychic process, only experience can teach him what may safely be neglected. The risk of mistaking something relevant for something trivial may be fatal to the logician's argument. Therefore the formal logician can never be the final judge of the value of an argument. His rules, the rules of the syllogism, the law of contradiction, and so on, never pronounce on its material worth. However formally perfect a syllogism may be, a fatal flaw may lurk in its actual application.

On the other hand, however grotesque its formal fallacy, it may still be a road to truth; it may still be good reasoning, for "good reasoning is that which leads us right and enables us to discover what we are willing to acclaim as truth" (*Studies in Humanism*, p. 92). One can never know therefore whether the proper answer to a logical claim should not take the form of a psychological explanation. Quite aside from mystic ecstasies and mental derangements, it is usually more effective, even in dealing with the sane, to persuade rather than to convince.

All actual thinking is inherently conditioned by psychological processes; it is all actuated by psychological interest; it has a motive and aim. If a rationalist claims that the specifically logical interest in validity and truth is *sui generis*, not to be confounded with other interests, he is merely issuing an arbitrary fiat. And this fiat is itself prompted by ulterior motives. The most fundamental conceptions of logic, e.g., necessity, self-evidence, certainty, and truth, are primarily descriptions of psychical processes. As the concepts of necessity and certainty, in necessary inferences, are the last refuge of the intellectualist, it is instructive to note his embarrassment in discriminating logical from psychological necessity. Does the conclusion necessarily and certainly follow the premises? We *feel* that it does. Certainty then is a psychological feeling. The logician tries to distinguish between psychological certainty and logical certainty. The former feeling often occurs before the logical proof is complete; and conversely even when a mathematical theorem has been demonstrated, a none too bright student fails to feel certain. The truth of the matter is that logical certainty is an extension of psychological certainty. Actually we stop thinking when we are psychologically satisfied; but we sometimes conceive other circumstances, ulterior purposes, or other minds which would require further evidence. This engenders the ideal of a complete proof capable of compelling the assent of all minds. Such an ideal is unattainable; but even if it could be attained, its certainty would still be psychological.

A further insuperable hurdle for rationalistic logic is a proposition's meaning. The meaning of a sentence depends on its context. Logicians recognize this fact, but they identify the context as the totality of knowledge. Hence, as is all too evident with Plato and Hegel, one must be omniscient to grasp the meaning of even a single sentence. This obviously rules out all *human* knowledge. To avoid this intellectual impasse, we must see that meaning is primarily psychological rather than logical. Questions of meaning are questions concerning what the person who made the assertion actually meant. This in turn is determined by the whole of his concrete personality (*Studies in Humanism*, p. 86). Or, to refer to another great philosopher: "When I use a word," Humpty Dumpty said, in rather a scornful tone, "it means just what I choose it to mean — nothing more or less." Alice had difficulty in guessing the meaning of some of Humpty Dumpty's words, for example, "impenetrable," which means "that we've had enough of that subject and it would be just as well if you'd mention what you mean to do next. . . ." The point is that words, as verbal symbols, are always ambiguous. They may mean whatever they can be used to mean. Leaving Humpty Dumpty behind in favor of a twentieth-century illustration, most of us are familiar with the fact that democracy means one thing when an American uses it and means quite another when used by a communist. Not only democracy and freedom, but all words are as it were blank forms to be filled with concrete meanings according to requirements. For this reason there is no guarantee that one will *take* the meaning that another *intends* to convey. Nor is it certain that a man will always intend the same meaning by the same word. Objectivity does not depend on the interrelation of absolute static truths in a supercelestial sphere, but on adaptation to the world of flux and on the congruousness of the opinions and aims of many people. Hence the determination of the significance of any judgment is a social problem, often of a very complicated character (*Studies in Humanism*, p. 90).

The Making of Truth

Truth too is ambiguous. A truth is a proposition to which the attribute *true* has somehow become attached. Unfortunately the adjective *true* is sometimes applied undeservedly and our truths prove false just as our goods prove bad. Therefore truth is ambiguous, for we must distinguish the initial claim from whatever subsequently verifies it. That is, truth may mean a claim which may or may not turn out to be valid; or it may mean a claim after it has been validated. This distinction is something the intellectualists have never grasped, from Plato on down to the most recent critics of pragmatism with their pathetic inability to do more than reiterate the confusions of the *Theaetetus*. At this point (*Studies in Humanism*, pp. 145–146) Schiller quotes and analyzes a paragraph from the *Theaetetus* with the purpose of showing that Plato unconsciously jumped back and forth from claim to validity so that his refutation of Protagoras is a confusion. Whether or not Plato, or even Protagoras, made Schiller's distinction, and if he did, whether Schiller's identification of the two meanings in the passage is correct or whether it is precisely the reverse, may be left to the pleasure of an interested student. At all events, it is unlikely that any intellectualist ever spoke of a claim to truth in Schiller's sense that all propositions, even the most ridiculous, claim to be true. That a truth lays claim to our recognition and acknowledgment is fair intellectualistic phraseology; but that the proposition "all triangles have four sides" claims to be true is an idea or expression foreign to Plato and his modern disciples.

However, as Schiller insists, the intellectualist must show how he distinguishes between a false statement (one that merely claims to be true) and a true statement (one that has been verified). This cannot be done by examining the statement itself, for every assertion is ambiguous, and as it shows no outward indication of what it means, we can hardly be said to know the meaning of any assertion whatever. Formal logic, which abstracts from all concrete application, is of no help, for the meaning of an assertion can be determined only in its concrete application. Meaning depends on purpose, on the use of words in actual knowing, on the varying connotations of words in common speech. With this, formal logic has nothing to do.

To describe how truth is made is not too difficult a task, at least in general outline. First we must admit that the sciences are actual knowledge. This is a fact that cannot be denied. What needs to be done therefore is simply to discover what procedures the several sciences have in common. Those procedures are the method of making truth. One common procedure is to disregard irrelevant factors. A true statement in any science must be relevant to the question which the science asked. That a physicist's statement reeks of crude realism and an engineer's calculations lack exactitude is of no importance provided they are right enough to serve the immediate purpose. Furthermore, every science (except psychology?) treats of a limited area of human experience. Sciences therefore come into being by the scientist's arbitrary selection of some standpoint; that is, a science depends on the scientist's purpose. Statements which serve this purpose are true. True statements are good statements, good for what they produce. This theory does not run the risk of subjective license, for a scientist does not work alone. The purposes that an individual chooses are restricted by the severe control of society, and he is prevented from making many truths he might wish to make. (Only a very great individual, like Stalin, can defy and then control social coercion.)

Further convergence toward objectivity is produced by the natural tendency to subordinate all purposes to the final or ultimate end, the Good. The truths of all sciences are finally unified and validated by their relation to the Supreme Good. The actual conflicts among values and purposes are not to be considered as final or absolute. Each value must be re-evaluated with reference to the highest conception of the ultimate good which for the time being seems attainable. There are therefore degrees of truth. Some truths satisfy but one or a few trivial purposes. Other truths satisfy more, and on up to "that ineffable ideal which would satisfy every purpose and unify all endeavors" (*ibid.*, p. 158). This "perfect harmony which forms our final aspiration" seems to require an optimistic, or at least a melioristic view of human resources. Schiller takes it as "evident" that purposive reaction upon the universe bestows dignity and grandeur upon the struggle of human life. But he did not always consider this so evident. Once he said that pessimism cannot be refuted and the choice between it and optimism is an act of pure will. Now, suppose that the progress toward the unification of all purposes is so slow as not to be worth the struggle; suppose success is so far in the future that I shall not live to enjoy it; or, worse, suppose the unification of all purposes is an evil and that social coercion has already produced too much unity; in such cases could a pragmatist persuade anyone but an irrational pragmatist to continue the struggle? Let us see if Dewey can.

DEWEY

John Dewey (1859–1952) wrote volumes — many volumes. His works on educational problems, both particular and general, altered the nature and purpose of the American public school system; he expressed himself on international affairs; *A Common Faith* gives his views on religion; there is a volume on aesthetics; he criticized the alleged miscarriage of justice in American courts; besides all of which there are more than enough books in which he explains his over-all philosophy. In these concluding pages it is entirely impossible to summarize such a mass of material. Since the post-hegelian era (and Dewey started out as an Hegelian) is typically anti-intellectual, this account of Dewey, in conformity with the chapter as a whole, will confine itself to an exposition and criticism of his fundamental ideas.

Pseudo-Problems

Dewey's basic irrationalism is seen as clearly as anywhere in his disparagement of epistemology. Although the philosophers from Plato to Hegel had divided into schools by their differing positions on this crucial problem, Dewey considers epistemology a pseudo-problem and a waste of time. It is true that just before his death Dewey collaborated with Arthur F. Bentley on a volume entitled *Knowing and the Known,* in which (p. 317) he asserts that his theory is "wholly and exclusively a theory of knowledge"; it is true also that his other works discuss knowledge, even at great length; but when his views are summarized, traditional epistemology, whether empirical, rationalistic, Platonic, or Hegelian, receives short shrift. For example (*Human Nature and Conduct,* Modern Library ed., p. 93), the dispute between Descartes and Locke or Hume and Kant as to whether there are innate ideas or whether a child is born with a blank mind is an evidence of an obtuseness that springs from a love of the status quo and an unwillingness to reform social institutions. Just how allegedly reactionary politics explain both Locke and Kant may not be quite clear; but Dewey is definite in his repudiation of both innate ideas and a blank mind. Instead of either of these the child must be assigned "the surging of specific native activities."

Another rather pertinent example of Dewey's dismissal of epistemological difficulties is his treatment of solipsism in *Experience and Nature* (pp. 278–279). Previous philosophers, e.g., Berkeley, attempted, perhaps awkwardly, to explain how one may come to a knowledge that other persons exist. Dewey's irrationalism is seen, not in that he rejects Berkeley's or Descartes' theory of this knowledge, but in that he refuses to acknowledge that there is a problem. For him it is incredible that such a pseudo-problem ever arose; for if every person has been born of parents, it is obvious beyond debate that other people exist. This is the viewpoint that has descended from Ludwig Feuerbach, and it begs the question. Presumably the most rationalistic of philosophers is not anxious to deny the existence of other persons, including parents; but the problem is, how do we arrive at this knowledge. To say that we know other people exist because we have parents is to by-pass the problem. In this case, and in many other cases, Dewey assumes the conclusion he should have argued for.

At this point the mention of Ludwig Feuerbach makes it convenient to relate Dewey in still further detail to Karl Marx as well, thus to show Dewey's continuity with the post-hegelian tradition. As indicated above, Marx anticipated Dewey in insisting that philosophy ought to be a forward-looking social activity. Dewey also follows Marx in criticizing the British empiricists for making man too passive. It was also mentioned that Dewey improved on Marx' terminology by speaking of the "taken" instead of the "given." And both men emphasize concrete events and overt actions. Then, finally, in the *Quest for Certainty* (p. 77), the idea that modern man is a divided personality because his actions are mundane and secular while his thoughts are still emotionally attached to the old creeds comes from Feuerbach. Dewey therefore is an heir of the irrationalist tradition. Now, to return to epistemology.

Dewey's disparagement of epistemology and the assumption of what needs to be proved is very evident in his treatment of Kantian themes. In *Knowing and the Known* (pp. 51–52, 55–56), Dewey and Bentley see no need of a Kantian synthesis of imagination. Kant, and St. Augustine too in his own way, had argued that the momenta of sensation must be synthesized, if we are to perceive houses and poetry. The various visual or auditory sensations must be held in memory and connected in order that the percipient may grasp the whole. But the passages referred to deny that it is necessary to explain how objects and men are connected; and they deny the necessity of synthesis on the ground that science pays no attention to it.

This reason reveals one of Dewey's most fundamental standpoints. He wished at all costs to be scientific; for him the processes of science are the most obvious and the most successful methods of knowing. Therefore if science neglects something, the something is nothing. That there could be problems to be solved before the natural sciences can start is unthinkable. The intellectualist naturally objects that Dewey is begging the question and dodging the problems. Dewey would reply that he has chosen a different starting point. What precisely this starting point is may at last be difficult to explain, but an attempt will be made by continuing a moment with Kant's synthesis of imagination. Locke had conceived sensations atomistically, and Kant's problem was to connect these disconnected bits of experience. However, argues Dewey in his *Reconstruction in Philosophy* (pp. 89–90, 138), when sensation is conceived as a continuous life process, there is no need of a synthetic faculty to connect them. It would appear that even disparate sensations, the consideration of which played an important part in Plato's refutation of Protagoras and led Aristotle to his theory of the common sense, do not need integration. If so, it becomes clear how little can survive of the thought of the earlier philosophers. For Dewey experience does not consist of "atomistic" sensations or separate qualities; on the contrary, the material of direct experience is or at least includes things (Schilpp, *The Philosophy of John Dewey*, p. 535). By things in this context Dewey must mean books, pieces of paper, pens, houses, and so on.

Now, there is some plausibility in starting with such things as these instead of separate qualities that need to be compounded or synthesized. Kant's admission that his synthesis was an unconscious function makes it suspect; and certainly in adult life we do not construct things by laboriously compounding separate qualities. Then why not make the starting point of knowledge the direct perception of things?

However, there are other passages in Dewey's writings that can be interpreted in a contrary sense, for the positing of things as the starting point throws us back to a chapter in Hegel's *Phenomenology* on The Thing and Deception, and back still further to the nominalism and realism of the Middle Ages. Such problems as these are for Dewey pseudo-problems. He rejects both nominalism and realism, though clearly he is more severe toward the latter. Classifications are not fixed in nature; they are humanly constructed for practical purposes. When we say that this thing is a book, we are making a classification — we are making this thing a book. Or, to use Dewey's example (*Reconstruction in Philosophy*, pp. 150–154), cherry trees are one thing to cabinet makers, another to artists, and still another thing to botanists. For Dewey, things are not so much *given* as *taken:* they are taken to be something in accordance with our purposes at the time. To ask what the thing really is and to contrast this reality with its appearances, or to discuss essence and accident, is to fall into another pseudo-problem.

Yet if this be so, can it be said that we start with the direct perception of things? Dewey may disown Kant's function of synthesizing sensations; but to account for the "takings" he must substitute what he calls "sensori-motor co-ordinations" (*ibid.,* p. 91). These, then, rather than things, are his starting point. But what are these co-ordinations? The prefix "sensori" seems to retain some of the old empirical consciousness; on the other hand the term "motor" suggests muscular motion and a behavioristic theory of knowledge. Earlier sections of this history of philosophy have discussed forms of behaviorism and have connected it with skeptical results. Here the question is whether or not Dewey has chosen behaviorism as the basis of his philosophy.

Behaviorism

William James had published an article in 1904 entitled, *Does 'Consciousness' Exist?*, in which he accepted the behavioristic view. The stream of thinking, he said, consists chiefly of the stream of breathing. The Kantian or Cartesian "I think" is in reality "I breathe." Of course James did not rigidly equate thinking and breathing; he included intracephalic muscular adjustments, etc.; but on the whole breath is the "essence out of which philosophers have constructed the entity known to them as consciousness. That entity is fictitious. . . . thoughts in the concrete are made of the same stuff as things are."

Now, in one place Dewey disclaims behaviorism by saying that he is no more behavioristic than mentalistic (Dewey and Bentley, *op. cit.*, p. 77, n. 15). The "no more" is perhaps a bit of exaggeration. Dewey is unremittingly anti-mentalistic, speaking in one place of the "malignant orientation" of some logicians towards a "fictive mental operator"; but his objection to behaviorism extends only to certain restricted forms of behaviorism. For example he has no objection to such phrases as, "language is of the essence of thought," and, "language is man himself in action" (*ibid.*, pp. 5, 33, 38); he refuses to separate mind from body or to suppose that mental mechanisms are different in kind from bodily operations; volition means habits and habits are adjustments *of* the environment, not merely *to* it; several passages imply the identification of consciousness as overt behavior; mind is the complex of bodily habits; habits formed in the exercise of biological aptitudes are the sole agents of observation, recollection, and judgment — a mind which performs these operations is a myth; concrete habits do all the perceiving and reasoning that is done; knowledge lives in the muscles, not in consciousness (*Human Nature and Conduct*, pp. 33, 52, 87, 175–177). This phraseology, though reproduced in a condensed rather than a verbatim form, is clearly behavioristic. If then Dewey and Bentley can in one place disclaim behaviorism, Dewey in other places explains his meaning. He is opposed to that form of behaviorism which locates thinking in the larynx or otherwise confines it "below the skin-surface of the organism" (*Experience and Nature*, p. 282). In fact, Dewey explicitly designates his theory as a form of Behaviorism (Schilpp, *op. cit.*, p. 555); he only wishes to avoid limiting behavior to the nervous system or to anything under the skin; behavior includes the environment, sometimes to a great distance, and sometimes involving other persons.

The restricted form of behaviorism preserves, if only to a small extent, the unfortunate notion of earlier confused philosophers that experience is private. It has long been held that no two persons can see, remember, or experience exactly the same thing. I cannot feel your toothache; and the effect of the sun on my retina or my brain is mine alone. Although this notion has seemed so obvious from the time of Protagoras to the present, Dewey is unable to see what stimulation of the retina has to do with the privacy of perception or with its mental character. The fact that the sun affects the retina shows, on the contrary, that perception is a complex objective event taking place in the objective world. The perception or interaction is no different, except in the complexity of factors, from the physical and chemical events that constitute the shining itself of the sun. To infer that the experience on the retina is private on the ground that two persons never have precisely the same event is no more valid than to conclude that the reaction in one test tube is private because it does not occur in another. Privacy and mentalism can be sustained only by a return to prescientific dualistic psychology. Schiller, it will be remembered, had a mentalistic, if not dualistic, position. He began with the mental processes of individual minds and accepted these actual knowings as empirical data. While Dewey discards the mentalism and the minds, for he wants no dualism of subject and object, he wishes still to retain knowing as an observable fact. Even though the word *knowledge* is No. 1 on the list of vague words, knowings and the knowing man are factual components of a factual cosmos. Dewey and Bentley (pp. 6, 47–48, 50) will take "talking organisms . . . as they come." The starting point then is the compound of men and things, and this compound may be called Experience.

Experience

In the post-hegelian reaction against the a priori and transcendental the standard appeal has been to experience; but if others did not notice it, Dewey recognizes that experience is a slippery weasel word. The particular ambiguity here indicated lies between the empirical methods of modern science and the purely private subjectivism of the earlier psychologists. As was mentioned above, Dewey rejects the meaning of experience as private and mental in favor of defining it as scientific method. Even though he has referred to the everyday things of practical life, he believes it safer not to begin with such gross and crude experience but with the refined selective and most authentic statements of commended methods of science (*Experience and Nature*, p. 2). From these latter we must eventually work back to the homely facts of daily existence. Otherwise even a scientist may employ, and professed scientific philosophers have employed the remoter findings of science in such a way as to pervert the immediate facts of gross experience. This is philosophical suicide. But if a philosopher begins with homely facts, he almost inevitably succumbs to earlier theories of subjectivism. In these, experience is supposed to be somebody's, to belong to an individual, and the individual is supposed to have sensations of brown, shape, etc., which he constructs into a chair. However, this approach does not, as its exponents claim, begin with gross experience but with a previously elaborated theory of psychology. Primary experience is not so much experience of browns as it is of chairs, and it stands closer to physics than to psychology. Therefore we must hold that experience is something quite other than consciousness. Contrary to James' earlier views, experience is not a stream; it includes the enduring banks of natural constitution and acquired habit as well as the feelings and ideas that flow on its surface. Experience should be assimilated to history rather than to the physiology of sensations: experience is sun, moon, stars, mountains, forests, rain and wind, as well as human attitude, interest, record, and interpretation.

Then does not experience mean everything; and if everything, has not the word become so all-inclusive as to be philosophically useless? The old meaning of private sensations was at least definite. Dewey rather welcomes this objection as showing that experience should not be equated with any special subject matter, but with a method of inquiry. The method begins and ends with denotation, with pointing; and this method is clearly distinguishable from that of rationalism with its logical deductions. Even logical deductions must be pointed to, so that the utmost in rationality receives its sanction from the sub-rational, or, as Dewey prefers to call it, the supra-rational. "Experience [is] the manifestation of interactions of an acculturated organism . . . with environment" (Schilpp, *op. cit.*, p. 535). Experience, then, is scientific method, and the word is used, despite its all-inclusiveness, to remind us that reality is not merely logical but includes whatever is denotatively found.

Does Science Discover Truth?

If knowledge begins with a denotative pointing to things and proceeds by laboratory experimentation, one might easily suppose that the end of the process, the finished knowledge, would be a knowledge of the things originally denoted. The scientist would first have his attention directed to water, then by electrolysis he would discover that water is H_2O, and this result would be the knowledge of what water is. Unfortunately, this is about as far removed from Dewey's view as anything could possibly be.

The notion that science discovers the real nature of things is a

holdover from the ancient ideal of speculation that separated knowing from doing. This in turn is a reflection of conservative politics
with its snobbish class distinctions. Even today the results of science
are controlled by the few for their selfish class interests. Society
should be reconstructed (*Quest for Certainty*, Chapter IV). Modern
science is not interested in mirroring what is or in discovering antecedent reality; it is chiefly interested in knowing how things change.
In all experiments the scientist initiates changes. Even in astronomy,
where he cannot change the stars, he alters the instruments. All this
is overt muscular action, and it should remove the old notion that
knowing is something superior to the practical arts. But the old dies
hard and philosophic journals still discuss epistemology and consciousness as if consciousness were something less obscure and more observable than the public procedures of science. The overt action of scientific experimentation puts the objects into different relations, not in a
random manner but in a planned procedure. We look at a crystal,
turn it over, put it in acid, cut it with a saw, pass an electric current
through it, grind it on a wheel, or anything else that might elicit
some previously unperceived quality. The consequences of these
planned operations form the objects that have the property of being
known. The original crystal presented itself as a problem; the newly
constructed object is the object that is known. Thus knowledge is a
mode of doing. Its ideal is not Aristotelian speculation, but the
production or control of qualities.

Modern mathematical and quantitative science, when combined
with the view that science discovers what reality really is, produces
the impression that perceived qualities and values of different sorts,
are not real. Water, they say, is not wet, is not transparent, is not a
drink; water is, *really* is H_2O. But when science is not taken as dealing with ultimate reality and when knowing is not given a preferred
position among our ways of experiencing the universe, then we can
maintain that wetness and value are as real as H_2O. And further, the
knowledge summarized in or implied by the formula H_2O enables us
to produce wet water to drink if we so desire. Science then is a search
for relations, among which mathematical relations are exceptionally
important, upon which the occurrence of concrete qualities depends.
With this knowledge we can regulate their occurrence. Science does

not inform us that true reality is nothing but an interplay of masses
in motion, devoid of sound, color, and the other qualities that make
life interesting. Science is the method of controlling their production. That is to say, knowledge is a way of operating with the things
of ordinary experience; it is a mode of practical action.

Operationalism

The older schools hold that thought is reflective rather than originative. Idealism may have its thought construct the ideal reality, but
concrete appearance, Herr Krug's pen, still remains obdurate. Sensa-
tional empiricism obviously denies that thought is originative; any
origination would be error. In contrast let us begin with the assumption that all we can possibly know about ideas is derived from their
use in experimental procedure (*Quest for Certainty*, p. 110). This is
the modern view of operationalism. For example, to find the length
of, say, a column of mercury, we must perform certain physical operations with our hands and eyes. Operationalism now asserts that the
concept length is synonymous with these particular operations. And
so of every concept. Mass is not a quantity of matter: mass is a set of
manipulations. Ideas are thus empirical, but they are acts performed
rather than the reception of sensations. Therefore the test of a new
idea is no longer a discovery of past antecedent being but its consequences in overt procedure. "Ideas are statements, not of what is or
has been, but of acts to be performed" (*ibid.*, p. 138).[4] "An idea or
conception is a claim or injunction or plan to *act* in a certain way as
the way to arrive at the clearing up of a specific situation" (*Reconstruction in Philosophy*, p. 156).[5]

Dewey extends this instrumentalism or operationalism to pure
mathematics and logic. The chief difference between physics and
logic seems to be that in the latter the operations are performed in
symbols. But otherwise logic is as functional and operative as physics.
"The status of mathematics is as empirical as that of metallurgy"
(*ibid.*, p. 137). Now, if Newtonian physics and all its concepts, as
Dewey explains at length, have been modified, exchanged, and re-

[4] Quotations from John Dewey, *The Quest for Certainty* (G. P. Putnam's Sons,
1929), by permission of the publisher.
[5] Quotations from *Reconstruction in Philosophy* (Henry Holt & Co., 1920), by
permission of the Beacon Press, Inc.

placed with those of Einstein, and if the task and progress of science is never finished, it would seem to follow that the concepts of logic, the law of contradiction, would be altered and replaced. Nietzsche and others denied the fixity of logical forms on the basis of biological evolution or on long-term anthropological history. In such a case the present logical forms will in all likelihood remain about the same for several generations at least. But if logic is to change with the rapidity of science, there is no assurance that the valid argument of today will remain valid for the next decade. Not only may the premises, now true, become false; but the implication, now valid, may be manipulated into a fallacy. Thus Dewey's arguments for instrumentalism may not be of value much longer. However, as the suicidal nature of relativism has been several times suggested, criticism may be directed to another point.

Dewey has said repeatedly that an idea is a plan of action to be performed and that knowledge is not a discovery of antecedent being. Knowledge is originative, not reflective. This instrumentalism, however, seems to conflict with what was designated as Dewey's starting point. His dismissal of solipsism amounted to the assertion that we begin with the knowledge of other people. In opposition to Locke's atomistic sensations, Dewey wishes to begin with books, mountains, and the homely facts of daily existence. Explicitly connected with the epistemological problem is his behaviorism. Mind, he said, is the complex of bodily habits, and knowledge lives in the muscles. But if ideas are plans of action, if knowledge looks to the future and never to the past, can these antecedent realities on which the process is based be known? Is this muscle, in which knowledge lives, itself a plan for future action? Undoubtedly all plans of action are ideas; but is it true that all ideas are plans of action? Or, has Dewey arbitrarily restricted the concept of knowledge? What reason is there for assuming that all we can ever know about ideas is derived from their use in experimentation? It may be that all science is practical and not speculative or reflective. Quite possibly H_2O is not water, but is a method for producing water. And a term might well be invented to designate these methods. The term could be science. However, if the term chosen is knowledge, and our everyday perception of wetness and water is not knowledge but is termed enjoyment or something else, all the old epistemological problems would still be found lurking behind enjoyment or whatever other unfamiliar names the theorist might use.

Ethical Implications

At various places in this volume the implications of science and epistemology for ethics and morality have been referred to. The sections on Plato, St. Augustine, Kant, and James are instances. Some of these, although the emphasis here has been epistemological throughout, suggest that morals, not knowledge, is the basic problem. And so it seems to be with Dewey, too. At least he suggests that the true problem of philosophy concerns the relation between science and values (*Quest*, p. 18; *Experience and Nature*, p. 394). Running through much of Dewey's writing is the theme that morality is or should be made continuous with science. The experimental method should be transferred from the technical field of physics and applied to the wider field of human life. Standards of conduct, he says (*Quest*, p. 273), are very largely to be had from the findings of the natural sciences. Education and morals are to advance along the same road that the chemical industry has travelled (*Reconstruction*, p. 73). And the success of science in limited fields is the promise of effecting integration in the wider field of collective human experience.

At the present time beliefs about values, according to Dewey, are in much the same state that beliefs about nature were before the rise of modern science. Two attitudes are prominent. First, there are those who distrust the capacity of experience to produce standards of conduct and appeal to a Supreme Being who has revealed eternal values. But this is old-fashioned. Today secular interests have enormously multiplied; the sense of transcendent values has become feeble; the authority of the church has been narrowed. Men may profess the old religion, but they act secularly. Belief in God therefore can safely be abandoned. The second attitude, perhaps characteristic of men who have half abandoned belief in God but who have not achieved a fully naturalistic viewpoint, is the enjoyment of values irrespective of the method used to produce them. This viewpoint is an irresponsible confusion not much better than theism. Value is not to be defined as enjoyments that happen just anyhow. The method of production is essential. Value is an enjoyment that is the consequence of intelligent action. One must consider the regulation of enjoyment by the reconstruction of economic, political, and religious institutions. In science we turned our backs on the immediately perceived qualities, *e.g.*, the wetness of water, and formed conceptions, *e.g.*, H_2O, by which we could produce more secure and more significant experiences of things. Things liked or enjoyed should be treated in the same way. They are possibilities of values to be achieved. The enjoyment becomes a value only after we discover its relations and causes.

Dare one translate this theory into an example that Dewey does not give? Suppose that Mr. Dewey in his younger days had, quite by accident, met Mr. James on the street. The Harvard professor on the spur of the moment invites Mr. Dewey home to dinner. Completely unknown to both of them, and certainly to Mr. Dewey, is the fact that Mrs. James has been roasting a handsome turkey all day. She has utilized the surest culinary methods to produce a gastronomical triumph. At the dinner table Mrs. James and Mr. Dewey enjoy the turkey; but for Mr. Dewey it is enjoyment only, while for Mrs. James it is a value. Now, if Dewey, the philosopher, wishes arbitrarily to limit the term *value* as he limited the term *idea*, no one can stop him; but Mrs. James, at least if she does not agree with the pragmatic men she is feeding, might feel that her enjoyment and value has been lessened by the hot actions of cooking and the steamy prospect of doing the dishes. She might envy Mr. Dewey and hope that sometime she could sit down to a meal she had not cooked. *The Quest for Certainty* gives the impression that the value of an enjoyment is proportional to the trouble of getting it. Could it not be inversely proportional?

Of course one should readily admit that enjoyments are more likely to occur by intelligent foresight than by reliance on mere accident. In caricature Dewey cleverly contrasts a mythical conquest of space by revising the Kantian concept with the scientific conquest by telephone and airplane. So much of what Dewey says is obvious. But Dewey goes far beyond the obvious. He hopes not only to invent means for gaining ends; he also argues that science can establish the ends or norms. The standards of conduct as well as the technical procedures are to be had from the methods of natural science. Almost uniformly throughout history this has been thought impossible and absurd. In two places at least (*Quest*, p. 269, and *Reconstruction*, p. 15) Dewey, referring to Plato, puts the problem as sharply as any one could wish. The physician with his medical knowledge can admittedly heal a sick man; but, Plato insists, medical knowledge can never decide whether it is good to do so. Let us construct a modern illustration. Suppose that Stalin in 1933 or 1943 had been seriously ill. Medical science presumably could have restored him to vigor. But might it not have been better to let him die? Clearly the standard by which the physicians would have governed their actions could only be political rather than medical. For all we know, perhaps someone in 1953 actually decided it was good to have Stalin die. Then was not Plato right when he denied that the methods of science could determine which ends are valuable, good, or right?

Although Dewey so pointedly puts the question, the pages that follow the last reference can hardly be judged to answer it. He insists again on the necessity of means for accomplishing the end; he talks about intelligent examination of consequences and the intentional modification of institutions and customs; and concludes that such is the significance of transferring scientific technique to the wider field of human life. The student will have to examine the text for himself to see whether the answer to Plato is somewhere hidden between the lines.

No Ultimate End

Two other elements are added to this theory, which, if they do not contribute to the missing answer, may at least help to disguise the fact that it is missing. Schiller had wished to organize the whole of life under one ultimate Good. The moral puzzle of choosing between two subordinate ends, incompatible but both desirable in isolation, was to be solved by discovering which one led the more effectively to the Summum Bonum. Dewey denies that there is a final end. Every end is a means. Even death, which in another sense is a final end for the individual, is not final from the standpoint of society, for institutions and customs are ends and means throughout successive generations. Hence, while Schiller can theoretically decide between two courses of action, the best that Dewey can do is to try each in turn and see what happens. Beliefs, beliefs as to what is good, should be tested in action; no belief is inherently true; no belief should be rigidly clung to; but like the beliefs of physics they should be relinquished when no longer useful. Moral laws are not something to swear by and stick to at all hazards; their soundness and pertinence to the specific situation are tested by what happens when they are acted upon (*Quest*, p. 278). Unfortunately there are some pairs of moral beliefs both of which cannot be experimentally tested. A young man might argue that health, vigor, and most of the good things of life are to be found before the age of twenty-five; afterward there are burdens of responsibility, decreasing strength, illness and pain. Would it not therefore be better to commit suicide and escape these misfortunes? Someone else suggests that the honors and experience of old age are better than the pleasures of youth. Here are two hypotheses for action. Which one, by Dewey's theory, should we try first? Obviously whichever one we try, we are debarred from trying the other. How then decide? If there were a determinable Supreme Good, as with Schiller, the question might be answered. Or if there were a knowable Supreme God, the question could be answered. But these beliefs are precisely the ones Dewey will not try.

There are many pairs of incompatible hypotheses; there are also alternatives which, though not logically incompatible, are nearly so practically. Should we try drug addiction for a time? Or, less extreme, should one be a physician for ten years and an orientalist for another decade? Or, since Dewey constantly talks of social problems and politics, should totalitarianism be developed or should an approach to anarchy be made? Hitler tried annihilating the Jews. Inasmuch as the standard of conduct is to emerge in the empirical attempt, it is difficult to see how on Dewey's theory one can choose his course otherwise than blindly.

Do We Agree?

However, the second element of the two hinted at above better disguises the fact of a missing answer and the resulting confusion. Explicitly in at least two passages and implicitly in several of his arguments Dewey assumes an almost world-wide uniformity of moral standards. No honest person, he says, can convince himself that murder would have beneficial consequences; and, again, a normal person will immediately resent and condemn an act of wanton cruelty (Dewey and Tufts, *Ethics*, revised edition, pp. 265, 292). Although this uniformity of belief is perilously close to the intuitionism that Dewey despises, and although it is inconsistent with Dewey's stress on variety and change, and with anthropological facts as well, and although these standards have not been produced by scientific method, some such uniformity seems indispensable if the theory is to avoid patent absurdity. If murder and therefore suicide could be known to be wrong a priori, one line of experimentation would automatically be closed. Since now Dewey cannot accept any intuitional a priori or any a priori divine command, he must assume this uniformity as a fact of experience. But clearly it is not a fact of experience. The communists consider murder and wanton cruelty desirable and satisfactory means for attaining their social ends. By torture and massacre they have reconstructed Russia's social institutions and habits. Their theory works in practice. Its success establishes the norms and standards of conduct. Similar cruelty worked equally well in antiquity also.

Apparently the conclusion is that Dewey cannot give a rational argument for or against any moral standard. He has no reason, applicable to all men, for opposing suicide or cruelty; he has no reason, valid for opponents, supporting the social ideals to which he is personally attached. Science must therefore be considered as purely a means of attaining a chosen end, and truth is the plan that gets me what I happen to want.

But if there is any criticism that aggravates Dewey, it is this charge of subjectivism. In his *Reconstruction* (pp. 146, 157) he emphatically asserts that instrumentalism does not mean that science exists for the purpose of attaining some private, one-sided advantage on which one has set one's heart. So "repulsive" is the conception of truth as a tool of private ambition that it is a wonder critics have attributed such a notion to sane men. A similar disavowal occurs in the *Problems of Men* (pp. 178–179). The good, he insists, is not to be defined as what I like. Now, these statements make it perfectly clear that Dewey recognizes the charge of subjectivism and that he believes it unfounded. But a disavowal, however explicit, is not a substitute for a rational argument, and instrumentalism will have to be judged on its own merits. The reference immediately above takes cognizance of subjective desires. Some of these are "large and generous"; others of course are private and narrow. To avoid a subjectivism of widespread disagreement as to ends of action Dewey cautiously hints at a type of ethical theory that would scientifically investigate the causes of desires. If such a theory could be constructed, it would be possible by its techniques to manipulate human nature as successfully as we now manipulate physical nature. Presumably Dewey was not anticipating the Red Chinese techniques of brainwashing. He disclaims a desire to alter human nature by external force. What he has in mind, he does not quite reveal. Possibly he means that a group of people, who already share his desires, could get control of public education and prevent the children from thinking along unapproved lines. Then in a generation or two morality would be objective because the population would have been habituated to desire just the social reconstruction Dewey demands.

Here again, one gains the impression that Dewey has imposed a foreign meaning on the term *objectivity*, as he did with the terms *knowledge* and *value*. The objectivity of public uniformity produced by political manipulation of human nature is not the objectivity that rationalists and theists have always demanded. Dewey's objectivity grows out of the personal subjective preferences of a few politicians or social reformers. As there are, however, in any historical situation, different preferences, plans, and desires, one is forced to ask whether there is any rational argument for choosing Dewey's ideal rather than another?. To some Dewey's idea is as repulsive as theirs is to him. And even to a "liberal," particularly if he is tired, success may not seem worth the effort. Why not just commit suicide and save oneself the bother? Why not!

CONCLUDING NOTE

The history of philosophy began with naturalism, and so far as this volume is concerned it ends with naturalism. The Presocratic naturalism dissolved into Sophism, from which a metaphysics arose; and the metaphysics lost itself in a mystic trance. Then under the influence of an alien source, Western Europe appealed to a divine revelation. In the sixteenth century one group put their complete trust in revelation, while another development turned to unaided human reason. This latter movement has now abandoned its metaphysics, its rationalism, and even the fixed truths of naturalistic science. It has dissolved into Sophism. Does this mean that philosophers and cultural epochs are nothing but children who pay their fare to take another ride on the merry-go-round? Is this Nietzsche's eternal recurrence? Or, could it be that a choice must be made between skeptical futility and a word from God? To answer this question for himself, the student, since he cannot ride very fast into the future and discover what a new age will do, might begin by turning back to the first page and pondering the whole thing over again. This will at least stave off suicide for a few days more.

SELECTED BIBLIOGRAPHY

HISTORIES OF PHILOSOPHY

Fuller, B. A. G., revised by Sterling M. McMurrin, A *History of Philosophy* (3rd ed.; Henry Holt & Co., 1955).

Jones, W. T., A *History of Western Philosophy* (Harcourt, Brace & Co., 1952).

Martin, S. G.; Clark, G. H.; Clarke, F. P.; and Ruddick, C. T., A *History of Philosophy* (F. S. Crofts & Co., 1941).

Windelband, W., translated by J. H. Tufts, A *History of Philosophy* (The Macmillan Company, 1893).

ANTIQUITY IN GENERAL

Burnet, John, *Early Greek Philosophy* (4th ed.; A. & C. Black, 1930).

Caird, Edward, *The Evolution of Theology in the Greek Philosophers* (James MacLehose & Sons, 1904).

Cornford, F. M., *Principium Sapientiae* (Cambridge University Press, 1952).

Diogenes Laertius, translated by R. D. Hicks, *Lives and Opinions of Eminent Philosophers*, in the Loeb Classical Library (G. P. Putnam's Sons, 1925).

Robin, L., *Greek Thought* (Kegan Paul, 1928).

Zeller, E., *Outlines of the History of Greek Philosophy* (13th ed., Henry Holt & Co., 1931).

CHAPTER 1. THE PRESOCRATICS

Beare, J. I., *Greek Theories of Elementary Cognition* (Oxford University Press, 1906).

Fuller, B. A. G., *History of Greek Philosophy: Thales to Democritus* (Henry Holt & Co., 1923).

Nahm, M., *Selections from Early Greek Philosophy* (F. S. Crofts & Co., 1934).

Verdenius, W. J., *Parmenides* (J. B. Wolters, 1942).

CHAPTER 2. THE SOPHISTS, SOCRATES, AND PLATO

Cornford, F. M., *Before and After Socrates* (The Macmillan Company, 1932).

——, *Plato's Theory of Knowledge* (Harcourt, Brace & Co., 1935).

Plato, *The Protagoras; The Phaedo; The Theaetetus; etc.*, in the Loeb Classical Library (G. P. Putnam's Sons).

Ritter, C., *The Essence of Plato's Philosophy* (The Dial Press, 1933).

Shorey, Paul, *What Plato Said* (University of Chicago Press, 1933).

——, *Platonism, Ancient and Modern* (University of California Press, 1938).

Stewart, J. A., *Plato's Doctrine of Ideas* (Oxford University Press, 1909).

Taylor, A. E., *Plato, the Man and his Work* (The Dial Press, 1927).

CHAPTER 3. ARISTOTLE

Grote, George, *Aristotle* (John Murray, 1872).

Mure, G. R. G., *Aristotle* (Oxford University Press, 1932).

Ross, W. D., *The Works of Aristotle* (Oxford University Press).

CHAPTER 4. THE HELLENISTIC AGE

Armstrong, A. H., *The Intelligible Universe in Plotinus* (Cambridge University Press, 1940).

Arnold, E. V., *Roman Stoicism* (Cambridge University Press, 1911).

Bailey, Cyril, *The Greek Atomists and Epicurus* (Oxford University Press, 1928).

Bevan, E. R., *Stoics and Skeptics* (Oxford University Press, 1913).

Cicero, *Academia; De finibus; etc.*, in the Loeb Classical Library, (G. P. Putnam's Sons).

Clark, G. H., *Selections from Hellenistic Philosophy* (F. S. Crofts & Co., 1940).

Hicks, R. D., *Stoic and Epicurean* (Charles Scribner's Sons, 1910).

Inge, W. R., *The Philosophy of Plotinus* (Longmans Green & Co., 1918).

Katz, Joseph, *Plotinus' Search for the Good* (King's Crown Press, 1950).

Lucretius, translated by Cyril Bailey, *De rerum natura* (Oxford University Press, 1910).

Merlan, Philip, *From Platonism to Neoplatonism* (Martinus Nijhoff, 1953).

Plotinus, translated by Stephen Mackenna, *The Enneads* (Charles T. Branford Co.).

Rosan, L. J., *The Philosophy of Proclus* (Cosmos, 1949).

Sextus Empiricus, *Adversus Mathematicos*, Vol. IV in the Loeb Classical Library (Harvard University Press, 1949).

Whittaker, Thomas, *The Neo-Platonists* (2nd ed.; Cambridge University Press, 1928).

CHAPTER 5. THE PATRISTIC PERIOD

St. Augustine, *De magistro; De libero arbitrio; De civitate Dei; Confessionum; etc.*, in *Basic Writings of St. Augustine*, edited by W. J. Oates, (Random House, 1948); or other editions.

Drummond, James, *Philo Judaeus* (Williams & Norgate, 1888).

Machen, J. G., *The Origin of Paul's Religion* (The Macmillan Company, 1921).

Warfield, B. B., *Studies in Tertullian and Augustine* (Oxford University Press, 1930).

Wolfson, H. A., *Philo* (Harvard University Press, 1947).

CHAPTER 6. THE SCHOLASTIC PERIOD

Anselm, translated by S. N. Deane, *Monologium; Proslogium* (Open Court Publishing Co., 1926).

Aquinas, Thomas, *Summa contra Gentiles; Summa theologica*, in *Basic Writings of St. Thomas Aquinas*, edited by A. C. Pegis (Random House, 1945).

Carré, M. H., *Realists and Nominalists* (Oxford University Press, 1946).

DeWulf, M., *The Spirit of Medieval Philosophy* (Charles Scribner's Sons, 1936).

———, *The History of Medieval Philosophy* (Longmans, Green & Co., 1935).

Gilson, E., *The Philosophy of St. Bonaventura* (Sheed & Ward, 1938).

———, *The Philosophy of St. Thomas Aquinas* (B. Herder Book Co., 1937).

Harris, C. R. S., *Duns Scotus* (Oxford University Press, 1927).

Moody, E. A., *The Logic of William of Occam* (Sheed & Ward, 1935).

CHAPTER 7. SEVENTEENTH–CENTURY RATIONALISM

Descartes, René, translated by John Veitch, *Meditations* (William Blackwood & Sons, 1897).

Joachim, H. H., *A Study of the Ethics of Spinoza* (Oxford University Press, 1901).

Leibniz, G. W., *The Monadology*, in *Selections*, edited by P. P. Wiener (Charles Scribner's Sons, 1951).

Spinoza, B., translated by W. Hale White, *Ethics* (Oxford University Press, 1923).

Wolfson, H. A., *Philosophy of Spinoza* (Harvard University Press, 1932).

CHAPTER 8. BRITISH EMPIRICISM

Berkeley, George, *Principles of Human Knowledge* (E. P. Dutton & Co., 1910).

Hume, David, edited by N. K. Smith, *Dialogues Concerning Natural Religion* (Oxford University Press, 1935).

———, edited by L. A. Selby-Bigge, *An Enquiry Concerning Human Understanding* (Oxford University Press, 1894).

Locke, John, *An Essay Concerning Human Understanding* (Oxford University Press, 1894).

CHAPTER 9. IMMANUEL KANT

Handyside, J., *Kant's Inaugural Dissertation* (Open Court Publishing Co., 1929).

Kant, I., translated by N. K. Smith, *Critique of Pure Reason* (The Macmillan Company, 1929).

———, translated by T. K. Abbott, *Critique of Practical Reason* (Longmans, Green & Co., 1909).

———, *Fundamental Principles of the Metaphysics of Morality* (Longmans, Green & Co., 1909).

———, edited by Paul Carus, *Prolegomena to Any Future Metaphysics* (Open Court Publishing Co., 1929).

Lindsay, A. D., *Kant* (Oxford University Press, 1934).

Paton, H. J., *Kant's Metaphysics of Experience* (The Macmillan Company, 1936).

Pritchard, H. A., *Kant's Theory of Knowledge* (Oxford University Press, 1909).

Smith, N. K., *A Commentary on Kant's Critique of Pure Reason* (The Macmillan Company, 1923).

CHAPTER 10. G. W. F. HEGEL

Caird, Edward, *Hegel* (William Blackwood & Sons, 1883).

Lowenberg, J., *Hegel: Selections* (Charles Scribner's Sons, 1920).

Mure, G. R. G., *An Introduction to Hegel* (Oxford University Press, 1940).

Stace, W. T., *The Philosophy of Hegel* (The Macmillan Company, 1924).

CHAPTER 11. CONTEMPORARY IRRATIONALISM

Dewey, John, *Experience and Nature* (Open Court Publishing Co., 1925).

———, *Human Nature and Conduct* (Henry Holt & Co., 1922).

———, *Logic, the Theory of Inquiry* (Henry Holt & Co., 1938).

———, *The Quest for Certainty* (Minton, Balch & Co., 1929).

———, *Reconstruction in Philosophy* (Henry Holt & Co., 1920).

Durkheim, E., translated by J. W. Swain, *The Elementary Forms of Religious Life* (The Free Press, 1947).

James, William, *A Pluralistic Universe* (Longmans, Green & Co., 1909).

———, *Pragmatism* (Longmans, Green & Co., 1907).

———, *Radical Empiricism* (Longmans, Green & Co., 1912).

———, *The Will to Believe*, in *Selected Papers on Philosophy* (E. P. Dutton, 1917).

Kierkegaard, Soren, translated by D. F. Swenson, *Concluding Unscientific Postscript* (Princeton University Press, 1941).

Marx–Engels, *The Communist Manifesto* (Charles H. Kerr & Co., 1945).

Martineau, H., *The Positive Philosophy of A. Comte* (The Macmillan Company, 1896).

Nietzsche, F., *Beyond Good and Evil* (The Tudor Publishing Co., 1931).

Schiller, F. C. S., *Humanism* (The Macmillan Company, 1912).

———, *Studies in Humanism* (The Macmillan Company, 1907).

Schleiermacher, F., translated by John Oman, *On Religion* (Ungar, 1955).

Schopenhauer, Arthur, *The World as Will and Idea* (Simon & Schuster, 1928).

Where is the wise man? Where is the scholar? Where is the philosopher of this age? Has not God made foolish the wisdom of the world? For since in the wisdom of God the world through its wisdom did not know him, God was pleased through the foolishness of what was preached to save those who believe. Jews demand miraculous signs and Greeks look for wisdom, but we preach Christ crucified: a stumbling block to Jews and foolishness to Gentiles, but to those whom God has called, both Jews and Greeks, Christ the power of God and the wisdom of God. For the foolishness of God is wiser than man's wisdom, and the weakness of God is stronger than man's strength.

I Corinthians 1:20-25

"Come to me, all you who are weary and burdened, and I will give you rest. Take my yoke upon you and learn from me, for I am gentle and humble in heart, and you will find rest for your souls. For my yoke is easy and my burden is light."

Matthew 11:28-30

INDEX

Abbott, T. K., 428
Abelard, 261, 265, 268, 271, 350, 371
Abraham, 3
Absolute, 69, 90, 439, 443, 444, 446–448, 453, 461, 463, 464, 466, 467, 471, 472, 474, 477–479, 485, 487, 489, 501, 502, 504, 507
Abstraction, 23, 24, 172, 185, 205, 217, 220, 221, 262, 265, 278, 279, 280, 293, 296, 363–365, 369, 371, 374, 375, 379, 381, 384, 389, 464, 465, 486
Achilles, 40, 41, 52
Ackermann, C., 192
Active intellect, 121, 135, 267, 268, 278, 280, 282, 283, 291, 294, 296, 438
Actuality and potentiality, 105, 106, 114, 124–126, 131, 133–135, 141–144, 159, 176, 274, 276, 282, 283, 329
Alaric, 234
Albertus Magnus, 268, 269, 270
Alcuin, 248
Alexander Aphrodisias, 135, 159, 160, 267
Alexander the Great, 46, 162, 195, 355
Al Gazali, 266, 392
Allegorical, 196–199
Ambrose, 218
Analogy, 34, 50, 57, 86, 118, 125, 135, 143, 205, 207, 208, 276, 277, 296, 338, 413, 414, 415
Anaxagoras, 32–35, 36, 62, 80, 82, 91, 105, 138
Anaximander, 10, 11, 12, 20, 34
Anaximenes, 10, 12, 13, 34
Anselm, 226, 252–259, 260, 261, 263,

269, 270, 271, 272, 284, 296, 317, 325, 335
Aquinas, 16, 133, 135, 246, 257, 263, 268–285, 287, 290–294, 296, 310, 371, 383, 435, 438
Archimedes, 304, 310
Aristarchus, 94, 146, 306, 307
Aristotle, 4, 5, 11, 13, 16, 20, 33, 34, 38, 85, 86, 92, 93, 96–146, 148, 158, 159, 162, 169, 170–173, 185, 187, 190, 195, 196, 198, 206, 210, 220, 222, 225, 230, 231, 236, 248, 250, 260–270, 273, 275, 277–279, 282–284, 290, 291, 294, 297, 303, 306, 318, 398, 399, 408, 415, 429, 438, 441–443, 497, 505, 520, 525
Arius, 216
Arnauld, 352
Arnim, J. von, 159, 160
Arnold, E. Vernon, 191
Athanasius, 213, 216, 217, 246
Atom, 8, 28, 30, 31, 35–37, 39, 41, 45, 49, 71, 94, 105, 123, 138, 147–150, 152, 154, 155, 157, 158, 160, 165, 237, 349, 351, 365, 393, 414, 437
Attraction and repulsion, 31, 32, 34, 39, 81, 379
Augustine, 104, 160, 165, 213, 217–248, 250–253, 260, 268, 270–272, 279, 284–286, 290, 292, 296, 310, 345, 413, 421, 435, 441, 495, 519
Averroes, 135, 266, 267, 268, 270, 282, 283, 438
Avicenna, 265, 266

Bacchus, 304
Bach, J. S., 361, 421
Bacon, Francis, 114

541

544

The Crisis Of Our Time

Historians have christened the thirteenth century the Age of Faith and termed the eighteenth century the Age of Reason. The twentieth century has been called many things: the Atomic Age, the Age of Inflation, the Age of the Tyrant, the Age of Aquarius. But it deserves one name more than the others: the Age of Irrationalism. Contemporary secular intellectuals are anti-intellectual. Contemporary philosophers are anti-philosophy. Contemporary theologians are anti-theology.

In past centuries secular philosophers have generally believed that knowledge is possible to man. Consequently they expended a great deal of thought and effort trying to justify knowledge. In the twentieth century, however, the optimism of the secular philosophers has all but disappeared. They despair of knowledge.

Like their secular counterparts, the great theologians and doctors of the church taught that knowledge is possible to man. Yet the theologians of the twentieth century have repudiated that belief. They also despair of knowledge. This radical skepticism has filtered down from the philosophers and theologians and penetrated our entire culture, from television to music to literature. *The Christian in the twentieth century is confronted with an overwhelming cultural consensus—sometimes stated explicitly, but most often implicitly: Man does not and cannot know anything truly.*

What does this have to do with Christianity? Simply this: If man can know nothing truly, man can truly know nothing. We

549

cannot know that the Bible is the Word of God, that Christ died for sin, or that Christ is alive today at the right hand of the Father. Unless knowledge is possible, Christianity is nonsensical, for it claims to be knowledge. What is at stake in the twentieth century is not simply a single doctrine, such as the Virgin Birth, or the existence of hell, as important as those doctrines may be, but the whole of Christianity itself. If knowledge is not possible to man, it is worse than silly to argue points of doctrine—it is insane.

The irrationalism of the present age is so thorough-going and pervasive that even the Remnant—the segment of the professing church that remains faithful—has accepted much of it, frequently without even being aware of what it was accepting. In some circles this irrationalism has become synonymous with piety and humility, and those who oppose it are denounced as rationalists—as though to be logical were a sin. Our contemporary anti-theologians make a contradiction and call it a Mystery. The faithful ask for truth and are given Paradox. If any balk at swallowing the absurdities of the anti-theologians, they are frequently marked as heretics or schismatics who seek to act independently of God.

There is no greater threat facing the true Church of Christ at this moment than the irrationalism that now controls our entire culture. Communism, guilty of tens of millions of murders, including those of millions of Christians, is to be feared, but not nearly so much as the idea that we do not and cannot know the truth. Hedonism, the popular philosophy of America, is not to be feared so much as the belief that logic—that "mere human logic," to use the religious irrationalists' own phrase—is futile. The attacks on truth, on revelation, on the intellect, and on logic are renewed daily. But note well: The misologists—the haters of logic—use logic to demonstrate the futility of using logic. The anti-intellectuals construct intricate intellectual arguments to prove the insufficiency of the intellect. The anti-theologians use the revealed Word of God to show that there can be no revealed Word of God—or that if there could, it would remain impenetrable darkness and Mystery to our finite minds.

Nonsense Has Come

Is it any wonder that the world is grasping at straws—the straws of experientialism, mysticism and drugs? After all, if people are told that the Bible contains insoluble mysteries, then is not a flight into mysticism to be expected? On what grounds can it be condemned? Certainly not on logical grounds or Biblical grounds, if logic is futile and the Bible unintelligible. Moreover, if it cannot be condemned on logical or Biblical grounds, it cannot be condemned at all. If people are going to have a religion of the mysterious, they will not adopt Christianity: They will have a genuine mystery religion. "Those who call for Nonsense," C.S. Lewis once wrote, "will find that it comes." And that is precisely what has happened. The popularity of Eastern mysticism, of drugs, and of religious experience is the logical consequence of the irrationalism of the twentieth century. There can and will be no Christian revival—and no reconstruction of society— unless and until the irrationalism of the age is totally repudiated by Christians.

The Church Defenseless

Yet how shall they do it? The spokesmen for Christianity have been fatally infected with irrationalism. The seminaries, which annually train thousands of men to teach millions of Christians, are the finishing schools of irrationalism, completing the job begun by the government schools and colleges. Some of the pulpits of the most conservative churches (we are not speaking of the apostate churches) are occupied by graduates of the anti-theological schools. These products of modern anti-theological education, when asked to give a reason for the hope that is in them, can generally respond with only the intellectual analogue of a shrug—a mumble about Mystery. They have not grasped—and therefore cannot teach those for whom they are responsible—the first truth: "And ye shall know the truth." Many, in fact, explicitly deny it, saying that, at best, we possess only "pointers" to the truth, or something "similar" to the truth, a mere analogy. Is the impotence of the Christian Church a puzzle? Is the fascination with pentecostalism and faith healing among members of conservative churches an enigma? Not when one understands the sort of studied nonsense that is purveyed in the name of God in the seminaries.

The Trinity Foundation

The creators of The Trinity Foundation firmly believe that theology is too important to be left to the licensed theologians—the graduates of the schools of theology. They have created The Trinity Foundation for the express purpose of teaching the faithful all that the Scriptures contain— not warmed over, baptized, secular philosophies. Each member of the board of directors of The Trinity Foundation has signed this oath: "I believe that the Bible alone and the Bible in its entirety is the Word of God and, therefore, inerrant in the autographs. I believe that the system of truth presented in the Bible is best summarized in the Westminster Confession of Faith. So help me God."

The ministry of The Trinity Foundation is the presentation of the system of truth taught in Scripture as clearly and as completely as possible. We do not regard obscurity as a virtue, nor confusion as a sign of spirituality. Confusion, like all error, is sin, and teaching that confusion is all that Christians can hope for is doubly sin.

The presentation of the truth of Scripture necessarily involves the rejection of error. The Foundation has exposed and will continue to expose the irrationalism of the twentieth century, whether its current spokesman be an existentialist philosopher or a professed Reformed theologian. We oppose anti-intellectualism, whether it be espoused by a neo-orthodox theologian or a fundamentalist evangelist. We reject misology, whether it be on the lips of a neo-evangelical or those of a Roman Catholic charismatic. To each error we bring the brilliant light of Scripture, proving all things, and holding fast to that which is true.

The Primacy of Theory

The ministry of The Trinity Foundation is not a "practical"

ministry. If you are a pastor, we will not enlighten you on how to organize an ecumenical prayer meeting in your community or how to double church attendance in a year. If you are a homemaker, you will have to read elsewhere to find out how to become a total woman. If you are a businessman, we will not tell you how to develop a social conscience. The professing church is drowning in such "practical" advice.

The Trinity Foundation is unapologetically theoretical in its outlook, believing that theory without practice is dead, and that practice without theory is blind. The trouble with the professing church is not primarily in its practice, but in its theory. Christians do not know, and many do not even care to know, the doctrines of Scripture. Doctrine is intellectual, and Christians are generally anti-intellectual. Doctrine is ivory tower philosophy, and they scorn ivory towers. The ivory tower, however, is the control tower of a civilization. It is a fundamental, theoretical mistake of the practical men to think that they can be merely practical, for practice is always the practice of some theory. The relationship between theory and practice is the relationship between cause and effect. If a person believes correct theory, his practice will tend to be correct. The practice of contemporary Christians is immoral because it is the practice of false theories. It is a major theoretical mistake of the practical men to think that they can ignore the ivory towers of the philosophers and theologians as irrelevant to their lives. Every action that the "practical" men take is governed by the thinking that has occurred in some ivory tower—whether that tower be the British Museum, the Academy, a home in Basel, Switzerland, or a tent in Israel.

In Understanding Be Men

It is the first duty of the Christian to understand correct theory—correct doctrine—and thereby implement correct practice. This order—first theory, then practice—is both logical and Biblical. It is, for example, exhibited in Paul's epistle to the Romans, in which he spends the first eleven chapters expounding theory and the last five discussing practice. The contemporary teachers of

Christians have not only reversed the order, they have inverted the Pauline emphasis on theory and practice. The virtually complete failure of the teachers of the professing church to instruct the faithful in correct doctrine is the cause of the misconduct and cultural impotence of Christians. The Church's lack of power is the result of its lack of truth. The *Gospel* is the power of God, not religious experience or personal relationship. The Church has no power because it has abandoned the Gospel, the good news, for a religion of experientialism. Twentieth century American Christians are children carried about by every wind of doctrine, not knowing what they believe, or even if they believe anything for certain.

The chief purpose of The Trinity Foundation is to counteract the irrationalism of the age and to expose the errors of the teachers of the church. Our emphasis—on the Bible as the sole source of truth, on the primacy of the intellect, on the supreme importance of correct doctrine, and on the necessity for systematic and logical thinking—is almost unique in Christendom. To the extent that the church survives —and she will survive and flourish—it will be because of her increasing acceptance of these basic ideas and their logical implications.

We believe that the Trinity Foundation is filling a vacuum in Christendom. We are saying that Christianity is intellectually defensible—that, in fact, it is the only intellectually defensible system of thought. We are saying that God has made the wisdom of this world —whether that wisdom be called science, religion, philosophy, or common sense—foolishness. We are appealing to all Christians who have not conceded defeat in the intellectual battle with the world to join us in our efforts to raise a standard to which all men of sound mind can repair.

The love of truth, of God's Word, has all but disappeared in our time. We are committed to and pray for a great instauration. But though we may not see this reformation of Christendom in our lifetimes, we believe it is our duty to present the whole counsel of God because Christ has commanded it. The results of our teaching are in God's hands, not ours. Whatever those results, His Word is never taught in vain, but always accomplishes the result that He intended it to accomplish. Professor Gordon H. Clark has stated our view well:

> There have been times in the history of God's people, for example, in the days of Jeremiah, when refreshing grace and widespread revival were not to be expected: the time was one of chastisement. If this twentieth century is of a similar nature, individual Christians here and there can find comfort and strength in a study of God's Word. But if God has decreed happier days for us and if we may expect a world-shaking and genuine spiritual awakening, then it is the author's belief that a zeal for souls, however necessary, is not the sufficient condition. Have there not been devout saints in every age, numerous enough to carry on a revival? Twelve such persons are plenty. What distinguishes the arid ages from the period of the Reformation, when nations were moved as they had not been since Paul preached in Ephesus, Corinth, and Rome, is the latter's fullness of knowledge of God's Word. To echo an early Reformation thought, when the ploughman and the garage attendant know the Bible as well as the theologian does, and know it better than some contemporary theologians, then the desired awakening shall have already occurred.

In addition to publishing books, of which *Thales To Dewey* is the twenty-sixth, the Foundation publishes a bimonthly newsletter, *The Trinity Review*. Subscriptions to *The Review* are free; please write to the address below to become a subscriber. If you would like further information or would like to join us in our work, please let us know.

The Trinity Foundation is a non-profit foundation tax-exempt under section 501 (c)(3) of the Internal Revenue Code of 1954. You can help us disseminate the Word of God through your tax-deductible contributions to the Foundation.

And we know that the Son of God is come, and hath given us an understanding, that we may know him that is true, and we are in him that is true, in his Son Jesus Christ. This is the true God, and eternal life.

John W. Robbins
President

Intellectual Ammunition

The Trinity Foundation is committed to the reconstruction of philosophy and theology along Biblical lines. We regard God's command to bring all our thoughts into conformity with Christ very seriously, and the books listed below are designed to accomplish that goal. They are written with two subordinate purposes: (1) to demolish all secular claims to knowledge; and (2) to build a system of truth based upon the Bible alone.

Works of Philosophy

Answer to Ayn Rand, John W. Robbins $4.95
The only analysis and criticism of the views of novelist-philosopher Ayn Rand from a consistently Christian perspective.

Behaviorism and Christianity, Gordon H. Clark $5.95
Behaviorism *is a critique of both secular and religious behaviorists. It includes chapters on John Watson, Edgar S. Singer Jr., Gilbert Ryle, B.F. Skinner, and Donald MacKay. Clark's refutation of behaviorism and his argument for a Christian doctrine of man are unanswerable.*

A Christian Philosophy of Education, Gordon H. Clark $8.95
The first edition of this book was published in 1946. It sparked the contemporary interest in Christian schools. Dr. Clark has thoroughly

revised and updated it, and it is needed now more than ever. Its chapters include: The Need for a World-View, The Christian World-View, The Alternative to Christian Theism, Neutrality, Ethics, The Christian Philosophy of Education, Academic Matters, Kindergarten to University. Three appendices are included as well: The Relationship of Public Education to Christianity, A Protestant World-View, and Art and the Gospel.

A Christian View of Men and Things, Gordon H. Clark $8.95
    No other book achieves what A Christian View *does: the presentation of Christianity as it applies to history, politics, ethics, science, religion, and epistemology. Clark's command of both worldly philosophy and Scripture is evident on every page, and the result is a breathtaking and invigorating challenge to the wisdom of this world.*

Clark Speaks From The Grave, Gordon H. Clark $3.95
    Dr. Clark chides some of his critics for their failure to defend Christianity competently. Clark Speaks *is a stimulating and illuminating discussion of the errors of contemporary apologists.*

Education, Christianity, and the State $7.95
J. Gresham Machen
    Machen was one of the foremost educators, theologians, and defenders of Christianity in the twentieth century. The author of numerous scholarly books, Machen saw clearly that if Christianity is to survive and flourish, a system of Christian grade schools must be established. This collection of essays captures his thought on education over nearly three decades.

Logic, Gordon H. Clark $8.95
    Written as a textbook for Christian schools, Logic *is another unique book from Clark's pen. His presentation of the laws of thought, which must be followed if Scripture is to be understood correctly, and which are found in Scripture itself, is both clear and thorough.* Logic *is an indispensable book for the thinking Christian.*

The Philosophy of Science and Belief in God $5.95
Gordon H. Clark
    In opposing the contemporary idolatry of science, Clark analyzes three major aspects of science: the problem of motion, Newtonian

science, and modern theories of physics. His conclusion is that science, while it may be useful, is always false; and he demonstrates its falsity in numerous ways. Since science is always false, it can offer no objection to the Bible and Christianity.

Religion, Reason and Revelation, Gordon H. Clark $7.95
   One of Clark's apologetical masterpieces, Religion, Reason and Revelation has been praised for the clarity of its thought and language. It includes chapters on Is Christianity a Religion? Faith and Reason, Inspiration and Language, Revelation and Morality, and God and Evil. It is must reading for all serious Christians.

Selections from Hellenistic Philosophy, Gordon H. Clark $10.95
   This is one of Clark's early works in which he translates, edits, and comments upon works by the Epicureans, the Stoics, Plutarch, Philo Judaeus, Hermes Trismegistus, and Plotinus. First published in 1940, it has been a standard college text for more than four decades.

Thales to Dewey, Gordon H. Clark $11.95
   The best one volume history of philosophy available. Clark analyzes secular philosophers in a clear and entertaining fashion.

Three Types of Religious Philosophy, Gordon H. Clark $6.95
   In this handbook on apologetics, Clark examines empiricism, rationalism, dogmatism, and contemporary irrationalism, which does not rise to the level of philosophy. He offers a solution to the question, "How can Christianity be defended before the world?"

William James, Gordon H. Clark $2.00
   America has not produced many philosophers, but William James has been extremely influential. Clark examines his philosophy of Pragmatism.

Works of Theology

The Atonement, Gordon H. Clark $8.95
   This is a major addition to Clark's multi-volume systematic theology. In The Atonement, Clark discusses the Covenants, the Virgin Birth and Incarnation, federal headship and representation, the rela-

tionship between God's sovereignty and justice, and much more. He analyzes traditional views of the Atonement and criticizes them in the light of Scripture alone.

The Biblical Doctrine of Man, Gordon H. Clark $5.95

Is man soul and body or soul, spirit, and body? What is the image of God? Is Adam's sin imputed to his children? Is evolution true? Are men totally depraved? What is the heart? These are some of the questions discussed and answered from Scripture in this book.

Cornelius Van Til: The Man and The Myth $2.45
John W. Robbins

The actual teachings of this eminent Philadelphia theologian have been obscured by the myths that surround him. This book penetrates those myths and criticizes Van Til's surprisingly unorthodox views of God and the Bible.

Faith and Saving Faith, Gordon H. Clark $5.95

The views of the Roman Catholic church, John Calvin, Thomas Manton, John Owen, Charles Hodge, and B.B. Warfield are discussed in this book. Is the object of faith a person or a proposition? Is faith more than belief? Is belief more than thinking with assent, as Augustine said? In a world chaotic with differing views of faith, Clark clearly explains the Biblical view of faith and saving faith.

God's Hammer: The Bible and Its Critics, Gordon H. Clark $6.95

The starting point of Christianity, the doctrine on which all other doctrines depend, is "The Bible alone is the Word of God written, and therefore inerrant in the autographs." Over the centuries the opponents of Christianity, with Satanic shrewdness, have concentrated their attacks on the truthfulness and completeness of the Bible. In the twentieth century the attack is not so much in the fields of history and archaeology as in philosophy. Clark's brilliant defense of the complete truthfulness of the Bible is captured in this collection of eleven major essays.

The Incarnation, Gordon H. Clark $8.95

Who was Christ? The attack on the Incarnation in the nineteenth and twentieth centuries has been vigorous, but the orthodox response has been lame. Clark reconstructs the doctrine of the Incarnation building and improving upon the Chalcedonian definition.

In Defense of Theology, Gordon H. Clark $12.95

There are four groups to whom Clark addresses this book: the average Christians who are uninterested in theology, the atheists and agnostics, the religious experientialists, and the serious Christians. The vindication of the knowledge of God against the objections of three of these groups is the first step in theology.

The Johannine Logos, Gordon H. Clark $5.95

In this book Clark answers the question: "How is Christ, who is the truth, related to the truths of the Bible?" He explains why John used the same word to refer to both Christ and his teaching.

Logical Criticisms of Textual Criticism, Gordon H. Clark $2.95

In this critique of the science of textual criticism, Dr. Clark exposes the fallacious argumentation of the modern textual critics and defends the view that the early Christians knew better than the modern critics which manuscripts of the New Testament were more accurate.

Pat Robertson: A Warning to America, John W. Robbins $6.95

The Protestant Reformation was based on the Biblical principle that the Bible is the only revelation from God, yet a growing political- religious movement, led by Pat Robertson, asserts that God speaks to them directly. This book addresses the serious issue of religious fanaticism in America by examining the theological and political views of Pat Robertson.

Predestination, Gordon H. Clark $7.95

Clark thoroughly discusses one of the most controversial and pervasive doctrines of the Bible: that God is, quite literally, Almighty. Free will, the origin of evil, God's omniscience, creation, and the new birth are all presented within a Scriptural framework. The objections of those who do not believe in the Almighty God are considered and refuted. This edition also contains the text of the booklet, Predestination in the Old Testament.

Scripture Twisting in the Seminaries. Part 1: Feminism $5.95
John W. Robbins

An analysis of the views of three graduates of Westminster Seminary on the role of women in the church.

The Trinity, Gordon H. Clark $8.95

Apart from the doctrine of Scripture, no teaching of the Bible is more important than the doctrine of God. Clark's defense of the orthodox doctrine of the Trinity is a principal portion of a major new work of Systematic Theology now in progress. There are chapters on the deity of Christ, Augustine, the incomprehensibility of God, Bavinck and Van Til, and the Holy Spirit, among others.

What Do Presbyterians Believe? Gordon H. Clark $6.95

This classic introduction to Christian doctrine has been republished. It is the best commentary on the Westminster Confession of Faith that has ever been written.

Commentaries on the New Testament

Colossians, Gordon H. Clark $6.95
Ephesians, Gordon H. Clark $8.95
First and Second Thessalonians, Gordon H. Clark $5.95
The Pastoral Epistles (I and II Timothy and Titus) $9.95
   Gordon H. Clark

All of Clark's commentaries are expository, not technical, and are written for the Christian layman. His purpose is to explain the text clearly and accurately so that the Word of God will be thoroughly known by every Christian. Revivals of Christianity come only through the spread of God's truth. The sound exposition of the Bible, through preaching and through commentaries on Scripture, is the only method of spreading that truth.

The Trinity Review

The Foundation's bimonthly newsletter, The Trinity Review, has been published since 1979 and has carried more than sixty major essays by Gordon H. Clark, J. Gresham Machen, Fyodor Dostoyevsky, Charles Hodge, John Witherspoon, and others. Back issues are available for 40¢ each.

Order Form

Name _____

Address _____

_____

Please: ☐ add my name to the mailing list for *The Trinity Review*. I understand that there is no charge for the *Review*.

☐ accept my tax deductible contribution of $ ___ for the work of the Foundation.

☐ send me _____ copies of *Thales to Dewey*. I enclose as payment $ _____.

☐ send me the Trinity Library of 30 books. I enclose $150 as full payment for it.

☐ send me the following books. I enclose full payment in the amount of $ _____ for them.

_____

_____

_____

_____

_____

_____

_____

Mail to: The Trinity Foundation
               Post Office Box 169
               Jefferson, MD 21755

Please add $1.00 for postage on orders less than $10. Thank you.
For quantity discounts, please write to the Foundation.